Environmental Science

We work with leading authors to develop the strongest
educational materials in environmental science, bringing
cutting-edge thinking and best learning practice to a
global market.

Under a range of well-known imprints, including Prentice
Hall, we craft high quality print and electronic
publications which help readers to understand and apply
their content, whether studying or at work.

To find out more about the complete range of our
publishing please visit us on the World Wide Web at:
www.pearsoneduc.com

Environmental Science
The Natural Environment and Human Impact
second edition
Andrew R. W. Jackson & Julie M. Jackson

Pearson Education Limited
Edinburgh Gate
Harlow
Essex CM20 2JE
England
and Associated Companies throughout the world

Visit us on the world wide web at:

http://www.pearsoneduc.com

_____

First published 1996
Second Edition 2000

© Pearson Education Limited 1996
© Andrew R. W. Jackson and Julie M. Jackson 2000

ISBN 0 582 41445 8

British Library Cataloguing-in-Publication Data
A catalogue record for this book is available from the British Library

Typeset by 32 in 8/12pt StoneSerif
Printed by Ashford Colour Press Ltd., Gosport

To   the memory of
Dr Eric Salvin Raper

Contents

Contents

Contents

Contents

Appendices

Preface to the second edition

Environmental science is a rapidly developing field. Since the publication of the first edition of this text, in 1996, a significant number of new environmental issues have come to the fore. This new edition of *Environmental Science* therefore includes a sizeable amount of new and topical material. Most notably, this takes the form of a new chapter (Chapter 10) that examines the exploitation of biological resources, together with four new case studies covering BSE, genetically modified crops, arsenic contamination of drinking water in the Ganges Delta, and the problems surrounding the disposal of radioactive waste. New material is also incorporated within other chapters, for example the El Niño–Southern Oscillation (ENSO), described in Chapter 4, and endocrine-disrupting substances, discussed in Chapter 14.

Additionally, other areas that were covered in the first edition have developed significantly since 1996 and consequently needed reappraisal. For example, the Montreal Protocol has been strengthened over recent years and its implementation is now resulting in noticeable effects (Chapter 15).

We also took the opportunity, afforded to us by the preparation of a new edition, to improve the overall accessibility of the book. We have sought to achieve this by incorporating a number of new features. These include learning objectives at the start of each chapter, colour plates, a glossary, a *Lecturers' guide* available to adopters from the publishers, and a supporting website (http://www.booksites.net).

ARW Jackson
JM Jackson
December 1999

Preface to the first edition

Modern techniques of environmental science allow us to explore our surroundings in ways that were unimaginable until relatively recently. These explorations have not only revealed the natural world in ever finer detail, they have also provided evidence to suggest that the activity of humans is, for the first time, causing changes to the environment on a global scale. Heightened interest in the nature and quality of our surroundings is reflected in the growing amount of published work concerning environmental issues, both in the press and in more specialist literature.

This book was written to provide a clear and authoritative introductory environmental science text. It strives to bridge the gap between the popularist and specialist environmental publications. It introduces the reader to the basic concepts and vocabulary necessary to explore complex environmental issues and problems.

Environmental science will primarily be of use to first-year undergraduate students of the environmental sciences, including environmental biology and environmental chemistry. However, it will also serve as a reference text for students of related disciplines such as environmental studies and environmental management. The text is constructed in a concise and coherent manner, making extensive use of boxed material, both to explain basic theory and to provide illustrative examples. In order to further enhance the student's learning experience, end of chapter problems and a selection of environmental case studies are included. The latter are intended to provide a starting point for further, independent, investigation into the environmental issues raised.

The book is divided into two main parts: **The Natural Environment** (Chapters 1–10) and **Human Impact on the Natural Environment** (Chapters 11–16). In the first of these, the nature and chemical behaviour of matter is explored, as are the major features and processes of the lithosphere, hydrosphere, biosphere and atmosphere, and the interactions between them. In the second part of the text, the impact of human activities upon the environment, through the exploitation of natural resources and the production of pollutants, is explored in depth. Attention is given in the final chapter to the issue of waste management.

Environmental science is concerned with the presentation of factual information and its scientific interpretation. It does not attempt to deal with either the ethical or legal problems associated with environmental issues. While techniques of environmental management are introduced where relevant in the latter part of this text, this is not a major theme of the book. Readers interested in this aspect of environmental science may wish to read Timothy O'Riordan's book *Environmental Science for Environmental Management* (second edition, Prentice Hall, 2000).

We would like to take this opportunity to explain some of the policies that we have adopted concerning specific units, nomenclature and symbolisms. When writing this book we have used SI units, except where other units are in more common usage in the general literature of environmental science. Conversion factors between SI units and their non-SI equivalents are given in Appendix 2. When referring to specific organisms, it has been our policy to refer to them by their common names, citing their Linnean Latin binomial at first mention only. When using half-cell equations we have represented oxidations as such, rather than as reverse reductions. We have done this to avoid the necessity for the subtraction of half-cell equations when generating full-cell equations. In accordance with convention, we use only reduction potentials when calculating cell potentials. In accordance with the convention used in physical chemistry, units and multiples appear after a solidus (/) in the column headings of tables and the labels on the axes of graphs.

ARW Jackson
JM Jackson
April 1995

Acknowledgements

There are a number of people to whom we are indebted for their help in the preparation of the second edition of *Environmental Science*. We would like to acknowledge colleagues Dr Kevin Reiling, for his helpful comments on part of the text, and Dr Dave Morman and Dr R Glynn Skerratt for the provision of material used in the composition of Case Study 3. We are particularly indebted to the ever-helpful staff of Alsager Library, Cheshire, for their assistance in obtaining information. Thanks are also due to the following people for supplying us with photographic material: Dr Julia Mayne, Professor Barbara Brown, Dr P Duncan Hywel-Evans, Dr Roman Kresinski and Mr Malcolm Rodgerson.

We wish to acknowledge the constructive criticism and helpful comments made by Professor Ian Spellerberg of Lincoln University, New Zealand, Dr Allan Jones of Dundee University, UK, and Dr Sheena Wurthmann of Glasgow Caledonian University, UK who reviewed the text when in draft form. Thanks are also due for the help given by members of staff at Pearson Education, particularly Alexandra Seabrook, Lynn Brandon, Shuet-Kei Cheung and Pauline Gillett. We are very grateful to the copy editor Mr Patrick Bonham and the proofreader Ms Annette Abel for their careful attention to detail. Also, we wish to thank all of those readers who took the time to inform the publishers of their impressions of the first edition and so helped to shape the second one.

A special mention must be made of our family for their support and encouragement. In particular, we would like to thank our sons, Tom and Hugh, for their patience and understanding during the writing of this new edition.

ARW Jackson
JM Jackson
December 1999

We would like to thank the following for permission to use copyrighted material:

Plate Section
NASA for plate 1; Geoscience Features picture library for plates 2, 3 and 8; Still Pictures for plates 4 and 6; Graham Bell for plate 7; Julia Mayne for plates 10, 11, 12, 18 and 19; Roman Kresinski for plate 13; ECOSCENE/Andrew D. R. Brown for plate 14; Barbara Brown for plate 15; Malcolm Rodgerson for plate 16; ECOSCENE/Cooper for plate 17; Panos Pictures/Marcus Rose for plate 20; ECOSCENE/Robert Walker for plate 22; P. Duncan Hywel-Evans for plate 23.

Plates 5 and 9 were photographed by Julie Jackson; plate 21 was photographed by Andrew Jackson.

The copyright of all photographic material remains with the individuals or organisations who supplied them, with the exception of plate 7 (Graham Bell), the copyright of which is now held by Andrew and Julie Jackson.

Chapter 1
National Radiological Protection Board for second figure in Box 1.6 from *Radon at a Glance* 2/e (1994); Oxford University Press for Fig. 1.8 from Wells, A.F. (1962). *Structural Inorganic Chemistry* 3/e; Thomson Learning Global Rights Group for Fig. 1.9(b) from Starr, C. and R. Taggart (1984) *Biology: the Unity and Diversity of Life* 3/e

Chapter 3
Kluwer Academic Publishers for figure in Box 3.3 from O'Neill, P. (1993) *Environmental Chemistry* 2/e; Longman Group Ltd. for Fig. 3.3 from Summerfield, M.A. (1991) *Global Geomorphology*; Macmillan Press Ltd. for Fig. 3.4 from Read, H.H. and J. Watson (1966) *Beginning Geology*; Longman Group Ltd. for Table 3.4 from Russell, E. W. (1973) *Soil Conditions and Plant Growth* 10/e; Blackwell Science Ltd. for Figs. 3.10 and 3.14 from White, R. E. (1979) *Introduction to the Principles and Practice of Soil Science*; also The Soil Survey and Land Research Centre for Fig. 3.10 from *Soil Survey of England and Wales* (1974); Longman Group Ltd. for Fig 3.16 from Simpson, K. (1983) *Soil*; Routledge for Figs. 3.17 & 3.18 from Briggs, D. and P. Smithson (1985) *Fundamentals of Physical Geography*; Edward Arnold for Figs. 3.20 & 3.21 and Table 3.7 from Raiswell, R.W., P. Brimblecombe, D.L. Dent and P.S. Liss (1980) *Environmental Chemistry: the earth-air-water factory*; the American Association for the Advancement of Science for Figs. 3.22 & 3.23 from Gibbs, R.J. (1970) *Mechanisms Controlling World Water Chemistry*, Science **170** pp1088–90; also Dr. R. J. Gibbs for Fig.3.22

Chapter 4
Routledge for second figure in Box 4.1 and Figs 4.16, 4.18 & 4.19 from Barry, R. and R.J. Chorley (1987) *Atmosphere, Weather and Climate* 5/e; also The University of Chicago Press for second figure in Box 4.1 from Sellers, W.D. (1965) *Physical Climatology*; also Dr. R.P. Beckinsale for Fig 4.18; also American Meteorological Society for Fig 4.19 from Boucher and Newcomb (1962) *in Journal of Applied Meteorology* Vol. 1 no.3 pp127–36; Intergovernmental Panel on Climate Change (IPCC) for third figure in Box 4.1 from Shine, Derwent, Wuebbles and Morcrette in *Climate Change: The IPCC Scientific Assessment* Houghton, J.T., G.J. Jenkins and J.J. Ephraums (eds) (1990); Routledge for first figure in Box 4.3 from Pickering, K.T. and L.A. Owen (1997*) An Introduction to Global Environmental Issues* 2/e; also Macmillan Magazines Ltd. for first figure in Box 4.3 redrawn from Street-Perrott, F.A. and R.A. Perrott (1990) 'Abrupt climatic fluctuations in the tropics: the influence of Atlantic Ocean circulation' in *Nature* **343** pp 607–12; Kluwer Academic Publishers for second figure in Box 4.3 from Tolmazin, D. (1985) *Elements of Dynamic Oceanography*; Wuerz Publishing Ltd. for Fig 4.2 from Bunce, N.J. (1990) *Environmental Chemistry*; also John Wiley & Sons Inc., Dr Barbara. J. Finlayson-Pitts and Dr James N. Pitts for Fig 4.2 from Finlayson-Pitts, B.J. and J.N. Pitts (1986) *Atmospheric Chemistry*; Longman Group Ltd. for Figs 4.5 & 4.17 from Henderson-Sellers, A. and P.J. Robinson, (1986) *Contemporary Climatology*; Kluwer Academic Publishers for Figs 4.6, 4.11 & 4.14 from White, I.D., D.N. Mottershead and S.J. Harrison (1992*) Environmental Systems: an introductory text* 2/e; also The University of Chicago Press for Fig 4.6 from Sellers, W.D. (1965*) Physical climatology*; also Methuen & Co. for Fig 4.11 from Lamb, H.H. (1972) *Climate Present, Past and Future*, Vol. 1; also The McGraw-Hill Companies for Fig 4.14 from Riehl, H. (1965) *Introduction to the Atmosphere* 3/e; Dr A..H. Oort for Fig 4.7 from Oort, A.H. (1983) *Global Atmospheric Circulation Statistics*, NOAA Prof. Paper 14; HMSO for Fig. 4.23 from DOE (1994) *Global Climate Change* 3/e (Crown copyright is reproduced with the permission of the controller of HMSO); World Meteorological Organisation (c/o The Press Syndicate of the University of Cambridge) for Fig. 4.24 from Houghton, J. T. (ed) (1984) *The Global Climate*

Chapter 5
Oxford University Press for Fig. 5.2 from Phillips, W.D. and T.J. Chilton (1989) *A-level Biology*; Kluwer Academic Publishers for Fig. 5.4 from White, I.D., D.N. Mottershead and S.J. Harrison (1992*) Environmental Systems: an introductory text* 2/e; Cambridge University Press for Fig. 5.7 from Houghton, J. T. (1997*) Global Warming: the Complete Briefing*

Chapter 7

Company of Biologists Ltd. for Fig. 7.3 from Gause, G.F. (1932) 'Experimental studies on the struggle for existence. I. Mixed populations of two species of yeast', *Journal of Experimental Biology* **9** pp389–402; The Ecological Society of America for Fig. 7.5 from Krebs, J. R. (1971) 'Territory and breeding density in the great tit (*Parus major*)', *Ecology* **52** pp2–22; Lippincott, Williams & Wilkins for Fig 7.9 from Gause, G.F. (1934) *The Struggle for Existence*; CSIRO Editorial Services for Fig. 7.10 from Caughley, G., G.C. Grigg, J. Caughley and G.T.E. Hill (1980) 'Does dingo predation control the densities of kangaroos and emus?', *Australian Wildlife Research* **7** pp1–12; Oxford University Press for Fig. 7.11 from Phillips, W.D. and T.J. Chilton (1989) *A-level Biology*; Blackwell Science Ltd. for Fig. 7.12 from Stafford, J. (1971) 'Heron populations of England and Wales 1928-1970', *Bird Study* **18** pp 218–21; John Wiley & Sons, Inc. for Fig. 7.13 from Marsh, W.M and J.M. Grossa, Jr. (1996) *Environmental Geography: Science, land use and Earth systems*; Kluwer Academic Publishers for Fig. 7.15 from Tolba, M.K., O.A. El-Kholy, E. El-Hinnawi, M.W. Holdgate, D.F. McMichael and R.E. Munn (eds) (1992) *The World Environment: 1972-1992:Two decades of challenge*

Chapter 8

Fig. 8.5 reprinted by permission of the publisher from *Ecology and Evolution of Communities* ed. M.L. Cody and J.M. Diamond, Cambridge, Mass.: The Belknap Press of Harvard University Press, Copyright © 1975 by the President and Fellows of Harvard College; Blackwell Science Ltd., for Fig. 8.7 from Horn, H.S. (1981) 'Succession' in *Theoretical Ecology*, May, R.M. (ed) pp 253-71

Chapter 9

Blackwell Science Ltd. for Fig 9.1 from Varley, G.C. (1970) 'The concept of energy flow applied to a woodland community' in *Animal Populations in Relation to their Food Resources*, Watson, A. (ed); Longman Group Ltd. for Fig. 9.6 from Macan, T.T. (1959) *A Guide to Freshwater Invertebrate Animals*; Franz Steiner Verlag GmbH, Wiesbaden for Fig. 9.7(a) from Lieth, H. (1964) *Geographisches Taschenbuch*; Fig 9.7(b) from Koblentz-Mishke, I.J., V.V. Volkovinsky and J.B. Kabanova (1970) 'Plankton primary production of the world ocean', *Scientific Exploration of the South Pacific*, Wooster, W.S. (ed) reprinted with permission from *Scientific Exploration of the South Pacific*, Copyright © 1968 by the National Academy of Sciences. courtesy of the National Academy Press, Washington, DC; Blackwell Science Ltd. for Fig. 9.10 from Swift, M.J., O.W. Heal and J.M. Anderson (1979) *Decomposition in Terrestrial Ecosystems*; Routledge for Fig. 9.12 from Park, C. (1997) *The Environment, Principles and Applications*; also John Wiley & Sons, Inc. for Fig. 9.12 from Marsh, W.M and J.M. Grossa, Jr. (1996) *Environmental Geography: Science, land use and Earth systems*; Fig. 9.13 and Table 9.4 from *Communities and Ecosystems* 2/e by Whittaker, R.H. 1975. Reprinted by permission of Prentice-Hall, Inc., Upper Saddle River, NJ

Chapter 10

World Conservation Monitoring Centre, Cambridge for Fig 10.1; Worldwatch Institute, Washington DC, USA for Fig. 10.2 from Worldwatch Institute (1996) *Vital Signs*; Gerald Duckworth & Co. Ltd. for Fig. 10.3 from Thorpe, H. (1978) 'The man-land relationship through time' in *Agriculture and Conservation*, Hawkes, J.G. (ed); The World Conservation Union (IUCN) for Table 10.4 from IUCN (The World Conservation Union)(1994) *Guidelines for Protected area Management Categories*

Chapter 11

Elsevier Science for Fig. 11.1 from Frissel, M.J. (ed) (1978) 'Cycling of mineral nutrients in agricultural systems', *Developments in Agriculture and Managed-forest Ecology* **3**; The Royal Society and Gerald Stanhill for Fig. 11.3 from Stanhill, G. (1986) 'Irrigation in arid lands', *Philosophical Transactions of the Royal Society*, London **A316** pp261–73; Professor A.C. Millington for Fig 11.4 from Soussan, J.G. and A.C. Millington 'Forests, Woodlands and Deforestation' in *Environmental Issues in the 1990s*, Mannion, A.M. and S.R. Bowlby (eds) (1992), John Wiley & Sons Ltd; Longman Group Ltd. for Fig. 11.5 from Mannion, A.M. (1991) *Global Environmental Change*; The McGraw-Hill Companies for Fig. 11.6 from Cunningham, W.P. and B.W. Saigo (1995) *Environmental Science: a global concern* 3/e

Chapter 12

Cambridge University Press for Fig. 12.1 (a) from Lambert, D. (1988) *The Cambridge Guide to the Earth*; Elsevier Science for Fig. 12.3 from Gore, A.J.P. (ed) (1983) *Ecosystems of the World- 4A Mires: swamp, bog, fen and moor*; Macmillan Press Ltd. for Fig. 12.4 from Read,

H.H. and J. Watson (1966) *Beginning Geology*; Chapman & Hall and UNEP for Fig. 12.6 from Tolba, M.K., O.A. El-Kholy, E. El-Hinnawi, M.W. Holdgate, D.F. McMichael and R.E. Munn (eds) (1992*) The World Environment: 1972–1992: Two decades of challenge*

Chapter 13

BP Amoco plc, London for Fig. 13.1 from *BP Amoco Statistical Review of World Energy* (1999); Michael Goodman for Fig. 13.2 from Reddy, A.K.N. and J. Goldemberg (1990) 'Energy for the Developing World', *Scientific American* **263 (3)** pp 63–72; Professor A. Porteous for Fig. 13.8 from Porteous A. (1991) *Dictionary of Environmental Science and Technology*; The McGraw-Hill Companies for Fig. 13.9 from McGraw-Hill (1987) *Encyclopedia of Science and Technology* 6/e; Longman Group Ltd. for Fig 13.14 from Summerfield, M.A. (1991) *Global Geomorphology*; also American Geophysical Union for Fig 13.14 from Vogt, P.R. (1981), p951, *Journal of Geophysical Research* **86**

Chapter 14

Professor H.B.N. Hynes and Liverpool University Press for Fig 14.1 from Hynes, H.B.N. (1960) *The Biology of Polluted Waters*

Chapter 15

Longman Group Ltd. for Fig. 15.1, Table 15.2 and Fig. 15.13 from Wellburn, A.R. (1994) *Air Pollution and Climate Change* 2/e; Ambio-Royal Swedish Academy of Sciences for Fig. 15.2 from Galloway, J.N. (1989) 'Atmospheric acidification projections for the future', *Ambio* **18** pp161–66; Dr. N. Sundararaman and the IPCC (Intergovernmental Panel on Climate Change) for Fig 15.5(a) from Houghton, J. T. (1997) *Global Warming; the complete briefing* and for Figs. 15.5(b), 15.14, 15.16, 15.17 & 15.18 from Houghton, J.T., L.G. Meira Filho, B.A. Callander, N. Harris, A. Kattenberg and K. Maskell (eds) (1996) *Climate Change 1995: the Science of Climate Change*; American Geophysical Union for Fig. 15.6 from Heidt, L.E., J.P. Krasnec, R.A. Lueb, W.H. Pollock, B.E. Henry and P.J. Crutzen (1980) 'Latitudinal distributions of CO and CH_4 over the Pacific', *Journal of Geophysical Research* **85** pp 7329-36; Wuerz Publishing Ltd. for Fig 15.10 from Bunce, N.J. (1990) *Environmental Chemistry*; Royal Meteorological Society for Fig. 15.11 from Wilkins, E.T. (1954) 'Air pollution aspects of the London fog of December 1952', *Quarterly Journal of the Royal Meteorological Society* **80** pp 267–71; World Meteorological Organisation (WMO) for Fig 15.15 from Houghton, J.T., G.J. Jenkins and J.J. Ephraums (eds) (1990) *Climate Change: The IPCC Scientific Assessment*

Case Study 7

The McGraw-Hill Companies for Fig. C7.1 from Cunningham, W.P. and B.W. Saigo (1995) *Environmental Science: a global concern* 3/e

Whilst every effort has been made to trace the owners of copyright material, in a few cases this has proved impossible and we take this opportunity to offer our apologies to any copyright holders whose rights we may have unwittingly infringed.

Introduction

Environmental science is the systematic study of the natural and man-made world. It is now a major discipline, reflecting our growing concern about the impact of human activity on the natural world.

The environment may be conceptualised as being composed of a number of interconnected processes and phenomena. These include the formation of rocks, the climate system, the cycling of biologically important elements and the interactions between organisms and their surroundings.

In part, environmental science involves the identification, measurement and classification of these processes and phenomena. Importantly, it also encompasses our attempts to rationalise their existence and to predict how they will alter in the future. Environmental science therefore, like all other sciences, involves detection, classification, measurement, the establishment of experimentally verified laws by hypothesis formulation and testing, and the generation of predictive models.

Environmental science is of importance, not only because it informs us about the world in which we live, but also because it enables us to address more effectively many of the pressing issues that confront the modern world. For this reason, environmental science is increasingly seen as a vital tool in establishing the ground rules by which the environment may be more effectively managed in the future.

The first part of this book (Chapters 1–9) explores the major attributes of the environment in the absence of human activity. It is largely devoted to a detailed examination of the salient characteristics and interactions of the lithosphere (rocks), hydrosphere (water), biosphere and atmosphere (Chapters 3–9). In recognition of the varied backgrounds of the readership, the basic scientific concepts that are required for an understanding of the chemical processes that are central to the environment are set out in Chapters 1 and 2.

The first nine chapters of the book not only describe the natural environment, they also form a firm foundation on which the second part of the book is built. Within the second part, the human impact on the natural environment is examined. In Chapters 10–13, the nature of both finite and renewable resources is explored, together with the processes and patterns of their exploitation. Specifically, we examine biological resources, agricultural land use, mineral extraction and energy production. The consequences of this exploitation are reviewed both within Chapters 10–13 and in Chapters 14 and 15 where the major types of water and atmospheric pollution are described. This part of the book closes with an introduction to the principles and practice of waste management (Chapter 16).

Within this book, the reader will find scientific explanations of the causes and potential ramifications of the major environmental issues that currently face us. For example, in Chapter 15, we explore the greenhouse effect and climate change, stratospheric ozone depletion and the phenomena of acid rain and smog. The environmental impact of agricultural land use, including deforestation, salinisation, soil erosion and desertification, are covered in Chapter 11. Also, the importance of the world's biological resources and the consequences of their exploitation are examined in Chapter 10.

This book aims to present a dispassionate, objective and authoritative introductory review of both the natural environment and the impact of human activity on it. It is designed to introduce the reader to the key concepts and vocabulary of environmental science. This learning experience is reinforced by the inclusion of boxes that expand on and illustrate the basic concepts introduced in the text. For ease of access, each of these boxes is assigned to one of the following categories: mini case studies, tool boxes, or further information boxes. To consolidate understanding, each chapter commences with a statement of objectives and closes with a series of problems. Topical case studies follow each of the chapters in the second part of the book (Chapters 10–16). These are designed to stimulate the reader to further investigate and evaluate specific environmental issues, thereby facilitating the development of independent study. A glossary is provided at the end of the text that contains a selection of key terms with which the reader may not be familiar. Additionally, a wider range of key terms is highlighted in the index, directing the reader to those parts of the main body of the text where the terms are either defined or described.

This text is primarily designed for first-year undergraduates of the environmental sciences, including environmental chemistry and environmental biology. However, it will also be of value as a source of background material to students of related disciplines, such as environmental management or environmental studies.

Part One

THE NATURAL ENVIRONMENT

The physical environment

An understanding of our physical surroundings is fundamental to environmental science. The living (biotic) and non-living physical (abiotic) worlds are inextricably interconnected. At one level, the physical world may be viewed as providing the life-support system for the biotic world. To emphasise this, it is worth noting that all of the forms of life that have evolved on Earth are composed of matter that has its origins in the abiotic world. Clearly, the relationship is more complex than this. During the time over which evolution has occurred, the physical environment has not only shaped life, but has been shaped by it. The chemical behaviour of biotic and abiotic systems is controlled by the same laws that determine the rate and extent of the reactions upon which they are based.

In the next five chapters, we explore:

- the nature of matter, how it is organised and the types of chemical and nuclear reactions that it undergoes (Chapter 1);

- the laws that govern how far and how fast chemical processes occur (Chapter 2);

- the salient features and processes that characterise the rocks, soils and waters of the Earth's surface (Chapter 3);

- the structure and composition of the atmosphere, and climate and climate change (Chapter 4);

- the cycles that move the biologically important elements through the biosphere, i.e. the life-supporting part of the world and the life within it (Chapter 5).

The nature and organisation of matter

After reading this chapter, you should be able to:

■ Define the terms matter, nuclide, isotope, element, compound, mixture and chemical species.

■ Describe atoms in terms of the arrangement of their constituent parts.

■ Understand the nature of ionic bonds and appreciate the link between the presence of these bonds and the properties of compounds that contain them.

■ Define the term molecule and understand the nature of the covalent bonds that bind together the constituent atoms of molecules.

■ Appreciate the relationship between the properties of compounds that contain covalent bonds and the nature and arrangement of the bonds that they contain.

■ Use the concepts of valency and oxidation state.

■ Understand the relationship between the valency of an element and the group of the Periodic Table in which it is found.

■ Use chemical formulae to represent compounds and chemical equations to represent chemical reactions.

■ Classify environmentally important chemical reactions.

■ Define and classify nuclear reactions.

■ Compare and contrast nuclear reactions and chemical reactions.

Introduction

As **matter** is anything that takes up space, an understanding of how it is organised and how it behaves is fundamental to an understanding of the environment. This chapter concentrates on the nature and organisation of matter. It is divided into sections that deal with atoms and elements; ions; molecules; valency and the Periodic Table; oxidation states; compounds, mixtures and chemical reactions; and nuclear reactions. The language, symbolism and concepts that are introduced here are used and developed throughout the book. The environmentally important features of the behaviour of matter are introduced both here and in Chapter 2.

1.1 Atoms and elements

Atoms are the smallest units of matter that are capable of entering into chemical reactions. They are themselves made up of three fundamental particles: electrons, protons and neutrons. Table 1.1 lists some of the properties of these subatomic particles.

Collections of atoms that all contain the same number of both protons and electrons are called **elements**. They are the simplest substances that can be isolated by chemical means. There are a total of about 109 elements known (Table 1.2). Ninety-two of these occur naturally on Earth, whilst the remainder have been made in nuclear reactors.

Atoms of any one element may vary from one another slightly in the number of neutrons that they contain. Atoms that vary from one another in this way are called **isotopes**: see Box 1.1.

Table 1.1 Properties of neutrons, protons and electrons:

Particle	Symbol	Charge[a]	Mass[b]
Neutron	n	0	1.0087
Proton	p	+1	1.0078
Electron	e^-	−1	5.5×10^{-4}

[a] Given as multiples of 1.602×10^{-19} C.
[b] Given in atomic mass units, u. $1\,u = 1.6605 \times 10^{-24}$ g.
Note: Atoms of all nuclides, except hydrogen, $_1^1H$, contain protons, neutrons and electrons. Each atom of $_1^1H$ contains a proton and an electron only.

Each atom has a very small and extremely dense nucleus. It is here that its protons and neutrons reside. An atom's electrons are found in a diffuse, yet ordered, cloud around its nucleus. The electrons are held in the atom because they are drawn to the nucleus. This occurs by virtue of the negative charge on the electrons and the positive charge on the nucleus. Charges of opposite sign attract one another.

The processes involved in chemical reactions underlie virtually all environmental phenomena. When atoms enter into chemical reactions they do so through their electron clouds. A knowledge of the structure of these clouds, referred to as 'the **electronic structure** of the atom', gives an insight into these vital processes.

It is now known that this structure is extremely complex. Fortunately, virtually all of the environmentally important chemical properties of atoms can be understood with the aid of a relatively simple model. In this model, electrons are imagined to reside in concentric shells about the nucleus. Each shell consists of a fixed number of orbits in which the electrons can be found. The shell closest to the nucleus is of lowest energy. It contains enough orbits to accommodate a maximum of two electrons. The next shell is of slightly higher energy and can hold eight electrons. The third and ensuing shells are of higher energy still. These are all capable of holding eight electrons, although this number can be

Table 1.2 The names and symbols of the elements.

Name	Symbol	Name	Symbol	Name	Symbol	Name	Symbol
Actinium	Ac	Erbium	Er	Neodymium	Nd	Silver	Ag
Aluminium	Al	Europium	Eu	Neon	Ne	Sodium	Na
or aluminum		Fermium	Fm	Neptunium	Np	Strontium	Sr
Americium	Am	Fluorine	F	Nickel	Ni	Sulphur or sulfur	S
Antimony	Sb	Francium	Fr	Niobium	Nb	Tantalum	Ta
Argon	Ar	Gadolinium	Gd	Nitrogen	N	Technetium	Tc
Arsenic	As	Gallium	Ga	Nobelium	No	Tellurium	Te
Astatine	At	Germanium	Ge	Osmium	Os	Terbium	Tb
Barium	Ba	Gold	Au	Oxygen	O	Thallium	Tl
Berkelium	Bk	Hafnium	Hf	Palladium	Pd	Thorium	Th
Beryllium	Be	Helium	He	Phosphorus	P	Thulium	Tm
Bismuth	Bi	Holmium	Ho	Platinum	Pt	Tin	Sn
Boron	B	Hydrogen	H	Plutonium	Pu	Titanium	Ti
Bromine	Br	Indium	In	Polonium	Po	Tungsten	W
Cadmium	Cd	Iodine	I	Potassium	K	Unnilennium	Une
Calcium	Ca	Iridium	Ir	Praseodymium	Pr	Unnilhexium	Unh
Californium	Cf	Iron	Fe	Promethium	Pm	Unniloctium	Uno
Carbon	C	Krypton	Kr	Protactinium	Pa	Unnilpentium	Unp
Cerium	Ce	Lanthanum	La	Radium	Ra	Unnilquadium	Unq
Cesium	Cs	Lawrencium	Lr	Radon	Rn	Unnilseptium	Uns
or caesium		Lead	Pb	Rhenium	Re	Uranium	U
Chlorine	Cl	Lithium	Li	Rhodium	Rh	Vanadium	V
Chromium	Cr	Lutetium	Lu	Rubidium	Rb	Xenon	Xe
Cobalt	Co	Magnesium	Mg	Ruthenium	Ru	Ytterbium	Yb
Copper	Cu	Manganese	Mn	Samarium	Sm	Yttrium	Y
Curium	Cm	Mendelevium	Md	Scandium	Sc	Zinc	Zn
Dysprosium	Dy	Mercury	Hg	Selenium	Se	Zirconium	Zr
Einsteinium	Es	Molybdenum	Mo	Silicon	Si		

Further Information Box

1.1   Isotopes

Atoms are made up of protons, neutrons and electrons (Table 1.1). Protons and neutrons are collectively known as **nucleons**. The total number of nucleons within an atom is referred to as its **mass number** (symbol A). The number of protons it contains is called its **atomic number** (symbol Z). An atom with given values of Z and A is called a nuclide. The full symbol of a nuclide takes the form $_Z^A E$ where E is the elemental symbol (Table 1.2). This is frequently given in an abbreviated form, $^A E$, as Z is implied by E and is hence redundant. Elements that are made up of more than one nuclide are said to be made up of isotopes. Each isotope is a nuclide with a mass number different from the other isotopes. For example, oxygen has three stable isotopes, oxygen-16, oxygen-17 and oxygen-18. These are given the symbols:

$$_8^{16}O \quad _8^{17}O \quad _8^{18}O \text{ or } ^{16}O \quad ^{17}O \quad ^{18}O$$

The only element that is given different names for its isotopes is hydrogen. Its most abundant isotope by far is $_1^1 H$, and this is simply called hydrogen. Its other isotopes ($_1^2 H$ and $_1^3 H$) are called deuterium (symbol D) and tritium (T) respectively.

exceeded. Indeed, the third shell is not completely full until it contains 18 electrons, the next is completely full after 32, and so on. In fact the maximum number of electrons per shell, X, accords with the following expression:

$$X = 2n^2$$

where $n = 1$ for the first shell, 2 for the second, etc.

Using this model, the electronic structure of an atom can be summarised by listing the number of electrons present in each of its shells. The attraction between the nucleus and the electrons ensures that the shells nearest the nucleus are generally filled in preference to those further out. Hence, lithium (atomic number 3) has two electrons in the shell closest to the nucleus and one in the next shell out. That is, it has an electronic structure of 2.1. Similarly, chlorine (atomic number 17) has an electronic structure of 2.8.7 (see Table 1.3 for the electronic structures of the common elements).

Table 1.3 The electronic structures of the more common elements.

Elemental symbol	Electronic structure
H	1
C	2.4
N	2.5
O	2.6
Na	2.8.1
Mg	2.8.2
Al	2.8.3
Si	2.8.4
P	2.8.5
S	2.8.6
Cl	2.8.7
Ar	2.8.8
K	2.8.8.1
Ca	2.8.8.2
Ti	2.8.10.2
Fe	2.8.14.2
Ni	2.8.16.2

The electron-containing shell that is furthest from the nucleus of any given atom is referred to as its **valence shell**, and the electrons it contains are known as **valence electrons**. These are important because when two atoms meet, their valence shell electrons come into closer contact than any other part of the atoms. Indeed, when atoms interact to make compounds they do so by either exchanging or sharing valence electrons (Sections 1.2 and 1.3 respectively). The electrons of an atom that are not in its valence shell are said to be **core electrons**.

1.2   Ions and ionic compounds

Electrons each carry a single negative charge. Protons each carry a single positive charge. Atoms contain equal numbers of electrons and protons. They have no net charge and are therefore electrically neutral.

Atoms become **ions** if they either lose or gain one or more electrons. Ions that are formed by atoms gaining one or more electrons are negatively charged because they contain more electrons than protons. Such ions are called **anions** (pronounced 'an ions'). Conversely, atoms that have lost electrons and therefore have fewer electrons than protons are positively charged. Such ions are known as **cations** (pronounced 'cat ions').

Ions of opposite charge attract one another strongly. Ions of like charge repel one another. An important consequence of this is that anions and cations are found together and in such proportions that the overall material has no net charge. The strong attraction between anions and cations is often referred to as an **ionic bond** and is an example of a **chemical bond**. Collections of atoms (or ions) of different elements, usually present in whole number ratios, that contain chemical bonds between the atoms (or ions) are called **compounds**. If ions are involved, the compounds are called **ionic compounds**.

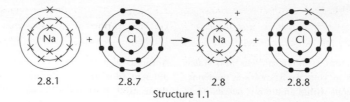

2.8.1   2.8.7   2.8   2.8.8

Structure 1.1

Many ions have eight electrons in their outermost shells. These ions are said to have **complete octets**. Complete octets may be achieved on ion formation from neutral atoms, either by the loss of all valence electrons or by the gain of sufficient electrons to fill the valence shell. Take, for example, the formation of sodium chloride, NaCl (common salt) from atoms of sodium (electronic structure 2.8.1) and atoms of chlorine (electronic structure 2.8.7). This can be represented as in Structure 1.1, where the electrons of the sodium atom are represented by crosses and those of the chlorine atom by dots.

During this process sodium has given up its valence electron, which has been accepted into the valence shell of the chlorine. By doing this, both atoms become ions and have eight electrons in their outermost shells.

The propensity of atoms to gain complete octets on ion formation has important implications. It means that there is a link between the number of valence electrons of an atom and its valency (see Section 1.4).

1.2.1   The structure and properties of ionic compounds

The structures of ionic compounds in the solid state can be extremely complex. However, such structures have in common an alternating pattern of anions and cations. Such an arrangement maximises the interactions between attracting pairs of ions (i.e. those of opposite charge) while minimising those between repelling pairs of ions. Figure 1.1 illustrates this principle with the structure of sodium chloride (one of the simplest structures known).

Many of the properties of ionic compounds can be predicted from a knowledge of the nature of the ionic bond. For example, because the ionic bond is very strong, one could predict that ionic compounds should be hard solids with high melting points. This prediction is borne out in the vast majority of ionic compounds.

The ability of water to dissolve ionic compounds is a vital part of many environmental phenomena, including chemical weathering (Chapter 3, Box 3.3) and many of the nutrient cycles (Chapter 5). Why should water be such a good solvent for so many ionic compounds? To answer this question, a knowledge of the structure of water is needed. This is described in some detail in Section 1.3.2. However, for the purposes of this discussion, a short summary now follows.

Water is made up of molecules (see Section 1.3), each containing a central oxygen atom covalently bonded to two hydrogen atoms. Each molecule is angular in shape and has an uneven distribution of charge such that the oxygen atom is slightly negative and the hydrogens are slightly positive (Figure 1.2).

This uneven distribution of charge means that cations will be attracted to the oxygen atoms of water, while anions will be attracted to the hydrogens. Hence, water is capable of dissolving ionic compounds by breaking up the ionic lattice and producing ions in solution surrounded by water

Figure 1.1 The structure of sodium chloride (NaCl) (sodium ions are shown dark shaded). Note that the rods are drawn between nearest neighbours of opposite charge.

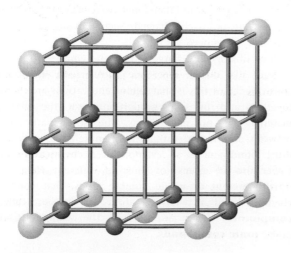

Figure 1.2 The water molecule ($\delta+$ = partial positive charge; $\delta-$ = partial negative charge).

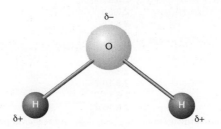

molecules. Water always dissolves a sufficient number of anions to balance the charge of the cations in solution and *vice versa*. This means that anions can be removed from solution only if they are either replaced by other anions or if cations are removed at the same time. Similarly, cations can be removed from solution only if they are either replaced by other cations or if anions are removed at the same time.

It is important to realise that given ions in solution always behave in the same way irrespective of the compounds from which they were dissolved. For example, acid rain can cause aluminium ions to dissolve in water. These then form insoluble aluminium hydroxides on the surface of fish gills, often resulting in the death of the fish. This will happen irrespective of the origin of the aluminium ions (more details of this mode of aluminium toxicity are given in Section 1.6.2).

1.3   Molecules and covalent compounds

Molecules are groups of atoms bonded together by shared electrons. Bonds of this type are called **covalent bonds**. The shared electrons spend most of their time in the region of space between the bonded atoms. It is the mutual attraction between the shared electrons and the nuclei of the atoms involved that binds the atoms together (see Figure 1.3). Compounds that contain atoms bonded together in this way are called **covalent compounds**.

The vast majority of covalent bonds are formed by the sharing of electron pairs between atoms.[1] If the bond consists of one such pair then it is referred to as a **single bond**. Multiple bonds, consisting of either two pairs (**double bonds**) or three pairs (**triple bonds**), are also common. Single bonds are represented by a single line joining the symbols for the atoms bonded together (e.g.

Figure **1.3** A schematic representation of a covalent bond showing the mutual attraction of the nuclei ($\bullet^+$) for the electrons of the bond (e^-). The volume enclosed by the shading on this diagram represents the region of space where the electrons spend 90% of their time.

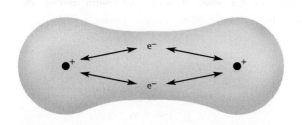

[1] There are molecules that contain covalent bonds that are formed by sharing less than a pair of electrons. Such molecules tend to be highly reactive and are therefore not found in the environment.

H—H), double bonds by a double line (e.g. $O=O$) and so on. It is important to realise that once the bond is formed, it is not possible to determine the origin of a given electron in a bond.

The use of dots and crosses to represent electrons, first encountered in Section 1.2, is also useful when trying to envisage covalent bond formation. Let us apply this approach to the oxygen molecule, O_2 (the vast majority of the oxygen within the atmosphere is found in this form). This can be considered to be formed from two atoms of oxygen (electronic structure 2.6), as in Structure 1.2. The electronic structures given in inverted commas are those envisaged when the shared electrons are counted in the valence shells of both atoms forming the bond.

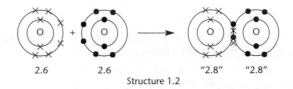

2.6   2.6   "2.8"   "2.8"

Structure 1.2

Note how, by sharing two pairs of electrons, both oxygen atoms have attained complete octets. This is roughly analogous to the idea of atoms attaining complete octets by ion formation, as introduced in Section 1.2. Because two pairs of electrons bond the atoms together in the oxygen molecule, it is often represented thus: $O=O$.

Water (H_2O), arguably the most environmentally important molecule, can also be represented by a dot and cross diagram. Hydrogen atoms *always* share a single pair of electrons when forming covalent bonds. Oxygen atoms, as already discussed, each need to gain two electrons for a complete octet and maximum stability. As shown in Structure 1.3, this can be achieved by sharing two pairs of electrons.

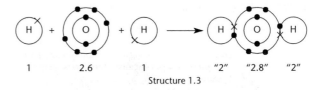

1   2.6   1   "2"   "2.8"   "2"

Structure 1.3

Note that the oxygen atom has two pairs of valence electrons that are not involved in covalent bond formation. Pairs of electrons such as these are called **lone pairs**.

Further illustrations of the use of dot and cross diagrams are given in Box 1.2. Included in this box is a dot and cross description of the bonding in methane, an important 'greenhouse gas' (see Chapters 4 and 15). Methane is an example of an organic compound. More information is given about this very important class of molecular compounds in Box 1.3.

Tool Box

1.2 An example showing the application of dot and cross diagrams to molecules

Dot and cross diagrams can be used to describe the bonding of many environmentally important molecules. For example:

1. Molecular nitrogen (N_2) (which makes up the bulk of the atmosphere) can be represented thus (note only valence shell electrons are shown):

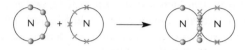

i.e., in shorthand: $N + N \rightarrow N \equiv N$.

2. Methane (CH_4) (an important fuel and major 'greenhouse gas') can be shown thus (again, only valence shell electrons are shown):

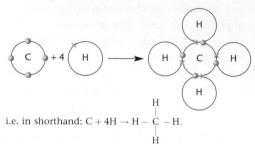

i.e. in shorthand: $C + 4H \rightarrow H - \overset{\displaystyle H}{\underset{\displaystyle H}{C}} - H$.

Further Information Box

1.3 Organic compounds

These are compounds that contain carbon and hydrogen covalently bonded together in molecules. They may also contain atoms of other elements, most commonly oxygen, nitrogen, sulfur, phosphorus or those of group 17 of the Periodic Table (called the halogens).

There are many organic compounds of high environmental significance. These include polyaromatic hydrocarbons (PAHs), polychlorinated biphenyls (PCBs), the vast majority of the components of crude oil, and most pesticides.

There are an enormous number of organic compounds known. This is because of the almost unique ability of carbon to **catenate;** that is to bond with itself to form chains or rings. In order to make sense of the almost bewildering array of organic compounds, they are put into classes that contain similar groups of atoms (such groups of atoms are called functional groups) (see the table below). This is useful, as compounds that contain a given functional group have similar chemical properties.

Some classes of organic compounds

Class	Distinguishing structural features[a]	Example, including name and structural formula, both in full and in short form
Alkane	R'—H	Propane H—C—C—C—H (with H's attached) ($CH_3CH_2CH_3$)
Alkene	R₂C=CR₂	Ethene H₂C=CH₂ (CH_2CH_2)

Class	Distinguishing structural features[a]	Example, including name and structural formula, both in full and in short form
Alkyne	R—C≡C—R	Ethyne H—C≡C—H (CHCH)
Aromatic compounds[b]		Benzene (ring structure) The aromatic C_6H_5 group is called the phenyl group
Alcohol	R—O—H	Methanol (CH_3OH) H—C—O—H The OH group is called the hydroxyl group
Aldehyde	R—C(=O)—H	Ethanal H—C—C—H (with O double bond) ($CH_3C(O)H$)
Ketone	R'—C(=O)—R'	Propanone H—C—C—C—H (with O double bond) ($CH_3C(O)CH_3$) The C=O group is called the carbonyl group

Further Information Box

1.3   (cont.)

Class	Distinguishing structural features[a]	Example, including name and structural formula, both in full and in short form
Carboxylic acid		Ethanoic acid (CH_3COOH) The COOH group is called the carboxyl group
Ether	$R'-O-R'$	Dimethyl ether (CH_3OCH_3)
Esters		Methyl propanoate ($CH_3OC(O)CH_2CH_3$)
Primary amines		Ethylamine ($CH_3CH_2NH_2$) The $-NH_2$ group is called the amino group

[a] Atoms that constitute a functional group are shown in **bold**.
[b] The majority, but not all, of this important group of compounds are based on the benzene ring.
R' = a chain of CH_2 groups of any length, i.e. $(CH_2)_n$ where n = 0 to infinity, terminating in a CH_3 group (such a chain is called an alkyl group).
R = an alkyl group or H.

You may have noticed when referring to the table above that the names of the examples often have common prefixes. Such prefixes indicate the number of carbon atoms in the R group. The remainder of the name, in many cases, indicates the class of compound (e.g. -ol indicates an alcohol, -ene an alkene, etc.). An explanation of the prefix meaning is given below.

A key to the prefixes to the names of organic compounds

Prefix	Number of C atoms in chain	Example
meth-	1	Methane (CH_4)
eth-	2	Ethane (CH_3CH_3)
prop-	3	Propane ($CH_3CH_2CH_3$)
but-	4	Butane ($CH_3CH_2CH_2CH_3$)
pent-	5	Pentane ($CH_3CH_2CH_2CH_2CH_3$)
hex- etc	6	Hexane ($CH_3CH_2CH_2CH_2CH_2CH_3$)

1.3.1   Dative bonds

In the examples considered so far, the electrons that form the bond come from *both* of the atoms that are bonded together. However, single covalent bonds may also be formed in which only *one* of the two atoms involved provides both of the bonding electrons. Such bonds are called **dative bonds** or **coordinate bonds**. Molecules that contain one or more of these bonds are called **complexes**. Compounds that contain complexes are called **coordination compounds**.

In order for a dative bond to form, there must be two atoms, either of which may be present as an ion, an atom or part of a molecule. One of these atoms must have a lone pair. The other atom must have sufficient space in a shell of suitably low energy to accept a share of this pair of electrons. Atoms of this type are called **Lewis acids**, most of which have suitable space in their valence shells.

As we have seen, the water molecule has two lone pairs on its oxygen atom, either of which can be used in the formation of dative bonds. Figure 1.4 illustrates the dative bond forming process with the example of the aluminium hexaquo ion, $[Al(H_2O)_6]^{3+}$, a complex found in highly acidic mine effluent. Here, the Al^{3+} ion (electronic structure 2.8) is using its vacant third shell to accept a share of the lone pairs donated by the water molecules.

Ions or molecules that have lone pairs are called **Lewis bases** or **ligands**. Some molecular ligands have more than one atom with a lone pair. These ligands are called **chelating agents**. The complexes they form are called **chelates**.

There are many natural and synthetic chelating agents of environmental importance. For example, the porphyrin ring system shown in Figure 1.5(a) forms the basis of the active sites in both chlorophyll 'a' (Figure 1.5(b)) and haemoglobin (essential in photosynthesis and mammalian respiration respectively).

The ethylenediaminetetraacetate ion (EDTA) (Figure 1.6(a)) is an example of a synthetic chelating agent. This is added to detergents, often in the form of ethylenediaminetetraacetic acid, to improve their efficiency. As a result, EDTA is now found in rivers and lakes, where it is causing some concern. This is because it forms soluble chelates with toxic metals such as mercury and lead (Figure 1.6(b)) making them available for uptake by living organisms.

Figure 1.4 The aluminium hexaquo ion, $[Al(H_2O)_6]^{3+}$. (The dative bonds are shown by arrows, pointing from the atom providing the electron pair for the bond. Non-dative bonds are represented by solid lines. Dotted lines show the overall octahedral shape of this species).

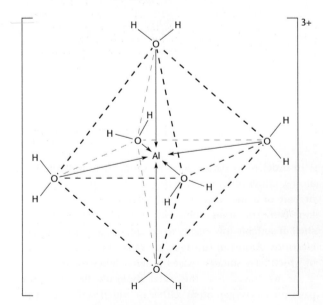

Figure 1.5 (a) The porphyrin ring, a natural chelating agent (lone pairs are shown as:). (b) Chlorophyll 'a', a natural chelate.

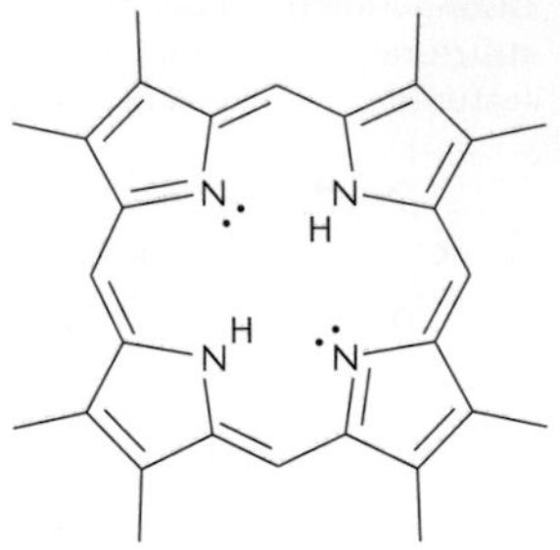

(a)

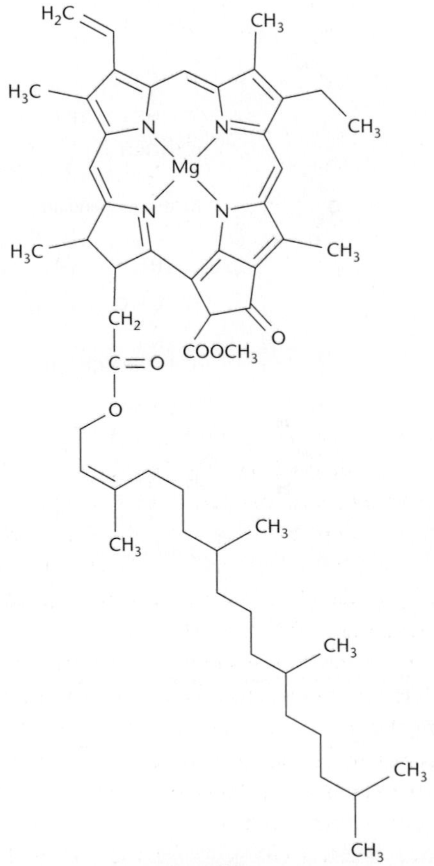

(b)

1.3.2 | Polar molecules

The electrons of a covalent bond between atoms of different elements are *rarely* evenly shared between the bonded atoms. One of the bonded atoms will have a greater attraction for the bonding electrons than the other. Elements whose atoms strongly attract the electrons of a covalent bond are said to be highly

Figure 1.6 (a) The ethylenediaminetetraacetate ion (EDTA). (b) The structure of the lead–EDTA chelate.

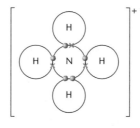

(a)

(b)

1.3.3   Molecular ions

There are molecules that carry a *net* overall charge. These are called **molecular ions**. These must not be confused with polar molecules, which merely have an uneven distribution of charge.

Molecular ions are either positively charged (cationic molecules) or negatively charged (anionic molecules). They are always found in association with ions of opposite charge in such proportions that the *overall material has no net charge*. Both anionic and cationic molecules are common in the environment; examples include CO_3^{2-} (the carbonate anion), SO_4^{2-} (the sulfate anion), NO_3^- (the nitrate anion) and NH_4^+ (the ammonium cation).

Molecular ions, like other molecules, can be represented by dot and cross diagrams (Figure 1.7).

1.3.4   Bonds within and between molecules

In addition to the strong covalent bonds *within* molecules (called **intramolecular bonds**), there are attractions between molecules in virtually all covalent compounds. These attractions are known as **intermolecular attractions**. With the exception of ionic bonds between anionic and cationic *molecules*, intermolecular attractions are weak.

electronegative. The most electronegative elements are, in order of descending electronegativity, fluorine, oxygen, nitrogen, chlorine and bromine. Molecules that involve the covalent bonding of atoms of these elements to atoms of less electronegative elements will be significantly **polar**. This means that they will have an uneven distribution of charge.

With this in mind, let us return to the water molecule and consider it in more detail. As seen in Figure 1.2, this is in fact angular in shape. It has an HOH angle of 104°30'. Oxygen is very much more electronegative than hydrogen. Hence, the oxygen atom draws the electrons in the two O—H bonds towards itself. As a result, the oxygen atom has a partial negative charge (given the symbol $\delta-$), and the hydrogen atoms have partial positive charges ($\delta+$).

As seen in Section 1.2.1, and elsewhere in this book, the polar nature of water has important environmental consequences.

The environmental properties of many other molecules are profoundly affected by their degree of polarity. For example, carbon dioxide (CO_2) and chlorofluorocarbons (CFCs) are polar molecules that are found in the atmosphere. It is the polar nature of their bonds that allows them to absorb infrared radiation, causing them to act as greenhouse gases (Chapters 4 and 15).

Figure 1.7 Dot and cross diagrams for (a) the ammonium ion (NH_4^+) and (b) the carbonate anion (CO_3^{2-}).

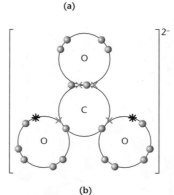

+ Valence electrons of N and H are shown as ◉ and × respectively. Note that although one of the N–H bonds is represented differently from the other three to show the origin of the electrons, they are in fact identical

(a)

2− Valence electrons of oxygen and carbon are represented by ◉ and × respectively and ✳ represents the electrons present by virtue of the overall 2− charge. Note that all of the C–O bonds are in fact indistinguishable from each other, and it is not possible to locate the position of the charges

(b)

Many compounds that contain small discrete molecules are either liquids or gases at normal temperatures and pressures, because the intermolecular attractions are easy to overcome. Examples of such compounds include carbon dioxide, water and methane.

There are solids that are made up of giant molecules that extend in all directions throughout the piece of material concerned. These are called three-dimensional network macromolecular solids, because each fragment of such a material contains one molecule *only*; it can have *only* intramolecular bonds. Hence, crushing, melting or dissolving these materials involves the breaking of strong bonds. Such materials are therefore hard and have high melting points and, unless they react with water, dissolve in it to a very limited extent. An example of such a material is silicon dioxide, otherwise known as silica. This is the material that most sand is made of. It has a giant molecular structure made up of SiO_4 units linked together in a three-dimensional network via shared oxygen atoms (Figure 1.8). As a result of its structure, it is highly resistant to weathering (Chapter 3).

There is one type of intermolecular attraction between molecules that, while still weak, is much stronger than others. This is the **hydrogen bond**. Hydrogen bonding occurs whenever hydrogen atoms are directly bonded to highly electronegative atoms in molecules that contain atoms with lone pairs of electrons. Hence, hydrogen bonding occurs in water.

Intramolecular hydrogen bonding is also known. For example, it is responsible for many of the structural details of DNA, the molecule that carries the genetic code (Figure 1.9 and see Chapter 6).

Figure 1.9 Examples of intermolecular and intramolecular hydrogen bonding. (a) Water, showing intermolecular hydrogen bonds (dotted lines); (b) DNA, showing intramolecular hydrogen bonds (dotted lines). (From *Biology: The Unity and Diversity of Life*, 3rd edition, by C. Starr and R. Taggart. © 1984. Reprinted with permission of Brooks/Cole Publishing, a division of Thomson Learning.)

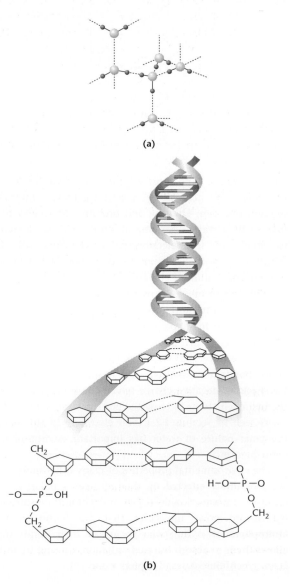

Figure 1.8 The structure of silicon dioxide (β-tridymite form). The silicon atoms are represented by the small black spheres (from Wells, 1962). Note that each silicon atom is bonded to four oxygen atoms by four single bonds (represented by rods) and that each oxygen atom is bonded, by single bonds, to two silicon atoms. This structure does not stop at the edges of the diagram but continues throughout the crystal of silicon dioxide. For clarity, bonds between atoms at the edges of this diagram and those just out of the picture have been omitted.

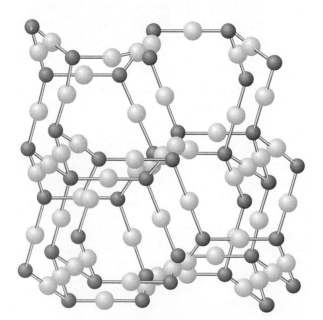

1.4   Valency and the Periodic Table of the elements

Valency is the combining power of an atom. In order to visualise this you may find it useful to think of atoms as having hands. A monovalent atom will have one hand, a divalent two, a trivalent three, etc. Whenever possible an atom will combine with other atoms so that it can use all of its hands to hold the hands of other atoms. This concept is useful as it allows predictions to be made about the ratios in which atoms will combine. These ratios are referred to as **stoichiometric ratios**.

Let us look at two examples. The first involves hydrogen and chlorine. Both of these have valencies of one. The compound they form, hydrogen chloride, is an acidic polluting gas that is produced when certain plastics are burnt. From a knowledge of the valencies of its constituent elements, we would expect it to have an $H:Cl$ ratio of $1:1$, which it does, as indicated in its formula HCl. The second example involves oxygen. This has a valency of two. It is therefore expected to combine with hydrogen to form hydrogen oxide with an $H:O$ ratio of $2:1$. This expectation is borne out: hydrogen oxide (better known as water!) has the formula H_2O.

We have already seen that in many compounds, be they covalent or ionic, the atoms or ions they contain have complete octets. To achieve these octets, the atoms of an element must, in general, either gain, lose or share electrons. The number of electrons that must be gained, lost or shared in this way is the same as the valency of the atom. There is therefore a link between the number of electrons in the valence shell of an atom and its valency. With the exception of hydrogen (which always has a valency of one), the valency (V) of an atom in compounds in which it has a complete octet is related to the number of electrons in its valence shell (N) by one of the following expressions:

$$V = N \text{ (as in sodium)}$$

or

$$V = 8 - N \text{ (as in chlorine)}$$

The **Periodic Table** is a means of listing the elements in such a way as to group together elements with similar properties. These properties include valency. This table is constructed by listing the elements in order of increasing atomic number, a new row being started whenever a new shell is occupied for the first time. By doing this, elements with the same numbers of valence electrons, and hence similar properties, are listed in vertical columns called **groups** (Table 1.4).

There is a relationship between the valency of an element and the group of the Periodic Table in which it is found. This may be expressed as follows:

1 For elements of groups 1 and 2, the valency is the same as the group number.
2 For elements of groups 13 to 18 inclusive, the valency is frequently given by one of the following expressions:

$$V = X - 10$$

or

$$V = 8 - (X - 10)$$

where V = valency and X = the group number of the element concerned.

Unfortunately, this convenient idea is a little too good to be entirely true! This is because there are many elements that form compounds in which they do not have complete octets. This is particularly true of elements in groups 4 to 11 inclusive. Many of these exhibit variable valency; some have such variable valencies as to make the concept useless as a predictive tool. What is worse, many of the elements of groups 13 to 18 that normally have predictable valencies will form compounds in which their valency is far from predictable.

Nonetheless, valency is a useful idea as most of the environmentally common elements have predictable valencies. Figure 1.10 shows the common valencies of the elements.

1.5   Oxidation states

The **oxidation state** of an element is either the actual charge on its atoms, or a notional charge. The oxidation state of an element in an elemental form (i.e. not in a compound) is zero. For a monoatomic ion, the oxidation state is the actual charge on the ion. For example, the chloride ion (Cl^-) has an oxidation state of -1 and the sodium ion (Na^+) has an oxidation state of $+1$.

In compounds (e.g. water, H_2O) or molecular ions (e.g. sulfate, SO_4^{2-}), the oxidation states of the constituent elements are notional charges based on the charge distribution that would occur if the electrons involved in bonding were placed on the most electronegative atoms present. In such cases, oxidation states are calculated using the following expression:

$$\Sigma o = c \qquad (1.1)$$

where Σo = the sum of the oxidation states of all of the atoms present and c = the overall charge of the compound or ion.

Like valencies, the oxidation states of some elements are essentially fixed. Table 1.5 lists these elements and their oxidation states.

Table 1.4 The Periodic Table of the elements.

Legend:

1	← Atomic number
H	
1.008	← Relative atomic mass (i.e. molar mass)

Group numbers (shown in bold italics)

Period	*1*	*2*	*3*	*4*	*5*	*6*	*7*	*8*	*9*	*10*	*11*	*12*	*13*	*14*	*15*	*16*	*17*	*18*
1	1 H 1.008																	2 He 4.00
2	3 Li 6.94	4 Be 9.01											5 B 10.81	6 C 12.01	7 N 14.01	8 O 16.00	9 F 19.00	10 Ne 20.18
3	11 Na 22.99	12 Mg 24.31											13 Al 26.98	14 Si 28.09	15 P 30.97	16 S 32.06	17 Cl 35.45	18 Ar 39.95
4	19 K 39.10	20 Ca 40.08	21 Sc 44.96	22 Ti 47.90	23 V 50.94	24 Cr 52.00	25 Mn 54.94	26 Fe 55.85	27 Co 58.93	28 Ni 58.71	29 Cu 63.54	30 Zn 65.37	31 Ga 69.72	32 Ge 72.59	33 As 74.92	34 Se 78.96	35 Br 79.91	36 Kr 83.80
5	37 Rb 85.47	38 Sr 87.62	39 Y 88.91	40 Zr 91.22	41 Nb 92.91	42 Mo 95.94	43 Tc 98.91	44 Ru 101.07	45 Rh 102.91	46 Pd 106.4	47 Ag 107.87	48 Cd 112.40	49 In 114.82	50 Sn 118.69	51 Sb 121.75	52 Te 127.60	53 I 126.90	54 Xe 131.30
6	55 Cs 132.91	56 Ba 137.34	57 La 138.91	72 Hf 178.49	73 Ta 180.95	74 W 183.85	75 Re 186.2	76 Os 190.2	77 Ir 192.2	78 Pt 195.09	79 Au 196.97	80 Hg 200.59	81 Tl 204.37	82 Pb 207.19	83 Bi 208.98	84 Po 210	85 At 210	86 Rn 222
7	87 Fr 223	88 Ra 226.03	89 Ac 227.03															

Lanthanides (see below)

Actinides (see below)

Lanthanides:

58 Ce 140.12	59 Pr 140.91	60 Nd 144.24	61 Pm 146.92	62 Sm 150.35	63 Eu 151.96	64 Gd 157.25	65 Tb 158.92	66 Dy 162.50	67 Ho 164.93	68 Er 167.26	69 Tm 168.93	70 Yb 173.04	71 Lu 174.97

Actinides:

90 Th 232.04	91 Pa 231.04	92 U 238.03	93 Np 237.05	94 Pu 239.05	95 Am 241.06	96 Cm 247.07	97 Bk 249.08	98 Cf 251.08	99 Es 254.09	100 Fm 257.10	101 Md 258.10	102 No 255	103 Lr 257

Note that the members of groups 3 to 12 inclusive are known collectively as the transition metals.

Figure 1.10 The common valencies of the elements (group numbers are shown in circles).

(1)	(2)													H 1	He 0					(13)	(14)	(15)	(16)	(17)	(18)
Li 1	Be 2																			B 3	C 4,2	N 1,2,3 4,5	O 2	F 1	Ne 0
Na 1	Mg 2																			Al 3	Si 4	P 3,5	S 2,4,6	Cl 1,2,3,4 5,6,7	Ar 0
		(3)	(4)	(5)	(6)	(7)	(8)	(9)	(10)	(11)	(12)														
K 1	Ca 2	Sc 3	Ti 2,3,4	V 2,3,4 5	Cr 2,3,6	Mn 2,3,4 6,7	Fe 2,3,6	Co 2,3	Ni 2,3	Cu 1,2	Zn 2									Ga 3	Ge 4	As 3,5	Se 2,4,6	Br 1,2,3 4,5,6	Kr 0
Rb 1	Sr 2	Y 3	Zr 2,3,4	Nb 3,5	Mo 2,3,4 5,6	Tc 7	Ru 3,4,5 6,8	Rh 2,3,4	Pd 2,4	Ag 1	Cd 2									In 1,3	Sn 2,4	Sb 3,5	Te 2,4,6	I 1,3,5 7	Xe 0
Cs 1	Ba 2	La 3	Hf 4	Ta 5	W 2,4,5 6	Re 2,4,5 6,7	Os 2,3,4 6,8	Ir 2,3,4 6	Pt 2,4,6	Au 1,3	Hg 1,2									Tl 1,3	Pb 2,4	Bi 3,5	Po 2,4	At —	Rn 0
Fr 1	Ra 2	Ac 3																							

Ce 3,4	Pr 3,4	Nd 3	Pm 3	Sm 2,3	Eu 2,3	Gd 3	Tb 3,4	Dy 3	Ho 3	Er 3	Tm 2,3	Yb 2,3	Lu 3
Th 3,4	Pa 4,5	U 3,4 5,6	Np 3,4,5 6	Pu 3,4,5 6	Am 3,4,5 6	Cm 3	Bk 3,4	Cf 3	Es 3	Fm 3	Md 3	No —	Lr —

By way of example let us use Table 1.5 and Equation 1.1 to calculate the oxidation states of sulfur in some of its environmentally important forms (we will return to these in Chapter 5, Section 5.5). The results of this exercise are give in Table 1.6.

Oxidation states are usually either quoted in parentheses after the name of the element concerned or superscripted to the right-hand side of the elemental symbol. For example, iron in the plus three oxidation state may be represented as either iron(III) or as Fe^{III}.

Table 1.5 The elements with essentially invariant oxidation states in their compounds.

Element	Oxidation state
Elements of group 1[a]	+1
Elements of group 2[a]	+2
Hydrogen in compounds with non-metals	+1
Hydrogen in compounds with metals	−1
Fluorine	−1
Oxygen	−2[b] unless combined with F or −1 in peroxides (O_2^{2-}) or −1/2 in superoxides (O_2^-) or −1/3 in ozonides (O_3^-)

[a] See Table 1.4 for a listing of the elements in these groups.
[b] −2 is by far the most common oxidation state for oxygen in compounds.

Table 1.6 Calculation of the oxidation states (OS) of sulfur in some of its environmentally significant forms.

Form	Where found	Oxidation state calculation
S_8	Crust	Elemental form OS = 0
SO_2	Atmosphere	$OS + (2 \times -2) = 0 = OS - 4$ $\therefore$ OS = 0 + 4 = 4
SO_3	Atmosphere	$OS + (3 \times -2) = 0 = OS - 6$ $\therefore$ OS = 0 + 6 = 6
SO_3^{2-}	Atmosphere and crust	$OS + (3 \times -2) = -2 = OS - 6$ $\therefore$ OS = 6 − 2 = 4
SO_4^{2-}	Atmosphere and crust	$OS + (4 \times -2) = -2 = OS - 8$ $\therefore$ OS = 8 − 2 = 6
S^{2-}	Crust	OS = −2
H_2S	Atmosphere	$OS + (2 \times 1) = 0 = OS + 2$ $\therefore$ OS = −2

1.6   Compounds, mixtures, chemical species and chemical reactions

Collections of atoms of different elements that are bonded together by chemical bonds are called **compounds**. Hence, a chemical reaction simply involves the breaking and making of chemical bonds. For a net change to have occurred, the atoms must be bound to different partners before and after the reaction. Collections of different compounds and/or elements that are not chemically bonded together are called **mixtures**.

Another term frequently used when talking about chemical reactions of environmental significance is **chemical species** (or simply species). This refers to an atom, ion or molecule with identifiable chemical properties. The collection of chemical species in which an element is found is referred to as its **chemical speciation** (or just speciation). For example, the speciation of sulfur in the atmosphere is extremely complex (Chapters 5 and 15). The major chemical species involved are sulfur dioxide (SO_2), sulfur trioxide (SO_3), sulfate ($SO_4{}^{2-}$), hydrogen sulfide (H_2S) and dimethyl sulfide ((CH_3)$_2$S). During chemical reactions, the atoms of the elements present change from one chemical species to another, changing the elements' speciation.

In this section, we concentrate on the symbolism and concepts used to describe and understand the nature of chemical species and their interactions. This is important because the bulk of matter in the environment is found as mixtures, the properties of which are largely determined by those of their individual constituent species.

1.6.1   Chemical formulae and chemical equations

Compounds are represented by **chemical formulae**. These formulae are made up of the symbols of the elements that are bonded together in the compound in question. For example, water is made up of molecules, each one of which contains one oxygen atom covalently bonded to two hydrogen atoms; its formula is therefore H_2O. In this formula, the 2 shows that there are twice as many atoms of hydrogen present as there are oxygen atoms in any sample of pure water.

Chemical reactions are represented by **chemical equations**. These equations use elemental symbols and/or chemical formulae to show the proportions in which chemicals react. For example, methane (CH_4) (the principal component of natural gas) on burning in air undergoes a reaction with oxygen molecules (O_2) (commonly called, simply, oxygen). This is represented by the following equation:

$$1CH_4 + 2O_2 \rightarrow 1CO_2 + 2H_2O$$

The components in front of the arrow are called the **reactants**, while those after the arrow are called the

products. The numbers in front of the formulae are coefficients, known as **coefficients of stoichiometry**. These show the proportions in which the different components react. In this case, for every molecule of methane burnt, two molecules of oxygen are consumed, while one molecule of carbon dioxide (CO_2) and two molecules of water are produced. It is usual to omit coefficients of stoichiometry of one, hence the above equation is usually represented thus:

$$CH_4 + 2O_2 \rightarrow CO_2 + 2H_2O$$

All chemical equations should be balanced. A chemical equation is balanced when there are as many atoms of reactants represented as there are atoms of products and when the net electrical charge on one side of the arrow is the same as on the other. In the above example, on either side of the arrow, carbon (C) appears once, while hydrogen (H) and oxygen (O) appear four times. The total charge on either side of the arrow is the same (in this case, zero). Hence, the equation is balanced.

Symbols representing the physical state of the reactants and products are frequently included in chemical equations. To continue with the current example, methane (a gas) reacts with oxygen (a gas) to give carbon dioxide (a gas) and water (a gas at the temperatures of combustion). This information can be conveyed in the chemical equation using the symbol g for a gas, thus:

$$CH_{4(g)} + 2O_{2(g)} \rightarrow CO_{2(g)} + 2H_2O_{(g)}$$

Other symbols used in this way are s for solid, l for liquid, c for a condensed phase (i.e. l or s), and aq for solution in water (i.e. aqueous solutions).

In a chemical reaction, the reactants react to form the products. Such reactions are reversible. This means that the products react together to produce the reactants. Let us write a general equation to represent the reaction between A and B to form C and D:

$$A + B \rightarrow C + D$$

From what has been said above the reaction represented by the following equation also occurs:

$$C + D \rightarrow A + B$$

So overall:

$$A + B \rightleftharpoons C + D$$

The extent to which the reverse reaction occurs varies enormously from one reaction to another (a point considered in detail in Chapter 2, Section 2.2). When oxygen and methane react on burning to produce water and carbon dioxide, the extent of the reverse reaction is negligible. Hence, it is legitimate to use a single arrow in the equation representing this reaction. On the other hand, the reaction between water (H_2O) and dissolved carbon dioxide (CO_2) to produce carbonic acid (H_2CO_3)

proceeds at an appreciable rate in both directions and is hence best represented thus:

$$CO_{2(aq)} + H_2O_{(l)} \rightleftharpoons H_2CO_{3(aq)}$$

1.6.2   Environmentally important chemical reactions

The major classes of chemical reaction of environmental importance are discussed below. It should be realised that it is possible for a given reaction to fall into more than one class.

Acid–base reactions

Arguably the most useful theory of acids and bases to the environmental scientist is that originally proposed by Brønsted and Lowry. The Brønsted–Lowry theory defines an **acid** as a donor of H^+ ions and a **base** as an acceptor of H^+ ions. As the hydrogen atom consists of a proton and an electron only, the H^+ ion is in fact a proton. Hence, an acid–base reaction is a proton transfer reaction.

Let us define an acid to be HA and a base to be B. The reaction between them can be represented thus:

$$HA + B \rightarrow A^- + HB^+$$

Some of the HB^+ molecules so produced will donate their protons to A^-; thus:

$$A^- + HB^+ \rightarrow HA + B$$

Hence, A^- is a base and HB^+ is an acid. The overall reaction between HA and B can therefore be represented as:

$$\underset{\text{acid 1}}{HA} + \underset{\text{base 1}}{B} \rightleftharpoons \underset{\text{base 2}}{A^-} + \underset{\text{acid 2}}{HB^+}$$

The double arrow indicates that the reaction proceeds in both directions. Base 2 (A^-) is referred to as the conjugate base of acid 1 (HA); acid 2 (HB^+) is called the conjugate acid of base 1 (B).

Let us look at some real examples. Nitric acid (HNO_3) is a component of acid rain. Its reaction with water (H_2O) can be written as:

$$\underset{\text{acid 1}}{HNO_3} + \underset{\text{base 1}}{H_2O} \rightleftharpoons \underset{\text{base 2}}{NO_3^-} + \underset{\text{acid 2}}{H_3O^+}$$

where NO_3^- is called the nitrate ion and H_3O^+ the hydronium ion.

HNO_3 is a very good proton donor (a good proton donor is called a **strong acid**). NO_3^- is a very poor proton acceptor (a poor proton acceptor is called a **weak base**). As a result, the forward (i.e. left to right) reaction represented in the above equation will predominate over the reverse reaction (right to left). It may therefore be represented thus:

$$HNO_3 + H_2O \rightarrow NO_3^- + H_3O^+$$

Nitrous acid (HNO_2) is another, but very minor, component of acid rain. It is a much weaker acid than HNO_3 and as a result will react with water as follows:

$$HNO_2 + H_2O \rightleftharpoons NO_2^- + H_3O^+$$

All of the acids referred to so far are capable of donating one proton per molecule and are therefore called monoprotic acids. Diprotic and triprotic acids can donate two and three protons respectively.

Water is not the only base encountered in the environment. However, the vast majority of environmentally important acid–base reactions occur in aqueous solution.

The main acidic component of most acid rain is sulfuric acid (H_2SO_4) (see Chapter 15, Section 15.2.2). It reacts with calcium carbonate ($CaCO_3$), a major constituent of limestones (including chalk) and marbles (Chapter 3, Section 3.1.3), causing the erosion of these rocks. The reaction concerned can be represented by the following equations:

$$H_2SO_{4(aq)} + 2H_2O_{(l)} \rightarrow 2H_3O^+_{(aq)} + SO_4^{2-}_{(aq)}$$

$$2H_3O^+_{(aq)} + CaCO_{3(s)} \rightarrow Ca^{2+}_{(aq)} + CO_{2(g)} + 3H_2O_{(l)}$$

The net reaction is the conversion of solid calcium carbonate to a gas (CO_2), a liquid (H_2O) and an aqueous solution of calcium sulfate, thus:

$$H_2SO_{4(aq)} + CaCO_{3(s)} \rightarrow$$
$$Ca^{2+}_{(aq)} + SO_4^{2-}_{(aq)} + CO_{2(g)} + H_2O_{(l)}$$

Note that calcium sulfate, $CaSO_4$, in solution can be shown as $Ca^{2+}_{(aq)} + SO_4^{2-}_{(aq)}$.

So far, we have considered water as a base. Water can also act as an acid. This is illustrated by its reaction with ammonia (NH_3), a gas which can be used as a nitrogenous fertiliser. The ammonia is so soluble in water that it can be directly injected into agricultural land without significant losses. This reaction is represented by the following equation:

$$NH_3 + H_2O \rightleftharpoons OH^- + NH_4^+$$

Note that the ammonium ion, NH_4^+, is a stronger acid than water, H_2O, and the hydroxide ion, OH^-, is a stronger base than ammonia, NH_3. Hence, the reverse reaction predominates as indicated by the differential length of the arrows.

Chemical species that are capable of acting as either an acid or a base depending on the nature of the other reactants are said to be **amphoteric**.

Table 1.7 shows some environmentally important acids and bases, listing them in order of their strength.

The reaction between an acid and a base is called a **neutralisation** reaction. An ionic compound that is

Table 1.7 Some environmentally important conjugate acids and bases listed in order of their strength (in water) (not to scale).

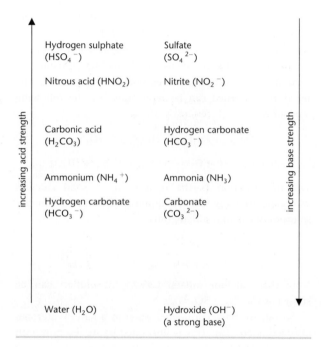

	Acids	Bases
strong acids	Sulfuric acid (H_2SO_4)	Hydrogen sulfate (HSO_4^-)
	Nitric acid (HNO_3)	Nitrate (NO_3^-)
	Hydronium ion (H_3O^+)	Water (H_2O)
increasing acid strength	Hydrogen sulphate (HSO_4^-)	Sulfate (SO_4^{2-})
	Nitrous acid (HNO_2)	Nitrite (NO_2^-)
	Carbonic acid (H_2CO_3)	Hydrogen carbonate (HCO_3^-)
	Ammonium (NH_4^+)	Ammonia (NH_3)
	Hydrogen carbonate (HCO_3^-)	Carbonate (CO_3^{2-})
	Water (H_2O)	Hydroxide (OH^-) (a strong base)

formed as a result of an aqueous neutralisation reaction is called a **salt**.

Environmentally important aspects of acid–base theory are discussed further in Chapter 2, Section 2.2 and in Box 1.4.

Precipitation reactions

These are reactions that occur in solution in which one or more of the products are insoluble in the solvent. Almost without exception, environmentally important reactions of this type involve water as the solvent.

By way of illustration, let us consider one of the impacts of acid rain. Many lakes and rivers affected by acid rain are entirely devoid of fish. This is thought to be caused primarily by a precipitation reaction. The aluminium concentration in the waters of acidified lakes and rivers can be relatively high compared with that in

unaffected but otherwise similar water bodies. If this acidified water meets with a source of OH^- ions the following reaction will take place:

$$Al^{3+}_{(aq)} + 3OH^-_{(aq)} \rightarrow Al(OH)_{3(s)}$$

The gills of fish represent such a source of OH^- ions. A gelatinous precipitate of aluminium hydroxide will therefore build up on the gill membranes, causing the fish to die of asphyxia.

The acid rain phenomenon is returned to in Chapter 15, Section 15.2.2, where it is dealt with in some detail.

Reduction–oxidation (or redox) reactions

Reactions that involve the complete transfer of one or more electrons from one chemical species to another are called reduction–oxidation reactions, or **redox reactions** for short. The species that gains the electrons is said to be *reduced* during this process, while the species that gives up electrons is *oxidised*. **Reducing agents** (also called reductants) are species that readily give up electrons, while **oxidising agents** (alternatively called oxidants) readily accept them.

Redox reactions are central to many environmentally significant systems. For example, they occur during the vital process of aerobic photosynthesis.

Aerobic photosynthesis enables green plants (and cyanobacteria) to use sunlight in the conversion of carbon dioxide (CO_2) and water (H_2O) into carbohydrate (CH_2O) and oxygen (O_2). This is responsible for the production of about 1×10^{17} grams of organic matter per year and the formation of virtually all of the oxygen present in the atmosphere. It is also one of the major sinks of carbon dioxide, a major greenhouse gas (see Chapter 15, Section 15.2.3).

Aerobic photosynthesis may be represented thus:

$$2H_2O^{-II} + C^{IV}O_2 \xrightarrow{\text{sunlight}} C^0H_2O + H_2O + O_2{}^0$$

where the superscripts indicate oxidation states (these have been calculated as outlined in Section 1.5).

It is important to realise that redox reactions involve the exchange of electrons; there is no net change in either the number of atoms or the net charge on either side of the arrow.

At first glance it is not apparent which of the species on the left-hand side of the arrow has been oxidised and which has been reduced. A close look at the oxidation states of the elements present on either side of the arrow is of considerable help in making this plain. This is because reduction is always accompanied by a *decrease* in oxidation state, while oxidation results in an *increase* in oxidation state.

During the aerobic photosynthesis reaction the oxygen that is originally present in water becomes molecular

1.4   The pH scale of acidity

The addition of an acid (HA) that is a stronger acid than H_2O to water will increase the concentration of the hydronium ion (H_3O^+). The reaction responsible for this is shown below:

$$HA + H_2O \rightarrow H_3O^+ + A^- \qquad (a)$$

The addition of a base (B) that is a stronger base than H_2O to water will increase the concentration of the hydroxide ion (OH^-). The reaction responsible for this is shown below:

$$B + H_2O \rightarrow OH^- + HB^+ \qquad (b)$$

Bases such as B are called alkalis and their aqueous solutions are said to be alkaline.

The pH scale is a scale of acidity. pH is defined according to the following expression:[1]

$$pH = -\log_{10}[H^+] \qquad (c)$$

where $[H^+] =$ the hydrogen ion (or, more precisely, the hydronium ion, H_3O^+) concentration in $mol\,dm^{-3}$ (see Box 2.4 for an explanation of these units). Note that p is the symbol used to stand for $-\log_{10}$; this will be used again in Chapter 2.

In the absence of an acid such as HA, or an alkali such as B, $[H_3O^+] = 1 \times 10^{-7}\,mol\,dm^{-3}$. Hence, the pH of pure water $= -\log(1 \times 10^{-7}) = 7$. Additions of acids of the type HA will increase the $[H_3O^+]$ and decrease the pH of the solution. Adding an alkali to water will increase the hydroxide ion concentration, which will decrease the hydronium ion concentration because of the reaction represented below.

$$H_3O^+ + OH^- \rightarrow 2H_2O$$

[1] Strictly speaking, $pH = -\log_{10}\{H^+\}$, where $\{H^+\} =$ the activity of H^+ (see Chapter 2, Box 2.5); however, as $\{H^+\}$ very closely approximates to $[H^+]$, Equation (c) is valid for most applications.

Hence, adding an alkali to an aqueous solution will increase its pH.

The table below shows the pH scale (note the scale is continuous, example concentrations have been taken for illustration).

$[H_3O^+]$ /mol dm^{-3}	pH	Examples
1	0	
1×10^{-1}	1	
1×10^{-2}	2	
1×10^{-3}	3	
1×10^{-4}	4	
1×10^{-5}	5	← Surface water polluted by acid rain ← Unpolluted rain
1×10^{-6}	6	
1×10^{-7}	7	← Pure water neutral ← Blood
1×10^{-8}	8	
1×10^{-9}	9	} Sea water
1×10^{-10}	10	
1×10^{-11}	11	
1×10^{-12}	12	
1×10^{-13}	13	
1×10^{-14}	14	

(increasing acidity upward, increasing alkalinity downward)

oxygen. In so doing, it changes its oxidation state from $-II$ to 0. While this is occurring, the carbon, originally present as carbon(IV) in carbon dioxide, becomes carbon(0) and is incorporated into the carbohydrate. It is now clear that the species being reduced (i.e. the one gaining electrons) is carbon dioxide, while water is the species being oxidised (i.e. the one losing electrons).

You will have noticed that in this example reduction and oxidation occur simultaneously. This is a universal observation. It is important to realise that these processes *cannot* happen independently. This is because it is the oxidation reaction that provides the electrons for the reduction reaction. Hence, reduction and oxidation reactions are referred to as half reactions (or half-cell reactions). The equations that represent them are called half equations (or half-cell equations).

Using a half-cell equation, the reduction of carbon dioxide can be represented by:

$$CO_2 + 4H^+ + 4e^- \rightarrow CH_2O + H_2O$$

Similarly, the oxidation of water can be represented thus:

$$2H_2O \xrightarrow{\text{sunlight}} 4e^- + O_2 + 4H^+$$

Adding these two half equations yields:

$$2H_2O + CO_2 + 4H^+ + 4e^- \xrightarrow{\text{sunlight}}$$
$$CH_2O + H_2O + 4e^- + O_2 + 4H^+$$

The electrons and hydrogen ions (H^+) can be cancelled as there are as many produced as consumed. Doing this cancellation generates the overall equation for photosynthesis:

$$2H_2O + CO_2 \rightarrow CH_2O + H_2O + O_2$$

The notion of half-cell reactions will be returned to in Chapter 2 (Section 2.1), where they will be used to predict the direction in which a redox reaction will occur in the absence of external stimuli.

There are many other examples of redox reactions of environmental importance and we will encounter many of these during the course of this book.

Complex formation reactions (also called complexation reactions)

These are reactions that result in the formation of dative bonds (Section 1.3.1). As a dative bond forms between a Lewis acid and a Lewis base, complex formation reactions may be considered as Lewis acid–base reactions. They are of considerable environmental significance. For example, many metal ions readily form complexes with both natural and synthetic ligands. Such reactions can radically alter the availability of metals to organisms. This is often because the solubility of the metal changes markedly on complexation. For instance, copper, a vital micronutrient, is often in short supply in peat-based soils. This is because it is rendered unavailable by complexation with the humic material in the peat (see Chapter 3, Section 3.2 for more information on peat and humic materials).

Hydrolysis reactions

These are reactions that involve water as one of the reactants. Hydrolysis reactions involving acidic solutions are called acid hydrolysis reactions. Similarly, base hydrolysis reactions are those involving basic solutions (basic solutions are said to be alkaline). As we will see, hydrolysis reactions are very common in the environment. They are responsible for a number of highly diverse and important phenomena. For example, they are responsible for much of the chemical weathering of rocks (Chapter 3, Section 3.2) and the degradation of pesticides.

Free radical reactions

Most molecules contain an even number of electrons, which behave as if they are present as pairs. For example, using ovals to enclose pairs of electrons, a molecule of water may be represented as in Structure 1.4.

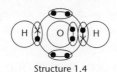

Structure 1.4

Structure 1.5

A fragment of a molecule that contains one or more unpaired electrons is called a **free radical**, or simply a radical. This is exemplified by the hydroxyl radical (OH), shown in Structure 1.5.

Radicals may be formed when a molecule breaks up on collision with another molecule or atom at high speed (a thermal reaction) or when it absorbs light (a photochemical reaction). Such fragments can also be formed when a molecule reacts with a species that has been energised (excited) in a previous interaction with light. For example, in the atmosphere molecules of the gas ozone (O_3) can absorb light (symbolised hv) to produce excited oxygen atoms:

$$O_3 + hv(\lambda < 310\,\text{nm}) \rightarrow O_2^* + O^*$$

where λ represents the wavelength of the light and asterisks denote excited states.

These may then fragment water, producing hydroxyl radicals:

$$O^* + H_2O \rightarrow 2OH$$

Most free radicals are highly reactive and are therefore generally found at low concentrations in the environment. Despite this, they are of considerable significance, particularly in atmospheric chemistry (Chapter 4, Box 4.2 and Chapter 15). This is primarily because most reactions that involve a free radical as a reactant also generate another as a product. The radical produced is then available to react with another molecule, and so on, producing a chain reaction. By this means, one free radical molecule or atom may cause many reactions to occur, consuming numerous molecules and producing many others in the process.

1.7   The atomic nucleus and nuclear reactions

The nucleus of any atom is made up of nucleons (protons and neutrons) (see Table 1.1). Processes that lead to a change in the number, nature or energy of these nucleons are called **nuclear reactions**, the main types of which are described in Box 1.5. As we will see, many nuclear reactions change nuclei of one element into those of another; such changes are called **transmutations**.

Further Information Box

1.5   Types of nuclear reaction

Nuclear reactions are reactions that involve changes to the nuclei of the atoms concerned. The main types of these reactions are full nuclear fission, nuclear fusion, spontaneous partial nuclear disintegration (nuclear decay) and other spontaneous decay processes. These are discussed below.

Full nuclear fission reactions

During nuclear fission, a heavy nucleus disintegrates to produce two or more nuclei of roughly similar mass. A few nuclides undergo fission without external stimulation. This is known as **spontaneous nuclear fission**. Others can be made to undergo fission by bombardment with neutrons, a process called **induced nuclear fission**. Materials that undergo induced nuclear fission are said to be **fissionable**. Most fissionable materials require fast moving neutrons to smash each nucleus apart. Others, however, will undergo fission on bombardment with slow neutrons. Such materials are said to be **fissile**. The process of induction in fissile materials may be considered to involve neutron capture. The fuels used in nuclear power generation, $^{235}_{92}$U, $^{233}_{92}$U and $^{239}_{94}$Pu, are all fissile (Chapter 13, Section 13.2.1). An example of an induced nuclear fission follows:

$$^{235}_{92}\text{U} + ^{1}_{0}\text{n} \rightarrow ^{90}_{38}\text{Sr} + ^{143}_{54}\text{Xe} + 3^{1}_{0}\text{n}$$

In general, the fission of a given nuclide will proceed via a suite of different reactions. The fission of $^{235}_{92}$U is no exception to this. Indeed the above equation represents one of about 50 similar reactions undergone by this isotope, each yielding different products.

Nuclear fusion reactions and nucleosynthesis

Nucleosynthesis is the name given to the production of elements. This occurs naturally in stars. It can also be made to occur artificially on Earth by colliding fast-moving nuclei or nucleons with the nuclei of other elements. For example bombardment of $^{14}_{7}$N with alpha particles (helium nuclei) results in the following overall reaction:

$$^{14}_{7}\text{N} + ^{4}_{2}\text{He}^{2+} \rightarrow ^{17}_{8}\text{O} + ^{1}_{1}\text{H}^{+}$$

The collision of the nuclei of two very fast moving light nuclides can result in nucleosynthesis via nuclear fusion. For example:

$$^{2}_{1}\text{H} + ^{2}_{1}\text{H} \rightarrow ^{3}_{2}\text{He} + ^{1}_{0}\text{n}$$

This reaction is of interest because it is one of those that may yet be harnessed in the production of nuclear power (Chapter 13, Section 13.2.1).

Spontaneous partial nuclear disintegration reactions (nuclear decay)

These are reactions in which a parent nucleus partially disintegrates, without external initiation, to yield a progeny called a **daughter nucleus**. The disintegration processes recognised are:

- *Alpha decay.*   These are reactions in which the parent nucleus emits a fast-moving helium nucleus (called an alpha particle, symbol α, $^{4}_{2}\alpha$ or $^{4}_{2}\text{He}^{2+}$, speed <10% of the speed of light). The daughter nucleus therefore has a mass number 4 less than the parent and an atomic number 2 less than the parent. This type of disintegration is rare for elements with mass numbers less than 200. An example of this type of decay is:

$$^{222}_{86}\text{Rn} \rightarrow ^{218}_{84}\text{Po} + ^{4}_{2}\text{He}^{2+}$$

- *Beta decay.*   In these reactions the parent nucleus ejects a fast-moving electron (called a beta particle, symbol β, β^{-} or $^{0}_{-1}\text{e}$, speed <90% of the speed of light). During this process a neutron is converted to a proton; the result is an increase in the atomic number by 1. A typical reaction of this type is:

$$^{14}_{6}\text{C} \rightarrow ^{14}_{7}\text{N} + ^{0}_{-1}\text{e}$$

- *Positron emission.*   A positron (symbol $^{0}_{+1}\text{e}$ or β^{+}) is a particle with the mass of an electron but of opposite charge. Such particles are emitted at high speed (<90% of the speed of light) from certain nuclei. The result is a decrease in the atomic number by one unit. For example:

$$^{43}_{22}\text{Ti} \rightarrow ^{43}_{21}\text{Sc} + \beta^{+}$$

Other spontaneous decay processes

- *Gamma decay.*   Both beta decay and alpha decay processes frequently leave the daughter nucleus in an excited state. Such daughter nuclei emit energy as gamma rays (symbol γ, a form of electromagnetic radiation). For example, excited $^{234}_{90}$Th, produced by the alpha decay of $^{238}_{92}$U, emits gamma rays with an energy of 0.05 MeV. Overall the reaction is:

$$^{238}_{92}\text{U} \rightarrow ^{234}_{90}\text{Th} + ^{4}_{2}\text{He}^{2+} + \gamma$$

- *Electron capture.*   During this process, the nucleus captures an orbital electron from its first shell. This results in a proton being converted to a neutron. Hence, the mass number is unchanged by this process but the atomic number decreases by one. The process is therefore broadly analogous to positron emission. For example:

$$^{44}_{22}\text{Ti} + ^{0}_{-1}\text{e} \rightarrow ^{44}_{21}\text{Sc}$$

As we have seen, many nuclear reactions change nuclei of one element into those of another; such changes are called **transmutations**.

The nature and organisation of matter

1.7.1 Nuclear binding energy and nuclear stability

The nucleons of an atom are held together by extremely strong, short-range forces. Hence, when a nucleus is formed from Z protons and $A–Z$ (i.e. N) neutrons, energy is released. This energy is called the **nuclear binding energy** and is so large that it can be detected as a loss in mass. This loss is related to the energy released by Einstein's famous formula:

$$E = mc^2$$

where E = the energy released (this is the mass equivalent energy) (in J)

m = the mass lost (in kg)

c = the speed of light ($3.00 \times 10^8 \, \mathrm{m \, s^{-1}}$).

Figure 1.11 shows how this energy varies as a function of the mass number. From this, it can be seen that the fusion (i.e. bringing together) of two light nuclei will result in the release of energy. Similarly, the fission (breaking apart) of a heavy nucleus to produce two or more nuclei of medium weight also releases energy. The nuclear fission reaction is the current basis of civilian nuclear power generation. Nuclear fusion has yet to be harnessed for the sustained controlled production of power. Details of these reactions are given in Box 1.5, while the production of nuclear power and its environmental consequences are discussed in detail elsewhere in this book, in Chapters 13 (Section 13.2), 14 (Section 14.7) and 16 (Section 16.4).

Given the large amounts of energy released in the formation of a nucleus, one might imagine that any combination of neutrons and protons could occur. There should therefore be an infinite number of elements, each with an infinite number of isotopes. However, this is not

the case. Only certain combinations of protons and neutrons are stable.

This phenomenon is illustrated in Figure 1.12. This shows a plot of mass number, A, against Z. The stable nuclei lie in the band shown on this plot. Nuclei outside this band are unstable and spontaneously undergo nuclear reactions (Box 1.5). Elements on the left of the band tend to decay by spontaneous beta ($_{-1}^{0}e$) or neutron emission. Elements on the right of this band are proton-rich and tend to decay by either positron ($_{+1}^{0}e$) emission or electron capture or possibly proton emission. By this means, unstable elements transmute to become stable elements. For example:

$$_{6}^{14}\mathrm{C} \rightarrow {}_{7}^{14}\mathrm{N} + {}_{-1}^{0}e + \gamma$$

and

$$_{15}^{29}\mathrm{P} \rightarrow {}_{14}^{29}\mathrm{Si} + {}_{+1}^{0}e$$

All elements with an atomic number greater than 83 are unstable and undergo spontaneous radioactive disintegration. This process is called **radioactive decay**. Such disintegration ceases when a stable element is reached; frequently this is an isotope of lead. In many cases, radioactive disintegration occurs in steps. Each step involves the ejection of an alpha or beta particle. Such step-wise transmutations are called radioactive series. These are named after the nuclide with which they start. Figure 1.13 shows the uranium-238 series. The numbers on

Figure **1.12** The mass number (A) of the stable nuclides plotted as a function of atomic number (Z). The continuous line shows the band in which the stable elements are found; the broken line shows the band in which the relatively stable elements with $Z > 83$ are found (all of which are radioactive).

Figure **1.11** A graph showing how the binding energy per nucleon (E_b/A) varies with mass number (A) for selected stable nuclei.

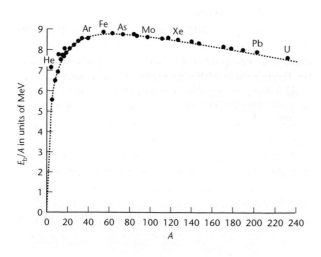

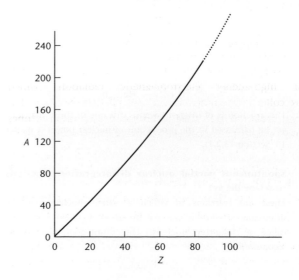

Figure 1.13 The uranium-238 series (the times are half-lives).

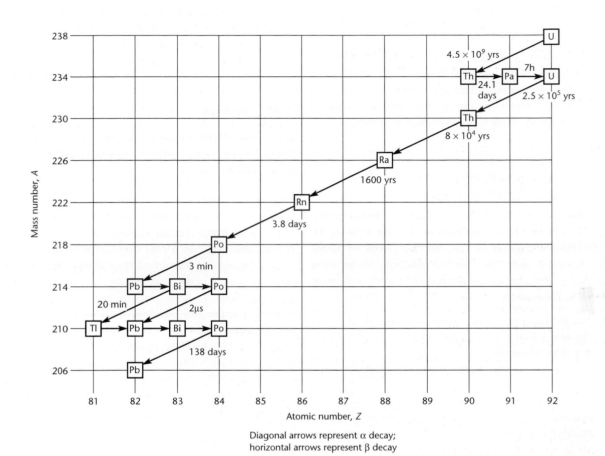

Diagonal arrows represent α decay;
horizontal arrows represent β decay

this figure are half-lives. These are characteristic of a given radioactive nuclide. They refer to the time taken for half of the nuclides within a given sample to disintegrate. This time is constant, irrespective of the number of nuclides originally present in a given sample.

1.7.2 Nuclear radiation

Nuclear reactions produce either high-speed particles and/ or high-energy electromagnetic radiation, which are collectively known as nuclear radiation. Nuclides that emit radiation are called **radionuclides** or **radioisotopes** and are said to possess **radioactivity**. The more common types of radioactive emissions are discussed in Box 1.5.

The interactions of such emissions with matter are potentially damaging. This is because nuclear radiation is sufficiently energetic to excite molecules, break chemical bonds and strip electrons from atoms and molecules. The free electrons produced by the electron-stripping process are themselves generally highly energetic and are capable of molecular excitation and bond cleavage. The chemical species that result from such interactions are frequently highly reactive and will form novel products.

Complicated chemical systems, such as biochemical processes, are particularly prone to disruption by radiation. Consequently, high doses of radioactivity can be fatal in the short term. Chronic low-level exposure may cause cancer and birth defects.

Fortunately, the human body is fairly well protected against certain forms of radioactivity. Alpha and moderately energetic beta radiation is stopped by the first few layers of skin, although highly energetic beta rays can cause severe burns. Gamma rays and neutrons are not stopped by the skin and can cause severe damage to internal organs. Ingestion, inhalation or wound contamination by radioisotopes can be particularly serious as the skin can then offer no protection. The radioisotope, once admitted, can remain in the body at high levels of activity for considerable lengths of time.

For example, plutonium-239, an alpha emitter with a radioactive half-life of 24 390 years, will remain active in the body for many years after deposition in bone as it has an assumed half-life of retention in this organ of about 50 years. Consequently, this radioisotope is considered to be one of the most toxic materials known. The maximum tolerated dose is estimated to be less than 10^{-6} g (i.e. one millionth of a gram) per person.

Case study 4 (page 304) describes some of the consequences of the accidental release of radioisotopes into the environment during the Chernobyl incident of 1986. Box 1.6 reports on the potential hazards caused by the naturally occurring radioactive element, radon.

1.7.3 The contrast between nuclear reactions and chemical reactions

Nuclear reactions are reactions that involve changes to the nuclei of atoms. Chemical reactions, on the other hand, only involve changes to the electron clouds of atoms (Sections 1.2 and 1.3). Nuclear reactions differ from chemical reactions in a number of other important respects. For example:

- Nuclear reactions are associated with radioactivity (Section 1.7.2). Chemical reactions can neither induce nor stop radioactivity.
- Nuclear reactions frequently involve changes either in the number of protons in the nucleus or in the mass number of the atoms concerned. However, chemical reactions never result in such changes. If the atomic number of the atom is altered it becomes an atom of another element. For examples, see Box 1.5. If the mass number of the atom changes without a change in the atomic number, a different isotope of the same element results. For example:

$$^{59}_{27}\text{Co} + ^{1}_{0}\text{n} \rightarrow ^{60}_{27}\text{Co}$$

- The energy changes involved in chemical reactions are much smaller than those involved in nuclear reactions. For example, the burning of methane (the main constituent of natural gas) in air liberates 890 kJ mol^{-1} (a mole (symbol mol) is 6.02×10^{23} particles of anything, in this case, methane molecules) compared with an energy of 9.66×10^{9} kJ mol^{-1} (i.e. nearly 10 000 million kJ mol^{-1}) liberated from the fission of $^{235}_{92}\text{U}$.
- Different isotopes of a given element are virtually identical in terms of the *chemical* reactions that they undergo, whereas different isotopes of the same element may well undergo very different *nuclear* reactions.
- The rate and nature of a nuclear reaction is largely independent of the chemical or physical form in which the atoms containing the reacting nuclei are found. Clearly, this is not the case with chemical reactions.

- Chemical reaction rates are highly sensitive to temperature and the presence or absence of a catalyst (Chapter 2, Section 2.3). Such rates may also be affected by changes in pressure. Nuclear reaction rates are, to all intents and purposes, independent of these factors.

1.8 Summary

Matter is anything that takes up space. It is made up of three fundamental particles: neutrons, protons and electrons. These are found in atoms and ions which, in turn, make up molecular and ionic compounds and mixtures. A nuclide is a collection of atoms each with the same number of both neutrons and protons. Elements are made up of atoms that all contain the same number of protons and electrons. Atoms that vary from one another only in the number of neutrons they contain are said to be different isotopes of the same element.

Atoms have a dense nucleus that is made up of neutrons and protons. This is surrounded by a diffuse, yet ordered, cloud of electrons. The arrangement of an atom's electrons within this cloud is called its electronic structure. This is important because the environmental chemistry of an atom is largely determined by its electronic structure. Atoms with similar valence shell electronic structures are placed in the same vertical group in the Periodic Table and have similar chemical properties.

In many compounds, atoms attain complete octets. This is done either by sharing electrons (forming covalent bond(s)) or by giving or receiving electrons (forming ionic bonds). Dot and cross diagrams are a useful means of visualising this bond formation process.

Ionic and covalent compounds have very different properties, which can be explained in terms of their mode of bonding.

Elements and compounds both enter into chemical reactions. Such reactions involve the breaking of old bonds and the making of new ones. Most chemical reactions of environmental importance are either acid–base, redox, complex formation, precipitation, hydrolysis, or free radical reactions.

Certain nuclides undergo nuclear reactions. The nuclear reactions may be subdivided into nuclear disintegration (nuclear decay), full nuclear fission, and nuclear fusion reactions. Nuclear fission and nuclear fusion reactions liberate large amounts of energy, the former being the current basis of nuclear power. Nuclear disintegration reactions are undergone by unstable nuclei called radionuclides or radioisotopes. These reactions involve the emission of harmful high-energy radiation. Such unstable nuclei are said to be radioactive.

Further Information Box

1.6   Radon

Radon (Rn) is a naturally occurring gas that forms as a result of the radioactive decay of radium (Ra), which in turn is formed as part of the radioactive decay series of elements such as uranium and thorium (see Figure 1.13). All 20 of its known isotopes are radioactive. Their decay series nearly all start with the emission of an alpha particle to yield an isotope of polonium (Po). A typical decay series for radon is given below:

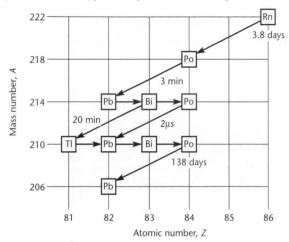

Diagonal arrows represent α decay;
horizontal arrows represent β decay

Members of such decay series are daughters of radon and most are radioactive with relatively short half-lives.

If an atom of radon is inhaled, it is unlikely to remain in the lung. This is because it is a noble gas, and as such it is non-polar and chemically unreactive. It will therefore probably be exhaled again without causing any harm. However, its daughters are metallic. These will oxidise rapidly on formation and will become adsorbed onto airborne particles which, in turn, may be inhaled and lodged on lung tissue. Clearly, a similar process will occur if a radon particle decays while inhaled.

The radioactive daughters, once in contact with the lung, can cause considerable damage to its sensitive tissues. This is particularly true of the alpha-emitting daughters. The Environmental Protection Agency (EPA) of the United States has estimated that for every 100 people living in homes with radon levels of $4\,pCi\,l^{-1}$ at an occupancy rate of 75%, between one and five persons will develop lung cancer attributable to exposure to radon and (especially) its daughters, over a 70-year life-span. If this risk is assumed to be linear, exposure to $200\,pCi\,l^{-1}$ will be equivalent to between 44 and 77 cases of lung cancer per 100 people similarly exposed. Radon levels in the home where this problem was first identified ranged as high as $2600\,pCi\,l^{-1}$!

High radon concentrations in buildings are noted only in certain geographical locations (see figure below). This is because there are only two significant building entry routes for radon. These are seepage of the gas through the foundation of the building from radon parent-containing rocks below the building and/or outgassing from water supplies that are derived from such rocks. Even in 'high radon areas' there is little of this gas outside confined spaces. What is more, in such areas, there is considerable variation in the radon levels between buildings and within any one building at different times. Buildings that are poorly ventilated and that have permeable foundations tend to be those that have elevated radon levels. Sealing the foundations of such buildings coupled with sub-foundation ventilation will ameliorate the problem.

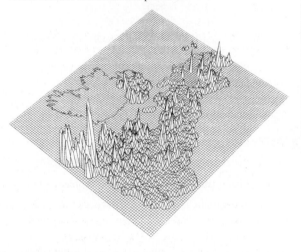

An illustration of the geographical dependence of radon levels. The outline represents the coastline of the British Isles, while the relative peak heights allow the radon doses at different locations to be compared (from the National Radiological Protection Board, 1994).

1.9   Problems

1 State the electronic structure of each of the following:
  (i) He
  (ii) C
  (iii) S
  (iv) N

2 Titanium dioxide (TiO_2) is a minor constituent of some soils. It can be considered to be an ionic solid. Use dot and cross diagrams to establish whether the ions present in this solid have attained complete octets.

3 Ethanol (CH_3CH_2OH) is a fuel that can be obtained from cropped plants (see Chapter 13, Section 13.3.8). Use a dot and cross diagram to establish the number of bonds that are present between each of its atoms.

4 (a) Under normal conditions, methane (CH_4) has a boiling point of $-161.5°C$, whereas water (H_2O) has a boiling point of $100°C$. Can you explain this anomaly? (Hint: Can methane form intermolecular hydrogen bonds?)

   (b) Which would you expect to have the higher boiling point under identical conditions, silane (SiH_4) or hydrogen sulfide (H_2S)?

5 Which of the following equations are not balanced? Attempt to balance those that are not balanced by increasing or decreasing coefficients of stoichiometry as required:

  (i) $CaCO_{3(s)} + H_2SO_{4(aq)} \rightarrow CaSO_{4(aq)} + H_2O_{(l)} + CO_{2(g)}$

  (ii) $MgCO_{3(s)} + H^+{}_{(aq)} \rightarrow Mg^{2+}{}_{(aq)} + H_2O_{(l)} + CO_{2(g)}$

  (iii) $2CO_{2(g)} + H_2O_{(l)} \rightarrow H_2CO_{3(aq)}$

  (iv) $SO_{2(g)} + O_{2(g)} \rightarrow SO_{3(g)}$

  (v) $SiO_4H_{4(aq)} \rightarrow SiO_{2(s)} + H_2O_{(l)}$

6 Calculate the oxidation states of the underlined element in the following:

  (i) $\underline{N}_2$

  (ii) $\underline{N}H_3$

  (iii) $\underline{N}H_4{}^+$

  (iv) $\underline{N}O_3{}^-$

  (v) $\underline{Fe}_2O_3$

  (vi) $\underline{Fe}O_2H$

7 Identify the equations in the following list that represent acid–base reactions in accordance with Brønsted–Lowry theory. For each equation identified, write down the acid and its conjugate base and the base and its conjugate acid.

  (i) $2HNO_{2(aq)} + O_{2(g)} \rightarrow 2HNO_{3(aq)}$

  (ii) $HNO_{2(aq)} + H_2O_{(l)} \rightarrow NO_2{}^-{}_{(aq)} + H_3O^+{}_{(aq)}$

  (iii) $Fe^{2+}{}_{(aq)} + H_2S_{(aq)} + 2H_2O_{(l)} \rightarrow FeS_{(s)} + 2H_3O^+{}_{(aq)}$

  (iv) $Na_2CO_{3(aq)} + H_2O_{(l)} \rightarrow Na^+{}_{(aq)} + OH^-{}_{(aq)} + NaHCO_{3(aq)}$

  (v) $O_{2(g)} + 2H_2O_{(l)} + 8OH^-{}_{(aq)} + 4Fe^{2+}{}_{(aq)} \rightarrow 4Fe(OH)_{3(s)}$

  (vi) $Cu(NO_3)_2 + 6H_2O \rightarrow Cu(H_2O)_6{}^{2+} + 2NO_3{}^-$

  (vii) $NH_3 + H_2O \rightarrow NH_4{}^+ + OH^-$

8 Identify the equations in the list given in problem 7 that represent redox reactions. For each equation identified, write down the identity of the reducing agent and the species reduced.

9 Identify the equations in the list given in problem 7 that represent precipitation reactions.

10 Identify the equations in the list given in problem 7 that represent hydrolysis reactions.

11 Identify the equations in the list given in problem 7 that represent complexation reactions.

12 A helium-4 nucleus ($^4_2He^{2+}$) is 0.0304 u less massive than predicted by simply summing the masses of the fundamental particles that make it up. Given that:

- $E = mc^2$ (where E = the mass energy equivalent in joules (symbol J), m= mass in kg, and cc= the speed of light = $3.00 \times 10^8\,m\,s^{-1}$)
- $1\,u = 1.66 \times 10^{-27}\,kg$
- $1\,MeV = 1.60 \times 10^{-13}\,J$
- $1\,mole = 6.022 \times 10^{23}\,particles$

calculate the binding energy of the helium-4 nucleus in:

  (i) J/nucleus

  (ii) kJ per mole of helium-4 nuclei

  (iii) MeV/nucleon.

1.10   Further reading

Atkins, P. W. and L. L. Jones (1997) *Chemistry: molecules, matter and change* (3rd edn). New York: W. H. Freeman.

Ebbing, D. D. and S. D. Gammon (1999) *General chemistry* (6th edn). Boston, MA: Houghton Mifflin.

Petrucci, R. and W. S. Harwood (1996) *General chemistry* (7th edn). Prentice Hall International.

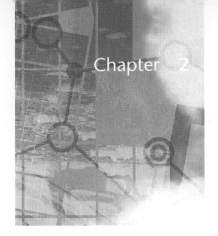

Energy flow, equilibrium and change

After reading this chapter, you should be able to:

■ Appreciate the importance of both thermodynamics and chemical kinetics to our understanding of the environment.

■ Define and use the laws of thermodynamics, especially the first and second laws.

■ Understand the concepts of dynamic equilibrium and spontaneous change.

■ Perform simple calculations based on equilibrium constants.

■ Use Le Chatelier's principle to predict the effect of perturbations of systems at dynamic equilibrium.

■ Appreciate the link between chemical kinetics and reaction mechanism.

■ Understand the concepts of half-life and pseudo order.

Introduction

Chemical and physical processes that cause materials to be changed from one form to another are at the heart of all environmental phenomena, whether they are biotic (biological) or abiotic (non-biological) in character. When these processes result in the transformation of all the material initially present into something else, they are said to go to completion.

To illustrate this, let us consider the radioactive decay of the naturally occurring isotope, radon-222 ($^{222}_{86}$Rn). This has a half-life of 3.823 days. It undergoes alpha decay (Chapter 1, Box 1.5) to yield the isotope polonium-218 ($^{218}_{84}$Po), in accordance with the following equation:

$$^{222}_{86}Rn \rightarrow\ ^{218}_{84}Po + ^{4}_{2}He^{2+}$$

After ten half-lives have elapsed (i.e. 38.23 days), less than 0.1% of the original sample of radon-222 remains. The process has virtually gone to completion. (See Chapter 1, Box 1.6 for more information on the properties of radon.)

Importantly, not all chemical and physical transformations do go to completion. Indeed, many reach a state, known as dynamic equilibrium, in which nothing appears to be happening and yet the process concerned is incomplete. This happens whenever the rate of a given chemical or physical transformation is matched by the rate of a process that reverses the transformation.

For example, when sea water evaporates in isolated rock pools, solid sea salt will eventually start to appear. However, this process of precipitation seems to stop prematurely, as it does not remove all of the salt from the water. Indeed, once precipitation has started the salinity of the water will remain very high and essentially constant, until all of the water has evaporated. The reason for this is that not only is salt leaving the water as a precipitate, it is also redissolving. At any one instant, the rates of solid salt formation and its dissolution will be in balance, thereby establishing a dynamic equilibrium that maintains the composition of the water by a process of two-way exchange.

Not only do natural processes vary in the extent to which they go to completion, they also differ in the speed with which they occur. Some processes, such as the weathering of rocks, are extremely slow, while others, including forest fires, are very rapid.

In this chapter, we briefly review the experimentally derived laws that allow an insight into these issues of extent and rate of transformation. The first two sections are concerned with an introduction to the laws of thermodynamics and the way that these determine the direction and extent of spontaneous change. The last section is concerned with the laws that govern the rates of transformation.

2.1   The laws of energy flow

The study of energy transformations is called **thermodynamics**. This is of importance to environmental scientists as it allows us to understand and predict much of the physical, chemical and biochemical behaviour of matter. It also enables us to predict the extent to which many processes occur and the amount of useful work that may be done by a given process (see below and Chapter 13, Box 13.1). However, a study of thermodynamics can *not* inform us about the speed with which a process will occur. In order to understand this we must use the principles of kinetics, particularly chemical kinetics, which are addressed in Section 2.3.

In thermodynamic analysis, it is convenient to consider the universe as being divided into a system and its surroundings (Figure 2.1). The **system** is the portion of the universe that is under consideration. It might be a pair of reacting molecules, a single cell of an organism, a whole organism, the oceans, the atmosphere or even the entire planet. The system is encapsulated by an imaginary or real **boundary** that separates it from its **surroundings**. If the system is **open**, both matter and energy can cross its boundary. A tree, or the atmosphere, would therefore be considered as an open system. (In the case of the tree, interactions with the atmosphere and soil allow matter and energy to cross its boundary; importantly, energy in the form of light also enters the tree, some of which is captured during the vital process of photosynthesis (Chapter 9, Section 9.2.1).) The boundary of a **closed system** may be traversed by energy, but *not* matter. The Earth, to a good

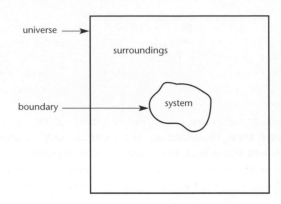

Figure 2.1 The segregation of the universe into a system and its surroundings.

approximation, is a closed system. There is little exchange of matter between it and space. However, energy in the form of both solar and terrestrial radiation crosses the Earth–space boundary. **Isolated systems** allow neither matter nor energy to cross their boundaries; such systems are mainly of theoretical value and few, if any, exist in nature.

It is important to understand what is meant by the term **energy**. It is the capacity to do work or supply heat. Whenever work is done or heat is supplied, an interaction occurs either between two parts of a system, or between a system and its surroundings. During an **interaction** an *observable* change in one part of the universe is correlated with a corresponding change in another. Heat and work are therefore the means by which the energy of a system may be altered, relative to its surroundings.

The **heat** interaction is what occurs when an object comes into contact with another that is either hotter or cooler than itself. Under these circumstances, the cool object is *observed* to become warmer (i.e. its temperature increases), and the warm object cooler.

Work is the name that is given to any interaction between two bodies, or any system and its surroundings, that is neither heat nor the transfer of matter. An electricity generating station may be considered to be a system. This produces a heat interaction with its surroundings, and may thereby be responsible for thermal pollution (Chapter 14, Section 14.8). However, it also exports electricity; this is neither matter nor heat and must therefore be work. All work interactions must, in theory, have the capacity to be entirely transformed into mechanical work. Mechanical work (w) is done whenever an object is moved by a force (F) over a distance (L); algebraically this is expressed as follows:

$$w = F \times L \qquad (2.1)$$

For instance, lifting a stone against the force due to gravity constitutes work. In the SI system the unit of force is the newton (N) (equivalent to $1\,kg\,m\,s^{-2}$); if this is sustained over 1 m, 1 joule (J) of work has been done. The joule is the unit used to express not only work but heat and energy also.

An important type of work is that done when a system contracts or expands against an external force. This is called pressure–volume work and is common in the environment. When any system that is open to the atmosphere enters into a chemical or physical process that either produces or consumes a gas, this type of work is done. In fact, these are somewhat special conditions, for under these circumstances the external force remains constant throughout the process as it is supplied by an essentially unchanging atmospheric pressure. Pressure–volume work under conditions of constant pressure is considered further in Box 2.1.

The laws of thermodynamics

The laws of thermodynamics are given in Table 2.1. These govern the way in which heat and work may transfer energy to systems from their surroundings. In this discussion, we will concentrate on the first and second laws, as these have greater utility in the environmental sciences.

The first law of thermodynamics

Energy has many forms, including those possessed by an object by virtue of its mass (see Chapter 1, Section 1.7.1), velocity (kinetic energy) and position relative to other objects (potential energy). Heat and work may facilitate the transformation of energy from one form to another, or its transfer in and out of a system. However, such processes cannot alter the total amount of energy in the universe; to do so would contravene the first law (Table 2.1).

The **internal energy**, U, of a system is the total energy of all of its constituent particles. Physical or chemical changes that involve either work or heat interactions between the system and its surroundings are therefore accompanied by a corresponding change in internal energy (ΔU):

$$\Delta U = q + w \qquad (2.2)$$

where q is the heat *added to* the system and w is the work *done on* the system. Equation 2.2 may therefore be seen as an alternative statement of the first law.

The change in internal energy, ΔU, can be measured by observing the heat interaction at constant volume (q_v). Under these conditions, pressure–volume work cannot be done. Therefore, unless some other type of work occurs, $w = 0$ and $\Delta U = q_v$.

Tool Box

2.1 Pressure–volume work at constant pressure

Let us consider pressure–volume work under conditions of constant pressure. In order to aid analysis, it is useful to consider the system to be the inside of a cylinder that is closed by a frictionless piston of area A and surrounded by a gas at constant pressure (P) (such as the atmosphere) (see figure opposite). If a reaction were to occur in the system that produced a gas, the piston would move out by a distance L against the force (F) exerted by P. It is now important to define w as the work *done on the system by its surroundings*. Production of a gas inside the cylinder would therefore result in a negative value for w as the system would do work on its surroundings.

Pressure is force per unit area, therefore:

$$F = P \times A$$

Substituting this into $w = F \times L$ (Equation 2.1), while noting the negative value for w that expansion of the system produces, results in:

$$w = -P \times A \times L$$

The change in volume[1] (ΔV) of the system that occurs during the reaction is given by:

$$\Delta V = A \times L$$

Therefore

$$w = -P \times \Delta V \text{ (often written } w = -P\Delta V)$$

The diagram shows the cylinder analogy used to understand the work done by a system on its surroundings by a change in its volume at constant pressure.

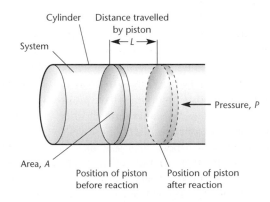

Cylinder

System

Distance travelled by piston

Area, A

Pressure, P

Position of piston before reaction

Position of piston after reaction

[1] The symbol Δ (pronounced 'delta') refers to a change in a parameter, p, in this case volume, V. It is, by convention, always calculated by subtracting the initial value of the parameter (p_i) from its final value (p_f), thus:

$$\Delta p = p_f - p_i$$

Table 2.1 The laws of thermodynamics.

Name	Statement[a]
Zeroth	Consider three bodies: A, B and C. If A and B are in thermal equilibrium with C, then A and B must also be in thermal equilibrium. A, B and C must therefore share a common temperature.
First	The energy content of the universe is constant.
Second	The entropy (disorder) of an isolated system can either remain constant or increase.
Third	At a temperature of absolute zero (0 K, $-273.15\,^\circ$C), a perfect crystalline material has zero entropy.

[a]All of these laws can be stated in a variety of ways. In the case of the first and second laws, this is explored in the text.

In the environment, alterations frequently occur in systems that allow expansion or contraction. If under these conditions a change in volume occurs, pressure–volume work will be done and ΔU can no longer be equated with the heat interaction. Under these conditions a more convenient parameter to monitor is the change in enthalpy (ΔH) that accompanies the alteration. **Enthalpy change** is defined by the following expression:

$$\Delta H = \Delta U + \Delta(PV) \tag{2.3}$$

or

$$\Delta H = q + w + \Delta(PV) \tag{2.4}$$

Under conditions of constant pressure:

$$\Delta(PV) = P\Delta V \tag{2.5}$$

and, if only pressure–volume work occurs (Box 2.1),

$$w = -P\Delta V \tag{2.6}$$

Therefore

$$\Delta H = q - P\Delta V + P\Delta V \text{ (constant pressure)} \tag{2.7}$$

Consequently measurement of the heat added to the system under these conditions (q_p) yields ΔH:

$$\Delta H = q_p \tag{2.8}$$

Chemical or physical changes that cause a system to absorb heat from its surroundings have positive values for ΔH and are said to be **endothermic**, while those that release heat are **exothermic** (ΔH is negative).

As one might expect, the size of ΔH is directly proportional to the amount of material undergoing change. Hence, values of ΔH are usually expressed in units of $J\,mol^{-1}$ (read as joules per mole), or, more commonly, $kJ\,mol^{-1}$ (the meaning of the symbol 'mol' is explained in Box 2.4, page 35). Enthalpy changes also vary with temperature and pressure. In order to allow comparisons, it is therefore useful to define a standard state, thus: any substance is in its **standard state** when it is pure and at 1

atmosphere pressure. This allows a standard reaction enthalpy (ΔH^o) to be defined as the enthalpy change that accompanies the conversion of reactants in their standard states to the products in their standard states. It is possible to cite standard reaction enthalpies for any temperature; however, this is commonly 298 K ($\sim$25°C).

Enthalpy change is a **function of state**. This means that its value is independent of the route taken. As shown in Box 2.2, this allows the standard reaction enthalpy for any reaction to be *calculated* from data taken from tables of standard enthalpies of formation (see Section 2.6, Further reading).

A special case of the standard reaction enthalpy is the **standard enthalpy of combustion** (ΔH_c^o). This is defined as the enthalpy change observed on the complete combustion of a substance in its standard state to yield the products also in their standard states. It is referenced to a particular temperature (usually 298 K) and is expressed in $kJ\,mol^{-1}$ of the substance that is burnt. Standard enthalpies of this kind are particularly valuable when the relative merits of different fuels are being discussed (Box 2.3).

The second law of thermodynamics

The first law of thermodynamics expresses the observation that although energy can be converted from one form to another, it can be neither created nor destroyed. To consider a specific example, on the combustion of a fuel, part of its internal energy is converted into other forms by heat interactions and/or work. The first law informs us that the energy liberated from the fuel has not been destroyed. Why, then, can this not be used to regenerate the fuel from its combustion products? This is the realm of the second law of thermodynamics.

The second law can be couched in several ways, one of which is given in Table 2.1. Alternative statements include:

1 The entropy (disorder, symbol S) of the universe is increasing, *or*
2 $\Delta S_{universe} = \Delta S_{system} + \Delta S_{surroundings} > 0$, *or*
3 For a spontaneous process to occur the entropy of either the system and/or its surroundings must increase.

The last of these alternatives is particularly informative in the context of the example outlined above. In order to explore this further, we need to understand what is meant by the term spontaneous. A spontaneous process is one that, once started, will continue without intervention from outside the system. Experience informs us that the burning of fuel clearly falls within this category. Once started, combustion will continue, unaided, until either the fuel or the oxidant (air) is exhausted.

Tool Box

2.2   Calculation of standard reaction enthalpies (ΔH^o) from standard enthalpies of formation (ΔH_f^o)

The standard enthalpy of formation (ΔH_f^o) of an element in its most stable form at 1 atmosphere pressure and a stated temperature (usually 298 K) is defined to be zero. Since elements are not compounds, this allows ΔH_f^o for any compound to be defined at a given temperature as the standard reaction enthalpy associated with its synthesis from its elements in their most stable form at a pressure of 1 atmosphere. This is expressed in units of $J\,mol^{-1}$ or, more commonly, $kJ\,mol^{-1}$ of the *compound*. Values of ΔH_f^o have been experimentally determined for many compounds and are available in several data books (see Section 2.6, Further reading).

This allows the value of ΔH^o for any reaction to be calculated using the following expression:

$$\Delta H = \Sigma \Delta H_f^o(products) - \Sigma \Delta H_f^o(reactants)$$

where Σ stands for 'sum of all of'.

To illustrate this, let us calculate the standard reaction enthalpy for the combustion of methane at 298 K (ΔH_{298}^o). The reaction concerned may be represented thus:

$$CH_{4(g)} + 2O_{2(g)} \rightarrow CO_{2(g)} + 2H_2O_{(l)}$$
$$\Delta H_{f298}^o/kJ\,mol^{-1} \quad -74.9 \quad 0 \quad -394 \quad -286$$

Therefore, using the equation given above,

$$\Delta H_{298}^o = (1 \times -394 + 2 \times -286)$$
$$- (1 \times -74.9 + 2 \times 0)$$
$$= -891.1\,kJ\,mol^{-1}$$

As expected, this is very similar to the value of ΔH_{298}^o obtained directly by measurement ($-890.4\,kJ\,mol^{-1}$).

It is important to realise that not all spontaneous processes are rapid. For example, under the conditions that prevail at the Earth's surface, conversion of diamond to graphite is a spontaneous process, but it is infinitesimally slow. The study of the speed of reactions is called chemical kinetics; we return to this subject in Section 2.3.

According to the second law, this process must be accompanied by an increase in the entropy of the system and/or its surroundings, otherwise it would not be spontaneous. In order to analyse this further let us examine the burning of a particular fuel, ethanol (CH_3CH_2OH), using the list of changes that generally lead to increases in entropy that is given in Table 2.2.

The reaction concerned may be represented thus:
$$CH_3CH_2OH_{(l)} + 3O_{2(g)} \rightarrow 2CO_{2(g)} + 3H_2O_{(l)} \quad (2.9)$$

The first point to note is that this is an exothermic process ($\Delta H_{c298}^o = -1371\,kJ\,mol^{-1}$ of ethanol). This heat interaction will normally cause a temperature rise; atoms and molecules will therefore move more rapidly, increasing their disorder. In addition, the total number of molecules after the reaction is greater than before by a factor of 5/4. This accompanies the breaking down of the relatively ordered substance, ethanol, into smaller, less-ordered species.

From this qualitative analysis, it is clear that, as expected, energy liberation by fuel burning causes an increase in the entropy of the universe (system plus surroundings). The opposite process, that is the use of this energy in the reconstitution of the fuel from its products, would therefore result in a *decrease* in entropy. It is therefore non-spontaneous and *could not* occur if the fuel, the oxidant and their reaction products constituted an isolated system.

In many systems, this type of qualitative analysis is insufficient to establish whether a process is spontaneous or not. Take for example the reaction depicted below:

$$CaCO_{3(s)} \longrightarrow CaO_{(s)} + CO_{2(g)} \quad (2.10)$$
calcium   calcium   carbon
carbonate   oxide   dioxide
(the main
constituent
of limestone)

This reaction is of considerable importance as carbon dioxide is a greenhouse gas. Therefore, if it were to proceed, highly significant global warming would be expected to ensue. Examination of this reaction in the light of the criteria for increases in entropy given in Table 2.2 leads to an ambiguous finding. The reaction as written leads to an increase in the total number of molecules and ions present, and the formation of a gas from a solid. Both of these phenomena will cause an increase in entropy. However, the reaction is endothermic ($\Delta H^o = +178.3\,kJ\,mol^{-1}$ of $CaCO_3$). This heat interaction will generally cause the temperature of the system to fall, decreasing entropy. Whether the reaction is spontaneous or not will therefore depend on the balance between these effects.

Therefore, the evaluation of the spontaneity of this reaction could be achieved if one could *quantify* the entropy change (ΔS, units $J\,K^{-1}\,mol^{-1}$) that accompanies the process in both the system and its surroundings. If the sum of these proved to be positive, the reaction would be spontaneous.

Quantitative evaluation of the entropy change in the system is relatively easy. Unfortunately, this is not common in the case of the entropy change of the surroundings. It is therefore convenient to define a new

Further Information Box

2.3 The enthalpy values of fuels

Combustible fuels are materials that are burnt to produce either heat and/or work interactions. While all fuels burn exothermically, the enthalpy of combustion varies from fuel to fuel. In order to aid comparison, different expressions of this enthalpy are used.

If the fuel is a pure element or compound, such as hydrogen, butane, methanol or octane, standard enthalpies of combustion (ΔH^o_{c298}), expressed in $kJ\,mol^{-1}$, are meaningful. However, most fuels (oil, coal, peat, wood, etc.) are mixtures of compounds, in which case, specific enthalpies of combustion are more appropriate. These are cited in $kJ\,g^{-1}$ ($MJ\,kg^{-1}$) and are also referred to as the calorific or heating values of the fuel. They assume a positive value for exothermic processes.

In general the most valued fuels are those with the highest specific enthalpies of combustion. However, for some applications, particularly transport, the volume of fuel required is also significant. In order to compare fuels on these grounds, enthalpy densities are used. The enthalpy density of a fuel is the heat interaction that occurs when a given volume is burnt at a constant pressure (usually 1 atmosphere). They are quoted in $kJ\,dm^{-3}$, at a specific temperature (usually 298 K) and defined as positive for exothermic processes.

Most fuels are based on hydrocarbons. These generate carbon dioxide (CO_2) as a product of combustion. This is a greenhouse gas and may therefore be contributing to global warming (Chapter 15, Section 15.2.3). When comparing the output of this gas from different fuels, the standard enthalpy of combustion expressed per mole of carbon is useful.

Great care must be exercised when using such data to compare the relative merits of fuels. Many factors other than enthalpy values influence the choice of fuel for a given application. These include the comparative cost of the different fuels available, the ease of handling of both the fuels and their combustion products, and an assessment of the differing environmental impacts of their use.

Let us briefly consider some of the relative advantages of three motor vehicle fuels: motor spirit (gasolene, petrol), ethanol (C_2H_5OH) and hydrogen (H_2). Unlike the others, the first of these is a complex mixture, primarily of hydrocarbons; however, its properties as a fuel approximate to those of octane (C_8H_{18}). The table following shows some of the relevant characteristics of these commodities.

Fuel	ΔH^o_{c298} /$kJ\,mol^{-1}$ of fuel	ΔH^o_{c298} /$kJ\,mol^{-1}$ of carbon	Specific enthalpy /$kJ\,g^{-1}$	Enthalpy density /$kJ\,dm^{-3}$
Motor spirit			42	2.5×10^4
Octane	−5512	−689	48	3.8×10^4
Ethanol	−1371	−685	30	2.4×10^4
Hydrogen	−286	infinite	141	13

From this it can be seen that hydrogen has two significant advantages over the other fuels. It has a high specific enthalpy and a zero production of carbon dioxide. However, it has several drawbacks; chief amongst these are its high cost and very low enthalpy density. It has not found commercial application as a motor fuel.

Currently motor spirit ($\sim$ octane) is the motor fuel of choice. It is relatively cheap to produce and has a large enthalpy density, hence obviating the need for huge fuel tanks. However, its use causes pollution problems. When burnt in an internal combustion engine, not only does it produce carbon dioxide, it also releases unburnt hydrocarbons and partially oxidised species, particularly carbon monoxide (CO). These unburnt and part-burnt materials are significant contributors to the problem of photochemical smog as are the oxides of nitrogen (NO_x), which are also generated during the combustion process (Chapter 15, Section 15.2.1).

The data shown above indicate that ethanol and motor spirit are roughly comparable fuels. They have similar enthalpy densities and specific enthalpies. However, ethanol has some distinct advantages that are not apparent from these data. Cars powered by this fuel generate 20 to 30% less carbon monoxide and about 15% less NO_x than those using motor spirit. In addition, any unburnt ethanol that escapes into the environment is relatively inactive and therefore does not contribute to the generation of photochemical smogs.

Motor spirit is a fossil fuel. In contrast, ethanol can be made by the fermentation of biomass, such as sugar cane. Once a fuel cycle based on ethanol production from biomass is established, the crop grown for fuel production absorbs as much carbon dioxide as is produced by fuel burning. The net production of carbon dioxide is therefore zero.

parameter that will allow calculations based *only* on the system to predict whether a given change is spontaneous. This is the Gibbs free energy (G). For reactions at constant temperature (T), changes in G (ΔG, units $J\,mol^{-1}$, commonly expressed as $kJ\,mol^{-1}$) can be calculated using:

$$\Delta G = \Delta H - T\Delta S \qquad (2.11)$$

Importantly, all of the parameters involved in the above equation relate to the *system*. What is more, it can be shown that:

$$\Delta G_{system} = -T\Delta S_{universe} \qquad (2.12)$$

Hence, if ΔG is *negative*, $\Delta S_{universe}$ must be *positive* and the reaction will be spontaneous. If ΔG is *positive*, $\Delta S_{universe}$

Table 2.2 Changes that, in general, increase entropy.

An increase in temperature

An increase in the number of molecules, atoms or ions

The formation of liquids from solids by either dissolution or melting

The formation of gases from liquids or solids

must be *negative* and the *reverse* reaction will be spontaneous.

Let us now re-examine the case of limestone decomposition represented by Equation 2.10.

Like enthalpy, entropy is a state function. Therefore, the change in entropy under standard conditions[1] (ΔS^o) for a given reaction may be calculated from S^o values for the reactants and products (available in tables; see Section 2.6, Further reading), using the following expression:

$$\Delta S^o = \Sigma S_f^o(\text{products}) - \Sigma S_f^o(\text{reactants}) \qquad (2.13)$$

In the case under examination:

$$CaCO_{3(s)} \rightarrow CaO_{(s)} + CO_{2(g)}$$

$S_{298}^o/\text{J K}^{-1}\text{mol}^{-1}$:   92.9   40   214

Therefore

$$\Delta S_{298}^o = (1 \times 40 + 1 \times 214) - (1 \times 92.9)$$
$$= 161.1\,\text{J K}^{-1}\text{mol}^{-1}$$

Noting that

$$\Delta H_{298}^o = +178.3\,\text{kJ mol}^{-1} = +178.3 \times 10^3\,\text{J mol}^{-1}$$

we obtain

$$\Delta G_{298}^o = 178.3 \times 10^3 - 298 \times 161.1$$
$$= 130\,292\,\text{J mol}^{-1} \simeq 130\,\text{kJ mol}^{-1}.$$

This is positive; therefore, under standard conditions at 298 K, the reaction as written is non-spontaneous, while its reverse is spontaneous.

There is an alternative means of establishing the ΔG^o values for any given reaction. This is based on the fact that, like enthalpy and entropy, Gibbs free energy is a state function. Therefore, where standard Gibbs free energy of formation (ΔG_f^o) data are available for all of the reactants and products in a given reaction, its ΔG^o value can be calculated using the following expression:

$$\Delta G^o = \Sigma \Delta G_f^o(\text{products}) - \Sigma \Delta G_f^o(\text{reactants}) \qquad (2.14)$$

Standard Gibbs free energy of formation data are available in reference works (see Section 2.6, Further reading).

[1] This is implied by the superscript ^{o}. This means that the reactants and products are in their standard states, i.e. pure and at 1 atmosphere pressure.

It is worth noting that neither ΔH nor ΔS vary greatly with temperature, whereas in most cases the same cannot be said of ΔG. We can write:

$$\Delta G_T \simeq \Delta H_{298} - T\Delta S_{298} \qquad (2.15)$$

From this, generalisations about the temperature dependence of spontaneity can be made; these are given in Table 2.3.

To consider a specific example, let us return to the reaction represented by Equation 2.10. This has positive values for both ΔH^o and ΔS^o, and therefore becomes spontaneous above a certain temperature. This temperature can be estimated, using the following reasoning.

There will be a temperature T at which ΔG^o is zero, under these conditions:

$$0 \simeq \Delta H_{298}^o - T\Delta S_{298}^o \qquad (2.16)$$

This can be rearranged to find T:

$$T\Delta S_{298}^o \simeq \Delta H_{298}^o \qquad (2.17)$$

Therefore if ΔH_{298}^o is expressed in J mol^{-1} and ΔS_{298}^o is given in J K^{-1} mol^{-1}, then:

$$T \simeq \frac{\Delta H_{298}^o}{\Delta S_{298}^o} = \frac{178.3 \times 10^3}{161.1} = 1107\,\text{K}$$

This is equivalent to $(1107 - 273)°C = 834°C$.

Above this temperature, ΔG^o will be negative and the process will become spontaneous under standard conditions. Temperatures above 834°C are very rarely met within the natural environment. Therefore, there is no possibility that this reaction will release catastrophically large amounts of carbon dioxide into the atmosphere.

The interaction between a system and its surroundings may include heat or work. The work interaction that is not pressure–volume work is called **useful work**. The parameter ΔG is a measure of the maximum amount of useful work that can be done by a system undergoing spontaneous change under conditions of constant temperature and pressure. These are the conditions that

Table 2.3 Generalisations on the temperature dependence of spontaneity, drawn from $\Delta G = \Delta H - T\Delta S$.

Sign of		**Interpretation**
ΔH	ΔS	
+	+	Process becomes spontaneous (ΔG negative) *above* a certain temperature
+	−	Process is non-spontaneous at all temperatures
−	+	Process is spontaneous at all temperatures
−	−	Process becomes spontaneous *below* a certain temperature

prevail in organisms, therefore the equality between ΔG and useful work is particularly relevant to biological systems. In practice, this maximum can never be realised as to do so the process would have to occur at an infinitesimal rate. There are non-biological systems, such as the internal combustion engine, that are capable of converting heat to work. These devices do not operate under conditions of constant temperature. The thermodynamic limitation on the efficiency of heat-to-work conversions is discussed in Chapter 13.

There are many processes of environmental significance that give the appearance of contravening the second law. Primary amongst these are the self-ordering biological systems including cells and complex organisms. While living, all such systems maintain, if not decrease their entropy with time. This can only be done at the expense of an increase in entropy in the surroundings.

At the level of biochemical reactions this is achieved by the coupling of non-spontaneous reactions with spontaneous processes, so that a net increase in entropy occurs. For example, during photosynthesis, green plants use the light energy that is *spontaneously* emitted by the sun. If the energy from the sun (or some other spontaneous process) were not supplied, photosynthesis could not occur as the reaction involved is endothermic (ΔH_{system} is positive) and involves a decrease in entropy (ΔS_{system} is negative).

$\Delta G°$ and redox systems

As explained in Chapter 1 (Section 1.6.2), reactions in which there is a complete transfer of one or more electrons are called redox reactions. During such reactions, the species that gains the electron(s) is said to be reduced, while the one that loses electron(s) is oxidised. These reduction and oxidation processes cannot occur in isolation, though it is possible to physically separate them. In order to see how this may be achieved, let us examine the reaction shown below:

$$Zn_{(s)} + 2H^+_{(aq)} \rightarrow Zn^{2+}_{(aq)} + H_{2(g)} \qquad (2.18)$$
zinc
metal

In districts that suffer from acid rain, this reaction is responsible for accelerating the breakdown in the corrosion protection afforded by the zinc plating of steel.

During this reaction, the metallic zinc ($Zn_{(s)}$, zero oxidation state) is oxidised to zinc ions in solution ($Zn^{2+}_{(aq)}$, oxidation state = +2). At the same time hydrogen ions (H^+, oxidation state = +1) are reduced to hydrogen molecules (H_2, zero oxidation state). These processes may be represented by half-cell equations, thus:

$$Zn_{(s)} \rightarrow Zn^{2+}_{(aq)} + 2e^- \qquad (2.19)$$

$$2e^- + 2H^+_{(aq)} \rightarrow H_{2(g)} \qquad (2.20)$$

Adding these and cancelling the electrons that are produced and consumed regenerates Equation 2.18:

$$Zn_{(s)} + 2e^- + 2H^+_{(aq)} \rightarrow Zn^{2+}_{(aq)} + 2e^- + H_{2(g)}$$

While it is impossible for the oxidation and reduction processes represented by Equations 2.19 and 2.20 to proceed either in isolation from one another, or at different times, it is possible for them to happen in different places. The apparatus shown in Figure 2.2 is designed to accommodate this. The oxidation of zinc in the left-hand beaker produces both zinc ions in solution and electrons. This allows electrons to travel to the platinum electrode in the right-hand beaker, via the electrical conductor. Once at this electrode, the electrons will reduce hydrogen ions present in solution. This process would not proceed in the absence of a salt bridge. This acts as a conduit, allowing ions to migrate between the beakers. It thereby stops the build-up of an excess of positively charged ions (cations) in the left-hand beaker, while making good the deficit in cations in the right-hand beaker.

A high-impedance voltmeter placed in the circuit at V will register an electromotive force (emf), called the cell potential (E_{cell}, units = volts, V). This is a direct measure of ΔG, for:

$$\Delta G = -nFE_{cell} \qquad (2.21)$$

where, n = the number of moles of electrons transferred in the reaction for each mole of the reactant of interest consumed (2 in this case) and F = the Faraday constant ($9.648 \times 10^4 \, C \, mol^{-1}$).

The value of E_{cell} will alter depending on the concentration of the solution in the beakers, the partial pressure of any gaseous reactants or products and the temperature of the system. It is therefore useful to define standard conditions. These are:

- aqueous solutions of unit activity (this approximates to a concentration of $1 \, mol \, dm^{-3}$, see Boxes 2.4 and 2.5);
- gaseous reactants or products are present at 1 atmosphere pressure;
- solids are present in their most stable form at 298 K;
- electrodes made of an inert material, such as platinum, are used whenever a solid does not appear in a half-cell equation;
- a temperature of 298 K.

Under these conditions the emf measured is the standard cell potential ($E°_{cell}$), and Equation 2.21 becomes:

$$\Delta G° = -nFE°_{cell} \qquad (2.22)$$

To continue with our example, the standard cell potential for the oxidation of metallic zinc by hydrogen

Figure 2.2 An electrochemical cell.

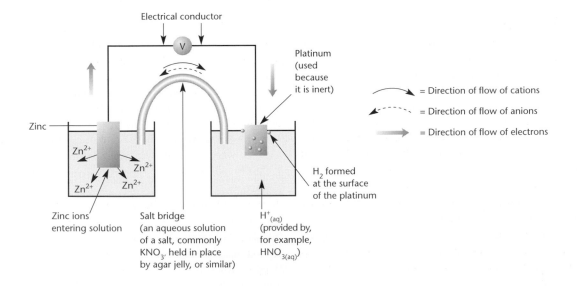

Tool Box

2.4 Concentration

The **concentration** of a substance is its amount in a given volume or amount of another substance. A very widely applicable expression of this parameter is moles of solute per dm^3 (or litre) of solution. This is known as **molar concentration** (or **molarity**), and its units are commonly abbreviated to mol dm^{-3} or M.

A **mole** (symbol, mol) is the amount of a substance that contains Avogadro's number ($6.022\,52 \times 10^{23}$) of particles, be they atoms, ions, radicals or molecules. It is possible to use mass to establish the number of moles of a chemically pure substance by using the concept of molar mass. The **molar mass** of an element is the mass, in grams, of one mole of its constituent atoms. Molar mass therefore has the units of g mol^{-1}, and for a chemically pure substance, moles = mass (in grams)/molar mass. The molar mass of any pure substance, given its formula, can be worked out by adding the molar masses of its constituent elements (see Chapter 1, Table 1.4 for these molar masses). For example, the molar mass of calcium chloride ($CaCl_2$) equals the molar mass of calcium plus two times the molar mass of chlorine, i.e. 40.08 g mol^{-1} + 2 × 35.45 g mol^{-1} = 110.98 g mol^{-1}. Note that 110.98 g of $CaCl_2$ will therefore contain one mole of calcium chloride, consisting of one mole of calcium ions (Ca^{2+}) and two moles of chloride ions (Cl^-).

The concentration in mol dm^{-3} of any chemically pure substance (X) of known mass can be calculated using the following expression:

$$[X] = \frac{m}{MM \times V}$$

where [X] = the concentration of X in mol dm^{-3}
m = the mass of X in g
MM = the molar mass of X in g mol^{-1}
V = the volume of the solution in dm^3.

1 g of $CaCl_2$ in 0.5 dm^3 of solution will therefore have a concentration of:

$$\frac{1}{110.98 \times 0.5} = 1.802 \times 10^{-2} \text{ mol dm}^{-3}$$

There are many other units of concentration in use; for example, it is frequently expressed in terms of mass of solute per unit volume of solution (e.g. g per 100 cm^3, or g dm^{-3}).

For trace concentrations the units '**parts per million**' **(ppm)** are commonly used. In solids, ppm stands for grams of substance per million grams of the solid (this is equivalent to mg kg^{-1}, or μg g^{-1}), while in solution ppm refers to grams of solute per million millilitres of solution (equivalent to mg l^{-1} or μg ml^{-1}). In the gaseous phase, ppm refers to litres of substance per million litres of gas (equivalent to μl l^{-1}), and is sometimes written as **ppmv** (parts per million, by volume). At ultra trace levels **parts per billion (ppb)** may be used, where, in each of the above applications, 1 ppm = 1000 ppb.

Tool Box

2.5 Activity

There are a number of physical and chemical properties of dilute solutions that are found to depend, in a simple way, on the concentration of the solute. However, in the vast majority of cases these relationships become more complex at higher concentrations. The main reason for this observation is that the effective concentration of the solute is lowered by the solute–solute interactions, which become increasingly significant as the solution becomes more concentrated. Similar observations are made of gaseous mixtures. Simple relationships between a given property of the mixture and the partial pressure of a trace constituent become more complex as the partial pressure of the constituent increases above trace levels. Again, the principal reason for this is that the effective partial pressure (analogous to effective concentration) is lowered by interactions between particles of the constituent concerned.

The name given to this effective concentration or effective partial pressure is **activity**. Algebraically, the relationship between activity (*a*) and concentration or partial pressure (*c*) takes the form shown below:

$$a = \frac{fc}{s}$$

where *f* is the activity coefficient and *s* is the standard concentration or partial pressure (1 mol dm^{-3} for a solute, 1 atm for a gas). As the units of *c* are mol dm^{-3} for a solute and atmospheres for a gas, this means that activities are dimensionless, and therefore have no units. By convention, chemically pure solids and liquids are given unit activity.

Activity coefficients vary considerably from species to species and with concentration. For electrolytes (compounds that form ions in solution) *f* is 1 at very low concentrations (say $<1 \times 10^{-6}$ mol dm^{-3}) but decreases fairly rapidly with increasing concentration, typically reaching between 0.9 and 0.5 at concentrations of 0.1 mol dm^{-3}. This decrease is particularly marked for solutions that contain multicharged ions such as sulfate ($SO_4{}^{2-}$), carbonate ($CO_3{}^{2-}$) or aluminium (Al^{3+}).

Activity coefficients must be calculated from experimentally derived data. This process is often tedious. There is a tendency therefore to use concentration or partial pressure as an approximation for activity, particularly at low concentrations and/or when highly accurate data are not required.

---

ions (Equation 2.18) is found to be 0.763 V. From this, ΔG° can be calculated:

$$\Delta G^{\circ} = -nFE^{\circ} = -2 \times 9.648 \times 10^4 \times 0.763$$

$$= -147\,228\,\text{J mol}^{-1} \text{ of zinc}$$

$$= -147.2\,\text{kJ mol}^{-1} \text{ of zinc}$$

The reaction is therefore spontaneous under standard conditions ($\Delta G^{\circ} < 0$).

Not only can standard cell potentials be measured, they can also be *calculated*. This is done by the combination of potentials attributable to individual half-cell reactions (see Boxes 2.6 and 2.7).

2.2 Dynamic equilibrium and spontaneous change

A system at equilibrium is one that exhibits no *net* change. This can be achieved by a balance of equal and opposite processes, resulting in a state known as **dynamic equilibrium.** For example, in a saturated solution of the sparingly soluble mineral gypsum ($CaSO_4 . 2H_2O$), both calcium (Ca^{2+}) and sulfate ($SO_4{}^{2-}$) ions continually leave and enter solution. However, as the rates of dissolution and precipitation are equal, the net concentration of these ions in solution does not alter with time.

In order to explore dynamic equilibria further, let us consider a reversible reaction represented by the following general equation:

$$aA + bB \rightleftharpoons cC + dD \qquad (2.23)$$

where A and B are the reactants, C and D are the products and a, b, c, and d are their coefficients of stoichiometry (Chapter 1, Section 1.6.1).

Near the start of the reaction A and B will be present at high concentrations and the rate of the forward process will be relatively rapid. As time goes by, the concentrations of A and B will fall and those of C and D will rise. The rate of the forward process will become slower, while the rate of the reverse process becomes more rapid. There will come a point when the rates of the two processes become equal and opposite. Under these conditions no net alteration in the concentration of either the reactants or the products will be observed. The reaction will have reached a state of dynamic equilibrium.

Once equilibrium has been reached, a parameter called the **equilibrium constant** (*K*) may be calculated using the following expression:

$$K = \frac{\{C\}^c \times \{D\}^d}{\{A\}^a \times \{B\}^b} = \frac{\frac{f\,[C]^c}{s} \times \frac{f\,[D]^d}{s}}{\frac{f\,[A]^a}{s} \times \frac{f\,[B]^b}{s}} \qquad (2.24)$$

where the symbols A, B, C, D, a, b, c and d have the same meaning as in Equation 2.23, the curly brackets represent the activity of the reactant or product that they enclose, [ ] represents the molar concentration of the species within

Tool Box

2.6 Calculation of standard cell potentials (E^o_{cell})

Background

As stated in the text (page 19), half-cell reactions, such as those represented by the two equations shown below, cannot occur in isolation.

$$Zn_{(s)} \rightarrow Zn^{2+}_{(aq)} + 2e^-$$

$$2e^- + 2H^+_{(aq)} \rightarrow H_{2(g)}$$

It is therefore impossible to establish, in an absolute sense, the potentials that they generate. However, relative values of this parameter can be established if all half-cells (known also as electrodes) are compared with one half-cell that is arbitrarily assigned a potential of zero. The half-cell chosen for this purpose is the standard hydrogen electrode (SHE), shown in the figure below.

Tables of the E^o_{cell} values obtained when different half-cells are connected to an SHE under standard conditions are available (see Section 2.6, Further reading). By convention, these tables represent each half-cell by a half-cell equation showing *reduction*. The E^o_{cell} values listed are therefore **standard reduction potentials** (E^o, or E^o_{red}), also called standard electrode potentials.

The sign of the potential attributed to a given half-cell must be reversed if the reaction is reversed. Reversal of a reduction reaction produces an oxidation reaction, the standard potential of which is merely $-E^o_{red}$. For example:

Reaction	Standard potential
$Zn^{2+}_{(aq)} + 2e^- \rightarrow Zn_{(s)}$	$E^o_{red} = -0.763\,V$
$Zn_{(s)} \rightarrow Zn^{2+}_{(aq)} + 2e^-$	$-E^o_{red} = 0.763\,V$

Electrode potentials and cell potentials are **intensive properties.** This means that they do not alter with the amount of material used. Therefore, any half-cell equation may be multiplied or divided throughout by any number without affecting the value of its standard potential. For example, the E^o_{red} for the reduction of $Zn^{2+}_{(aq)}$ to $Zn_{(s)}$ remains at $-0.763\,V$, whether the half-cell equation is written:

$$2Zn^{2+}_{(aq)} + 4e^- \rightarrow 2Zn_{(s)}$$

or even

$$0.5Zn^{2+}_{(aq)} + e^- \rightarrow 0.5Zn_{(s)}$$

Method of calculation

The procedure used to calculate the standard cell potential (E^o_{cell}) of any redox reaction is as follows:

1   The equation representing the redox reaction is split into half-cell equations, one representing the oxidation process, the other the reduction.

2   Tabulated data are used to find the standard reduction potentials for the reduction half-cell reaction and the reverse of the oxidation half-cell reaction.

3   The sign of the latter of these reduction potentials is reversed to give the standard potential of the oxidation process.

4   The standard potentials are summed, yielding E^o_{cell}.

For example, consider the oxidation of metallic zinc ($Zn_{(s)}$) by hydrogen ions ($H^+_{(aq)}$):

$$Zn_{(s)} + 2H^+_{(aq)} \rightarrow Zn^{2+}_{(aq)} + H_{2(g)}$$

This is equivalent to:

$$2e^- + 2H^+_{(aq)} \rightarrow H_{2(g)}\,(E^o_{red} = 0\,V \text{ by definition})$$

plus

$$Zn_{(s)} \rightarrow Zn^{2+}_{(aq)} + 2e^-\,(-E^o_{red} = 0.763\,V)$$

giving on addition:

$$Zn_{(s)} + 2e^- + 2H^+_{(aq)} \rightarrow Zn^{2+}_{(aq)} + 2e^- + H_{2(g)}$$

Therefore $E^o_{cell} = 0 + 0.763 = 0.763\,V$.

A further example of this process is given in Box 2.7.

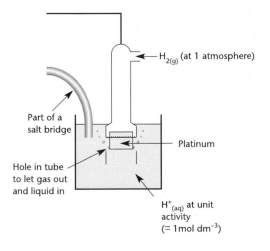

The standard hydrogen electrode (SHE).

the brackets, and f and s stand for activity coefficient and standard concentration respectively. (See Box 2.5 for more on activities and their relationship to concentration.)

At low concentrations, f approaches 1 and we can write:

$$K \simeq \frac{[C]^c \times [D]^d}{[A]^a \times [B]^b} \tag{2.25}$$

It has been found, by experiment, that for any given reaction, at any given temperature, K remains unaltered

---

Tool Box

2.7 An example of the calculation of ΔG° using standard reduction potentials

When acid mine drainage enters a river, copious amounts of a bright orange precipitate form. This cuts light penetration and smothers the river bottom, killing many of the organisms present. The orange deposit is formed by the hydrolysis of iron(III) salts. One source of these could be the aerial oxidation of any iron(II) present. It is possible to use reduction potentials to establish whether this is thermodynamically possible under standard conditions.

The reaction concerned may be represented thus:

$$4Fe^{2+}_{(aq)} + O_{2(aq)} + 4H^+_{(aq)} \rightarrow 4Fe^{3+}_{(aq)} + 2H_2O_{(aq)} \qquad (a)$$

This may be considered to be the sum of two half-cells, depicted by the following equations:

$$O_{2(aq)} + 4H^+_{(aq)} + 4e^- \rightarrow 2H_2O_{(aq)} \qquad (b)$$

plus

$$4 \times (Fe^{2+}_{(aq)} \rightarrow Fe^{3+}_{(aq)} + e^-) \qquad (c)$$

giving Equation a on addition and cancellation of e^-:

$$4Fe^{2+}_{(aq)} + O_{2(aq)} + 4H^+_{(aq)} + \cancel{4e^-} \rightarrow$$
$$4Fe^{3+}_{(aq)} + 2H_2O_{(aq)} + \cancel{4e^-} \qquad (a)$$

The standard reduction potentials for the corresponding half-cell reactions, obtained from tabulated data (see Section 2.6, Further reading) are:

$$O_{2(aq)} + 4H^+_{(aq)} + 4e^- \rightarrow 2H_2O_{(aq)} \quad E^\circ = +1.23V$$
$$Fe^{3+}_{(aq)} + e^- \rightarrow Fe^{2+}_{(aq)} \qquad\qquad E^\circ = +0.771\,V \qquad (d)$$

(note that this is the reverse of Equation c).

The standard cell potential (E°_{cell}) may now be calculated by *reversing the sign of the second of these* and summing the result:

$$E^\circ_{cell} = (+1.23) + (-0.771) = 0.459\,V$$

Notice that the stoichiometry of the overall reaction requires that each time the half-cell reaction b occurs, reaction c happens four times. It is important to realise that this multiplier is *not* applied when calculating the standard cell potential, for the reasons outlined in the text.

ΔG° can now be calculated:

$$\Delta G^\circ = -4 \times 9.648 \times 10^4 \times 0.459$$
$$= -177\,137\,J\,mol^{-1}\ of\ oxygen\ (O_2)$$
$$= -177.1\,kJ\,mol^{-1}\ of\ oxygen\ (O_2)$$

As ΔG° is negative the reaction is spontaneous under standard conditions. As would be expected, this is in keeping with observation. This reaction is indeed responsible for much of the iron(III) present in the outfall from mine drains. What is more, the reaction is microbially mediated, the organisms concerned utilising the energy released, much in the same way as we do when we oxidise carbohydrates.

---

irrespective of the starting concentrations of either the reactants or the products.

The partial pressure (P) of an ideal gas is proportional to its concentration in $mol\,dm^{-3}$. Therefore, the partial pressures of any gaseous reactants and/or products may be used in Equations 2.24 and 2.25 instead of their concentrations (s now stands for standard partial pressure). However, care must be exercised as, in general, the value of K obtained using partial pressures will be different numerically from that based on concentrations.

There are many reactions during which the concentration of one or more of the reactants and/or products remains essentially unaltered. This happens if the reaction involves more than one phase and if one of these phases is made up of a pure material. It also occurs when the solvent takes part in reactions that proceed in solution. In both cases, the result is a simplified equilibrium constant expression. This happens because activity of chemically pure phases is defined as unity, and the activity of a solvent closely approximates to unity.

To illustrate this, let us consider the dissolution of calcium carbonate:

$$CaCO_{3(s)} \xrightleftharpoons{+water} Ca^{2+}_{(aq)} + CO_3^{2-}_{(aq)} \qquad (2.26)$$

Noting that by definition, $\{CaCO_{3(s)}\} = 1$, the equilibrium constant expression for this takes the form:

$$K = \frac{\{Ca^{2+}_{(aq)}\} \times \{CO_3^{2-}_{(aq)}\}}{1}$$
$$= \{Ca^{2+}_{(aq)}\} \times \{CO_3^{2-}_{(aq)}\} \qquad (2.27)$$

In cases such as this, where the reaction concerned is the dissolution of a sparingly soluble salt, the equilibrium constant is referred to as a **solubility product** (symbolised K_{sp}). As indicated in Table 2.4, this is not the only equilibrium constant to be given a specific name.

There are many occasions when an overall reaction can be expressed as the sum of two, or more, reactions for which equilibrium constant data are known. Under these circumstances the equilibrium constant of the net reaction can be calculated. It is numerically equal to the product of the equilibrium constants for the part reactions.

Let us consider a specific example. Sulfur dioxide is a major component of acid rain (Chapter 15, Section 15.2.2). It dissolves in water and undergoes the following reaction:

$$SO_{2(g)} + 2H_2O_{(l)} \rightleftharpoons HSO_3^-_{(aq)} + H_3O^+_{(aq)} \qquad (2.28)$$

This may be considered as the sum of the following:

Table 2.4 Named equilibrium constants.

Name	Symbol	Reaction type	Expression
Solubility product	K_{sp}	Dissolution of poorly soluble salts: $A_xB_{y(s)} \rightleftharpoons xA^{y+} + yB^{x-}$	$K_{sp} = \{A^{y+}\}^x\{B^{x-}\}^y$
Henry's law constant	K_H or k_H or H	Dissolution of gases in solvents: $X_{(g)} \rightleftharpoons X_{(solv)}$	$K_H = \dfrac{[X_{(solv)}]}{P_{X_{(g)}}}$
Stability (or formation) constants	K_{stab}	Formation of complexes (species with dative bonds): $M^{n+} + xL^{y-} \rightleftharpoons ML_x^{(n-y)+}$	$K_{stab} = \dfrac{\{ML_x^{(n-y)+}\}}{\{M^{n+}\}\{L^{y-}\}^x}$
Ionic product of water	K_w	Auto-ionisation of water: $2H_2O \rightleftharpoons H_3O^+ + OH^-$	$K_w = \{H_3O^+\}\{OH^-\} = 1 \times 10^{-14}$ at $25°C$
Acid ionisation constant	K_a	Dissociation of weak Brønsted acids: $HA + H_2O \rightleftharpoons H_3O^+ + A^-$	$K_a = \dfrac{\{H_3O^+\}\{A^-\}}{\{HA\}}$
Base ionisation constant	K_b	Ionisation of weak Brønsted bases: $B + H_2O \rightleftharpoons BH^+ + OH^-$	$K_b = \dfrac{\{BH^+\}\{OH^-\}}{\{B\}}$
Partition coefficient	K	Distribution of a solute (So) between two immiscible solvents (solv$_1$ and solv$_2$): $So(solv_1) \rightleftharpoons So(solv_2)$	$K = \dfrac{[So(solv_2)]}{[So(solv_1)]}$
Octanol–water partition coefficient	K_{ow}	Distribution of a solute (So) between water (aq) and octanol (oct): $So(aq) \rightleftharpoons So(oct)$	$K_{ow} = \dfrac{[So(oct)]}{[So(aq)]}$

Notes: P stands for partial pressure measured in atmospheres, while square brackets, [], represent molar concentration. The curly brackets, {}, represent activity based on molar concentration. In dilute solutions the activity of a solute approximates to its molar concentration.

Unlike the other equilibrium constants in this table, the Henry's Law constant is not dimensionless; it therefore has units. These are usually given as $mol\,dm^{-3}\,atm^{-1}$.

When an equilibrium constant (K) has a very small value it is often convenient to cite it as a pK value, where $pK = -\log_{10} K$.

Note that, as activity is dimensionless (Box 2.5), equilibrium constants derived from equations based on activities are also dimensionless and therefore have no units.

While most equilibrium constant equations are, by definition, based on activities, there are some important exceptions. These include those that yield Henry's Law constant, partition coefficients and octanol–water partition coefficients. These exceptions use concentrations and/or partial pressures in place of activities. The constants that these generate will exhibit a degree of concentration dependence.

$$SO_{2(g)} + H_2O_{(l)} \xrightarrow{\; + \text{solvent water} \;} SO_2.H_2O_{(aq)} \qquad (2.29)$$

$$K_H = 1.24\,mol\,dm^{-3}\,atm^{-1}$$

$$SO_2.H_2O_{(aq)} + H_2O_{(l)} \rightleftharpoons HSO_3^-{}_{(aq)} + H_3O^+{}_{(aq)}$$

$$K_a = 1.7 \times 10^{-2} \qquad (2.30)$$

Adding these equations and cancelling the term that is both produced and consumed gives:

$$SO_{2(g)} + \cancel{SO_2.H_2O_{(aq)}} + 2H_2O_{(l)} \rightleftharpoons$$
$$\cancel{SO_2.H_2O_{(aq)}} + HSO_3^-{}_{(aq)} + H_3O^+{}_{(aq)} \qquad (2.31)$$

The equilibrium constant (K) for the total reaction is therefore given by:

$$K = K_H \times K_a = 1.24 \times 1.7 \times 10^{-2} = 2.1 \times 10^{-2}$$

This value of K is used in Box 2.8 to estimate the pH of water in equilibrium with atmospheric sulfur dioxide at a concentration of 0.2 ppm.

The relationship between ΔG and K

It is possible to *calculate* the value of K for any process, physical or chemical, for which the value of ΔG^o is either known or can be calculated. The equation used is:

$$\Delta G^o = -RT \ln K \qquad (2.32)$$

where R is the gas constant ($8.314\,41\,J\,K^{-1}\,mol^{-1}$), T is the temperature in kelvin, and ΔG^o is expressed in $J\,mol^{-1}$.

Perturbation of systems in dynamic equilibrium

A chemical system in a state of dynamic equilibrium may be perturbed if it experiences a change in temperature, pressure or the concentration of one or more of its reactants or products. It is highly probable that immediately after perturbation, the system will no longer be at equilibrium, in which case the concentrations of the reactants and products will then shift to new values, ultimately restoring equilibrium.

Qualitative predictions about the direction of these shifts can be made on the basis of **Le Chatelier's principle**, which may be stated thus:

> If a system at dynamic equilibrium is perturbed
> by changes in concentration, pressure or
> temperature, it will alter its composition so as to minimise
> the change.

In order to explore the effects of concentration further,

2.8 Acidity due to sulfur dioxide

When fuels that contain either inorganic or organic sulfides are burnt, sulfur dioxide ($SO_{2(g)}$) is formed. This gas dissolves in water to yield an acidic solution (i.e. pH < 7) that is in part responsible for the phenomenon of acid rain (Chapter 15, Section 15.2.2). The main reaction responsible for this may be represented thus:

$$SO_{2(g)} + 2H_2O_{(l)} \rightleftharpoons HSO_3^-{}_{(aq)} + H_3O^+{}_{(aq)} \qquad (a)$$

The equation giving the overall equilibrium constant, K, for this process is:

$$K = \frac{\{HSO_3^-\} \times \{H_3O^+\}}{P_{SO_2}} = 2.1 \times 10^{-2}$$

Let us use this to estimate the pH of water that is in equilibrium with air at atmospheric pressure that contains 0.2 ppm sulfur dioxide.

Assuming ideal gas behaviour, 0.2 ppm SO_2 is equivalent to a partial pressure (P_{SO_2}) of 0.2×10^{-6} atm. If one assumes also that the reaction represented by Equation (a) is the only source of $H_3O^+{}_{(aq)}$ and $HSO_3^-{}_{(aq)}$, then:

$$[H_3O^+] = [HSO_3^-]$$

and

$$[H_3O^+] \times [HSO_3^-] = [H_3O^+]^2$$

Therefore, using the approximation that concentration equals activity:

$$K = \frac{[H_3O^+]^2}{P_{SO_2}}$$

Rearranging:

$$[H_3O^+]^2 = K \times P_{SO_2}$$

and taking square roots:

$$[H_3O^+] = \sqrt{K \times P_{SO_2}}$$
$$= \sqrt{2.1 \times 10^{-2} \times 0.2 \times 10^{-6}}$$
$$= 6.48 \times 10^{-5} \simeq \{H_3O^+\}$$

Noting that $pH = -\log_{10}\{H_3O^+\}$, then

$$pH \simeq -\log_{10}(6.48 \times 10^{-5}) = 4.19$$

let us reconsider the equilibrium represented by the following generalised equation:

$$aA + bB \rightleftharpoons cC + dD \qquad (2.23)$$

If a change occurs that increases the concentration of one or more of the *reactants* (i.e. A and/or B), the system will no longer be at equilibrium. Le Chatelier's principle informs us that the system will alter so as to minimise this change, that is some of the *reactants* will be removed by the formation of more *products*. Conversely, if the perturbation is mediated via an increase in the concentration of one or more of the *products* (i.e. C and/or D), it will be followed by the formation of more *reactants*, again minimising the change, in this case by removing *products*.

In order for changes in pressure to bring about perturbations from equilibrium, the volume of the products must be different from that of the reactants. This is most marked when the reaction either produces or consumes a net amount of gas. Application of Le Chatelier's principle under these circumstances is straightforward. An increase in pressure brought about by a decrease in the volume of the system will favour reactions that produce a net decrease in the amount of gas present as these will tend to reduce the pressure. Conversely, reactions that generate a net increase in the amount of gas are enhanced by a decrease in pressure caused by an increase in the system's volume.

As indicated by Le Chatelier's principle, qualitative predictions of the effect of temperature changes on a system at equilibrium can also be made. To do this one must know whether the reaction is endothermic ($\Delta H > 0$) or exothermic ($\Delta H < 0$). Temperature increases favour endothermic processes as these absorb heat and therefore tend to lower the temperature. Conversely exothermic reactions are favoured by temperature decreases.

To illustrate the application of this principle, let us consider the reaction used in the Haber process for the artificial fixation of atmospheric nitrogen for use in fertilisers, plastics and explosives:

$$N_{2(g)} + 3H_{2(g)} \rightleftharpoons 2NH_{3(g)} \qquad (2.33)$$
$$\Delta H^o_{298} = -92.2 \, kJ \, mol^{-1}$$

As indicated by this equation, a mixture of nitrogen and hydrogen placed in a sealed container at constant temperature will produce ammonia (NH_3) until equilibrium is ultimately reached. Further net reaction will not occur unless the equilibrium is perturbed. Le Chatelier's principle indicates the types of perturbation that will be successful in increasing the yield of ammonia. These are:

1 a drop in the temperature (the reaction is exothermic and is therefore favoured at low temperatures);
2 an increase in the pressure (this favours the forward reaction as it generates a net reduction in the total amount of gas; a total of four moles of gaseous reactants produce two moles of gaseous products);
3 addition of reactants and withdrawal of products.

Commercial production is in keeping with items 2 and 3 on this list. The reaction is carried out at pressures between 150 and 600 atmospheres with the continual addition of reactants and removal of products. However, contrary to the indication given by Le Chatelier's principle, commercial production does not employ low temperatures. Indeed, the reaction is carried out at between 400 and 600°C. Undoubtedly, as predicted by Le Chatelier's principle, these high temperatures militate against high yields. However, they are required because at lower temperatures the reaction is too slow to be commercially viable, even in the presence of the catalyst used in this process.

This is a reminder of an important point: *thermodynamic arguments (such as those based on Le Chatelier's principle) can give information about the position of equilibrium and the equilibrium concentrations of reactants and products. However, they give no indication about the rate at which equilibrium is achieved.* This is the realm of chemical kinetics and is considered in the next section.

2.3   Chemical kinetics

So far in this chapter our discussions have centred around the information that can be gained from the application of thermodynamics to systems of environmental importance. This has allowed us to explore the notion of *how far* a process will go towards completion before dynamic equilibrium becomes established. However, such knowledge is of limited applicability unless we also know *how fast* the process occurs. This is addressed in this section.

Reaction rates, rate laws and rate constants

Consider again the general reaction represented by the equation:

$$aA + bB \rightleftharpoons cC + dD \qquad (2.23)$$

The speed of this process is called the **rate of reaction.** This is defined as the rate, with respect to time (t), of disappearance of the reactants or appearance of the products, each divided by their coefficient of stoichiometry, thus:

$$\text{rate} = -\frac{d[A]}{a \times dt} = -\frac{d[B]}{b \times dt}$$
$$= +\frac{d[C]}{c \times dt} = +\frac{d[D]}{d \times dt} \qquad (2.34)$$

where d stands for 'infinitesimal change in', $[\,]$ = concentration of the species in the brackets, and a, b, c and d are the coefficients of stoichiometry in the above equation. A minus sign indicates loss of reactant, while a plus sign represents a gain of product.

Experimentally, it is found that the rate of any given reaction is related to the concentration of its reactants and products by an equation of the following type, known as the **rate law:**

$$\text{rate} = k \times [A]^e \times [B]^f \times [C]^g \times [D]^h \qquad (2.35)$$

where the powers e, f, g and h are commonly 0, 1 or 2, although fractions and negative numbers are also found. The proportionality constant, k, is called the **rate constant**. Different reactions have different values of k.

The size of k is an indication of the rapidity of a given reaction; the larger its value, the faster it is. For any one reaction, the size of the rate constant is increased if the temperature is raised. In general, near room temperature, an increase of 10°C will approximately double the rate of reaction.

The rate constant will also be increased if a catalyst is added. These species speed up a reaction by providing a new, more rapid pathway by which it can proceed. Importantly, the amount of catalyst remains constant throughout the process. This is possible because it is both consumed and regenerated during the reaction.

In reactions that essentially go to completion (i.e. the equilibrium constant K is very large), or reactions in their initial stages when very little product has been produced, the rate law generally simplifies to:

$$\text{rate} = k \times [A]^e \times [B]^f \qquad (2.36)$$

The powers define the **order of the reaction**. If e is 1, the reaction is first order with respect to A; if e is 2, then it is second order with respect to A, and so on. The sum of all the powers in the rate law is the overall order of the reaction. For example, if both e and f are 1, overall the reaction is second order. Clearly, the units of k must depend on the order of the reaction (see Table 2.5 for details).

Reaction mechanisms

All reactions proceed via a mechanism that consists of one or more indivisible steps known as *elementary reactions*. At a molecular level, these generally involve either the break-up of one particle, in which case they are said to be

Table 2.5 The units of the rate constant, k.

Order of reaction	Phase of reaction	
	Solution	Gas
First	s^{-1}	s^{-1}
Second	$dm^3\,mol^{-1}\,s^{-1}$	$cm^3\,molecule^{-1}\,s^{-1}$
Third	$dm^6\,mol^{-2}\,s^{-1}$	$cm^6\,molecule^{-2}\,s^{-1}$

unimolecular, or the collision and reaction of two particles, when they are called *bimolecular*. Termolecular reactions, that is those involving three particles, are relatively rare, although they are of considerable importance in many atmospheric reactions. Examples of each of these types of elementary reaction are given in Figure 2.3.

If the mechanism involves only one elementary reaction, then the powers e and f (Equation 2.36) generally equal the coefficients of stoichiometry, a and b respectively (Equation 2.23). Unfortunately, most reactions proceed via a sequence of elementary reactions, in which case the connection between e and f and a and b is broken. However, a link remains between the mechanism and the experimentally observable rate law. This is important as it allows rate laws to be used to formulate suggested reaction mechanisms. This is useful information for it allows more accurate models to be made of the fate of both natural and man-made chemicals in the environment.

An example, illustrating how rate law information can shed light on reaction mechanisms, is given in Box 2.9.

Integrated rate equations and half-lives

Many reactions that involve a single reactant species (X) proceed via simple first or second order kinetics. The rate laws associated with these processes are rate $= k[X]$ and rate $= k[X]^2$ respectively. It is possible to use calculus to derive integrated rate equations from these expressions. These express the concentration of the reactant as a function of time (t) as shown in Table 2.6.

The time taken for the concentration, or amount, of a species to drop to half its original value is called its **half-**

life ($t_{1/2}$). Consider again single reactant processes that proceed via first or second order kinetics. For these, expressions that relate the half-life of the reactant to the rate constant can be readily derived from the integrated rate equations.

For a first order process,

$$t_{1/2} = \frac{0.6931}{k} \tag{2.37}$$

Importantly, this demonstrates that in the case of first order processes the half-life depends only on the value of k. Therefore, it remains constant throughout the process, even though the concentration, or amount, of the reactant becomes smaller with time, along with the rate of reaction. First order reactions that essentially go to completion are largely complete after ten half-lives, as after this time less than 1% of the original reactants will still be present.

For a single-reactant second order process:

$$t_{1/2} = \frac{1}{k[X]_0} \tag{2.38}$$

where $[X]_0$ is as defined in Table 2.6. In this case the half-life depends on both the value of k and $[X]_0$. It therefore varies during the course of the reaction.

The half-life concept is also of some utility when considering second and third order processes of the type shown in Equations 2.39 and 2.40 below. In each case, the expression for the half-life of X ($t_{1/2}^X$) is *only* applicable while the concentrations of the other reactants remain constant. For second order processes (X + Y → products),

$$\text{rate} = k[X][Y]; \quad t_{1/2}^X = \frac{0.6931}{k[Y]} \tag{2.39}$$

and for third order processes (X + Y + Z → products),

$$\text{rate} = k[X][Y][Z]; \quad t_{1/2}^X = \frac{0.6931}{k[Y][Z]} \tag{2.40}$$

Figure 2.3 Examples of elementary reactions: (a) unimolecular, (b) bimolecular and (c) termolecular. All these reactions take part in the chemistry of the atmosphere (Chapter 15). In reaction (c), M is often N_2 or O_2. In most reactions that involve a third body of this type its purpose is to remove excess energy from the product. If this were not done, the product would spontaneously disintegrate, reforming the reactants.

(a)

$CH_3CO.O_2.NO_2 \rightarrow CH_3CO.O_2 + NO_2$
peroxyacetyl → peroxyactyl + nitrogen
nitrate (PAN)   radical   dioxide

(b)

$CH_3O + O_2 \rightarrow HO_2 + HCHO$
methoxy + oxygen → hydroperoxyl + formaldehyde
radical   radical   (methanal)

(c)

$CH_3 + O_2 + M \rightarrow CH_3O_2 + M$
methoxy + oxygen + third → peroxymethyl + third
radical   body   radical   body

Pseudo order

Many environmental reactions of significance occur between species that are present in large concentrations (such as molecular oxygen, O_2, in the atmosphere) and molecules, ions or atoms that are present only at trace levels. Under these conditions, as the reaction proceeds, the concentration of the trace constituent falls, while that of the bulk component remains essentially constant. Observations made under these conditions will therefore find that the rate of reaction depends on the concentration of the trace species only. This may give an apparent order for the reaction that is less than the true order; this apparent order is known as a **pseudo order**.

Let us illustrate this with an example:

$$2NO + O_2 \rightarrow 2NO_2 \tag{2.41}$$

Tool Box

2.9 Rate law information and the study of mechanisms

To illustrate how rate law information can be used in the elucidation of mechanisms, let us consider the reaction represented by the following equation:

$$2O_3 \rightarrow 3O_2$$

This is in part responsible for the natural breakdown of ozone (O_3) in the upper atmosphere (stratosphere) by the action of light with a wavelength $(\lambda) < 325$ nm (Chapter 15, Section 15.2.4).

One possibility is that the reaction occurs via a single bimolecular elementary reaction, i.e.:

$$O_3 + O_3 \rightarrow 3O_2$$

This would lead to a rate law of the form:

$$\text{rate} = k[O_3]^2$$

However, the experimentally observed rate law is:

$$\text{rate} = k[O_3]^2[O_2]^{-1} \tag{a}$$

The fact that this is more complex than can be accounted for on the basis of a single step implies that a more complex mechanism must be operating. One possibility is the sequence of reactions given in the following table, which shows a suggested mechanism for the stratospheric reaction, $2O_3 \rightarrow 3O_2$:

Elementary reaction	Predicted rate law	Observed relative rate
Step 1		
$O_3 \underset{\xleftarrow{\hspace{1cm}}}{\overset{\text{light}\,(\lambda < 325\,\text{nm})}{\xrightarrow{\hspace{1cm}}}} O_2 + O$	Forward reaction: rate $= k_1[O_3]$	Very fast
	Reverse reaction: rate $= k_1'[O_2][O]$	Very fast
Step 2		
$O_3 + O \leftrightarrows 2O_2$	Forward reaction: rate $= k_2[O_3][O]$	Slow
	Reverse reaction: rate $= k_2'[O_2]^2$	Very slow

The net forward process (cancelling common terms) is:

$$2O_3 + \emptyset \rightarrow \emptyset + 3O_2$$

To demonstrate that this mechanism is consistent with the observed rate law we will initially concentrate on the second step. The *reverse* reaction in this step is extremely slow. This means it will have very little effect on the overall forward rate; it can therefore be ignored. Step 2 also contains the slowest *forward* elementary reaction in this sequence. A slow reaction

such as this is called a **rate determining step** (RDS). It acts in much the same way as a traffic jam in a journey; it dictates the overall rate of progress. Therefore, in general, it is reasonable to expect the overall rate law to equal the rate law of the RDS. In this case this is:

$$\text{rate} = k_2[O_3][O] \tag{b}$$

This appears to be at variance with the observed rate law (Equation a). Notice, however, that the oxygen atoms (O) that feature in Equation b are both created and destroyed during the overall reaction. Species that behave like this are called **reaction intermediates** and do not appear in overall rate laws.

In order to explore the link between Equation b and the observed rate law, we need to examine the reactions of step 1, as these control the concentration of oxygen atoms. Under conditions of constant light flux, the very fast forward and reverse reactions of this step rapidly reach dynamic equilibrium. Under these circumstances, the rates of these opposing reactions are equal; therefore:

$$k_1[O_3] = k_1'[O_2][O]$$

Rearranging this to make the concentration of oxygen atoms the subject of the equation yields:

$$[O] = \frac{k_1[O_3]}{k_1'[O_2]}$$

Substituting this into Equation b produces:

$$\text{rate} = \frac{k_2[O_3]k_1[O_3]}{k_1'[O_2]} \tag{c}$$

Noting that, in all cases:

$$\frac{1}{x^y} = x^{-y}$$

Equation c can therefore be rewritten as:

$$\text{rate} = k_2[O_3]k_1[O_3]k_1'^{-1}[O_2]^{-1} = k_2k_1k_1'^{-1}[O_3]^2[O_2]^{-1}$$

If we define $k = k_2k_1k_1'^{-1}$, then:

$$\text{rate} = k[O_3]^2[O_2]^{-1} = \text{observed rate law} \tag{a}$$

It is worth noting that rate law information alone cannot *prove* that a particular mechanism is in operation; it can merely exclude other possibilities. In the case under study, rate law information allows a mechanism consisting of a single bimolecular elementary reaction to be discounted. The suggested two-step mechanism is in agreement with observations and is widely accepted as accurate. However, there remains a possibility that it is not the mechanism that actually operates. Other possibilities that are in agreement with the rate law also exist and cannot be discounted without further investigation.

Table 2.6 Integrated rate equations for first and second order reactions of the type A → products.

First order process	Second order process
$\ln[X]_t = -kt + \ln[X]_0$	$\dfrac{1}{[X]_t} = kt + \dfrac{1}{[X]_0}$

Note: ln stands for natural logarithm (i.e. to base e); $[X]_0$ is the concentration of X at a given time, defined as time=0; and $[X]_t$ is its concentration after a given time, t, has elapsed from time = 0.

The above equation represents the direct thermal oxidation of nitrogen(II) oxide (NO), also called nitric oxide, with oxygen (O_2) to form nitrogen(IV) oxide (NO_2), known also as nitrogen dioxide. Laboratory experiments, where the concentration of oxygen can be varied, show that overall this is a third order process with the following rate law:

$$\text{rate} = k[NO]^2[O_2] \qquad (2.42)$$

In the atmosphere, where the concentration of oxygen is essentially constant, this becomes a pseudo second order reaction for which the apparent rate law is:

$$\text{rate} = k^*[NO]^2 \qquad (2.43)$$

2.4 Summary

The first law of thermodynamics informs us that there are no known processes in the universe that either create or destroy energy. However, it is possible for energy to be changed from one form to another. Consequently, a non-isolated system may enter into either heat and/or work interactions with its surroundings. The heat interaction at constant pressure, when only pressure–volume work is done, is called the enthalpy change, symbolised ΔH. This is defined to be positive for any process that is endothermic (i.e. causes the system to absorb heat from its surroundings).

The second law of thermodynamics allows us to assess the conditions required for spontaneous (i.e. unforced) change. Algebraically, these can be defined as

$$\Delta G = \Delta H - T\Delta S$$

If ΔG is negative, the process is spontaneous; if $\Delta G = 0$, the system is in equilibrium; and if ΔG is positive, the reverse process is spontaneous.

In the case of redox systems, there is a direct measure of ΔG, for $\Delta G = -nFE_{\text{cell}}$, or under standard conditions $\Delta G^o = -nFE_{\text{cell}}^o$. E_{cell}^o can be calculated from tabulated data.

ΔH, ΔS and ΔG are all functions of state. This means that for any reaction their values, under standard conditions, can be calculated from tabulated data, using expressions of the form

$$\Delta X^o = \Sigma X_f^o(\text{products}) - \Sigma X_f^o(\text{reactants})$$

where X = ΔH or ΔG, or

$$\Delta S^o = \Sigma S_f^o(\text{products}) - \Sigma S_f^o(\text{reactants})$$

Dynamic equilibria are sustained because of continual equal and opposite change. At any one temperature, a dynamic equilibrium is characterised by its equilibrium constant K. A reaction in equilibrium may be represented thus:

$$aA + bB \rightleftharpoons cC + dD$$

for which

$$K = \frac{\{C\}^c \times \{D\}^d}{\{A\}^a \times \{B\}^b}$$

The relationship between ΔG^o and K is as follows:

$$\Delta G^o = -RT \ln K$$

Predictions about the response to perturbation of a system at equilibrium can be made on the basis of Le Chatelier's principle, which may be stated thus:

> If a system at dynamic equilibrium is perturbed by changes in concentration, pressure or temperature, it will alter its composition so as to minimise the change.

While the arguments summarised above inform us about the direction of change, they cannot predict or explain the rate at which change will occur. This can be achieved by a study of chemical kinetics.

Experimentally it is found that for reactions of the type

$$aA + bB \rightleftharpoons cC + dD$$

rate laws can be written that take the form

$$\text{rate of reaction} = k \times [A]^e \times [B]^f \times [C]^g \times [D]^h$$

where the powers e, f, g and h are commonly 0, 1 or 2, although fractions and negative numbers are also found. The sum of the powers is known as the overall order of the reaction. The rate of a given reaction will be increased either if the temperature is raised or if a catalyst is added.

Reactions occur via one or more indivisible elementary reactions. The sequence of these that lead to the overall reaction is called the reaction mechanism. If the rate law of a reaction is known, it can be used as a tool in the elucidation of its mechanism.

Integrated rate equations express the relationship between the concentration of a reactant and time. The half-life of a reactant is the time taken for either its concentration or its amount to fall to half of its original value. Integrated rate equations can be used to derive expressions that define the half-life of a reactant in terms of k.

Under conditions where one or more of the reactants are in great excess, the observed rate law may assume a pseudo order that is less than its true order.

Problems

1 (a) Use the data below to calculate ΔH°, ΔS° and ΔG° at 298 K associated with the complete combustion of ethane ($C_2H_{6(g)}$).

(b) What is the specific enthalpy of ethane? If it were burnt in an internal combustion engine with exactly the same efficiency as octane, which of these fuels would produce more carbon dioxide on a joule for joule basis?

Compound	$\Delta H^{\circ}_{f\,298}$/kJ mol^{-1}	$\Delta S^{\circ}_{f\,298}$/J K^{-1} mol^{-1}
$C_2H_{6(g)}$	−84.7	230
$O_{2(g)}$	0	205
$CO_{2(g)}$	−394	214
$H_2O_{(g)}$	−242	189

2 Calculate the enthalpy density of methanol (CH_3OH) from the following data. Express your answer in kJ dm^{-3}.

Substance	$\Delta H^{\circ}_{f\,298}$/kJ mol^{-1}
$CH_3OH_{(l)}$	−239
$CO_{2(g)}$	−349
$H_2O_{(l)}$	−286

Assume the density of methanol to be 0.791 g cm^{-3}.

3 (a) Under standard conditions, at what temperature will pure liquid water spontaneously freeze? Use the data below to justify your answer.

For the reaction: $H_2O_{(l)} \rightarrow H_2O_{(s)}$ (2.44)

$\Delta H^{\circ}_{273.15} = -6.02$ kJ mol^{-1}

$\Delta S^{\circ}_{273.15} = -22.0$ J K^{-1} mol^{-1}

(b) If the process represented by Equation 2.44 were endothermic, would water freeze at any temperature?

4 All gases dissolve in water exothermically. Use Le Chatelier's principle to decide whether the solubilities of gases increase or decrease as temperature increases. How does this relate to the phenomenon of thermal pollution introduced in Chapter 14 (Section 14.8)?

5 (a) Use the information given below to calculate the equilibrium constant for the reaction represented by Equation 2.45:

$$CaCO_{3(s)} + H_3O^{+}_{(aq)} \rightleftharpoons Ca^{2+}_{(aq)} + HCO_3^{-}_{(aq)} + H_2O_{(l)} \qquad (2.45)$$

(b) Limestone is essentially calcium carbonate. Would you expect this to dissolve more appreciably in acid rain (pH $\lesssim 5$) or clean rainwater (pH $\simeq 5.6$)? Justify your answer.

(c) Calculate the concentration of calcium ions that would be present in water at equilibrium with solid calcium carbonate at a pH of 4.5. Express your answer in both ppm and mol dm^{-3}.

Information:

$$HCO_3^{-}_{(aq)} + H_2O_{(l)} \rightleftharpoons CO_3^{2-}_{(aq)} + H_3O^{+}_{(aq)}$$

$$K_a = 4.8 \times 10^{-11}$$

$$CaCO_{3(s)} \rightleftharpoons Ca^{2+}_{(aq)} + CO_3^{2-}_{(aq)}$$

$$K_{sp} = 6 \times 10^{-9}$$

6 Use the data presented in Box 2.8 to calculate the pH of rainwater that is in equilibrium with air that contains 1 ppm of sulfur dioxide.

7 The thermal decomposition of PAN occurs by the elemental reaction shown in Figure 2.3(a). Given that the rate constant for this process is 3.6×10^{-4} s^{-1} in the atmosphere, calculate the half-life of this species in the environment.

8 What is the mathematical relationship between k and k^* given in equations 2.42 and 2.43 respectively?

9 What is the ratio of $[O_2]:[N_2]$ in water equilibrated with air at 20°C? The Henry's law constants for the dissolution of oxygen (O_2) and nitrogen (N_2) in water at this temperature are 1.34×10^{-3} and 6.79×10^{-4} mol dm^{-3} atm^{-1} respectively. Note, information on the composition of the atmosphere is given in Chapter 4 (Section 4.1).

2.6   Further reading

Atkins, P. W. and L. L. Jones (1997) *Chemistry: molecules, matter and change* (3rd edn). New York: W. H. Freeman.

Aylward, G. and T. Findlay (1998) *SI chemical data* (4th edn). Milton, Australia: Jacaranda Wiley (A useful, almost 'pocket sized' data book)

Ebbing, D. D. and S. D. Gammon (1999) *General chemistry* (6th edn). Boston, MA: Houghton Mifflin.

Lide, D. R. (1998) *CRC handbook of chemistry and physics* (79th edn). Boca Raton, FL: CRC Press. (A superb data book, but definitely not pocket sized)

Chapter 3

The Earth's surface

Chapter Objectives

After reading this chapter, you should be able to:

- Understand the essential features of the theory of plate tectonics.

- Define the terms rock and soil.

- Understand the categorisation of rock into igneous, metamorphic and sedimentary forms and the interconversion of these types of rock during the rock cycle.

- Describe the components of soils, and what is meant by the terms soil textural class and soil structure.

- Describe the processes of soil formation and the factors that control soil development, and appreciate how these lead to the features seen in soil profiles.

- Appreciate the environmental importance of water.

- Compare and contrast the salient features of rainwater, river water, lake water and sea water.

Introduction

Life has evolved at the surface of the Earth in the environment formed at the interface between the land, sea and air. An understanding of the nature of this environment and the processes that have produced it is essential if we are to ensure the continued existence of the human species. In this chapter we are concerned with the thin skin of the Earth, called the crust, the waters found on it and the soils generated from it. Chapter 4 is dedicated to the atmosphere.

3.1 The crust

3.1.1 The position of the crust

As shown in Figure 3.1, the Earth may be divided into three zones, the core, mantle and crust. The crust represents less than 1% of the Earth's total mass and only about 0.5% of its radius. It does not, however, have a uniform thickness, varying from an average of about 35 km in the continental regions to about 5–10 km under the oceans.

The high points of the crust are continually being worn away by the processes of weathering (Section 3.2) and erosion. The low points of the crust are being infilled with the debris generated by these destructive processes. As this has been happening since the formation of the crust between 3.9×10^9 and 4.5×10^9 years ago, one might expect it to be smooth, and yet it is not. This is because the crust is also subjected to earth-building processes, which have their origin in forces that are generated within the planet. Land-forming processes that have their origin within the Earth are said to be **endogenic**, while surface processes (such as erosion) are said to be **exogenic**.

Figure 3.1 A schematic representation of the major components of the Earth. (The depths of the outer two layers are not to scale.)

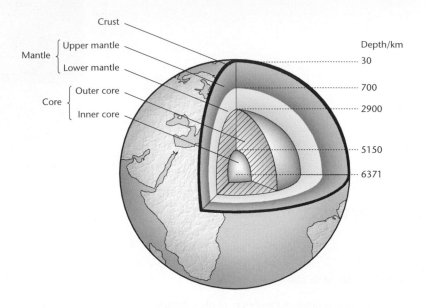

The crust and the upper part of the mantle form a coherent solid layer known as the **lithosphere**. This lies above a relatively soft region of the mantle called the **asthenosphere** (Figure 3.2).

Figure 3.2 The relationship between the lithosphere and the asthenosphere (showing a subduction zone). The arrows show the direction of plate movement.

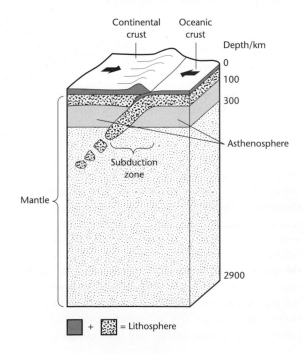

Plate tectonics

The term **tectonics** refers to the major structural features of the crust and the processes that form them. According to the widely accepted theory of **plate tectonics**, the surface of the Earth is divided into a series of essentially rigid plates of lithosphere (Figure 3.3). The fact that the asthenosphere can deform allows these plates to move relative to one another. The plates meet at **plate boundaries**, three major types of which are recognised: transform boundaries, divergent boundaries and convergent boundaries. A **transform boundary** occurs when two plates move, one past the other, along a transform fault, without either moving apart or colliding. Alternatively, plates may move apart forming a **divergent boundary**. Such boundaries occur in mid oceans and are associated with the addition of new crustal material from below, leading to the formation of characteristic mid-ocean ridges. Although much less common, continental divergent boundaries also occur, forming rift valleys. When two plates moving towards one another meet, a **convergent boundary** is formed. If one of the plates is continental and the other oceanic, the oceanic plate moves below the continental one, a process called **subduction** (Figure 3.2). This results in the melting of the subducted plate. The less dense material within it rises, causing volcanoes and mountain building (a process called **orogeny**). When two continental plates converge (as occurs at the Himalayas) plate thickening occurs without significant subduction. The intense and wide-ranging activity associated with convergent plate

Figure 3.3 The major lithospheric plates (from Summerfield, 1991).

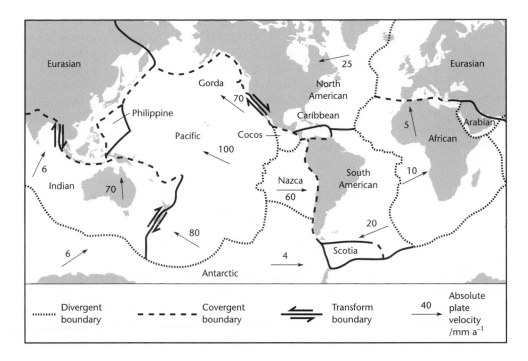

Figure 3.4 The current mobile belts of the Earth's surface (after Read and Watson, 1966).

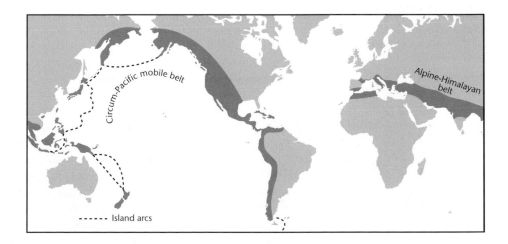

boundaries gives rise to areas known as mobile belts (Figure 3.4).

The driving mechanism behind the movement of the lithospheric plates is not fully understood. The most widely accepted theory suggests that the extremely slow cooling of the interior of the Earth is the primary motivator in this process. The inner core of the Earth is solid. This is increasing in size, at a very low rate, as the liquid outer core solidifies onto it[1]. As this occurs, heat is transferred from the core to the mantle where it is believed

[1] The absolute rate of solidification is estimated to be 3×10^{13} kg of iron per year. This is equivalent to <10 ppb per year of the outer core.

to sustain enormous convection currents within the asthenosphere. As shown in Figure 3.5, it seems probable that these currents drive the plates into one another at convergent boundaries, facilitating volcanism and mountain building, while pulling them apart at divergent ones. They also provide the magma that adds to the crust at the mid-ocean ridges. The heat that is supplied to the underside of the lithosphere by these currents is ultimately lost to space as terrestrial (i.e. long-wave) radiation (see Box 4.1 for more information on the nature of terrestrial radiation).

There is an alternative explanation for the initiation of plate movement. According to this, the subsiding portions of the oceanic plates that are subducted beneath the continental regions at convergent boundaries sink by virtue of their high density. In so doing, they pull the oceanic plates with them, leading to the formation of mid-ocean divergent boundaries, allowing magma to fill the gap and form the mid-ocean ridges. The movement of the lithospheric plates over the asthenosphere would encourage the establishment of convection currents as shown in Figure 3.5.

It is noteworthy that the two theories outlined above are not mutually inconsistent. It is possible that both mechanisms are in action, possibly in conjunction with others yet to be formulated.

3.1.3 The composition of the crust

The non-living, naturally occurring solid materials that form the crust are called **rocks**. Rocks need not be hard; the term encompasses such materials as clay and sand. Most rocks are composed of **minerals**. Each mineral has recognisable properties and a distinct chemical composition and atomic structure. Over 2000 minerals are known. However, there are ten mineral types to which the most common minerals are related; these are given in Table 3.1.

Over 80% of the mass of the crust is made up of only three of the one hundred plus elements known, namely oxygen, silicon and aluminium (Table 3.2). It is not surprising, therefore, that these elements dominate the composition and structural framework of most minerals. Such minerals are called silicates if they contain a structural framework consisting of silicon and oxygen and aluminosilicates if the framework also contains aluminium (Box 3.1).

Rocks can be conveniently categorised into one of three groups, namely igneous, sedimentary and metamorphic.

Igneous rocks form on the solidification of molten rock material, called **magma**, that has its origins in the mantle or in the lower part of the crust. Such rocks are nearly all made up of interlocking crystalline minerals

Figure 3.5 A theoretical model of the origin of the forces that cause the lithospheric plates to move. Heat, escaping from the core of the Earth, in the direction of the dashed arrow on the diagram, causes enormous convection currents to be established in the asthenosphere. Friction between the top of the asthenosphere and the bottom of the lithosphere drags the oceanic plates apart, forcing them into the continental ones.

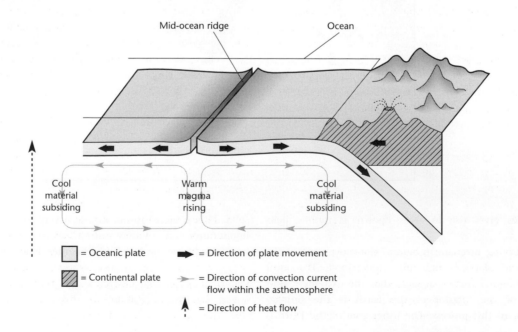

Table 3.1 The major rock-forming minerals.

| Mineral | Average abundance in rock types selected/% | | | |
	Limestone	Sandstone	Basalt	Granite
Amphiboles	0.0	0.0	0.0	2.4
Carbonates	92.8	10.6	0.0	0.0
Chlorites	0.0	1.1	0.0	0.0
Clay minerals	1.0	6.9	0.0	0.0
Feldspars	2.2	8.4	46.2	52.3
Iron ores	0.3	0.3	2.8	0.5
Micas	0.0	1.2	0.0	11.5
Olivine	0.0	0.0	7.6	0.0
Pyroxenes	0.0	0.0	36.9	trace
Quartz	3.7	69.8	0.0	31.3

Table 3.2 The major chemical elements of the Earth's crust.

Element	% (w/w)	Element	% (w/w)
Oxygen	47	Calcium	4
Silicon	28	Potassium	3
Aluminium	8	Sodium	3
Iron	5	Magnesium	2

with few voids. As a result they are generally impervious and frequently have considerable mechanical strength.

There are two major factors that determine the nature of igneous rocks: the composition of the magma from which they are made and the rate at which the magma cooled. The composition of the magma is determined, at least in part, by the content of the rocks that it melted and dissolved on its way to its point of solidification. The rate at which it cools is largely determined by where it solidifies.

Extrusive igneous rocks form on the solidification of magma that reaches the surface as a liquid; such magma is called **lava** (Plate 2). Lava tends to cool rapidly, allowing little time for crystal formation, so producing fine-grained rock (i.e. rock made up of mineral grains of small size).

Intrusive igneous rocks form when magma cools within the crust. **Batholiths** are large intrusions that cut across the features of the country rock (Figure 3.6); they have steep sides and no apparent base. During the formation of these features the magma cools slowly, allowing large crystal growth, resulting in coarse-grained rocks.

Minor intrusions called **dykes** and **sills** also occur (Figure 3.7). Both of these features are sheet-like and vary in thickness from a few centimetres to hundreds of metres. Dykes tend to be vertical, or nearly so, and cut across the strata of the country rock. In contrast, sills tend to be essentially horizontal and follow the strata of rock into which they intrude. Rocks in these features tend to have medium textures, reflecting the moderate rate of cooling experienced during their formation.

Sedimentary rocks form in one or more of the following ways:

- from the fragments produced during weathering and erosion;
- as a result of dissolved material precipitating from water;
- as a consequence of biological activity.

Sedimentary rocks that form from the solid debris of erosion and weathering are said to be **clastic** rocks; other sedimentary rocks are therefore **non-clastic**.

The loose material produced during weathering may become consolidated, a process known as **lithification**. This can occur by a variety of mechanisms including drying, compaction and cementation. The last of these may be mediated by the precipitation of materials from water percolating through the sediment. Silica (SiO_2), compounds of aluminium, calcium carbonate ($CaCO_3$) and various metal oxides often act as cements.

The debris produced by erosion and weathering is sorted on the basis of particle size (texture) by the action of gravity, running water and wind. In general, fine-textured material is transported further from the point of erosion than is coarse-textured material. As a result, rocks that form near to the point of the erosion tend to have coarser textures than those further away. Many clastic rocks contain particles of quartz as it is highly resistant to weathering.

Rock gypsum ($CaSO_4.2H_2O$) and rock salt (halite, NaCl) and *some* limestones (essentially $CaCO_3$) are examples of sedimentary rocks that have been formed by precipitation from water. Such materials are clearly non-clastic and are collectively called **evaporites**.

Many limestones, including chalk, are rocks formed by the biological precipitation of calcium carbonate ($CaCO_3$). This material is secreted by many aquatic organisms, being used in the formation of their skeletal structures. Limestones made from the calcareous material left after the death and decay of these organisms are clearly non-clastic.

Peat, lignite, bituminous coal and anthracite all result from the accumulation of plant material in bogs or

Further Information Box

3.1   Silicate and aluminosilicate minerals

The structural basis of silicate and aluminosilicate minerals

All silicate minerals are based on the silica tetrahedron (see representations 1 and 2 below). A tetrahedron is a three-dimensional geometric form that has four faces (each one an equilateral triangle) and four points; it is a regular triangular-based pyramid. The silica tetrahedron has the centre of an oxygen atom at each of its points and a silicon atom at its centre. It may be considered to consist of a silicon cation (Si^{4+}) residing within the hole left in the centre of four close-packed oxide (O^{2-}) ions, the net charge on the unit therefore being 4−. Alternatively, it can be thought of as a silicon atom bonded by single covalent bonds to four oxygen atoms, disposed towards the corners of a tetrahedron. In this case, each oxygen atom requires an electron from outside to complete its octet, again giving the overall unit a 4− charge. Neither of these models is completely accurate; in fact the bond between the silicon and oxygen atoms in this unit is about half-way between these two extremes, exhibiting about 52% covalent character.

Oxygen atoms may bridge silica tetrahedra. In this way each silica tetrahedron may be linked to one, two, three or four other tetrahedra by *shared* corners, so building up a variety of silicate frameworks. Unlike unshared oxygens, bridging atoms do not carry a net negative charge. Silica tetrahedra do not link via shared edges or faces.

In all silicate minerals the net negative charges carried by the unshared oxygen atoms of the silicate framework are balanced by metallic cations such as Ca^{2+}, Na^+, Fe^{2+}, or Mg^{2+}. These cations bond the silicate framework units of the mineral together by electrostatic forces.

Representations of the silica tetrahedron

1 A close-packed arrangement of oxygens (large spheres) with a central silicon (small sphere). The middle oxygen lies in the depression made by the three other oxygens, which are beneath it.

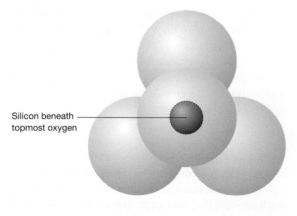

Silicon beneath topmost oxygen

2 A 'ball and stick' model, where light rods = the edges of the tetrahedron, large spheres = oxygen, small sphere = silicon and dark rods = the Si—O bond.

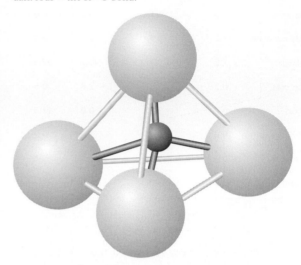

The classification of silicate and aluminosilicate minerals

The classification of silicate minerals is based on the complexity of their silicate framework, as shown in the table. Minerals in which some of the silicon atoms of the silicate framework have been substituted by aluminium atoms are called aluminosilicates. The framework then carries an extra negative charge for each such substitution by virtue of the replacement of a tetravalent silicon atom (Si^{4+}) with a trivalent aluminium atom (Al^{3+}).

Silicate class	Framework unit	Example
Nesosilicates	Isolated $SiO_4{}^{4-}$ tetrahedra	Forsterite, Mg_2SiO_4, an olivine
Sorosilicates	Short chains or rings of silica tetrahedra	Beryl, $Be_3Al_2Si_6O_{18}$
Inosilicates	Infinite chains of silica tetrahedra	Diopside, $CaMgSi_2O_6$, a pyroxene; tremolite, $Ca_2Fe_5Si_8O_{22}(OH)_2$, an amphibole
Phyllosilicates	Infinite sheets of silica tetrahedra	Talc, $Mg_3(Si_4O_{10})(OH)_4$
Tectosilicates	3-D network of silica tetrahedra	Quartz, SiO_2

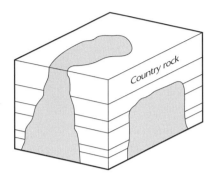

Figure 3.7 Dykes and sills.

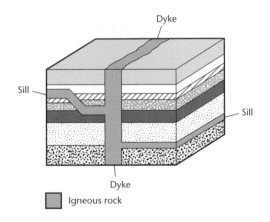

hydrostatic pressure, when in combination with thermal metamorphism, will favour the formation of denser minerals over less dense alternatives. Unlike hydrostatic pressure, directed pressure or stress tends to distort rocks, producing dynamic metamorphism. When this occurs in isolation, the structure of the rock alters but its mineralogical composition remains essentially unchanged. The movement of hot gases or liquids through a rock may alter its bulk elemental composition, leading to changes in the rock's mineralogical composition, a process called **metasomatic metamorphism**. This occurs because such fluids can act as transport media, importing and/or exporting mineral-forming material to and from the parent rock.

It is convenient to categorise metamorphism into one of three types: contact metamorphism, dislocation metamorphism and regional metamorphism.

Contact metamorphism occurs as the result of magma intrusions. The scale of the phenomenon depends to a large degree on the size of the intrusion. Sills and dykes will typically induce metamorphism to a depth of 2 to 3 cm in the neighbouring rocks. In contrast, a batholith may induce alteration in rocks 1 to 2 km from its boundary, so producing a contact aureole of metamorphic rocks. High pressures and temperatures are generated in the locality of a major igneous intrusion; in addition the magma will exude large amounts of gas and liquid. Contact metamorphism is therefore most intense on the boundary of the intrusion and is both thermal and metasomatic in nature.

Dislocation metamorphism occurs in the vicinity of major earth movements. Here, directed pressure is the main cause of the alteration, hence dynamic metamorphism predominates.

Regional metamorphism occurs over the large areas of mobile belts (Figure 3.4 shows the location of modern mobile belts). Thermal, dynamic and metasomatic metamorphism all occur. These often leave rocks whose constituent minerals show preferential orientation, having been reconstituted and recrystallised under directed pressure. Slate is a familiar and typical result of such processes.

An outline of the classification of igneous, sedimentary and metamorphic rocks is given in Box 3.2.

swamps. In such locations, the very high moisture content of the ground causes anaerobic (oxygen deficient) conditions to arise. Under such conditions the decay of plant material is arrested, leading to the formation of peat. While both bogs and swamps may produce peat, most coals are believed to be derived from ancient deltaic swamps (i.e. swamps formed in river deltas). These swamps became submerged either by a rise in the sea level or by subsidence of the land. In either case, this killed the plant life and the peat was covered by sedimentary silts or muds. Depending on the severity and longevity of the resulting compaction and desiccation, the peat was transformed initially into lignite (brown coal), then to bituminous coal and ultimately to anthracite (hard coal).

Metamorphic rocks form by the alteration of existing rock (called **parent rock**) by the action of extreme heat and/or pressure and/or permeating hot gases or liquids. The action of heat alone causes **thermal metamorphism**. This is often characterised by the presence of new minerals formed when high temperatures cause the parent rock to melt and recrystallise. Non-directional confining or

3.1.4   The rock cycle

If a long enough time-scale is chosen, it is clear that the rocks of the crust are not static but are created, destroyed and recreated in sequence, thereby producing the **rock cycle** (Figure 3.8). This cycle is driven by three principal sources of energy, namely the cooling of the interior of the

Further Information Box

3.2   The classification of rocks

Rocks are classified as being either igneous (if they are derived from magma), sedimentary (if they are formed by the deposition of debris or are the result of biological or chemical activity) or metamorphic (if they have been altered by severe pressure and/or high temperatures); see main text for details. Each of these major classes of rock is subdivided, generally in the manner shown in the tables below.

The classification of igneous rocks

Grain size	Silica (SiO_2) content[a]				
	>66% (acid)	52–66% (intermediate)		45–52% (basic)	<45% (ultra-basic)
Coarse	Granite	Granodiorite	Diorite	Gabbro	Peridotite
Medium	Micro-granite	Micro-granodiorite	Micro-diorite	Dolerite	
Fine	Rhyolite	Dacite/rhyolite	Andesite	Basalt	

[a] Note that the idea of acidity and basicity based on the silica content came from the nineteenth-century notion that silica was derived from silicic acid. This terminology has held, even though it is now known that the silica content is not a measure of acidity.

The classification of sedimentary rocks

Clastic

Grain size	Examples
Fine	Greywacke, siltstone, mudstone, shale
Medium	Arkose, orthoquartzite, sandstone, grit
Coarse	Tillite, conglomerate, breccia

Non-clastic

Biological origin	Examples
Phosphatic	Some phosphate rock
Carbonaceous	Peat and coal
Calcareous	Limestone of biochemical origin, oolitic and pisolitic limestone (in part)

Chemical origin	Examples
Phosphatic	Some phosphate rock
Ferruginous	Ironstone
Saline	Gypsum, rock salt
Siliceous	Chert, flint
Calcareous	Dolomite, calcareous mudstone, oolitic and pisolitic limestone (in part)

Earth, radioactive processes within the lithosphere and, finally, the sun.

As described in Section 3.1.2, the cooling of the Earth's interior is thought to bring about massive convection currents within the mantle that drive the movement of the lithospheric plates that cover the surface of the globe. Plate movement allows magma to be added to the crust both at the divergent boundaries (i.e. where the plates move apart) and during the igneous activity associated with orogeny (i.e. mountain building) at the convergent boundaries. This magma cools, forming igneous rock. When it is exposed at the surface of the Earth, this rock is altered by the processes of weathering and denuded by erosion. Deposition allows the products of weathering to accumulate in the margins of the oceans and other sediment traps (such as lake basins and river flood plains). Lithification of these materials leads to the formation of sedimentary rocks. These may later be exposed by uplift

3.2   continued

The classification of metamorphic rocks

Rocks formed by regional metamorphism

Original rock	Metamorphic rock: grade of metamorphism[b]		
	Low	Medium	High
Dolerite/basalt	Greenschist	Amphibolite	Amphibolite, charnockite, eclogite
Greywacke	Schist	Schist	Gneiss, granulite
Pure limestone	Marble	Marble	Marble
Impure limestone	Calcareous schist	Calc-silicate rock	Gneiss
Quartz sandstone	Quartz schist	Quartzite	Quartzite
Shale/mudstone	Slate/phyllite	Schist	Gneiss, granulite

Rocks formed by contact metamorphism

Original rock	Metamorphic rock
Dolerite/basalt	Basic hornfels
Pure limestone	Marble
Impure limestone	Calcareous hornfels
Quartz sandstone	Quartzite
Shale/mudstone	Hornfels

[b] High-grade metamorphism is greater in degree than medium-grade, which is higher than low-grade.

and/or denudation and consequently weathered and eroded, thus completing a loop within the rock cycle.

Metamorphic rock can be formed when any rock is altered by intense heat, high pressure and/or permeating fluids. In extreme cases, high temperatures result in the reformation of magma, which may be returned to the Earth's interior or solidified within the lithosphere or at the surface, completing other loops within the rock cycle. A further loop is completed when metamorphic rocks are exposed at the surface, as a consequence of uplift and/or denudation, and are consequently subject to the processes of weathering and erosion.

3.2   Soils

Soils are clearly of enormous environmental importance, being the media that support virtually all higher plant life. They are developed at the interface between the crust and the atmosphere by the action of biological, chemical and physical processes. These are the processes that are responsible for the breakdown of the rocks at the surface of the crust, a process known as **weathering** (Box 3.3). It is the presence of biological activity that differentiates a soil from merely weathered rock. Hence, a **soil** may be defined as a region of the terrestrial crust that has been altered by biological activity.

3.2.1   The components of soil

The vast majority of soils have four recognisable components: inorganic matter, organic matter, soil water and soil atmosphere. These are generally intimately mixed and may be difficult to separate. In poorly drained areas, such as bogs and swamps, the decay of plant material is delayed by the anaerobic (oxygen deficient) conditions that prevail. Under these conditions 80–95% of the soil solids may be organic. Organic soils such as these, while they may be of considerable economic and environmental importance, are not the norm. Most soils are termed inorganic (or mineral); these contain 1–10% organic matter (Figure 3.9, page 60).

The surface of virtually all rocks is covered with a layer of unconsolidated material called the **regolith**. It is from this that the inorganic fraction of a soil is generally derived. The regolith is either formed by the chemical and physical

Figure 3.8 Two representations of the rock cycle: (a) general overview

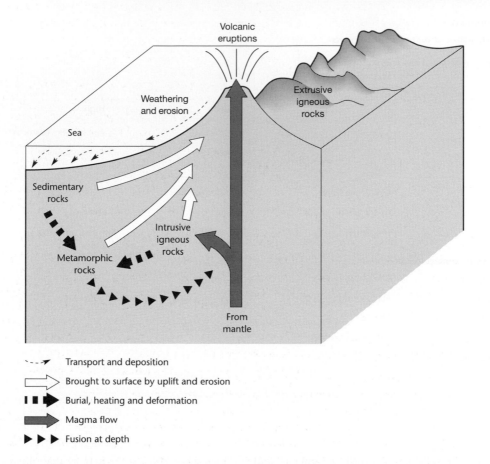

weathering of the bedrock (Box 3.3) or has been brought in from outside by the action of wind or moving water or ice.

The particle size distribution of the inorganic fraction of a soil is of considerable importance in determining its ability to support higher plant life and productive agriculture. For example, soils with a high proportion of fine particles (called **fine-textured** soils) have high moisture and nutrient holding capacities but have a tendency to be poorly drained, and are slow to warm in the spring. Conversely, **coarse-textured** soils have a high proportion of larger sized particles. Such soils are generally free draining and quick to warm, while often suffering from low nutrient and moisture holding capacities. Soils that contain a fairly even mixture of particles of various sizes are said to be **medium-textured**. These tend to share the advantageous properties of both fine and coarse-textured soils and are therefore ideal for the growth of many plants.

Any one soil will contain inorganic particles with a variety of sizes. These particles may be grouped according to the size range into which they fall. Table 3.3 (page 60) shows the various classification schemes of particle size in current use. While varying in detail, all of these share the recognition of

four gross size ranges, namely, in order of decreasing particle size: gravel, sand, silt and clay. The particle size distribution of a particular soil is indicated by allocating it to the appropriate textural class. This is done according to the proportion of sand, silt and clay sized particles that it contains (collectively known as the fine earth), the grit having been removed and ignored (Figure 3.10, page 61). Hence, a soil that contains 20% clay, 40% sand and 40% silt in its fine earth fraction will be a clay loam, a medium-textured soil.

Soil organic matter is a mixture of partially decayed plant and animal remains and material synthesised by micro-organisms. In many soils, it is a major source of the essential elements sulfur and phosphorus. For plants that are not capable of nitrogen fixation from the atmosphere (Chapter 5, Box 5.3), soil organic matter is essentially the only source of this element.

Humus is the organic matter that is more resistant to microbial decay. The structure of humus is complex and not fully understood. However, certain features have been established; these are explored in Box 3.4 as are the processes of humus formation and the types of humus

Figure 3.8 (b) with details of processes and the flow of energy and matter.

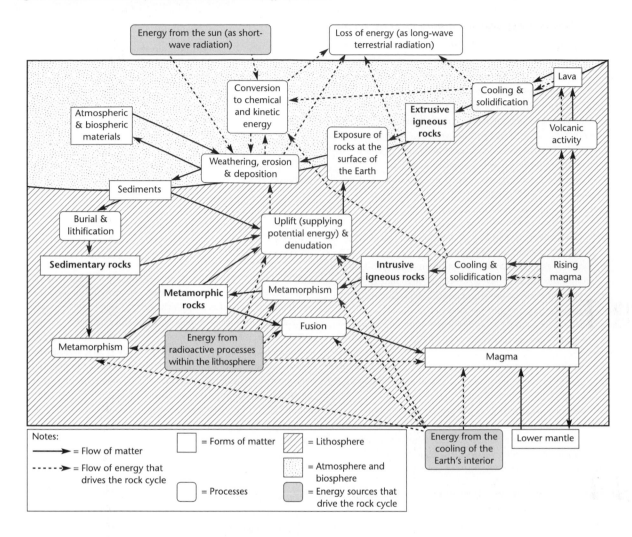

found. Humus has a very important role in the determination of the fertility of a given inorganic soil. It has a very high nutrient and water holding capacity compared with the inorganic fraction. For example, humus may be responsible for one-third of the moisture retaining ability of a medium-textured soil while representing only 5% of its mass. In addition, it acts as an adhesive, causing the particles of the inorganic fraction of the soil to be bound together into relatively robust pellets called **peds**. The formation of peds is generally accompanied by the appearance of voids. These provide pathways for effective drainage and the ingress of air from above. Thus relatively fine-textured soils can be free draining and well aerated if their humus content is sufficiently high.

Water that is lost from a soil sample on maintaining it at 105°C for at least 24 hours is defined as **soil water**. Water that is bound within the structure of the soil

minerals (i.e. water of crystallisation) is not lost under these conditions and is therefore *not* considered to be soil water. Distinction is also made between soil water and **groundwater**, the latter being the water that is below the water table. Soil water together with the dissolved salts it contains is called the **soil solution**.

Plants are not necessarily capable of utilising all of the soil water. The water that is lost by drainage from a saturated soil is not available, nor is the water that is held in very small voids or tightly bound to the surface of soil solids. Once all of the available water has been removed the plants lose turgor and wilt. The water content of the soil at this stage is termed the **wilting point** (WP). The water content of a soil after drainage is its **field capacity** (FC). The difference between FC and WP is called the **available water capacity** (AWC). Soils with high values of AWC are less prone to drought than those with low AWC values. As can be seen from Figure 3.11, medium to fine-

3.3 Weathering and secondary mineral formation

Weathering

Most rocks form at high temperatures and pressures in the absence of air, water and biological activity. These conditions are very different from those that prevail at the surface. As a result, surface rocks are not in equilibrium with their surroundings and are therefore thermodynamically unstable. The process of change that this initiates is called **weathering**. It has three recognisable elements, physical, chemical and biological weathering, which are discussed below.

Physical weathering (also called **mechanical weathering**) does not alter rock chemically, it merely fragments it. This occurs as a result of crack formation due to:

- rock expansion in response to unloading (the removal of the material above a rock by erosion);
- cycles of expansion and contraction on heating and cooling during the day–night cycle, or wetting and drying;
- pressure due to the growth of crystals (especially ice crystals) trapped within the rock;
- physical abrasion by wind or flowing water or ice and the particles swept along within these fluids.

The net result is a material with a high surface area to volume ratio that is therefore more open to surface chemical attack by air and water.

Chemical weathering is a process during which the chemical composition of the weathering material changes. Water has a vital role in this process, acting as a solvent, a transport medium and a catalyst. The major classes of reaction that are responsible for chemical weathering are as follows.

Oxidation. Some minerals contain reduced species such as Fe^{II} or S^{-II}. These may be oxidised on exposure to air. For example:

$$10H_2O_{(l)} + O_{2(g)} + 2Fe_2^{II}SiO_{4(s)} \rightarrow$$
$$2H_4SiO_{4(aq)} + 4Fe^{III}(OH)_{3(s)}$$

Dissolution. Water is an excellent solvent for minerals held together by ionic bonds, particularly if the ions are univalent. Hence, halite (sodium chloride) does not remain in the weathering zone for long except in arid conditions.

Hydrolysis. This is a reaction in which water is one of the reactants. For example:

$$CaCO_3 + 2H_2O \rightarrow Ca(OH)_2 + H_2CO_3$$

As the result is a relatively strong base (calcium hydroxide, $Ca(OH)_2$) and a very weak acid (carbonic acid, H_2CO_3), the resulting solution is therefore alkaline. The production of a weak acid and a strong base is a common consequence of hydrolytic weathering reactions.

Acid hydrolysis. This is hydrolysis by acidified water; it is more potent than ordinary hydrolysis. An acidic species that is ubiquitous on the surface of the Earth is carbonic acid, as it is formed by the dissolution of atmospheric carbon dioxide in rain, thus:

$$CO_2 + H_2O \rightleftharpoons H_2CO_3$$

This is acidic as it enters into the following equilibria (see main text for more details):

$$H_2CO_3 \underset{H_2O}{\rightleftharpoons} H_3O^+ + HCO_3^- \underset{H_2O}{\rightleftharpoons} 2H_3O^+ + CO_3^{2-}$$

Carbonic acid enters into a number of important weathering reactions, for example:

$$CaCO_{3(s)} + H_2CO_{3(aq)} \rightarrow Ca^{2+}{}_{(aq)} + 2HCO_3^-{}_{(aq)}$$

Acid hydrolysis is an example of a neutralisation reaction and results in the increase of the pH of the acidic medium involved.

Biological weathering is weathering that occurs as a consequence of biological activity. It can result in the mechanical fragmentation of rock, such as may result on root penetration. However, it may also produce changes in the chemical composition of the rock.

Organisms modify the chemistry of their surroundings by both excretion and secretion. This can have consequential effects on the weathering processes. For example, the excretion of carbon dioxide into the soil atmosphere by the respiratory action of a root will increase the level of carbonic acid-mediated chemical weathering. Acid hydrolysis is also favoured by the presence of acidic species such as carboxylic acids (ROOH) and phenols (ArOH), which result from the partial breakdown of soil organic matter.

In addition, some micro-organisms are capable of oxidising inorganic species. For example, the aerial oxidation of iron pyrites (FeS_2), as represented by the following equation, is much more rapid when micro-organisms are involved:

$$2FeS_2 + 2H_2O + 7O_2 \rightarrow 2FeSO_4 + 2H_2SO_4$$

The resulting strong acid (sulfuric acid) readily promotes acid hydrolysis reactions.

Secondary mineral formation

The minerals within unaltered rock are called **primary minerals**. **Secondary minerals** are those that form after the rock has formed and include those products by weathering reactions. Such secondary minerals are more resistant to weathering than primary minerals and therefore build up in soil profiles. The vast majority of these secondary minerals have dimensions less than $2\,\mu m$ and are therefore classed as clays.

The majority of secondary minerals in soils are either hydrated metal oxides (mostly of iron and aluminium) or one of many silicate minerals known as clay minerals. Clay minerals form either as a result of the alteration of primary silicate minerals, without their complete dissolution, or as a result of the recrystallisation of dissolved species.

3.3 continued

The vast majority of clay minerals contain layers of silica tetrahedra and are therefore phyllosilicates. In addition, they contain layers of either aluminium or divalent cations such as magnesium in octahedral arrangements of oxygen atoms (some of which are protonated and are therefore hydroxyl groups). The tetrahedral and octahedral layers are bound together by *shared* oxygens (see figure below).

Clay minerals all exhibit **isomorphous replacement**, that is the replacement of atoms or ions of the lattice with atoms or ions of a different element without structural change. This happens during the formation of the mineral and is therefore permanent. The most frequent types of isomorphous replacement occur when Al^{3+} ions take the place of Si^{4+} ions in the tetrahedral layer or where Al^{3+} ions of the octahedral layer

are replaced by M^{2+} ions (where M^{2+} is a divalent cation, commonly Mg^{2+}).

Isomorphous replacement of this type means that the lattice gains a permanent overall negative charge and is therefore attractive to cations in solution. These cations adhere to the surface. However, they readily undergo exchange with other cations in solution. This phenomenon is known as **cation exchange**, and is of vital significance. If soils did not have cation exchange capacities, the many nutrient species that are cationic (e.g. K^+, Ca^{2+}, Mg^{2+}, NH_4^+, Na^+) would be rapidly leached from the reach of plants by percolating water. The extent to which a material can exchange cations is referred to as its **cation exchange capacity** (or **CEC**).

An 'end-on' view of the layer structure of a typical clay mineral (kaolinite). *Source*: O'Neill, 1993.

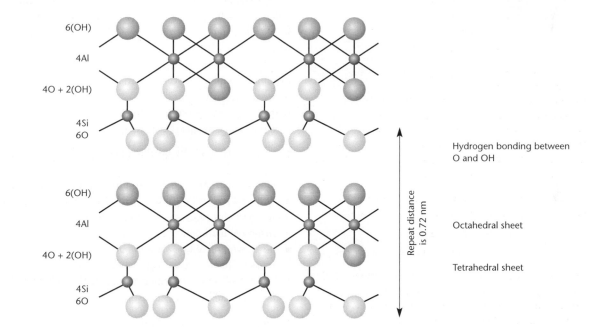

textured soils are much less prone to drought than are coarse-textured soils.

As discussed in Chapter 4 (Section 4.1), the major constituents of the atmosphere are nitrogen, N_2 (78%), oxygen, O_2 (21%), argon, Ar (1%) and carbon dioxide, CO_2 (0.03%) (all percentages are on a volume basis and refer to dry air). The air entrained within the soil is referred to as the **soil atmosphere**; it is in slow exchange with the bulk atmosphere above. The respiratory activity of organisms within the soil, coupled with the low rate of exchange, ensures that the soil atmosphere has a different

composition from that of the bulk atmosphere. In particular, in comparison with the bulk atmosphere, its oxygen levels are depleted and carbon dioxide levels are enhanced (Table 3.4). Under waterlogged conditions this alteration can become severe; oxygen concentrations can drop to zero, whilst those of carbon dioxide may increase by a factor of greater than 20. Such oxygen deficient conditions (referred to as anaerobic) provoke considerable changes in the soil environment. Micro-organisms capable of utilising respiratory oxidants other than oxygen (micro-organisms called **anaerobes**) multiply in numbers. Their

Figure 3.9 The components of soil. This diagram relates to an inorganic soil; the figures shown in parentheses are typical of those obtained from a silt loam topsoil. The proportion of voids occupied by water is extremely variable.

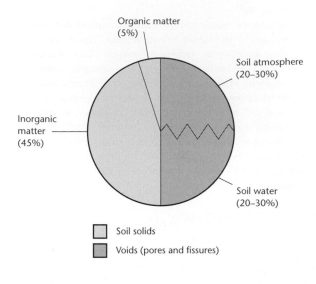

Organic matter (5%)

Soil atmosphere (20–30%)

Inorganic matter (45%)

Soil water (20–30%)

☐ Soil solids
▨ Voids (pores and fissures)

Table 3.3 Soil particle size classification schemes.

Size class	Size range (diameter/mm)		
	a	b	c
Clay	<0.002	<0.002	<0.002
Silt	0.002–0.02	0.002–0.05	0.002–0.06
Sand	0.02–2	0.05–2	0.06–2
Gravel	>2	>2	>2

Size ranges:
  a = the international or Atterberg system (this also divides sand into fine sand and coarse sand).
  b = USDA system (this divides sand into fine sand, medium sand, coarse sand and very coarse sand).
  c = system adopted by the Soil Survey of England and Wales, British Standards, and the Massachusetts Institute of Technology (this divides sand into fine sand, medium sand and coarse sand and refers to gravel as stones).

activity, when coupled with the changed redox potential of the soil environment, promotes increasing concentrations of reduced forms of nitrogen (N_2 is produced, as is N_2O), iron (e.g. $Fe^{2+}_{(aq)}$), manganese (e.g. $Mn^{2+}_{(aq)}$) and sulfur (e.g. H_2S). In addition, volatile organic species that either would not be produced under aerobic conditions, or would be oxidised in the presence of oxygen, accumulate. These include methane, ethene and various volatile fatty acids. The roots of many plants are damaged in waterlogged soils as a consequence of both the low oxygen levels and the presence of highly toxic species such as hydrogen sulfide (H_2S).

3.2.2 Soil structure

The arrangement of voids, individual soil particles and aggregates of these particles is referred to as the **soil structure**. This has both macroscopic and microscopic manifestations. The former of these can be seen with the naked eye or with the aid of a hand lens, while the latter only become evident with the application of optical or electron microscopy and will not be discussed here.

The solid material in most soils is aggregated at least to some extent. The greater the degree and stability of the aggregation, the more developed the structure is said to be. Soils that do not contain aggregated material have structures that are described as either **massive** if the material is consolidated or **single-grain** if it is not. Soils with highly developed structures, consisting of small (1–5 mm), stable aggregates and interconnecting voids will be less prone to waterlogging than their massive equivalents.

Aggregates of soil solids may be of several different types. Of these, **peds** are the most significant in natural soils. These are relatively robust aggregates, capable of withstanding several cycles of wetting and drying. They are clearly visible and easily identifiable, being separated from one another by voids or lines of weakness. Peds may be categorised into one of four groups according to their shapes; these are given in Figure 3.12.

Other macroscopic structural units recognised are:

■ **fragments**, made by breaking peds *across* natural lines of weakness;
■ **clods**, which are lumps of soil formed by tillage;
■ **concretions** and **nodules**, both of which are groups of soil particles permanently cemented together by insoluble material;
■ **pans**, which are horizontal regions in which the soil particles have become aggregated over considerable areas. They may be formed by mechanical action or by the accumulation of cementing materials washed from higher in the soil;
■ **pores**, which are cylindrical voids;
■ **fissures**, which are voids that are approximately planar.

3.2.3 The soil profile

A vertical section through a soil is referred to as a **soil profile**. Most soil profiles exhibit pronounced horizontal banding. Each band, called a **horizon**, is distinguishable from its neighbours on the basis of differences in one or more of colour, texture, structure, hardness or other tangible property.

Clearly, different soils have different profiles. However, the generation of many soils includes the processes

Figure 3.10 Soil textural classes (from White, 1979, after SSEW, 1974).

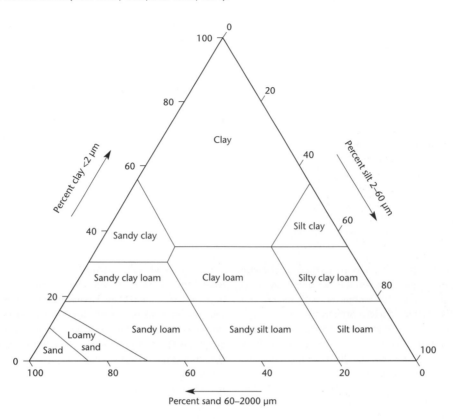

associated with the addition of organic matter from above and the translocation of material by percolating water from the upper part of the profile to the lower. As illustrated in Plate 3 this frequently produces a soil profile with:

- a layer of organic matter at the surface (often labelled the L horizon);
- a horizon from which material has been washed, hence described as **eluvial** (the A horizon);
- a horizon into which the material has been washed, hence described as **illuvial** (the B horizon);
- a layer of unconsolidated chemically and physically weathered parent material (the C horizon);
- unweathered bedrock (the R horizon).

Of these, the A and B horizons are virtually ubiquitous in mineral soils.

3.2.4 The processes of soil formation

The soil profile may be considered to be an open system (Figure 3.13). Material inputs to this system result from aqueous precipitation (rain, snow, hail, etc.), natural organic matter input (e.g. litter fall), deposition of debris eroded from elsewhere, lateral inflow from adjacent soils, the input of weathered material from the parent material, and man-made additions including fertilisers and other agrochemicals. Material outputs result from leaching, lateral outflow, evapo-transpiration, plant uptake, erosion and gaseous losses from the soil atmosphere. Within the system, soil-forming chemical, biological and physical processes occur that result in the alteration and translocation of material. These include biological activity, including humus formation (Box 3.4), mineral dissolution and secondary mineral formation (Box 3.3), *leaching, gleying, lessivage, podzolisation, upward translocation* and *physical mixing*. Of these processes, those shown in italics are explored below, while those in roman type are detailed in boxes as indicated.

Leaching is a process by which percolating water moves matter from one place to another. In its early stages it will move material down the profile, concentrating it in the lower horizons, while at a later stage it may remove the material from the soil altogether. There are two principal factors that determine the rate at which a given material is leached, its solubility and rainfall. In general, the more soluble a material is, the greater is its susceptibility to leaching and the more mobile it appears

3.4   Humus

The formation, nature and properties of humus

Plant and animal remains that are found in the soil decompose to produce water, carbon dioxide and a residue, called humus, that is highly resistant to further breakdown. This decomposition occurs as a result of:

- mechanical breakdown caused by, for example, ice crystal growth or the abrasive action of wind and moving water;
- chemical reactions with air and water including hydrolysis, oxidation and hydration;
- the activity of detritivores such as woodlice (Crustacea, Isopoda), earthworms (Annelida, Lumbricidae) and eelworms (Nematoda);
- the action of decomposer organisms such as fungi and bacteria.

These processes occur in parallel; however, the relative importance of those higher up the above list becomes less important as the decomposition progresses. The actions of decomposers and detritivores are dealt with in Chapter 9, Section 9.5.

Humus is an insoluble, highly heterogeneous polymeric material. It is believed to be formed by the condensation of amino acids with microbially oxidised simple aromatic compounds of both plant and microbial origin. It contains a high density of phenolic (ArOH), carbonyl ($R_2C{=}O$) and carboxylic acid (RCOOH) functional groups. These groups allow humus to bind metal ions, by virtue of both chelation and a high, but pH dependent, cation exchange capacity.

Humus is found in particles of colloidal size (i.e. $< 2\,\mu$m). It is tightly bound to the inorganic compounds of the soil's clay fraction by a combination of hydrogen bonds, Van der Waals' forces, and coordination to cations held by the negative charge on the mineral fraction. The results of this are called **clay–humus complexes**.

Types of humus

Humified organic matter that is well incorporated into a mineral soil is referred to as **mull** humus. This forms in soils that are moist, well-aerated and neutral or mildly acidic. In such soils the rapid rate of humification, coupled with the mixing of organic matter and mineral matter by detritivores, means that little or no surface accumulation of organic matter occurs.

Such accumulation is favoured, however, in environments where the activity of detritivores and/or aerobic micro-organisms is limited. These environments may prevail in soils that are waterlogged, have low temperatures and/or are highly acidic. Waterlogging over extended periods of time will arrest the rate of organic matter breakdown, leading to the formation of peat, an organic soil. Highly acidic conditions, such as are generated under coniferous woods, inhibit the incorporation of organic matter into the inorganic part of the soil. This can lead to the build-up of organic matter, called **mor** humus, on the surface of an essentially inorganic soil.

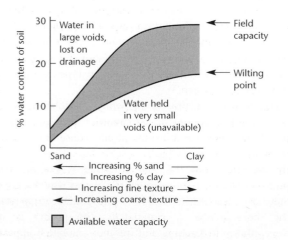

Figure 3.11 The generally observed relationship between soil texture and soil moisture characteristics. Note that the available water capacity of a given mineral soil will be markedly increased by a modest rise in humus content.

in the soil environment. The highly soluble sodium chloride, for instance, is rarely found in soils except in the most arid areas. In contrast, the sparingly soluble calcium carbonate, present in calcareous parent materials, may remain in the profile for thousands of years, even in humid climates. The behaviour of calcium carbonate also serves to illustrate the rule that higher rainfall leads to more rapid leaching, the trend shown in Figure 3.14 being typical.

Different compounds that contain the same element may have strikingly different solubilities. It follows that the chemical form of a given element will have a considerable influence on its susceptibility to leaching (elements in different chemical forms are said to be in different chemical species). For example, leaching of calcium becomes more rapid as the percolating water becomes more acidic. This can be understood when it is realised that sparingly soluble calcium carbonate ($CaCO_3$) may be converted to the more soluble calcium hydrogen carbonate ($Ca(HCO_3)_2$) and aqueous calcium ions by the following reaction:

Table 3.4 The composition of the soil atmosphere in well-aerated soils (Russell, 1973).

Soil and land use	Usual composition (% by volume)	
	O$_2$	CO$_2$
Arable land:		
fallow	20.7	0.1
unmanured	20.4	0.2
manured	20.3	0.4
Sandy soil, manured and cropped with:		
potatoes	20.3	0.6
serradella	20.7	0.2
Pasture land	18–20	0.5–1.5

Figure 3.12 The classification of peds by shape.

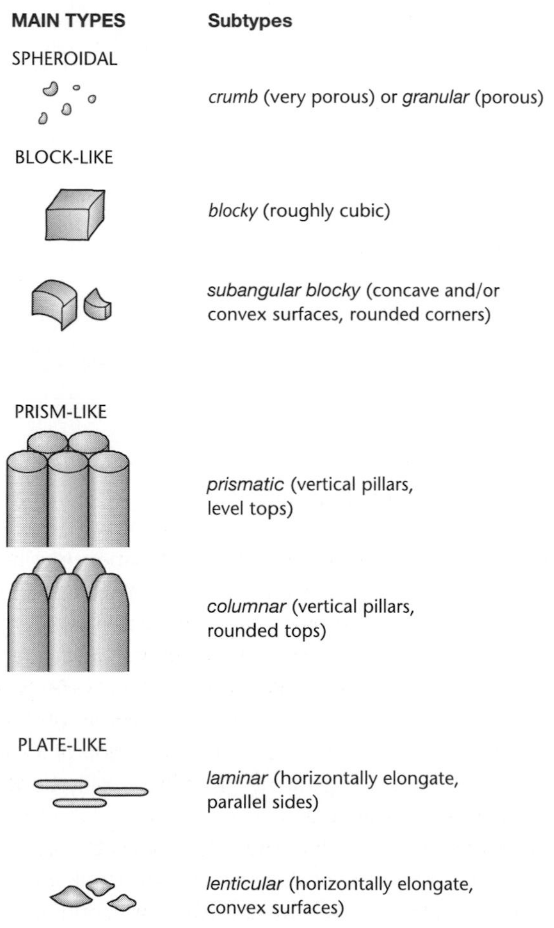

MAIN TYPES — **Subtypes**

SPHEROIDAL — *crumb* (very porous) or *granular* (porous)

BLOCK-LIKE — *blocky* (roughly cubic); *subangular blocky* (concave and/or convex surfaces, rounded corners)

PRISM-LIKE — *prismatic* (vertical pillars, level tops); *columnar* (vertical pillars, rounded tops)

PLATE-LIKE — *laminar* (horizontally elongate, parallel sides); *lenticular* (horizontally elongate, convex surfaces)

$$2CaCO_{3(s)} + 2H^+_{(aq)} \rightarrow Ca^{2+}_{(aq)} + Ca(HCO_3)_{2(aq)}$$

Gleying is a process that involves changes in chemical speciation that result in changes in solubility. It is characterised by the reduction and subsequent partial solubilisation and leaching of iron. It occurs in waterlogged mineral soils that nonetheless contain some organic matter. Under the anaerobic conditions that prevail in such soils any iron(III) present may be reduced to iron(II). This occurs by a combination of purely chemical and microbiologically mediated reactions, the latter being dominant. Most of the iron(II) produced is in the form of either soluble complexes or solid blue–green–grey coloured mixed hydroxides of iron(II) and iron(III). A gleyed horizon may therefore be identified by the presence of blue–green to blue–grey colours. These are frequently accompanied in the more aerobic areas, such as root channels, by the orange–brown colours of insoluble iron(III) compounds. These compounds form and precipitate when the soluble iron(II) complexes formed on gleying are transported to the more aerobic areas by leaching.

The solubilisation of iron as iron(II) complexes is not unique to gleying. Similar, while not identical, phenomena occur in the processes of lessivage and podzolisation. Let us consider these in turn.

Lessivage is the eluvation of clay and iron oxides from the A horizon. This is essentially a mechanical leaching process. However, it is probable that the destabilisation of soil aggregates within the A horizon is a necessary prerequisite of this process. It is likely that this happens by the removal of cementatious iron oxides by the formation of transient, soluble iron(II) complexes with phenolic leaf leachates.

Podzolisation may be considered to be a more extreme form of lessivage. Here, polycarboxylic acid humic compounds and polyphenolic leaf leachates form chelates with aluminium cations and iron(II) respectively. These soluble complexes are leached from the A horizon. As a result of the removal of coloured iron and organic matter, this horizon becomes characteristically pale in colour, and is redesignated as an E horizon (E horizons are eluvial horizons that are low in organic matter). Once translocated to the B horizon the iron complexes break down and the aluminium complexes precipitate. The resulting deposits of iron(III) hydroxides and organic matter cause a darkening of this horizon. The process in the B horizon is complex. However, it is primarily a consequence of microbial oxidation of the organic chelating agents and the flocculating effect of relatively high concentrations of polyvalent cations such as Ca^{2+}, Mg^{2+} and Al^{3+} found near the weathering parent material. The end product of this phenomenon is a soil called a **podzol**, the characteristics of which are the presence of mor humus, a leached E horizon and an accumulation of iron, aluminium and humic material in the B horizon.

Upward translocation is a feature of arid soils where

Figure 3.13 The systems view of soil.

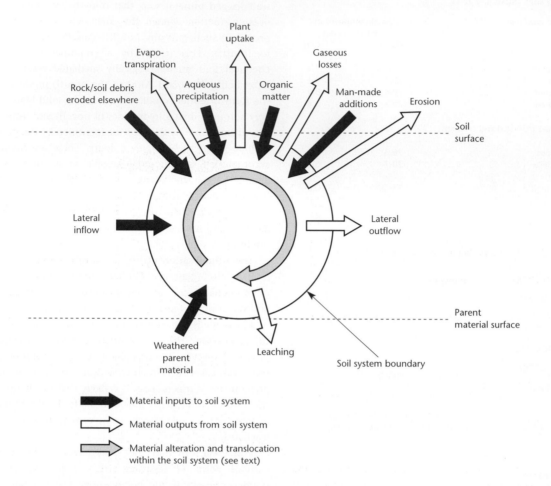

the rate of evapo-transpiration exceeds rainfall. Under these conditions water is moved up through the profile by capillary action. Its evaporation at the surface leads to the precipitation of the dissolved materials it contained. The net result is the upward movement of soluble and sparingly soluble material. When sodium compounds dominate the material translocated (which they frequently do) the process is called salinisation.

Physical mixing of materials within the profile may be mediated by biological, chemical, physical and/or human activity, all of which serve to disrupt horizon development and maintenance. The most significant of these processes are probably those associated with tillage (ploughing, etc.), root growth, burrowing animals and frost action. The last of these is a feature of climates that facilitate the repeated freezing and thawing of water within the soil. During freezing, growing water crystals may disrupt structural features. On melting, the space occupied by any large crystals may be filled with fine-textured material. The net result is frequently one of mixing.

3.2.5   The control of soil development

The major processes involved in soil formation (outlined in Section 3.2.4) are under environmental control. The environmental factors that exert greatest control are parent material, climate, vegetation and relief (topography); the influence of each of these varies with time. The complex nature of the interaction of these controls and processes has led to the generation of a wide variety of soil types. Below are given two examples that illustrate these interactions.

The first example illustrates the influence of time, showing the sequence of development of a soil from its infancy to maturity. It concerns the formation of the brown earths, typical mature soils of the deciduous woodlands of cool humid areas of Europe, North America and Asia.

In the early stages of development (Figure 3.15) the soil consists of little more than a mantle of poorly humified organic matter over a shallow layer of

Figure 3.14 The relationship between rainfall and depth of the calcium carbonate layer in soils derived from calcareous loess (a wind-blown parent material) (after White, 1979, after Jenny, 1941).

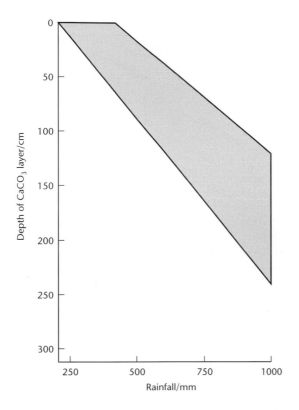

Figure 3.15 The stages in the development of a brown earth.

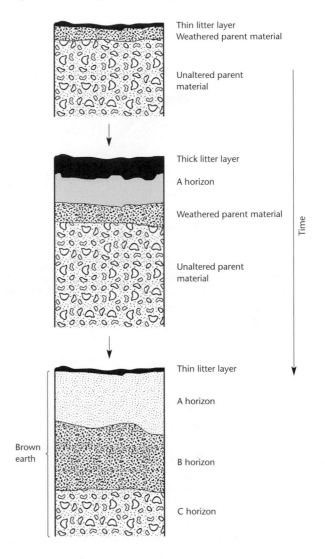

weathered parent material. Typically, such soils support pioneer communities of plants including liverworts, mosses and lichens. During the next two to three hundred years species diversity increases and the vegetation gradually transforms until it is dominated by grasses, sedges and shrubs. The soil is now much deeper (typically 20 to 30 cm) and consists of a thick litter layer over a recognisable A horizon that contains large amounts of well-humified organic matter with a gradual transition to weathered parent material below. The species diversity continues to increase over the next few centuries, and the vegetation becomes dominated by deciduous woods, the climax community. The numbers of burrowing animals, such as earthworms, increase, resulting in the incorporation of the organic matter into the mineral horizons, producing a very thin litter layer. A, B and C horizons are well developed in the mature soil, although the boundaries between them are gradual (Plate 3).

The second example concerns a specific location: a valley in south-east Scotland. This area has a cool temperate climate. Figure 3.16 shows a section across the valley concerned. This example is useful as it allows the

roles of parent material, topography and vegetation to be illustrated, together with those of local changes in climate.

The soils of the hill-tops are typical podzols. These soils have formed under the influence of a combination of moderately high rainfall (1000 mm per year), adequate drainage, and vegetation that produces chelating polyphenolic leachates.

The impervious fine-textured glacial till that dominates the parent material in the valley bottom has created an area of poor drainage. This has facilitated the formation of gleys and peats.

Interestingly, there is an asymmetry evident across this transect. This is attributable to local differences in climate, the south-facing slope being warmer and drier than the north-facing one. There are two distinct consequences of this difference. Firstly, podzolisation extends further down the north-facing slope as there is more water here to

Figure 3.16 The soils of a valley in south-east Scotland (from Simpson, 1983).

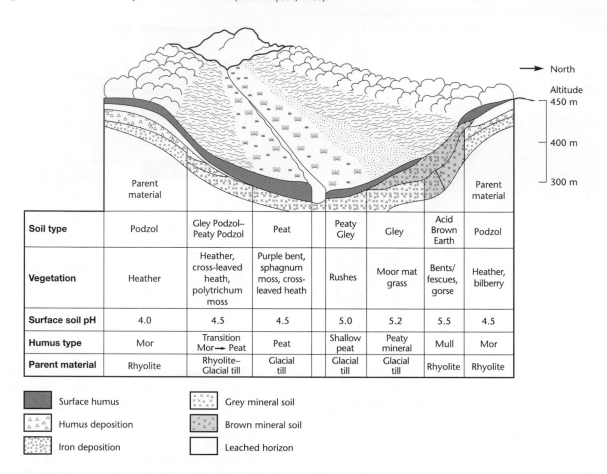

Soil type	Podzol	Gley Podzol–Peaty Podzol	Peat	Peaty Gley	Gley	Acid Brown Earth	Podzol
Vegetation	Heather	Heather, cross-leaved heath, polytrichum moss	Purple bent, sphagnum moss, cross-leaved heath	Rushes	Moor mat grass	Bents/ fescues, gorse	Heather, bilberry
Surface soil pH	4.0	4.5	4.5	5.0	5.2	5.5	4.5
Humus type	Mor	Transition Mor → Peat	Peat	Shallow peat	Peaty mineral	Mull	Mor
Parent material	Rhyolite	Rhyolite–Glacial till	Glacial till	Glacial till	Glacial till	Rhyolite	Rhyolite

- Surface humus
- Humus deposition
- Iron deposition
- Grey mineral soil
- Brown mineral soil
- Leached horizon

facilitate leaching. Secondly, peat formation is less advanced on the south-facing slope as there is less moisture available for waterlogging.

It is noteworthy that in this example there is a strong relationship between natural vegetation cover and soil type. While these relationships are common, particularly in mature soils, caution is required in their interpretation. It is not always possible to ascribe a direct causal relationship between soil type and vegetation. It is true that the soil type can influence the plants that are able to thrive in a particular locality. It is also true that the plants growing in a particular place will determine some of the characteristics of the soil in which they grow. However, the role of climate, topography, parent material and time must not be overlooked. A second and more pragmatic need for caution follows from the fact that a given plant species will generally thrive on more than one type of soil. Therefore, the boundary between soil types does not always coincide with a change in the vegetation.

While the examples chosen above were taken from temperate zones, the processes of soil formation are essentially the same the world over. However, the rate and extent of soil formation vary considerably. Higher temperature and higher rainfall favour rapid development, while stable conditions favour maturity. Full soil development may take only tens to hundreds of years in highly permeable deposits in the humid tropics, while requiring several thousand years in cool, dry climates. In either extreme, soil maturity will not be achieved under unstable conditions engendered by, for example, high rates of erosion or rapidly changing vegetation.

Attempts have been made to develop predictive models of soil development. One approach is to identify the combination of environmental conditions that optimises each of the individual soil-forming processes. Once this has been done it is possible to predict the combination of soil-forming processes that are dominant under a given set of environmental conditions. On this basis it is possible to predict the soil type that should be formed.

By way of illustration of this approach, Figure 3.17 shows the environmental conditions that favour maximal upward translocation, biological activity, gleying and leaching, four of the most important soil-forming processes. The predictive tool based on this information is shown in Figure 3.18. The reader may find it useful to evaluate the success of this model using the second example discussed above and illustrated in Figure 3.16.

3.3   The hydrosphere

The waters of the Earth's surface constitute the **hydrosphere**. About 70% of the surface of the globe is covered with liquid water, and about 10% of the land is covered in ice. About 97% of the mass of the hydrosphere is oceanic and 2% is ice, leaving only approximately 1% that is fresh water. These figures remain remarkably constant. This is because water is cycled through the hydrosphere, by the processes of evaporation, condensation and run-off. More details of this phenomenon are given in Chapter 5, Section 5.1.1.

The ubiquitous nature of water, when coupled with its remarkable properties, ensures that it has a role in virtually all environmental phenomena. For example, it plays pivotal roles in the regulation of climate (Chapter 4), the cycling of nutrients (Chapter 5), biochemical reactions and the processes of weathering (Box 3.3). Water's properties of environmental significance include:

■ higher melting and boiling points than would be expected on the basis of its molar mass, while having appreciable vapour pressures both when solid and liquid (allowing water to be present on Earth

simultaneously in all three phases, i.e. vapour, solid and liquid);
■ high enthalpies of melting and vaporisation and high specific heat capacity;
■ low thermal conductivity;
■ being less dense as a solid than as a liquid (virtually all other substances become more dense on solidification);
■ being an excellent solvent, especially for ionic compounds that contain singly charged ions and organic compounds that contain nitrogen or oxygen atoms.

Many of these properties have their origins in the polar nature of the water molecule and/or the three-dimensional hydrogen bonding network that is found in bulk water (Figures 1.2 and 1.9(a)). For instance, it is hydrogen bonding that is responsible for the high melting and boiling points of water, while its ability to dissolve ionic compounds can be related to the polarity of its molecules (Figure 3.19).

3.3.1   Rainwater

The compositions of the dissolved solids in rainwater, river water and sea water are compared in Figure 3.20. The main points to notice are:

1 With respect to total dissolved solids (TDS), rainwater is about 4.8×10^3 less concentrated than sea water. This is despite the fact that 83% of rainwater is generated by evaporation from the oceans. This is possible because on evaporation the water is purified as dissolved solids remain in the sea water.
2 While the concentrations of dissolved solids in rain and sea water are very different, the *proportions* of the different constituents in each are remarkably similar. The dissolved solids in both cases are dominated by sodium and chloride. The evaporation of sea water *spray* produces particles of sea water solids in the atmosphere; these are then dissolved by falling raindrops. This produces, with respect to dissolved solids, rainwater that appears to be very dilute sea water.

In addition to dissolved solids, rainwater contains dust particles that have been washed out of the atmosphere together with dissolved gases. The solubility of the various atmospheric gases in water is related to their atmospheric concentration and to their Henry's law constants by the following expression (see Chapter 2, Section 2.2 and Table 2.4):

$$P_{X_{(g)}}K_H = [X_{(aq)}] \tag{3.1}$$

Figure 3.17 The relationship between environmental factors and the soil-forming processes of leaching, biological activity, gleying and upward translocation. The zones show the optimal conditions for each of these processes (from Briggs and Smithson, 1985).

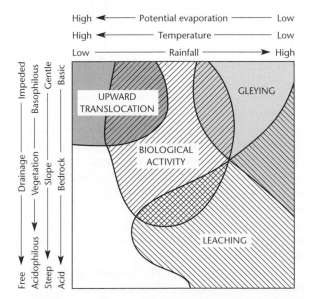

Figure 3.18 The relationship between environmental factors and soil type (from Briggs and Smithson, 1985).

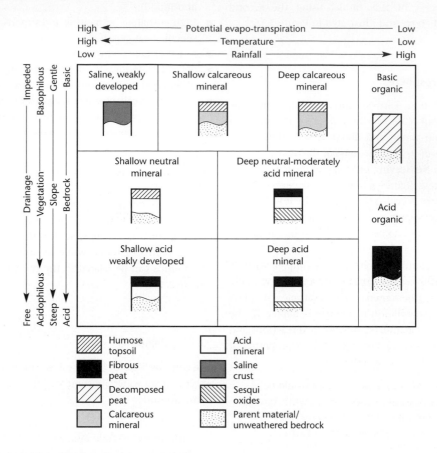

where X is a given atmospheric gas, e.g. O_2, Ar, etc.; K_H is the Henry's law constant for X; $P_{X(g)}$ represents the partial pressure (in atmospheres) of $X_{(g)}$, and $[X_{(aq)}]$ is the molarity of $X_{(aq)}$.

Table 3.5 gives the Henry's law constants for the major atmospheric gases. Of the gases listed in this table, one of them, carbon dioxide, reacts with water to give an acidic solution (i.e. pH < 7). This is important because it means that even unpolluted rainwater is a more potent weathering agent than pure water (which has pH = 7) (Box 3.3).

It is possible to predict the pH of unpolluted rainwater via the following argument.

The reaction between carbon dioxide and water may be represented as follows:

$$CO_{2(aq)} + H_2O_{(l)} \rightleftharpoons H_2CO_{3(aq)}$$

While this reaction lies to the left a significant amount of H_2CO_3 (carbonic acid) is present, and *aqueous carbon dioxide may be treated as if it were carbonic acid.* This undergoes reactions of the type:

$$H_2CO_{3(aq)} + H_2O \rightleftharpoons HCO_3{}^-{}_{(aq)} + H_3O^+{}_{(aq)} \quad (3.2)$$

for which

$$K_1 = 4.5 \times 10^{-7} \simeq \frac{[HCO_3{}^-][H_3O^+]}{[H_2CO_3]} \quad (3.3)$$

and

$$HCO_3{}^-{}_{(aq)} + H_2O \rightleftharpoons CO_3{}^{2-}{}_{(aq)} + H_3O^+{}_{(aq)}$$

for which

$$K_2 = 4.7 \times 10^{-11} \simeq \frac{[CO_3{}^{2-}][H_3O^+]}{[HCO_3{}^-]} \quad (3.4)$$

As a result of the involvement of $H_3O^+{}_{(aq)}$ in these reactions, the relative proportions of the various carbonate species (i.e. carbonic acid, H_2CO_3, hydrogen carbonate, $HCO_3{}^-$, and carbonate, $CO_3{}^{2-}$) will be pH dependent. This dependence is shown in Figure 3.21, from which it can be seen that the contribution from the carbonate ion only becomes significant at pH values > 8.5. For most natural water bodies it can therefore be ignored, as can Equation 3.4, and the total dissolved carbon dioxide concentration may be treated as the sum of the molar concentrations of $H_2CO_{3(aq)}$ and $HCO_3{}^-{}_{(aq)}$.

From Equation 3.1 and the statement given in italics earlier it follows that:

Figure 3.19 The dissolution of an ionic solid in water. Note how the polar nature of the water molecule allows both the dissolved cations and anions to be surrounded by solvent molecules (a process called solvation). It is the water molecules involved in solvation that keep the ions apart and stop them from reforming the solid.

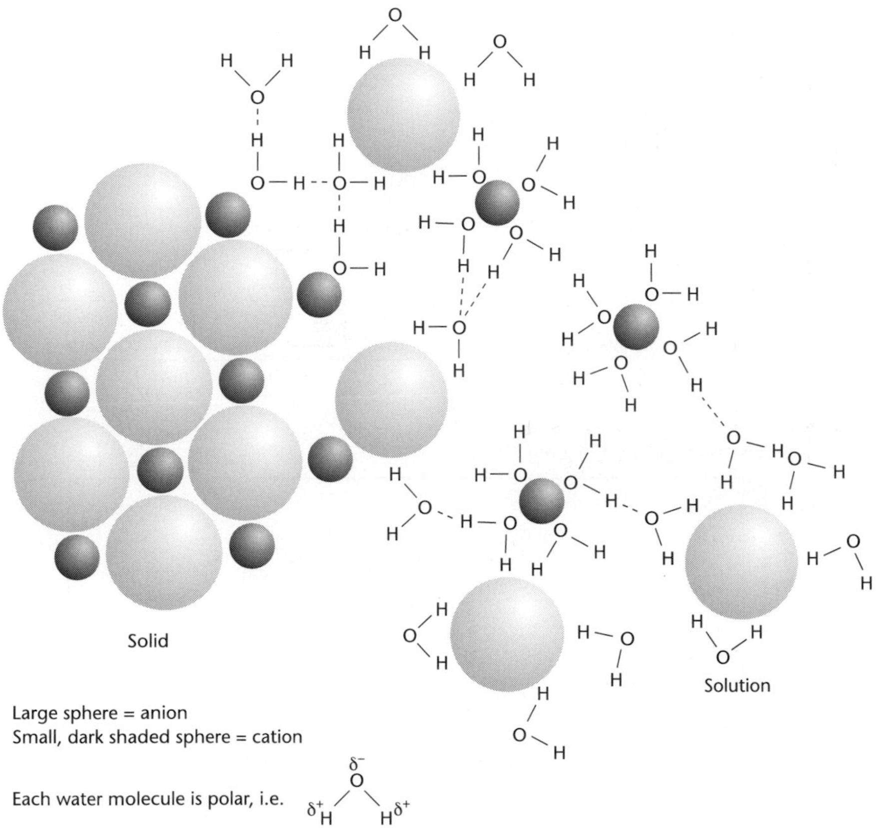

Solid

Large sphere = anion
Small, dark shaded sphere = cation

Solution

Each water molecule is polar, i.e.

$$P_{CO_2(g)}K_{H,CO_2} = [H_2CO_{3(aq)}] \quad (3.5)$$

while from Equation 3.3:

$$[HCO_3^-][H_3O^+] \simeq K_1[H_2CO_3] \quad (3.6)$$

Combining Equations 3.5 and 3.6 gives:

$$[HCO_3^-][H_3O^+] \simeq K_1 K_{H,CO_2} P_{CO_2(g)} \quad (3.7)$$

Noting that if the $[H_3O^+]$ from the auto-ionisation of water is ignored, Equation 3.2 implies that $[H_3O^+] = [HCO_3^-]$, therefore Equation 3.7 becomes:

$$[H_3O^+]^2 \simeq K_1 K_{H,CO_2} P_{CO_2(g)}.$$

Taking square roots,

$$[H_3O^+] \simeq \sqrt{K_1 K_{H,CO_2} P_{CO_2(g)}}$$

and, as $P_{CO_2(g)} = 3.6 \times 10^{-4}$ atmospheres,

$$[H_3O^+] \simeq \sqrt{4.5 \times 10^{-7} \times 3.79 \times 10^{-2} \times 3.6 \times 10^{-4}}$$
$$= 2.478 \times 10^{-6}.$$

Therefore, as $pH = -\log_{10}\{H_3O^+\} \simeq -\log_{10}[H_3O^+]$,

$$pH \simeq 5.61$$

This is in close agreement with measured values of the pH of unpolluted rainwater, suggesting that its pH is indeed controlled by dissolved carbon dioxide.

3.3.2   River water

River water is derived from rainwater that has either run off or run through its surrounding rocks. When rainwater hits the ground and percolates through rock its composition changes. Its total dissolved solids content increases and the proportions of its individual dissolved constituents alter. As a result, river water tends to be markedly more concentrated than rainwater and to have calcium rather than sodium as its dominant cation (Figure 3.20).

However, the situation is more complicated than this simplistic picture would suggest. When the weight ratio

Figure 3.20 The dissolved solids content of rain, river and sea water. Note 1. the different scales used for each histogram; 2. TDS = total dissolved solids. (from Raiswell *et al.*, 1980).

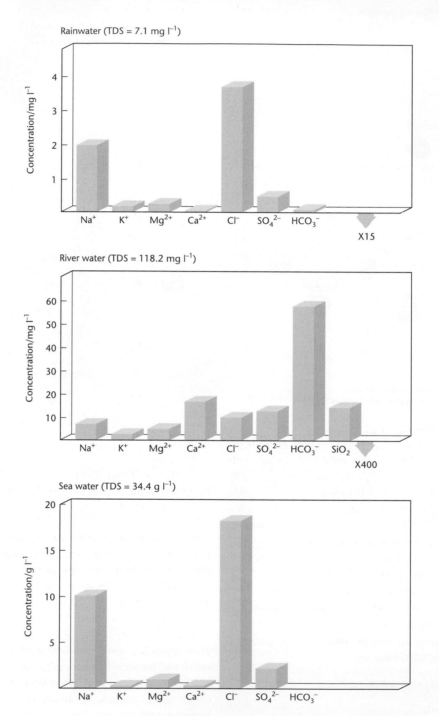

of $Na^+/(Na^+ + Ca^{2+})$ of the world's rivers is plotted against the logarithm of their total dissolved salts content, a distinct pattern emerges (Figure 3.22).

The water in rivers with catchment areas that are highly weathered tends to be only slightly different from rainwater. This is because the surrounding rocks contain little material that is easily leached. These rivers are said to be under **precipitation dominance** (Figure 3.23) and have characteristically low dissolved salts contents and $Na^+/(Na^+ + Ca^{2+})$ weight ratios close to unity.

Table 3.5 Henry's Law constants (K_H) for the major gases of the atmosphere in pure water at 20°C.

Gas	$K_H/\mathrm{mol\,dm^{-3}\,atm^{-1}}$
Nitrogen (N_2)	6.79×10^{-4}
Oxygen (O_2)	1.34×10^{-3}
Argon (Ar)	1.43×10^{-3}
Carbon dioxide (CO_2)	3.79×10^{-2}

Figure 3.21 The relationship between carbonate speciation and pH (from Raiswell *et al.*, 1980). ...... = H_2CO_3, ——— = HCO_3^-, - - - - - = CO_3^{2-},

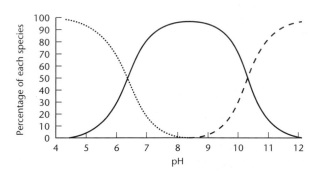

Figure 3.22 A plot of the weight ratio $Na^+/(Na^+ + Ca^{2+})$ against total dissolved salts for waters of the hydrosphere. The world's rivers, lakes and oceans are nearly all found within the shaded zone (after Gibbs, 1970). Figures 3.22 and 3.23 from *Science* **170** pp 1088–90 reprinted with permission from American Association for the Advancement of Science.

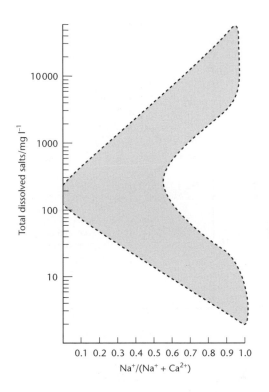

Rivers whose drainage basins contain rocks that are actively being weathered are said to be under **rock dominance**. These have intermediate dissolved salts contents and $Na^+/(Na^+ + Ca^{2+})$ weight ratios of about 0.55 and below.

Some rivers have dissolved salts contents higher than those under rock dominance. This can arise only in very arid areas, where the rate of evaporation considerably exceeds that of precipitation. Under these conditions the dissolved salts content increases. Eventually, the solubility of calcium carbonate is exceeded and this salt precipitates, leaving a solution with a high dissolved salts content and $Na^+/(Na^+ + Ca^{2+})$ weight ratio. Such rivers are under the control of **evaporation precipitation**.

3.3.3 | Lake water

Here we consider fresh water lakes, the dissolved solids content of which is largely determined by the river water that flows into them (see Section 3.3.2). However, compared to rivers, lakes are calm. This means, as we will see, that unlike rivers their behaviour is determined to a very great extent by the fact that pure water has a density maximum at 4°C.

If sufficiently deep, lakes in temperate zones develop a distinctly layered or **stratified** pattern during the summer months (Figure 3.24). An upper layer of warmer, less dense water, called the **epilimnion**, floats on a cooler, denser layer, called the **hypolimnion**; these are separated by a zone of rapid temperature change called the **thermocline** or **metalimnion**. Photosynthetic biological activity tends to deplete the epilimnion of nutrients; while breakdown of detritus in the hypolimnion depletes it of oxygen. On cooling in the autumn, the temperature of the epilimnion falls to that of the hypolimnion. At this point the water is the same density throughout and wind-induced vertical mixing is possible, a process called **turnover**. This facilitates the oxygenation of the deeper parts of the lake, while bringing nutrients to the upper waters. In the winter, stratification may also occur, with water at less than 4°C floating on water at 4°C in the depths. If the water freezes, the lower density of ice ensures that it does so from the top down. The insulating properties of the ice layer retard cooling so inhibiting the complete solidification of the lake. In the spring, the upper layers

Figure 3.23 The location of rivers under precipitation dominance, rock dominance and the influence of evaporation precipitation on a plot of the weight ratio $Na^+/(Na^+ + Ca^{2+})$ against total dissolved salts for waters of the hydrosphere (after Gibbs, 1970).

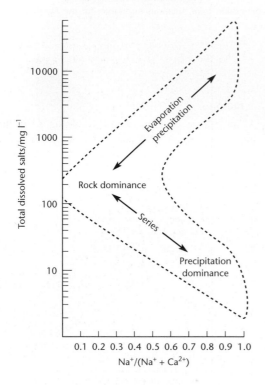

Figure 3.24 The stratification and mixing of temperate lakes.

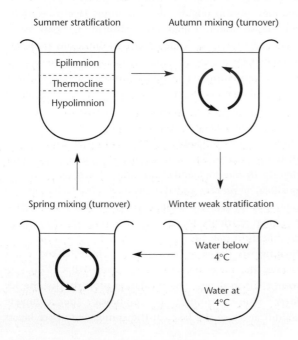

warm until the waters of the lake are all at the same temperature and density, therefore turnover can once again occur. Continued warming of the upper layers leads to the reintroduction of the summer stratification.

In contrast, lakes in the polar and subpolar regions that are frozen for most of the year do not show stratification in the summer, but exhibit turnover for the duration of this season.

Stratification occurs in tropical and subtropical lakes. In comparison with temperate lakes the temperature of the waters of the epilimnion and hypolimnion is higher, whilst the temperature difference between these strata is less marked. Turnover on cooling is relatively easily induced in these warm water lakes. As a result, those in subtropical zones tend to have a winter circulation period, while those in tropical climates with little seasonality may either turn over frequently or have rare or irregular periods of turnover.

3.3.4 Sea water

Sea water contains both dissolved and suspended solids. The concentration of total dissolved solids is, on average, $35\,g\,l^{-1}$; however, this varies between about 33 and $37\,g\,l^{-1}$ depending on climate, location and season. As shown in Figure 3.20, the dissolved solids composition of sea water is dominated by chloride anions and sodium cations.

Water, dissolved solids and particulate matter are perpetually added to the oceans by the action of rivers, rain, marine volcanoes, and ice and underground water flow (Table 3.6). This material is lost from the oceans, in the case of water by evaporation, and in the case of solids by precipitation and loss to the atmosphere of fine particles formed on the evaporation of sea spray.

Geological evidence suggests that the composition of sea water has changed little over the past 10^8 to 10^9 years. This implies either that change is very slow or that the inputs of water and solids must be matched by their outputs; in general the latter proposition is accepted as true. The inputs and outputs of water are discussed in Chapter 5, Section 5.1. The fate of suspended solids is, in the main, straightforward as these merely sink to be deposited as sediments. The mechanisms by which dissolved solids are removed from sea water are not all fully understood. However, physical, biological and chemical reactions all play a role. Table 3.7 itemises the main categories of reaction by which dissolved solids are believed to be removed from sea water, together with a numerical indication of their relative importance.

Table 3.6 Estimated rates of inflow of suspended and dissolved solids into the oceans.

Source	Suspended solids/kg a^{-1}	Dissolved solids/kg a^{-1}
Atmosphere	6×10^{11}	2.5×10^{11}
Ice	20×10^{11}	$< 7 \times 10^{11}$
Marine erosion	2.5×10^{11}	
Rivers	183×10^{11}	39×10^{11}
Subsurface waters	4.8×10^{11}	4.7×10^{11}
Volcanic activity	1.5×10^{11}	

3.4 Summary

The extremely thin, outer layer of the Earth is called the crust, below which is found the mantle. The crust and the upper part of the mantle are fused together to form a solid layer called the lithosphere. The surface of the Earth is made up of a series of interlocking pieces of lithosphere, each referred to as a plate. These come together at plate boundaries, of which there are three major types, namely transform, divergent and convergent boundaries. Mountain ranges form at convergent boundaries.

The crust is made up of rocks. These are non-living naturally occurring solids that are commonly composed of silicate and/or aluminosilicate minerals. Rocks may be classified as being either igneous, sedimentary or metamorphic, according to their origin. The processes of mountain building and igneous activity cause new igneous and metamorphic rocks to form and the land to be uplifted. The processes of erosion and weathering wear away at the uplifted land, and provide the material for new sedimentary rocks. The rocks of the crust are therefore part of a rock cycle.

Soils are the upper parts of the terrestrial crust that have been not merely weathered, but also altered by biological activity. Soils are open systems. They form under the influence of material inputs and outputs and a range of internal processes under the control of a number of environmental factors.

The hydrosphere encompasses all of the waters of the Earth's surface. The dissolved solids of both rainwater and sea water are dominated by sodium and chloride ions; in this respect rainwater appears to be very dilute sea water. In addition to dissolved solids, rainwater contains particles and dissolved gases.

The dissolved solids content of river water tends to be much higher than that of rainwater. What is more, the dominant cation in river water is generally calcium rather than sodium.

Table 3.7 A budget showing proposed mechanisms of removal of dissolved solids that enter the oceans by river discharge (after Raiswell *et al.*, 1980). Note carbonate and silicate formation are largely biologically mediated, while the other processes are either chemically mediated, or in the case of evaporative processes, physically mediated.

	Balance of constituents/10^{10} mol							
	SO_4^{2-}	Cl^-	Ca^{2+}	Mg^{2+}	Na^+	K^+	SiO_2	HCO_3^-
Annual addition by rivers	382	715	1220	554	900	189	710	3118
Removal processes:								
Evaporative processes $715Na^+ + 715Cl^- \rightarrow 715NaCl$ $382Ca^{2+} + 382SO_4^{2-} \rightarrow 382CaSO_4$			838	554	185	189	710	3118
Carbonate formation $838Ca^{2+} + 1676HCO_3^- \rightarrow 838CaCO_3 + 838CO_2 + 838H_2O$ $44Mg^{2+} + 88HCO_3^- \rightarrow 44MgCO_3 + 44H_2O + 44CO_2$				510	185	189	710	1354
Silica formation $360H_4SiO_4 \rightarrow 360SiO_2 + 360H_2O$				510	185	189	350	1354
Interactions between clays and sea water $Ca\text{-clay} + 189K^+ \rightarrow 95K_2\text{-clay} + 95Ca^{2+}$ $Ca\text{-clay} + 185Na^+ \rightarrow 93Na_2\text{-clay} + 93Ca^{2+}$ $188Ca^{2+} + 376HCO_3^- \rightarrow 188CaCO_3 + 188CO_2 + 188H_2O$ $10Mg^{2+} + 20HCO_3^- \rightarrow 10MgCO_3 + 10CO_2 + 10H_2O$				500			350	958
Reverse weathering $100Al_2Si_2O_5(OH)_4 + 500Mg^{2+} + 100SiO_2 + 1000HCO_3^-$ $\rightarrow 100Mg_5Al_2Si_3O_{10}(OH)_8 + 1000CO_2 + 300H_2O$							250	-42

The dissolved solids content of fresh water lakes is largely determined by the nature of the river water that feeds them. At any one time, the waters of deep lakes tend to be either stratified (layered) or subjected to vertical mixing (turnover). The occurrence of these two phenomena shows a marked dependence on both season and the climatic regime of the locality of the lake.

Sea water has high levels of both suspended and dissolved solids. The rate of addition of suspended and dissolved solids to sea water as a consequence of the influx of river water is matched by the rate of removal by deposition. The mechanisms by which dissolved solids are removed from sea water are not fully understood; however, physical, biological and chemical reactions all play a part.

3.5 Problems

1 How many oxygen atoms of each silica tetrahedron in a phyllosilicate are shared with other silica tetrahedra?

2 Arrange the following minerals in order of ease of chemical weathering: hornblende (an amphibole, a type of inosilicate), biotite (a phyllosilicate), olivine (a neosilicate), quartz (a tectosilicate).
   (Hints: (i) water is generally better at breaking ionic bonds than it is at breaking covalent bonds; and (ii) the Si—O bond is more covalent than the bond between the silicate framework and the metal ions in silicate minerals.)

3 (a) To what textural classes do soils with the following proportions of sand, silt and clay belong?
     (i) 80% sand, 10% silt, 10% clay
     (ii) 40% sand, 50% silt, 10% clay
     (iii) 10% sand, 40% silt, 50% clay
   (b) State the maximum and minimum proportions of sand, silt and clay that may be possessed by soils of each of the following textural classes:
     (i) clay loam
     (ii) silty clay
     (iii) sand

4 Explain, as far as you can, the formation of the pattern shown in Figure 3.25.

5 The soil atmosphere content of a soil at its field capacity is referred to as its air capacity (C_a). With this in mind answer the following, in each case explaining your reasoning:
   (a) In general terms, how would you expect C_a to vary with soil texture?
   (b) What truth, if any, do you think the following statement holds: 'A soil with a high air capacity will be less prone to the development of anaerobic conditions than one with a low air capacity'?
   (c) Do you think that a soil with a given humus content will have a higher or lower air capacity than a soil of identical texture but lower humus content?

6 In a soil sample, the soil atmosphere was found to contain 20 times the concentration of carbon dioxide found in the bulk atmosphere. Calculate the pH of soil water assuming that it is in equilibrium with the soil atmosphere and that it is controlled by dissolved carbon dioxide alone.

7 The mere evaporation of river water and consequent precipitation of calcium carbonate is not sufficient to produce sea water. Nonetheless, when sea water is placed on the plot shown in Figure 3.23 it appears within the envelope drawn to encompass the rivers. Shade the area of this diagram where you expect sea water to lie. Explain the reasoning that enabled you to decide which area to shade.

8 What is the minimum temperature of the hypolimnion? Explain your answer.

9 Warming in the spring can cause temperate lakes to turn over. Would you expect this to occur in tropical or subtropical lakes if they were to experience a period of warming of similar magnitude? Justify your answer.

Figure 3.25 The proportion of soil atmosphere, water, organic and inorganic solids down a typical profile.

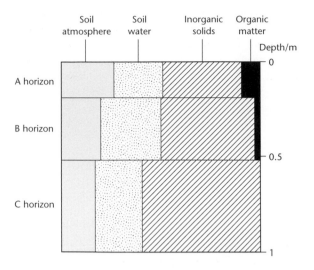

3.6   Further reading

Fitzpatrick, E. A. (1986) *An introduction to soil science* (2nd edn). Harlow: Longman.

O'Neill, P (1998) *Environmental chemistry* (3rd edn). Cheltenham: Stanley Thornes.

Raiswell, R. W. , P. Brimblecombe, D. L. Dent and P. S. Liss (1980) *Environmental chemistry: the earth–air–water factory*. London: Edward Arnold/Hodder Headline.

Rowell, D. L. (1994) *Soil science: methods and applications*. Harlow: Longman. (An excellent guide to the practical aspects of soil science)

Summerfield, M. A. (1991) *Global geomorphology; an introduction to the study of landforms*. Harlow: Longman.

White, I. D., D. N. Mottershead and S. J. Harrison (1992) *Environmental systems; an introductory text* (2nd edn). London: Chapman & Hall. (Especially Chapters 5, 6, 11 and 22; considers the structure and circulation of the atmosphere in Chapters 3, 4, 6, 8 and 9)

White, R. E. (1997) *Principles and practice of soil science: the soil as a natural resource* (3rd edn). Oxford: Blackwell Science.

The atmosphere

After reading this chapter, you should be able to:

- Describe the structure and composition of the atmosphere.

- Differentiate between the terms weather and climate.

- Demonstrate an understanding of the main features of the Earth's radiation and energy budgets.

- Describe the larger-scale features of tropospheric airflow and understand the processes that lead to these features.

- Compare and contrast the climates of the tropical, mid-latitude and polar regions of the globe.

- Appreciate that, when viewed over the long term, it is evident that large-scale climate changes have occurred in the past, and that such changes can be expected in the future.

- Recognise that the mechanisms that mediate climate change are not fully understood but that models of the climate system can be devised that have both predictive and interpretative value.

Introduction

The envelope of gas that surrounds the Earth is called the **atmosphere**. The boundary between it and space is not sharp. However, virtually all of the atmosphere is within 80 000 km of the Earth's surface and the bulk of it (99% by mass) is found in the lower 50 km.

This thin layer of gas has many functions that are central to the continued existence of life on Earth. It acts as a filter, removing DNA-destroying high-energy ultraviolet radiation; it traps infrared radiation that is given out by the Earth and transforms it into thermal motion, so warming the surface of the Earth; and it forms a conduit through which life-sustaining energy and matter move.

In the first section of this chapter the origins of the contemporary atmosphere, its composition and its structure are explored. The second section is concerned with weather, climate and the energy flows and atmospheric circulation systems that are responsible for the global climate.

4.1 The structure and composition of the atmosphere

The primitive atmosphere that enveloped the early Earth, prior to the evolution of life, was formed as a result of outgassing from the interior of the planet. This atmosphere was probably dominated by nitrogen (N_2), water (H_2O) and carbon dioxide (CO_2). It is likely that ammonia (NH_3) and methane (CH_4) would have been present also, but at lower concentrations. Oxygen (O_2), which accounts for about one-fifth of the volume of the current atmosphere, would have been present only at trace levels (10^{-8} to 10^{-12}% v/v).

Irradiation of this prebiotic atmosphere with ultraviolet light from the sun would have facilitated the following photochemical reactions:[1]

$$H_2O_{(g)} + hv \ (\lambda < 240 \, nm) \rightarrow H_{(g)} + OH_{(g)}$$
$$CO_{2(g)} + hv \ (\lambda < 240 \, nm) \rightarrow CO_{(g)} + O_{(g)}$$

where hv represents a photon of light and λ stands for wavelength.

The products of these reactions are free radicals. Such species contain unpaired electrons and are generally highly reactive. The following reactions would then have occurred, releasing energy as heat and warming the atmosphere:

$$2H + M \rightarrow H_2 + M$$
$$2OH \rightarrow H_2O + O$$
$$2O + M \rightarrow O_2 + M$$
$$O_2 + 2H_2 \rightarrow 2H_2O$$

where M represents a third body.

It is thought that the atmosphere underwent a dramatic change with the evolution of photosynthetic organisms. These convert carbon dioxide and water into carbohydrate and oxygen with the aid of light (Chapter 6, Section 6.4 and Chapter 9, Section 9.2.1). They release the oxygen into the atmosphere and retain the carbohydrate. The bulk of the carbohydrate is later oxidised back to carbon dioxide and water during respiration (Chapter 6, Section 6.3) or other forms of oxidative decay (Chapter 5, Section 5.1.2). However, some becomes buried in sediments and is therefore effectively permanently removed from the atmosphere. The net result is a decrease in the carbon dioxide content of the atmosphere and, perhaps more importantly, an increase in its oxygen levels.

Early life is believed to have evolved in water at a depth of 10 m or more below the surface. At these depths the water column would have been sufficiently deep to remove the DNA-damaging ultraviolet light ($\lambda \sim 302 \, nm$) arriving from the sun. Molecular oxygen (O_2) and its relative, ozone (O_3), can also remove this lethal ultraviolet radiation (see later in this section). Hence, the increase in the molecular oxygen content of the atmosphere brought about by the advent of photosynthesis would have facilitated the development of life in shallow waters and eventually on land.

[1] **Photochemical reactions** are chemical reactions that either will not occur in the absence of light, or are assisted or accelerated by the presence of light.

Table 4.1 The major components of dry air.[a]

Component	% (v/v)	% (w/w)
Nitrogen, $N_{2(g)}$	78.09	75.51
Oxygen, $O_{2(g)}$	20.95	23.15
Argon, $Ar_{(g)}$	0.93	1.23
Carbon dioxide, $CO_{2(g)}$	0.03[b]	0.05[b]

[a] The figures given refer to air in the lower part of the atmosphere, called the troposphere; this extends up to about 15 km, Figure 4.2. However, the proportions of the *major* components of the air vary very little, both horizontally and vertically, up to about 80 km. Note that the air also contains variable amounts of trace gases, water (H_2O, up to 4% by volume of moist tropospheric air) and particulates (aerosols).
[b] Variable.

The Earth's current atmosphere is a complex mixture of gases and suspended particles. This mixture is dominated by two gases, nitrogen (N_2) and oxygen (O_2), which together account for 99% of the volume of dry air (Table 4.1). The composition of the atmosphere is remarkably stable given that it is not isolated from its surroundings. Indeed, it is an *open system*, being subjected to both matter and energy inputs and outputs (Chapter 2, Section 2.1) (Figure 4.1).

There is a small and largely insignificant exchange of matter between the atmosphere and space. In contrast,

Figure 4.1 Inputs to and outputs from the atmospheric system. Notes: 1. Sensible heat is heat that is associated with a change in temperature. 2. Latent heat is heat that is associated with changes of state (e.g. evaporation of water).

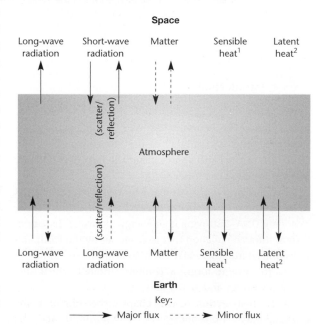

there is a substantial two-way flow of matter between the Earth (particularly the oceans) and the atmosphere. Most importantly, water, nitrogen, oxygen and carbon dioxide continually enter and leave the atmosphere as part of their biogeochemical cycles (Chapter 5). In the absence of human intervention, the rates of addition of these and other materials to the atmosphere are approximately equalled by their rates of removal. The overall composition of the atmosphere has therefore remained essentially constant over recent geological time by virtue of a dynamic steady state.

Human intervention appears to be removing this steady state condition with respect to several important trace gases including carbon dioxide, carbon monoxide (CO), oxides of nitrogen (NO_x), chlorofluorocarbons (CFCs),[2] oxides of sulfur (SO_x) and methane (CH_4). In some cases, the levels of these gases in the atmosphere are increasing very rapidly. For example, methane concentrations are rising by about 1% per year. These changes and their consequences are discussed in Chapter 15.

The energy inputs to the atmosphere arise as a result of irradiation from both the sun and the Earth (Box 4.1), from convection and conduction of thermal energy from the Earth's surface (sensible heat) and in the form of latent heat of vaporisation from the evaporation and condensation of water. The atmosphere also loses energy to its surroundings as a result of radiation. These processes are largely responsible for the layered structure of the current atmosphere (Figure 4.2).

The thermosphere has a very low density and pressure ($<10^{-5}$ atm). In this region, the atmosphere is predominantly made up of atoms and ions. These are formed when high-energy, short-wavelength, solar radiation ($\lambda \ll 200$ nm) is absorbed, typical reactions being:

$$N_{2(g)} + h\nu \rightarrow 2N_{(g)}$$

$$N_{(g)} + h\nu \rightarrow N^+_{(g)} + e^-_{(g)}$$

$$O_{2(g)} + h\nu \rightarrow O_2^+_{(g)} + e^-_{(g)}$$

The species produced are reactive and tend to recombine, reforming the reactants and releasing energy. As this energy is principally released in the form of thermal motion of the molecules, atoms or ions involved, the net effect is a warming of the thermosphere.

The temperature of the thermosphere decreases with decreasing altitude until the mesopause is reached at about 90 km (Figure 4.2). This is because the particles in the upper thermosphere absorb the short-wave radiation responsible for the warming effect described above.

[2] There are no natural sources of CFCs. These gases were therefore absent from the atmosphere prior to 1930, when they were first introduced by General Motors in the United States of America.

Relatively little of this radiation penetrates to the lower thermosphere and, as a result, this is not warmed to the same extent.

The population of molecular species *increases* with decreasing altitude. Below the mesopause, in the mesosphere and stratosphere, this facilitates warming by the absorption of solar radiation with wavelengths between 200 and 300 nm. This warming phenomenon reaches a maximum at the stratopause (the boundary between the mesosphere and the stratosphere). Below this altitude, the population of molecules continues to rise but the amount of the radiation in the 200 to 300 nm region decreases as it has been removed by molecules at higher levels. As a result, the temperature of the stratosphere *decreases* with decreasing altitude.

Like the warming observed in the thermosphere, mesospheric and stratospheric warming is based on the conversion of solar radiation into thermal motion via absorption and chemical reaction. Pivotal in this process are the natural reactions involved in the production and destruction of stratospheric ozone (O_3). These may be represented thus:

$$O_2 + h\nu \; (\lambda < 240 \text{ nm}) \rightarrow 2O \qquad (4.1)$$
ozone production
$$O + O_2 + M \rightarrow O_3 + M \qquad (4.2)$$

$$O_3 + h\nu \; (\lambda < 325 \text{ nm}) \rightarrow O_2 + O \qquad (4.3)$$
ozone destruction
$$O + O_3 \rightarrow 2O_2 \qquad (4.4)$$

Note that the reactions represented by Equations 4.2 and 4.4 are energy releasing (exothermic) as are the reactions shown by Equations 4.1 and 4.3 *if* the energy of the radiation absorbed is taken into account.

The reaction represented by Equation 4.4 occurs at significant rates in the atmosphere, by both catalytic and non-catalytic mechanisms. The following naturally occurring odd electron species have all been shown to catalyse this reaction: Cl, NO, H and OH. In each case, catalysis is facilitated by the sequence shown below, in which X is used to represent the odd electron species involved:

$$O_3 + X \rightarrow O_2 + XO \qquad (4.5)$$

$$O + XO \rightarrow O_2 + X \qquad (4.6)$$

Note that when Equations 4.5 and 4.6 are added and species that are *both* consumed and produced are cancelled, Equation 4.4 results. Note also that the reaction represented by Equation 4.6 regenerates the catalyst, X, consumed in Equation 4.5. Hence, one atom or molecule of a catalyst may destroy many molecules of ozone before it is removed from the atmosphere by reaction with a non-ozone species.

Despite the considerable amounts of ozone generated within the atmosphere (3.5×10^8 kg per day), the

4.1 Black bodies, grey bodies; solar and terrestrial radiation

A body that absorbs all electromagnetic radiation that falls on it is called a **black body**. One can construct a nearly perfect black body merely by punching a hole in the top of a tin can. The hole acts as the 'surface' of a black body. Any light falling on it will pass into the can where it is absorbed by the internal surfaces of its walls. Black bodies neither reflect nor transmit any of the radiation that they intercept.

Not only is a black body a perfect absorber, it is also a perfect radiator of electromagnetic radiation. This means that the relative intensities of the different frequencies that it radiates are dependent only on its temperature (see figure below). This can be understood when it is realised that the radiation is generated by the oscillations of the particles that make up the body. The hotter the body, the faster these particles oscillate and therefore the higher the frequency of the radiation that they emit.

The temperature dependence of black body radiation

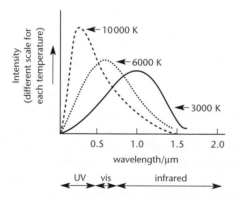

To a good approximation, the sun behaves as a black body with a surface temperature of 6000 K. At this temperature, the radiation emitted (i.e. **solar radiation**) reaches a maximum intensity in the visible part of the electromagnetic spectrum (see next figure).

In contrast, the Earth with its atmosphere only *very roughly* approximates to a black body. It is neither a perfect absorber nor a perfect radiator and is therefore referred to as a **grey body**.

The Earth intercepts about 0.002% of the total electromagnetic output of the sun. Of this, about 36% is reflected back into space; the remainder is absorbed, warming the Earth.

As well as absorbing and reflecting radiation, the Earth also emits radiation. The third figure compares the Earth's electromagnetic emission spectrum with that expected from a black body of the same temperature.

The solar spectrum (redrawn from Barry and Chorley, 1987, after Sellers, 1965)

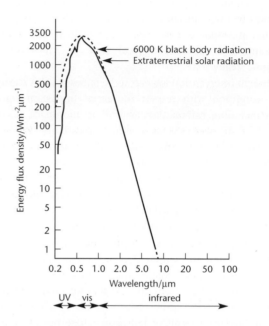

Notice that, as expected from its temperature, the emission spectrum of the Earth reaches a maximum in the infrared. This maximum is at a much longer wavelength than the peak of the solar spectrum. For this reason, solar radiation is often referred to as short-wave radiation, whereas that from the Earth (**terrestrial radiation**) is called long-wave radiation.

The net flux at the tropopause at mid-latitude with clear sky conditions and a surface temperature of 294 K (solid line) compared with the spectrum expected from a black body at this temperature (dotted line) (after Shine *et al.*, 1990)

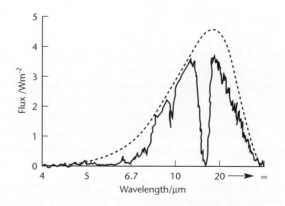

Further Information Box

4.1   continued

Notice also that the terrestrial spectrum is not smooth (unlike that of a black body). This is because the Earth's atmosphere contains trace components that absorb specific parts of the infrared spectrum. Particularly important in this regard are the gases carbon dioxide (CO_2), water (H_2O) and methane (CH_4). For example, the deep trough in the emission spectrum of the Earth at about $15\,\mu m$ is caused by carbon dioxide. Carbon dioxide is sufficiently good at absorbing in this region that natural atmospheric levels of this gas make the atmosphere practically opaque at around $15\,\mu m$. Hence, virtually none of the terrestrial radiation with this wavelength escapes into space. This is important because the energy possessed by this radiation is not immediately lost from the atmosphere; if it were, the Earth's surface would be significantly cooler. By this means the Earth's atmosphere acts as a blanket, keeping the surface warm. This is the so-called **greenhouse effect**.

Figure 4.2 The structure of the atmosphere (from Bunce, 1990, after Finlayson-Pitts and Pitts, 1986, *Atmospheric Chemistry*, reprinted by permission of John Wiley & Sons, Inc.).

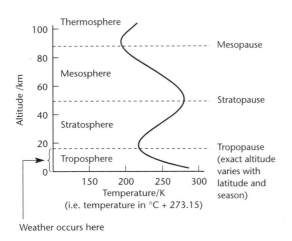

Figure 4.3 Ozone (O_3) levels in the atmosphere.

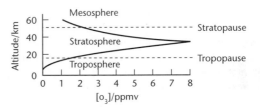

concentration of ozone within any one region of the atmosphere remains remarkably constant. This is because the rates of production and removal of ozone are roughly in balance.

Ozone is found at *trace levels* at all altitudes below the stratopause, reaching a maximum concentration of about 8–10 ppm within the stratosphere (Figure 4.3). This stratospheric band of relatively concentrated ozone is sometimes referred to as the **ozone layer**, although this is clearly a misnomer given the low absolute concentration of this gas.

It is worth emphasising that ozone is not a major constituent of any part of the atmosphere. Indeed, if all of the ozone within the atmosphere were concentrated at sea level it would produce a layer only about 3 mm thick.

Despite its relatively low abundance, the importance of ozone must not be underestimated. Stratospheric ozone absorbs harmful ultraviolet light principally in the region 230–320 nm. It does this by virtue of the photochemical reaction represented by Equation 4.3. Molecular oxygen (O_2) also absorbs harmful ultraviolet radiation, but in a different region, near 200 nm. There is considerable evidence to suggest that human activity is leading to an increase in the rate of stratospheric ozone destruction. This phenomenon may have far-reaching consequences, as discussed in Chapter 15 (Section 15.2.4). In contrast to ozone within the stratosphere, ozone at ground level is not welcome and is considered to be a pollutant; this is also discussed in Chapter 15 (Section 15.2.1).

Beneath the stratosphere lies the troposphere. This contains about 90% of the mass of the atmosphere and the majority of the trace gases. The reactions into which these trace gases enter are highly complex and of considerable importance. Key to many of these processes are the hydroxyl (OH) and nitrate (NO_3) radicals; the formation of these is briefly reviewed in Box 4.2.

Within the troposphere, absorption of *terrestrial* radiation causes warming near the surface of the Earth; this is the so-called **greenhouse effect**. Without this effect, the mean temperature of the atmosphere at the surface of the Earth would fall from its current value of 15°C to about −17°C or lower, probably making the world uninhabitable.

As explained in Box 4.1, the Earth radiates in the infrared region of the electromagnetic spectrum. Only molecules that have vibrational states with different dipole moments can absorb this radiation. The major

4.2   Tropospheric hydroxyl and nitrate radicals

Many reduced species enter the lower atmosphere (called the troposphere) by virtue of both natural and/or artificial (**anthropogenic**) processes. These species include hydrocarbons (the most important of which is methane, CH_4), carbon monoxide (CO), hydrogen sulfide (H_2S), dimethyl sulfide (($CH_3)_2S$), sulfur dioxide (SO_2) and oxides of nitrogen (most importantly nitric oxide, NO, and nitrogen dioxide, NO_2). Some of these reduced species will be physically removed from the troposphere, by transfer to either the crust, the oceans or the stratosphere. Those that remain are, in general, readily oxidised *in situ*.

The ability of tropospheric reactions to oxidise reduced species is of great importance, as without these reactions the atmosphere would rapidly become polluted. This ability is ultimately due to the presence of a high concentration of oxygen (O_2, 20.95% by volume of dry air). However, oxygen itself is rarely directly involved in these reactions, as more reactive oxidants derived from photochemical transformations of oxygen are present. The most important of these are the hydroxyl radical (OH) and the nitrate radical (NO_3).[1]

The hydroxyl radical (OH)

The formation of hydroxyl radicals in unpolluted tropospheric air primarily involves three species, ozone (O_3), methane (CH_4) and water (H_2O).

Ozone is a trace constituent of the troposphere. It enters this region of the atmosphere from the stratosphere (part of the upper atmosphere) where it is generated photochemically from oxygen (O_2). It is also generated photochemically within the troposphere when NO_2 is present:

$$NO_2 + h\nu \ (\lambda < 400\,nm) \rightarrow NO + O \tag{a}$$

$$O + O_2 + M \rightarrow O_3 + M \tag{b}$$

where M represents a 'third body' required to stabilise the product.

Ozone itself is subject to photolysis:

$$O_3 + h\nu \ (\lambda < 310\,nm) \rightarrow O^* + O_2^* \tag{c}$$

The products of this reaction are in electronically excited states (as indicated by the asterisks) and are therefore chemically distinct from their ground state counterparts. Of particular

---

[1] Note that the hydroxyl radical and the nitrate radical should not be confused with the hydroxide ion (OH^-) and the nitrate ion (NO_3^-). The chemistry of these ions is very different from that of the radicals discussed here.

importance is the ability of the excited atomic oxygen produced to react with methane or water to generate hydroxyl radicals:

$$O^* + CH_4 \rightarrow OH + CH_3 \tag{d}$$

$$O^* + H_2O \rightarrow 2OH \tag{e}$$

The hydroxyl radicals generated are highly reactive and are rapidly reduced. In clean air, reaction with carbon monoxide (CO) accounts for about 70% of these radicals while the vast bulk of the remainder react with methane.

The tropospheric oxidation of methane by hydroxyl radicals is a complex process, particularly in the presence of NO. Under these conditions, a variety of products is produced including NO_2 and, importantly, hydroxyl radicals. The NO_2 generated also leads to the replenishment of the tropospheric OH via the photochemical production of ozone and subsequent reactions (reactions a to e above).

The high reactivity of the hydroxyl radical ensures that it is removed from the atmosphere at a high rate. At sunset, the photochemical reactions that are responsible for the production of the vast bulk of this species stop. As a result, the tropospheric hydroxyl radical concentration falls rapidly at night. Hence, nocturnal oxidation reactions involving the hydroxyl radical are of little importance compared with those occurring during daylight.

The nitrate radical (NO_3)

The concentration of the nitrate radical in the troposphere during the day-time is minimal. This is because this species is subject to photochemical destruction. However, it can be formed in the troposphere in the absence of light by the reaction between ozone and nitrogen dioxide (NO_2):

$$O_3 + NO_2 \rightarrow NO_3 + O_2 \tag{f}$$

Hence the concentration of this species rises appreciably at night. Indeed, its night-time concentration can be up to three orders larger than the day-time concentration of the hydroxyl radical. As a result, the nitrate radical is a significant oxidant even though its reactivity toward tropospheric organic substances is generally lower than that of the hydroxyl radical.

It would be a mistake to assume that the production of the nitrate radical was independent of photochemistry. Reaction f is not a photochemical reaction, but the ozone that it consumes is of photochemical origin (see page 79 and reactions a and b above).

---

components of dry air, namely nitrogen (N_2), oxygen (O_2) and argon (Ar) (Table 4.1), do not have this characteristic and are therefore incapable of absorbing terrestrial radiation; consequently, they are not greenhouse gases. In contrast, water (H_2O) and many of the trace gases,

including carbon dioxide (CO_2) and methane (CH_4), are greenhouse gases as they are capable of absorbing in the infrared region.

Figure 4.4 shows the infrared *absorption* spectra of water, carbon dioxide and methane. Each of these

Figure 4.4 The infrared absorption spectra of (a) water, (b) carbon dioxide and (c) methane.

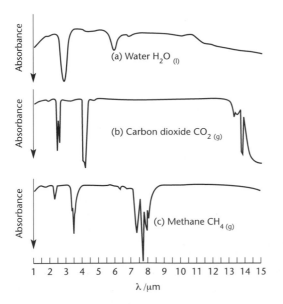

spectra consists of several relatively narrow bands of wavelength over which absorption occurs. These bands are typically separated by relatively large regions of the spectrum within which little radiation is absorbed; these regions are called **windows**. For example, water absorbs strongly at $2.91\,\mu$m and again at $6.09\,\mu$m; between these peaks in the absorption spectrum is a window (Figure 4.4).

It is instructive to note that many of the peaks in the infrared spectra of water, methane and carbon dioxide do not coincide. For example there is a peak at $4.3\,\mu$m in the spectrum of carbon dioxide, while neither water nor methane absorbs significantly at this wavelength. The peaks in one spectrum tend to 'fill' the windows in the others. This means that a mixture of methane, carbon dioxide and water is capable of absorbing a greater range of the infrared spectrum than any one of these gases alone. In general, therefore, mixtures of infrared-absorbing gases have the potential to generate a greater greenhouse effect than any one gas alone.

Interestingly, the presence of greenhouse gases does not cause warming in all situations. This is because these gases not only absorb infrared radiation, they also emit it. When the density of greenhouse gases is sufficiently low, radiation emitted by one molecule is unlikely to be absorbed by a neighbour and may escape into space. This can occur in the upper atmosphere, cooling it down. Conversely, in regions of the atmosphere where there is a high density of greenhouse gases the absorption process dominates and a net warming occurs. For this reason, the greenhouse effect is most pronounced in the lower parts of the troposphere. Hence, within this region temperature *increases* with decreasing altitude (Figure 4.2). This has two important consequences.

Firstly, there is a temperature minimum at the tropopause (Figure 4.2). This acts as a cold-trap, condensing out many of the less volatile components of the troposphere, greatly inhibiting their transfer into the stratosphere. For example, very little water crosses the tropopause and consequently the stratosphere is relatively dry. What is more, much of the water that it does contain is produced within the stratosphere as a result of the oxidation of volatile hydrogen-containing species such as methane (CH_4).

Secondly, the warming of the lower parts of the troposphere causes it to expand, decreasing its density and causing it to rise. This produces turbulence and relatively rapid mixing. In contrast, the stratosphere is calm. This is because a **temperature inversion** exists within this zone, that is, warmer air lies over cooler, denser air (Figure 4.2). Under certain climatic conditions *temporary* temperature inversions can also be found within the troposphere. As will be seen in Chapter 15 (Section 15.2.1), such inversions can entrap pockets of highly polluted air.

4.2   Weather and climate

Weather is the physical condition of the atmosphere (particularly the troposphere) at a specific time and place with regard to wind, temperature, cloud cover, fog and precipitation (the collective word for rain, hail, snow, etc.).

Typically, weather is highly variable and somewhat unpredictable. As a result, a longer term view of the weather patterns of a particular locality is frequently more useful as an environmental tool. This longer term view is called **climate**. The climate of a particular area is generally defined in terms of either its average weather conditions or the frequency of occurrence of a particular atmospheric feature, such as thunderstorms.

Clearly, weather and climate are important components of the environment. It follows therefore, that in order to understand the environment and the possible impact of human activity on it, a basic knowledge of the origins of weather and climate are required. In this section, the major forces that bring about the more important weather patterns and climates of the contemporary world will be reviewed. Attention will also be given to patterns of past climate change.

4.2.1 | Radiation and energy budgets

The Earth is bathed in short-wave electromagnetic radiation from the sun (Box 4.1). About 36% of this radiation arriving at the top of the atmosphere is reflected back into space; the remainder is absorbed. This absorption occurs both within the atmosphere and at the Earth's surface. Of these two sites of absorption, the Earth's surface is the more important, accounting for about 73% of the total solar radiation absorbed by the Earth–atmosphere system. The Earth's surface is therefore warmed by the absorption of solar radiation. This is highly significant as it acts as a source of energy, warming the air and driving atmospheric motion (Section 4.2.2).

The Earth–atmosphere system not only absorbs and reflects electromagnetic radiation, it also emits it. The radiation emitted is of a longer wavelength than that received from the sun (Box 4.1).

If the Earth is observed for a sufficiently long time, the overall energy budget of the globe is seen to be in balance. In other words, the total energy absorbed as radiation from the sun is matched by the total energy emitted as radiation by the Earth–atmosphere system. Algebraically this may be represented thus:

$$K - L = 0$$

where K is the total solar radiation flux absorbed by the Earth–atmosphere system, and L is the total terrestrial radiation flux emitted by the same system (note that radiation flux is the energy flow per unit time and its units are $J\,s^{-1} = W$).

This is an example of a radiation budget, so called because all of the energy fluxes involved are in the form of electromagnetic radiation. If this budget were not in balance, the Earth would either warm up (i.e. if $K > L$) or cool down (if $K < L$), and climate change would ensue.

The radiation budget is *not* in balance at a *local* level, even when averaged over a substantial time period (Figure 4.5). At low latitudes (i.e. at or near the equator) more energy is absorbed than emitted (i.e. $K > L$), the inverse being true at high latitudes (i.e. $K < L$). This implies that there must be mechanisms that allow energy to be moved from the equatorial regions toward the poles. These mechanisms involve the circulatory movement of matter in both the lower atmosphere and the oceans (Figure 4.6). Together these circulatory systems are responsible for many of the features of the global climate. The circulation of the lower atmosphere is discussed in Section 4.2.2. The influence of ocean circulation on climate is discussed in Boxes 4.3 and 4.4, whilst its role in climate change is explored in Section 4.2.6.

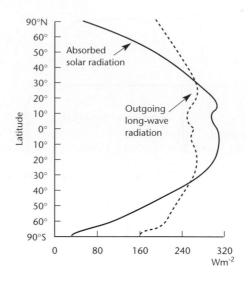

Figure 4.5 The variation in absorbed solar and emitted long-wave radiation with latitude (derived from satellite data) (from Henderson-Sellers and Robinson, 1986, NOAA-NESS, Washington, DC).

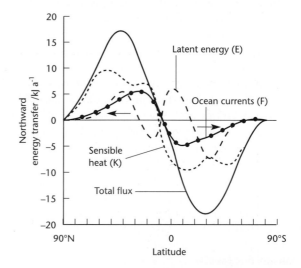

Figure 4.6 The poleward transfer of energy by the atmosphere (E and K) and the oceans (F) (from White *et al.*, 1992, after Sellers, 1965). Note: sensible heat is associated with temperature change; latent heat is associated with changes of state (e.g. evaporation of water).

There is an overall decrease in the mean surface temperature with increasing latitude (Figure 4.7). If there were no poleward movement of energy within the atmosphere this trend would be more pronounced. The lower latitudes would be hotter than they are, while the poles would be cooler. Consequently, much of the Earth would be appreciably less hospitable than it is.

While the radiation budget of the Earth–atmosphere system is in balance, when taken as a whole, this is not

4.3   The climatic influence of ocean currents

The oceanic conveyor belt

The water of the oceans is in a perpetual state of circulatory motion driven by convection. As we will see, this flow, known as the **oceanic conveyor belt**, has a profound influence on climate, particularly in Europe.

   This motion is in part initiated by the subsidence of water in the North Atlantic. This water sinks because it has a relatively high density by virtue of its low temperature and high salinity. It then moves at depth, forming part of a current system that eventually pushes deep waters to the surface in the Indian and Pacific Oceans, where they are warmed by the sun (see figure). These waters form surface currents that ultimately return to the North Atlantic, completing the circulation of the 'conveyor belt' and transporting warm water into otherwise cold seas.

   Winds blowing across the North Atlantic transfer a significant degree of warmth to the surrounding countries. The annual amount of heat absorbed from the conveyor belt by this process is almost one-third as much as that received from the sun in this location. Consequently, the lands of the North Atlantic region are about 6°C warmer than they would be in the absence of the conveyor belt. Europe is the main beneficiary of this effect as the prevailing winds across the North Atlantic are westerly (Figure 4.11 on page 92).

Wind-blown surface currents

As prevailing winds blow across the oceans, some of their kinetic energy is transferred to the water, producing the great surface currents of the world (see second figure). The rotation of the Earth influences the paths taken by these currents, producing essentially circular flows within each of the major ocean basins. South of the equator, the movement is essentially anti-clockwise, while to the north it is clockwise.

   The translocation of thermal energy within wind-blown surface currents can have a significant impact on the climate at a regional level. For example, the shores of northern Europe are bathed in warm waters that have their origin in the Gulf of Mexico. Prevailing westerly winds transfer some of this warmth onto the land. This is in part responsible for the relatively mild conditions experienced within maritime northern Europe. For example, the mean annual temperature of Edinburgh, UK (55.9°N, 3.2°W) is 8.6°C, whereas that of Moscow, Russia (55.7°N, 37.6°E) is only 4.4°C.

The oceanic conveyor belt (from Pickering and Owen, 1997; redrawn after Street-Perrott and Perrott, 1990).

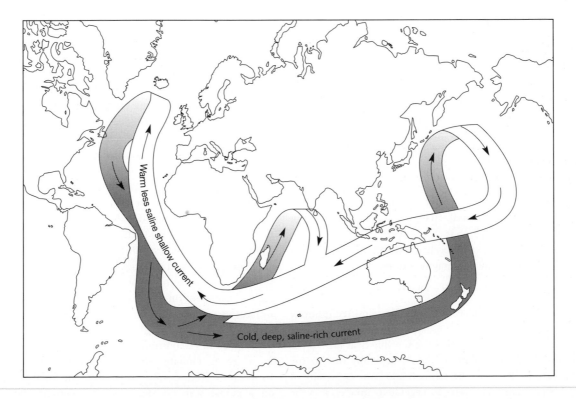

Further Information Box

4.3 continued

The great surface currents of the world (from Tolmazin, 1985).

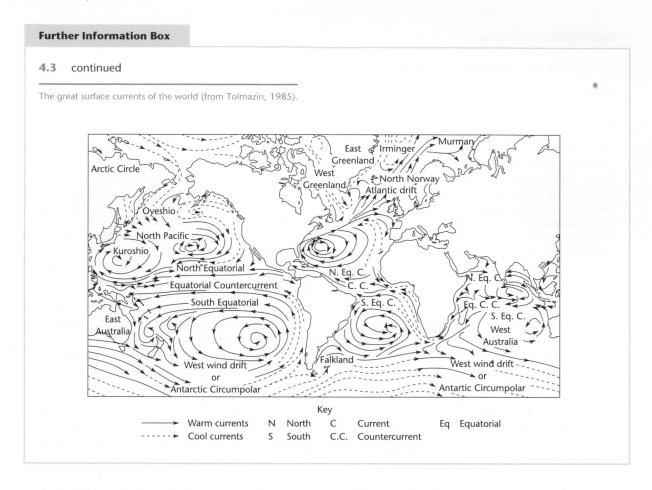

Key

→ Warm currents	N	North	C	Current	Eq Equatorial
----► Cool currents	S	South	C.C.	Countercurrent	

true of its two principal components, the atmosphere and the Earth's surface. The surface of the Earth absorbs more radiative energy than it emits, while the reverse is true of the atmosphere. Nonetheless, the global annual mean surface temperature remains essentially constant with time, implying that both the surface and the atmosphere must be in a state of overall energy balance. For this to be the case, there must be non-radiative mechanisms of energy transfer from the Earth's surface to the atmosphere. These mechanisms involve the transfer of energy as both sensible and latent heat. Sensible heat is heat that produces temperature change. Latent heat affects something without changing its temperature; for example, melting ice at $0°C$ involves latent heat as no temperature change will occur until all of the ice has melted. Algebraically this may be expressed as:

$$Q^* = G + H + LE + P + C \qquad (4.7)$$

where Q^* is the net radiation absorbed or emitted (positive for surfaces in net receipt of radiative energy), G is the heat flux into the sub-surface, H is the sensible heat flux to the air, and LE is the latent heat flux, generally due to the evaporation of water. The terms P and C are generally of lesser significance and refer to vegetated surfaces. P is the energy trapped during photosynthesis while C is a term that includes absorption of heat by the vegetation.

Equation 4.7 implies a balance between the radiative and non-radiative energy fluxes, even at a local scale. While this balance is maintained in the relatively long term, this is rarely the case over short time periods, such as hours or days. For example, early morning sunshine will cause Q^* to become positive, exceeding the total outputs from the surface represented by the other terms in the equation. Under these conditions, the temperature of the surface will rise. As the temperature rises, so long-wave emission increases, as do the fluxes from the surface represented by G, H and, if water is present, LE, tending to regain balance. If no other changes occur, a new equilibrium temperature will therefore become established and Equation 4.7 will hold again.

Many of the terms that make up Equation 4.7 are highly dependent on the nature of the surface. As a result, surfaces vary considerably in their temperature response to a given change in energy input. This is of considerable importance in establishing the temperature characteristics of a given climate and the global distribution of temperature (Figure 4.7). Most important in this respect, on a global scale, is the difference between land and

Further Information Box

4.4   El Niño-Southern Oscillation (ENSO)

Alterations in the ocean current–atmosphere system can have dramatic effects on climate. This is well illustrated by the phenomenon known as the El Niño–Southern Oscillation (ENSO).

A current of warm water, flowing from north to south along the coasts of Ecuador and Peru, appears around Christmas each year and was named the current of El Niño (the boy child (Jesus)) by local sailors. The term El Niño later became restricted to the much more intense warming of the seas off the tropical South American Pacific coast that occurs every few years, on an irregular cycle. This warming is now known to be one phase of a cyclic pattern called the El Niño–Southern Oscillation, or ENSO. The Southern Oscillation is a see-sawing of sea-level atmospheric pressures across the International Date Line. The El Niño part of the ENSO (also referred to as an El Niño event, the warm phase of ENSO, or an ENSO warm event) is characterised by anomalously warm sea surface temperatures (SSTs) in the central and eastern equatorial Pacific. This is correlated with sea-level atmospheric pressures that are unusually low in the south-eastern tropical Pacific and unusually high in the western tropical Pacific and Indian Ocean regions.

In the years between successive El Niño events, normal conditions can prevail. These are characterised by cooler waters off the western coast of tropical South America. In many ENSO cycles, however, there is a period during which the surface waters of the central and eastern equatorial Pacific are exceptionally cold. These periods are known variously as La Niña, cold phase of ENSO, ENSO cold event, El Viejo or anti-El Niño. They are associated with unusually high sea-level atmospheric pressures to the east of the International Date Line and unusually low pressures to its west.

During normal conditions, the trade winds blow strongly across the Pacific from the tropical coast of South America towards Indonesia (see figure (a) below). Friction between the moving air and the water transfers kinetic energy to the ocean and a surface current flows in essentially the same direction as the trade winds. The water on the western side of the Pacific is piled up by the wind and the sea level on this side is approximately 0.6 m higher than on the eastern coast. The thermocline (the interface between the warm surface waters and the cold waters below) is pushed down in the west to a depth of approximately 150 m and pulled upwards in the east to approximately 30 m beneath the surface.

The proximity of the thermocline to the surface off the tropical coast of South America allows cold, nutrient-rich waters to upwell in the eastern Pacific. This injection of nutrients into the photic zone (i.e. that part of the ocean illuminated with sunlight) boosts primary productivity, thus allowing high population densities of fish to develop. These fish, particularly the anchoveta, sustain both seabirds and a thriving fishing industry off the tropical coast of South America.

As a consequence of the upwelling of cold water, the air above the eastern Pacific remains relatively cool and does not rise sufficiently to produce high rainfalls on the western seaboard of tropical South America. In contrast, the warm surface waters of the western side of the Pacific, around Indonesia, heat the air above them and laden it with moisture. This warm air rises and cools. The rising air encourages the trade winds to blow across the Pacific, to replace the air that has moved aloft. Simultaneously, the cooling of the rising moist air produces rain clouds leading to the characteristically wet climate of the region.

Figure (a) Normal conditions

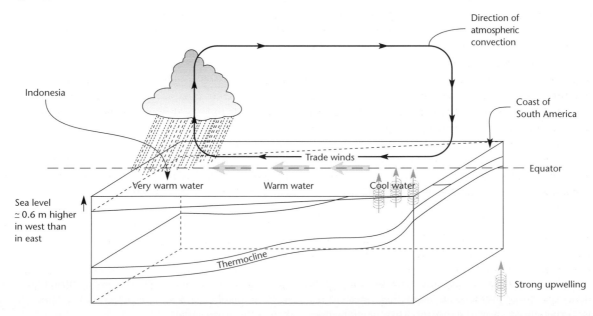

Further Information Box

4.4 continued

During an El Niño event (see figure (b) below), the Pacific trade winds that normally blow towards the west slacken and might even be reversed. The pool of warm water around Indonesia moves eastwards, as does its associated rain cloud. The sea level and thermocline flatten out across the Pacific, suppressing the upwelling of cold, nutrient-rich waters in the east. This has dramatic effects on both climate and ecology, with consequent economic costs. While these effects are most keenly felt in the tropical Pacific region, they have worldwide ramifications.

Each El Niño event is different in its severity and in the details of the impacts that it has. However, typical effects include:

- massive declines in the fish, seabird, fur seal and sea lion populations off the coast of tropical South America;
- drought, especially in the countries on the western, tropical margins of the Pacific but also further afield (e.g. Africa, Brazil, India and Sri Lanka were badly affected by drought in the extreme El Niño of 1982–1983);
- high rainfall in the normally arid coastal regions of Peru;
- an increase in the frequency of typhoons and hurricanes in the South China Sea and the western part of the Pacific;
- wet, cool summers in Europe;
- forest fires in Indonesia (Chapter 10, Box 10.8);
- damage to Pacific coral reefs, caused by abnormal water temperatures and/or indirect effects of forest fires.

Human activity often exacerbates the ecological and economic effects of El Niño events by, for example:

- in areas suffering from drought linked with El Niño, initiating forest fires (as occurred in Indonesia during the El Niño event that started in 1997) or overgrazing with cattle (as occurred in the Low Veldt area of Zimbabwe in the El Niño of the early 1990s);
- early resumption of commercial fishing off the Pacific coast of tropical South America after an El Niño event has finished, thereby giving little respite to the depleted fish and seabird populations.

There is some evidence to suggest that the frequency, longevity and severity of El Niño events are increasing. Typically, ENSO warm events, each lasting 8 to 10 months, can be expected to appear once every 2 to 7 years (although an interval of 3–5 years between El Niños is more the norm) with La Niña events in between. Between January 1982 and June 1998 there were four El Niño events but only one La Niña (1988–89). Of the warm events, two were extremely severe (the 1982–83 and the 1997–98 events) and one lasted for five years (ending in June 1995). While it is possible that these observations have a natural cause, it appears to be more likely that they are attributable to global warming (Chapter 15, Section 15.2.3).

Figure (b) Conditions during an El Niño event.

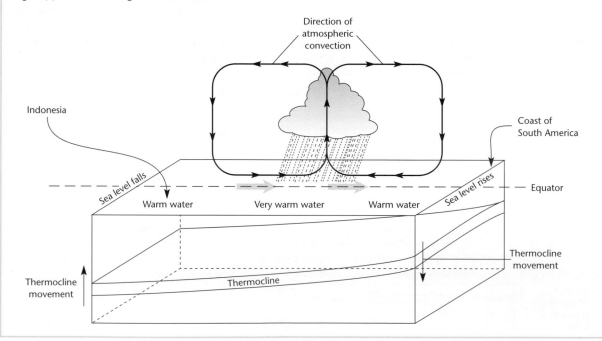

ocean. The temperature ranges and rates of temperature change experienced over land are many times greater than those experienced over the ocean. This phenomenon, when viewed on a large scale, is called **continentality**. It arises, primarily, because G is lower at the land surface than at the ocean surface.

Figure 4.7 Mean sea-level temperatures (°C) during (a) the southern hemisphere summer (December, January, February) and (b) the northern hemisphere summer (June, July, August) (from Oort, 1983).

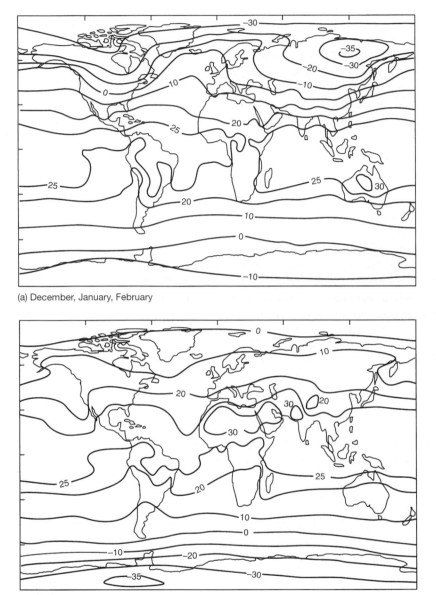

(a) December, January, February

(b) June, July, August

4.2.2 | Tropospheric airflow

The troposphere (i.e. the lower atmosphere, Figure 4.2) is turbulent. Within this layer, air is circulated by large-scale movements that make up the **primary circulation of the atmosphere**. Secondary and tertiary circulation systems are also recognised. These constitute fine structure that is superimposed on the primary circulation system. Secondary circulation is made up of features that are typically the size of the countries of Europe or the larger states of the US. Tertiary circulation consists of yet smaller-scale phenomena, usually covering distances under 160 km.

In this section, we are mainly concerned with the primary circulation system. While some discussion of phenomena leading to secondary circulation is also given, consideration of this and tertiary circulation is largely beyond the scope of this book. The interested reader is directed to the further reading given at the end of the chapter for further information on this topic.

Air circulates within the atmosphere under the influence of three forces that operate in the horizontal plane. Each of these will be considered in turn.

The pressure gradient force. Consider two places on the same horizontal surface that are at different atmospheric pressures. Under these circumstances, a force is established that accelerates air from the high-pressure area to the low-pressure one. The resulting airflow will cease when the pressure is equalised across the surface.

The frictional force. As the air passes over the surface of the Earth, it transfers some of its energy to the surface and, in so doing, its velocity is reduced. This phenomenon can therefore be envisaged as a force operating in direct opposition to the direction of movement. Clearly, the effect is most evident in the lowest part of the atmosphere. At altitudes greater than about 1 km above the surface, the frictional force is negligible.

The Coriolis force. Figure 4.8 shows a disc that is rotating about an axis that is perpendicular to its surface. Consider an object that, *when viewed from a stationary point above the disc*, is seen to be traversing its surface in a straight line. The same object *when viewed from the rotating disc* will be seen to follow a curved path. Put slightly differently, an object that is moving across the surface of a spinning disc will, when viewed from the disc, experience an apparent force at right angles to the direction of motion of the object. This is the Coriolis force; it operates to the right over a surface that is rotating anti-clockwise and to the left over a clockwise rotating surface.

The northern hemisphere of the Earth, when viewed from space along its axis, approximates to an anti-clockwise rotating disc. When viewed from the Earth, air moving over its surface therefore experiences a movement to the right. Similarly, air moving across the southern hemisphere will be deflected to the left. The spinning disc approximation is best at the poles. It becomes progressively less accurate as the globe is traversed in an equatorial direction. The Coriolis force is therefore maximal at the poles and zero at the equator. Figure 4.9 summarises the influence of the Coriolis force on the direction of deflection of air flow over the Earth's surface.

Of the three forces described above, the pressure gradient force is the principal driving force producing horizontal airflow. The other forces modify its speed and direction. The combined effect of these forces is illustrated in Figure 4.10.

In addition to these forces, airflow is controlled by the requirement to conserve both mass and, in the absence of an external couple, angular momentum (Box 4.5).

The global circulation of the atmosphere, under the control of the factors outlined above, produces an extremely complex and variable pattern of airflow, the more subtle variations in which are yet to be fully

Figure 4.8 The Coriolis force.

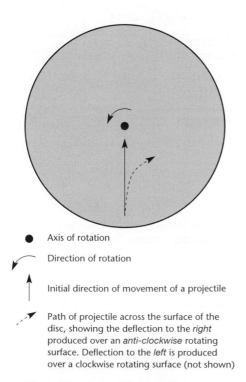

● Axis of rotation

╭ Direction of rotation

↑ Initial direction of movement of a projectile

↗ Path of projectile across the surface of the disc, showing the deflection to the *right* produced over an *anti-clockwise* rotating surface. Deflection to the *left* is produced over a clockwise rotating surface (not shown)

Figure 4.9 The direction of airflow deflection as a consequence of the Coriolis force.

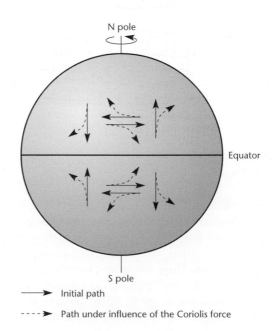

——▶ Initial path

----▶ Path under influence of the Coriolis force

Figure 4.10 The result of the three forces causing airflow.

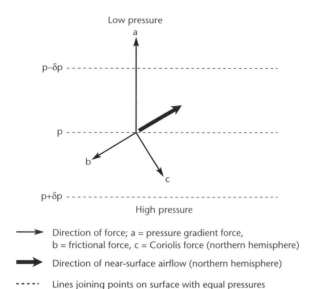

Direction of force; a = pressure gradient force, b = frictional force, c = Coriolis force (northern hemisphere)

Direction of near-surface airflow (northern hemisphere)

Lines joining points on surface with equal pressures (called isobars)

understood. However, many of the major features of the global atmospheric circulation have now been accounted for by the use of theoretical models.

Figure 4.11 shows the average wind directions across the surface of the Earth. While these winds differ considerably in their variability, it is possible to discern a definite overall pattern of polar easterlies, mid-latitude westerlies and trade winds. Any model of primary atmospheric circulation has to account for this pattern, as well as a net poleward redistribution of energy from the equator, without changing the planet's mass balance or angular momentum.

It is possible to explain these gross observations, and some other major climatic features, by envisaging three circulatory cells in each hemisphere. These cells are called the Hadley cell, the Ferrel cell (or mid-latitude cell) and the polar cell (Figure 4.12). Arguments based on this *three-cell model* may be couched in the following terms.

Hadley cell operation (Figure 4.13). Air warmed by the surface at the equator becomes buoyant and rises, generating a zone of low pressure. Surface airflow then

Further Information Box

4.5 Angular momentum and its conservation

Angular momentum is a property possessed by a body as a result of its rotation about a point. The angular momentum (A) of a particle in the atmosphere at a given altitude will be dependent on its mass (m), its distance from the Earth's axis (r) and the angular velocity of the point (ω), such that:

$$A = mr^2\omega$$

The angular momentum of the particle will not alter unless it is subjected to an external couple[1] that acts about the Earth's axis.

If the particle were to move poleward conserving altitude, r would decrease (see figure) and hence ω must increase. Conversely, an equator-bound particle at constant altitude must suffer a decrease in ω.

Consequently, a particle of air at the equator, initially moving at the same angular velocity as the Earth's surface at a given altitude, will have to move towards the east if it is subjected to a force that moves it in a poleward direction. This is to a large part responsible for the maintenance of the westerly (eastward) winds that typify the airflow of the mid-latitudes (Figure 4.11).

[1] A couple is the rotational analogue of a force in linear motion. When a force acts on a particle of fixed mass it causes it to undergo linear acceleration. When a couple acts on a particle of fixed mass and radius from its axis of rotation it brings about an angular acceleration.

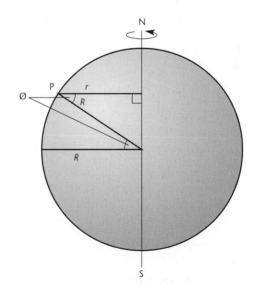

The figure shows the relationship between the perpendicular distance (r) of a given particle (P) from the Earth's axis and the angle of latitude ϕ, where: R is the distance from the Earth's centre to P, and $r = R\cos\phi$.

Figure 4.11 Average surface wind directions (1900–50) (from White *et al.*, 1992, after Lamb, 1972).

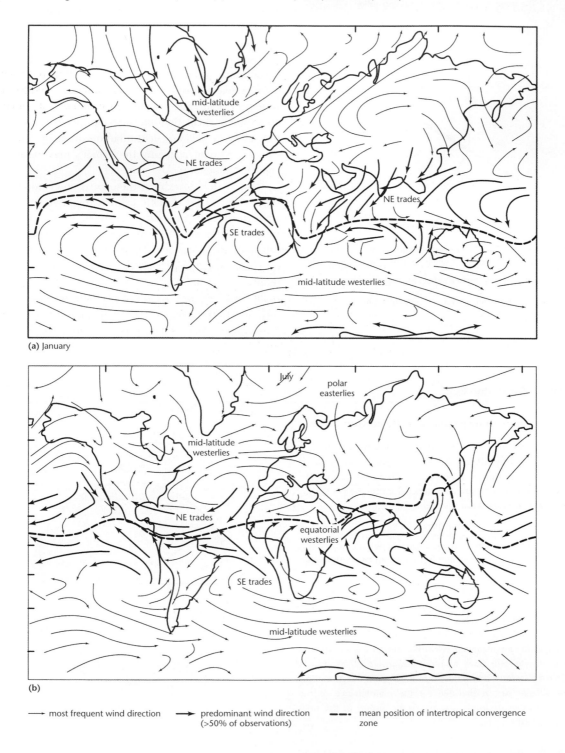

(a) January

(b)

→ most frequent wind direction → predominant wind direction (>50% of observations) ▬ ▬ ▬ mean position of intertropical convergence zone

occurs equatorwards under the influence of the pressure gradient generated. The direction of the airflow produced is modified by the need to conserve angular momentum and, to a lesser extent, the Coriolis force. The net result is the formation of the trade winds, converging on the **intertropical convergence zone** (ITCZ). The air aloft moves poleward, losing energy by radiative cooling. It becomes dense, falls and is warmed by adiabatic compression (Box 4.6). This generates two areas of high pressure at latitudes of about 30°N and 30°S. Approaching

Figure 4.12 The three-cell model of primary atmospheric circulation. Note that latitudes are approximate; wind directions and convergence/divergence statements refer to *surface* conditions.

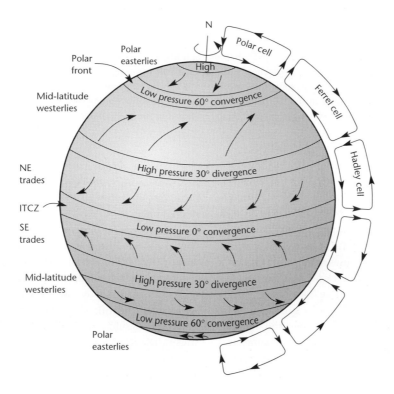

Figure 4.13 The Hadley cell.

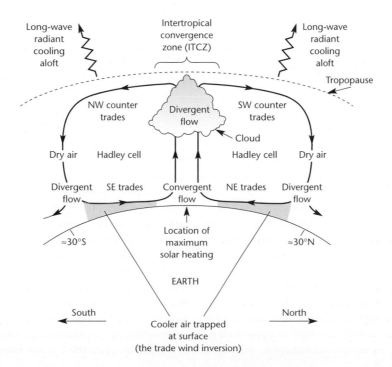

Further Information Box

4.6 Adiabatic cooling and warming of air

Adiabatic means without the gain or loss of *heat*.

If a portion of air within the atmosphere is forced to increase in altitude it will experience a decrease in pressure and hence it will expand. Under adiabatic conditions, this requires the conversion of some of its internal energy into work. Consequently, there will be a decrease in the thermal motion of the atoms and molecules that make up the portion of air

and a corresponding temperature fall. This process is called **adiabatic cooling**. If the portion of air is forced to decrease in altitude the opposite will occur and its temperature will rise (**adiabatic warming**).

Adiabatic cooling of water-saturated air will cause condensation to occur. This may ultimately lead to cloud formation and precipitation.

---

surface level, a portion of this relatively warm air moves towards the ITCZ, trapping a layer of cooler air near the ground and forming the trade winds. This cooler air picks up moisture and, being unable to rise, cannot lose it until it reaches the ITCZ. At the ITCZ it is raised aloft; the adiabatic cooling that ensues causes its moisture burden to condense. This produces a wide cloud and precipitation band at the ITCZ that is clearly visible from space (Plate 1).

Polar cell operation. Cold air at the poles sinks, generating two areas of high pressure (one at each pole) and divergent flow at the surface. This air moves equatorwards, becoming easterly under the influence of the Coriolis force, until it reaches the poleward moving westerlies. Here the cold polar air is warmed, becomes buoyant and rises, returning to the poles aloft.

Ferrel cell operation. A portion of the surface divergent flow generated at the higher latitude extremes of the Hadley cell moves polewards (Figure 4.13). These mid-latitude poleward airflows are deflected, by both the Coriolis force and the conservation of momentum, into westerly winds. On meeting the equatorward extremes of the polar cell, these winds are borne aloft, where they return equatorward, completing the cell.

In this model, the polar and Hadley cells are driven by air ascending over relatively warm areas and descending over cool ones; they are therefore termed 'thermally direct'. Conversely, the Ferrel or mid-latitude cell is thermally indirect and is therefore driven by the other two cells.

While this model is in general accordance with many observations, particularly in the equatorial regions, it is now known to be a gross over-simplification. What is worse, there are strong indications that in the mid-latitude regions it is largely *incorrect*.

The three-cell model requires that within each cell, the flow aloft must be in the opposite direction to that on the ground. Upper airflows within the Ferrel (mid-latitude) cell must therefore be in an easterly direction, in opposition to the westerly surface flow. In contradiction with this

prediction, measurements have shown that the predominant airflow of the upper troposphere within the mid-latitudes is *westerly*. These westerly upper winds are now known to be present in both hemispheres in both winter and summer. These winds reach very high speeds, particularly within narrow ribbon-shaped bands high in the troposphere, called the **jet streams**. Although not necessarily continuous, two essentially circumpolar jet streams are identifiable within the mid-latitude region. These are the subtropical jet stream and the polar front jet stream. The relative positions of these within the northern hemisphere are shown in Figure 4.14.

The strong upper level circumpolar mid-latitude westerly airflow described above is not truly circular about either pole. This is particularly true in the northern hemisphere, where a greater proportion of the land is located. Here, the airflow is best described as wave-like. These waves, called **Rossby waves**, vary with time in their number, position and amplitude, taking as little as one or two months to form and decay (Figure 4.15). These horizontal wave-like motions and their associated eddies are now thought to be central to the poleward movement of energy above latitudes of 30° (Figure 4.16).

Overall, the primary circulation of the atmosphere can be understood in terms of three divisions, namely the Hadley cell, the Rossby waves and the polar cell. While there is evidence for the existence of a mid-latitude cell, this is now known to be weak and of relatively little significance.

Let us now consider three features of high significance in the secondary circulation of the atmosphere: air masses, extratropical cyclones and anticyclones. These features are of particular importance in the determination of the climates of the mid-latitudes (Section 4.2.4).

An **air mass** is part of the atmosphere that shows relatively little horizontal variation in temperature. Air masses develop over several days under conditions of relative calm. During this time, an air mass develops temperature and moisture characteristics that are dictated by the surface over which it has formed. Once formed, air

Figure 4.14 Northern hemisphere mid-latitude jet streams. The symbol A indicates the mean position of the axis of the subtropical jet stream in winter. The zone in which the polar front jet stream is most active is shown by B (from White *et al.*, 1992, after Riehl, 1965).

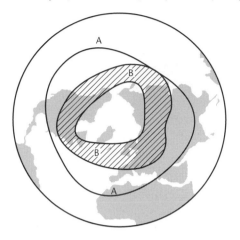

masses may be moved away from their source regions by the general circulation of the atmosphere (Figure 4.17).

Where two air masses meet that have differing temperature characteristics, a **front** is formed. A front is therefore a zone in which there is a rapid change in temperature across the horizontal plane.

The polar front, where polar maritime and tropical maritime air masses most commonly meet, is of considerable significance to mid-latitude weather and climate (Section 4.2.4). This feature is mobile but is commonly found around the 40° to 60° latitudes.

Extratropical cyclones (depressions or lows) are areas of low pressure that develop at fronts (Figures 4.18 and 4.19). The polar front is particularly important in this regard. Depressions are approximately circular features, 150 to 3000 km in diameter. They last for 4 to 7 days. They are associated with the Rossby waves that extend, in a highly variable fashion, over the mid-latitudes (Figure 4.15). Consequently, depressions are common features of the atmosphere in many regions of the mid-latitudes.

Within extratropical cyclones, there is convergent surface flow and rising air. The adiabatic cooling of the rising air commonly causes cloud formation (Box 4.6). Consequently, these features are sources of relatively copious precipitation, particularly if they originate over oceans.

Importantly, lows move eastwards as a result of the westerly airflow that dominates the mid-latitudes.

Anticyclones (or highs) are areas of high pressure. Here surface airflow is divergent, supplied by subsiding (i.e. falling) air (Figure 4.20). The pressure gradient within an anticyclone is less than in a depression. As a result, wind speeds are lower in these high pressure features than in extratropical cyclones.

The subsiding air within an anticyclone is warmed adiabatically (Box 4.6) and so the formation of precipitating clouds is inhibited. Anticyclones are therefore frequently associated with clear skies.

Figure 4.15 The northern hemisphere showing the cycle of development and decay of the Rossby waves.

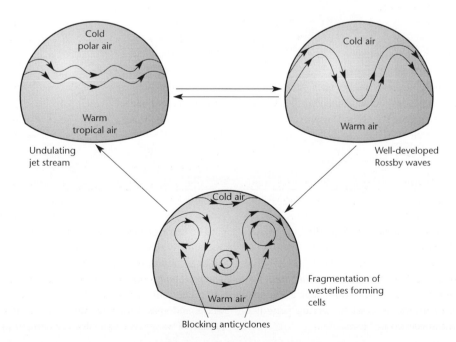

Figure 4.16 The movement of energy poleward (from Barry and Chorley, 1987). Note meridional flux is that associated with direct movement parallel to imaginary lines drawn from pole to pole. Such movement is expected within circulatory cells, such as the Hadley cells.

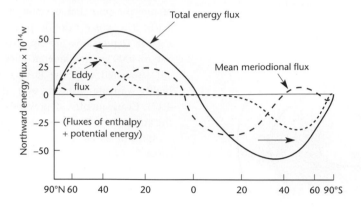

Figure 4.17 The major air mass sources (from Henderson-Sellers and Robinson, 1986).

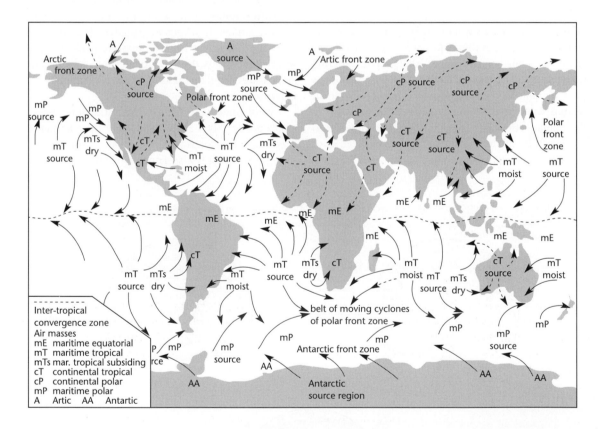

Anticyclones may be small scale (similar in size to depressions), or large scale (of roughly continental proportions). Let us consider these in turn.

Small anticyclones, like lows, can form at fronts, particularly the polar front. Anticyclones that are formed in this way tend to follow depressions, giving periods of clear skies within a succession of lows.

The cycle of Rossby waves illustrated in Figure 4.15 can also directly produce anticyclonic features of small size. These highs are essentially static, moving eastward slowly, if at all. These features, known as blocking anticyclones, can deflect the movement of lows poleward. They can last for several weeks and may therefore significantly disrupt the normal pattern of successive depressions arriving from the west.

Figure 4.18 The sequence of development of an extratropical cyclone (idealised) (after Barry and Chorley, 1987, after Strahler, 1951). Note that in the open stage (b) the cold front moves more rapidly than the warm front. This results in the meeting of the two fronts at the occluded stage (c).

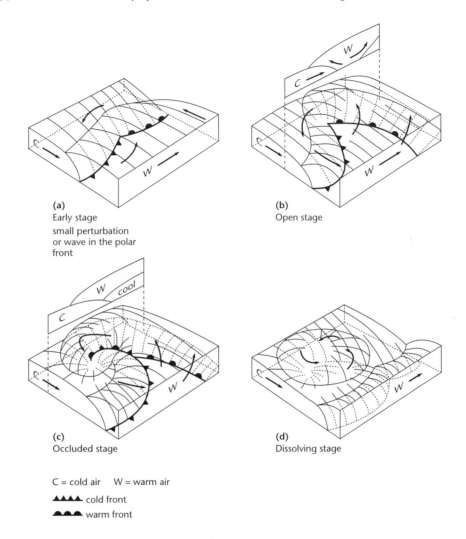

(a)
Early stage
small perturbation
or wave in the polar
front

(b)
Open stage

(c)
Occluded stage

(d)
Dissolving stage

C = cold air   W = warm air

▲▲▲▲ cold front

●●● warm front

Large anticyclones tend to be long-lived phenomena; some are present virtually throughout the year, while others are seasonal in their occurrence.

The poleward ends of the Hadley cells provide essentially permanent anticyclonic features. These extend over large areas of the globe at latitudes around 30°N and 30°S. They are evident from the surface to the tropopause.

High-pressure zones covering large areas for extended periods are also generated over high- to mid-latitude continental interiors. These occur during the winter months over large areas of Canada and central Asia. The origin of these anticyclones is quite different from those associated with the Hadley cells and is seated in continentality. Radiative cooling from the surface of these continental regions leads to an increase in the density of the near-surface air, causing subsidence. This brings about a pressure increase near the ground, producing anticyclonic conditions that dominate the weather of the region. Unlike Hadley cell anticyclones, these seasonal highs are vertically shallow, extending no more than about 2 km from the Earth's surface.

The strength of the model of tropospheric circulation outlined above is testified by its ability to explain many of the features of the regional climates of the world. These are briefly considered in the following sections.

4.2.3   Tropical climates

Tropical climates are those in which there is no discernible winter/summer seasonal change in temperature. Such

Figure 4.19 The cloud sequence associated with the development of an extratropical cyclone (idealised) (from Barry and Chorley, 1987, after Boucher and Newcomb, 1962).

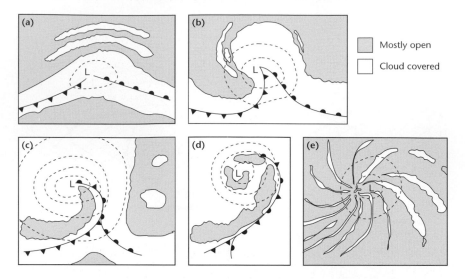

Mostly open

Cloud covered

(a), (b), (c) and (d) refer to the stages in the idealised development of an extratropical cyclone as shown in Figure 4.18.

Figure 4.20 A vertical section showing air movement in anticyclones.

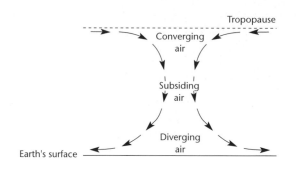

climates tend to be located between the latitudes of 30°N and 30°S.

The main features of many tropical climates are those imposed by the Hadley cells that dominate the primary circulation of the atmosphere in the lower latitudes (Section 4.2.2, Figure 4.13). Of particular importance is the presence of cloud and precipitation at the intertropical convergence zone (ITCZ) and the dry, hot, high-pressure zones created at the poleward extremes of the Hadley cells.

As a consequence, two distinct regional tropical climates develop. Areas covered by the ITCZ are typically hot with high rainfall, whereas those located about the outer limbs of the Hadley cells (~30°N and 30°S) tend to be hot deserts.

It is worth noting that the ITCZ is not static, but moves seasonally, roughly in coincidence with the place of maximal solar heating (Figure 4.11, page 92). Consequently, for many locations this produces a distinct summer rainy season.

The presence of a rainy season within a tropical climate can also be produced by a different phenomenon, that of the monsoon climate. This is driven by a summer circulation pattern that is superimposed on the Hadley circulation. It dominates the climate over much of the tropical part of the eastern hemisphere and is characterised by a seasonal reversal in the direction of airflow (Figure 4.21).

During the rainy season, which occurs in summer, moist onshore winds blow. These rise over the land, causing cooling, cloud formation and rain. In essence, the cause of this summer wind is a thermally direct cell caused by the differential heating of the land and ocean (Figure 4.22). When autumn arrives, this cell is weakened by a reduction in the contrast between terrestrial and maritime surface temperatures. This allows the cell to be easily disrupted. In the northern hemisphere this happens primarily by the encroachment over the Himalayas of the equatorward migrating westerlies. This allows winter surface airflow patterns to become established, primarily consisting of northerly or north-easterly dry winds from inland. These conditions continue into early summer, the onset of the rainy season being suppressed until the westerlies have retreated behind the Himalayas. Once this has occurred, the summer thermally direct cell becomes re-established and the rainy season frequently starts very rapidly as a characteristic monsoon 'burst'.

Figure 4.21 The monsoon region (as defined by surface-based observations).

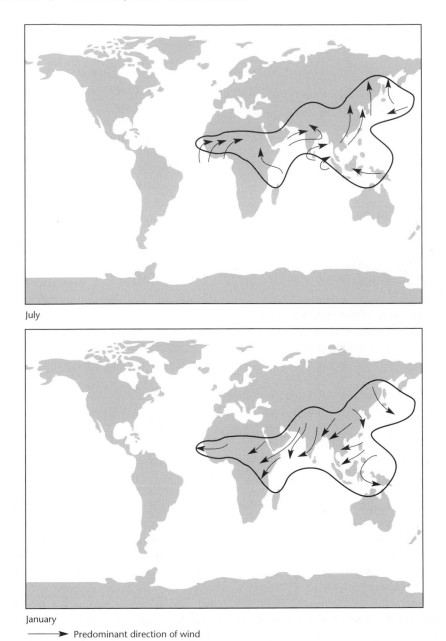

July

January

→ Predominant direction of wind

4.2.4   Mid-latitude climates

The climates of the mid-latitudes (30–60°N and 30–55°S) can be divided according to both latitude and east–west location. In essence, western coastal areas are wetter than their eastern counterparts, while those remote from the ocean are drier still. Superimposed on this is a tendency towards lower mean surface temperatures with increasing latitude. This picture is complicated by greater temperature fluctuations within continental interiors

when compared with those of their margins (a phenomenon called continentality, Section 4.2.1). Additionally, the west coast climates of the lower latitudes tend to have greater seasonality in their rainfall patterns than do those nearer the poles, winter being the wetter season.

The wet weather that typifies the climates of the western coasts is attributable to the prevailing westerly airflow. This sweeps precipitating extratropical cyclones over these areas from the Atlantic and Pacific Oceans,

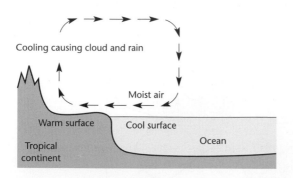

Figure 4.22 The basis of the monsoon circulation.

where they are formed throughout the year under the influence of the polar front.

Nearer the equator, the west coast mid-latitude climate is modified by the influence of the outer, subsiding, portions of the Hadley cells. These anticyclonic features sweep polewards in the summer months bringing warm dry weather. Consequently, west coast areas located at the equatorial end of the mid-latitudes tend to have dry, warm to hot summers and wet, cool winters. Climates such as these are called *mediterranean* after their archetype and are found in several parts of the world (Chapter 9, Figure 9.12).

Poleward of the mediterranean climates are found the *marine west coast climates* and, further poleward still, the *cold west coast climates*. The latter are distinguished from the former by their lower mean temperatures and shorter growing seasons. These climates are out of the reach of the Hadley cells and hence tend to have fairly even distributions of precipitation throughout the year. Nonetheless, the summers tend to be drier than the winters, as summer depressions tend to be less intense than their winter counterparts.

Inland of the west coasts, precipitation lessens and temperature fluctuations increase as the maritime influence decreases. Ultimately this leads to the formation of *interior desert climates*. This will only happen if the continent is sufficiently large and/or if there is a mountain range extending along a north–south axis. The influence of such a mountain range is particularly noticeable in North America, where the Rocky Mountains form a hurdle inland of the western seaboard. Eastbound precipitating systems rarely pass over this obstacle. Hence, interior desert climates are formed within its lee.

Climates of the eastern portions of continents within the mid-latitudes are influenced by air mass movements. Much of the eastern half of North America is traversed by air masses from both polar continental and tropical maritime areas (Figure 4.17). The latter contain moist air and are the main source of precipitation in this part of the world. Fluctuations in the Rossby waves allow the boundary between these very different air masses to pass over much of this part of the continent. The climates of these regions therefore incorporate rapid and substantial fluctuations in temperature.

The east coast of Asia is also bathed in both moist maritime and dry continental air. While the climates generated are broadly similar to those of eastern North America, they tend to have a more marked seasonality to their rainfall regimes. During winter, a sustained large-scale high-pressure feature forms over the Eurasian interior, centred over Mongolia (Section 4.2.2). This causes frequent, dry, essentially north-westerly winds to flow over the surface of the eastern part of mid-latitude Asia. This wind flow pattern tends to be reversed in the summer months, bringing moist maritime winds and greater rain.

The lands of the southern hemisphere are under essentially the same climatic influences as those in the north. However, the land masses in the southern mid-latitudes are much less extensive than their northern counterparts. Consequently, continental interior and east coast climates are less well developed. By way of partial exception, eastern South America, under the lee of the Andes mountains, shows some similarities to continental North American climates.

4.2.5 | Polar climates

A polar climate may be defined as one in which the average temperature of the warmest month does not exceed 10°C. Such climates cover much of the globe at latitudes greater than about 60°N and 55°S.

In these regions, much of the ground is permanently frozen, a condition known as **permafrost**. In the warmer permafrost areas, the surface may thaw during the summer, supporting some plant growth over a very limited growing season (Chapter 9, Section 9.7.1).

Not only are polar climates cold, they are frequently arid. This aridity is particularly marked away from the margins of the polar area. Here, the low levels of precipitation may be attributed to the low moisture-carrying capacity of the cold air and the stable atmospheric conditions found in areas covered by the polar cell (Section 4.2.2). Despite this aridity, much of the land is covered with surface water (generally frozen). This is primarily because what precipitation there is largely remains at the surface, as losses by evaporation and infiltration through the permafrost are low.

The interior of the northern polar region is generally calm. In contrast, the interior of the south polar region is blustery as strong winds of topographic origin are common over the mountainous continent of Antarctica.

As would be expected, mid-latitudinal influences are

felt at the edges of the polar districts. Particularly important are the depressions that frequently encroach on the *margins* of both polar regions. These alter the climates of these marginal polar areas as they bring both wind and precipitation.

4.2.6   The climate system and climate change

Little climatic alteration is apparent over time-scales of decades. However, it would be a mistake to think of climate as an unchanging phenomenon. When viewed over periods of thousands or tens of thousands of years, it becomes clear that the world has experienced a series of highly significant climatic changes. On this long-term time-scale, a pattern of alternating cold periods (called ice ages or **glacials**) and warm periods (**interglacials**) is apparent (Figure 4.23). Superimposed on this are more subtle variations that become noticeable over periods of several decades or centuries. Such variations include the cool period, known as the Little Ice Age, that was experienced in northern Europe between the sixteenth and nineteenth centuries.

The mechanisms that mediate climate change are not fully understood. However, it is possible to build models of the climate that enhance this understanding and that have both predictive and interpretative value. Within such models, the climate is considered to be the product of the interplay between the various components of the climatic system (Figure 4.24). Alterations that modify this interplay are seen as instrumental in producing climate change.

The nature and extent of the climate change brought about by a given alteration in the climate system is often dependent on the operation of *feedback mechanisms*. Mechanisms that enhance an initial change in climate are said to be positive, while those that decrease the size of change are negative.

For example, an increase in the amount of solar energy absorbed at the surface would cause an increase in surface temperature. This would be accompanied by a decrease in the proportion of the surface that was covered with snow. Snow is more reflective than the land, vegetation or water on which it lies. A decrease in the snow cover will therefore allow more solar radiation to be absorbed so initiating positive feedback.

Knowledge gained from a study of the past few thousand years may lead to the expectation that any future changes in climate would be gradual. However, this view may well be wrong. Recent evidence suggests that, in the more distant past, major changes have occurred very rapidly, possibly over periods as short as 15 to 30 years.

The end of the last ice age (about 15 000 BP) appears to have been accompanied by significant, sudden fluctuations in the temperature regime experienced by the North Atlantic region. One explanation of such events is linked to the operation of the oceanic conveyor belt described in Box 4.3. This currently warms the North Atlantic relative to the North Pacific. However, this conveyor belt could equally well operate in reverse, warming the North Pacific. Were this to occur, the North Atlantic would become significantly cooler, initiating glaciation. Any future reversal of the oceanic conveyor belt may act as a 'switch', rapidly changing the climate from its current form to a new, stable, but highly different one.

4.3   Summary

The contemporary atmosphere has formed, under the influence of both photosynthetic activity and photochemical reactions, from gases evolved from the Earth.

The atmosphere has a layered structure. In order of increasing altitude, these layers are called the troposphere, stratosphere, mesosphere and thermosphere. Each layer is different from the others in terms of composition and/or temperature profile.

The main constituents of the troposphere and stratosphere are nitrogen (N_2, 78.09% v/v), oxygen (O_2, 20.95% v/v) and argon (Ar, 0.93% v/v) (percentages are for dry tropospheric air). The troposphere also contains a significant amount of water (H_2O, 0.5 to 4% v/v moist air). The atmosphere contains trace gases of great importance, including carbon dioxide (CO_2) (a greenhouse gas) and ozone (O_3) (a gas found mainly in the stratosphere; it absorbs harmful ultraviolet light).

The absorption of solar energy at the Earth's surface provides a source of heat that warms the atmosphere from below. This gives the energy that is responsible for driving the weather and climate patterns of the globe. It causes turbulent mixing of the troposphere, allowing a net redistribution of energy away from the equator, where it is most intensely absorbed. The primary circulation of the atmosphere that results can be represented by a three-division model. The divisions are as follows: the Hadley cells, located either side of the equator; the Rossby waves in the mid-latitudes; and the high-latitude polar cells.

The major surface wind patterns and climates of the world can be understood in terms of this model. The Hadley cells are responsible for the trade winds, the precipitation associated with the intertropical convergence zone (ITCZ) and the aridity caused by the high-pressure zones at their outer edges. In certain parts of the world, this situation is modified by monsoon wind patterns.

The Rossby waves, and their associated westerly surface

Figure 4.23 Trends in past average global temperatures (from DOE, 1994).

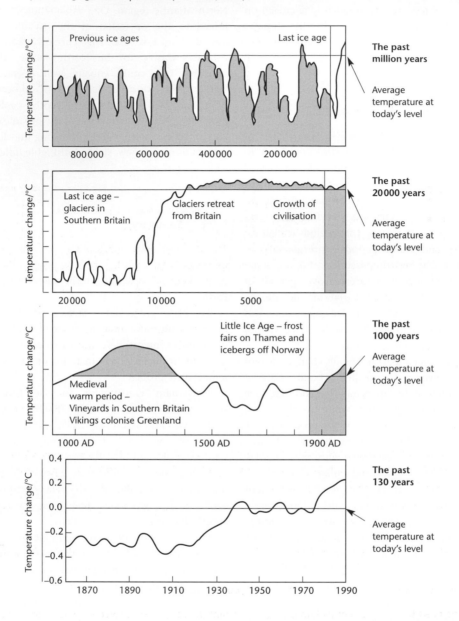

winds and eastward-migrating depressions, are responsible for the wet weather that typifies west coast mid-latitude climates. East coast mid-latitude locations are therefore comparatively dry, while interior continental regions are drier still.

The polar regions are typically cold and arid under the influence of the polar cells. This basic polar climate is modified in places, particularly by the influences of topography (causing high winds in the south polar region) and encroaching mid-latitude airflows (causing enhanced precipitation at the polar margins).

The climate is in a constant state of change. This can clearly be seen if the past climate is viewed over a sufficiently long time-scale (centuries, thousands of years or tens of thousands of years). The mechanisms of climate change are not fully understood. However, informative models have been devised that are based on the concept of the climate system, including feedback mechanisms.

While recent climate change has been gradual, there are suggestions that there have been periods of rapid transformation in the past. It is possible that such events were initiated by alterations in the operation of the oceanic conveyor belt. Similar changes in the future may also be possible.

Figure 4.24 The climate system (from Houghton, 1984).

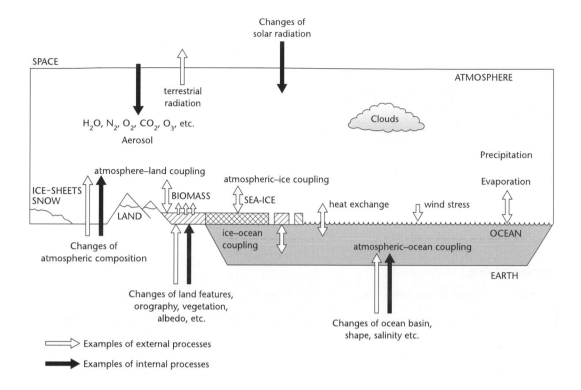

Problems

1 The oxidation of methane in the stratosphere generates a significant amount of the water contained in this part of the atmosphere. From which region of the atmosphere does this methane originate? Could water directly enter the stratosphere from this region? Justify your answer.

2 Contrast the mechanisms that lead to an increase in temperature with decreasing altitude in the mesosphere and troposphere.

3 Oxygen atoms are highly reactive. With this in mind, explain why the ozone concentration of the stratosphere at night is approximately the same as at sunset (refer to Equations 4.1 to 4.4).

4 Would you expect the mesosphere to be turbulent? Justify your answer.

5 Explain why the need to conserve momentum is more important than the Coriolis force in generating an easterly direction to the trade winds.

6 Imagine an object moving across the surface of the Earth at $30\,\mathrm{m\,s^{-1}}$. The magnitude of the acceleration (a) that it experiences as a consequence of the Coriolis force is related to the speed of the object (u), the rotation rate of the Earth in radians $\mathrm{s^{-1}}$ (ω) and the latitude of the object (ϕ) in accordance with the following expression:

$$a = (\omega \sin \phi)u$$

What is the value of a at each of the following latitudinal locations?
   (a) the equator
   (b) the North Pole
   (c) the South Pole
   (d) 20°N

7 Use the concept of continentality to explain why in the summer the ITCZ reaches higher latitudes over the interior of the Asian continent than over the oceans.

8 Consider the monsoon climates of south-east Asia. Does the mean winter surface airflow pattern of these climates accord with that predicted on the basis of the Hadley cell circulation? Explain your answer.

9 Radiative cooling from the ground is more effective under clear skies. With this in mind, are night-time frosts more likely in the mid-latitude winters under extratropical cyclonic or anticyclonic conditions?

10 The rate of temperature change with respect to altitude brought about by adiabatic cooling or warming is called the adiabatic lapse rate. Its value for unsaturated air is $9.8^\circ C\,km^{-1}$. Would you expect the adiabatic lapse rate for air saturated with water vapour to be higher or lower than this? Justify your answer.

11 Write, in your own words, an account of the origin of the mediterranean climatic type. Explain how its characteristics determine the nature of the fauna and flora that it supports (further information about this is given in Chapter 9, Section 9.7.4).

12 Ice is more effective at reflecting incoming solar radiation than are other Earth surfaces. If the Earth were to receive less solar radiation than it does currently, would the ensuing increase in surface ice initiate a positive or negative feedback mechanism?

4.5   Further reading

Barry, R. G. and R. J. Chorley (1998) *Atmosphere, weather and climate* (7th edn). London: Routledge.

Bunce, N. J. (1990) *Environmental chemistry* (2nd edn). Winnipeg: Wuerz. (This considers the structure and chemistry of the atmosphere and its pollutants in its first three chapters)

Houghton, J. T., L. G. Meira Filho, B. A. Callander, N. Harris, A. Kattenberg and K. Maskell (eds) (1996) *Climate change 1995: The science of climate change*. Published for the IPCC by Cambridge University Press. (Explains the basis and outcomes of climate modelling)

Robinson, P. J. and A. Henderson-Sellers (1999) *Contemporary climatology* (2nd edn). Harlow: Longman.

Wayne, R. P. (1991) *Chemistry of atmospheres* (2nd edn). Oxford: Oxford University Press.

White, I. D., D. N. Mottershead and S. J. Harrison (1992) *Environmental systems; an introductory text* (2nd edn). London: Chapman & Hall. (Considers the structure and circulation of the atmosphere in Chapters 3, 4, 6, 8 and 9)

Bioelement cycling

After reading this chapter, you should be able to:

■ Define the terms nutrient, bioelement, macro-nutrient element, biogeochemical cycle, reservoir, flux, dynamic steady state and residence time.

■ Use box models to aid your understanding of bioelement cycling.

■ Recognise the importance of biogeochemical cycles in the sustenance of life on Earth and the pivotal role played by solar energy in the maintenance of these cycles.

■ Appreciate the highly significant part played by biological processes in many of the biogeochemical cycles of the macro-nutrient elements.

■ Understand that all of the biogeochemical cycles are interlinked.

■ Report, in some detail, the salient features of the cycles entered into by oxygen (including the water cycle), carbon, nitrogen, phosphorus, sulfur, sodium, potassium, calcium and magnesium.

Introduction

A **nutrient** is a chemical species that is actively taken up by an organism and used to maintain its bodily functions. Nutrients supply the chemical elements that are necessary for the normal growth of organisms. These are known as the **essential elements** or **bioelements** (Figure 5.1). There are strikingly few of these, given the enormous number of chemical reactions that are needed to support life.

Nine of the bioelements are needed in greater quantities than the rest. These are sometimes referred to as the **macro-nutrient elements**. They are oxygen (O), hydrogen (H), carbon (C), nitrogen (N), calcium (Ca), phosphorus (P), sulfur (S), potassium (K), and magnesium (Mg). The bulk of any one organism is made up of a combination of some or all of these macro-nutrient

elements. For example, 99% of the body mass of a human is attributable to the first six of these elements (Figure 5.2).

The Earth is a closed system (Chapter 2, Section 2.1). This means that the supply of bioelements is finite. Despite this, on a global scale, the supply of these elements appears to be inexhaustible. This is because these elements are recycled through the environment. The atoms that make up the food we eat have been eaten many times before!

For each of the bioelements it is possible to trace a closed circuit through which it cycles. All of these circuits have both a **biotic phase** in which the bioelement is within organisms, and an **abiotic phase** in which it is in the geochemical (i.e. physical)

Figure 5.1 The bioelements.

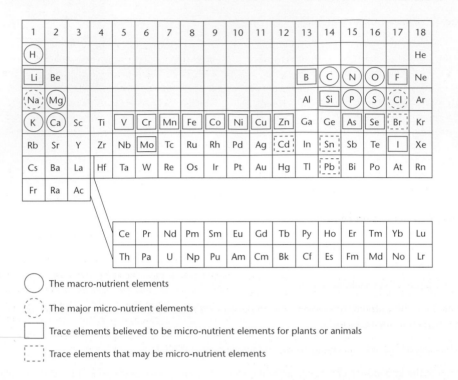

⬡ The macro-nutrient elements

⬡ The major micro-nutrient elements

☐ Trace elements believed to be micro-nutrient elements for plants or animals

⌐ ⌐ Trace elements that may be micro-nutrient elements

Figure 5.2 The percentage composition by mass of a human being (from Phillips and Chilton, 1989).

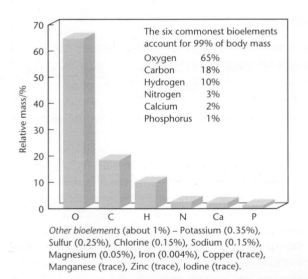

The six commonest bioelements account for 99% of body mass

Oxygen	65%
Carbon	18%
Hydrogen	10%
Nitrogen	3%
Calcium	2%
Phosphorus	1%

Other bioelements (about 1%) – Potassium (0.35%), Sulfur (0.25%), Chlorine (0.15%), Sodium (0.15%), Magnesium (0.05%), Iron (0.004%), Copper (trace), Manganese (trace), Zinc (trace), Iodine (trace).

environment. For this reason such circuits are called **biogeochemical cycles**. The continuation of these cycles is dependent on a sustained energy supply. Much of this is provided by the sun, the remainder comes from the internal energy of the Earth. An important feature of the biogeochemical cycles is that they are interlinked. As we

will see, the cycling of one element is often profoundly affected by the cycling of others.

The relative importance of biological and geochemical transformations are not the same for all cycles. In some cases, transformations that occur within the biotic phase are of great significance to the operation of the cycle. This is true for the nitrogen, sulfur, carbon and oxygen cycles. Other cycles are essentially geochemical in nature. These would carry on, with little change, even if life on Earth were to cease. This is true of the phosphorus, sodium, potassium and magnesium cycles.

This chapter concentrates on the biogeochemical cycles of the macro-nutrient elements. Emphasis is placed on the discussion of the main processes and transformations that are involved in these cycles. Where appropriate, mention is made of human impacts on these cycles; these topics are expanded on in Part Two of this book (especially Chapters 11 to 15). For convenience, considerable use will be made of box models when discussing nutrient cycles. The essential features of these models are given in Box 5.1.

5.1 The oxygen cycles

We live on an oxygen-rich planet. On a weight for weight basis, oxygen accounts for 46.6% of the crust, 85.8% of the

5.1 Box models of bioelement cycling

Box models are used to portray the cycling of bioelements through the environment. These are useful as they give insight into the impact of human activities on these vital processes.

In these models, the cycles are depicted as a series of boxes linked by arrows (see the atmospheric oxygen and carbon cycles, Figures 5.5 and 5.6 later in this chapter, for examples). The boxes represent reservoirs of the bioelement concerned, while the arrows represent the direction of movement of material from one reservoir to another.

In this context, a **reservoir** is a 'store' of material that is *separate* from other such stores on the grounds of physical location or chemical speciation.

For example, carbon is found in the atmosphere, the Earth's crust and the oceans. These three reservoirs are distinct on the basis of location. Reservoirs based on chemical speciation may also be identified within the carbon cycle. Concentrating on the atmosphere, carbon is found to be present in many chemical species. The most important of these are carbon dioxide (CO_2), methane (CH_4) and carbon monoxide (CO); each constitutes a separate reservoir of carbon.

It is possible to estimate the size of the major reservoirs within a given cycle. This size is generally expressed in kilograms (symbol kg) or moles (mol). It is also possible to estimate the rate of movement of material from one reservoir to another, a parameter called **flux**. Fluxes are usually expressed in kilograms per annum ($kg\,a^{-1}$) or moles per annum ($mol\,a^{-1}$).

There is considerable evidence to suggest that the sizes of the main reservoirs of the major nutrient cycles have remained essentially constant for many millions of years. This is despite the natural continuous addition and removal of material. This implies that the total flux out of any one reservoir must be equalled by the total flux into it. Such reservoirs are said to be in a **dynamic steady state**.

It would be highly useful to know whether a particular human activity is likely to have a significant impact on the size of a reservoir. A parameter called **residence time** (symbol τ, occasionally referred to as 'turnover time', 'average transit time' or 'lifetime') is of some use in this respect. It is the ratio of the amount of material in a reservoir to the total flux in or out of it. Hence, the residence time of carbon as carbon dioxide in the atmosphere is:

$$\frac{59.9 \times 10^{15}}{10.39 \times 10^{15} + 8.30 \times 10^{15}} = 3.2 \, \text{years}$$

while that of molecular oxygen (O_2) in the atmosphere can be seen to be:

$$\frac{3.8 \times 10^{19}}{5.0 \times 10^{15}} = 7.6 \times 10^3 \, \text{years}$$

Residence time gives an indication of the fragility of a given reservoir to change. Reservoirs with large residence times are robust, whereas those with small residence times are fragile.

In many circumstances, the removal processes of a given species (X) from a reservoir, such as the atmosphere, obey either first order or pseudo first order kinetics (Chapter 2, Section 2.3). That is, for each process:

$$\text{rate} = k[X]$$

where k is the first order rate constant and square brackets stand for molar concentration. When this occurs:

$$\tau = \frac{1}{\Sigma k}$$

where Σ stands for 'sum of all'. Under these circumstances,

$$[X]' = \frac{[X]}{e^n}$$

where $[X]'$ equals the concentration of X after n residence times, $[X]$ is the initial concentration of X, and e is the base of natural logarithms (i.e. 2.718 28, approx.).

---

oceans and 23.2% of the atmosphere. Let us briefly review oxygen speciation in each of these reservoirs before exploring the oxygen cycles.

Oxygen in the crust. Most of the oxygen in the crust is present as silicate and aluminosilicate minerals, both of which are based on the SiO_4 tetrahedral unit (Chapter 3, Box 3.1). The remainder is present either as water (H_2O) or as oxygen-containing non-silicate minerals. These include minerals based on the oxide anion (O^{2-}) and those based on the oxygen-containing molecular anions (called oxyanions), including phosphate (PO_4^{3-}), carbonate (CO_3^{2-}) and sulfate (SO_4^{2-}).

Oxygen in the oceans. The vast majority of oxygen in the oceans is present as water (H_2O). However, dissolved in this, there is a very small, but biologically significant, amount of oxygen-containing species. These include molecular oxygen (O_2), silicate (SiO_4^{4-}), sulfate, nitrate (NO_3^-) and carbonate.

Oxygen in the atmosphere. The speciation of oxygen in the atmosphere is complex. It involves molecular oxygen, carbon dioxide, water, ozone (O_3), the oxides of sulfur (SO_2 and SO_3, collectively known as SO_x) sulfate (SO_4^{2-}), the oxides of nitrogen (NO and NO_2, collectively known as NO_x, and N_2O) and nitrate. Of these, the dominant species are molecular oxygen (20.95% by volume of dry air), carbon dioxide (0.03% by volume of dry air) and, to a varying extent, water (0.5 to 4% by volume of moist air) (Chapter 4, Section 4.1).

The bulk of the oxygen in all of these reservoirs moves

through one of three essentially separate cycles. These are the rock cycle (discussed briefly in Chapter 3, Section 3.1.4), the water cycle and the atmospheric oxygen cycle. The latter two are described below.

The water cycle

Without the continued circulation of water through the environment, much of the life on Earth would cease. This is because water plays many roles in the sustenance of life. For example, it acts as a solvent and transport medium, allowing nutrients to be absorbed by organisms and to be moved within them. In addition, water plays a major role in the maintenance of a world climate that is compatible with continued life. It does this by trapping and redistributing a significant proportion of the solar energy arriving at the Earth (Chapter 4, especially Section 4.2.1). Finally, water is central to the process of aerobic photosynthesis by which higher plants convert carbon dioxide into carbohydrate (Chapter 6, Section 6.4).

The circulation of water through the environment is referred to as the **water cycle** or the **hydrological cycle**. This is shown in simplified form in Figure 5.3.

The major reservoirs in this cycle are the oceans, the atmosphere, ice and land-based water bodies including rivers, lakes and ground waters. There are two types of

process by which water is transferred between these reservoirs. The first type includes those associated with translocation such as surface run-off and wind. The second comprises those concerned with changes in phase, including evaporation and condensation (Figure 5.4).

Transpiration and evapotranspiration are special cases of evaporation; these are explored in Box 5.2.

The water cycle is driven by solar energy, the absorption of which powers the key processes of evaporation and translocation by wind. As can be seen in Figure 5.3, the bulk of evaporation occurs from the oceans. However, not all of the water so evaporated is returned to the oceans directly by **precipitation** (the collective word for rain, hail and snow). The remainder is transported to be precipitated over the land. Hence, more water enters the land via precipitation than leaves it by evaporation. The excess water eventually returns to the oceans by surface run-off (predominantly in rivers) and ground water seepage.

On a global scale, human activity has little impact on the hydrological cycle. However, extraction of fresh water either from rivers or from the ground can have severe local consequences (Chapter 12, Section 12.5). In the future, large-scale perturbations in the hydrological cycle may occur if predictions based on the enhanced greenhouse effect are borne out (Chapter 15, Section 15.2.3).

Figure **5.3** The hydrological cycle.

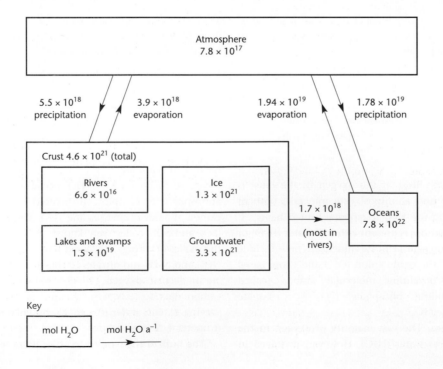

Figure 5.4 Processes in the hydrological cycle: (a) the hydrological system; (b) changes in phase occurring in the hydrological cycle (from White *et al.*, 1992).

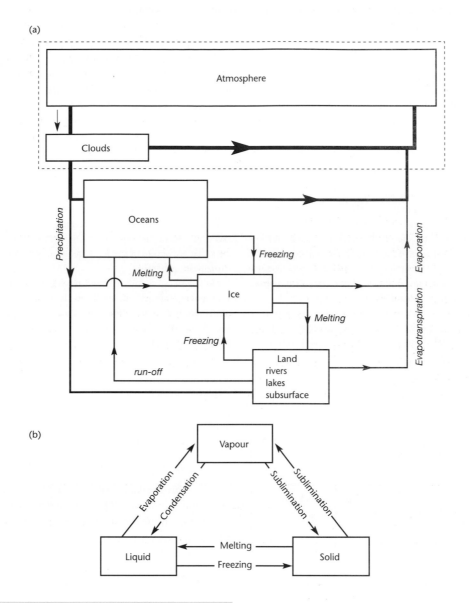

5.1.2   The atmospheric oxygen cycle

As discussed in Chapter 4 (Section 4.1), the presence of oxygen (O_2) in the atmosphere can almost wholly be ascribed to the activity of higher plants. These release this gas as a by-product during the photosynthesis of carbohydrates. This process consumes carbon dioxide and requires sunlight. It may be represented thus:

$$2H_2O_{(l)} + CO_{2(g)} \xrightarrow{\text{sunlight}} CH_2O_{(s)} + H_2O_{(l)} + O_{2(g)}$$

where CH_2O represents carbohydrate.

Much of the carbohydrate produced is later oxidised during respiration (a process vital to continued life on Earth: Chapter 6, Section 6.3) and similar but non-biological oxidation reactions. These processes are collectively known as **oxidative decay**. They consume oxygen and release carbon dioxide back into the atmosphere:

$$CH_2O_{(s)} + O_{2(g)} \rightarrow CO_{2(g)} + H_2O_{(l)}$$

Carbon dioxide is also produced at the expense of oxygen during similar reactions when ancient organic sediments such as coal and oil are exposed to the air.

Atmospheric oxygen and carbon dioxide are therefore linked in a cycle that is largely biologically mediated and that requires the input of solar energy. This is the atmospheric oxygen cycle and is shown in Figure 5.5.

5.2 The evaporation, transpiration and evapotranspiration of water

Evaporation of water involves the net transfer of molecules from the liquid to the gas phase.

To explore this further, it may be useful to imagine a pool of water in contact with still, dry air. The molecules of water that make up the pool are in a constant state of random motion by virtue of the kinetic energy that they possess. At the surface of the pool, some of the molecules will have sufficient kinetic energy to break free of the hydrogen bonds that bind them to the liquid. These molecules will enter the gas phase and become part of the air.

After some time, there will be a significant number of water molecules in the gas phase, some of which will re-enter the liquid phase. As time progresses, the population of water molecules in the gas phase will increase as will the rate at which molecules re-enter the liquid phase. Eventually, the rate at which the molecules leave the liquid phase will equal that at which they re-enter. At this point, evaporation will cease as there is no longer a net loss of molecules from the liquid phase, and the air is said to be **saturated**.

Evaporation can be restarted either by supplying heat to increase the kinetic energy of the water molecules and/or by replacing the saturated air with drier air. By such means the evaporation can be made to continue until the supply of liquid water to the surface is exhausted and the pool is dry.

Clearly, exhaustion of liquid water does not happen in the open oceans. Here, evaporation is controlled by the heat available, the degree of saturation of the air, the wind speed and the salinity of the water (for a given set of conditions, a 1% increase in salinity results in approximately a 1% decrease in evaporation).

On bare land, the rate at which water is supplied to the surface of the ground is often the limiting factor. However, on vegetation-covered surfaces the plants form another pathway by which water from the soil can enter the atmosphere. Water that is passed from the liquid to the gas phase by this means is said to have undergone **transpiration**. This can be highly significant. In densely vegetated humid areas transpiration can account for in excess of 60% of the water lost to the atmosphere. In semi-arid areas that are devoid of surface water, transpiration accounts for virtually all such losses.

Most land is partially covered by vegetation. Here, land to atmosphere transfer of moisture is brought about by a combination of evaporation and transpiration. These transfers are frequently lumped together and given the term **evapotranspiration**.

Figure 5.5 The atmospheric oxygen cycle.

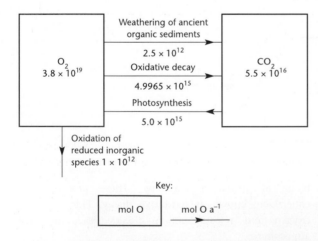

As can be seen from Figure 5.5, oxygen is also removed from the atmosphere by reaction with reduced inorganic species. These include metals in reduced states exposed by weathering, such as iron(II) and manganese(II), and gases released by volcanoes such as carbon monoxide (CO), hydrogen (H_2) and hydrogen sulfide (H_2S). Reactions of oxygen with reduced inorganic species rarely yield carbon dioxide as a product. Hence, they represent a net loss of oxygen from the atmospheric oxygen cycle. For example, iron(II)-containing minerals may be oxidised to yield a variety of iron(III) species. A general expression may be written for this oxidation using $Fe(OH)_{3(s)}$ to represent the iron(III) products, thus:

$$O_{2(g)} + 4Fe^{2+}_{(aq)} + 10H_2O_{(l)} \rightarrow 4Fe(OH)_{3(s)} + 8H^+_{(aq)}$$

Despite this 'leakage' of oxygen from the cycle, the molecular oxygen (O_2) reservoir remains in an approximately steady state condition. This is because the rate of molecular oxygen production by photosynthesis, i.e. 5000×10^{12} mol a^{-1} (Figure 5.5), equals the *total* rate of its depletion (i.e. $4996.5 \times 10^{12} + 2.5 \times 10^{12} + 1 \times 10^{12}$ mol a^{-1}).

The enhanced consumption of molecular oxygen as a result of fossil fuel combustion has little impact on the atmospheric reservoir of this gas. Primarily, this is because this reservoir and the residence time of the oxygen within it are both large.

5.2 The carbon cycle

It is convenient to consider the carbon in the carbon cycle (Figure 5.6) to be either inorganic or organic. Carbon dioxide (CO_2) and the related species carbonate (CO_3^{2-}) and hydrogen carbonate (HCO_3^-, also called bicarbonate) constitute the vast bulk of the inorganic carbon, while

Figure 5.6 The carbon cycle.

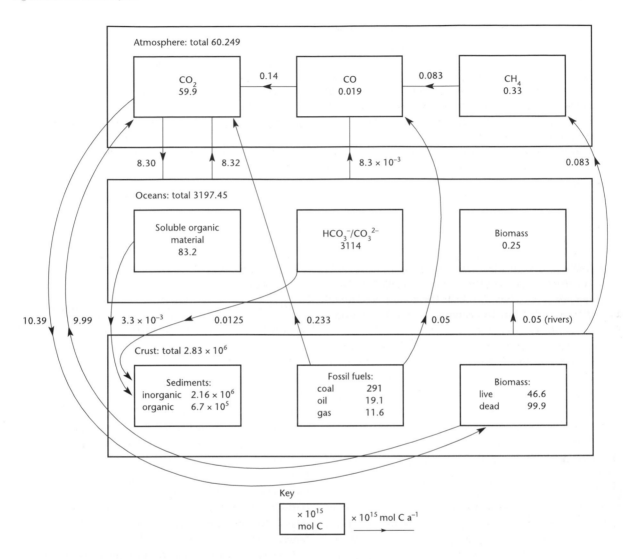

organic carbon is that found in organisms (living or dead), fossil fuels, finely dispersed organic deposits in rocks and organic molecules dissolved in water or dispersed in the atmosphere.

There is a continuous two-way flow of carbon between the inorganic and organic forms. Inorganic carbon is in an oxidised state. This is reduced to organic carbon during photosynthesis (Chapter 6, Section 6.4). This process occurs in green plants and requires energy in the form of sunlight.

As organic carbon is in a reduced state, it is susceptible to oxidation by atmospheric oxygen (O_2). This process can occur in the absence of living organisms. However, it is generally biologically mediated, in which case it is called respiration (Chapter 6, Section 6.3). As the oxidation of organic carbon is exothermic, respiration can be thought

of as the liberation of the solar energy trapped as chemical energy during photosynthesis. Both green plants and the animals that they support require the energy liberated during respiration for the maintenance of their bodily functions. Hence, the continued existence of these organisms is dependent on the continued solar-powered cycling of carbon between its inorganic and organic forms.

From the foregoing discussion it is clear that the carbon cycle and the atmospheric oxygen cycle (Section 5.1.2) are interlinked. The processes of photosynthesis and respiration are central to both.

In excess of 99% of all of the matter in the carbon cycle is found in the crust, where it is present in both inorganic and organic forms. The rates of flux to and from this reservoir are small. Hence, the vast majority of carbon in the crust is essentially unavailable for cycling. This is reflected in the extremely long mean residence time for crustal carbon (2.7×10^5 years).

Carbon in the crust is largely of biological origin. Most of the carbon in this reservoir is inorganic. This is deposited as the remains of the many marine organisms that use calcium carbonate ($CaCO_3$) as the principal component of their skeletal structures. On consolidation and/or metamorphism, these remains produce limestones and related rocks (Chapter 3, Section 3.1.3).

Organic carbon is deposited in sediments when the rate of photosynthesis is greater than the combined rates of respiration and non-biological oxidation. For example, this happens in stagnant waters where biological oxygen demand outstrips the rate at which molecular oxygen (O_2) is supplied from the atmosphere. The removal of organic carbon from the environment by this means is of great significance. If this process were to stop, more carbon would be available for oxidation. As a consequence, the oxygen levels in the atmosphere would drop significantly, and the carbon dioxide levels would rise.

The bulk of organic carbon in the crust is present as fine dispersions in sedimentary rocks such as shales. Deposits in which organic carbon compounds are the major constituent also occur, but they are rare. However, such deposits are of great economic and environmental importance as they constitute the fossil fuels (oil, gas and coal). More information is given on the formation of these fuels in Chapter 12 (Section 12.4).

The mean residence time of carbon dioxide in the atmosphere is relatively small (3.2 years). This is close to the time taken for the lower atmosphere to mix. Thus, local variations in the carbon dioxide levels of the atmosphere may be expected. What is more, relatively small perturbations in either the outward or inward flux of atmospheric carbon would be expected to alter the size of this reservoir. Both of these phenomena are observed.

Figure 5.7 shows the levels of carbon dioxide in the atmosphere measured in the northern hemisphere (at the Mauna Loa Observatory in Hawaii). The sawtooth pattern is essentially a consequence of seasonal variations in the net ratio of photosynthesis to respiration. An inverse of this pattern is seen in the opposite hemisphere. The general upward trend shows a removal of the dynamic steady state condition from this reservoir. This is due to human activity, particularly fossil fuel burning. It has been suggested that this removal of the steady state may have important consequences for the world's climate, possibly bringing about global warming (Chapter 15, Section 15.2.3).

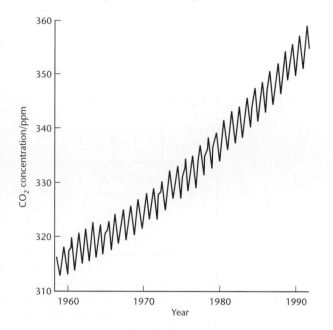

Figure 5.7 Atmospheric levels of carbon dioxide (measured at the Mauna Loa Laboratory, Hawaii) (from Houghton, 1997).

5.3 The nitrogen cycle

Nitrogen is essential to life. It is a fundamental component of the class of molecules called amino acids. These are vital as they are the 'building blocks' of proteins (Chapter 6, Section 6.6). Proteins have a variety of functions including those of natural catalysts (called **enzymes**), chemical messengers within an organism (**hormones**) and the transport and storage of small molecules, such as oxygen (O_2). Proteins also have a tissue structure-forming function.

Nitrogen is an essential component of the bases that make up DNA. This is the molecule that carries the genetic code of all living creatures (Chapter 6 , Section 6.5).

Nitrogen has other biologically significant roles. For instance, there are organisms that are capable of utilising nitrogen in its oxidised forms as a substitute for oxygen (O_2) during respiration, while there are others that can oxidise reduced nitrogen with oxygen, to liberate energy.

In fact, nitrogen has many biologically available oxidation states (Figure 5.8). This means that biologically mediated redox reactions are central to the nitrogen cycle (Figure 5.9). Alterations in chemical speciation that such reactions bring about often result in the movement of nitrogen from one reservoir to another in a different physical location.

A great deal of effort has been expended in attempts to understand the processes involved in the nitrogen cycle.

Figure 5.8 Nitrogen speciation in the environment.

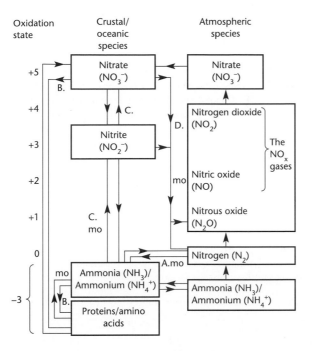

mo = reactions that involve microbial activity, A. = nitrogen fixation,
B. = assimilation C. = nitrification, D. = denitrification

This is particularly true of those processes that relate directly to crop growth. This is because nitrogen supply is frequently the limiting factor in crop yields. Despite the large amount of work completed and the considerable progress that has been made, there still remain unanswered questions. For instance, the magnitude of many of the fluxes in the cycle are little more than intelligent guesses.

Nitrogen is not a major component of either the crust or the oceans. However, 76% of the mass of the atmosphere is molecular nitrogen (N_2). This means that this atmospheric gas is the most significant single reservoir in the nitrogen cycle (Figure 5.9).

The process by which atmospheric nitrogen is reduced to ammonia (NH_3) and subsequently incorporated into amino acids is called **nitrogen fixation**. This is carried out by a limited number of prokaryotic micro-organisms only. These may be free-living or in symbiotic association with plants (Box 5.3).

The energy for nitrogen fixation is supplied by the oxidation of carbohydrate and therefore is ultimately supplied by photosynthesis (Chapter 6, Section 6.4). Hence, sunlight is the prime source of energy that drives the nitrogen cycle. The nitrogen, oxygen and carbon cycles are therefore closely interlinked.

Figure 5.9 The nitrogen cycle.

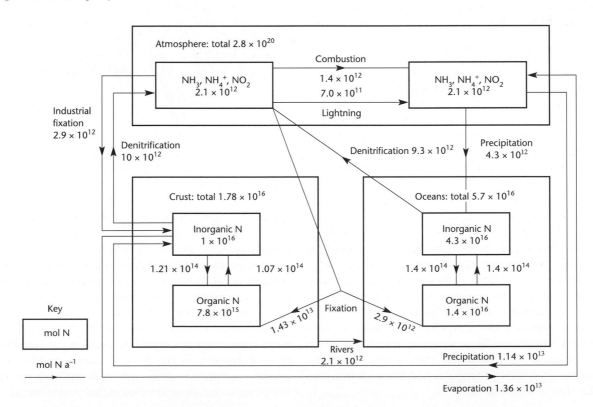

Further Information Box

5.3 Biological nitrogen fixation

Nitrogen fixation is the process by which atmospheric nitrogen (N_2) is reduced and incorporated into biological tissues. Higher plants cannot do this, though some prokaryotic organisms can. Blue-green algae and some bacteria are nitrogen fixers. They may be free living or in symbiotic relationships with plants. For example, legumes (peas, beans, clover, etc.) are capable of hosting bacteria such as *Rhizobium* spp. within their roots, forming nitrogen-fixing nodules (see figure below).

All nitrogen fixers have in common the ability to reduce molecular nitrogen (N_2) to form ammonia (NH_3). This is not a simple matter, as nitrogen is particularly unreactive. This inertness is attributable to the very strong triple bond between the two atoms of the nitrogen molecule, the complete breakage of which must be achieved if the nitrogen is to be made available for use in biological systems. The energy required to do this is considerable ($950 \, kJ \, mol^{-1}$).

Nitrogen fixers ultimately derive both the energy and the electrons necessary for the reduction of molecular nitrogen to ammonia from the oxidation of carbohydrate. The half-cell reactions involved may be represented thus:

$$3H_2O + 3CH_2O \rightarrow 3CO_2 + 12H^+ + 12e^- \qquad (a)$$

$$12H^+ + 2N_2 + 12e^- \rightarrow 4NH_3 \qquad (b)$$

Therefore, overall (adding a and b and cancelling electrons and H^+ terms that appear on both sides of the arrow), the process may be represented thus:

$$3H_2O + 3CH_2O + 2N_2 \rightarrow 3CO_2 + 4NH_3$$

While this process can be summarised in simple equations, it is in fact highly complex.

Nitrogen fixation is made possible by the presence of an enzyme called nitrogenase. This facilitates the half-cell reaction represented by Equation b above. Nitrogenase is a complex of two protein molecules, one larger than the other. Both of these contain iron while the larger one also contains two atoms of molybdenum. During the catalytic cycle, molecular nitrogen (N_2) is bound to the molybdenum, where it is reduced by electrons fed through the iron atoms, and is ultimately released as two molecules of ammonia. The energy for this process is supplied by the conversion of ATP to ADP on the smaller protein molecule. The ATP for this process is synthesised

elsewhere in the organism during the oxidation of carbohydrate.

Nitrogen fixation is energy intensive. It consumes considerable quantities of carbohydrate. Indeed, it has been suggested that as much as 12% of photosynthetic activity is used in this process. However, under most circumstances, this process is not a net drain on productivity. This is because nitrogen is frequently a limiting nutrient and biological nitrogen fixation is the only natural low-temperature way in which atmospheric nitrogen (N_2) is made available for use by higher plants.

The process of nitrogen fixation also consumes nitrous oxide (N_2O), as nitrogenase can use it as a substrate instead of molecular nitrogen.

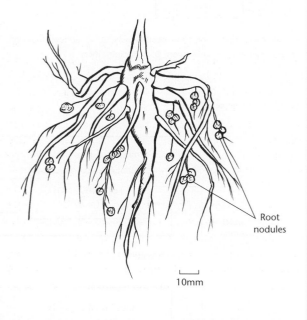

Root system of the scarlet runner bean (*Phaseolus multiflorus*) showing nitrogen-fixing root nodules.

Root nodules

10mm

It is known that microbially fixed nitrogen becomes available to terrestrial higher plants by a number of pathways. Those higher plants that form symbiotic relationships with nitrogen fixers are supplied with amino acids directly by the micro-organisms concerned.

Most higher plants, however, obtain their nitrogen from the soil solution in an inorganic form. This is either ammonium (NH_4^+) or nitrate (NO_3^-). The process by which this inorganic nitrogen is transformed into amino acids is called **assimilation**.

The biological process by which reduced inorganic nitrogen species are oxidised in the soil to nitrate is known as **nitrification**. In the absence of human intervention, it is this process that is very largely responsible for the presence of nitrate in the soil solution.

Nitrification is mediated by the activity of nitrifying micro-organisms; these derive energy from the oxidation of fixed nitrogen in the form of ammonia (NH_3) (or ammonium, NH_4^+) to nitrite (NO_2^-) and then to nitrate. The principal organisms involved in this process belong to the genera *Nitrosomonas* and *Nitrobacter*. *Nitrosomonas* is responsible for the oxidation of ammonium, thus:

$$2NH_4^+ + 3O_2 \rightarrow 2NO_2^- + 4H^+ + 2H_2O$$

whilst *Nitrobacter* carries out the oxidation of the nitrite produced, thus:

$$2NO_2^- + O_2 \rightarrow 2NO_3^-$$

During nitrification, small amounts of the gas nitrous oxide (dinitrogen oxide, N_2O) may be liberated as a consequence of incomplete oxidation of ammonium to nitrite.

The nitrogen in living terrestrial organisms is returned to the soil via excretion and death. The nitrogen held within the decaying matter so produced represents the major store of fixed nitrogen in the soil. This is broken down by organisms (called **saprophytes**) that live on dead organic matter, and is ultimately released as ammonia and ammonium. This process is called **ammonification** or **mineralisation**. The ammonia produced is either returned to the atmosphere, temporarily held as ammonium within the cation exchange capacity of the soil (Chapter 3, Boxes 3.3 and 3.4), taken up by plants, or subjected to nitrification.

Not all of the nitrified nitrogen is subsequently taken up by plants. Some of the crustal nitrate is leached from the soil by percolating waters and is ultimately washed to the ocean. In addition, nitrified nitrogen is returned to the atmosphere from both the land and the oceans via the process of **denitrification**. This process involves the reduction of nitrate to nitrogen (N_2) and/or nitrous oxide (N_2O).

Denitrification of a purely chemical form has been observed even in well-aerated soils. However, microbially mediated denitrification is generally of much greater importance. This occurs under anaerobic conditions when the micro-organisms involved use nitrate as a substitute for molecular oxygen (O_2) as the oxidant during respiration. The half-cell reaction for the reduction of nitrate during this process may be represented thus:

$$2NO_3^-{}_{(aq)} + 12H^+{}_{(aq)} + 10e^- \rightarrow N_{2(g)} + 6H_2O_{(l)}$$

Nitrous oxide is produced as an intermediate in this process and this gas may be released in significant quantities if the rate of denitrification is high. High rates are favoured by spatial or temporal fluctuations in the degree of soil aeration, coupled with high levels of mineral nitrogen and decomposable organic matter.

Nitrous oxide is a fairly inert gas and is therefore removed from the atmosphere at a low rate. Other than molecular nitrogen (N_2), this is the most abundant nitrogen species in the atmosphere. Microbially generated nitrous oxide survives long enough in the atmosphere to enter the upper atmosphere (i.e. the stratosphere). Here it

enters into processes that are involved in the determination of the concentration of ozone (O_3) (Chapter 15, Sections 15.1.2 and 15.2.4).

Soil systems therefore represent an important sub-cycle within the larger nitrogen cycle (Figure 5.10). The processes of assimilation, ammonification and nitrification facilitate circulation within this sub-cycle, while the processes of fixation, leaching and denitrification represent inputs and outputs from and to the larger nitrogen cycle.

There are non-biological routes by which atmospheric nitrogen (N_2) may become available for use by organisms. At high temperatures, nitrogen oxides can be formed by the direct reaction of nitrogen with oxygen. This happens naturally in lightning and artificially during the burning of fuels in air. A significant proportion of the oxides produced are ultimately converted into nitrates. These are readily removed from the atmosphere by rain, as they are highly soluble. On entering the soil or surface waters, these nitrates become available for uptake by plants.

As mentioned previously, terrestrial plant growth is frequently limited by the supply of nitrogen. This is despite the considerable quantities of nitrogen fixed by natural processes (Figure 5.9). As a result, the use of nitrogenous fertilisers has allowed farmers to substantially increase crop yields. The bulk of these fertilisers are made by the Haber process, developed by Haber and Bosch during 1910–14 (Chapter 2, Section 2.2). This has played a major part in the maintenance of adequate food supplies. Overall, the world's food supply has kept pace with demand. If this were not the case, the current exponential growth in the human population would not have been sustained thus far (Chapter 7, Section 7.3).

The use of nitrogenous fertilisers is not without its problems. The amount of nitrogen fixed industrially for application as fertilisers is enormous. Indeed the levels of terrestrial bio-fixation and industrial fixation are now broadly similar (1.43×10^{13} mol N a^{-1} and 2.9×10^{12} mol N a^{-1} respectively, Figure 5.9). As a result, industrial fixation has disrupted the dynamic steady state of the crustal nitrogen reservoir.

The application of nitrate fertilisers and the nitrification of ammonia-based fertilisers have led to an increase in the levels of nitrate in soil waters. As nitrates are highly soluble, they are leached from the soil into neighbouring surface and ground waters. The pollution problems associated with these nutrients are considerable; these are discussed in Chapter 14 (Section 14.2 and Box 14.3).

The denitrification of nitrate derived from artificial fertilisers has caused the atmospheric levels of nitrous oxide to rise. This is of concern as nitrous oxide is a greenhouse gas, and therefore may be contributing to

Figure 5.10 The soil-based nitrogen sub-cycle.

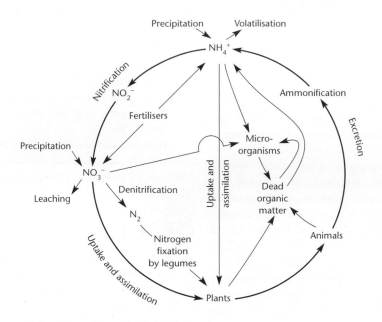

global warming. What is more, elevated concentrations of this gas in the upper atmosphere may lead to alterations in the concentration of stratospheric ozone (O_3) (Chapter 15, Sections 15.1.2 and 15.2.4).

5.4 The phosphorus cycle

Phosphorus is an essential element. It plays a central role in both cell metabolism and reproduction. It is contained in the energy-transferring molecules adenosine triphosphate (ATP), adenosine diphosphate (ADP) and adenosine monophosphate (AMP) (Chapter 6, Section 6.3). It is also a key component of DNA (deoxyribonucleic acid) and RNA (ribonucleic acid), the molecules that contain and transfer the genetic code (Chapter 6, Section 6.5).

The phosphorus cycle is shown in simplified form in Figure 5.11. In essence, this is a geochemical cycle. It follows the pattern seen in the rock cycle (Chapter 3, Section 3.1.4) of weathering, transport, sedimentation and uplift, followed by renewed weathering, and so on.

The largest reservoir within this cycle is the crust. This is because naturally occurring phosphorus-containing compounds are of low solubility and extremely low volatility. Therefore, comparatively little phosphorus is present in solution in lakes, rivers or oceans and virtually none is found in the atmosphere. The fluxes between reservoirs largely result from the movement of solid particles, borne either aerially or in

suspension in water. The magnitudes of these fluxes are not accurately known because the transport processes vary with time and from place to place, as does the phosphorus content of the particulate matter in which it is transported.

The low solubility of phosphorus-containing minerals means that much of the phosphorus in soils and sediments beneath water bodies (such as lakes) is unavailable to plants and other organisms. Hence, even in environments where phosphate minerals are relatively abundant, the low concentration of phosphorus in solution may limit growth. This is particularly true for organisms that are capable of fixing nitrogen (Box 5.3) as the growth of these species is not limited by the supply of nitrogen. Therefore, the addition of phosphorus fertiliser to a soil supporting leguminous crops will often increase the rate of nitrogen fixation.

The importance of phosphorus as a crop nutrient has meant that a great deal of work has been done on the behaviour of this element in the soil environment. Within this context, three types of phosphorus are readily identified. Firstly, there is phosphate in the soil solution. Secondly, there is phosphorus that is part of the soil organic matter. Lastly, there are several forms of solid inorganic phosphate, most of which are of very low solubility. The first category is generally tiny compared with the other two. Nonetheless, it is highly important as it is probably the only form in which this nutrient is readily available for uptake by plants. The

Figure 5.11 The phosphorus cycle.

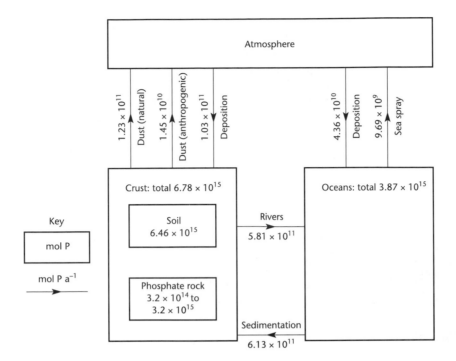

latter two forms represent the store of phosphorus within the soil.

The proportion of the total phosphorus content of a soil that is in the organic fraction varies considerably both from soil to soil and with depth within a given soil (Figure 5.12). Typically the organic fraction accounts for 30 to 85% of the total soil phosphorus. This store is of least significance in soils that have received heavy applications of inorganic phosphate fertiliser. Conversely, it is of greatest significance both in natural soils that contain little inorganic material (e.g. peat-based soils) and in unadulterated mineral soils that are highly weathered, which occur in some tropical areas. Removal of the upper horizons[1] from such tropical mineral soils reveals a subsoil that is so deficient in phosphorus (and frequently other nutrients) that it can only support poor plant growth.

The chemical speciation of phosphorus in the organic fraction of soils is not fully understood. However, it has been established that, in general, plants absorb very little of their phosphorus directly from this store.

The inorganic fraction of most soils contains both films of phosphate materials and definite phosphate compounds. The solubility of virtually all of the solid

inorganic phosphates found in soils is extremely low. What is more, soluble phosphate compounds added as fertilisers are readily precipitated within the soil environment (Chapter 11, Box 11.1).

Figure 5.12 The distribution of soil phosphorus (P) down a soil profile.

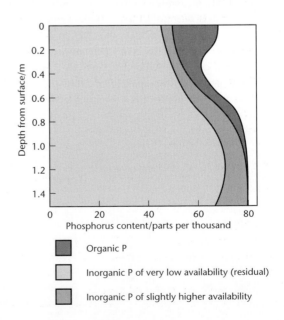

[1] The horizontal layers within soils are called horizons: see Chapter 3.

Human activity has significantly increased the flux of phosphorus from the crust, into both inland waters and the oceans.

In most cases, the anthropogenic influx of phosphorus into inland waters has happened as a result of the addition of phosphate water softeners to detergents. These enter sewerage systems and, unless specific steps are taken to remove them, pass into the water body used to accept the sewage outfall. Such additions can lead to **algal blooms**, that is rapid growths of algae, and subsequent stagnation (Chapter 14, Section 14.2).

The increased phosphorus flux into the oceans has a different origin. It is mainly the result of increased soil erosion caused by modern farming and deforestation practices (Chapter 11, Section 11.5). It has been estimated that this has produced an increase in the rate of movement of phosphorus from the land to the oceans in the form of suspended solids from about $1.6 \times 10^{11}\,\mathrm{mol\,P\,a^{-1}}$ to approximately $4.5 \times 10^{11}\,\mathrm{mol\,P\,a^{-1}}$.

5.5 The sulfur cycle

Sulfur is necessary for life. It has several important biochemical functions. For example, like nitrogen, sulfur has a key role in the structure and function of proteins. However, unlike nitrogen, it is not found in all amino acids (the 'building blocks' of proteins, Chapter 6, Section 6.6). It is present, however, in the amino acid cysteine, which contains a thiol (−S−H) group (Figure 5.13). Proteins that contain such sulfur-containing amino acids are endowed with the ability to form disulfide linkages (Figure 5.14). These can be *within* a protein molecule, that is *intra*molecular; or *between* protein molecules, that is *inter*molecular. Intramolecular linkages of this type ensure that each protein has an appropriate shape for the function it is to perform. In contrast, intermolecular disulfide links are used to join protein molecules together. By virtue of such links, proteins can be used to form relatively rigid structures, such as hair and nails.

Figure 5.13 Cysteine, a sulfur-containing amino acid.

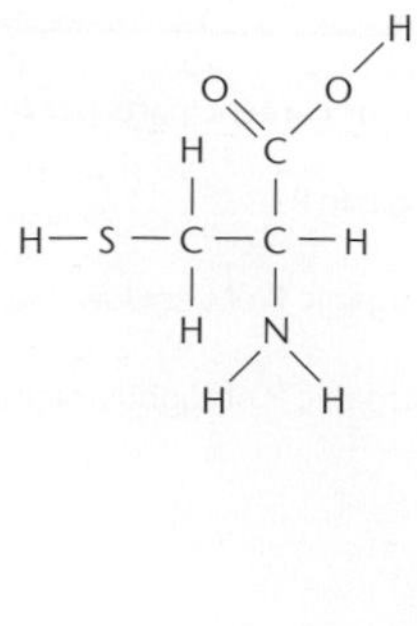

Figure 5.14 Disulfide linkage formation.

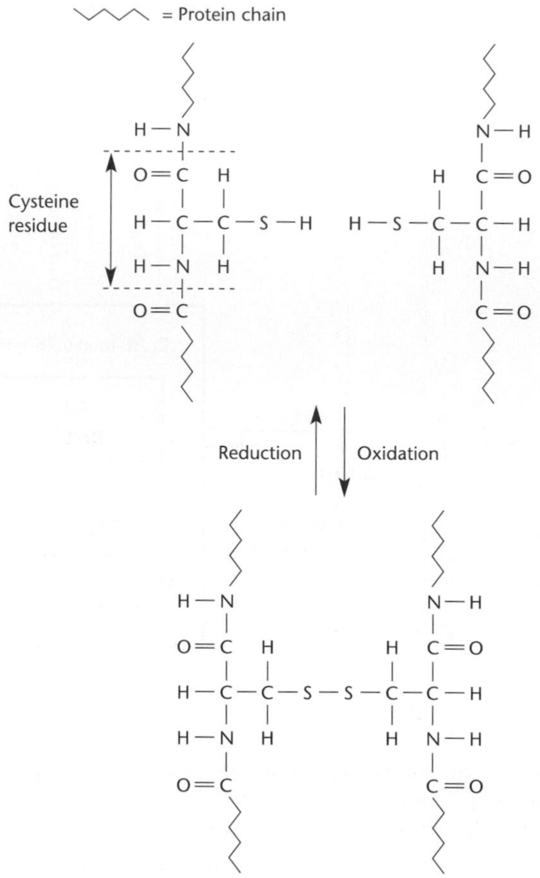

Sulfur has several biochemically accessible oxidation states (Figure 5.15). This means that micro-organisms can bring about the reduction of oxidised sulfur and, under different conditions, the oxidation of reduced forms of this element. The changes in speciation brought about by such biochemical transformations are frequently responsible for the translocation of sulfur from one reservoir to another in a physically different location. Indeed, biochemically mediated redox reactions involving sulfur are of great significance in the cycling of this nutrient. It must be borne in mind, however, that purely chemical redox reactions involving sulfur also occur in nature. These are of particular significance in the atmosphere.

The sulfur cycle is shown in simplified form in Figure 5.16. From this it can be seen that the major reservoirs of this element are crustal and oceanic, in comparison with which the atmospheric reservoir is tiny, though highly important.

Let us consider the key processes that occur in the atmospheric sulfur reservoir before reviewing those that characterise its crustal and oceanic reservoirs.

Figure 5.15 The main environmental species of sulfur.

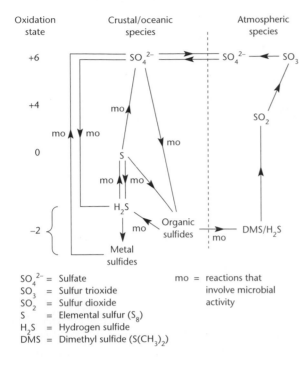

SO$_4^{2-}$ = Sulfate
SO$_3$ = Sulfur trioxide
SO$_2$ = Sulfur dioxide
S = Elemental sulfur (S$_8$)
H$_2$S = Hydrogen sulfide
DMS = Dimethyl sulfide (S(CH$_3$)$_2$)

mo = reactions that involve microbial activity

At first glance, the small size of the atmospheric reservoir may seem a little surprising. After all, sulfur is found in several highly volatile chemical species that are produced in large quantities by both natural and man-made processes (Figure 5.16). The reservoir remains small because these species not only rapidly enter the atmosphere, they also rapidly leave it. In other words, the mean residence time of sulfur in the atmosphere is extremely short.

The most important sulfur-containing species entering the atmosphere are sulfur dioxide (SO$_2$), dimethyl sulfide ((CH$_3$)$_2$S, known as DMS), hydrogen sulfide (H$_2$S), and carbonyl sulfide (OCS) (Figures 5.16 and 5.17).

Large amounts of hydrogen sulfide are generated under anaerobic conditions by micro-organisms, particularly in marine environments (see below). However, in the presence of excess iron and/or similar metals it reacts to yield insoluble sulfides of extremely low volatility. Therefore, much of the sulfur present initially as hydrogen sulfide enters the crustal reservoir rather than the atmosphere. Indeed, the liberation of hydrogen sulfide from marine sediments is now considered to be of minor significance.

DMS is generated in the top 50 m of the marine environment by the activity of phytoplankton. Within

Figure 5.16 The sulfur cycle.

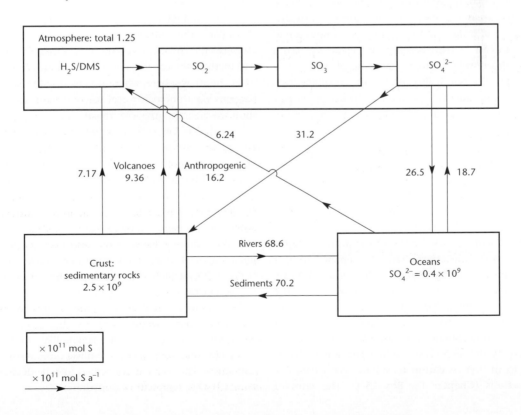

Figure 5.17 The fate of sulfur species in the atmosphere. Horizontal arrows represent chemical reactions; the remainder represent physical translocations. Sulfur dioxide is removed from the atmosphere by dry deposition (DD) or oxidation to sulfate (SO_4^{2-}). Sulfate is mainly removed by wet deposition (WD).

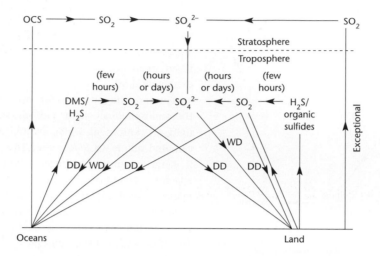

these organisms is found a sulfur-containing salt, dimethylsulfoniopropionate (DMSP). It is possible that this serves as an osmotic pressure regulator, stopping water from migrating out of the cells of the organisms concerned. On entering sea water DMSP degrades, forming DMS, some of which escapes into the atmosphere. The concentration of DMS in sea water is low and the flux per unit area of this compound into the atmosphere is small. However, the areas involved are vast; consequently the total evolution of DMS from the oceans is enormous (up to ~5.6×10^{11} mol S a^{-1}). This accounts for about one-tenth of the total flux of sulfur entering the atmosphere.

Carbonyl sulfide (OCS) also enters the atmosphere from the marine environment. It is produced in the upper part of the oceans by the action of sunlight on a number of organic compounds.

Sulfur dioxide enters the atmosphere as a result of essentially abiotic processes. Of particular importance are those processes associated with volcanic activity, the burning of fossil fuels and the roasting of sulfide ores (Chapter 15, Section 15.1.1, and Chapter 12, Section 12.1).

Figure 5.17 summarises the fate of the principal sulfur species that enter the atmosphere. As depicted in this diagram, atmospheric hydrogen sulfide and DMS are rapidly oxidised in the lower atmosphere (the troposphere: Chapter 4, Section 4.1). This forms sulfur dioxide, adding to that already present from other sources. Some atmospheric sulfur dioxide is removed by the process of dry deposition, while the remainder is subjected to further oxidation to sulfate, via a complex set of reactions (Chapter 15, Box 15.1). The rates of

deposition and oxidation of sulfur dioxide are dependent on conditions, both being more rapid in humid than in dry air. However, they are generally both in the range 1 to 10% per hour.

In the exceptional circumstances of a major volcanic eruption (such as El Chichon in the spring of 1982), sulfur dioxide may be directly injected into the upper atmosphere (the stratosphere: Chapter 4, Section 4.1). Here it is oxidised to sulfate, as in the lower atmosphere.

Unlike the other sulfur species entering the atmosphere, carbonyl sulfide is resistant to oxidation within the troposphere. It survives for sufficient time to enter the stratosphere, where it is oxidised to sulfate. This happens via a photochemical reaction pathway, involving short wavelength ultraviolet radiation.

Despite the low concentration of sulfur species in the atmosphere (as low as 0.6 ppb), they are highly important. They play key roles in the nutrition of higher plants (see below) and the incidence of acid rain (Chapter 15, Section 15.2.2). Sulfur species may also play a part in the regulation of climate by providing particles around which water can condense, allowing cloud formation to occur over the remote oceans. It has also been suggested that sulfate-induced stratospheric haze may accelerate the rate of ozone (O_3) depletion in the upper atmosphere (Chapter 15, Section 15.2.4).

Let us now consider the key processes that occur in the crustal and oceanic sulfur reservoirs.

Under anaerobic conditions, sulfate like nitrate, may be utilised by micro-organisms to oxidise carbohydrate during respiration. The reaction concerned may be depicted thus, using CH_2O to represent carbohydrate:

$$2CH_2O + 2H^+ + SO_4{}^{2-} \rightarrow H_2S + 2CO_2 + 2H_2O$$

Similar reactions utilising partially reduced sulfur species such as sulfite ($SO_3{}^{2-}$), thiosulfate ($S_2O_3{}^{2-}$) and elemental sulfur (S_8) in place of sulfate also occur.

The sulfide (S^{-II}, present in H_2S) generated in these reactions will form precipitates with many metals, particularly the late transition metals and those immediately after them in the Periodic Table (Chapter 4, Table 1.4). The ubiquitous nature of iron means that iron sulfides are frequently formed in sediments in which sulfate reduction is occurring. The reactions form troilite (FeS) and iron pyrites (FeS_2, known as fool's gold), and may be represented thus:

$$3H_2S + 2Fe(OH)_3 \rightarrow 2FeS + S + 6H_2O$$

$$S + FeS \rightarrow FeS_2$$

The reduction of sulfate to sulfide by carbohydrate does not liberate as much energy as does the oxidation of carbohydrate with nitrate to form ammonia. Consequently, in anaerobic environments with appreciable nitrate concentrations, sulfate-reducing micro-organisms will be out-competed by those that reduce nitrate. Under these conditions, ammonia and not sulfide, will be the principal reduced species formed. Such conditions prevail in the deep waters and/or sediments of many fresh water lakes and in most waterlogged surface soils of humid regions.

The situation is different in deep marine waters and/or sediments or soils submerged beneath brackish or sea water. Here the nitrate content is relatively low and the supply of sulfate from the sea water is essentially limitless. In such sediments, the onset of anaerobic conditions generates a brief period of nitrate reduction, followed by a sustained period of sulfate reduction. The bulk of the sulfide generated is precipitated as iron sulfides with a minimal evolution of gaseous hydrogen sulfide (H_2S). This process therefore results in a net flux of sulfur from the oceanic to the crustal reservoir.

Under aerobic conditions, sulfur in its reduced states (primarily sulfide, S^{-II}) can be oxidised by micro-organisms, including several bacteria of the genus *Thiobacillus*. This happens at the expense of molecular oxygen (O_2) in aerobic soils, sediments and water bodies. The ultimate product of these reactions is sulfate ($SO_4{}^{2-}$), in which the sulfur is in the plus six oxidation state. These processes are thermodynamically favourable and result in the liberation of energy that can be utilised by the organisms concerned. The following equation represents an example of this type of reaction:

$$H_2S + 2O_2 \rightarrow H_2SO_4$$

Note that the sulfate is produced in the form of sulfuric acid (H_2SO_4). This means that exposure to the air of

material with a significant sulfide content results in its rapid acidification. When soils that have been flooded for appreciable lengths of time with brackish or sea waters are drained, their pH values drop to as low as 1 or 2. Soils of this type are known as **cat-clays**. They cover significant areas of land in south-east Asia and in tidal areas of other parts of the world. Unless these soils are kept submerged, they soon become too acidic to support higher plant growth.

Sulfuric acid acidification can also be a significant problem in mining areas, where reduced sulfur species are oxidised in spoil heaps (Chapter 14, Section 14.3.2).

The redox reactions considered in the foregoing discussions have considerable implications in plant nutrition. This is because the availability of soil sulfur for uptake by higher plants is highly dependent on its chemical speciation. In general, plants exclusively absorb sulfur from the soil as sulfate. In most surface soils of humid regions this is a small fraction of the total sulfur present, even under aerobic conditions. The major soil reservoir of this bioelement is the organic fraction. Sulfur in this store becomes available when it is mineralised by soil organisms.

Overall, most plants are supplied with adequate amounts of sulfur, particularly in industrialised regions. In many cases this is due, in part at least, to the ability of plants to absorb sulfur from the atmosphere. This can occur to a significant extent even in soils with sufficient sulfate. Plants grown in such soils can obtain 25–35% of their sulfur directly from the air.

The most significant human intervention into the sulfur cycle occurs as a product of the combustion of fossil fuels. These fuels contain a small but significant amount of sulfur, which is liberated as sulfur dioxide when they are burnt. This rapidly oxidises in the atmosphere and is deposited as acid rain (Chapter 15, Section 15.2.2). The implementation of pollution control and abatement measures designed to control the acid rain problem will reduce atmospheric concentrations of this bioelement. This may well necessitate an increase in the use of sulfur-based fertilisers in the future.

5.6 Sodium, potassium, calcium and magnesium cycles

Potassium, magnesium and calcium are needed by organisms in relatively large amounts: they are macro-nutrient elements. In comparison, sodium is needed in lesser amounts: it is a micro-nutrient element. These ions have several biological functions, the more important of which are summarised in Table 5.1.

Table 5.1 The main biological functions of sodium, potassium, calcium and magnesium in human beings and plants.

Element	Main functions	
	Plants	Human beings
Sodium (Na)		Control of the balance of electrical potentials across cell membranes. Involved in nerve impulses.
Potassium (K)	Main cation within cells. Key role in guard cell operation. Acts as a cofactor for some enzymes.	Control of the balance of electrical potentials across cell membranes. Involved in nerve impulses.
Calcium (Ca)	Acts as a cofactor for some enzymes. Formation of middle lamella (the 'gum' between adjacent cell walls).	Bone formation. Cell membrane stabilisation. Involved in blood clotting. Involved in muscle contraction. Acts as a cofactor for some enzymes.
Magnesium (Mg)	Key component of chlorophyll. Acts as a cofactor for some enzymes.	Involved in nerve impulses. Acts as a cofactor for some enzymes.

Sodium and potassium are members of group 1 of the Periodic Table, whereas calcium and magnesium are members of group 2 (Figure 5.1). These elements have no redox chemistry in the environment. Sodium and potassium are found in the plus one oxidation state only (i.e. as Na^+ and K^+), while calcium and magnesium are exclusively in the plus two oxidation state (i.e. as Ca^{2+} and Mg^{2+}).

The geochemical cycles entered into by sodium, potassium, calcium and magnesium are depicted in Figure 5.18. From this it can be seen that there are many similarities in the environmental behaviour of these elements. They all enter into an essentially sedimentary cycle of weathering, transport, sedimentation and uplift followed by renewed weathering, and so on. In this respect, their environmental behaviour is similar to that of phosphorus (Section 5.4).

While the cycles of sodium, potassium, calcium and magnesium are essentially similar, there are important differences in detail. These are largely attributable to the influences of biological activity, differences in solubility of some of their salts and the differing ability of these ions to be entrapped within clays.

With this in mind, it is interesting to contrast the relative concentrations of these ions in typical sea and river waters (Table 5.2). The dominant cation in river water is calcium, while that in sea water is sodium.

The dominance of calcium over sodium in river water is essentially a reflection of the fact that more calcium than sodium is dissolved by percolating waters prior to their entry to rivers. This occurs for two reasons. Firstly, calcium minerals are more susceptible to weathering than are sodium silicates. Secondly, the concentration of calcium in the crust is higher than that of sodium (Ca is 3.6% w/w of the crust, while Na is 2.8% w/w).

In contrast to river water, sea water contains a much higher content of dissolved solids (typical total dissolved solids values being $34.4\,g\,dm^{-3}$ for sea water and $0.118\,g\,dm^{-3}$ for river water). Significantly, the concentrations of carbonate and calcium species within sea water are sufficient to exceed the solubility product of calcium carbonate. Consequently, this may precipitate from solution, ultimately forming limestones (this is usually a biomediated process: Chapter 3, Section 3.1.3). There is no similar mechanism for sodium precipitation in open waters, hence the dominance of sodium over calcium in the oceans.

During limestone formation, magnesium carbonate is frequently precipitated along with the calcium carbonate. However, the solubility of magnesium carbonate is greater than that of calcium carbonate. Hence, much less magnesium than calcium is precipitated in this way and limestones are predominantly calcium carbonate. Consequently, sea water contains more magnesium than calcium, even though the rivers flowing into the oceans supply more calcium than magnesium.

The dominance of magnesium over calcium in sea water is maintained under conditions of evaporite[2] formation. Evaporite deposits contain both calcium salts (e.g. anhydrite, $CaSO_4$ and gypsum, $CaSO_4.2H_2O$) and magnesium salts (e.g. $MgCl_2.6H_2O$ and $MgSO_4$). However, of these the calcium sulfate salts are of lowest solubility and hence precipitate first, thus ensuring the dominance of magnesium over calcium in the remaining water.

Of the four ions discussed in this section, potassium has the lowest concentration in both river and sea waters. This is, in part at least, due to the relatively high concentration of this ion in biological material, typically being 15 times that of sodium. In addition, outside biological systems, potassium is strongly absorbed onto negatively charged clays and humic materials. It is also relatively easily entrained into new silicate minerals, a trait it shares with magnesium.

Human interventions in the cycles discussed here are primarily deliberate. These are intended to increase agricultural productivity.

[2] Evaporites are rocks formed by the evaporation of water that contains dissolved solids.

Figure 5.18 The geochemical cycles of sodium (Na), potassium (K), calcium (Ca) and magnesium (Mg).

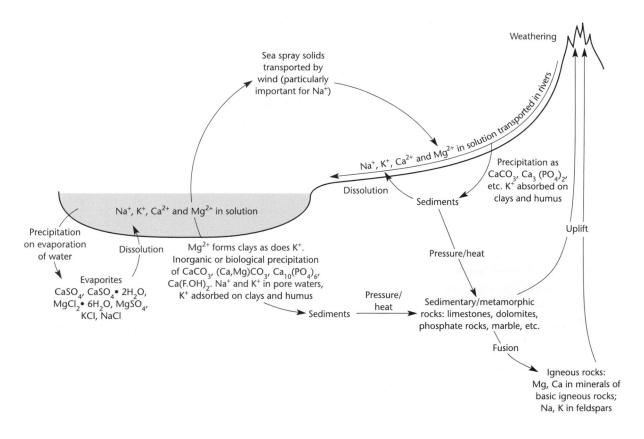

Table 5.2 The dissolved sodium (Na), potassium (K), calcium (Ca) and magnesium (Mg) content of typical sea and river waters.[a]

Nature of E	River water		Sea water	
	[E]/mM	$\dfrac{[E]}{\Sigma[E]}$	[E]/mM	$\dfrac{[E]}{\Sigma[E]}$
Na^+	0.274	0.31	470	0.88
K^+	0.059	0.067	1.02	1.9×10^{-3}
Ca^{2+}	0.375	0.43	10.2	0.019
Mg^{2+}	0.171	0.19	53.6	0.10

$$\Sigma[E]/mM(\text{river}) = 0.274 + 0.059 + 0.375 + 0.171 = 0.879$$
$$\Sigma[E]/mM(\text{sea}) = 470 + 1.02 + 10.2 + 53.6 = 534.82$$

[a] Note that river waters are more variable in their dissolved solids contents than are sea waters. For a discussion of this see Chapter 3, Section 3.3.2.

Potassium is commonly a limiting plant nutrient. This is a consequence of the relatively high demand that plants have for this element, coupled with its propensity to be bound to, and within, clays. Potassium deficiency is particularly common on heavily cropped land, where it is removed in large amounts with the harvest. Under these conditions, additions of potassium fertilisers are necessary for the maintenance of soil fertility.

Calcium and magnesium are also deliberately added to agricultural land. These are added in the form of oxides, hydroxides or carbonates, materials known as **lime**. Clearly, such additions increase the concentrations of the nutrients calcium and magnesium. Perhaps more importantly, they also have indirect beneficial effects associated with the decrease in acidity that liming brings about. For example, raising the pH of a highly acidic soil to about 6.5 by the addition of lime will enhance the availability of phosphorus and molybdenum while decreasing the concentrations of iron, aluminium and manganese to sub-toxic levels. Without liming, the fertility of many soils in humid regions could not be maintained.

5.7   Summary

Of the 92 naturally occurring elements, only *nine* make up the bulk of all organisms. These are oxygen (O), hydrogen

(H), carbon (C), nitrogen (N), calcium (Ca), phosphorus (P), sulfur (S), potassium (K), and magnesium (Mg). These are known as the macro-nutrient elements. In addition to these, there are a few other elements, known as the micro-nutrient elements, that are needed in smaller quantities for the maintenance of healthy life. The micro- and macro-nutrient elements are collectively called the essential elements or bioelements (Figure 5.1).

On a global scale, the supply of bioelements is apparently limitless. This is because they are circulated through the environment in biogeochemical cycles. These cycles are powered by the sun and the internal energy of the Earth. It is possible to construct a relatively simple box model to represent these cycles (Box 5.1). In this, each bioelement is seen to move through a series of reservoirs, represented as boxes.

During circulation, all of the bioelements enter into both biotic and abiotic phases, the relative importance of which is not the same for all cycles. It is important to realise that the individual biogeochemical cycles do not exist in isolation, but are interlinked.

Human activity has a considerable impact on many of the biogeochemical cycles. This is particularly true of the nitrogen, carbon and sulfur cycles, where human intervention has already brought about changes of global dimensions.

5.8 Problems

1 Review the processes that interlink:
   (a) the atmospheric oxygen and water cycles;
   (b) the nitrogen and phosphorus cycles.

2 It has been suggested that, on a geological time-scale, there has been a greater amount of photosynthetic activity than respiratory activity. Do you agree? Justify your answer.

3 In recent years, a steady increase in the levels of atmospheric carbon dioxide has been observed (Figure 5.7). There is some evidence that this has led to an increase in the levels of primary productivity. Is this what you would expect? Justify your answer.

4 The process of denitrification involves the reduction of nitrate to molecular nitrogen (N_2) and/or nitrous oxide. The nitrate is part of the crustal reservoir, whereas the products of this process are part of the atmospheric reservoir. Therefore, denitrification results in the movement of nitrogen between two reservoirs that are in physically different locations. Give two further examples where nitrogen movement from one reservoir to another at a different physical location is dependent on changes in chemical speciation.

5 Write balanced half-cell equations to represent the oxidation and reduction reactions that occur when *Nitrosomonas* bacteria oxidise ammonium to nitrite.

6 The half-cell equations for the reduction of nitrate to molecular nitrogen and the oxidation of carbohydrate to carbon dioxide and water are given below. Write a balanced equation that represents the overall reaction that occurs upon denitrification when the nitrogen-containing product is N_2.

$$2NO_3^- + 12H^+ + 10e^- \rightarrow N_2 + 6H_2O$$
$$H_2O + CH_2O \rightarrow CO_2 + 4H^+ + 4e^-$$

7 When nitrogenous fertilisers are added to lowland paddy rice, the additions are made directly into the anoxic zone beneath the surface of the flooded soil. Ammonium fertilisers are used in preference to nitrate fertilisers. Explain why the fertilisers are not broadcast over the surface of the water and why nitrate-based fertilisers are inferior to those based on ammonium under these conditions.

8 On the basis of concentration data, the limiting nutrient in many fresh water lakes appears to be carbon. However, even among apparently carbon-deficient lakes the rate of algal growth is determined by the levels of phosphorus in solution. In practice, then, the limiting nutrient is phosphorus. Explain this apparent anomaly.

9 Calculate the volume of water in a lake that has the following characteristics:
   (i) a residence time of 9.3 years for the water within it;
   (ii) a total influx of phosphorus of $1.8 \times 10^{11}\,mg\,P\,a^{-1}$, all in the form of soluble phosphate in river water with a phosphorus content of $0.06\,mg\,dm^{-3}$;
   (iii) a phosphorus content of $0.06\,mg\,dm^{-3}$.

Assume that the lake is in a dynamic steady state with respect to both phosphorus and water and that the sole influx of water and phosphorus is from river water.

10 Study Figure 5.12. Explain the changes with depth in the distribution of soil phosphorus between the organic, residual inorganic and more readily available inorganic forms.

11 Calculate the approximate residence time of atmospheric nitrogen (N_2), then compare it with the approximate residence time of sulfur dioxide (SO_2).
    (a) Which is more robust to human activity, the nitrogen reservoir or the sulfur reservoir?
    (b) Which of these molecules (N_2 or SO_2) would you expect to be unevenly distributed in the atmosphere?

12 The oxidation of sulfur dioxide in the atmosphere is a pseudo first order process. The rate constant for this process is generally in the range 0.01 to 0.1 hour^{-1}.
    (a) In what range would you expect the half-life of this species to fall, assuming the absence of other mechanisms of SO_2 removal (such as dry deposition)?
    (b) If all inputs of sulfur dioxide into the atmosphere were to cease instantaneously, how long would it take until the concentration of this species effectively dropped to zero? Again assume that oxidation is the only mechanism of SO_2 depletion.
    (See Chapter 2, Section 2.3 for help.)

13 Why is carbonyl sulfide not oxidised in the troposphere in the same way that it is in the stratosphere?

14 Given that the iron in both troilite (FeS) and iron pyrites (FeS_2) is in the plus two oxidation state, what is the oxidation state of sulfur in these species?

15 On a weight for weight basis 3.6% of the crust is calcium. What is the mean crustal concentration of this element in $mol\,kg^{-1}$ and $mol\,dm^{-3}$ (the mean density of the crust is $2.9\,g\,cm^{-3}$).

16 The oceanic residence time of calcium is 1×10^6 years. Would you expect the residence time of magnesium in the oceans to be greater or less than this?

17 (a) Consider a species that is removed from a reservoir solely by first order or pseudo first order processes. What is the mathematical relationship between its half-life ($t_{1/2}$) and residence time (τ)? (See Chapter 2, Section 2.3 for more on half-lives.)
    (b) Assume that the removal processes of carbon dioxide (CO_2) from the atmosphere all obey either first order or pseudo first order kinetics. If all fluxes into the atmosphere were to cease and all outward fluxes were to remain constant, approximately how long would it take for the atmospheric concentration of this gas to fall to 75% of its current value of 0.03% v/v?

5.9   Further reading

General background

O'Neill, P. (1998) *Environmental chemistry* (3rd edn). Cheltenham: Stanley Thornes.

Raiswell, R. W., P. Brimblecombe, D. L. Dent and P. S. Liss (1980) *Environmental chemistry: the earth–air–water factory*. London: Edward Arnold.

On transformations in the soil environment

Brady, N. and R. Weil (1998) *Nature and properties of soils* (12th edn). Prentice Hall.

White, R. E. (1997) *Principles and practice of soil science: the soil as a natural resource* (3rd edn). Oxford: Blackwell Science.

Wild, A. (ed.) (1988) *Russell's soil conditions and plant growth* (11th edn). Harlow: Longman.

On chemical transformations in the environment

Bunce, N. J. (1990) *Environmental chemistry*. Winnipeg: Wuerz.

The biological environment

The study of living organisms and the way in which they interact with each other and with their physical environment may be approached at a number of different levels. At the microscopic level, we are interested in the structure and functioning of cells, especially as carriers of the organism's genetic code. At the other extreme, the biological environment may be examined at the level of the biome, vast areas which, in the case of the terrestrial biomes, span continents, each characterised by a particular climate and vegetation type.

In the next four chapters, we explore the biological environment at the level of the cell, the population, the community, the ecosystem and the biome. Together with the physical environment (Chapters 1–5), these chapters not only describe the natural environment in the absence of human activity, they also form a firm foundation upon which the rest of the book is built.

Chapter 6

The cellular basis of life

Chapter Objectives

After reading this chapter, you should be able to:

- Compare and contrast prokaryotic and eukaryotic cells.

- Outline the main characteristics of eukaryotic plant and animal cells.

- Distinguish between the chemical reactions of aerobic and anaerobic cell respiration.

- Understand the process of photosynthesis, including the role played by chloroplasts.

- Outline the structure of DNA.

- Explain the mechanism of protein synthesis.

- With the aid of diagrams, outline the processes of mitosis and meiosis.

- Appreciate how the experimental work of Gregor Mendel has contributed to our present understanding of genetics (heredity).

- Describe, briefly, the techniques of recombinant DNA technology, and their role in the genetic modification of plants and animals.

Introduction

All living organisms are made up of cells. They may be **unicellular** (consisting of a single cell) or **multicellular** (made up of many cells). Protozoans, such as *Amoeba*, and bacteria are examples of unicellular organisms whilst, at the other extreme, humans are made up of a minimum of 10^{12} cells!

Two types of cells are recognised: prokaryotic and eukaryotic. Most unicellular organisms are prokaryotes, for example bacteria, although some, such as protozoans and yeasts, are eukaryotes. All multicellular organisms, plants and animals, are composed of eukaryotic cells.

This chapter commences with a comparison between these two basic cells types and proceeds to examine the differences (and similarities) between eukaryotic plant and animal cells. The processes of cell respiration, photosynthesis (plant cells only) and protein synthesis in eukaryotic cells are all discussed in detail in this chapter. The structure of DNA (deoxyribonucleic acid) and RNA (ribonucleic acid) are described as necessary preliminaries to the understanding of protein synthesis and, in the case of DNA (the genetic material in cells), the replication of chromosomes prior to cell division.

The second half of the chapter deals with how cells divide and, through simple Mendelian genetics, the promotion of individual variability within populations. This concept is fundamental to the process of natural selection discussed in Chapter 8, Section 8.2.1. The chapter ends with a section on recombinant DNA technology, a new and powerful technology potentially capable of altering the genetic make-up of organisms.

6.1 Prokaryotes and eukaryotes

Cells may be divided into two basic types: **prokaryotes** and **eukaryotes**. Although these share three basic structural characteristics, namely a plasma (cell) membrane, cytoplasm and a nucleus or nuclear material, they differ in a number of important respects.

Prokaryotic cells are small (1–10 μm) and simple. They are *always* unicellular and include blue-green algae (cyanobacteria) and bacteria (Figure 6.1). Most living organisms are made up of eukaryotic cells (Figures 6.2 and 6.3). These cells are larger (10–100 μm) and structurally much more complex. All multicellular organisms are made up of eukaryotic cells and some unicellular organisms are also eukaryotes, for example yeasts and protozoans.

Figure **6.1** Schematic diagram of the ultrastructure of a prokaryotic bacterial cell.

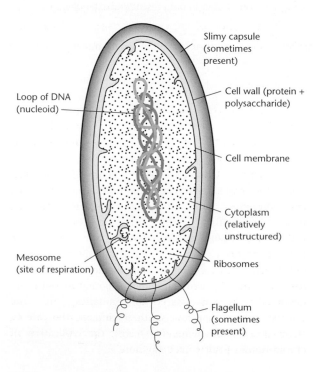

Figure **6.2** Schematic diagram of the ultrastructure of a generalised eukaryotic animal cell.

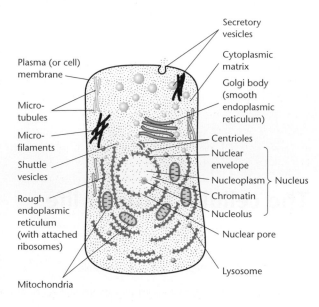

Figure **6.3** Schematic diagram of the ultrastructure of a generalised eukaryotic plant cell.

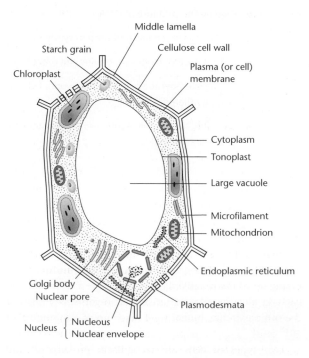

Perhaps the most striking difference between prokaryotic and eukaryotic cells is the nature of the 'nucleus', which contains the cell's genetic information. In eukaryotes, the nucleus is a distinct membrane-bound organelle containing DNA (deoxyribonucleic acid) and RNA (ribonucleic acid) (Figures 6.2 and 6.3). In prokaryotes, there is no membrane-bound nucleus, only diffuse areas of nucleoplasm. The nuclear material itself consists of strands of DNA arranged in the form of a ring (Figure 6.1).

Eukaryotic cells have specialised membrane-bound organelles to carry out specific cell functions, for example mitochondria (aerobic respiration) and, in plant cells, chloroplasts (photosynthesis). These organelles are not present in prokaryotes. Membrane systems such as the endoplasmic reticulum and Golgi body are also confined to eukaryotic cells. In evolutionary terms, the prokaryotic cell is thought to have given rise to the eukaryotic cell about 1500 million years ago.

6.2   A comparison between the ultrastructure of eukaryotic plant and animal cells

The ultrastructures of generalised plant and animal cells are shown schematically in Figures 6.2 and 6.3. A number of membrane-bound organelles and membrane systems are clearly apparent within the cells. The appearance and function of these cell structures are presented in summary form in Table 6.1. Further details of the mitochondria (respiration), the chloroplasts (photosynthesis) and the ribosomes (protein synthesis) are given in Sections 6.3, 6.4 and 6.6 respectively.

Eukaryotic plant and animal cells share a number of common features (Figures 6.2 and 6.3). However, there are some basic structural differences between them (Table 6.2). For example, plant cells are unique in possessing a cellulose cell wall *as well as* a cell membrane. Chloroplasts, the organelles responsible for photosynthesis, are also confined to plant cells (Section 6.4).

The shape, form and content of eukaryotic cells are highly variable, producing an enormous diversity amongst cells (Figure 6.4, page 133). The structural characteristics of particular cell types are strongly correlated with their functions. For example, in human reproduction, the sole function of the male spermatozoon cell is to reach the female egg cell first and fertilise it. The whole structure of the sperm cell is adapted to give it high motility. Spermatozoa are single cells each with a long tail or flagellum (Figure 6.4). Powerful undulations of the flagellum propel the sperm cell forward. The high energy requirements of this process are provided by an unusually high density of mitochondria present in the sperm cell.

6.3   Mitochondria and the process of cell respiration

Mitochondria are found in virtually all eukaryotic cells. They are organelles of vital importance as they constitute the site of cell respiration, producing energy-rich molecules of adenosine triphosphate (ATP).

The structure of mitochondria

Mitochondria are rod-shaped organelles with a diameter of approximately 1μm and a length of approximately 2.5μm (Figure 6.5, page 134). They are surrounded by a pair of membranes separated by a very narrow fluid-filled space. The outer membrane is smooth but the inner one is highly folded to form a series of irregular partitions known as cristae. These extend into the internal matrix and serve to greatly increase the surface area of the inner membrane. The cristae themselves are densely covered with stalked particles of protein, each with a diameter of 0.8 nm. These are believed to contain the respiratory enzyme molecules needed for the production of ATP.

The number of mitochondria in individual eukaryotic cells varies from only 50 to in excess of 2000. High numbers of mitochondria are found in cells with high energy requirements. For example, liver cells can contain up to 2500 mitochondria, which in total may occupy as much as 20% of the cell's volume! In addition, such mitochondria tend to have more cristae and therefore more respiratory enzyme molecules. Within cells, mitochondria are located next to sites of highest energy demands; for example, in sperm cells they are packed into the middle region of the modified flagellum (Figure 6.4, page 133).

Cell respiration

The process of cell respiration is an extremely complex one. Figure 6.6 (page 134) illustrates the main steps involved in **aerobic cell respiration**. This process can be split into two basic parts, only the second stage requiring the presence of oxygen. If no oxygen is available, **anaerobic respiration** occurs, producing lactic acid in the case of animals and ethanol in the case of plants and yeast (Box 6.1, page 135).

The first stage of cell respiration occurs in the cytoplasm. The starting material is glucose, from stored glycogen in the case of animal cells or stored starch in the case of plant cells. Each glucose molecule (containing six carbon atoms) is broken down in a series of steps to produce *two* molecules of pyruvic acid, each containing three carbon atoms (Figure 6.6(a)). This process is known as **glycolysis** (literally 'sugar splitting').

Table 6.1 Cell ultrastructure: organelles and membrane systems.

Structure	Description	Functions
Organelles		
Mitochondria	Usually rod-shaped; ~1 μm in diameter and ~2.5 μm in length; inner membrane convoluted to form irregular partitions called cristae; carries respiratory enzymes	Production of energy-rich ATP (adenosine triphosphate)
Chloroplasts (plants only)	Variable in size, 4–10 μm in diameter; double unit membrane; contains chlorophyll and enzymes involved in photosynthesis	Photosynthesis
Nucleus	Major cell organelle; 20 μm in diameter; contains chromatin (DNA and proteins)	Control centre for activities of cell; contains genetic material of cell; vital role in cell division
Nucleolus	Specialist part of nucleus; ~2 μm in diameter	Manufacture of ribosomes and RNA
Ribosomes	Small cytoplasmic granules composed of 50% ribosomal RNA (rRNA) and 50% protein; 25 nm in diameter	Site of protein synthesis
Lysosomes	Dark spherical bodies containing enzymes, mostly hydrolases; 0.2–0.5 μm in diameter	Intracellular digestion; release of enzymes outside cell; destruction of unwanted or worn-out cell organelles or whole cells (autolysis)
Microfilaments	Solid protein filaments; ~5 nm in diameter; occur in bundles in cytoplasm	Associated with cell motility, e.g. in muscle contraction
Microtubules	Hollow tubes of protein; ~20 nm in diameter; occur either singly or in bundles in cytoplasm	Intracellular transport and support
Cilia	Fine hair-like extensions from cell surface; <0.3 μm in diameter and 5–10 μm in length; arrangement of nine peripheral and two central microtubules inside cilia	Cell locomotion, wafting material along ducts and tubules, e.g. mucus in respiratory tracts of mammals
Flagella	Similar in structure to cilia but much longer, ~100 μm in length	Cell locomotion
Centrioles (animal cells only)	Two rod-like structures found at right angles to each other; 0.2 μm in diameter; ring of nine peripheral microtubules present	Formation of spindle at cell division; role in formation of cilia and flagella
Cellulose cell wall (plant cells only)	Layered structure made up of microfibrils of cellulose; ~5 μm thick; often impregnated with other polysaccharides, e.g. pectin and lignin	Provides support in herbaceous plants; acts as waterproof layer if lignin for example is present
Granules	Variable in appearance	Food storage: glycogen in animal cells and starch grains in plant cells
Vacuoles	Fluid-filled sacs surrounded by membranes; variable in appearance	Storage of waste materials and food
Membrane systems		
Rough ER (endoplasmic reticulum)	Network of membranes enclosing a series of interconnected flattened cavities (cisternae); encrusted with ribosomes; continuous with outer nuclear membrane	Transportation of proteins synthesised by ribosomes
Smooth ER	Network of membranes, not continuous with rough ER; no ribosomes present	Synthesis and transport of lipids and steroids
Golgi body	Stack of flattened cavities (cisternae) lined with smooth ER; vesicles associated with Golgi body	Production of glycoproteins by addition of carbohydrate to proteins made in channels of rough ER; packaging and secretion of many of these glycoproteins; production of lysosomes
Nuclear envelope	Double unit membrane around nucleus; contains nuclear pores each ~40–100 nm in diameter	Regulation of material exchange between nucleus and cytoplasm
Plasma membrane	Considered to be a protein/lipid mosaic about 7 nm thick; partially permeable; may be thrown into folds known as microvilli where cells need a large surface area for absorption or exchange of materials	Acts as selective barrier regulating entry and exit of substances in and out of cell

Table 6.2 General characteristics of plant and animal cells.

Plant cells	Animal cells
Cell membrane *and* cellulose cell wall	Cell membrane only
Several features associated with cell wall: pits, middle lamella and plasmodermata (cytoplasmic connections through walls of adjacent cells)	
Large central vacuole containing cell sap	No large central vacuole; many small vacuoles scattered throughout cell
Membrane surrounding vacuole (known as the tonoplast)	No such membrane
Cytoplasm, organelles and nucleus usually peripheral	Cytoplasm throughout cell; nucleus often central
Cilia and flagella absent in higher plants	Cilia often present in higher animals
Centrioles absent in higher plants	Centrioles present
Chloroplasts with chlorophyll (in photosynthetic cells)	No chloroplasts
Autotrophic nutrition	Heterotrophic nutrition
Food stored in form of starch grains	Food stored in form of glycogen granules
Comparatively large (50 μm in diameter)	Comparatively small (20 μm in diameter)
Rarely motile (i.e. not able to move)	Often motile

Figure 6.4 The diversity of eukaryotic cells.

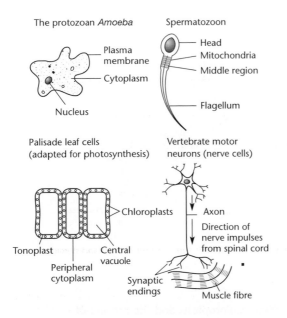

The initial phase of glycolysis involves the addition of phosphate groups to the sugar molecules, a process known as phosphorylation. Two molecules of adenosine triphosphate (ATP) each donate their terminal phosphate groups for attachment to each sugar molecule. Phosphorylation makes the sugar molecule more reactive and also prevents it from leaving the cell.

The phosphorylated sugar is then split into two molecules of 3-carbon sugar. In this process, two hydrogen atoms are initially removed and accepted by the respiratory carrier NAD (nicotinamide adenine dinucleotide) in the cytoplasm. These hydrogen atoms are then shunted into a mitochondrion, where they enter a hydrogen carrier system and eventually produce three molecules of ATP (Box 6.2, page 136). The 3-carbon sugar is then converted into pyruvic acid, with the direct production of two molecules of ATP.

In the presence of oxygen, the pyruvic acid enters into a mitochondrion and is converted into acetyl coenzyme A (acetyl CoA). This forms a very important link between the process of glycolysis, which took place in the cytoplasm, and the second major stage, the citric acid cycle, which takes place in the mitochondrion itself (Figure 6.6(b)). Carbon dioxide is given off by this reaction and two hydrogen atoms are lost from the pyruvic acid. These enter the hydrogen carrier system with the production of three molecules of ATP (Box 6.2).

Acetyl CoA (two carbon atoms) reacts with oxaloacetic acid (four carbon atoms) to form citric acid (six carbon atoms). This citric acid is then converted back to oxaloacetic acid by a complex series of reactions. This process was worked out by Sir Hans Krebs and is hence referred to as the **Krebs citric acid cycle**. Figure 6.6(b) shows a very simplified version of this cycle.

Figure 6.5 The structure of a mitochondrion: (a) longitudinal section; (b) transverse section.

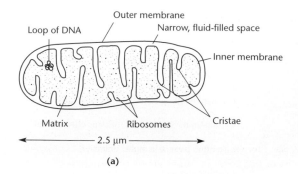

(a)

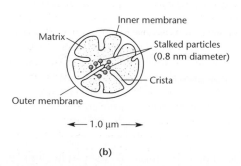

(b)

Figure 6.6 Aerobic cell respiration: (a) glycolysis (in cytoplasm); (b) the citric acid cycle (in mitochondrion). Asterisks indicate ATP molecules produced via the hydrogen carrier system (Box 6.2) as opposed to those produced directly. *Note*: There is a net gain of two ATP molecules in the cytoplasm during glycolysis. Eighteen molecules of ATP are produced in the mitochondrion for *each* molecule of pyruvic acid. As one molecule of sugar gives *two* molecules of pyruvic acid, the *maximum* number of ATP molecules which can be produced by aerobic cell respiration is $(2 \times 18) + 2 = 38$ per molecule of sugar.

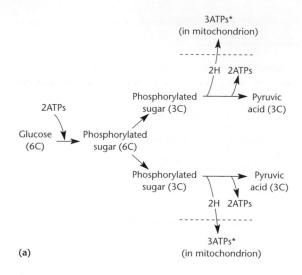

(a)

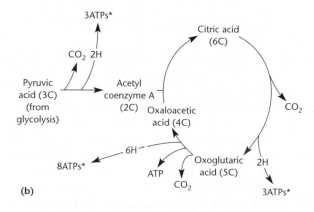

(b)

Of the many intermediate steps, two involve the loss of carbon dioxide and four involve the removal of hydrogen atoms, which are subsequently passed through carrier systems with the production of ATP (Box 6.2). Three of these carrier systems produce three molecules of ATP from every two hydrogen atoms whilst the fourth produces only two molecules of ATP per pair of hydrogen atoms. One of the steps in the citric acid cycle produces one molecule of ATP directly (Figure 6.6(b)). Within the mitochondria, the citric acid cycle appears to occur in the matrix whilst the hydrogen carrier systems span the inner mitochondrial membrane.

The citric acid cycle is the most important source of energy in cell metabolism. By donating hydrogen atoms to the carrier systems, packets of energy in the form of ATP molecules can be produced. Complete oxidation of one molecule of glucose can yield a maximum of 38 ATP molecules (Figure 6.6). The ATP can then be broken down in the cell by the enzyme ATPase to provide energy wherever and whenever it is required. For this reason, ATP is sometimes referred to as the 'universal energy currency' of the cell.

Although glucose has been cited as the starting material in the process of cell respiration, it should be noted that there are other respiratory substrates, which do not need to be initially converted into carbohydrate, such as fat and, as a last resort, protein.

| 6.4 | Chloroplasts and the process of photosynthesis |

Chloroplasts are cell organelles found in the tissues of green plants and in unicellular algae. They contain a number of light-sensitive pigments, the most important of which is chlorophyll 'a'. The main function of chloroplasts is to trap light energy from the sun, needed for the process of photosynthesis.

Further Information Box

6.1   The chemical reactions of aerobic and anaerobic cell respiration

In aerobic respiration, 'energy-rich' glucose molecules are completely oxidised to form carbon dioxide and water:

$$C_6H_{12}O_6 + 6O_2 \rightarrow 6CO_2 + 6H_2O$$

glucose   oxygen carbon water

dioxide

$\Delta G°$, the standard free energy change of this reaction, is $-2870\,kJ\,mol^{-1}$. The negative value of $\Delta G°$ shows that free energy has been released during this reaction. Such reactions are termed **exergonic**. Reactions which need a continuous external supply of free energy to keep them going are known as **endergonic**, i.e. free energy consuming.

In anaerobic respiration, where no molecular oxygen (O_2) is available, the pyruvic acid molecules formed by glycolysis cannot enter the citric acid cycle (Figure 6.6). Instead, the pyruvic acid may be converted into lactic acid (in the case of animals) or ethanol (in the case of plants and yeasts). These two reactions, represented below, are both exergonic, but produce much less free energy than aerobic respiration.

Lactic fermentation (animals):

$$C_6H_{12}O_6 \rightarrow 2C_3H_6O_3\ (\Delta G° = -150\,kJ\,mol^{-1})$$

glucose   lactic acid

Alcoholic fermentation (plants and yeasts):

$$C_6H_{12}O_6 \rightarrow 2C_2H_5OH + 2CO_2\ (\Delta G° = -210\,kJ\,mol^{-1})$$

glucose   ethanol   carbon

dioxide

Both types of anaerobic respiration produce toxic waste products which will eventually halt the process of anaerobic respiration. For example, in humans, anaerobic respiration can occur in muscle cells during extreme exertion, when the demand for oxygen outstrips its supply. However, the build-up of lactic acid eventually causes muscle fatigue.

It is worth noting that in aerobic respiration, a maximum of 38 molecules of ATP can be produced per molecule of glucose. These yield a total of 1178 kJ of free energy per mole of glucose ($38 \times 31\,kJ$ per mole of ATP). The first reaction in this box shows that the complete oxidation of glucose yields 2870 kJ of free energy per mole. Therefore the efficiency of conversion from free energy released to free energy stored in ATP is about 41%. The remainder of the energy is in the form of heat.

In comparison, the production of ATP molecules during anaerobic respiration is small. In alcoholic fermentation, only two molecules are produced directly during glycolysis (the two hydrogen atoms produced are used to produce ethanol). Therefore, only 62 kJ of usable energy is trapped in the form of ATP from a potential of 2870 kJ per mole of glucose. The efficiency of this process is therefore only about 2%.

The structure of chloroplasts

Chloroplasts are large organelles, varying in length from 4 to 10 μm and with an approximate diameter of 1 μm. A comparison between the structure of a chloroplast (Figure 6.7) and a mitochondrion (Figure 6.5) reveals a number of similarities. Both organelles are surrounded by a double membrane but in the case of the chloroplast *both* membranes are smooth. Mitochondria and chloroplasts both contain their own DNA and ribosomes and are capable of some protein synthesis. They are both able to divide and reproduce independently of the remainder of the cell. These characteristics have given rise to the hypothesis that mitochondria and chloroplasts were originally free-living prokaryotic cells that were ingested by primitive eukaryotic cells.

The internal structure of chloroplasts consists largely of a complex membrane system, not connected to the paired membrane surrounding the chloroplast. Stacks of disc-like cavities called thylakoids make up structures known as grana, which are interconnected by lamellae (Figure 6.7). The membranes of the thylakoids contain the light-sensitive pigments needed to absorb light energy from the sun. The fluid interior of the chloroplast is known as the stroma. Starch grains and lipid globules are clearly visible within the stroma.

The process of photosynthesis

In photosynthesis, carbon dioxide and water are converted into glucose using light energy from the sun. The *overall* equation for this reaction can be summarised thus:

$$6CO_2 + 6H_2O \xrightarrow{\text{energy from sunlight}} C_6H_{12}O_6 + 6O_2 \qquad (6.1)$$

carbon   water   glucose   oxygen

dioxide

Experiments have shown that the process of photosynthesis has two distinct phases, the first consisting of a series of photochemical reactions (**light reactions**) and the second consisting of a series of non-photochemical reactions, controlled by enzymes (**dark reactions**) (Figure 6.8).

In the light reactions, energy from the sun is absorbed by chlorophyll and used to split water molecules into

6.2 The hydrogen carrier system and the production of ATP (adenosine triphosphate)

The breakdown of glucose molecules during respiration produces energy which can be used to synthesise ATP. The most important source of energy comes from the removal of hydrogen atoms (dehydrogenation) from various intermediate compounds during the gradual breakdown of sugar.

These hydrogen atoms are initially accepted by the hydrogen carrier NAD, present in the matrix of the mitochondria, which is consequently reduced to NADH. There are three more carrier molecules involved in the hydrogen carrier system and these are all firmly attached to the inner membrane of the mitochondrion. The hydrogen atoms from the NADH are accepted by the first of these carriers, which is reduced as a result, whilst the NADH is reoxidised to NAD. The energy released during this transfer is sufficient for the synthesis of one molecule of ATP.

This hydrogen transfer is repeated twice more with the third and fourth carrier molecules, producing two further molecules of ATP. For each pair of hydrogen atoms, a total of three molecules of ATP can be produced through the hydrogen carrier system.

As this entire process involves the oxidation of compounds (through the removal of hydrogen) coupled with the linking of phosphate groups to ADP (adenosine diphosphate) to form ATP, it is described as **oxidative phosphorylation**.

The hydrogen atoms finally combine with oxygen molecules to form water. It is only at this final stage that molecular oxygen is directly involved in aerobic respiration. However, if it is not available to accept the hydrogen atoms then the hydrogen carrier system and the citric acid cycle cannot function and aerobic respiration cannot proceed.

Figure 6.7 The structure of a chloroplast.

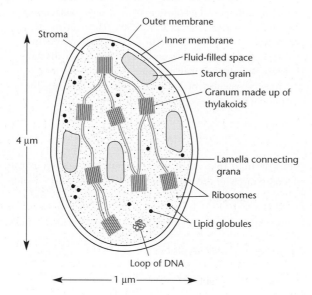

Figure 6.8 The process of photosynthesis.

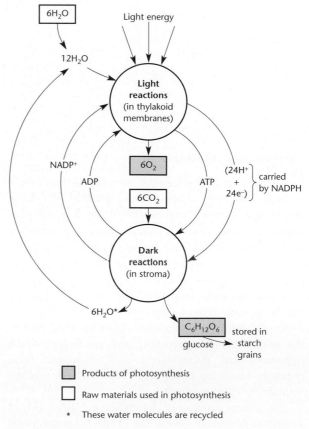

hydrogen ions (H⁺), electrons (e⁻) and molecular oxygen (O_2). This process is known as photolysis. The energy from this process has two effects. Firstly, ATP is produced from ADP (adenosine diphosphate) and inorganic phosphate by the enzyme ATP synthesase. Secondly, hydrogen ions and electrons are transferred to the hydrogen carrier NADP⁺ (nicotinamide adenine dinucleotide phosphate) to form NADPH (Figure 6.8). These light reactions occur in the thylakoid membranes of the chloroplast, where the light-sensitive pigments are located.

The second set of reactions are known as the dark reactions and these take place in the stroma of the chloroplast. Energy from ATP and NADPH is used to build up glucose molecules from the raw material, carbon dioxide (Figure 6.8). The glucose is stored in the form of starch grains and provides the starting material for the process of cell respiration (Section 6.3).

6.3   A comparison of C_3 and C_4 plants

Most temperate plants, including economically important crop species such as rice (*Oryza sativa*), wheat (*Triticum aestivum*) and sugar beet (*Beta vulgaris*), are termed C_3 plants. This means that, during photosynthesis, carbon dioxide initially reacts with ribulose-1,5-bisphosphate to form a 3-carbon compound, 3-phosphoglycerate. These 3-carbon compounds can subsequently be used to construct larger molecules, such as glucose. This pathway is known as the C_3 pathway.

In some desert and tropical plants, an alternative pathway of carbon dioxide fixation, the C_4 pathway, is used. Although C_4 species comprise less than 5% of the world's flora, they include a number of economically important crop species such as sugar cane (*Saccharum officinarum*), maize (*Zea mays*) and sorghum (*Sorghum* spp.). In this mechanism, carbon dioxide is incorporated into a series of 4-carbon molecules, initially oxaloacetic acid, then malic acid and aspartic acid. The 4-carbon molecules constitute a temporary store of carbon dioxide within the plant. Once transported to the chloroplasts in the bundle sheath cells, they are broken down to release carbon dioxide (CO_2), which is then used in the normal C_3 type of fixation.

The potential growth of C_4 plants is more rapid than that of C_3 plants, for a number of reasons. The enzyme PEP-carboxylase (phosphoenolpyruvate carboxylase) used in the initial fixation of CO_2 in C_4 plants is more efficient than its counterpart, rubisco, in C_3 plants. This enables C_4 plants to grow at lower ambient CO_2 concentrations than C_3 plants. In addition, C_4 plants are able to photosynthesise at higher light intensities and at higher temperatures. The efficiency of the C_4 mechanism also means that these plants are able to close their stomata for a greater percentage of the time, thus minimising water loss through the process of transpiration. C_4 plants are therefore generally well suited to hot, dry climates.

There is considerable interest in how C_4 plants will fare compared with C_3 plants under conditions of global warming. It is feasible that C_4 plants will be favoured by the higher temperatures, and that it will be possible to grow crop species of this group at higher latitudes than at present.

It should be appreciated that the biochemistry of photosynthesis is very complex and beyond the scope of this book. However, one important point that should be made here is that three different photosynthetic pathways – C_3, C_4 and CAM (crassulacean acid metabolism) – are recognised on the basis of physiology. The first two of these are briefly described and compared in Box 6.3; the third, CAM, is explained in Box 9.12 on page 210.

6.5   The structure of DNA and RNA

In order to understand the mechanisms of protein synthesis and the replication of chromosomes prior to cell division, it is necessary first to be familiar with the structure of DNA (deoxyribonucleic acid) and, in the case of protein synthesis, RNA (ribonucleic acid).

DNA and RNA are both nucleic acids, made up of sub-units called **nucleotides**. Nucleotides are made up of three different chemical groups, namely a phosphate group, a 5-carbon sugar and an organic base (Figure 6.9). The sugar molecule is always ribose in the case of RNA and deoxyribose in the case of DNA. In DNA, the organic bases are adenine (A), guanine (G), cytosine (C) and thymine (T), whilst in RNA, thymine is replaced by uracil (U). Adenine and guanine are both purine bases with a double-ring structure, whilst cytosine, thymine and uracil are pyrimidine bases with a single-ring structure. In both cases, the rings contain nitrogen atoms in addition to carbon atoms.

Figure 6.9 The structure of nucleotides.

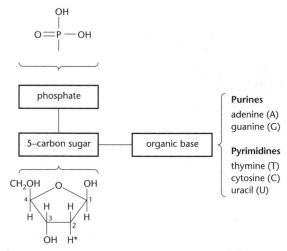

Deoxyribose (DNA nucleotides)

* In ribose (the sugar group found in the nucleotides of RNA), this H is replaced with OH

In nucleic acids, the sub-units of nucleotides are linked together to form a long chain. The linkages are formed between the phosphate group of one nucleotide and the sugar group of the next. This results in a sugar–phosphate backbone to the molecule of nucleic acid (Figure 6.10). Ribonucleic acid (RNA) is usually composed of a *single strand* of nucleic acid. It occurs in all cells in the form of messenger RNA (mRNA), transfer RNA (tRNA) and ribosomal RNA (rRNA). These are all involved in the synthesis of proteins (Table 6.3 and Section 6.6).

The structure of DNA is much more complex than that of RNA. It is enormously long and composed of millions of nucleotide sub-units. It is always *double-stranded* and consists of two parallel strands of nucleic acid whose sugar–phosphate backbones run in opposite directions. These two strands are held together by hydrogen-bonding between pairs of organic bases (Figure 6.10). This base-pairing can only occur between certain bases, namely adenine and thymine (with two hydrogen bonds) and guanine and cytosine (with three hydrogen bonds).

In DNA, *all* the nucleotides are held together by base-pairing and the resultant three-dimensional structure is very stable. The two strands of nucleic acid are twisted to form a double helix. The structure of DNA was elucidated by James Watson, Francis Crick and colleagues in 1953 using the technique of X-ray crystallography.

The fully complementary nature of the base pairs in DNA means that each strand can act as a blueprint (or template) for the other. Assisted by the enzyme DNA polymerase, the DNA molecule can be 'unzipped' and replicate itself exactly by the assemblage of new nucleotides from the cell's pool. This process is known as **semiconservative replication** since the two identical DNA molecules produced consist of one original and one new strand of DNA. The ability of DNA to replicate itself is essential to the process of cell division. It enables an exact copy of the cell's genetic instructions to be handed on to the new daughter cells (Section 6.7).

The long molecules of DNA occur within the nucleus of individual cells. It is thought that each DNA molecule corresponds to a single **chromosome**. There are a characteristic number of chromosomes for individual species, for example 46 in the case of humans. These carry the hereditary information of the individual on a series of shorter sections of the nucleic acid known as **genes** (Section 6.7).

6.6 Protein synthesis

The process of protein synthesis is an extremely important one. Through it, the cell manufactures many essential biochemical compounds, including all the biological catalysts (enzymes) needed to control metabolism. The actual sites of protein production are the ribosomes, which in eukaryotic cells are associated with rough endoplasmic

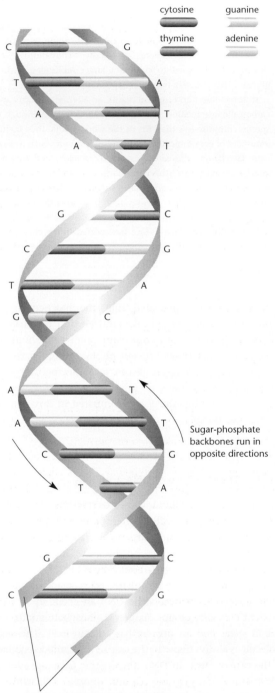

Figure 6.10 The double helix structure of DNA (deoxyribonucleic acid). The capital letters C, G, T and A represent the organic bases cytosine, guanine, thymine and adenine respectively.

cytosine   guanine

thymine   adenine

Sugar-phosphate backbones run in opposite directions

The two parallel strands of nucleic acid are held together by hydrogen-bonding between pairs of organic bases

Table 6.3 The different types of RNA (ribonucleic acid).

Type	Structure	Function
Messenger RNA (mRNA)	75–3000 nucleotides long; not folded in any special way; produced in nucleus by DNA	Carries coded instructions from DNA in nucleus to ribosomes in cytoplasm where it initiates the process of protein synthesis
Transfer RNA (tRNA)	Small molecules of 75–90 nucleotides; 20 different types each corresponding to one of the 20 amino acids; forms clover-leaf shape due to regions of base-pairing; manufactured in nucleus by DNA	Transport of amino acids from 'pool' to mRNA in ribosomes; anticodons of tRNA lock onto codons of mRNA, assembling amino acids in sequence specified by original DNA instructions
Ribosomal RNA (rRNA)	Very large molecules with thousands of nucleotides; can fold back on itself to form regions of base-pairing; major components of ribosomes; made in nucleus by DNA	Correct functioning of ribosomes during protein synthesis

reticulum (ER) found in the cell's cytoplasm (Table 6.1). The process of protein synthesis is controlled by nuclear DNA and mediated through the activities of different types of RNA. It occurs in two major stages, transcription and translation (Figure 6.11).

Transcription

The first stage of protein synthesis occurs in the nucleus and involves the **transcription** of coded instructions carried on the DNA molecule onto strands of messenger RNA (mRNA) (Figure 6.11(a)).

The DNA molecule is made up of a series of shorter sections known as genes. Each gene carries the instructions for making a particular protein. Proteins are made up of amino acids, of which there are 20 different types. As there are only four organic bases present in the DNA molecule, *triplets* of bases code for the specific types of amino acids. There are 64 different possible combinations of the triplet code and only 20 types of amino acids found in proteins. Some amino acids therefore have more than one triplet code. In addition, some triplets of bases do not code for any amino acids. These constitute the codes which effectively separate the instructions for one protein from the next.

In transcription, the DNA unwinds at the point which codes for the requisite protein, breaking the hydrogen bonds between the DNA base pairs. Only one of the DNA strands acts as a template for transcription and is known as the **anticoding strand**. Free nucleotides match themselves to the base pairs on the anticoding strand and form mRNA, through the action of the enzyme RNA polymerase (Figure 6.11(a)). In mRNA, the base uracil replaces the base thymine and combines with adenine. Each triplet of bases on mRNA is known as a **codon**. Once assembled, the mRNA becomes detached from the DNA and diffuses out of the nucleus into the cytoplasm.

Translation

The mRNA carries the coded instructions for protein synthesis from the nuclear DNA to the ribosomes attached to the rough endoplasmic reticulum in the cytoplasm. In the second major stage of protein synthesis, known as **translation**, these instructions must be 'translated' into a sequence of amino acids which will make up the required protein (Figure 6.11(b)).

The mRNA molecule is held in position by a series of ribosomes. These are small cell organelles, containing equal parts of proteins and ribosomal RNA (rRNA) (Table 6.3). The amino acids needed to construct the protein are brought to the mRNA by molecules of transfer RNA (tRNA). These tRNA molecules differ in the sequence of the three bases present at one end of the molecule (known as the **anticodon**, Figure 6.11(b)) and are amino acid-specific. The amino acid becomes attached to the opposite end of its particular tRNA molecule, with the help of energy derived from ATP.

Starting at one end of mRNA, two mRNA codons attract a complementary pair of tRNA anticodons. Once attracted, these tRNA anticodons are held together by a ribosome and a peptide bond is formed between their amino acids. The ribosome moves along the mRNA, sequentially lining up amino acids until a polypeptide of the requisite length and composition is built up. Several ribosomes proceed along the mRNA in this manner forming a number of polypeptide molecules. Together with other different polypeptides and prosthetic groups, these form completed proteins.

Once formed by the ribosomes, the proteins pass through the membrane of the rough endoplasmic reticulum into its cisternal space. Many of these proteins are destined for export from the cell (Figure 6.12).

Vesicles containing protein (known as shuttle vesicles) are budded off from the rough ER and become fused with the cisternae of the Golgi body, an intracellular membrane system made of smooth ER (Table 6.1). In the Golgi body, a carbohydrate prosthetic group is added to the protein

Figure 6.11 The synthesis of proteins: (a) transcription; (b) translation.

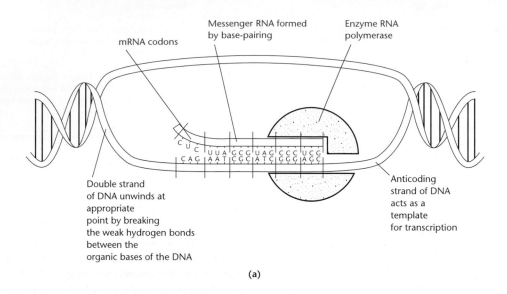

(a)

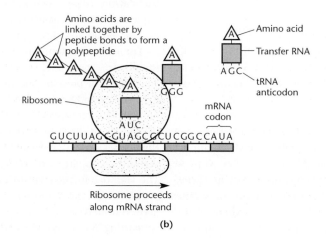

(b)

molecules to form glycoproteins such as mucus, a lubricating secretion found in animals. Secretory vesicles are then budded off from the Golgi body. These eventually fuse with the plasma membrane of the cell and discharge their contents to the outside, a process known as **exocytosis** (Figure 6.12).

6.7 Chromosomes and cell division

In eukaryotic organisms, the genetic information of the cell is carried on chromosomes found in the nucleus. There are a characteristic number of chromosomes for each species and these are present as homologous pairs. The chromosomes are central to the process of cell division, enabling genetic information to be passed from one generation to the next. There are two types of cell division, mitosis and meiosis.

Mitosis

In **mitosis**, the daughter cells produced contain exactly the same number of chromosomes as the parent cell and are *genetically identical* to it and to each other. Mitosis occurs in asexual reproduction and in the growth of body tissues.

The main stages of mitosis are shown in Figure 6.13. The stage where the cell is preparing to divide is known as **interphase**. This stage occupies about 90% of the **cell cycle** (measured from one cell division to the next) (Figure 6.14). During this stage, the chromosomal DNA replicates by the process of semiconservative replication so

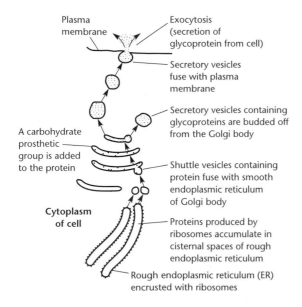

Figure 6.12 The progression of proteins, from synthesis to secretion.

Plasma membrane

Exocytosis (secretion of glycoprotein from cell)

Secretory vesicles fuse with plasma membrane

Secretory vesicles containing glycoproteins are budded off from the Golgi body

A carbohydrate prosthetic group is added to the protein

Shuttle vesicles containing protein fuse with smooth endoplasmic reticulum of Golgi body

Cytoplasm of cell

Proteins produced by ribosomes accumulate in cisternal spaces of rough endoplasmic reticulum

Rough endoplasmic reticulum (ER) encrusted with ribosomes

that each daughter cell will eventually receive an identical set of chromosomes (Section 6.5). The cell's centrioles duplicate, possibly in preparation for spindle formation, although their exact function is not known. Energy supplies are built up and new cell organelles are made to supply the daughter cells.

The division of the nucleus itself occupies only a small part of the cell cycle and is followed immediately by the division of the cell's cytoplasm (a process known as **cytokinesis**) (Figure 6.14). Nuclear division is a continuous process but, for descriptive purposes, four main stages – prophase, metaphase, anaphase and telophase – are recognised here (Figure 6.13).

In **prophase**, the chromosomes shorten and thicken (i.e. condense) and become visible under the light microscope. Each chromosome can then be seen to be composed of sister **chromatids** joined by a structure called the **centromere**. The nucleoli of the nucleus disappear and the **mitotic spindle** composed of microtubules starts to develop.

In the next stage, **metaphase**, the chromosomes occupy a central position, with their centromeres near the equator of the cell. Metaphase is followed by **anaphase**. During anaphase, the chromatids are actively pulled apart at the region of their centromeres and travel to opposite poles of the spindle.

In the final phase of mitosis, known as **telophase**, the chromosomes start to decondense. At each pole, nuclear membranes start to reform around the chromosomes and nucleoli start to reappear. During telophase, the cell's cytoplasm starts to divide by cleaving in the region of the

equator. Eventually this process of cytokinesis leads to the formation of two separate daughter cells, each genetically identical to the parent cell.

Meiosis

The second type of cell division is called **meiosis**. Meiosis involves *two separate meiotic divisions* and results in the formation of four daughter cells, each with *half* the normal complement of chromosomes (Figure 6.15). Meiosis takes place in the formation of gametes (sex cells) during sexual reproduction.

Normal cells of a particular species contain a fixed number of chromosomes arranged in homologous pairs. Cells which contain pairs of chromosomes are said to be **diploid** and are represented by the symbol 2n. These pairs need *not* be genetically identical. In the case of humans, there are 46 chromosomes arranged in 23 homologous pairs. Of these pairs, 22 are autosomes and the remaining pair are the sex chromosomes (XY in males, XX in females).

The normal cell condition is one of interphase, which is the same as described previously for mitosis. Meiosis itself involves two successive cell divisions, the first to separate homologous chromosomes and the second to separate the chromatids (Figure 6.15).

The initial phase of the **first meiotic division** is known as **prophase I**. This usually lasts for several days. In prophase I, the nucleolus disappears, the spindle starts to form and the chromosomes (each consisting of two chromatids joined at the centromere) appear. Homologous pairs of chromosomes link up to form bivalents by a process known as synapsis. After synapsis, **crossing-over** occurs between homologous chromatids, facilitating the exchange of genetic material (Figure 6.16). This random event is extremely important as it allows new combinations of genes to form.

In the next stage, **metaphase I**, homologous pairs of chromosomes align themselves along the equator of the spindle. These chromosome pairs then separate and travel to opposite poles of the spindle (**anaphase I**). In **telophase I**, the chromosomes reach the poles. The cell membrane invaginates to produce two daughter cells, each with the adult complement of chromosomes (2n) (remember that prior to cell division, the chromosomes have replicated themselves).

In the **second meiotic division**, new spindles form in each of the daughter cells, usually at right angles to the one formed in meiosis I (**prophase II**). In **metaphase II** the chromosomes arrange themselves along the equator, and in **anaphase II**, the chromatids pull apart and move to opposite poles of the spindle. In **telophase II**, cleavage

Figure 6.13 Mitosis in a generalised animal cell.

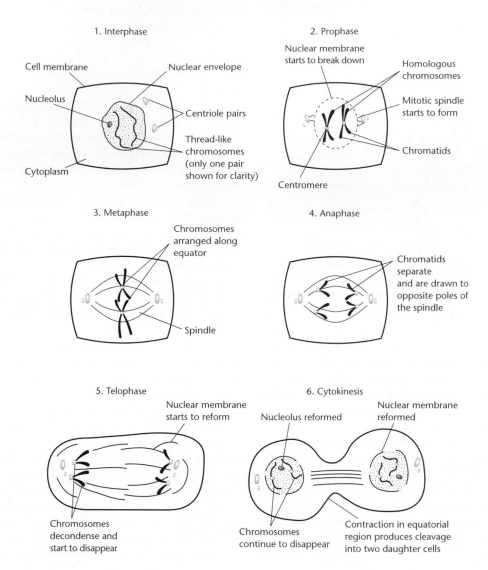

1. Interphase

Cell membrane
Nuclear envelope
Nucleolus
Centriole pairs
Thread-like chromosomes (only one pair shown for clarity)
Cytoplasm

2. Prophase

Nuclear membrane starts to break down
Homologous chromosomes
Mitotic spindle starts to form
Chromatids
Centromere

3. Metaphase

Chromosomes arranged along equator
Spindle

4. Anaphase

Chromatids separate and are drawn to opposite poles of the spindle

5. Telophase

Nuclear membrane starts to reform
Chromosomes decondense and start to disappear

6. Cytokinesis

Nucleolus reformed
Nuclear membrane reformed
Chromosomes continue to disappear
Contraction in equatorial region produces cleavage into two daughter cells

produces two new daughter cells. The nucleolus and nuclear membranes reform and the chromosomes become thread-like and indistinct as the cell enters interphase.

The gametes (sex cells) formed by meiosis contain only half the number of chromosomes found in the original parent cell. They are therefore **haploid** (n). When the nuclei of two gametes fuse at fertilisation, the normal diploid (2n) condition of chromosomes is restored. Although the new offspring have the same *number* of chromosomes as their parents, they are genetically different. Each one has received a set of chromosomes from each of its parents.

The great advantage of sexual reproduction is the genetic variation produced amongst the offspring. This provides the 'raw material' upon which the forces of natural selection can act (Chapter 8, Section 8.2). The study of patterns of inheritance is known as **heredity** or, more usually, **genetics**. The mechanism of how characteristics are passed down from one generation to the next is examined in the next section.

6.8 The study of genetics (heredity)

The first scientific study of heredity was carried out by an Austrian monk, Gregor Mendel (1822–84). Beginning in 1856, Mendel carried out a long series of experiments, using the garden pea (*Pisum savitum*). The pea plants were ideal subjects for study as they had a number of

Figure 6.14 The cell cycle.

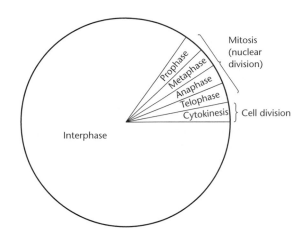

contrasting characters which were easily recognisable, for example long or short stems, smooth or wrinkled seeds. The peas were normally self-fertilising. Therefore characters of the parent plants were passed down from

generation to generation without alteration and thus maintained as **pure-breeding** lines.

In his first experiments, Mendel investigated the inheritance of a single pair of contrasting characteristics (now termed **monohybrid inheritance**). He crossed pea plants from pure-breeding lines, taking care to ensure that no self-fertilisation occurred.

Figure 6.17 summarises the results he obtained from crossing plants with long stems (tall) with plants with short stems (dwarf). All the seeds produced by this cross gave rise to tall plants in the **first filial generation** (F1). These tall F1 pea plants were then self-pollinated (selfed) and the resultant seeds sown. The plants of the next generation (known as the **second filial** (F2) **generation**) were found to be a mixture, consisting of tall and dwarf plants in a ratio of approximately 3:1. No pea plants intermediate in height between the tall and dwarf forms were obtained.

Mendel obtained similar results from other monohybrid crosses. On this basis, he formulated his first generalisation about the nature of inheritance (now

Figure 6.15 Meiosis in a generalised animal cell.

The first meiotic division

1. Prophase I

Chromatids of chromosome
Plasma membrane
Centriole pair
Centromere
Homologous chromosomes form bivalents
Nuclear membrane starts to break down

2. Metaphase I

Equator
Spindle
Homologous chromosomes

3. Anaphase I

Homologous chromosomes part and migrate to opposite poles of the cell

4. Telophase I

Centrioles replicated
Cell constricts at equator producing two daughter cells

The second meiotic division

5. Prophase II

New spindle forms at right angles to the first
One of the daughter cells from the first meiotic division

6. Metaphase II

Spindle
Chromosomes arrange themselves along equator

7. Anaphase II

Chromatids separate and migrate to opposite poles of the cell

8. Telophase II

Chromosomes become thread-like and disappear
Cleavage produces two daughter cells
Nucleolus reforms
Nuclear membrane reforms

Interphase

Figure 6.16 Crossing-over: the exchange of genetic material.

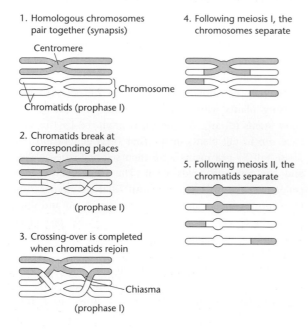

1. Homologous chromosomes pair together (synapsis)

Centromere

Chromosome

Chromatids (prophase I)

2. Chromatids break at corresponding places

(prophase I)

3. Crossing-over is completed when chromatids rejoin

Chiasma

(prophase I)

4. Following meiosis I, the chromosomes separate

5. Following meiosis II, the chromatids separate

Figure 6.17 Monohybrid inheritance: Mendel's cross between tall and dwarf pea plants.

Parental generation (P)	tall × dwarf
First filial generation (F1)	all tall (selfed)
Second filial generation (F2)	tall × dwarf (787) (277)
Actual ratio	2.84 : 1

known as Mendel's First Law or Mendel's Law of Segregation). Essentially, he stated that an organism's characteristics are controlled by factors; these are normally carried in pairs but occur singly in the gametes. The character which was expressed in the F1 generation, Mendel termed **dominant**, whilst the character which was masked in the F1, he called **recessive**.

The 'factors' which Mendel hypothesised correspond to the genes, which were not discovered until a century later. There are many genes and these occur in pairs, one on each chromosome of a homologous pair. Their positions correspond to one another and occur at a definite point along the length of the chromosome known as the **locus** (Figure 6.18). The alternative forms of a particular gene, for example tall and dwarf in the previous example, are known as **alleles**.

A pea plant may contain the same alleles for a particular characteristic (**homozygous genotype**) or two different ones (**heterozygous genotype**). The **phenotype** describes the appearance of the pea plant. It is the product of both the plant's genetic make-up (its genotype) and its environment.

Mendel's First Law can be explained by meiosis (Section 6.7). In meiosis, homologous chromosomes come together and then segregate from each other (Figure 6.15). As a result, the gametes receive only one of each type of chromosome. As mentioned previously, the pairs of alleles are carried on homologous pairs of chromosomes. Therefore, they are also segregated at gamete formation and each gamete receives only one of each pair of alleles. The chromosomes, and hence the alleles, recombine when the gametes randomly fuse at fertilisation. Figure 6.19 interprets the cross summarised in Figure 6.17 in terms of these alleles.

Mendel next proceeded to investigate the inheritance of *two* pairs of characteristics (**dihybrid crosses**). The results of one such cross, between pure-breeding pea plants with smooth yellow seeds and pure-breeding plants with wrinkled green seeds, are summarised in Figure 6.20. The F1 generation all produced seeds which were both smooth

Figure 6.18 Meiosis: the segregation of homologous chromosomes and their alleles.

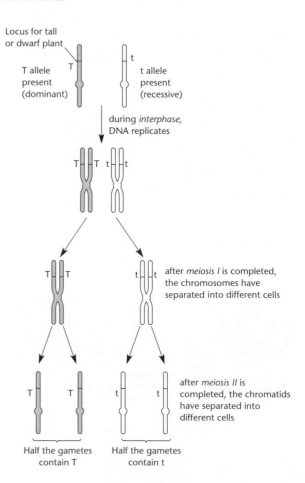

Locus for tall or dwarf plant

T allele present (dominant)

t allele present (recessive)

during *interphase*, DNA replicates

after *meiosis I* is completed, the chromosomes have separated into different cells

after *meiosis II* is completed, the chromatids have separated into different cells

Half the gametes contain T

Half the gametes contain t

and yellow, showing that these two factors were dominant. In the F2 generation, new combinations of characteristics appeared, i.e. peas with smooth green seeds and peas with wrinkled yellow seeds. These are known as **recombinant types**. The genetic explanation of this cross is given in Figure 6.21. The ratio of F2 phenotypes predicted (9:3:3:1) is almost exactly what Mendel observed.

On the basis of a number of similar results obtained from different dihybrid crosses, Mendel put forward his second generalisation (now known as Mendel's Second Law or the Law of Independent Assortment). Essentially, this law states that each of a pair of contrasted characters (alleles in modern terms) may be combined with either of another pair. Again, the explanation lies with meiosis. Very briefly, the genes for two different characteristics segregate and assort independently because the separate chromosomes which carry them behave in that fashion.

Figure **6.19** Genetic explanation of Mendel's monohybrid cross between tall and dwarf pea plants (Fig. 6.17), where T represents the tall allele (dominant) and t represents the dwarf allele (recessive) of the gene determining the height of pea plants. (Use is made of the Punnett square, a conventional representation used to calculate the proportion of different genotypes in the progeny of a genetic cross.)

Parental generation (**P**)

	Phenotype	tall		dwarf
			×	
	Genotype	TT		tt

Using the Punnett square:

	T	T
t	Tt	Tt
t	Tt	Tt

First filial generation (**F1**)   Phenotype: all tall
Genotype: all Tt

Self-cross between plants of the F1 generation

	Phenotype	tall		tall
			×	
	Genotype	Tt		Tt

Using the Punnett square:

	T	t
T	TT	Tt
t	Tt	tt

Second filial generation (**F2**)   Phenotype: $\frac{3}{4}$ tall, $\frac{1}{4}$ dwarf
Phenotypic ratio 3:1
Genotype: $\frac{1}{4}$ TT, $\frac{2}{4}$ Tt, $\frac{1}{4}$ tt

Figure **6.20** Dihybrid inheritance: Mendel's cross between pea plants with smooth yellow seeds and pea plants with wrinkled green seeds.

P	smooth yellow seeds	×	wrinkled green seeds	
F1	all with smooth yellow seeds (selfed)			
F2	smooth yellow seeds (315)	smooth green seeds (108)	wrinkled yellow seeds (101)	wrinkled green seeds (32)
Actual ratio	9.85 :	3.38 :	3.16 :	1

6.9 Recombinant DNA technology

The study of genetics was greatly advanced in the 1950s and 1960s by two very important discoveries concerning DNA, namely its chemical structure (Section 6.5) and its role as the genetic material of the cell. In the 1970s, a further advance of enormous magnitude was made. It became possible for the first time to isolate, analyse and manipulate individual genes found on the chromosomal DNA. These techniques are known under the umbrella term of **recombinant DNA technology**.

The role of the restriction endonucleases

The myriad techniques of recombinant DNA technology would not be possible without the **restriction endonucleases**, discovered in bacterial cells. The function of these enzymes in the bacteria cell is to destroy any foreign DNA, such as viral DNA, by cutting it up. The key to their importance in recombinant DNA technology is the *precision* with which these cuts are made.

Each type of restriction endonuclease only cuts the DNA at a specific point within a short specific sequence of nucleotides, known as the restriction site (Figure 6.22). Hundreds of these enzymes have now been discovered, providing an extensive array of 'molecular knives' with which molecular geneticists can carve up DNA. The cuts made by these restriction endonucleases are usually staggered, resulting in an overhang at each end (Figure 6.22).

The separation and identification of restriction fragments

The restriction fragments of DNA can be separated according to size by the technique of **gel electrophoresis**. Essentially, their movement through an agarose gel (or other medium) in an electric field is dependent on their length, with smaller fragments travelling further. The fragments separate out into bands in the gel and their actual size can then be determined

Figure 6.21 Genetic explanation of Mendel's dihybrid cross (Fig. 6.20) where S represents the smooth allele (dominant) and s represents the wrinkled allele (recessive) of the gene determining seed appearance, and where Y represents the yellow allele (dominant) and y represents the green allele (recessive) of the gene determining seed colour. (Use is made of the Punnett square, a conventional representation used to calculate the proportion of different genotypes in the progeny of a genetic cross.)

Parental generation (**P**)

	Phenotype	Smooth, yellow		Wrinkled, green
			×	
	Genotype	SSYY		ssyy

Using the Punnett square:

	SY	SY
sy	SsYy	SsYy
sy	SsYy	SsYy

First filial generation (**F1**) Phenotype: all have smooth, yellow seeds
Genotype: all Ss Yy

Self-cross between plants of the F1 generation

	Phenotype	Smooth, yellow		Smooth, yellow
			×	
	Genotype	SsYy		SsYy

Using the Punnett square:

	SY	Sy	sY	sy
SY	SSYY	SSYy	SsYY	SsYy
Sy	SSYy	SSyy	SsYy	Ssyy
sY	SsYY	SsYy	ssYY	ssYy
sy	SsYy	Ssyy	ssYy	ssyy

Second filial generation (**F2**) Phenotype: $9/16$ smooth, yellow seeds (shaded background)
$3/16$ smooth, green seeds (dotted background)
$3/16$ wrinkled, yellow seeds (cross-hatched background)
$1/16$ wrinkled, green seeds (blank background)

Phenotypic ratio 9:3:3:1
Genotype: see Punnet square above

by comparison with the movement of fragments of known length. The accuracy of this method is such that fragments which differ by only one nucleotide can be successfully separated.

The restriction fragments can be identified either at this stage by screening the gel or at a later stage when a group of identical DNA fragments have been produced by cloning. This is done by the use of nucleic acid probes. First, the relatively weak hydrogen bonds between the double DNA strand are induced to break, either by gentle heating or by suitable chemical treatments. This separation into two single strands is a natural phenomenon of DNA, facilitating its replication prior to cell division (Section 6.7) and its transcription by messenger RNA (mRNA) during protein synthesis (Section 6.6).

The probes of nucleic acid used for identification are short lengths of DNA or RNA of known composition. These are labelled chemically or radioactively for subsequent ease of detection. These probes pair up with complementary base sequences on the DNA fragment to produce a double strand in that region. This identification technique is known as **nucleic acid hybridisation** and is central to recombinant DNA technology. It enables individual genes (short stretches of DNA which specify the production of particular proteins) to be isolated from a mixture of DNA fragments.

Gene cloning

The next step in recombinant DNA technology is usually the cloning of desired DNA fragments i.e. genes, and the

Figure 6.22 The formation of recombinant DNA.

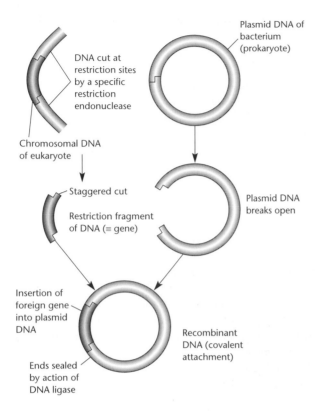

DNA cut at restriction sites by a specific restriction endonuclease

Plasmid DNA of bacterium (prokaryote)

Chromosomal DNA of eukaryote

Staggered cut

Restriction fragment of DNA (≡ gene)

Plasmid DNA breaks open

Insertion of foreign gene into plasmid DNA

Recombinant DNA (covalent attachment)

Ends sealed by action of DNA ligase

The uses of gene clones

Gene clones produced in the manner described above have a number of uses. They provide large quantities of eukaryotic and prokaryotic genes for detailed investigation. Moreover, the gene clones can be made to produce large quantities of their specific protein by the use of expression vectors. For a number of reasons, many eukaryotic genes do not express successfully in prokaryotic bacterial cells. The protein, if it is produced at all, may not be in a fully functional form. To overcome this incompatibility, such eukaryotic genes can be expressed in eukaryotic cells, usually yeast or mammalian cells. Mammalian cells are used for the commercial production of a number of recombinant proteins of medical importance, for example insulin and interferon.

The genetic modification of plants and animals

Man has sought to improve the quality and performance of crops and domestic livestock by selective breeding since the beginnings of farming, thousands of years ago. Over the last century, the practice of selecting for desirable attributes, such as disease resistance and improved reproductive performance, has gathered pace with the implementation of many intensive breeding programmes.

The advent of recombinant DNA technology has the potential to revolutionise plant and animal breeding. Essentially, it provides a direct method by which the genetic make-up of an organism can be altered. The introduced gene can then be passed down to future generations in the usual way (Section 6.7). Animals and plants which contain genes introduced from other species are known as **transgenic**.

In animals, the new gene must be directly introduced into the fertilised egg or very early embryo for the technique to be successful. To date, a number of transgenic animals have been bred including mice, pigs, sheep, goats and cows. This work is currently at the experimental stage.

In plants, new genes can be introduced using a plasmid vector. Figure 6.23 illustrates this procedure using the bacterium *Agrobacterium tubefaciens*. This bacterium normally infects dicotyledonous plants such as tobacco, tomatoes and potatoes. It contains a Ti (tumour-inducing) plasmid. This becomes incorporated into the infected plant's own DNA and subsequently causes the plant to form a tumour known as a crown gall.

Plant molecular geneticists have taken advantage of this pathway to incorporate desirable genes, for example glyphosate resistance, into dicotyledonous plants using *Agrobacterium* as the carrier. The desired gene, obtained from gene cloning, is spliced into the Ti plasmid to form

production of large quantities for further investigation. In order to clone the DNA fragment, it must be introduced into a host cell, usually a bacterial (prokaryote) cell. However, this cannot be done directly as the fragment of 'foreign' DNA will be broken down and destroyed by the bacterium's own nucleases. Therefore, the DNA fragment must first be incorporated into the DNA of a suitable vector or carrier in order to be transformed into the host.

Bacterial plasmids and phages are commonly used as vectors. A **plasmid** is a circle of DNA which replicates independently of the cell's chromosomes and a **phage** is a bacterial virus. The use of a restriction endonuclease usually produces DNA fragments with staggered ends. If the same restriction enzyme is used on plasmid DNA, for example, the foreign DNA fragment can easily be inserted (or spliced) into it. This forms **recombinant DNA** (Figure 6.22). The ends join by base-pairing and are sealed by the action of the enzyme ligase.

The plasmid or phage vector carrying the foreign DNA is then taken up by a host, where it produces clones by replication of the plasmid. The most commonly used bacterial host is *Escherichia coli*. Pre-treatment with a concentrated solution of a calcium salt renders the cell membranes of *E. coli* permeable and enables the recombinant DNA to be taken up relatively easily.

Figure 6.23 The production of a transgenic dicotyledonous plant using the carrier *Agrobacterium*.

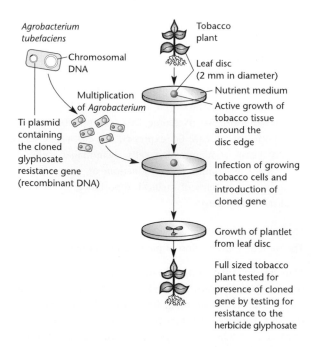

nitrogen fixation and those which endow resistance to various insects, viruses and herbicides. Unfortunately, *Agrobacterium* does not normally infect monocotyledonous plants. This route cannot therefore be used in the genetic engineering of many crop plants such as rice, wheat and maize.

Case study 1 (page 240) examines the main environmental issues associated with genetically modified (GM) crops.

6.10 Summary

Cells may be classified as prokaryotic or eukaryotic. Eukaryotic cells are more sophisticated, with a highly organised internal structure made up of organelles and membrane systems. The nucleus of the eukaryotic cell is membrane-bound and contains DNA in the form of chromosomes. This chromosomal DNA plays a central role in the functioning of the cell. It directs protein synthesis and carries the genetic (hereditary) material of the cell. The chemical structure of DNA was determined in the 1950s and represented a milestone in the study of genetics.

Only 20 years later, the advent of recombinant DNA technology revolutionised genetics. For the first time, specific genes could be isolated, analysed and manipulated in various ways. One application of recombinant DNA technology is the introduction of 'desirable' genes directly into crop plants. This can bypass the need for the more traditional methods of selective breeding programmes.

recombinant DNA. This is naturally transformed into the DNA of some of the cells of the infected plant. A whole new plant can then be raised by culturing the transformed cells. Subsequent testing will reveal if the new plant is indeed transgenic, i.e. contains the introduced gene (Figure 6.23).

There are a number of genes which interest plant molecular geneticists, including those which control

6.11 Problems

1 What are the major differences between prokaryotic and eukaryotic cells? Illustrate your answer.

2 Compare and contrast the ultrastructure of eukaryotic plant and animal cells.

3 How is the structure of a mitochondrion adapted to its function as the site of cell respiration in eukaryotic cells? Include in your answer a brief account of aerobic cell respiration.

4 Outline the process of photosynthesis in plants, remembering that it occurs in two distinct stages.

5 Describe the chemical structure of DNA. How is it able to replicate itself and why is this ability essential?

6 Briefly distinguish between mitosis and meiosis. What is the genetic outcome of each type of cell division? Using annotated diagrams, outline *one* of these processes.

7 In a monohybrid cross between pea plants with smooth seeds and pea plants with wrinkled seeds, all the first filial (F1) generation had smooth seeds. What results would you expect when the F1 generation was self-fertilised? What does the answer tell you about the genotypes of the F1 and parental generations?

8 In the context of recombinant DNA technology, what is meant by the following terms: restriction endonucleases, nucleic acid hybridisation, recombinant DNA, vectors, gene cloning, transgenic organisms?

6.12   Further reading

Alberts, B., D. Bray, J. Lewis, M. Raff, K. Roberts and J. D. Watson (1994) *Molecular biology of the cell* (3rd edn). New York: Garland Publishing.

Smith, C. A. and E. J. Wood (1996) *Cell biology* (2nd edn). London: Chapman & Hall.

Weaver, R. F. and P. W. Hedrick (1992) *Genetics* (2nd edn). William C. Brown.

Chapter 7

Population dynamics

Chapter Objectives

After reading this chapter, you should be able to:

- Define the term 'population' and discuss the factors that govern population size.

- Understand how life tables are constructed and used.

- Explain what is meant by survival (survivorship) curves, and outline the three main types, with examples.

- Compare and contrast the main characteristics of *r*-species and *K*-species.

- Describe the possible outcomes of both intraspecific and interspecific competition, with reference to specific examples.

- Appreciate the role of predation in population regulation and be familiar with the types of experiments that have led to the production of predator–prey models.

- Evaluate the global pattern of human population growth over historic time and give reasons for its upsurge in the latter half of the twentieth century.

- Discuss the main differences in population statistics (e.g. average life expectancy, birth rates, etc.) between 'more-developed' and 'less-developed' countries.

Introduction

A **population** may be defined as a group of individuals belonging to the same species which live in a given area at a given time. In studying populations, we are concerned not only with their size but with the way in which populations change over time. The study of population change is known as **population dynamics**. Environmental scientists are interested in this subject because it is when the combined effects of individual responses to change become manifest at the level of the *population* that the environmental implications of change become significant.

In this chapter, the growth of populations and the factors which serve to regulate population growth, including competition and predation, are examined in detail. This discussion includes a number of classic experiments which have contributed greatly to our understanding of the mechanisms which underlie population growth and regulation.

The study of plant and animal populations has very important ecological applications, for example in the conservation of threatened wildlife (see Box 10.10, page 234) and in the biological control of pests (see Box 11.2, page 249). Many of the concepts which apply to such populations apply equally to *human* populations. However, there are some features of human populations which are unique, for example our ability to largely control our own environment. An understanding of human population dynamics is extremely important when considering the impact of various human activities upon the environment. Therefore, the dynamics of human populations are discussed, as a special case, in the concluding section of this chapter.

7.1 Population growth

7.1.1 Factors governing population size

For organisms which do not move, it is possible to determine the size of a population *directly* by counting all the individuals present. However, such an approach is rarely undertaken because of its laborious nature. It is more usual to make estimates of population density by taking representative samples of known size, usually at random. **Population density** may be expressed as the number of individuals of the population per unit area or per unit volume, as appropriate. There are a number of techniques used to measure population density, for example the capture–mark–recapture technique (Box 7.1). If the *total* volume or area occupied by a population is

known, then population density can be converted to an estimate of population size by multiplication.

When the density of a population is recorded over a period of time, changes in the size of that population are usually observed. Populations grow and decline, and even if they are maintained at a more or less constant level, small fluctuations will still occur. These patterns occur in response to changes in the environment and interactions with other living organisms (Section 7.2). Changes in population size are governed by four main parameters. These are birth rate, death rate, immigration and emigration.

Populations may increase in size as a result of **immigration** (the arrival of individuals from neighbouring populations) or natality. **Natality** is a broad term which encompasses the production of new individuals by germination, hatching, fission and live birth. In mammals, natality is equivalent to the **birth rate**. This can be expressed as a percentage, or numbers per thousand, of new individuals being produced each year. For example, if an original population of 400 individuals gives rise to 60 new individuals within one year, then the birth rate is said to be 15%.

Populations may decrease in size as a result of **emigration** (the dispersal of individuals from the original population to new areas) or **mortality** (death rate). Mortality, like natality, is usually expressed in terms of a percentage, or numbers per thousand, dying each year. Under optimum conditions, all organisms would live to the end of their natural life-span and die of senescence. In reality, very few organisms reach this advanced stage. They

Tool Box

7.1 The estimation of population density: the capture–mark–recapture method

It is unusual to be able to count the number of individuals in a particular population directly. Methods for estimating population density are therefore needed. For animals which are mobile, the capture–mark–recapture method, of which there are several models, is an appropriate one.

The simplest of these models, which will be examined here, is the Petersen (or Lincoln) method. This involves only two sampling periods. At the first sampling, captured individuals are marked appropriately and released back into the population. At the second sampling, the proportion of marked individuals within the random sample is counted. This proportion is assumed to be representative of that of the population as a whole. Estimates of the total size of the population (N) can be made using the following formula:

$$N = \frac{nM}{x}$$

where n = the total number of individuals in the second sample

M = the total number of individuals originally marked in the first sample

x = the number of marked individuals recaptured in the second sample.

In the following example, 148 trout were taken from a small lake and marked. Several days later, a random sample was taken which yielded 186 trout, of which 25 were marked. Using the formula above:

$$N = \frac{186 \times 148}{25} = 1101$$

In this example, it is assumed that the population size has not changed during the brief interval between the two sampling periods. The reliability of such estimates can be tested using standard statistical procedures for the estimation of errors.

Capture–recapture techniques in general make a number of assumptions which may not always be valid. For example, it is assumed that marked and unmarked animals are captured randomly. However, marked field mice, having been trapped once, may avoid traps in future.

are cut down prematurely by disease, starvation or predators.

It should be noted that immigration and emigration are rarely measured in population studies. The usual assumption behind this omission is that these two types of dispersal, which operate in opposite directions, cancel each other out. Alternatively, the population under study may be in an isolated habitat, for example on an island, where dispersal, one way or the other, is not thought to be significant.

7.1.2 Survival curves

Measurements of population size alone do not take into account other important characteristics of populations such as the age distribution and sex ratio of individuals. The probability of an individual producing offspring or dying varies with these factors. The age distribution of mortality can be represented in the form of a life table (Box 7.2). These were originally developed by demographers interested in the life expectancy of human populations, usually for the purposes of life insurance. The l_x column of the life table (Box 7.2), representing the proportion of individuals surviving, can be plotted (on a logarithmic scale) against age to produce **survival** or **survivorship curves**. Three main types of survival curve are recognised (Figure 7.1).

In Type I curves, greatest mortality occurs in older individuals. This type of curve is typical of mammals such as elephants. They are long-lived and produce few

---

Tool Box

7.2   The construction and use of life tables

The age-specific mortality of a population can be presented in the form of a life table. These were originally developed by human demographers interested in forecasting how long people could be expected to live. Life tables have subsequently been used in a small number of studies on animal populations. For example, Lowe (1969)[1] followed the fate of the 1957 cohort of red deer (*Cervus elaphus*) stags on the Isle of Rhum in Scotland.

In order to explain clearly how a life table is constructed, a hypothetical example is given. The age interval x is set at one year and n represents the number of organisms in the starting cohort. The values for n_x, the number alive at the start of age interval x, are set at 165, 98, 43, 16 and 0. From these data, all the other columns in the life table can be calculated. The methods of calculating l_x, d_x and q_x are shown below the table. The calculation of e_x is more complicated and is explained in the subsequent text.

x	n_x	l_x	d_x	q_x	e_x
0	165	1.000	67	0.406	1.453
1	98	0.594	55	0.561	1.104
2	43	0.261	27	0.628	0.874
3	16	0.097	16	1.0	0.505
4	0	0.0	—	—	—

l_x = proportion alive at start of age interval x (i.e. n_x/n).
d_x = number dying *during* the age interval x to $x + 1$ (i.e. $n_x - n_{x+1}$).
q_x = rate of mortality during the age interval x to $x + 1$ (i.e. d_x/n_x).
e_x = mean expectation of life for organisms alive at start of interval x (see text).

[1] Lowe, V. P. W. (1969) Population dynamics of the red deer (*Cervus elaphus* L.) on Rhum. *Journal of Animal Ecology*, 38, 425–57.

The calculation of e_x involves a number of steps. Firstly, the average number of organisms alive during each age interval (L_x) must be calculated using the formula

$$L_x = (l_x + l_{x+1})/2$$

Using the life table, the average number of individuals alive in age class 0 to 1 years is

$$L_0 = (1.0 + 0.594)/2 = 0.797$$

Once all the L_x values have been calculated, T_x, the number of animal-years remaining in each cohort, can be worked out. This is obtained by adding together all the L_x values between the x in question and the bottom of the table. For example:

$$T_1 = (0.428 + 0.179 + 0.049 + 0) = 0.656$$

Finally, e_x (the mean expectation of life for organisms alive at the start of age interval x) can be obtained by dividing T_x by l_x. For example:

$$e_2 = 0.228/0.261 = 0.874$$

The resulting values are shown in the second table.

x	l_x	L_x	T_x	e_x
0	1.000	0.797	1.453	1.453
1	0.594	0.428	0.656	1.104
2	0.261	0.179	0.228	0.874
3	0.097	0.049	0.049	0.505
4	0.0	—	—	—

This is an example of a 'cohort' life table where data on the number of individuals in the starting cohort and surviving to each subsequent age interval are available. Life tables can also be derived from the age structure of a population at a particular point in time. These are known as 'static' life tables.

Figure 7.1 Hypothetical survivorship curves. The Type I curve represents a population in which older individuals are most at risk of dying, whilst the Type III curve represents a population in which greatest mortality occurs amongst young individuals. The Type II curve represents a population in which individuals have an equal chance of dying, regardless of age.

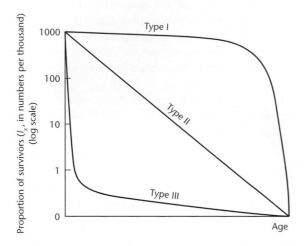

Figure 7.2 Exponential growth of bacteria in laboratory culture.

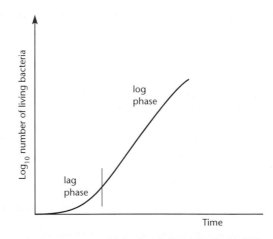

offspring, towards which they exhibit parental care. In Type III curves, highest mortality occurs in the early juvenile stages. This curve is typical of most plant and invertebrate populations. These organisms are short-lived and produce vast numbers of offspring, which are left to fend for themselves. Only a few offspring survive to reproduce and repeat the cycle. The last curve, Type II, represents organisms which have an equal chance of dying at any age. This is a rare situation in nature but does occur in the hydrozoan *Hydra*. The types of survival curve shown by human populations are discussed in Section 7.3.2.

7.1.3 Exponential growth

In optimum conditions of unlimited food and space, populations can grow at an explosive rate. This phenomenon has been demonstrated in a number of laboratory experiments. Organisms such as bacteria and yeast are particularly suitable subjects as their reproductive rate is very rapid. Flour beetles (*Tribolium* spp.) and wheat beetles (*Calandra* spp) have also been used extensively in growth experiments. Basically, the experimental organisms are introduced into optimum conditions of food and space and their subsequent growth rate recorded.

Figure 7.2 shows the type of curve produced when bacteria are introduced into a sterile medium. Initially, there is little increase in the bacterial population (the lag phase). However, because the cell numbers are doubling

with each generation, the growth rate increases progressively, producing the steep curve shown in Figure 7.2. This growth curve is known as the **exponential**, **logistic** or **log curve**. In the natural world, this type of growth is exhibited by opportunist species which colonise new habitats and then move on when conditions deteriorate (Section 7.1.6 and Chapter 8, Section 8.4).

All populations have the *capacity* to increase exponentially. They each have a maximum rate of increase known as the **intrinsic rate of increase** (r). This is dependent on the longevity and fertility of individuals and the time taken between generations. It is characteristic for each particular species. The *actual rate of increase* of populations can be represented algebraically by the following equation:

$$\frac{dX}{dt} = rX \qquad (7.1)$$

where dX/dt = rate of change of numbers (X) with time (t)

X = number of individuals in the population

r = intrinsic rate of increase.

This equation can be integrated into another form which can be used to *predict* the growth of populations (Box 7.3).

7.1.4 Types of growth curves

Populations cannot continue to grow exponentially. This fact was recognised in the nineteenth century by Darwin and recorded in his book 'On the Origin of Species by Natural Selection' (1859). There comes a point after which conditions for growth become progressively less favourable. Figure 7.3 shows the overall growth curve for yeast cells grown in laboratory culture. After the lag and exponential phases, the growth rate slows down as food

7.3   Using the exponential equation to predict future population size

The following form of the exponential equation can be used to make projections of population growth:

$$X_t = X_0\,e^{rt}$$

where X_t = the population after a certain time (t)

  X_0 = the number of individuals in the starting population

  e = the constant that is the base of natural logarithms (i.e. approx 2..72)

  r = the intrinsic rate of increase.

Laboratory experiments using populations of yeast cells under ideal conditions give an r value of approximately 0.5/

hour. If the number of individual yeast cells in the starting population (X_0) is also known, predictions about the size of the population after certain time intervals (X_t) can be made.

If, for example, an initial population of 20 yeast cells was allowed to grow for a period of 10 hours, the number of individuals in the 'final' population can be calculated thus:

$$X_t = 20 \times e^{(0.5 \times 10)}$$
$$= 2968$$

Therefore, in this example, the number of yeast cells after a ten-hour period is almost 3000.

Figure 7.3 Sigmoidal growth of pure cultures of the yeasts *Saccharomyces* and *Schizosaccharomyces* (from Gause, 1932).

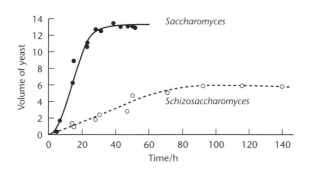

Figure 7.4 J-shaped growth curve of planktonic algae.

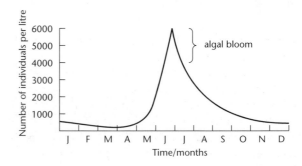

resources become limited and mutual poisoning by the build-up of toxic waste products occurs.

Eventually an equilibrium is reached where there is no appreciable change in the population size. This is known as the stationary phase, where the birth rate is equalled by the death rate. This is ensued by the decline phase. In this stage, the death rate exceeds the birth rate as food supplies continue to diminish and the level of toxicity increases. This type of growth curve is known as **S-shaped** or **sigmoid**.

Another type of growth curve is exhibited by populations of organisms which grow exponentially and then crash to very low numbers. This produces a **J-shaped growth curve** and is typical of organisms with many generations per year. Figure 7.4 illustrates this type of 'boom-or-bust' curve for planktonic algae. In summer months, the algae can reach very high densities. This phenomenon is known as an **algal bloom**. The presence of such blooms can have very serious consequences for aquatic ecosystems (Chapter 14, Section 14.2).

7.1.5   Environmental resistance

In the case of yeast grown in laboratory culture (Section 7.1.4), the factors which limit exponential growth are a combination of diminishing food resources and the build-up of toxic waste products, principally ethanol. These factors are caused by the rapid growth of the population itself and are therefore known as **density-dependent factors**. In natural populations, external factors, for example temperature and food availability, also limit population growth. These are called **density-independent factors**.

The term **environmental resistance** encompasses all factors (internal and external) which limit the growth of particular populations. It means that for any particular species in a given habitat, there is a *limit* to the number of individuals which can be supported. This is known as the **carrying capacity of the environment** (K).

Environmental resistance can be incorporated into Equation 7.1 by the introduction of the growth realisation factor (g):

$$g = \frac{K - X}{K} \qquad (7.2)$$

where K is the carrying capacity of the environment. This results in

$$\frac{dX}{dt} = \frac{rX(K - X)}{K} \qquad (7.3)$$

This equation can be used to model the growth of laboratory populations, often with reasonable accuracy. As the population increases in size, the feedback from the effects of intraspecific competition (represented by the term $(K - X)/K$) becomes ever stronger. The net rate of increase declines until the carrying capacity (K) is reached. At this point, the population has reached equilibrium and there is no further change in population size (dX/dt).

7.1.6 | Population strategies

The terms r (the intrinsic rate of increase) and K (the carrying capacity of the environment) have already been introduced in this chapter in the equations for population growth (Sections 7.1.3 and 7.1.5 respectively). These terms may also be applied to different species depending on the 'strategies' they adopt in order to maximise their chances of long-term survival.

At one extreme of the continuum of population strategies are the **r-species** (also known as **r–strategists**). Some of their main characteristics are summarised in Table 7.1. The r-species are so called because they reproduce very rapidly and therefore have a high r value. They generally have a survival curve approximating to Type III (Section 7.1.2 and Figure 7.1). The r-species include the pioneer species which exploit new or disturbed habitats and are typical of the early stages of ecological succession (Chapter 8, Section 8.4).

The r-species quickly exhaust the resources of the habitats they colonise and can exceed the carrying capacity of the environment (K) if they remain too long. This would result in a population crash similar to the one illustrated in Figure 7.4. When local conditions start to deteriorate, r-strategists usually disperse to colonise other unexploited habitats. They are poor competitors. Bacteria, annual weeds and aphids are all good examples of r-species.

K-species (also referred to as **K-strategists**) are good competitors (Table 7.1). They occupy more stable habitats than those favoured by r-strategists. As their name suggests, they exist at levels close to the carrying capacity of the environment (K). They have low values of r and their reproductive rate is sensitive to population density. Their survival curves are generally Type I (Section 7.1.2 and Figure 7.1). In ecological succession, K-species are

Table 7.1 Some characteristics of r- and K-species.

r-species	K-species
Rapid reproduction	Slow reproduction
Many offspring	Few offspring
No parental care	Parental care
Short generation time	Long generation time
High r value	Low r value
Reproduction rate not sensitive to population density	Reproduction rate sensitive to population density
Population size may exceed K and then crash	Population size tends to stay close to K
Good dispersal	Poor dispersal
Poor competitors	Good competitors
Exploit temporary habitats	Found in stable habitats
Small size	Large size
Short-lived	Long-lived
Examples	
Annual plants	Trees
Flour beetles	Albatrosses
Bacteria	Man

r = intrinsic rate of increase.
K = carrying capacity of the environment.

typical of the later, more mature communities (Chapter 8, Section 8.4). The wandering albatross (*Diomedea exulans*) is a good example of a K-strategist. It takes several years to reach maturity and, when it does, only lays a single egg every two years.

In reality, most species exhibit a mixture of r and K characteristics and therefore occupy intermediate positions on the r–K continuum. Nonetheless, this concept is a useful one in population and community ecology.

7.2 Population regulation

Natural populations do not increase in size indefinitely but encounter, in due course, environmental resistance, which places a ceiling on population size (Section 7.1.5). There are several factors which can produce environmental resistance and these will each be examined in turn. Only the first, intraspecific competition (Section 7.2.1), originates from within the population itself. It is known therefore as an intrinsic factor and acts in a density-dependent fashion. All other factors originate from outside and are termed extrinsic factors. These may involve interactions with other populations, i.e. interspecific competition (Section 7.2.2), or predation (Section 7.2.3), or may be physical effects of climate (Section 7.2.4).

It should be noted at this early stage that the factors responsible for population regulation rarely operate singly. Usually a combination of factors are involved. However, amongst these, there is often one factor deemed to be the most influential. This is known as the **key factor** and in most cases it exerts its effect through increased mortality, rather than decreased natality (Section 7.1.1).

7.2.1 Intraspecific competition

Intraspecific competition occurs between individuals belonging to the same species. In single-species laboratory experiments, intraspecific competition over dwindling food supplies and the build-up of toxic waste products are responsible for the eventual levelling out of population size (Section 7.1.4). These intrinsic factors act in a density-dependent fashion. This means that as the population size increases, so too does the pressure on food supply and the deleterious production of toxic wastes.

In natural populations, intraspecific competition over space can regulate population size on a local scale. This may result from either territorial behaviour or overcrowding.

Territorial behaviour occurs in a wide range of animals. A **territory** is an area of suitable habitat which is defended by the occupant(s) against intruders of the same species. Territories may be occupied permanently.

For example, breeding pairs of tawny owls (*Strix aluco*) stay within a fixed exclusive area for the whole of their adulthood. In other territorial animals, territories are only occupied on a temporary basis. This is common in birds, for example great tits (*Parus major*), when territories are established for the duration of the breeding season only. In yet other animals, territorial behaviour occurs sporadically and appears to be correlated with the availability of food, for example in the iiwi (*Vestiaria coccinea*), a species of Hawaiian honeycreeper (Box 7.4). To individuals holding territories, the benefits in terms of individual fitness (Chapter 8, Section 8.2) must outweigh the costs of defending it. The benefits are usually ones of adequate food supply and/or attracting mates. The size of occupied breeding territories must be just large enough to provide sufficient food for the rearing of the offspring. The costs are mainly ones involving defence. Box 7.5 discusses the methods of defence shown by the European robin (*Erithacus rubecula*).

In a particular habitat, for example a mixed woodland, the territorial behaviour of a particular species will result in a mosaic pattern of defended patches. In a number of studies, nearest neighbour analysis has shown that individuals are not distributed in a random fashion but are spaced out by their territorial behaviour, for example in great tits (Figure 7.5).

Such behaviour serves to limit the population density within a given area. This has been demonstrated in a number of studies, where territories have become available through the natural death or experimental removal of their occupants. New individuals quickly establish

Mini Case Study

7.4 The costs and benefits of territoriality in the iiwi, a Hawaiian honeycreeper

The iiwi (*Vestiaria coccinea*), a species of Hawaiian honeycreeper, is a nectar-feeding bird. It sometimes displays territorial behaviour, actively defending patches of flowers. However, at other times, it is non-territorial, presumably because the costs of defending a territory are higher than the benefits accrued.

Carpenter and MacMillen (1976)[1] directly quantified the costs and benefits of territoriality in the iiwi. On this basis, they were able to predict when it was beneficial to honeycreepers to hold territories and when a change to non-territorial behaviour was favoured.

Essentially, territorial defence should occur between two thresholds. At one extreme, the abundance of the food supply

is so great that the honeycreeper can obtain all its needs without defending a territory. At the other extreme, the food supply is generally so low that the extra food accrued by being territorial is still insufficient to support the honeycreeper. In these circumstances, the bird would do better to find another patch of flowers.

The predictions of this model were tested for ten honeycreepers, three non-territorial and seven territorial. In nine cases out of ten, the birds' behaviour concurred with the predictions of the model. Although this simple model has its limitations, it represents one of the few studies to try and quantify the costs and benefits involved in feeding territoriality. Changes between territorial behaviour and non-territorial behaviour in the honeycreeper are rapid, responding to the rapid fluctuations in the availability of their nectar food supply.

[1] Carpenter, F. L. and R. E. MacMillen (1976) Threshold model of feeding territoriality and test with a Hawaiian honeycreeper. *Science*, **194**, 639–42.

7.5   Territorial defence in the European robin

The European robin (*Erithacus rubecula*) is a small songbird which belongs to the thrush family. It is found throughout Europe. Male robins are territorial throughout the year, whilst females only defend territories in the winter. In the breeding season, the female pairs up with a male in his territory.

Male robins (and, in winter, female robins) sing to advertise their presence in a territory. This may be viewed as 'long-range' territorial defence. Potential intruders are warned in advance that the territory is already occupied, without actually seeing the occupant.

If a resident robin encounters another robin intruding into its territory, it adopts a 'threat' posture. It stretches itself up and fluffs up the vivid red feathers on its chest. Such a posture is usually sufficient to deter the intruder.

It has been demonstrated that a combination of singing and threatening displays by a caged resident robin was sufficient to drive away a potential intruder. However, when the caged robin was placed into another robin's territory, it shrank back and would have fled if possible. This ritualised behaviour between resident and intruder takes the place of real aggression, which could involve actual bodily harm to one or both participants.

Figure 7.5 Distribution of great tits (*Parus major*) in Wytham Woods, Oxfordshire, UK (from Krebs, 1971).

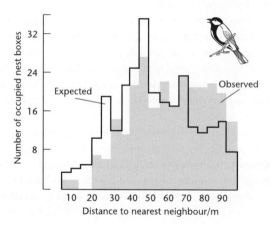

themselves in the unoccupied territories. In the case of red grouse (*Lagopus lagopus scoticus*), replacements were non-territorial grouse which otherwise would have failed to breed. The possession of a territory therefore conveys a selective advantage to the occupant (Chapter 8, Section 8.2). From the population dynamics point of view, territoriality regulates population density on a local scale. It is important to emphasise that this is a product, and not a function, of territorial behaviour.

Overcrowding within populations can also result in population regulation through a variety of mechanisms. In laboratory conditions, brown rats (*Rattus norvegicus*) show a very marked decline in fecundity when the population reaches a certain critical density. This occurs despite the presence of adequate food supplies. Hormonal changes adversely affect the reproductive behaviour of the rats. They may fail to breed at all, or if they do they may eat their young or abandon them prematurely. These changes are accompanied by an increase in aggression. This type of

regulation may prevail in natural populations under similar conditions of overcrowding, for example in voles (*Microtus* spp.).

7.2.2   Interspecific competition

Interspecific competition occurs when individuals from two or more *different* species compete over limited resources, for example of food and water.

The classical model for two-species competition was put forward, independently, by Lotka (1925)[1] and Volterra (1926).[2] They assumed that each species on its own would increase in accordance with the model represented by Equation 7.3 (Section 7.1.5). However, together they would interact in accordance with the following equations:

$$\frac{dX}{dt} = \frac{r_x X(K_x - X - \alpha Y)}{K_x}$$

for species X, and

$$\frac{dY}{dt} = \frac{r_y Y(K_y - Y - \beta X)}{K_y}$$

for species Y, where α and β are the **competition coefficients**.

In Equation 7.3, the rate of change dX/dt is zero when $X_t = K$. In the above equations, dX/dt is zero in species X when $X + \alpha Y = K_x$ and in species Y when $Y + \beta X = K_y$.

The Lotka–Volterra model for two-species competition predicts four possible outcomes (Figure 7.6). The points at which there is no change in numbers of individuals in population X or Y (i.e. where $dX/dt = 0$ and $dY/dt = 0$

[1] Lotka, A. J. (1925) *Elements of physical biology*. Baltimore, MD: Williams and Wilkins.
[2] Volterra, V. (1926) [Translation in] Chapman, R. N. (1931) *Animal ecology*. New York: McGraw-Hill.

Figure 7.6 Four types of outcome for the Lotka–Volterra two-species competition model.

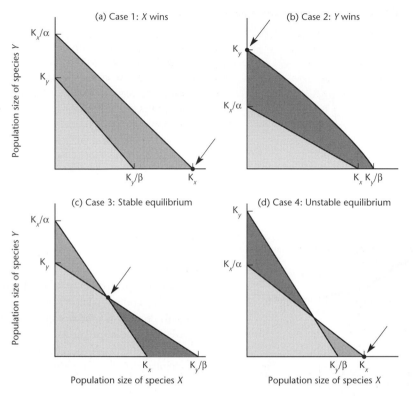

Diagonal lines are zero growth isoclines. Arrows show equilibrium points.

respectively) are represented on the graphs by the zero growth isoclines. It is the relative position of these lines and whether or not they intersect which determines the outcome of the model.

If the isoclines do not intersect, the two species cannot reach an equilibrium. The species whose isocline is underneath the other becomes extinct (Figure 7.6(a) and (b)). If the isoclines do intersect, then the two populations can coexist at that point. The equilibria reached may be stable or unstable (Figure 7.6(c) and (d) respectively).

Theoretically, models of two-species competition predict that either one species becomes extinct or that the two species may be able to coexist. Laboratory experiments have used a range of organisms, namely protozoans, yeasts, insects and plants, to examine the effects of interspecific competition between pairs of similar species. In most experiments, one of the species became extinct.

In the late 1940s, Park performed a series of competition experiments using the flour beetles *Tribolium confusum* and *Tribolium castaneum*. At a temperature of 29.5°C, *T. confusum* became extinct (Figure 7.7(a)). However, in later experiments, Park was able to alter the outcome of the competition by varying external physical factors of temperature and humidity. For example, at temperatures above 29°C, *T. confusum* was driven to extinction, whereas below 29°C, *T. castaneum* died out.

A further complication which affected the outcome of these experiments was the presence or absence of the parasite *Adelina*, a protozoan which attacks flour beetles. *T. castaneum* was more severely affected by the parasite. Park was therefore able to reverse the outcome of the experiment performed at 29.5°C (Figure 7.7(a)). In the presence of *Adelina*, *T. castaneum* usually became extinct (Figure 7.7(b)).

Park continued his investigations using different genetic strains of the two *Tribolium* species and found that this factor too could influence the outcome of competition experiments. It should be noted here that the outcome of all these experiments was not absolute; rather the probability of one species outcompeting the other was higher depending on the experimental conditions.

In some laboratory experiments, coexistence between two species has been reported. Such an outcome seems to hinge on there being some slight difference between the requirements of the two species concerned. For example,

Figure 7.7 Competition between two species of flour beetle, *Tribolium confusum* and *T. castaneum*, at 29.5°C (from Hassell, 1976; data from Park, T. (1948) Experimental studies of interspecies competition, *Ecological Monographs*, **18**: 265–308, The Ecological Society of America).

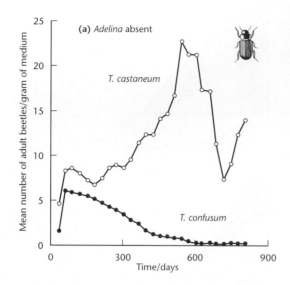

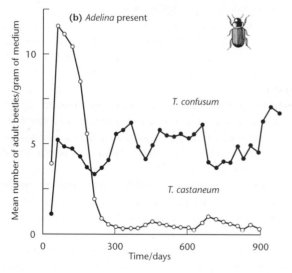

Gause (1935)[3] found that coexistence between the protozoans *Paramecium bursaria* and *Paramecium aurelia* in a tube of yeast was possible because of a difference in their feeding habits: *P. bursaria* utilised the bottom yeast layers whilst *P. aurelia* fed on the yeast suspension at the top of the tube.

In laboratory experiments, two-species competition often leads to the extinction of the 'inferior competitor' by

the 'superior competitor'. However, in the field situation, instances of the coexistence of similar species have been recorded, for example the many herbaceous species found living in intimate proximity in meadows. If resources are not limited in nature, then a lack of competition between the species could explain their coexistence. Alternatively, the explanation could be that intense competition in the past has caused slight differences between species to evolve, thus accounting for their current coexistence.

In some natural populations, interspecific competition has been demonstrated to occur. One example is the competition between two species of barnacle, *Chthamalus stellatus* and *Balanus balanoides* (Box 7.6). The role of competition in natural populations is discussed further in Chapter 8, Section 8.1.1.

7.2.3 | Predation

Predation is the term used to describe the killing and eating of animals (known as **prey**) usually by other animals (known as **predators**). There are in fact about 500 species of predatory plants, including sundews (*Drosera* spp.) and pitcher plants. These use a variety of different mechanisms to trap and then digest small invertebrates, usually insects. However, predation occurs predominantly amongst animals. These exhibit a wide range of different strategies for the procurement of prey (more general information on predation is given in Chapter 8, Section 8.1.2).

Included within the category of predators are the **insect parasitoids**, which differ from 'true parasites' in that they usually *kill* their hosts. These usually belong to the order Diptera (true flies) or the order Hymenoptera (bees, wasps and ants). Host organisms belong mainly to other insect orders and are mostly attacked in the pre-adult stages. Insect parasitoids are very widespread, accounting for about 10% of all known insect species. They are of enormous ecological and economic importance, especially in the biological control of insect pests.

In the 1920s, the first theoretical model for predator–prey interactions was presented, independently, by Lotka (1925)[1] and Volterra (1926).[2] The Lotka–Volterra model, as it is known, predicted that predator and prey populations would oscillate out of phase (Figure 7.8). Oscillations would be of the same amplitude and the size of that amplitude would depend on the initial densities of the predator and prey populations.

The first test of this purely deductive model was made by Gause in the 1930s. He used two ciliate protozoans: *Paramecium caudatum* as the prey and *Didinium nasutum* as the predator. An oatmeal medium provided nutrition for the bacteria upon which the *Paramecium* fed.

[3] Gause, G. F. (1935) Experimental demonstration of Volterra's periodic oscillation in the numbers of animals. *Journal of Experimental Biology*, **12**, 44–8.

7.6   Interspecific competition between two species of barnacle

The barnacles *Chthamalus stellatus* and *Balanus balanoides* often occur together on the rocky Atlantic shores of north-west Europe. They were studied in their natural rocky shore habitat in Scotland by Connell (1961).[1] He observed that adult *Chthamalus* occurred in the intertidal zone, whilst adult *Balanus* occupied a zone lower down the shore, even though young *Chthamalus* were observed to settle there too.

Connell recorded the fate of young *Chthamalus* in the *Balanus* zone, keeping some areas artificially free from *Balanus*

by deliberately removing them. He found that in the areas devoid of *Balanus*, *Chthamalus* were successful colonisers. However, where *Balanus* occurred naturally, *Chthamalus* failed to gain a foothold. It appears that it is direct competition over space by *Balanus* which excludes *Chthamalus* from the lower shore zone. Direct observations confirmed that *Chthamalus* was indeed crushed and undercut by *Balanus*.

It seems that the lower tolerance of *Balanus* to conditions of periodic desiccation prevents it from extending its range to the intertidal zone of the rocky shore. Here, in the absence of interspecific competition from *Balanus*, *Chthamalus* is able to survive.

[1] Connell, J. H. (1961) The influence of interspecific competition and other factors on the distribution of the barnacle *Chthamalus stellatus*. *Ecology*, **42**, 710–23.

Figure 7.8 Outcome of the Lotka–Volterra predator–prey model.

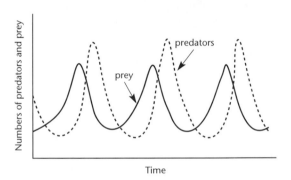

In Gause's first experiment, the *Didinium* simply ate all the *Paramecium* and then itself died of starvation (Figure 7.9(a)). In his second experiment, Gause provided a sediment substrate. The *Didinium* ate all the *Paramecium* in the clear fluid and then died as before. The portion of *Paramecium* in the sediment *refuge* then multiplied in the absence of the predatory *Didinium* (Figure 7.9(b)). Neither of these two experiments produced the classic oscillations predicted by the Lotka–Volterra model. In yet another experiment, Gause was at last able to produce repeated oscillations, but only by adding one *Didinium* and one *Paramecium* every three days (immigration) (Figure 7.9(c)). He concluded therefore that predator–prey oscillations were not an *inherent* property of the interaction itself, as predicted by Lotka and Volterra, but depended on 'interference' from outside the system.

Gause's conclusions were challenged by Huffaker

(1958)[4] who felt that the system Gause used was much too simple. Huffaker set out to try and produce the oscillations predicted by the Lotka–Volterra model in his laboratory experiments. He used two species of mites: *Eotetranychus sexmaculatus*, which feeds on oranges, as the prey and *Typhlodromus occidentalis* as the predator.

In his *simple* systems, both populations became extinct. However, Huffaker was eventually able to produce repeated predator–prey oscillations by constructing an enormously complex experimental system consisting of 252 oranges with multiple petroleum-jelly barriers! He demonstrated that it was possible to maintain a predator–prey relationship in the laboratory but that the system had to provide a high degree of environmental heterogeneity to be successful. Within his system, local emigration and immigration allowed *Eotetranychus* to evade the predatory *Typhlodromus*. Since Huffaker's experiments, stable predator–prey oscillations have been produced in a number of laboratory systems.

Does this pattern of repeated oscillations in predator and prey densities occur in the field situation? Relevant data are not plentiful because of the laborious nature of data collection and the long time-scale involved. However, there is some evidence that such oscillations do occur. The difficulty lies in ascribing these oscillations to the *interaction* between the predator and its prey. In the case of the snowshoe hare (*Lepus americanus*) and the Canada lynx (*Lynx canadensis*), coupled cycles in their densities seemed to provide evidence of classical predator–prey oscillations in the field. However, this may not be as simple as was first thought: see Box 7.7.

It is very difficult to apply predator–prey models to the field situation. The models themselves, in order to be workable, must be relatively simple. They make a number

[4] Huffaker, C. B. (1958) *Hilgardia*, **27**, 343–83.

Figure 7.9 Predator–prey interactions between the protozoans *Didinium nasutum* (predator) and *Paramecium caudatum* (prey) (from Gause, 1934).

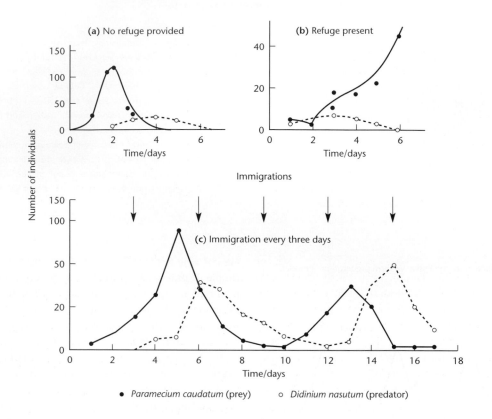

● *Paramecium caudatum* (prey)   ○ *Didinium nasutum* (predator)

of assumptions which are simply not true of natural populations. To take just one example, the search for prey by predators is assumed to be random. However, this is usually not the case. If prey populations are aggregated or clumped in their distribution, predators will concentrate their search in areas of high prey density. This type of behaviour (an example of optimal foraging) obviously maximises their chances of encountering more prey organisms per unit time.

In the laboratory, the interaction under test is usually

Mini Case Study

7.7 Predator–prey interactions: the Canada lynx and the snowshoe hare

Populations of the Canada lynx (*Lynx canadensis*) undergo cyclic oscillations in density, reaching a peak every 9 or 10 years. This pattern can be traced back as far as the early nineteenth century by examining the records of lynx pelts kept by the Hudson's Bay Company in Canada. The main prey of the Canada lynx is the snowshoe hare (*Lepus americanus*). This also follows an approximately 10-year cycle. This would seem to provide evidence for a classic predator–prey interaction occurring in natural populations.

However, further examination of the field situation has shown that the cycles of density shown by the snowshoe hare populations are more likely to be correlated with the availability of their food supply, the terminal twigs of shrubs

and trees. The snowshoe hare is the dominant herbivore in the boreal forests of North America and in times of high hare densities, food shortages result in a decline in numbers.

The densities of the Canada lynx populations apparently *follow* those of the snowshoe hare, rather than generate them. This is not therefore a classic predator–prey oscillation as predicted by the Lotka–Volterra model.

References: Elton, C. and M. Nicholson (1942) The ten-year cycle in numbers of the lynx in Canada. *Journal of Animal Ecology*, **11**, 215–44.

Keith, L. B. (1963) *Wildlife's ten-year cycle*. Madison, WI: University of Wisconsin Press.

Figure 7.10 Comparison of the density of red kangaroos (*Macropus rufus*) across the border between New South Wales and South Australia (from Caughley *et al.*, 1980).

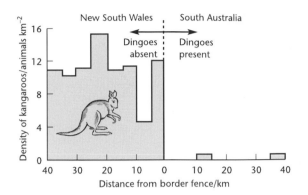

Figure 7.11 Growth curves of populations of the water flea *Moina macrocopa* at different temperatures (from Phillips and Chilton, 1989).

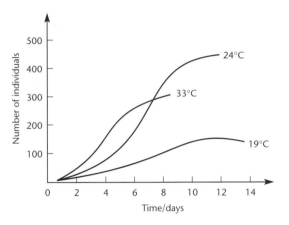

between a single species of predator and a single species of its prey (although there is an increasing interest in systems involving more than two species). This is in itself an oversimplification of what occurs naturally. Predators usually have several different prey types, often selecting those whose abundance is currently the highest (a process known as **prey switching**). In addition, the predator–prey interaction does not occur in isolation but is complicated by other interactions, for example competition, and influenced by environmental change.

Having said all this, there is evidence that, in some cases, predators do influence the density of their prey. This evidence is provided either by removal experiments or by the biological control of insect pests, often by insect parasitoids. One striking example of the effect of removing natural predators can be found in Australia. The predator in question is the dingo (*Canis familiaris dingo*). In order to exclude this large carnivore from sheep country in New South Wales, a dingo fence was erected along the state border with South Australia. The density of another of the dingo's prey species, the red kangaroo (*Macropus rufus*), subsequently reached very high levels in New South Wales in comparison with South Australia, where dingoes were still present (Figure 7.10).

In summary, it can be said that the theoretical models of predator–prey relationships (of which the Lotka–Volterra model is one very important example), though oversimplified, are useful in showing the tendency of such relationships to produce coupled oscillations. This pattern has been produced in several laboratory experiments. Such cyclic oscillations have been observed in some predator–prey populations in the field. However, the difficulty here is pinpointing predation as the key factor influencing predator density and vice versa.

7.2.4 Physical factors

Physical factors, for example of temperature, water and light, also play a part in influencing the population dynamics of organisms. In laboratory experiments, physical factors can influence the growth curves of single species. Figure 7.11 illustrates the effect of temperature on the growth curves of *Moina macrocopa* (a species of water flea).

Changing physical parameters can also influence the outcome of population interactions. For example, in Gause's extensive experimentation with the flour beetles *Tribolium confusum* and *T. castaneum*, both temperature and humidity were shown to be instrumental in determining the outcome of competition between the two species.

In laboratory experiments, under controlled conditions, the effect of extrinsic physical factors can be clearly demonstrated. In contrast, in natural populations, it is often difficult to separate the influence of physical parameters on population density from other extrinsic effects. However, there are a number of examples where sudden changes in the environment are mirrored by sudden changes in the abundance of a particular species. For example, in a classic study on the population of the grey heron (*Ardea cinerea*) in England and Wales between 1928 and 1970, the population showed a significant decline in the aftermath of severe winters (Figure 7.12). However, the heron population was able to recover after these periodic crashes and regain its former level.

7.3 Human population dynamics

The growth pattern of the world's human population is treated in this section as a special case. It is unusual in that

Figure 7.12 Changes in the abundance of grey herons (*Ardea cinerea*) in England and Wales, 1928–70 (from Stafford, 1971).

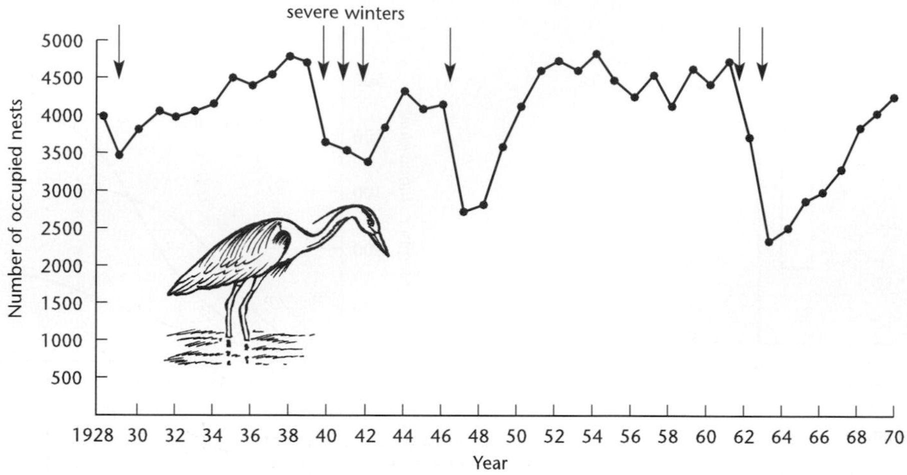

it remains in a state of exponential growth (Section 7.1.3). The implications of such a massive expansion in numbers upon the finite resources of the Earth are enormous. In this section, the past patterns, present situation and future trends in the growth of human populations are examined. General comparisons are made between the 'more-developed' countries (MDCs) and the 'less-developed' countries (LDCs).

The statistical study of human populations is called **demography**. Demographers take into account the age distribution and sex ratio of human populations, as well as their size, in order to make future predictions about population growth. Ignoring migration, the growth rate (r) of a population is the birth rate (b) minus the death rate (d). In human populations, both birth rates and death rates are usually expressed as numbers per thousand head of population per year.

7.3.1 The global pattern of human population growth

Figure 7.13 illustrates the growth of the world's human population. The species *Homo sapiens* is thought to have appeared about 100 000 years ago. Like their hominid ancestors, *Homo sapiens* were originally hunter–gatherers. For thousands of years, the level of the world's human population remained relatively constant.

Around 12 000–10 000 BP (before present), there is evidence that *Homo sapiens* began to cultivate crops and domesticate animals. A roaming hunter–gatherer existence was exchanged for a settled, more stable lifestyle. With this transition came a steady increase in the growth rate of the population. This was due to a

combination of increased birth rates and decreased death rates, although where the balance lies can only be a matter of conjecture.

This trend, related largely to agricultural developments, continued steadily until the middle of the eighteenth century. At this point, the Industrial Revolution triggered a second and much more dramatic increase in the rate of growth of the world's population (Figure 7.13). In Europe and North America, the death rate continued to decline for a number of reasons. There was a general improvement in living conditions. For example, enormous improvements were made in public sanitation with the provision of sewerage systems and the purification of water supplies. By the end of the nineteenth century, in Europe and North America, birth rates had followed death rates in decline.

Today, the global trend of human population growth continues to be one of accelerating increase (Figure 7.13). At present, there are 6 billion human beings living on Earth (late-1999 figure). Table 7.2 shows how many years it has taken to add each extra billion people to the world's population. The figures speak for themselves. The first billion mark was reached in 1800 and the second billion mark in 1930. However, whilst it took 130 years to add the second billion, it took only 30 years to add the third billion (by 1960), 15 years to add the fourth (by 1975), 12 to add the fifth (by 1987) and 12 to add the sixth (by 1999). It is projected that the next 2.9 billion will be added in approximately 50 years' time (Table 7.2).

Factors like starvation, disease and wars, which have devastating 'local' effects on human populations, do not affect the overall global trend of population increase.

Figure 7.13 The growth of the world's human population over the last 12 000 years (from Marsh and Grossa, 1996).

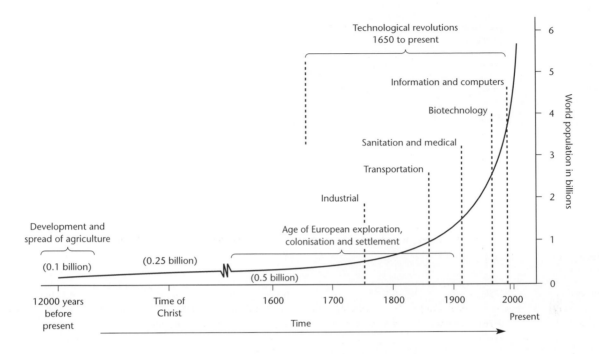

Table 7.2 The time taken to add each extra billion to the world's human population.

Billion reached	Year	Years to add 1 billion
First	1800	All of human history
Second	1930	130
Third	1960	30
Fourth	1975	15
Fifth	1987	12
Sixth	1999	12
Projected Seventh	2013	14
Eighth	2025–30	12–17
8.9 billion	2050	20–25

Source: Information for first to sixth billion from the World Population Reference Bureau; projected figures (medium projection) from *World Population Prospects: The 1998 Revision* of the United Nations Population Division.

Only the bubonic plague (Black Death), spread to humans by fleas infesting black rats (*Rattus rattus*), caused a significant decline in the growth rate. Between 1348 and 1350, about 25% of the population of Europe is thought to have perished as a result of this terrible plague.

7.3.2   A comparison between 'more-developed' and 'less-developed' countries

More-developed countries (MDCs)

About one-fifth of the world's 6 billion population live in countries classed as 'more developed'. This category is largely confined to the northern hemisphere and includes the United States, Canada, the countries of Europe, New Zealand and Australia. These modern, industrialised societies are typified by low birth rates and low death rates (Table 7.3). The survivorship curves of such populations are Type I (Figure 7.1, Section 7.1.2) with the majority of the population reaching old age. The average life expectancy for the inhabitants of MDCs is 75 years. Infant mortality is much lower in MDCs but is still large enough to cause a dip in the survivorship curve. The rate of population increase is low and, in the case of Europe, is actually negative (Table 7.3, Figure 7.14).

Less-developed countries (LDCs)

It is salutary to realise that only 150 years ago, the more-developed countries listed above would have been placed in this category. Today, the 133 countries classed as LDCs are found largely in the southern hemisphere, in Africa, Latin America and Asia. They account for about four-fifths of the world's current population. Such countries

Table 7.3 Population statistics.

Region	Population estimate, mid-1998 (millions)	Natural increase (annual, %)	Annual birth rate (per 1000 population	Annual death rate (per 1000 population)	Per capita GNP, 1996 (US$)
Africa	763	2.5	40	15	650
Latin America and Caribbean	500	1.8	25	7	3710
Asia (including China)	3604	1.5	23	8	2490
Oceania (including Australia and N.Z.)	30	1.1	18	7	15 430
North America	301	0.6	14	8	27 100
Europe	728	−0.1	10	11	13 710
World	5926	1.4	23	9	5050

Source: Data from the 1998 World Population Data Sheet; world totals and means by calculation.

experience many problems, including food shortages and infectious diseases such as malaria, cholera and tuberculosis. Birth rates and death rates are usually high (Table 7.3). The survivorship curves of such populations approximate to Type III (Figure 7.1, Section 7.1.2), with a high infant mortality. The average life expectancy for people living in LDCs is 63 years.

The transition from *high* birth and death rates to *low* birth and death rates is known as the **demographic transition** and is usually associated with the general modernisation and industrialisation of a society.

However, the export of modern drugs and technology from MDCs to LDCs has often meant a relatively swift and significant drop in their death rate. This occurs without the progressive modernisation of that society. The concomitant decline in birth rates which usually follows the decline in death rates in a demographic transition does not therefore take place. As a result, there is a high rate of increase in the growth of such populations (Table 7.3, Figure 7.14).

7.3.3 The future of the world's human population

In Section 7.3.1, it was stated that it took only 12 years to add the fifth billion to the world's population, from 1975 to 1987. A further billion people were added by 1999, bringing

the population to six billion. A comparison between MDCs and LDCs (Section 7.3.2) shows that whilst growth rates are low in MDCs, they are high in LDCs (Table 7.3, Figure 7.14). The vast majority of future population increase will therefore occur in the less-developed countries (Figure 7.15, and Plate 4). Even a low rate of increase in LDCs would add an enormous number of extra people because the base populations are so large. For example, in 1998, China had an estimated 1.24 billion individuals, i.e. approximately one-fifth of the world's population. An annual growth rate of only 1% would add an extra 12.4 million people to the Chinese population in the space of one year.

The increasing pressure of the world's human population on its resources is an issue of paramount importance. However, it should be borne in mind that this is not just a question of simple numbers but also of the level of per capita consumption. There is a very marked divide between the consumption levels in the more-developed countries when compared with those in less-developed ones, a point referred to later in chapters concerned with human impact on natural resources, namely Chapters 11, 12 and 13. The figures for *per capita* gross national product (GNP) for the major regions of the world are given in Table 7.3; these show clearly the vast gulf between the developed and developing world.

In countries where the annual rate of population increase is high, the only humanitarian approach to

Figure 7.14 World map showing the annual rate of increase in human populations (data from 1998 World Population Data Sheet).

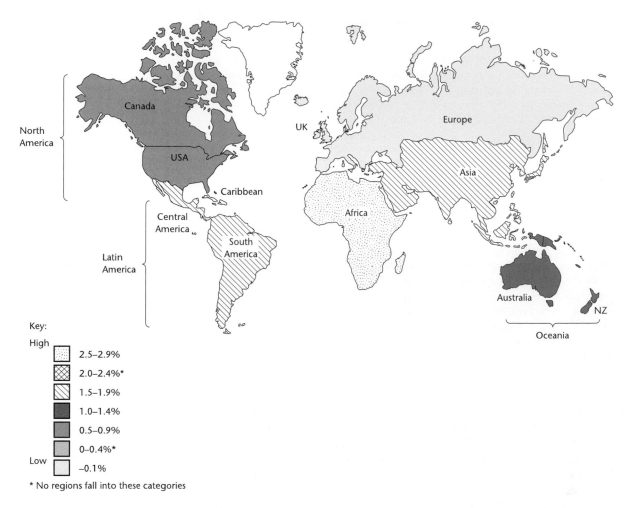

Key:

High

2.5–2.9%

2.0–2.4%*

1.5–1.9%

1.0–1.4%

0.5–0.9%

0–0.4%*

Low   –0.1%

* No regions fall into these categories

Figure 7.15 Population age pyramids for developed and developing countries, 1985 and 2025 (from Tolba *et al.*, 1992; data from UN Population Division, 1990).

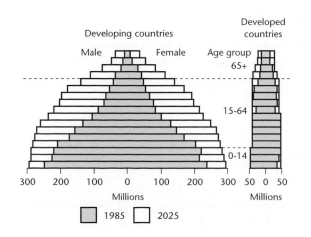

reversing this trend is to encourage families to have fewer children. However, this often runs contrary to religious beliefs and social and cultural traditions. For example, in peasant-type cultures, a large family is favoured because it means more help on the land and care for the parents in their old age.

State-run programmes of birth control have met with some success, for example in India and China. Box 7.8 examines the situation in China in some detail.

However, even if women were to begin bearing children at the **replacement level** only (i.e. at a level where the population would exactly replace itself), the human population would still continue to increase. The reason for this is that in most countries, especially LDCs, the number of women in the pre-reproductive and reproductive age groups is disproportionately large. This is apparent from the population age pyramid representing the 'developing countries' illustrated in Figure 7.15.

Mini Case Study

7.8   Limiting population growth: the Chinese approach

China has about one-fifth of the world's population, with a population size of 1.24 billion (mid-1998 figure). Between 1950 and 1980, the population grew by about 400 million. However, it was not until the late 1970s that the Chinese policy of 'more people, more production' was replaced by a government programme aimed at reducing the growth rate of the Chinese population.

The first steps of this programme included free birth control devices, medical abortions and sterilisations. Throughout China, literature promoted the advice of 'Later Longer Fewer', encouraging citizens to start families later, to leave longer gaps between children and to have fewer children.

The Chinese government programme to curb population growth became progressively more severe. Today men and women are not allowed to marry until aged 27 and 25 respectively. Couples are actively encouraged to have only one child. Couples who pledge to restrict their families to just one are given free medical care and education for that child, together with preferential treatment in obtaining a job when the child reaches adulthood. Other benefits to the couple include better housing, higher pay and greater chances of promotion at work.

In contrast, newly-wed couples who refuse to sign such a pledge must pay for all the healthcare and education of their children. They receive no benefits such as promotions at work and have to pay additional income tax. If a couple sign and then exceed the agreed limit of one child, severe penalties are incurred.

The effect of this austere programme, possible only under a totalitarian regime, was immediate. The growth rate of the Chinese population declined rapidly and, by 1981, the annual natural increase was only 1.2%. Although this annual figure has wavered slightly in subsequent years, the latest figure available (mid-1998) is 1.0%.

Reference: H. Yuan Tien (1992) *China's Demographic Dilemmas*. Washington, DC: Population Reference Bureau.

The future of the world's population is uncertain. Predictions have been made that it will level off in about 100 years' time, after the addition of the twelfth billion. However, the exact level at which the population would become 'stationary' will depend on the rate of population growth in the future and how quickly it can be slowed down to the replacement level. Without concerted action, it is possible that the human population will continue to increase rapidly, with calamitous results.

7.4   Summary

The study of population dynamics is concerned primarily with changes in populations over time. In ideal conditions, populations increase exponentially but, as demonstrated by laboratory experiments, such an increase cannot be sustained indefinitely. A variety of factors, grouped under the umbrella term 'environmental resistance', act to curtail the growth of populations. These may arise from within the populations themselves, for example intraspecific competition, or from the outside, for example interspecific competition and predation. Usually a combination of these factors is involved and the challenge is to identify the key factor responsible. Although much work has been done in producing mathematical models and testing them in the laboratory, information on the population dynamics of natural populations is much scarcer.

This chapter concludes with a discussion of the growth of human populations (past, present and future) and compares the population dynamics of the more-developed countries with those of the less-developed ones. Man's dominion over the environment means that the world's human population is now in a phase of exponential growth, with no sign of abatement.

7.5   Problems

1 With reference to Box 7.1, estimate the population of field mice in a wheat field, given that 25 individuals were initially marked and of these six were recaptured in a total recapture of 37 individuals.

2 What are 'survivorship curves' and how are they constructed? Sketch the three main types and, with reference to examples, explain how these three patterns are produced.

3 With reference to Box 7.3, estimate the population of yeast cells at 5, 10 and 15 hours, given an initial starting population of ten cells.

4 Sketch a graph showing the two main types of growth curve. With reference to examples, explain what is occurring in each case.

5 What is meant by the term 'environmental resistance'? What are the factors which may be involved and where may they originate?

6 What is meant by the term 'interspecific competition'? In natural populations of territorial birds, explain how it regulates population size on a local scale. Illustrate your answer with specific examples.

7 Competition between two species may have different outcomes. Discuss these with reference to laboratory and field experiments.

8 What did the purely deductive Lotka–Volterra model for predator–prey interactions predict? Has this pattern been produced in laboratory experiments? Does it occur in natural populations in the field? Refer to specific examples in your discussion.

9 Describe the global pattern of human population growth from the appearance of *Homo sapiens* to the present day, giving reasons for any sudden increases in the rate of population growth.

10 The world's human population is in a state of exponential growth, a trend which looks set to continue. Explain why the less-developed countries (LDCs) will be the major contributors of new individuals in the future and what steps have been taken to slow down the rate of population growth.

<h2>7.6 Further reading</h2>

Begon, M., J. L. Harper and C. R. Townsend (1996) *Ecology: individuals, populations and communities* (3rd edn). Oxford: Blackwell Science.

Begon, M., M. Mortimer and D. Thompson (1996) *Population ecology*. Oxford: Blackwell Science.

Krebs, C .J. (1993) *Ecology: the experimental analysis of distribution and abundance* (4th edn). Harlow: Addison Wesley Longman Higher Education.

Moss, R., A. Watson and J. Ollason (1982) *Animal population dynamics*. Kluwer Academic.

Stiling, P. (1998) *Ecology*. New York: Prentice Hall.

World Population Data Sheet (1998) Population Reference Bureau, 1875 Connecticut Ave., NW, Suite 520, Washington, DC 20009-5728, USA.

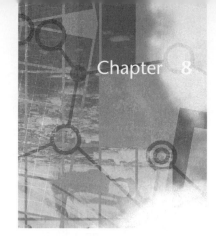

Chapter 8

Biological communities

Chapter Objectives

After reading this chapter, you should be able to:

■ Outline the five main interactions that can take place between species, namely competition, predation, parasitism, mutualism and commensalism.

■ Understand the concepts of habitat and niche.

■ Explain the mechanism of natural selection and the various factors (both abiotic and biotic) which may act as selection pressures on populations.

■ Define the term 'speciation' and outline the routes by which this process may operate.

■ Distinguish between the terms 'species richness' and 'species diversity', and discuss the factors which govern species richness.

■ Describe the process of ecological succession, together with suggested mechanisms, and the concept of the climax state.

■ Compare and contrast the process of primary succession with that of secondary succession.

Introduction

Biological communities consist of an assemblage of different species which interact with each other in various ways. Understanding the functioning of communities as a whole, through the interactions of their constituent species, is an important prerequisite to the preservation of their biodiversity. The concept of biodiversity is returned to in Chapter 10 of this book, where it is discussed in some detail.

In the first part of this chapter, the major types of species interaction are discussed. This is followed by a section in which the role of natural selection in shaping communities through the adaptation of

individual species and the process of speciation is examined.

In the next section, trends in the species richness (i.e. number of species) of biological communities are explored. Particular reference is made in this section to the huge number of species observed in the tropics compared with that of temperate and polar regions. This chapter concludes with a section on ecological succession, a process which involves a series of transitional biological communities. This process is of particular environmental relevance as it may be instigated by a number of human activities, for example the clearing of large areas of native forest.

8.1 Interactions between species

This section presents a brief résumé of the major types of relationships which exist between organisms within a community. These are competition, predation, parasitism, mutualism and commensalism. The last three are all examples of **symbiosis**, which is defined as a close relationship between individuals of two species. However, in some texts the terms symbiosis and mutualism are used synonymously.

8.1.1 Competition

Competition is a negative interaction between species where both suffer as a result (Table 8.1). It may occur between members of the same species (**intraspecific competition**) or between members of two or more different species (**interspecific competition**). In plants, competition may occur over water, nutrients or light. In animals, competition may be for water, food, mates or the space needed for such things as breeding, over-wintering or predator avoidance.

Intraspecific or interspecific competition can be of two basic types. In **resource/scramble competition**, organisms compete over resources which are in short supply. In this case, competitors do not interact directly with one another but are affected by the depletion of the resource after others have exploited it.

In **contest/interference competition**, organisms seek to actively exclude their competitors from resources. One example of this type of competition is found in red deer (*Cervus elaphus*), where stags fight each other in a contest over mates. The resource in this case is the right to mate with all the females in the herd.

In laboratory experiments designed to study competition between closely related species, the superior competitor often drives the inferior one to extinction (Chapter 7, Section 7.2.2). However, in nature, many species, apparently similar in their requirements, coexist. How widespread is competition in the real world? Does it act as a major evolutionary pressure? Or are resources seldom limiting? These are some of the questions which challenge ecologists.

The survival of the superior competitor to the detriment of its rival in laboratory experiments illustrates the '**competitive exclusion principle**'. Put simply, this states that 'complete competitors cannot coexist' or 'no two competitors can occupy the same niche' (Box 8.1). If the contested resource is food, for example, a species can avoid a superior competitor by either utilising a different part of the habitat (Box 8.1) or altering its diet. Thus competition is acting as an evolutionary pressure.

Close study of the coexistence of similar species often reveals subtle differences in their niche requirements (Box 8.2). However, it cannot be proved that it is past competition which has led to this diversity.

8.1.2 Predation

Predation is the consumption of one organism by another. Such a broad definition will encompass herbivores grazing on plants, parasites and parasitoids (Section 8.1.3) as well as **carnivores**, i.e. animals which kill and eat other animals. In this section, discussion is restricted to carnivores or 'true predators'.

Carnivores may be invertebrates, for example dragonfly nymphs (order Odonata), or vertebrates, for example the African lion (*Panthera leo*). Predators differ in the variety of prey types which they locate and consume. Some predators have very restricted diets of only a few prey types or even just one and are known as **specialists**. However, most predators have a broad diet and are known as **generalists**. This has the advantage that predators can switch from one prey type to another depending on their relative abundance.

Prey switching illustrates the principle of **optimal foraging**. This concept predicts that carnivores (in this case) will select prey which will provide the greatest net energy gain, once the energetic costs involved in capturing and consuming the prey have been taken into account. Clearly, the density of the prey populations will affect the energetic costs of predators locating and capturing prey. Ease of capture means that predators usually take the more vulnerable members of the prey population. Individuals which are either old, very young or weakened by disease are

Table 8.1 Interaction between species.

Type of interaction	Description	Effects on participants
Competition	Neither species benefits; both species suffer	−/−
Predation	One species kills another for food	+/−
Parasitism	One species (the parasite) benefits to the detriment of the other (the host)	+/−
Mutualism	Both species benefit from this close association	+/+
Commensalism	One species benefits from this association whilst the other is unaffected	+/0

+ = beneficial effect.
− = detrimental effect.
0 = slight or no effect.

Further Information Box

8.1   Habitat and niche

The **habitat** of an organism, be it micro-organism, plant or animal, may be defined as the place where it lives. Habitat must be seen from the point of view of the organism in question. For example, within a deciduous wood, a beetle may be confined to a small area of bark on a single tree, whilst for a squirrel, the whole wood and beyond may be viewed as its habitat. Bearing this in mind, one way of classifying habitats is to look at their distribution, in both time and space (see table). Of the twelve resultant habitat types, only two are uninhabitable.

Within any particular habitat, there are a range of ecological niches which can be exploited by different species. The niche concept is an abstract and complicated concept but one very central to ecology. For a particular species, certain conditions of external parameters, for example temperature and humidity, and resources, for example food and space, must exist for that species to survive, grow, reproduce and maintain a viable population.

A single parameter, such as temperature, can be envisaged in the figure as having an upper limit (u) and a lower limit (l) beyond which the species in question cannot survive. This can be represented linearly (a). If another parameter, such as humidity, is added, the niche may be represented by an *area* (b). If a further parameter (nutrients) is added, the niche is represented by a *volume* (c).

Space	Time			
	Constant	Predictably seasonal	Unpredictable	Ephemeral
Continuous	H	H	H	UH
Patchy	H	H	H	H
Isolated	H	H	H	UH

H = habitable   UH = uninhabitable

All necessary parameters of the physical environment, together with resources, can be added until the niche is represented by a model said to be of '*n-dimensional*' *hypervolume*. This model represents the *fundamental niche* of a particular species.

Theoretically, if a habitat has all the necessary conditions, then the particular species could occur. However, two further points must be considered. Firstly, can the habitat be colonised or is it too remote? Secondly, the species in question will not exist in isolation but will be affected by the presence of other species. These may restrict its niche by competition and predation. Thus the fundamental niche for a particular species is not the same as its *realised niche*.

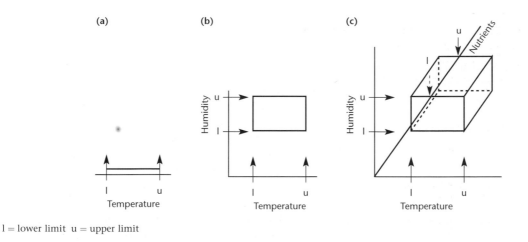

(a)   (b)   (c)

l = lower limit   u = upper limit

usually the ones which are taken preferentially (Figure 8.1).

What effect do predators have on prey populations (and vice versa)? Little is known about the predator–prey relationship in nature since it is obscured by the influence of many other environmental factors (Chapter 7, Section 7.2.3). However, some studies have shown that the accidental or deliberate introduction of predators has significantly affected the abundance of their prey populations in the field. For example, the sea lamprey

(*Petromyzon marinus*), a marine species which migrates into fresh water to spawn, invaded the Great Lakes in North America in the early 1920s. Within the space of only 20 years, this voracious predator had virtually eliminated the lake trout population.

The interaction between predator and prey populations fuels a coevolutionary race. Since the prey individuals taken tend to be those unable to reproduce, the breeding potential of prey populations is not usually significantly

Mini Case Study

8.2 The coexistence of closely related species

In a number of field studies, closely related species, often of birds, have been observed to coexist. Usually, subtle differences between the niche requirements of the individual species concerned enable them to occupy the same habitat.

In a classic study of coexistence, MacArthur (1958)[1] observed five insectivorous species of the warbler genus *Dendroica*. These small birds inhabit the tree canopy of coniferous forests in New England, USA. MacArthur documented small differences between the five *Dendroica* species in terms of their feeding positions, the way in which they fed and their nesting times.

MacArthur ascribed the coexistence of the bay-breasted warbler (*D. castanea*), the black-throated green warbler (*D. virens*) and the blackburnian warbler (*D. fusca*) to observed differences in their feeding zones within the tree canopy. The fourth species, the Cape May warbler (*D. tigrina*), fluctuated in abundance in association with occasional outbreaks of insects, whilst the fifth, the myrtle warbler (*D. coronata*), was more of a generalist and less common than the other species.

[1] MacArthur, R. H. (1958) Population ecology of some warblers of northeastern coniferous forests. *Ecology*, **39**, 599–619.

reduced by predation. Through the process of natural selection (Section 8.2), predators are selected for their ability to hunt whilst prey are selected for their ability to avoid predation. Prey species may reduce their vulnerability to predation by using refuges, by living in groups or by aposematic coloration (Box 8.3).

8.1.3 Parasitism

A **parasite** is an organism which obtains its nutrients from another organism, known as the **host**. The host organism derives no benefit from this relationship (Table 8.1).

The degree of intimacy between a parasite and its host varies widely. A mosquito such as *Anopheles gambiae* is an example of an external or **ectoparasite**. From time to time, it locates a human host and takes a blood meal, with little damage to the host. However, the mosquito itself may be infected with the malarial parasite *Plasmodium*, which enters the vertebrate host's bloodstream as the female mosquito feeds. This protozoan is an internal or **endoparasite**. It lives permanently in the host's tissue, causing considerable damage and often death. Figure 8.2 illustrates the life-cycle of *Plasmodium vivax*. A parasite which causes disease is known as a **pathogen**.

Figure **8.1** Age distribution of adult moose (*Alces alces*) killed by timber wolves (*Canis lupus*) on Isle Royale, Lake Superior, 1958–74 (from Peterson, R. O. (1977) Wolf ecology and prey relationships on Isle Royale. *US National Park Service Scientific Monographs*, Series II, US Department of the Interior, National Park Service).

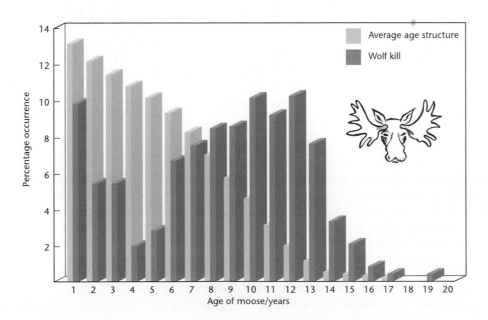

Mini Case Study

8.3 Prey defence by aposematic coloration in the monarch butterfly

The monarch butterfly (*Danaus plexippus*) uses **aposematic** or 'warning' coloration as a form of prey defence. Its bright colours and bold patterns warn potential predators that it is poisonous to eat and therefore best left well alone.

The poison present in the monarch butterfly is obtained in the caterpillar stage from its food plant, milkweed (*Asclepias curassavica*). This plant contains cardiac glycosides which affect the vertebrate heartbeat and are therefore poisonous to mammals and birds, for example. However, the caterpillar of the monarch butterfly is able to feed on these poisonous milkweeds with no ill effects. The cardiac glycosides obtained are stored and passed on to the adult butterfly stage.

Insect-eating birds, for example blue jays (*Cyanocitta cristata*), quickly learn that such monarch butterflies are distasteful and avoid them after a single unpleasant experience. Experiments have shown that monarch butterflies raised on cabbage are eaten by blue jays with no ill effects. However, those raised on poisonous milkweeds cause the birds to vomit violently and to subsequently reject all monarch butterflies.

It is interesting to observe that not all milkweed species contain cardiac glycosides and therefore not all monarch butterflies are poisonous. These edible monarchs benefit from the association of their aposematic coloration with distastefulness acquired by those insect-eating birds which have experienced a noxious monarch butterfly. The monarch butterfly is also mimicked by other species which are themselves palatable, for example the viceroy butterfly (*Limenitis archippus archippus* Cram). This is an example of **Batesian mimicry**.

Reference: Brower, L. P. (1969) Ecological chemistry. *Scientific American*, **220**(2), 22–29.

Figure 8.2 Life cycle of the malarial parasite *Plasmodium vivax*.

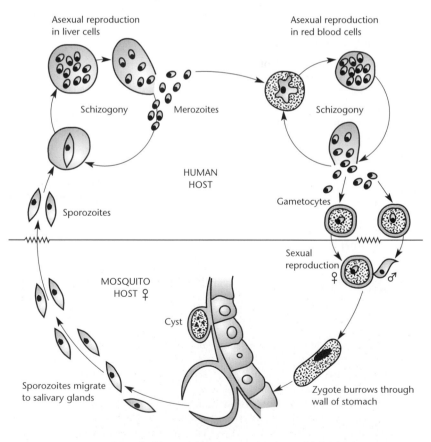

The example given above is also an illustration of **vector transmission**. The mosquito acts as an agent or vector spreading the malarial parasite between final hosts. In some cases, direct transmission occurs between host organisms. The spread of parasites in a host population depends on many factors, including the density of both. This has important implications for the monoculture of crops (Chapter 11, Section 11.3.3).

In parasitism, as in predation (Section 8.1.2), the parasite and its host tend to evolve together (coevolve). Through the process of natural selection (Section 8.2), parasites best able to locate and exploit potential hosts are favoured. Concomitantly, potential hosts best able to avoid or resist attack are those which tend to survive. Parasites, including insect parasitoids (which kill their hosts), are used as agents of biological control (Box 11.2, page 249).

8.1.4 Mutualism

The term **mutualism** is usually reserved for symbiotic relationships where there is evidence of mutual benefit to both participants (Table 8.1). The benefits accrued usually involve help in obtaining food or avoiding predation.

Mutualism is a very widespread phenomenon which encompasses many important relationships. Examples include the alga/fungus association in lichens (Box 8.4), the **mycorrhizal association** between fungi and the roots of higher plants (Box 8.5), the nitrogen-fixing bacteria found in leguminous plants (Chapter 9, Section 9.2.3) and the cellulose-digesting microbes found in the stomachs of ruminants (Chapter 9, Box 9.6).

8.1.5 Commensalism

Commensalism describes the symbiotic relationship between two organisms which is beneficial to one (known as the commensal) whilst the other is relatively unaffected

(Table 8.1). The association between the sharksucker fish (*Remora remora*) and sharks is an example of commensalism. The sharksucker fish, the commensal, is dependent on the shark for food scraps. Its dorsal fin is modified to form a suction pad which it uses to cling onto the belly of the shark. For its part, the shark is relatively unaffected by the presence of the sharksucker fish, except for a slight loss in streamlining.

8.2 Natural selection

The theory of natural selection was put forward by Charles Darwin (1809–82) in his book 'On the Origin of Species by Natural Selection', published in 1859. This theory suggests a mechanism by which species can adapt to changes in their environment. It has also been proposed that, under certain circumstances, natural selection can lead to the production of new species (**speciation**). However, the role of natural selection in the process of *evolution* has recently been challenged and the interested reader is referred to S. J. Gould's collection of essays on the subject in Section 8.7, Further reading.

8.2.1 The mechanism of natural selection

The key points which underlie the proposed mechanism of natural selection may be listed as follows:

1 The reproductive potential of populations is very high and many offspring are produced.
2 However, population sizes tend to remain constant because many offspring die before reaching maturity ('survival of the fittest').
3 Individuals in a population vary and much of this variation has a genetic basis (Chapter 6, Section 6.7).
4 Many traits of individuals can therefore be inherited by their offspring (Chapter 6, Section 6.8).

Further Information Box

8.4 Lichens

Lichens are dual organisms. They consist of fungal hyphae and photosynthetic algal cells in such close association that they behave as one organism. This relationship is a good example of mutualism, whereby both participants benefit. The fungal component provides structural support and absorbs water and minerals. The alga provides organic food materials, which it manufactures by photosynthesis.

This intimate association enables lichens to colonise inhospitable environments where neither organism on its own could survive. They are **pioneer organisms**, able to colonise newly created habitats such as cooled volcanic lava. Lichens are, therefore, very important in the initial stages of primary succession. They reproduce asexually; tiny fragments containing undifferentiated fungal and algal cells break off and are dispersed by the wind. In this way, lichens spread to colonise new habitats.

Further Information Box

8.5 Mycorrhizal associations

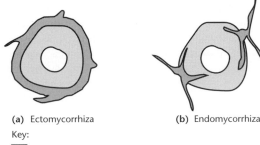

(a) Ectomycorrhiza   **(b)** Endomycorrhiza

Key:

▨ Mycorrhizal material

▨ Root cortex

☐ Vascular tissue of plant root

The mutualistic association between fungi and plant roots is known as **mycorrhiza** (literally 'fungus root'). There are many different types of mycorrhizal association but they are usually classified into those which form a sheath around the plant roots, known as ectomycorrhizae (a), and those where the fungal hyphae actually penetrate the root tissue, known as endomycorrhizae (b).

Ectomycorrhizae are widespread, especially amongst trees such as conifers, beech (*Fagus* spp.) and oak (*Quercus* spp.). They usually involve basidiomycete or ascomycete fungi. Their presence greatly increases the uptake of nutrients by the trees. This may be of particular importance where soils are poor and nitrogen-deficient. The advantage to the fungi of this association appears to be the derivation of carbohydrates and vitamins from the tree roots. Endomycorrhizae occur in a larger variety of plants but less is known about them.

5 Favourable traits (i.e. those which enhance the chances of survival) will be selected for, since individuals possessing them will be more likely to reach reproductive maturity and produce offspring.

6 The genetic composition of populations changes over time, refining the adaptation of organisms to their environments.

Central to this theory of natural selection is the notion of 'individual fitness'. **Fitness** is a measure of the contribution which individuals make to the genetic make-up of future generations. Individuals which are well adapted to their environments are those which will be more likely to survive and reproduce. The genotypic traits which favour their survival over other members of the population will be passed on to their progeny. 'Less fit' individuals will be less successful and tend to die before attaining reproductive maturity. In this way, less suitable traits are eliminated from the population whilst traits favourable to survival come to predominate in the gene pool.

8.2.2   Selection pressures

There are a variety of factors, both abiotic and biotic, which may act as selection pressures on populations of organisms. Abiotic factors include the physical and chemical environment of plants and animals. Biotic factors are the interactions which take place between the organisms themselves, such as predation, competition and parasitism (Section 8.1). Box 8.6 illustrates the effect of predation on the peppered moth (*Biston betularia*).

There are three types of selection which are recognised (Figure 8.3). In **directional selection**, phenotypes at one extreme are selected for. This type of selection is thought to operate in many predator–prey relationships. Thus, in the case of the impala (*Aepyceros mel-ampus*) and the cheetah (*Acinonyx jubatus*), fleetness of foot is selected for in both. The impala must run fast to escape whilst the cheetah must run even faster in order to capture its prey. This is an example of coevolution where two interacting species have a reciprocal selective effect.

Directional selection produces genotypic change more quickly than the other types. Therefore, it is the type most frequently used in artificial selection. Applied over many generations, artificial selection can enhance attributes deemed desirable by humans, for example a high oil content in maize (*Zea mays*) and increased yields in paddy rice (*Oryza sativa*).

Stabilising selection is very common in natural populations. In this type of selection, phenotypic characteristics at both extremes of a continuum are selected against and so the mean value of the phenotypic trait tends to remain fairly constant in the population. This is best illustrated by example.

In many species of plants, flowers tend to be produced at a particular time of the year when the likelihood of pollination by bees is high. Since bees collect nectar preferentially from flowers whose density is high, flowers of a particular species which bloom too early or too late are selected against. Thus the bees are acting as a selective pressure favouring synchrony of flowering within species.

The third type of selection is known as **disruptive selection**, where extreme phenotypes are actually favoured over intermediates. If the two extreme phenotypes become

Mini Case Study

8.6 The peppered moth

The normal form of the peppered moth (*Biston betularia*) has speckled grey-white wings. This coloration provides effective camouflage for the moth when it rests during the day against lichen-covered trees. Such markings are referred to as **cryptic coloration**.

In 1848, a single specimen of a black or melanic form of peppered moth was captured near Manchester. By 1895, 98% of the peppered moths found in Manchester were of this melanic type. Against the soot-blackened trees of heavily polluted industrial areas the black form provided better camouflage. This phenomenon is known as **industrial melanism** and is shared by other moths and insects.

Breeding experiments showed that melanism is an inheritable Mendelian trait controlled by a dominant mutant gene. Starting in the early 1950s, H. B. D. Kettlewell and his co-workers investigated the role of natural selection in the spread of this gene in populations of peppered moths.

For his field studies, he chose two sites: a heavily polluted woodland in Rubery, Birmingham, and an unpolluted woodland (Dead End Wood) in rural Dorset. Using the mark–release–recapture method, Kettlewell recaptured a higher percentage of the black melanic form in the polluted woodland (27.5%) compared with the normal light form (13.1%). However, in the unpolluted woodland, more of the light form were recaptured (12.5%) compared with the dark melanic form (6.3%). This reversal in the relative rates of recapture reflects the differential rates of survival of the two forms of peppered moth in the two different situations.

Direct observation revealed that predation by insectivorous birds, including robins (*Erithacus rubecula*) and song thrushes (*Turdus philomelos*), was responsible for the differential survival rates. In unpolluted woods, 164 melanic moths were taken compared with only 26 light ones. In polluted woods, birds were observed to take 43 light moths and only 15 black ones. In this instance, predation is acting as an agent for natural selection.

Reference: Kettlewell, H. B. D. (1968) Industrial melanism in moths and its contribution to our knowledge of evolution. *Proceedings of the Royal Institution of Great Britain*, **36**, 616–35.

Figure 8.3 Three types of selection.

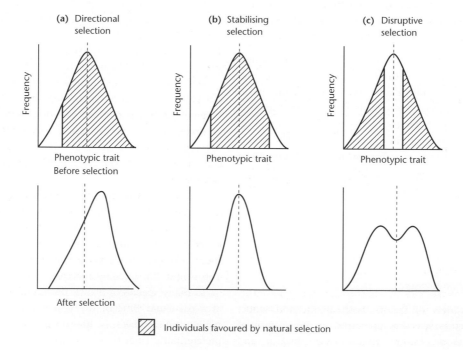

reproductively isolated, then disruptive selection can form the basis for speciation (Section 8.2.3).

Natural selection results in the adaptation of organisms. However, it can only operate on the phenotypes available and therefore fitness is only relative.

8.2.3 Speciation

A **species** may be best defined as a group of populations capable of interbreeding with each other but reproductively isolated from other groups. If two similar types of organism do not interbreed in nature (as opposed to captivity) or the resultant offspring are sterile, then, in accordance with the definition above, they do not belong to the same species. **Speciation** is the term given to the process which gives rise to new species. This may occur in a number of different circumstances.

Speciation which occurs as a result of geographic isolation is known as **allopatric speciation.** Initially, two (or more) populations of the same species become physically separated from each other and therefore reproductively isolated. In time, these populations evolve independently to become adapted to their own separate habitats. If these populations are incapable of interbreeding should they come into contact again, then the process of speciation may be regarded as complete.

One example of this type of speciation concerns the desert pupfish (*Cyprinodon* spp.), which inhabits the hot springs of California's Death Valley. During the last Ice Age, these springs were interconnected, but since then the aquatic passages have dried up, leaving populations of the pupfish isolated from each other. This has resulted in the evolution of four separate species.

Another type of speciation is **parapatric speciation.** This occurs between populations of the same species found in adjacent areas. It may occur, for example, when a population of a widespread species exploits a new habitat. It is not the same as allopatric speciation as no physical barrier exists to impede the exchange of genes between the two populations.

The third and final type of speciation is known as **sympatric speciation**. This occurs without any geographical isolation. Within a population occupying the same place, two or more groups become reproductively isolated from each other. However, this type of speciation is very rare in nature.

In summary, it may be said that, of the three types of speciation distinguished above, allopatric speciation is by far the most widespread.

8.3   Species richness

Species richness refers to the *number* of species present in a particular community. However, this measure does not take into account the *relative abundance* of the individual species present. In other words, it gives the same weighting to rare species as it does to those which are common. **Species diversity** takes both species richness and the relative abundance of the constituent species into account. The species composition of a particular community can be described when the identities of all its constituent species are known.

8.3.1   Patterns in species richness

There are several distinct patterns of species richness which have been identified. Probably the most well known of these trends is the increase in species richness from the poles to the tropics, which has been recognised for over a century. A similar trend of increasing species richness accompanies the process of ecological succession (Section 8.4). One further example involves island communities. Islands which are remote or small have, for some taxonomic groups, fewer species than those which border continents or have a larger area.

8.3.2   The factors which govern species richness

The existence of major patterns of species richness is widely accepted. However, explaining why such patterns should exist is fraught with difficulties. There are a number of factors which, in different combinations, could be influential in determining these patterns of species richness. However, correlation does not necessarily imply a causal relationship.

In this section, the factors deemed to be important in determining patterns of species richness will be examined in turn. Reference will be made mainly to the enormous number of species which exist at the tropics compared with temperate and polar regions.

Productivity

The level of terrestrial primary productivity (Chapter 9, Section 9.2.2) is greatest at the tropics and generally decreases towards the poles. This decrease is caused by climatic factors, i.e. decreases in average temperature, amount of available light and length of growing season, as latitude increases.

This broad pattern is interrupted locally where areas of high altitude (mountain ranges) and high aridity (desert regions) decrease productivity. Other exceptions occur where areas of high productivity support few animal species, for example salt marshes. In such instances, other factors must be more important in determining species richness, for example lack of structural heterogeneity in the case of salt marshes.

Could increased primary productivity be responsible for the huge numbers of species observed at the tropics? Evidence is mixed and inconclusive, especially if increased productivity simply means more of the same. However, if it means a widening of the range of resources available, then new species could conceivably be supported in such a situation, thus increasing species richness (Figure 8.4).

Figure 8.4 Species accommodation along a resource continuum.

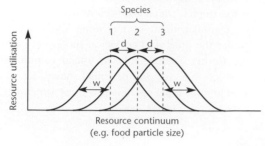

(a) Broad niches with a large overlap (i.e. d < w); interspecific competition is relatively intense

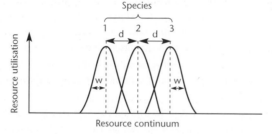

(b) Narrow niches with a little overlap (i.e. d > w); increasing specialisation reduces interspecific competition

d = distance between peaks of adjacent curves
w = standard deviation of the curves

Figure 8.5 The relationship between bird species richness and the structural diversity of vegetation in mediterranean-type habitats (from Cody, 1975).

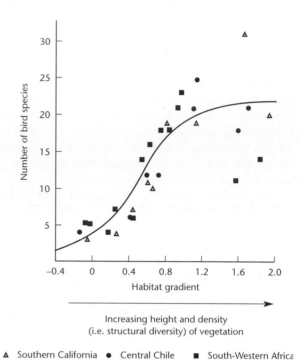

Increasing height and density
(i.e. structural diversity) of vegetation

△ Southern California   ● Central Chile   ■ South-Western Africa

Spatial heterogeneity

Spatial heterogeneity describes the complexity of a habitat. In the case of plants, species richness may be related to the number of different soil types present and the topographical variation of the habitat. For animals, it is the structural diversity of the plant species themselves which is important, rather than the number of plant species present. Many studies have shown a correlation between the number of animal species present and the structural diversity of the vegetation present (Figure 8.5).

Increased spatial heterogeneity, i.e. patchiness of the habitat in terms of resources, effectively increases the number of niches (Box 8.1) available and thus promotes species richness. The range of resources is increased, allowing new species to be accommodated.

Time-scale

One theory for the increased species richness in plants and animals in the tropics is the time hypothesis. The tropics have existed without major perturbations longer than the temperate and arctic regions, which have been subjected to periods of glaciation. The last Ice Age ended about 10 000 years ago and it is thought that affected regions are

still recovering. Plants and animals have had a much longer uninterrupted period of time in which to evolve and speciate in the tropics.

In addition, rapid evolution is favoured in the tropics. Climatic conditions favour an increased number of generations per year and the sedentary nature of populations in the tropics restricts gene flow and promotes genetic differentiation between sub-populations. The importance of the time factor in increasing species richness is supported by the results from studies of Lake Baikal in Siberia (Box 8.7).

Environmental stability

Another factor, closely linked to the time factor, is that of environmental stability. The tropics are perceived to be areas of high environmental stability. There is no seasonality as experienced by temperate and arctic regions. Temperature and day length are constant, though rainfall can be erratic. This constancy allows animals to 'fine-tune' to their environment, to become increasingly specialised through adaptation (Section 8.2), thus allowing more species to be accommodated along the resource continuum (Figure 8.4).

The ocean floor also represents a stable environment which has existed over a long time-span. Bottom samples reveal a surprisingly high number of species in some

8.7   The time factor and species richness in Lake Baikal

Lake Baikal in Siberia is an example of a very ancient lake which existed before the end of the Tertiary period (2 million years ago). Only a few lakes have such ancient origins; the majority of lakes originated much more recently, in the Pleistocene, which ended 10 000 years ago.

Lake Baikal has a remarkably rich fauna. In its deep waters, 580 species of benthic (bottom-living) invertebrates have been recorded. In contrast, another temperate lake, the Great Slave Lake in northern Canada, has only four species of benthic invertebrates. This lake was formed after the last Ice Age and is therefore much younger than Lake Baikal.

Lake Baikal is a vast lake (33 000 square km) and a very deep one (1522 m). In the last Ice Age, only its surface waters froze, leaving its deeper layers relatively unaffected by glaciation. In this region of the lake at least, time has had the opportunity to play an important role in generating the large number of benthic species observed in Lake Baikal today.

benthic invertebrate groups. These results support the time-stability explanation of increased species richness.

Competition

Competition between species for resources is thought by many naturalists to be of greater importance in the tropics compared with temperate and polar regions, where natural selection is thought to be governed mainly by physical factors. Competition could favour a greater number of species in the tropics by either narrowing the niche breadth or increasing the niche overlap of different species (Figure 8.4). However, such predictions are very difficult to test.

Predation

Predation is thought to play an important role in increasing the species richness of a community in some situations by reducing competition. If predators reduce the populations of their prey to below the carrying capacity of the environment, then additional species, hitherto excluded, may be able to coexist (Box 8.8). Such new species may in turn support their own predators.

According to this theory, predation increases species richness by reducing competition. Interestingly, this is in contrast with the hypothesis presented in the previous section whereby *increased competition* is thought to lead to an increase in species richness. The role of predators and parasites, present in greatest numbers in the tropics, in ostensibly reducing competition and thus increasing species richness is unclear.

In summary, it can be said that, in most cases, no *single* factor can be identified as the sole explanation for the high level of species richness observed in particular situations. A combination of all of the six factors outlined above probably operates to produce the enormous number of plant and animal species which exist in the tropics.

8.8   The effect of predation on the species richness of a community

The starfish *Pisaster ochraceus* is a top predator in the intertidal rocky-shore communities of the North American Pacific coast. In his pioneering work, Paine (1966)[1] studied its influence on community structure by removal experiments.

P. ochraceus feeds mainly on sessile, filterfeeding barnacles and mussels. In its presence, a total of 15 species of invertebrates and macroscopic algae usually occurred together in these rocky-shore communities. However, removal of the starfish led to a dramatic change in community structure. The number of species present dropped to only eight and the community became dominated by the mussel *Mytilus californianus*.

This is an example of predation increasing the species richness of a community. In this case, the different species compete for space on the rocks to attach themselves. *M. californianus*, however, is the dominant competitor. Without predation by *P. ochraceus* to cut tracts in the mussel beds and allow other species to obtain suitable attachment sites, *M. californianus* monopolises the available space.

In the presence of *P. ochraceus*, *M. californianus* is not eradicated because individuals become too large to be eaten by the starfish. A species, like *P. ochraceus*, which determines community structure is known as a **keystone species**.

[1] Paine, R. T. (1966) Food web complexity and species diversity. *American Naturalist*, **100**, 65–75.

8.4   Ecological succession

Ecological succession is the change over time of biological communities until a stable, climax community is reached. Each discrete transitional stage is known as a **seral stage** and the entire process in a particular habitat is known as a **sere**. Succession occurs in newly created habitats (primary succession) and in situations where there has been an abrupt removal of the existing vegetation, either by natural disasters or by human activities (secondary succession).

8.4.1   Primary succession

The process of **primary succession** is initiated when new uncolonised habitats are created, either through human activities or by natural phenomena. Such habitats have little or no soil and contain no reserves of seeds or spores. Examples of primary succession may be found when mining creates waste heaps, when sand dunes are formed and when volcanoes spew out molten lava which then cools. Box 8.9 describes the process of primary succession on the volcanic islands of Krakatau in Indonesia and Surtsey near Iceland.

Such newly created habitats are characterised by a lack of soil (Chapter 3, Section 3.2). Only a very few organisms are able to grow without soil, namely bacteria and lichens (Plate 5). These are able to survive by utilising nutrients which have dissolved out of the rock itself, together with nutrients available in the rainwater. Lichens are in fact dual organisms consisting of an alga and a fungus in intimate association (Box 8.4).

As time progresses, small weathered fragments of rock accumulate in tiny crevices. Together with wind-blown dust and dead organic matter from the lichens themselves, this provides a new type of substrate where mosses and ferns can take hold. These eliminate the lichens and dominate the next seral stage in the successional process.

The mosses break up the rock surface further and themselves add organic material when they die. Eventually the seeds of small rooted plants are able to germinate and become established, eliminating the mosses. This process, whereby each seral stage is replaced by another, usually proceeds until a mature climax community, often dominated by deciduous trees, is reached. This process may take hundreds of years to complete. The mechanisms underlying succession are examined in Section 8.4.3.

8.4.2   Secondary succession

Secondary succession occurs when the existing vegetation is abruptly removed. This can be caused by natural disasters or by human activities such as deforestation and strip mining (Chapter 11, Section 11.5.1, and Chapter 12, Section 12.4.1 respectively). Whatever the cause, the net result is the same. The mature biological community is replaced by an earlier successional stage and the process of secondary succession begins.

The main distinction between this type of succession and primary succession is that soil, containing organic matter (and often some seeds and spores), is already present. The eventual recovery of devastated habitats depends on the availability of surviving patches of the original habitat, which will act as a reservoir of plants, seeds and animals. Box 8.10 examines the process of secondary succession in the Old Fields of North Carolina, USA.

Mini Case Study

8.9   Primary succession on volcanic islands: Krakatau and Surtsey

In 1883, the volcanic island of Krakatau in what is now Indonesia erupted. All life on the island was destroyed. The nearest sources of recolonising flora were neighbouring islands, 19 and 40 km distant.

In its first year after the eruption, Krakatau remained barren. Then blue-green algae and mosses started to colonise the laval rocks. After three years, some higher plants became established. These were mainly ferns, spread by spores, and flowering plants belonging to the beach flora. After 50 years, Krakatau was covered by forest. Colonisation of Krakatau was initially by seeds and spores spread by the wind and ocean currents. Later, they were introduced by birds and finally by man.

The eruption of the volcanic island of Surtsey, near Iceland, in 1965–66, provided a more recent opportunity to study the process of recolonisation and primary succession on bare volcanic rock. The nearest potential source for recolonisation was a small island, 5.5 km distant from Surtsey.

By 1968, over 100 species of algae were recorded on Surtsey. One of these, *Mastigocladus laminosus*, must have come from Iceland, 75 km away. The first lichens were found in 1970. However, the most important pioneers were the mosses, which thrived in the cool, moist climate. The first moss was found in 1967, and by 1972, 63 species had been recorded, of which 12 were common. In 1971, the first fern, *Cystopteris fragilis*, was found, together with four species of flowering plants belonging to the beach flora. Around this time, species of insects, migratory birds and shore birds were also recorded.

Mini Case Study

8.10   Secondary succession in the 'Old Fields' of North Carolina, USA

In the nineteenth century, the opening up of the frontier led many of the farmers of North Carolina to abandon their farms and move west. Since the date of abandonment is recorded in many instances, these so-called 'Old Fields' have provided an excellent opportunity to study the process of secondary succession.

The first stage in this succession is usually dominated by horseweed (*Erigeron canadensis*), which germinates immediately and overwinters as a rosette plant. As it is an annual, it dies the next summer after blooming. In the second year after the field's last cultivation, the perennial aster (*Aster pilosus*) outcompetes the horseweed and dominates the next seral stage. The aster itself is then outcompeted in the third year by the drought-resistant perennial broomsedge (*Andropogon virginicus*). These early stages in 'old field' succession occur very rapidly. They are governed by competition and are therefore a

good example of the inhibition mechanism of succession (Section 8.4.3).

In the next successional stage, the abandoned farmland is invaded by large numbers of shortleaf pine (*Pinus echinata*). Their seeds are able to germinate in bare soil. This seral stage lasts for about 20 years until the accumulation of pine litter changes the soil in such a way as to facilitate the germination of oak seedlings. This part of the succession seems to fit best with the classical mechanism of succession (Section 8.4.3).

Hardwoods such as oaks (*Quercus* spp.) and hickories (*Carya* spp.) make up the final or climax community in this example of secondary succession. To reach this final stage takes between 50 and 150 years.

Reference: Krebs, C. J. (1994) *Ecology: The experimental analysis of distribution and abundance* (4th edn). London: Harper Collins, Chapter 22.

The plants which initially colonise the denuded habitat are typically annuals. These are characterised by high numbers of light wind-borne seeds which disperse effectively to colonise such habitats (Table 8.2). They are tolerant of full sunlight and grow rapidly. Such plants are known as **pioneer** or **fugitive species**. These are replaced by herbaceous perennial plants, which in turn given way to seral stages dominated by shrubs, then pines and finally deciduous trees.

In the two types of succession examined to date, the process of succession has been driven by changes wrought within the successive biological communities by the organisms themselves. These are examples of **autogenic succession**. Sometimes, the process of succession is caused by factors external to the community in question and this is known as **allogenic succession**.

For example, a lake can undergo allogenic succession when rivers, laden with silt, deposit material in the lake. This causes the lake to eventually change into a marsh or bog. The marsh itself becomes a terrestrial habitat in time (Figure 8.6). This particular example of allogenic succession can be inadvertently speeded up by human activities. Deforestation is one cause of soil erosion which results in an increased silt-load of the rivers feeding the lake.

A similar type of succession can be stimulated when large amounts of phosphates from agricultural sources and domestic sewage effluent enter the lake via rivers and surface run-off (Chapter 14, Section 14.2). As a result, vegetative growth is significantly increased. The build-up of dead organic debris gradually fills in the lake from the margins to the centre and again the lake eventually becomes solid land.

Table 8.2 Some characteristics of plants typical of early and late successional stages.

Characteristic	Early stage	Late stage
Seeds produced:		
number	many	few
size	small	large
Seed dispersal:		
agent	wind	animals
dispersion	good	poor
Rate of growth	rapid	slow
Eventual size	small	large
Shade tolerance	poor	good
Type of competitor	poor	good

8.4.3   The mechanisms of succession

There are three theories concerning the mechanisms which underlie and propel succession (Figure 8.7). The classical explanation for the process of succession is known as the **facilitation theory**. In this hypothesis, species replacement occurs because existing species modify their habitat making it less suitable for themselves. The environment so modified favours other species which then outcompete and replace the existing plants. Thus succession proceeds in a predictable, orderly manner until the final climax community is reached.

The second theory is the **inhibition theory**. In this theory, which species succeed in establishing themselves

Figure 8.6 Allogenic succession: from lake to land.

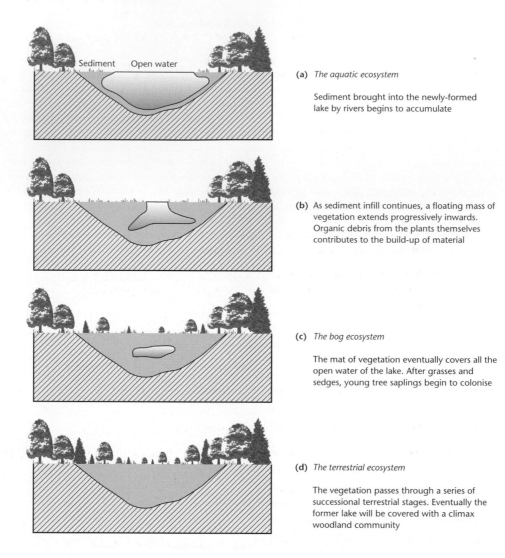

(a) *The aquatic ecosystem*

Sediment brought into the newly-formed lake by rivers begins to accumulate

(b) As sediment infill continues, a floating mass of vegetation extends progressively inwards. Organic debris from the plants themselves contributes to the build-up of material

(c) *The bog ecosystem*

The mat of vegetation eventually covers all the open water of the lake. After grasses and sedges, young tree saplings begin to colonise

(d) *The terrestrial ecosystem*

The vegetation passes through a series of successional terrestrial stages. Eventually the former lake will be covered with a climax woodland community

depends entirely on which arrives first. No one species is competitively superior to another. Succession does not proceed in an orderly manner. Short-lived species are eventually replaced by longer-lived species.

The final model is known as the **tolerance model** and may be viewed as intermediate between the other two. In this model, any species can colonise initially but some are competitively superior and come to dominate the mature community.

<table>
<tr><td>8.4.4</td><td>Characteristics of plants of early and late successional stages</td></tr>
</table>

Table 8.2 has illustrated the main features of plant species which characterise early and late successional stages. These represent two extremes of a continuum of characteristics. It can be readily seen that the plant species are adapted to very different situations.

The pioneer plants are efficient colonisers which are able to utilise harsh physical habitats. They grow rapidly and produce large quantities of light seeds which are wind-dispersed. They are poor competitors and shade-intolerant.

Plant species characteristic of mature communities are adapted to competition. The average height of plant species tends to increase as succession proceeds because of competition for the light needed for photosynthesis. Species richness (Section 8.3) tends to increase with each seral stage, although it often falls off slightly in the climax community. Interspecific competition replaces the intraspecific competition characteristic of the earlier stages of succession.

Figure 8.7 Three models of succession (from Horn, 1981). A, B, C and D represent four species; the arrows mean 'is replaced by'.

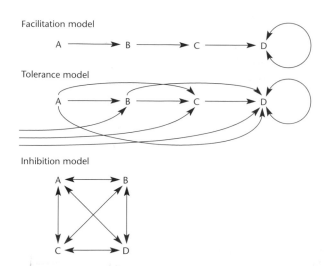

Facilitation model

Tolerance model

Inhibition model

Most studies of ecological succession concentrate on the plant communities present since their make-up determines to a great extent the composition of the animal community which they support.

8.4.5   The concept of the climax state

In the discussion to date, the climax community or state has been repeatedly referred to. How do we identify when this 'final' stage has been reached? The answer could be when the rate of change is so slow as to be imperceptible to man. However, care should be taken with this definition as the process of succession usually occurs over hundreds of years whilst the average life-span of humans is about 70 years.

The key here is the *persistence* of the community, which is self-perpetuating in its composition. However, gradual changes will still occur even in communities thought to be in the climax state as they follow climatic fluctuations. In addition, micro-successions will occur within communities, for example when a tree falls to the ground, giving even a stable community a mosaic pattern. Therefore, the climax community in any absolute sense is probably regarded as a useful but essentially abstract concept.

It used to be thought that climate was the sole determinant of the composition of the climax community. Therefore, in a particular climatic zone, every sere would eventually end up as the climax state characteristic of that region. This was known as the **monoclimax theory.**

This theory has been superseded by the **polyclimax theory**. This states that whilst climate is the major determinant, there are a number of possible climax states depending on local conditions of topography, soil conditions and animal activity.

In some habitats, the expected climax community is never achieved due to the periodic interruption of some natural disturbance, for example fire. The plant species able to withstand fire come to dominate the community because fire eliminates potential competitors. Examples of these so-called 'fire-maintained' communities are the pine forests of the southern and western United States. These should be regarded as climax communities even if they do appear as transitional stages elsewhere.

In some instances, natural succession is halted or perturbed by the selective grazing of herbivores. A striking example of this occurred in the 1950s in Great Britain when the introduction of the virus myxoma (a relative of smallpox) devastated the population of the European rabbit (*Oryctolagus cuniculus*). This resulted in a dramatic increase in the number of flowering plants, and shrub and tree seedlings.

8.5   Summary

Biological communities are made up of different species which occur together, in variable proportions, in time and space. Individual species within a community do not exist in isolation. They interact with each other in a number of different ways, for example through competition and predation. Biological communities are not static entities. They change in composition as environmental conditions alter. This change is mediated through the process of natural selection. This process shapes the populations which make up the community by operating on the individuals of each constituent species.

The number of species present in a community (i.e. its species richness) varies. A number of distinctive trends of increasing species richness have been identified, for example from the poles to the tropics. Another such trend accompanies ecological succession, a process often initiated as a result of human activities. Ecological succession may occur when new habitats are created (primary succession) or when the existing vegetation of a habitat is abruptly removed (secondary succession). The successional process involves a series of transitional biological communities before the final stage, the climax community, is reached.

8.6 Problems

1 Using the following notation:
   + = beneficial effect
   − = negative effect
   0 = little or no effect
   describe the interaction between species in the following: competition, predation, parasitism, mutualism and commensalism. Use at least two examples for each type of interaction to illustrate your answer.

2 What is meant by cryptic and aposematic coloration? How may each help prey species to avoid predation? Illustrate your answer with examples.

3 How does natural selection enable species to adapt to a changing environment? What is meant by directional and stabilising selection? Give an example of each.

4 What is meant by the terms 'species' and 'speciation'? With reference to the role of natural selection, describe how speciation may occur in populations which have become geographically isolated.

5 What is meant by 'species richness'? With reference to the pattern of species richness observed from the tropics to the poles, briefly discuss each of the factors which may influence this trend.

6 What is 'ecological succession'? Distinguish between primary and secondary succession. Give examples where human activities have instigated the successional process.

7 In ecological succession, what is meant by pioneer and climax communities? Compare and contrast the characteristics of plants typical of each stage and discuss how these attributes adapt them to their respective situations.

8.7 Further reading

Begon, M., J. L. Harper and C. R. Townsend (1996) *Ecology: individuals, populations and communities* (3rd edn). Oxford: Blackwell Science.

Gould, S. J. (1994) *Eight little piggies: reflections in natural history*. London: Penguin.

Krebs, C .J. (1993) *Ecology: the experimental analysis of distribution and abundance* (4th edn). Harlow: Addison Wesley Longman Higher Education.

Krebs, J. R. and N. B. Davies (1997) *Behavioural ecology: an evolutionary approach* (4th edn). Oxford: Blackwell Science.

Pianka, E. R. (1993) *Evolutionary ecology* (5th edn). Harlow: Addison Wesley Longman Higher Education.

Ricklefs, R. E. (1990) *Ecology* (3rd edn). New York: W. H. Freeman.

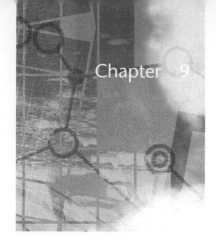

Chapter 9

Ecosystems and biomes

Chapter Objectives

After reading this chapter, you should be able to:

- Understand the concept of a food web, and appreciate how this is relevant to the environmental fate of certain toxic substances, such as DDT.

- Explain clearly the process of aerobic photosynthesis.

- Define primary productivity and outline the factors that may limit this process (in both terrestrial and aquatic ecosystems).

- Appreciate the inefficiency of energy transfer between different trophic levels and understand how this relates to energy pyramids.

- Describe the process of decomposition, with particular reference to the role played by detritivores and decomposers.

- Understand the concept of ecosystem stability and how this relates to the response of an ecosystem to perturbations (both natural and man-made).

- Outline the main characteristics (of climate, vegetation, primary productivity, etc.) of the eight terrestrial biomes featured here.

- Compare and contrast the marine and freshwater biomes.

Introduction

The term **ecosystem** is an abbreviated form of 'ecological system'. Ecosystems consist of organisms (biotic/'living' factors), their environment (abiotic/'non-living' factors), and all the interactions which take place between them. An ecosystem is therefore a complex and dynamic system, constantly in motion. Nutrients are continually recycled within the ecosystem, whilst energy flows through it.

The boundary of an ecosystem is usually 'in the eye of the beholder'. At one extreme, the biosphere may be regarded as a global ecosystem. The land masses of the world may be divided into areas of similar climate and vegetation. These vast areas are referred to as terrestrial ecosystems or biomes. On a more localised scale, a pond or wood may be considered to be an ecosystem for the purposes of practical study.

In this chapter, the organisation of ecosystems in terms of the feeding relationships between plants and animals is established first. This is followed by a discussion of primary productivity, including the effect of limiting factors in both terrestrial and aquatic ecosystems. In Section 9.3, the flow of energy through ecosystems receives detailed attention. This is followed by a brief discussion of secondary productivity.

The role of decomposition in the recycling of nutrients within ecosystems is examined in Section 9.5 (detailed accounts of the cycling of biologically important elements are given in Chapter 5). In Section 9.6, the concept of ecosystem stability is explored. This is of particular relevance when considering the impact of human activities on the environment.

The chapter concludes with a systematic résumé of the terrestrial and aquatic biomes of the world, many of which are illustrated in the colour plate section.

9.1 Food chains and food webs

In ecosystems, the feeding relationships between animals and plants are of fundamental importance to the functioning of the system as a whole, facilitating the flow of energy and the cycling of nutrients. Very simply, plants and animals may be arranged in a hierarchy based on 'who eats whom', known as a **food chain**. This concept was first introduced in 1927 by the ecologist

Charles Elton. An example of a simple food chain is shown below:

Phytoplankton → Krill → Blue whale + other predators
(tiny, free- (small
floating plants) crustaceans)

where → denotes 'is consumed by'.

In practice, given the enormous complexity of the natural world, simple food chains like this are rare. The situation is usually very much more complex, and the myriad feeding relationships that exist between animal and plant species within an ecosystem are more accurately described by the term **food web**. Figures 9.1 and 9.2 give examples of food webs taken from actual studies on a terrestrial and an aquatic ecosystem respectively.

The interconnections between different members of the food web within a particular ecosystem mean that when one group is affected, the implications can spread throughout the ecosystem. This assumes a particular relevance when considering the fate of toxic substances released into the environment by human activities. Some environmentally persistent pollutants do not pass naturally through the bodies of animals but are taken up selectively by bone and fat tissues. Each individual consumer within a food web eats large numbers of organisms, thereby ingesting all of the toxicants that these

Figure 9.1 A simplified food web from Wytham Woods, Oxfordshire, UK (after Varley, 1970).

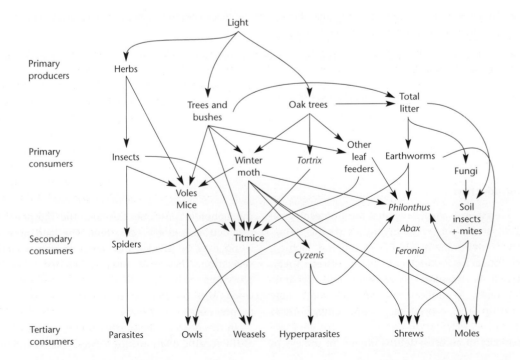

Figure 9.2 A food web from a freshwater habitat (after Popham, E. J. (1955) *Some aspects of life in fresh water*. London: William Heinemann Ltd.

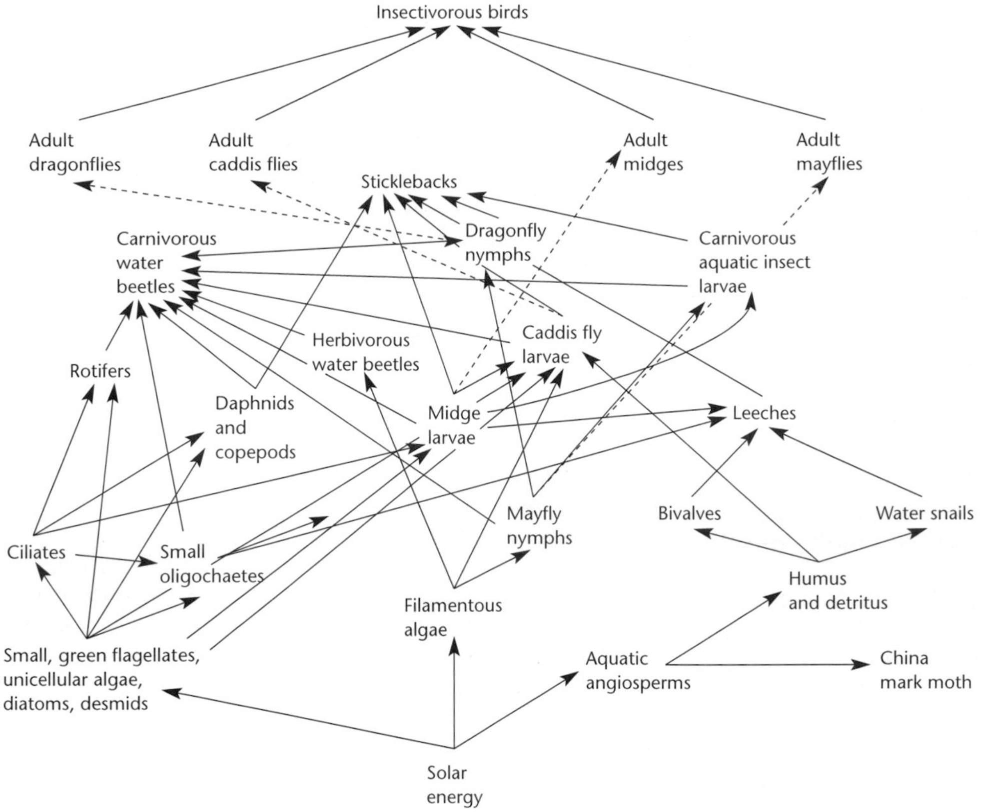

The arrows ⟶ mean 'is consumed by', thereby showing the various pathways of energy flow through the ecosystem

organisms contain. If these toxicants are not excreted or broken down, they will accumulate within the individual. In this way, the toxic substance becomes progressively more concentrated with each successive link in the food chain, reaching a peak in those predators at the top of the food web. The organochlorine pesticide DDT is just one example of a toxic substance that undergoes this process of **biomagnification** (Chapter 14, Section 14.5).

Another example that illustrates the importance of the links between the different members of the ecosystem involves the New Zealand flatworm (*Artioposthia triangularis*), which was accidentally introduced into the UK. This predator has destroyed huge numbers of earthworms (e.g. *Lumbricus terrestris*) in Scotland and Northern Ireland and is beginning to establish colonies in England. A significant decline in the earthworm population could have serious repercussions both for the various bird species that feed directly on them, and for their predators in turn. In addition, the soil structure itself could be adversely affected by the lack of earthworms.

9.1.1 Trophic levels

In order to understand the pathways for energy flow and nutrient cycling within ecosystems, ecologists have assigned groups of plants and animals to various feeding levels. These are called **trophic levels**, a term derived from the Greek *trophos*, meaning nourishment (Table 9.1).

In terrestrial ecosystems, green plants occupy the first trophic level. Plants are almost unique in their ability to harness the radiant energy of the sun to make their own food (Section 9.2.1). They are called **autotrophs** (literally 'self-feeders', Greek) and also **primary producers**. Upon their activities, the other members of the food web, the **heterotrophs** (literally 'other-feeders', Greek), are directly or indirectly dependent. In certain aquatic ecosystems, for example deep lakes and open seas, phytoplankton (microscopic floating plants, mainly algae and diatoms) fulfil the role of primary producers.

The second trophic level is occupied by the **herbivores** ('plant-eaters'), which are sometimes referred to as **primary consumers** (Table 9.1). The third trophic level is

Table 9.1 The trophic levels of food webs and equivalent terms.

Trophic level	Producer/ consumer	Autotroph/ heterotroph	Herbivore/ carnivore
First	Primary producer	Autotroph	
Second	Primary consumer	Heterotroph	Herbivore
Third	Secondary consumer	Heterotroph	Carnivore 1
Fourth	Tertiary consumer	Heterotroph	Carnivore 2

occupied by the **carnivores** ('meat-eaters'), which prey directly on the herbivores and are therefore termed **secondary consumers**. Carnivores that prey on these carnivores fill the fourth trophic level and are called **tertiary consumers**. A fifth trophic level of top carnivores may exist but this is usually the limit to the number of levels found in nature.

The concept of trophic levels is undoubtedly very useful in attempting to understand the complex organisation of food webs. However, examples of food webs found in the literature can oversimplify the situation, clumping disparate groups of animals together as 'feeding types' or ignoring the presence of parasites (organisms which feed on the tissues of other organisms) and **omnivores** ('everything-eaters').

In some instances, it is difficult to assign animals to just one trophic level. Some animals, the omnivores, take food from a variety of different sources, for example the red fox (*Vulpes vulpes*) (Box 9.1) and the grizzly bear (*Ursus americanus*) (Plate 6). In others, the type of food taken is dependent on the stage of an animal's life-cycle. The tadpoles of the common frog (*Rana temporaria*) are at first herbivorous, grazing on algae, but later become carnivorous, feeding mainly on water fleas. The adult frogs are carnivorous, feeding on slugs, worms and flies.

9.1.2 Grazer- and detritivore-based food webs

In the discussion of food webs so far, we have concentrated on those based mainly on the autotrophic production of green plants and phytoplankton. These pathways within a food web are termed **grazer** food chains. Distinct from them, but linked to them, are other types of food chains known as **decomposer** food chains (Figure 9.3). Dead organic matter in the form of plant and animal remains and faecal waste provides an alternative food source utilised by a vast array of **decomposers** (bacteria and fungi) and **detritivores** ('dead matter-eaters').

In some ecosystems, such as woodlands and shaded streams, where the autotrophic production of food by plants and the level of herbivorous grazers supported are low, dead organic matter becomes the main source of food and energy and supports a large population of detritivores and their predators. The decomposition process is vital to the functioning of the ecosystem as it facilitates the recycling of nutrients (Section 9.5).

9.2 Primary production

Primary production is the term used to describe the generation of biological material by autotrophic green plants via the process of photosynthesis. These primary producers occupy exclusively the first trophic level in grazer food webs (Table 9.1). A few plants are not autotrophs but heterotrophs. The carnivorous sundew (*Drosera* spp.), for example, feed on insects, which they trap on their sticky leaves.

Further Information Box

9.1 The feeding habits of the red fox (*Vulpes vulpes*)

The red fox (*Vulpes vulpes*) is found throughout Europe, North America and the former Soviet Union. It is a good example of an omnivore, an animal which takes its food from a variety of different sources. The table shows that it may be assigned to any one of a number of trophic levels, depending on what it is consuming at the time. The red fox can act as a scavenger, feeding on the dead bodies of animals (carrion). In this instance, it becomes part of the decomposer food chain, which is based on dead organic matter, instead of a grazer food chain based on the autotrophic production of green plants.

Trophic level	Grazer food chains		Decomposer food chain	
First	Berries	Grass	Algae	Carrion
Second	**Red fox**	Rabbits	Slugs	**Red fox**
Third		**Red fox**	Frogs	
Fourth			**Red fox**	

Figure 9.3 The link between grazer and decomposer food chains.

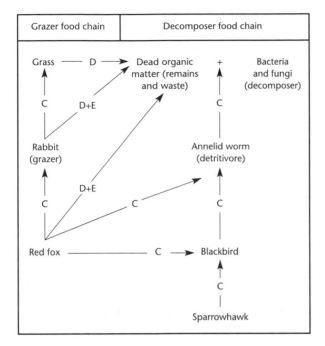

D = Death
C = Consumption
E = Egestion of faecal waste

9.2.1 The process of aerobic photosynthesis

Autotrophs are unique in their ability to use the radiant energy of the sun to convert simple inorganic molecules of carbon dioxide and water into complex organic molecules of glucose. This process is called **photosynthesis**. There are two types, namely aerobic photosynthesis and anaerobic photosynthesis. Of these, the former is more important. It is a redox reaction (Chapter 1, Section 1.6.2) and can be represented by the following chemical equation:

$$6H_2O + 6CO_2 \xrightarrow{\text{solar energy}} C_6H_{12}O_6 + 6O_2$$

water · carbon dioxide · glucose · oxygen

The photosynthetic process converts radiant energy into chemical energy. This is consistent with the first law of thermodynamics, which states that although energy cannot be created or destroyed, it can be converted from one form to another (Chapter 2, Section 2.1). This chemical energy is, in effect, stored in the glucose molecules, which may themselves be used to make other storage and structural compounds like starch and cellulose (Figure 9.4). The stored energy can be released on the oxidation of these photosynthetic products. This process is called **respiration** and the reaction may be represented thus:

Figure 9.4 The chemical structure of (a) glucose, (b) starch and (c) cellulose.

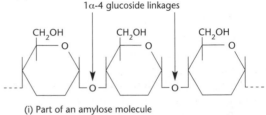

(i) α-glucose (ii) β-glucoside

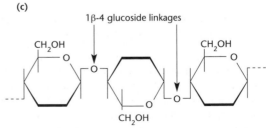

(i) Part of an amylose molecule

(ii) Part of an amylopectin molecule

(c)

Part of a cellulose molecule

9.2 The process of transpiration

Transpiration is defined as the loss of water from the leaves and other aerial parts of the plant. The water is first absorbed from the soil by the roots and then conducted through a series of continuous tubes, the xylem vessels, to the leaf veins. Most of the water is lost by evaporation from the surfaces of the leaf mesophyll cells and subsequent diffusion of the water vapour through the stomata. Only a small percentage, about 1%, is used for photosynthesis.

The upward flow of water and nutrients in the xylem vessels is caused by the suction pressure exerted by transpiration and is known as the transpiration stream. The water column can be drawn up without breaking because of the attraction between the water molecules themselves (cohesion) and the attraction between the water molecules and the sides of the capillary xylem tubes (adhesion).

Transpiration is strongly influenced by ambient atmospheric conditions; for example, high temperatures increase transpiration whilst high humidity decreases it. Transpiration can be controlled by the opening and closing of the stomatal pores.

$$C_6H_{12}O_6 + 6O_2 \longrightarrow 6CO_2 + 6H_2O$$

glucose   oxygen   carbon   water
dioxide

Photosynthesis takes place mainly in the leaves of green plants. Specialist organelles called chloroplasts are found in the leaf cells. They are responsible for the green coloration of plants and are the actual sites of photosynthetic activity, absorbing sunlight in the blue and red regions of the spectrum. A more detailed account of the role of chloroplasts in the process of photosynthesis is given in Chapter 6, Section 6.4.

The carbon dioxide needed for photosynthesis is freely available in the atmosphere and enters the leaves via special pores called stomata. It is then absorbed into the surrounding cells by diffusion. Water, the other inorganic molecule required, is absorbed from the soil by the root system and is transported to the leaves via the xylem vessels by the process of transpiration (Box 9.2).

Although the process of aerobic photosynthesis is almost universally the one used in the production of glucose, there are some minor exceptions: some groups of organisms are able to make simple sugars using alternative biochemical pathways (Box 9.3).

9.2.2 Primary productivity

We can estimate the **standing crop** of plants in a particular ecosystem by measuring their **biomass** (weight of living material) per unit area. This can be expressed in units of either energy (e.g. $J\,m^{-2}$) or dry organic matter (e.g. $kg\,m^{-2}$). However, this is a static measurement taken at a particular time. To gain a more accurate picture, it is better to estimate the rate at which new biomass is being produced per unit area. This is known as the **primary productivity** of a community and it can be expressed in units of either energy or dry organic matter per unit area per unit time. It may be used to compare the primary productivity of different ecosystems (Section 9.2.4).

The total fixation of energy by photosynthesis is called the **gross primary productivity** (GPP). However, the plant requires some of this energy for its own maintenance activities. This portion is subsequently lost to the community as respiratory heat (R). The productivity that remains is called the **net primary productivity** (NPP) and it is this that is available for consumption by the next trophic level. To summarise:

$$GPP - R = NPP$$

9.3 Photosynthetic sulfur bacteria

Members of this group of bacteria are able to produce glucose by the process of anaerobic photosynthesis. The reaction is different from that found in aerobic photosynthesis, where water is used as the reducing agent. In contrast, these bacteria use hydrogen sulfide as their source of electrons. Sulfur, and not oxygen, is produced as a by-product of this reaction. However, the process is still a photosynthetic one as sunlight is used as the energy source.

The equation for this reaction can be written thus:

$$12H_2S + 6CO_2 \xrightarrow{\text{solar energy}} C_6H_{12}O_6 + 6H_2O + 12S$$

hydrogen   carbon   glucose   water   sulfur
sulfide   dioxide

Members of the genus *Chromatium*, which belong to the group of 'purple bacteria', are examples of anaerobic photosynthetic bacteria. They occur in many lakes and are able to make use of the hydrogen sulfide present in the bottom sediments.

Tool Box

9.4   The measurement of primary productivity in aquatic habitats using the light and dark bottle technique

In aquatic habitats, primary productivity can be measured by gas exchange. The concentration of dissolved oxygen in water is typically low, therefore oxygen from photosynthesis adds significantly to the amount present. For short-term measurements of phytoplankton productivity, the light and dark bottle technique can be satisfactorily applied.

Sealed bottles containing samples of phytoplankton are suspended at the desired depth(s) in the water body for a standard period of time. In the light bottles, sunlight is admitted and photosynthesis, as well as respiration, can occur. In the dark bottles, however, light is excluded, preventing photosynthesis.

From the measurement of the level of oxygen in the light bottle, the net primary productivity can be obtained.

To summarise:

$$P_{light} - R_{light} = NPP$$

oxygen produced by photosynthesis (light bottle) — oxygen used by respiration (light bottle) = net primary productivity

By adding the amount of oxygen removed in the dark bottles to the left-hand side of the above equation, the gross primary productivity can be measured:

$$P_{light} - R_{light} + R_{dark} = GPP$$

(light bottle)   (light bottle)   (dark bottle)   gross primary productivity

---

There are a variety of techniques used for the measurement of primary productivity. Box 9.4 gives one example in some detail.

9.2.3   Factors which limit primary productivity

In order to grow and reproduce at an optimum rate, primary producers need certain physical and chemical conditions, for example of light, nutrients and temperature (Table 9.2). Should any one of these essential abiotic factors be scarce, its effect will be to limit the level of primary productivity, no matter how profuse the others

are. It becomes therefore a **limiting factor**. This concept can be illustrated using the analogy of a barrel of water. Each stave represents an abiotic factor essential to the growth and reproduction of primary producers. The level of water held in the barrel represents primary productivity and is determined by the height of the lowest stave. This is analogous to the situation where the level of primary productivity is restricted by the abiotic factor that is in shortest supply.

Limiting factors in terrestrial ecosystems

In terrestrial ecosystems, carbon dioxide is rarely a limiting factor; it is freely available in the atmosphere (0.03% of atmospheric gases). However, light can often be a limiting factor to the productivity of green plants. This is evident when examining the situation in tropical rainforests. Here the dense, multi-layered tree canopy removes the vast majority of radiant energy (up to 98%) before it reaches ground level. Few green plants flourish in the deep shade beneath.

The ability of trees and plants to capture light efficiently is influenced by the density and arrangement of their leaves. Day length has an important influence on primary productivity as it determines the period of time when plants can be photosynthetically active. The length of the growing season (the period of the year when plants bear photosynthetically active foliage) is determined by latitude.

Lack of water leads to an overall decrease in primary productivity, partly because individual plants become less photosynthetically active and partly because it leads to a general decrease in vegetation cover, for example as seen in deserts.

An increase in temperature causes an increase in the rate of gross primary production. However, the rate of

Table 9.2 Abiotic factors that can limit primary productivity.

Ecosystem type	Physical factors	Chemical factors
Aquatic	Light penetration (level of suspended solids)	Level of dissolved nutrients (especially nitrate and phosphate)
	Temperature	Level of dissolved oxygen
	Water currents	Salinity
Terrestrial	Light	Level of dissolved nutrients in soil water (especially nitrate and phosphate)
	Temperature Water (precipitation) Soil fertility Wind	

Table 9.3 The mineral-derived macro-nutrient elements needed for healthy plant growth.[a]

Element	Ions absorbed	Functions	Symptoms of deficiency
Nitrogen (N)	Nitrate (NO_3^-), ammonium (NH_4^+)	Component of proteins and nucleic acids	Stunted growth, yellow leaves (chlorosis)
Phosphorus (P)	Phosphate (PO_4^{3-}), orthophosphate ($H_2PO_4^-$)	Component of nucleic acids and ATP, essential for flowering, fruiting and root growth	Stunted growth, especially of roots
Potassium (K)	Potassium (K^+)	Enzyme cofactor, main intracellular cation	Stunted growth, premature death, yellow leaves (chlorosis)
Sulfur (S)	Sulfate (SO_4^{2-})	Component of protein	Reduced root growth, yellow leaves (chlorosis)
Calcium (Ca)	Calcium (Ca^{2+})	Enzyme cofactor, formation of middle lamella	Stunted growth, death of apical buds
Magnesium (Mg)	Magnesium (Mg^{2+})	Enzyme cofactor, component of chlorophyll	Yellow leaves (chlorosis)

[a] The micro-nutrient elements needed for healthy plant growth and development are boron, chlorine, copper, iron, manganese, molybdenum and zinc.

respiration also increases with temperature and there comes a point where there is no increase in net primary production because of respiratory losses. Temperature also accelerates the rate of transpiration (Box 9.2) and may therefore cause water to become a limiting factor.

Table 9.3 lists the principal mineral nutrient elements essential for plant growth. Phosphorus is most likely to be the element in short supply, followed by nitrogen. Members of the pea family (Leguminosae) have overcome the problem of nitrogen deficiency by forming symbiotic relationships with the nitrogen-fixing bacteria *Rhizobium*. These bacteria, present in the soil, induce the legume to form special root nodules. By fixing atmospheric nitrogen (N_2), *Rhizobium* bacteria make nitrogen available to the plant in the form of the ammonium ion (NH^{4+}) and in return are able to utilise the sugars produced by the plant.

Limiting factors in aquatic ecosystems

The contribution of green plants and attached algae to the total primary production of aquatic ecosystems is usually limited, as they are generally restricted to the shallower margins of water bodies. In the deep waters of lakes and oceans, phytoplankton, minute free-floating plants (Figure 9.5), take over the role of primary producers.

The primary productivity of phytoplankton is determined by three main factors: the availability of light, the availability of nutrients and the intensity of grazing by zooplankton (minute free-floating animals (Figure 9.6)).

The depth of light penetration determines the zone of primary production and is dependent on the clarity of the water. This region is known as the **photic zone**. Below this is the **aphotic zone**, where lack of sunlight for photosynthesis becomes a limiting factor.

The lack of essential nutrient elements (Table 9.3), principally nitrogen and phosphorus, severely limits primary productivity in tropical and sub-tropical seas. In some areas of very low productivity, for example the Sargasso Sea (a sub-tropical part of the Atlantic Ocean), iron appears to be the critical limiting factor.

In areas of upwelling where nutrients are brought from the bottom sediment to the surface by vertical currents, primary productivity is high and it is in these fertile areas where the rich fishing grounds of the world are to be found, for example the Antarctic Convergence.

The density of phytoplankton and therefore the level of primary productivity may be greatly reduced by the intense grazing of zooplankton. Temperature does not appear to influence the primary productivity of marine ecosystems; arctic oceans are as productive as tropical seas.

9.2.4 Global comparison of primary productivity

Figure 9.7 shows the global pattern of net primary productivity (NPP) in (a) land masses and (b) oceans. A comparison between the two maps shows that the NPP of the oceans is very much lower than that of the land masses. The most productive terrestrial ecosystems have an NPP of $>800\,g\,C\,m^{-2}\,a^{-1}$, almost a magnitude higher than the most productive ocean areas at $>90\,g\,C\,m^{-2}\,a^{-1}$. Estimates of the NPP of terrestrial ecosystems are likely to be underestimates. Below-ground productivity, for example of roots and storage organs, is usually ignored, as measuring it is technically so difficult. The actual difference between NPP levels on land and in the sea is therefore very likely to be even more magnified.

Figure **9.5** Typical members of the microscopic freshwater phytoplankton community.

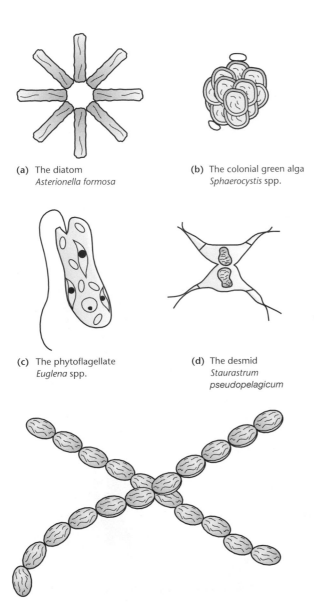

(a) The diatom
Asterionella formosa

(b) The colonial green alga
Sphaerocystis spp.

(c) The phytoflagellate
Euglena spp.

(d) The desmid
Staurastrum pseudopelagicum

(e) Threads of the blue-green alga
Anabaena flos-aquae

In terrestrial ecosystems, NPP is highest in the tropics ($>800\,\mathrm{g\,C\,m^{-2}\,a^{-1}}$) and decreases with increasing latitude. This suggests that day length (the period of time when light is available for photosynthesis), length of growing season and temperature are the main factors constraining net primary productivity. This pattern, however, is interrupted by desert areas, where lack of precipitation limits NPP. For example, in the Great Victoria Desert of Australia at $\sim28°$S, NPP is only 0–$100\,\mathrm{g}$ $\mathrm{C\,m^{-2}\,a^{-1}}$.

Figure **9.6** Typical members of the freshwater zooplankton community (from Macan, 1959).

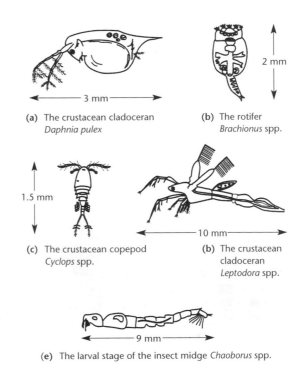

(a) The crustacean cladoceran
Daphnia pulex

(b) The rotifer
Brachionus spp.

(c) The crustacean copepod
Cyclops spp.

(b) The crustacean cladoceran
Leptodora spp.

(e) The larval stage of the insect midge *Chaoborus* spp.

In the oceans, the areas of highest NPP ($>90\,\mathrm{g\,C\,m^{-2}\,a^{-1}}$) occur around the continental shelves and in the areas of upwelling in the deep oceans, irrespective of temperature and latitude. As discussed in Section 9.2.3, a scarcity of essential nutrient elements (Table 9.3) is the principal factor that limits primary productivity in the open oceans ($<35\,\mathrm{g\,C\,m^{-2}\,a^{-1}}$). For this reason, although the oceans cover two-thirds of the Earth's surface, they contribute only one-third of its net primary productivity.

9.3 Energy flow in ecosystems

The energy needed for the functioning of most ecosystems comes from an external source, the sun. Unlike nutrients which are continually recycled (Chapter 5), energy flows through the ecosystem only once and must therefore be continuously replenished.

9.3.1 The efficiency of energy transfer between trophic levels

The efficiency with which energy is transferred from one trophic level to the next is known as the **ecological efficiency** or **Lindeman efficiency**. Ecological efficiencies between trophic levels are typically low. In

Figure 9.7 Global comparison of net primary productivity: (a) on land (after Leith, 1964) and (b) in the oceans (after Koblentz–Mishke *et al.*, 1970).

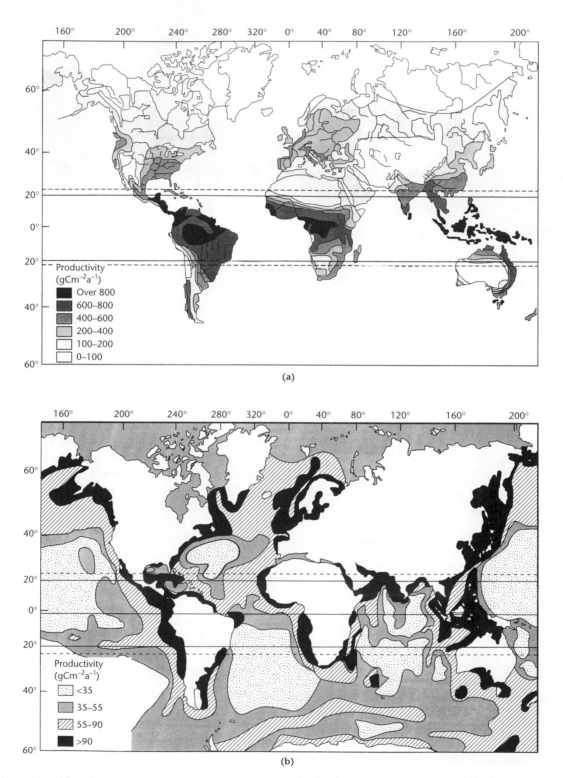

(a)

(b)

Figure 9.8 Schematic diagram showing the partitioning of energy as it passes from one trophic level ($n-1$) to the next (n). Bold arrows represent energy passing through trophic levels, dashed arrows represent energy lost from trophic levels $n-1$ and n, and plain arrows represent energy entering the decomposer pathway.

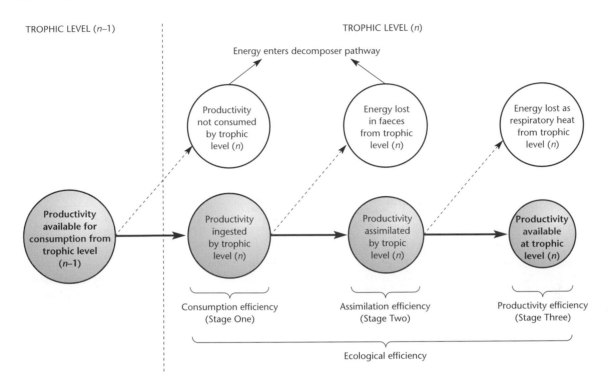

other words, a large proportion of the energy available at one trophic level ($n-1$) is lost during the process of transfer to the next trophic level (n). Figure 9.8 illustrates the three main stages at which energy may be lost during the transfer process. Each of these stages will be dealt with in turn in the text. This model may be equally applied to the transfer of energy between any consecutive pair of trophic levels.

Consumption efficiency (Stage 1)

Not all of the net productivity (NP) available at one trophic level is consumed by the next. The percentage of NP that is actually ingested is known as the **consumption efficiency** (CE). This can be represented by the following equation:

$$CE = \frac{I_n}{P_{n-1}} \times 100 \qquad (9.1)$$

where I_n is the productivity ingested at trophic level n, and P_{n-1} is the net productivity available at trophic level ($n-1$).

The consumption efficiency of herbivores is low, about 25% for grasslands and only about 5% for forests. There are several reasons for this. Some of the plant biomass

available will inevitably die without being grazed and enter the decomposer pathway (Section 9.5), for example the autumnal leaf-shed of deciduous trees. Some of the plant biomass may be in a form that is unavailable or unpalatable to herbivores. This is particularly true in forests, where a large proportion of the plant biomass is in the form of roots and trunks. This partially explains the very low consumption efficiency (~5%) recorded for herbivores in forest ecosystems. In aquatic ecosystems, the consumption efficiency of herbivorous zooplankton is much higher, between 50% and 90%, because the phytoplankton on which they graze lack thick resistant cell walls. Plants themselves may have evolved defence mechanisms to protect them from herbivore attack, therefore reducing the consumption efficiency of their consumers (Box 9.5).

Finally, the consumption efficiency of herbivores in a particular ecosystem will be strongly influenced by their density (numbers per given area). There is evidence that their numbers are not governed by the availability of their food supply but are kept down by predation. Little appears to be known about the consumption efficiency of carnivores. It is probably at this stage that there is greatest inefficiency due to the difficulties involved in locating and capturing prey.

9.5 Plant defence mechanisms

Plant defence mechanisms can be divided into the following categories.

1 Physical defences
  (a) Mechanical structures present on the surface of the plant to deter herbivore attack, e.g. the spines (modified stem tips) of gorse (family Leguminosae).
  (b) Structural mechanisms for reducing the digestibility of plants to herbivores, e.g. the presence of complex polymers such as cellulose, lignin or tannin, and the presence of silica in many plants of the family Gramineae (grasses).

2 Chemical defences
  (a) Alkaloids. These are the best known and most virulent of the many groups of poisons present in plants. Examples

are the atropine found in deadly nightshade (family Solanaceae) and the coniine found in hemlock (family Umbelliferae).
  (b) Cyanide. The production of cyanide in response to tissue damage by grazing animals is widespread in plants, e.g. in white clover (family Leguminosae).

The majority of plant species have evolved a combination of plant defence mechanisms. In response, herbivores have co-evolved a whole range of adaptations to overcome them. This phenomenon explains why so many insects, such as butterflies, have specific food plants.

Assimilation efficiency (Stage 2)

At this second stage during the transfer of energy (Figure 9.8) more energy is lost because not all of the net productivity ingested is broken down and assimilated by the trophic level in question. A variable proportion of material passes undigested through the gut to be ejested as faecal waste. This waste then enters the decomposer pathway (Section 9.5). The percentage of net productivity ingested that is actually assimilated is called the **assimilation efficiency** (AE). This can be represented by the following equation:

$$AE = \frac{A_n}{I_n} \times 100 \qquad (9.2)$$

where A_n is the food energy assimilated across the gut wall in trophic level n, and I_n is the productivity ingested at trophic level n.

The assimilation efficiency of different types of consumers varies enormously and is largely a result of how

similar the biochemical make-up of the consumer is to that of its food source or prey. Plant material is very different in its nutritional composition from the herbivores that consume it. It contains large quantities of fixed carbon from the process of photosynthesis (Section 9.2.1) and as such is potentially a rich source of energy. However, much of that energy is bound up in cellulose (Figure 9.4(c)) and lignin, which form the walls of cells in trees and higher plants. Most herbivores lack the specific enzymes necessary for the breakdown of these substances. The assimilation efficiency of these types of herbivores usually varies between 30% and 40%.

A higher assimilation efficiency of up to 60% is recorded for herbivores which form a mutualistic association (Chapter 8, Section 8.1.4) with cellulase-secreting bacteria present in their guts. Their guts are specially adapted to facilitate the cellulose-digesting activities of these microbes, for example the rumen of deer and cattle (Box 9.6). Rabbits also increase their

9.6 Ruminant metabolism

In ruminants, such as sheep, cattle and deer, the foregut is extensively modified to form an elaborate four-chambered compartment to facilitate the cellulose-digesting activities of symbiotic bacteria and protozoans. Ruminants swallow their food, mainly grass, with minimal chewing. It enters the first two compartments, the reticulo-rumen (often referred to as simply the rumen), where the cellulose undergoes extensive breakdown by microbes. These microbes, namely bacteria and protozoans, ferment the ingested food anaerobically to produce fatty acids.

The food is then regurgitated, rechewed and reswallowed. On

its second descent, it bypasses the rumen and enters the third chamber, the omasum, where it is physically reworked. From there it is passed into the fourth and final chamber, the abomasum, where the fatty acids are absorbed for use by the ruminant.

The assimilation efficiency of ruminants depends on three main factors: the volume of microbial fluid present, the retention time for partially digested food, and the percentage of indigestible material present in the ingested food. These factors are all interrelated and more complete digestion is favoured by larger ruminant size.

assimilation efficiency by reingesting soft faecal pellets that still contain significant levels of protein, despite having passed through the gut already. This is known as **coprophagy**.

The assimilation efficiencies of predatory animals are greater than those of herbivores and sometimes reach values greater than 90%. This is because, biochemically, the tissues of carnivores are very similar to those of their prey.

Net production efficiency (Stage 3)

During this stage, the productivity previously assimilated is converted into biomass (Figure 9.8). This process involves the conversion of the simple molecular products of assimilation into complex biological structures (e.g. proteins, cells, organs, etc.). This produces an increase in order (i.e. a decrease in entropy) within the organisms concerned. This process must be accompanied by an increase in the entropy of the universe, in accordance with the second law of thermodynamics (Chapter 2, Section 2.1). Organisms achieve this, in part, by releasing some of the chemical energy of their assimilated food as heat, so increasing the random thermal motion of the molecules that make up their immediate surroundings. Furthermore, some of the chemical energy in the assimilated productivity is required by the consumers themselves for movement. For these reasons, the transfer of chemical energy from assimilated productivity to the productivity at a given trophic level can never be 100% efficient.

The percentage of chemical energy assimilated that is converted into new biomass is known as the **net production efficiency** (PE) and can be represented by the following equation:

$$PE = \frac{P_n}{A_n} \times 100 \qquad (9.3)$$

where P_n is the net productivity available at trophic level n, and A_n is the food energy assimilated across the gut wall in trophic level n.

It should be noted that production is a composite term encompassing energy destined for growth of the individual and energy destined for reproduction. The latter often involves huge investments of energy by the female.

The production efficiency of an animal is inversely related to its level of activity. Even at rest, some energy is required by the animal to support its vital body functions, for example heartbeat, kidney function and breathing. This is known as the **basal metabolic rate**.

Taking a general view, the production efficiencies of animals seem to be strongly associated with the taxonomic class to which they belong. Invertebrates are fairly efficient in converting assimilated energy into new biomass and have a relatively high production efficiency of 30–40%. In contrast, the production efficiencies of vertebrates are generally much lower. This is especially true of **endotherms** (i.e. animals that must maintain a constant internal body temperature by the metabolic generation of heat). Moreover, the maintenance of constant body temperature becomes increasingly problematic with decreasing body size (Box 9.7).

Tool Box

9.7   Surface area to volume ratio

The surface area to volume ratio of animals directly affects the amount of heat loss from their bodies. This is of particular importance to endotherms, which maintain a constant internal body temperature by the metabolic generation of heat. The relationship between surface area and volume can be demonstrated by the use of cubes (see figure).

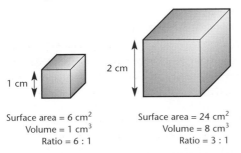

Surface area = 6 cm^2
Volume = 1 cm^3
Ratio = 6 : 1

Surface area = 24 cm^2
Volume = 8 cm^3
Ratio = 3 : 1

The total surface area of a cube can be found by measuring the surface area of one side, i.e. length × breadth, and multiplying it by the total number of sides, i.e. 6. The volume of a cube is the product of its length × breadth × height.

The results for the two cubes illustrated are tabulated below.

Length of cube side/ cm	Area of one side/ cm^2	Total area of all sides/ cm^2	Volume of cube/ cm^3	Area to volume ratio
1	1	6	1	6 : 1
2	4	24	8	24 : 8 or 3 : 1

The smaller cube has a much higher surface area to volume ratio (6 : 1) than the larger one (3 : 1). This illustrates why small endothermic animals are particularly vulnerable to heat loss. Members of the Soricidae (shrew family) have to consume at least their own body weight in food every 24 hours to stay alive. They must maintain a high metabolic rate in order to make good the large amount of heat lost from their tiny bodies.

The reasons why the efficiency of energy transfer from one trophic level to the next, i.e. the ecological or Lindeman efficiency, is so low have been examined in some detail. By multiplying the efficiencies at each of the three stages, we can obtain a value for the ecological efficiency (EcE). This can be represented by the following equation:

$$EcE = CE \times AE \times PE \qquad (9.4)$$

where EcE = ecological or Lindeman efficiency

  CE = consumption efficiency

  AE = assimilation efficiency

  PE = net production efficiency.

Ecologists traditionally assumed an ecological efficiency of 10% (known as the 10% rule) but it is now recognised that its value may vary between 5% and 20%. The result of this inefficiency of transfer is that the amount of energy available decreases with each successive trophic level. Represented diagrammatically, this forms a pyramidal arrangement known as a **pyramid of energy** (Figure 9.9(a)).

These energetic constraints were once thought to be a sufficient explanation for the perceived limitation to the number of trophic levels observed in food webs, but this classical view is currently out of favour. Other possible explanations include size and other design constraints. Predators, in order to catch their prey, are usually larger, stronger and faster. However, there should come a point where the energy costs of being larger and more mobile are not balanced by the energy obtained from capturing prey.

A similar pyramidal arrangement is usually obtained when measurements of numbers or biomass are used instead of energy (Figure 9.9(b)(i) and (c)(i)). The relative

increase in size and decrease in abundance with each successive trophic level was first recognised by the British ecologist Charles Elton in 1927. His pioneering ideas underpin much of modern-day research into food webs. As with all rules, however, there are exceptions. For example, in aquatic ecosystems, an inverted pyramid of biomass is obtained because the phytoplanktonic algae (primary producers) are shorter-lived than the zooplankton (primary consumers) which predate on them (Figure 9.9(c)(ii)). Similarly, pyramids of numbers may be inverted, for example when one host supports many hyperparasites (a **hyperparasite** is a parasite that lives on, or in, another parasite) (Figure 9.9(b)(ii)).

9.4 Secondary productivity

Secondary productivity is a measurement of the rate at which new biomass is produced per unit area by the animal community. However, such measurements, unlike those of primary productivity (Section 9.2.2), are extremely difficult to make. To obtain a reasonably accurate picture, population size, age structure, and rates of birth (natality), death (mortality), emigration and immigration must all be taken into account (Chapter 7).

Estimations of secondary productivity are usually restricted to a few or perhaps just a single species, often studied in laboratory conditions. The results obtained are then used to estimate the field situation and should therefore be treated with caution. Information about secondary productivity is very sparse (with the exception of some data available for marine and freshwater fish). The International Biological Programme (IBP) (1964–74) paid particular attention to the study of productivity in terrestrial and aquatic ecosystems. It was reasonably successful in assessing levels of primary productivity in different communities but was unable to achieve similar success in its various studies on secondary productivity. It is therefore impossible to construct a global map of comparative secondary productivity of the sort presented for primary productivity (Figure 9.7).

The factors that limit secondary productivity in different ecosystems are little understood. They are likely to be several and interrelated and probably include the effects of predation and of low levels of primary productivity.

Figure 9.9 Pyramids of (a) energy, (b) numbers and (c) biomass.

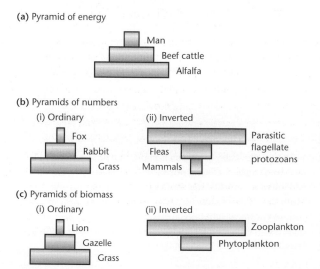

(a) Pyramid of energy

Man
Beef cattle
Alfalfa

(b) Pyramids of numbers

(i) Ordinary

Fox
Rabbit
Grass

(ii) Inverted

Fleas
Mammals
Parasitic flagellate protozoans

(c) Pyramids of biomass

(i) Ordinary

Lion
Gazelle
Grass

(ii) Inverted

Zooplankton
Phytoplankton

9.5 Decomposition

The process of **decomposition** may be defined as the gradual breakdown of dead organic matter. It involves a combination of physical and biological forces. Two main 'groups' of organisms are active in the biological disintegration of dead organic matter: the **detritivores** (detritus-eating invertebrates from a wide range of taxonomic groups) and the **decomposers** (bacteria and fungi).

The process of decomposition is integral to the functioning of the ecosystem. The breakdown of dead organic matter results in the release of inorganic nutrients that are thus made available for uptake by higher plants. The cycle is completed, enabling nutrients to be constantly recycled within the ecosystem (Chapter 5).

9.5.1   The origin of dead organic matter

Dead organic matter may be of plant or animal origin. When animals die, as a result of old age or disease, their carcasses are usually quickly exploited by scavengers which feed on this carrion. The bulk of dead organic matter, however, is of plant origin, consisting of either whole individuals (e.g. dead trees) or parts of them (e.g. the autumnal leaf-fall of deciduous trees). Dead organic matter is also formed underground, where parts of roots, such as root hairs and root caps, are continuously shed into an area of the soil known as the rhizosphere. The faeces of heterotrophic organisms are also an important source of dead organic matter.

9.5.2   The process of decomposition

In this section, we make particular reference to a deciduous woodland ecosystem.

Whatever its origin, dead organic matter is broken down by a combination of physical processes and the biological activities of detritivores and decomposers. The example chosen to illustrate the decomposition process, the deciduous woodland, receives large amounts of dead plant matter annually. The quantity of this dead organic matter will vary spatially and temporally (i.e. in space and time) but will reach a peak in autumn when the trees shed their leaves. It should be noted, however, that the dead organic matter in deciduous woodlands is not restricted to the annual leaf-fall. Other parts of the parent tree, such as twigs and branches, may be broken off by high winds. Storm conditions can bring down entire trees, often those already weakened by age or disease.

Unless prematurely stripped by wind action, the leaves die on the tree in autumn and the forces of decomposition become active. The leaves can be colonised immediately by bacteria and fungal spores (the decomposers) ever-present in the air. Already, the physical forces of decay will be at work as the leaves lose their moisture content

(desiccate) and start to change structurally. In addition, the action of rainwater will start to leach soluble materials from the dead leaves.

Once detached from the parent tree, the leaves fall to the woodland floor and become part of the litter layer. The process of decomposition continues apace. Physical processes such as freezing/thawing and the trampling of animals accelerate the mechanical breakdown of the dead leaves. Soluble materials continue to be leached. Decomposers and detritivores together complete the process of decomposition. Each of these two important groups of organisms will now be examined in a little more detail.

The decomposers

The decomposer group of organisms consists of bacteria and fungi, both of which feed in a similar way. They secrete extracellular digestive enzymes that break down the complex structural molecules of organic detritus into simple ones that they are then able to utilise. Organisms that feed in this way are called **saprophytes**. Shelf fungi are particularly important in the decomposition of wood (Box 9.8).

The nature of the extracellular digestive enzymes secreted by different decomposer organisms is usually fairly specific to a particular component of the dead organic matter under attack. Colonisation of detritus usually occurs in waves. Fresh detritus is first colonised by sugar fungi, for example *Mucor* and *Penicillium*. These feed on soluble materials, mainly sugars and amino acids, which are freely diffusible. The sugar fungi are then replaced in succession by colonies of decomposer organisms, each able to make use of progressively more resistant substances in the dead organic matter. These substances may be placed in the following approximate sequence:

Sugars < starch < hemicelluloses, pectins, proteins < cellulose < lignins < suberins < cutins

where the symbol '<' means 'less resistant than'.

The detritivores

The rate of decomposition is greatly accelerated by a second group of organisms, the detritivores. These detritus-feeding invertebrates come from a wide range of taxonomic groups, for example Myriapoda (centipedes), Annelida (earthworms), Nematoda (nematodes) and Isopoda (woodlice). Terrestrial detritivores are usually classified on the basis of size (Figure 9.10), whereas aquatic detritivores are usually classified according to their mode of feeding.

9.8 Shelf fungi

Shelf fungi belong to the class Basidiomycetes. They obtain their food from the dead organic remains of trees. The parts of the fungi which are visible are known as the brackets or fruiting bodies. These produce light-resistant spores which can be dispersed effectively to colonise fresh sources of dead organic matter.

Most of the fungal structure occurs within the dead wood itself. It consists of a tangled mass of thread-like filaments called hyphae, which are known collectively as the mycelium. The hyphae have rigid cell walls of chitin and are not divided into true cells, a feature that facilitates a continuous flow of protoplasm. The hyphal tips produce extracellular enzymes that can break down complex organic molecules, for example cellulose, into simple sugars that they can then absorb. The fungal hyphae of shelf fungi are very effective in penetrating wood. Their activities enable bacteria to gain access to the interior of the wood and thus accelerate its decomposition.

The figure shows the shelf fungus *Trametes versicolor* on rotting wood.

Detritivores are consumers in the sense that they consume their food source, the detritus, for nutrients and energy just like any other type of consumer. However, their feeding activities inadvertently assist the process of decomposition by breaking down coarse particulate organic matter (>2 mm) and egesting it in a more fragmented form known as fine particulate organic matter (<2 mm). This digestive breakdown of particles greatly increases the surface area exposed to attack by microbial decomposers, both inside and outside the gut. In the absence of detritivores, the rate of microbial breakdown of dead organic matter is suppressed. This effect has been demonstrated by a number of exclusion experiments such as the one illustrated in Figure 9.11.

The activities of detritivores and decomposers are intricately bound and difficult to disentangle. Dead organic matter may pass several times through the guts of detritivores, whose assimilation efficiency (Section 9.3.1) is usually low, around 15%.

The net result of the decomposition process is the release of nutrients locked up in dead organic matter to the 'nutrient pool', a process known as **mineralisation**. These nutrients are therefore made available for uptake by higher plants. Some of the nutrients are used by the decomposers themselves and become temporarily locked in their protoplasm until their demise, a process known as **immobilisation**.

Complete decomposition of organic detritus is rare, relying as it does on a wide array of decomposers and detritivores. In practice, some plant residues persist and these form the humus content of soils (Chapter 3, Section 3.2). Conditions of low temperature, poor aeration and acidity all reduce the diversity, density and activity of decomposers and detritivores. Such conditions result in the build-up of dead organic matter. Peat is formed in this way over thousands of years.

9.6 Ecosystem stability

The concept of stability is a very important one in the study of ecosystems. Ecosystems are not static entities but dynamic ones, constantly shifting and altering. The **stability** of an ecosystem describes its capacity to return to an equilibrium state after being temporarily disturbed.

The term **resilience** is used to describe the speed with which an ecosystem returns to its original state, having been displaced from it by perturbations. Recovery is usually rapid in ecosystems where nutrients are easily cycled and the efficiency of nutrient capture is high, for example ponds and meadows. A second term, **resistance**, introduced subsequently, describes the ability of the ecosystem to resist being displaced in the first place and is a measure of how effectively it is buffered against change.

Ecosystems that are able to persist only within a narrow range of environmental conditions are described as **dynamically fragile**. Such ecosystems tend to be complex and to exist in very stable environments where conditions are relatively constant, for example the tropical rainforests. They are particularly vulnerable to any change or disturbance, natural or man-made. On the other hand, ecosystems that are able to tolerate a wide range of

Figure 9.10 Size classification by body width of organisms in terrestrial decomposer food webs (after Swift *et al.*, 1979).

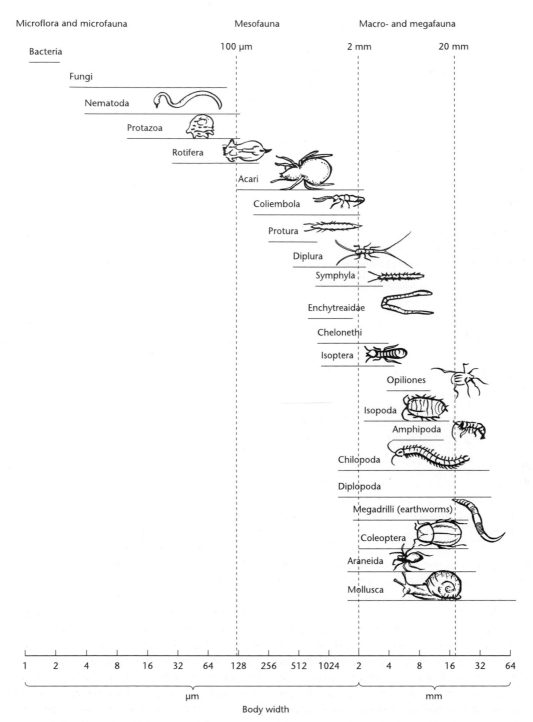

The following groups are wholly carnivorous:
Opiliones (harvest spiders), Chilopoda (centipedes), Araneida (spiders)

Figure 9.11 Decomposition of leaf discs by soil animals (from Edwards, C. A. and G. W. Heath (1963) The role of soil organisms in breakdown of leaf material. In Doiksen, J. and J. Van der Drift (eds) *Soil organisms*. Oxford: Elsevier Science).

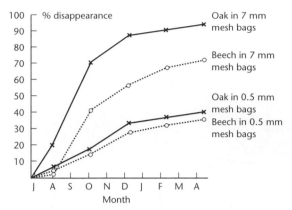

Leaf discs were enclosed in mesh bags with either large (7 mm) or small (0.5 mm) openings. Most of the large detritivores, such as earthworms and millipedes, were excluded from the bags with 0.5 mm openings but bacteria, fungi and small arthropods were still admitted

environmental conditions are termed **dynamically robust**. These tend to be found in seasonal climates where physical conditions vary over the year.

The response of ecosystems as a whole to change is dependent on and paralleled by the individual responses of their constituent species. Therefore, adaptations at the species level play an important role in determining the relative stability of the ecosystem of which they are part.

9.6.1 The nature of perturbations

The origin of perturbations affecting ecosystems may be biotic, for example the deliberate introduction of predators to control pest populations, or abiotic, for example a period of exceptionally low rainfall. They may be natural or caused by human activities and their magnitude and duration varies. In some instances, ecosystems are perturbed to such an extent that they are unable to recover and are destroyed and lost. Natural catastrophes such as volcanic eruptions and monsoonal floods, and human activities such as deforestation and mining, can all have this disastrous effect. The barren ground thus created is usually colonised by opportunistic plant species and the process of secondary succession commences (Chapter 8, Section 8.4.2). However, the mature (climax) ecosystem originally lost may take centuries to re-establish, if at all.

If disturbance to an ecosystem occurs on a sufficiently

regular basis, the species present may become adapted. Thereafter, the disturbance becomes essential to the maintenance of that ecosystem. For example, in the chaparral biome (Section 9.7.4), fires periodically destroy the evergreen shrub vegetation. However, many of the chaparral species are able to grow again from their root systems. The regular occurrence of fire therefore helps to maintain the characteristic chaparral vegetation by preventing the encroachment of other species.

9.6.2 The relationship between ecosystem stability and complexity

Before 1970, the generally accepted view amongst ecologists was that ecosystem stability was positively correlated with its complexity. The complexity of an ecosystem can be measured in many ways, for example by the number of species present (Chapter 8, Section 8.3) or by the number of interactions taking place between the species present (Box 9.9).

However, in the early 1970s, the use of mathematical models of food webs showed a decrease in ecosystem stability when the number of species present or the number of interactions was increased. Such a result ran contrary to the widely held pre-1970s belief. However, as there is some conflict between the results obtained from a number of similar studies and as the predictive models used may be based on food webs assembled at random (which is not the case in nature and is clearly an approximation), it would be inappropriate to replace one general view with another. Thus the relationship between ecosystem stability and complexity remains unresolved.

9.7 Terrestrial and aquatic biomes

The land masses of the world may be divided into large regions known as terrestrial biomes (Figure 9.12). These major biogeographical divisions, based on climate, flora and fauna, provide a useful and commonly used framework for classifying the terrestrial environment. Similarly, the water bodies of the world (the aquatic biome) may be subdivided into marine and freshwater biomes, within which a number of different ecosystem types may be conveniently recognised. It should be appreciated that there are no sharp divisions between different biomes; they usually merge gradually into each other. These transitional zones share characteristics from each of the bordering biomes.

In this section, the eight major terrestrial biomes – tundra, taiga, temperate deciduous forest, chaparral, temperate grasslands, tropical grasslands, deserts and

Tool Box

9.9   Connectance

The complexity of food webs can be expressed by a measure called **connectance**. This can be found using the following equation:

$$connectance = \frac{actual \text{ number of interspecific interactions}}{potential \text{ number of interspecific interactions}}$$

A higher connectance value indicates a more complex food web. Where there are n species, the potential number of interspecific interactions is:

$$\frac{n(n-1)}{2}$$

Therefore in the food web shown in the figure, the number of potential interspecific interactions is $9 \times 8 \div 2 = 36$. The actual number of interspecific interactions, found by counting the arrows, is 14. The connectance of this food web is therefore:

$$\frac{14}{36} = 0.39$$

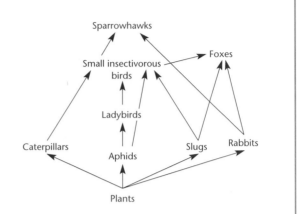

One important generalisation which can be made about food webs is that as the number of species involved (i.e. the species richness) increases, connectance is observed to fall.

Figure **9.12** A simplified map showing the major terrestrial biomes of the world (from Park, 1997, after Marsh and Grossa, 1996).

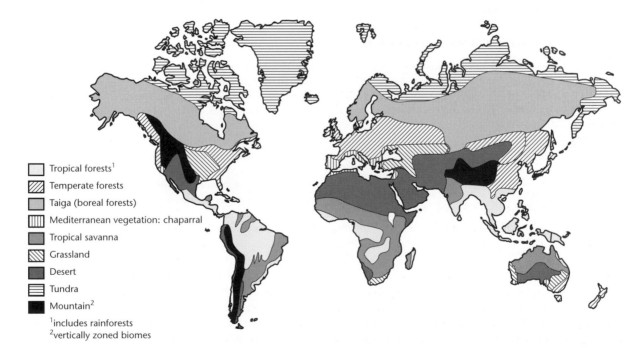

Tropical forests[1]

Temperate forests

Taiga (boreal forests)

Mediterranean vegetation: chaparral

Tropical savanna

Grassland

Desert

Tundra

Mountain[2]

[1]includes rainforests
[2]vertically zoned biomes

tropical rainforests – are described in turn. This is followed by a review of the marine and freshwater biomes, and the chapter concludes with a section on wetland ecosystems. Where appropriate, mention is made of the major human impact on specific biomes and the reader is referred forward to the relevant chapters in the second part of this book.

With reference to the terrestrial biomes, Figure 9.13 illustrates how the eight major types listed above relate to mean annual temperature and mean annual precipitation, whilst Box 9.10 gives details of latitudinal and altitudinal trends. Another interesting feature of terrestrial biomes is the remarkable similarities that can be exhibited by animal species of different continents

Figure 9.13 The relationship between the eight major terrestrial biomes and mean annual temperature and mean annual precipitation (after Whittaker, 1975).

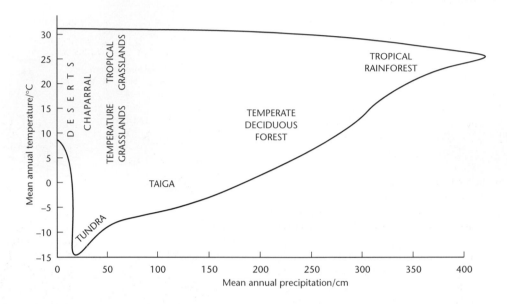

Further Information Box

9.10 Latitudinal and altitudinal gradients

Terrestrial biome type is usually determined by mean annual temperature and mean annual precipitation. An examination of Figure 9.13 shows that changes in biome type are broadly correlated with latitude. A typical gradient from the equator to the arctic could proceed as follows:

Tropical rainforest → temperate deciduous forest
→ coniferous forest (taiga) → tundra

Gradients of vegetational change are sometimes called **ecoclines**. In general terms, a decrease in ground cover and a decrease in the height of the dominant plants accompany the progression from the tropical rainforest through to the tundra.

Increasing altitude has a similar effect on biome type as increasing latitude. Every 600 m of vertical ascent is equivalent to a 1000 km trek poleward in the northern hemisphere. Temperature decreases with increasing altitude, and precipitation is also affected. In general, the majority of precipitation falls on the windward side of mountains, leaving the leeward side with very little.

In the Rocky Mountains in Canada, temperate deciduous woodland occupies the foothills. As altitude increases, this changes to taiga. Above the tree line, beyond which trees cannot grow, is a region of alpine tundra. The mountains are topped with permanent ice and snow, a situation analogous to the arctic region. This altitudinal gradient mirrors the latitudinal gradient seen when journeying north in Canada.

that occupy similar habitats within the same biome. Such similar pairs are known as ecological equivalents (Box 9.11).

9.7.1 Tundra

The **tundra** biome covers over 5% of the total land surface (Table 9.4). It is confined to the northern hemisphere, where it occupies a vast circumpolar tract, separating the polar icecap in the north from the coniferous forests to the south (Figure 9.12). Very little rain falls in the tundra (<25 cm per year), much of it during the summer months. The long winters are very cold and the growing season is short. Net annual primary productivity is low, 10–400 g m^{-2}) (Table 9.4).

The tundra is practically treeless, with the exception of some dwarf willows (*Salix* spp.). The vegetation consists of an assemblage of mosses, lichens and herbaceous plants such as heather and sedges. The soil surface often has a

Further Information Box

9.11   Ecological equivalents

Different species that fulfil the same ecological role in different communities are known as **ecological equivalents**. Such similarities of form and function are not the result of sharing a common ancestor but are produced by adaptation to the same type of ecological conditions. This process, when shown by species that are geographically isolated and taxonomically unrelated, is known as **convergent evolution**.

There are many examples of ecological equivalents. Australia became a separate land mass 60 million years ago. It was originally part of the single land mass known as Pangaea, which started to break up 200 million years ago. In the rest of the world, placental mammals outcompeted the more primitive mammals, the marsupials and monotremes. However, in Australia, there were no placental mammals and, in isolation, evolutionary change produced a whole spectrum of specialised marsupials.

A comparison between these specialised marsupials and placental mammals found on other continents reveals many instances of ecological equivalence, for example between the Tasmanian wolf (*Thylacinus cyanocephalus*) and placental wolves (e.g. *Canis lupus*) and between the marsupial mole (*Notoryctes typhlops*) and placental moles (e.g. *Talpa europaea*).

Examples of convergent evolution can be found in the tropical rainforests of South America and Africa. Examples include the African pygmy hippopotamus (*Cheoropsis liberiensis*)

and the South American capybara (*Hydrochaeris hydrochaeris*), and the African potto (*Perodicticus potto*) and the South American three-toed sloth (*Bradypus tridactylus*) (see figure).

Pygmy hippopotamus
(*Cheoropsis liberiensis*)

Capybara
(*Hydrochaeris hydrochaeris*)

Potto
(*Perodicticus potto*)

Three-toed sloth
(*Bradypus tridactylus*)

hummocked appearance due to the process of successive freezing and thawing (Plate 7).

The subsoil in the tundra is permanently frozen, a condition known as permafrost. Even in the summer, only the surface few centimetres of soil thaw out. Since the permafrost prevents this water from draining away, a landscape of shallow lakes, bogs and marshes is created each summer. At this time of year, insects flourish, providing food for millions of migratory birds, and visiting caribou (*Rangifer tarandus*) come to graze. The tundra biome has been relatively unexploited by humans, a notable exception being for oil extraction. It is very vulnerable to physical damage, taking decades to recover from disturbance.

9.7.2   Taiga

South of the tundra lies a band of coniferous (evergreen) forest known as **taiga**. This broad belt of boreal forest extends across North America, Europe and Asia, covering about 8% of the world's total land surface. The climate of the taiga is not quite as harsh as that of the tundra. The average daily temperature is higher and the growing season is longer. Net annual primary productivity is also higher than that of

the tundra, in the range 400–2000 g m^{-2} (Table 9.4). In the taiga, the subsoil thaws completely in summer. Precipitation is higher than that of the tundra, and much of it falls as snow in the long cold winters.

The species richness of the coniferous forest is very low, with usually only one or two dominant species. These may be spruce (*Picea*), firs (*Pseudotsuga* or *Abies*) or pines (*Pinus*). Conifers are adapted to survive the long snowy winters. For example, their conical shape helps to shed snow, so preventing tree damage (Plate 8). Beneath the dense canopy of the taiga, little grows. Needles are shed continuously in small quantities. Decomposition is slow and a layer of acidic, partly decomposed plant material builds up on the forest floor. The soils of the taiga are typically acidic and poor in nutrients.

Considering the hostility of the environment, the fauna of the taiga is surprisingly rich. For example, over 50 species of insects that feed on conifers have been recorded. These include the pine sawfly (*Diprion pini*) and the spruce budworm (*Choristoneura fumiferana*). Populations of such insects can reach very high densities and cause extensive damage to trees. The principal human use of the taiga is as a source of timber, and such insect pests can pose a serious problem to the forestry industry.

Table 9.4 Net annual primary productivity and standing crop biomass estimates for contrasting communities of the world (from Whittaker, 1975).

Ecosystem type	Area (10^6 km^2)	Net primary productivity, per unit area (g m^{-2} or t km^{-2})		World net primary production (10^9 t)	Biomass per unit area (kg m^{-2})		World biomass (10^9 t)
		Normal range	Mean		Normal range	Mean	
Tropical rainforest	17.0	1000–3500	2200	37.4	6–80	45	765
Tropical seasonal forest	7.5	1000–2500	1600	12.0	6–60	35	260
Temperate evergreen forest	5.0	600–2500	1300	6.5	6–200	35	175
Temperate deciduous forest	7.0	600–2500	1200	8.4	6–60	30	210
Boreal forest	12.0	400–2000	800	9.6	6–40	20	240
Woodland and shrubland	8.5	250–1200	700	6.0	2–20	6	50
Savanna	15.0	200–2000	900	13.5	0.2–15	4	60
Temperate grassland	9.0	200–1500	600	5.4	0.2–5	1.6	14
Tundra and alpine	8.0	10–400	140	1.1	0.1–3	0.6	5
Desert and semi-desert scrub	18.0	10–250	90	1.6	0.1–4	0.7	13
Extreme desert, rock, sand and ice	24.0	0–10	3	0.07	0–0.2	0.02	0.5
Cultivated land	14.0	100–3500	650	9.1	0.4–12	1	14
Swamp and marsh	2.0	800–3500	2000	4.0	3–50	15	30
Lake and stream	2.0	100–1500	250	0.5	0–0.1	0.02	0.05
Total continental	149		773	115		12.3	1837
Open ocean	332.0	2–400	125	41.5	0–0.005	0.003	1.0
Upwelling zones	0.4	400–1000	500	0.2	0.005–0.1	0.02	0.008
Continental shelf	26.6	200–600	360	9.6	0.001–0.04	0.01	0.27
Algal beds and reefs	0.6	500–4000	2500	1.6	0.04–4	2	1.2
Estuaries	1.4	200–3500	1500	2.1	0.01–6	1	1.4
Total marine	361		152	55.0		0.01	3.9
Full total	510		333	170		3.6	1841

9.7.3 Temperate deciduous forest

Temperate deciduous forest is found mainly in Europe, the United States and China, covering over 4.5% of the world's total land surface. Annual rainfall is abundant, usually between 75 and 200 cm per year, and the long growing season is warm and mild. Temperatures can fall below freezing in winter but do not usually drop below −12°C. The net annual primary productivity of this biome ranges between 600 and 2500 g m^{-2} (Table 9.4).

The vegetation consists largely of broad-leaved deciduous trees, such as oak (*Quercus*), maple (*Acer*), hickory (*Carya*) and beech (*Fagus*) (Plate 9). The species richness of the tree flora is very low, with only one or two dominant species in a particular locality. Trees can reach heights of 40–50 m when mature. However, the canopy is less dense than that found in the taiga or in tropical rainforests. Light filters through to the forest floor, even when the trees are in full leaf. Shrubs and herbaceous plants are therefore able to form an extensive ground cover.

Unlike the soils of the northern coniferous forests (taiga), the soils of temperate deciduous woodlands are rich in nutrients. Each autumn, the annual leaf-fall covers the forest floor with a layer of dead organic matter. The action of decomposers and detritivores rapidly breaks down the fallen leaves so releasing nutrients back into the soil. The temperate deciduous forest biome has been extensively exploited. Much of the original vegetation has now been cleared, often to make land available for agriculture.

Mediterranean vegetation: chaparral

Chaparral is the name given to temperate evergreen scrubland. This biome is not extensive and has a patchy distribution worldwide (Figure 9.12). It occurs mainly in South Australia, Chile, South Africa (where it is called fynbos), California and around the Mediterranean coast. The climate of the chaparral is usually termed 'mediterranean' and is characterised by summer drought and mild, wet winters. The vegetation consists of evergreen thickets, together with small oaks or eucalyptus trees (Plate 10). This hard-leaved scrub vegetation is adapted to survive the summer drought conditions. Dominant forms, for example the Californian chamise (*Adenostoma fasciculatum*), are also able to regenerate from their root systems after fires. The frequent occurrence of fires in the chaparral biome helps to maintain the typical scrub vegetation.

9.7.5 Temperate grasslands

The temperate grassland biome is fairly extensive, covering an area of about 6% of the total land surface (Table 9.4). It is found in areas with a fairly dry continental climate, primarily in the United States (prairie), former Soviet Union (steppe) and Argentina (pampas) (Figure 9.12). Annual rainfall is higher than that of the chaparral but still low, between 25 and 75 cm. The climate is characterised by summer drought. Net annual primary productivity falls in the range 200–1500 g m^{-2} (Table 9.4).

The vegetation is dominated by a variety of native grasses (Plate 11). These are able to survive the drought by using their deep roots to take up water from the subsoil. The grassland soil has a high humus content compared with forest soils and is therefore ideal for growing staple food crops such as wheat (*Triticum aestivum*). Grasslands are also used by people as natural pastures for the rough grazing of cattle, sheep and goats. However, both intensive cultivation and overgrazing by domestic livestock has resulted in severe soil erosion in parts of the temperate grassland biome.

9.7.6 Tropical grasslands

Tropical grassland, or **savanna** as it is known, covers about 10% of the world's total land surface. It occurs mainly in Africa but is also found in South America, southern Asia and Australia (Figure 9.12). Savanna vegetation varies from pure grassland to grassland sprinkled with a few trees and shrubs (Plate 12).

Like the temperate grasslands, tropical grasslands experience seasonal drought. However, the annual rainfall is higher, up to 120 cm. The soil is fertile and, in the rainy season, tropical grasslands are very productive. Net annual primary productivity ranges between 200 and 2000 g m^{-2} (Table 9.4). The fauna of the savanna is characterised by large mammals. In Africa, herbivores include wildebeest (*Connochaetes taurinus*), Thomson's gazelle (*Gazella thomsoni*) and zebra (*Equus burchelli*). These are hunted by other large mammals such as lions (*Panthera leo*) and cheetahs (*Acinonyx jubatus*).

In both temperate and tropical grasslands, the composition of the vegetation is determined by the grazing of herbivores rather than by the climate itself. Fire plays a key role in the maintenance of both types of grassland biome, preventing the establishment of forests in regions where the climate is suitable for trees.

9.7.7 Desert

The **desert** biome covers nearly a quarter of the Earth's land surface (Figure 9.12). Desert regions occur mainly around the latitudes of 30°N and 30°S, as a result of global atmospheric circulation (Chapter 4, Section 4.2.3). The desert climate is arid, with <25 cm of rainfall per year. When the rain does come, it is often torrential, producing flash floods and severe soil erosion. Daytime temperatures in the desert are very high. At night, the heat absorbed by the desert sand and rock during the day is rapidly lost by radiant cooling, causing temperatures to drop very rapidly.

The sparse desert flora can be split into three main groups. In the first group are the fast-growing annuals whose brief life cycle is synchronised with the infrequent rain showers. The second group is made up of tough, stunted shrubs such as the mesquite (*Prosopis glandulosa*). The last group consists of succulents (including all cacti), that are able to survive periods of drought by storing water in their tissues (Box 9.12 and Plate 13).

Desert animals show a range of adaptations to conditions of high temperature and aridity. Water is conserved by the production of dry excretory products such as uric acid. Desert animals usually avoid temperature

Further Information Box

9.12 Adaptation to desert conditions: cacti

Cacti (family Cactaceae) are examples of **xerophytes**, plants that are specialised for life in habitats where water is scarce. Cacti are all succulents. They are able to store water in their stem tissues during periods of drought. They usually have extensive root systems that either penetrate deeply into the groundwater or are spread laterally over a wide area to intercept as much rainfall as possible. Wide spacing between cacti reduces competition for the available water.

Water is lost from plants through pores called stomata, by the process of transpiration. Cacti show a number of adaptations to slow down the rate of water loss. For example, the number of stomata is reduced and the external surface of cacti is covered

with a thick, waxy cuticle. The leaves are reduced to form non-photosynthetic spines. Together with hairs or wool, these spines help to baffle the dehydrating effects of the sun and wind by trapping a layer of moisture around the plant.

One final and very important modification of cacti is their type of photosynthesis. Presumably to restrict water loss during high daytime temperatures, the stomata are open only during the night. The carbon dioxide necessary for photosynthesis is absorbed and stored as malic acid. During the day, it is used to complete photosynthesis. This modification of photosynthesis is called crassulacean acid metabolism (CAM) and it is clearly of advantage to the cacti.

extremes by living in burrows, only venturing forth to feed at dawn and dusk or during the night. The desert jerboa (*Jaculus jaculus*), found in North Africa and central Asia, is nocturnal. This small rodent extracts vital water from its diet of seeds, roots and insects.

The net annual primary productivity of deserts is very low, ranging from zero to a maximum of $250\,\mathrm{g\,m}^{-2}$ in semi-desert scrub (Table 9.4). However, with copious irrigation, deserts can be turned into productive agricultural land (Chapter 11, Section 11.3.3). The peripheries of the world's deserts are continuously expanding, turning millions of hectares into desert. This process has been greatly accelerated by the use of inappropriate agricultural practices (Chapter 11, Section 11.5.4).

9.7.8 Tropical rainforest

Tropical rainforest covers over 11% of the Earth's land surface (Table 9.4). It occurs in the equatorial regions of Africa, Central America, South America, south-east Asia and northern Australia, between the Tropics of Cancer (23°N) and Capricorn (23°S) (Figure 9.12). Many islands in the Indian and Pacific Oceans are also covered with tropical rainforest.

The climate is wet, with an annual rainfall of between 200 and 400 cm, and the average temperature of the coldest month is 18°C or higher. There is no marked seasonality in the tropical rainforests; conditions are constantly warm and usually wet. Net annual primary productivity is high, ranging from 1000 to $3500\,\mathrm{g\,m}^{-2}$ (Table 9.4).

The species richness of plants and animals in the tropical rainforests is enormous (Chapter 8, Section 8.3). It is thought that as many as half of the plant and animal

species on Earth occur in this biome. Between 50 and 100 different tree species may be recorded within a single *hectare* of tropical rainforest, and the record stands at almost 300!

The trees of the tropical rainforest grow to a height of 50–60 m, forming a dense canopy layer through which little light can penetrate (Plate 14). The root systems of the trees tend to be shallow. They often have wide bases called buttresses in order to balance them. Other features of the tropical vegetation include the presence of trailing vines called lianas, and parasitic (or commensal) plants called epiphytes. These live high up in the branches of trees and obtain moisture and nutrients from the surrounding air.

Little in the way of autotrophic vegetation grows on the forest floor due to the lack of light. The soils themselves are impoverished. Decomposition of dead plant and animal material is very rapid under the conditions of high temperature and high humidity. As a result, there is no accumulation of organic matter such as occurs in grasslands and temperate deciduous forests. Nutrients are found only in the surface layers of the soil. These are quickly taken up by the trees and 'locked' within the vegetation.

The fauna of the tropical rainforest includes an enormous array of birds, insects and other animals. Many of these live in the canopy layer, although a wide variety of invertebrates inhabit the forest floor, along with numerous fungi.

The tropical rainforest ecosystem is very fragile and vulnerable to any disturbance. It is being extensively exploited for its rich resources, for example of hardwood timber and minerals, and to provide cleared land for agricultural development. The deforestation of tropical rainforests is discussed in more detail in Chapter 11, Section 11.5.1.

Figure 9.14 Schematic diagram (not drawn to scale) showing the major marine zones and corresponding features of the continental margin.

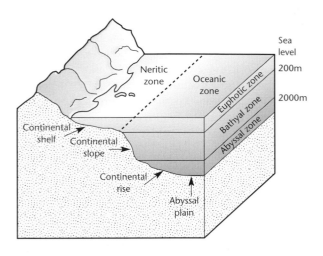

9.7.9 The marine biome

The marine biome is made up of the world's five oceans, namely the Antarctic, Arctic, Atlantic, Indian and Pacific. A distinction is usually made between the open ocean and coastal waters. The boundary between these two regions occurs at the outer edge of the continental shelf (Figure 9.14).

Open ocean

The open ocean covers approximately 70% of the Earth's surface and can reach depths in excess of 10 000 metres. Its salinity is relatively constant (with a salt concentration of about 3.5% w/v) and it is buffered against extremes of temperature. Within the open ocean, phytoplankton (minute, free-floating photosynthetic organisms) fulfil the role of primary producer and form the basis of marine food webs.

Net primary productivity (NPP) in the open ocean is influenced by two main factors: the availability of light and nutrients. Light, necessary for the process of photosynthesis, is restricted to the surface layers of the ocean, a region known as the **photic** (or **euphotic**) **zone**. The exact depth of this zone is determined by the clarity of the water but is generally less than 200 m. Generally speaking, the availability of essential plant nutrients is very restricted within the open ocean ecosystem. This factor is largely responsible for the low value of net annual primary productivity recorded for the open oceans (between 2 and 400 g m^{-2}, Table 9.4). However, there are regions within the open sea where vertical currents bring nutrients from the bottom sediments into the photic zone

and net annual primary productivity is much higher as a result (between 400 and 1000 g m^{-2}, Table 9.4). These upwelling zones, as they are known, account for only 0.1% of the total area of the marine biome. However, they are of considerable economic importance, providing rich fishing grounds for human populations.

The ocean ecosystem can be divided into the neritic zone, the region of coastal influence where it overlies the continental shelf, and the oceanic zone beyond the influence of adjacent land masses (Figure 9.14). Within the open ocean (oceanic) ecosystem, a number of different zones are distinguished on the basis of depth (Figure 9.14), each with a characteristic biota (although there is some migration of organisms between the zones). The euphotic zone extends to a depth of ~200 m and extends into the neritic zone over the continental shelf. Below the euphotic zone is the bathyal zone, which extends from the outer edge of the continental shelf (~200 m depth) to a depth of ~2000 m, and corresponds to the continental slope region of the continental margin. This is underlain by the abyssal zone, which extends from 2000 m to the seafloor (~4000–6000 m below sea level) and corresponds to the continental rise of the continental margin. The seafloor itself is a flat, extensive area known as the abyssal plain. However, such plains are not generally featureless but are dotted with seamounts (submerged volcanic mountains) and traversed by deep-sea trenches. The waters of these trenches, below 6000 m, make up the final marine zone, known as the hadal zone.

In general, the deep ocean bed supports few living organisms – less than 0.5 g (wet weight) m^{-2}. However, in 1977, a new type of benthic community, composed largely of tubeworms (e.g. *Riftia pachyptila*) and bivalve molluscs, was discovered in the vicinity of deep hydrothermal vents present in the mid-ocean ridges. These unique communities, which had evolved largely in isolation, were found to be based not on photosynthetic organisms but on chemosynthetic bacteria, capable of obtaining energy from the oxidation of hydrogen sulfide emitted from the volcanic vents.

Coastal waters

The coastal waters of the marine biome are confined to the continental shelf regions of the continental landmasses (Figure 9.14). These shallow waters (not exceeding 200 m in depth) occupy approximately 7% of the total area of the marine environment. Both light and nutrients are more readily available in coastal waters than in the open oceans. Consequently, this ecosystem is more productive, with a net annual primary productivity of 200–600 g m^{-2} (Table 9.4). Continental shelf waters provide a valuable source of

Figure 9.15 Three basic types of coral reef formation.

(a) Fringing reef
(directly attached
to the land)

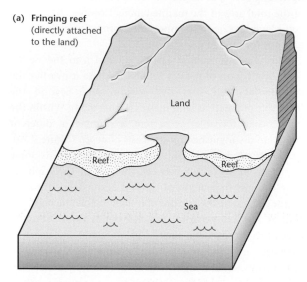

(b) Barrier reef
(separated from the
land by a belt of
shallow water)

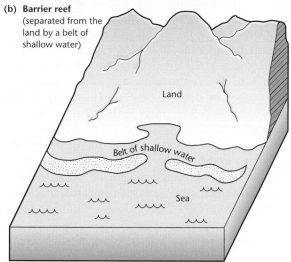

(c) Atoll
(ring-like coral reef, enclosing a central lagoon,
which develops in association with a subsiding volcanic island)

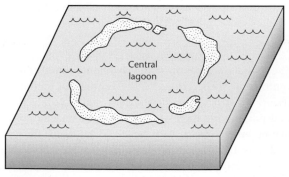

seafood for human consumption. In addition, the majority of marine oil and mineral deposits are located in this region.

Within the coastal waters of the marine environment, coral reef communities deserve a special mention. Coral reefs are widely distributed in shallow tropical and sub-tropical waters (Plate 15). They occur in three basic formations: fringing reefs, barrier reefs and atolls (Figure 9.15). The reef structure itself is formed by the deposition of calcium carbonate by the coral colony. Corals are animals that contain algae called zooanthellae within their tissues. This mutualistic association enables the coral to live in nutrient-poor waters. The net annual primary productivity of coral reefs may reach as high as $4000\,g\,m^{-2}$ (Table 9.4) and, in terms of species richness, they are comparable with the tropical rainforests. However, coral reefs face a number of serious threats from human activities (Chapter 10, Section 10.5.1).

9.7.10 The freshwater biome

In comparison with landmasses and oceans, the total area occupied by the freshwater biome is tiny (Table 9.4). Nevertheless, freshwater ecosystems are extremely important to humans and are used for a variety of purposes, e.g. fresh water supply, irrigation, transportation, recreation, fish production and waste disposal. Moreover, they form an integral part of the hydrological cycle (Chapter 5, Section 5.1.1).

Freshwater ecosystems may be divided into two main groups: those with standing water, like lakes and ponds (known as **lentic** ecosystems), and those with flowing water, such as rivers and streams (known as **lotic** ecosystems).

Lentic ecosystems

Lentic ecosystems form in depressions on the Earth's surface and are entirely surrounded by land. They range in size from small ponds to large permanent lakes. Most natural lakes were formed when the Pleistocene ice sheets retreated, about 10 000 years ago, and are therefore, in a geological sense, relatively young. Many of these glacial lakes can be found in northern Europe and North America (Plate 16). There are a few very ancient lakes which date back beyond the Quaternary period (which commenced 2 million years ago) into the Tertiary period, for example Lake Baikal in Siberia. Lakes have also been created artificially, for example to provide reservoirs for domestic water supply.

The net primary productivity of lakes is determined by a number of factors including the availability of light, dissolved oxygen and nutrients. The concentration of dissolved solids is lower than that of seawater, with the actual composition determined by the nature of the surrounding soils and rocks. Lakes with a scarcity of dissolved nutrients, and consequently a low productivity, are classed as **oligotrophic** whilst those rich in plant nutrients, and therefore usually highly productive, are classed as **eutrophic**. Eutrophic lakes tend to suffer from frequent algal blooms. These occur in temperate lakes in spring and in autumn when thorough mixing of the stratified layers (present in summer and winter) takes place (Chapter 3, Section 3.3.3). Nutrients, previously locked in the bottom sediments, are brought to the surface, causing an explosive growth in algal populations. This phenomenon can also be caused by human activities. The addition of excessive quantities of plant nutrients, e.g. through agricultural run-off, can result in the progressive eutrophication of lakes (Chapter 14, Section 14.2). Lakes may also undergo changes in pH as a result of human activities. For example, the production of acid rain from power station emissions (Chapter 15, Section 15.2.2) has had a devastating effect on the flora and fauna of many lakes (Chapter 14, Section 14.3).

Lotic ecosystems

The property of water that is important in the study of lakes is its density at different temperatures. In rivers and streams, its dominant characteristic is its downhill flow. Permanent rivers usually originate in upland regions, where a number of tributaries, bearing water from direct precipitation and surface run-off, join to form a channel. In its early stages, the stream is primarily an agent of erosion. However, as it proceeds on its course to the sea (or lake), it tends to become wider and slower, depositing progressively more of the sediment load it acquired in its earlier stages. When the river eventually meets the ocean, a delta may form. Such depositional features, composed of alluvial sediments, are typically very fertile and often used for crop cultivation.

Although the one-way movement of water dominates the lotic ecosystem, habitat suitability for different groups of aquatic organisms will vary within the river. In those stretches of the river where flow is rapid, organisms must be adapted to withstand the strong current or be washed away. Overall, the nutrient content of rivers and streams tends to be low, due to the flow of water. However, they are usually well aerated. Conditions, however, can deteriorate significantly in natural watercourses as a consequence of human activities. The input of pollutants from industrial, domestic and agricultural sources has created an unacceptably high pollution burden in many rivers, with serious consequences for the aquatic biota (Chapter 14).

9.7.11 Wetland ecosystems

Wetlands are areas habitually saturated with water, which may be partly or wholly covered permanently, periodically or occasionally by fresh, brackish or salt water (static or flowing) up to a depth of 6 metres. Many wetlands are found in coastal locations and include river estuaries, intertidal mudflats and saltmarshes (Plate 17). Other wetlands are freshwater ecosystems, for example bogs (lowland and upland), fens, swamps, marshes and water meadows (Table 9.5).

With the exception of acidic bogs, nutrient levels in wetland ecosystems tend to be high and, as a result, they

Table 9.5 Wetland ecosystems.

Type	Brief description
Estuary	Semi-enclosed body of water, formed when a river flows into a sea. Salinity is variable due to the mixing of fresh and salt water but increases towards the mouth of the estuary.
Intertidal mudflat	Large expanse of muddy land exposed at low tide but covered at high tide. Found, e.g., in the vicinity of sheltered estuaries.
Saltmarsh	Type of intertidal mudflat that is colonised by salt-tolerant plants and supports a characteristic plant and animal community. Formed, e.g., behind a spit (narrow tongue of sediment that extends from the beach into open water).
Bog	Wet area, usually upland, which supports a characteristic plant community including sphagnum moss and carnivorous plants such as sundews (*Drosera* spp.). Acidic conditions lead to the eventual formation of peat.
Fen	Area of low-lying, marshy ground, on alkaline, neutral or slightly acid peat or mineral soil, covered with shallow, usually stagnant, water originating from groundwater. Characteristic plant community consisting of tall herbaceous plants, such as reeds.
Swamp	Area of ground that is permanently waterlogged and dominated by woody plants. May experience periodic flooding. No surface accumulation of peat.
Marsh	Lowland area of poorly drained land that is occasionally flooded. Plant community dominated by sedges, reeds and rushes, with no or few woody plants; develops on the wet (but not peaty) soil.
Water meadow	Area of grassland bordering a river that regularly floods in winter.

are highly productive. For example, estuaries constitute one of the most productive ecosystems in the world, with a net annual primary productivity of $200-3500\,g\,m^{-2}$ (Table 9.4). As well as supporting a rich biodiversity of plant and animal species, wetlands perform important ecological functions, primarily the regulation of water regimes. However, in the past the unique role played by wetland ecosystems and their value as a resource (cultural, economic, scientific and recreational) have not been fully appreciated. By 1985, an estimated 1.6 million km^2 of wetlands worldwide had been drained, usually for conversion to agriculture or forestry, or for urban development. Wetlands have also been used for landfill and as toxic waste dumps.

Growing international concern about the rapid decline in the number of wetland habitats (and the status of remaining ones) led to the adoption, and subsequent enforcement, of the Convention on Wetlands of International Importance Especially as Waterfowl Habitat (commonly known as the Ramsar Convention) (Chapter 10, Section 10.6.3). Under this treaty, the conservation and wise use of wetland ecosystems was, and is, actively promoted, through both national schemes and international cooperation.

9.8 Summary

Ecosystems are dynamic systems. They consist of living organisms, their environment, and all the interactions that take place between them. The feeding relationships between animals and plants are fundamental to the organisation and functioning of ecosystems, facilitating the through-flow of energy and the recycling of nutrients via the process of decomposition. They also assume a particular importance when considering the environmental fate of toxic substances such as DDT.

The primary productivity of ecosystems, i.e. the rate at which autotrophic green plants can generate new biomass by the process of photosynthesis, is highly variable. Limiting factors such as scarcity of light or nutrients play a key role in influencing productivity at this level. Much less is known about the levels of secondary productivity, i.e. the rate of production of new biomass by the animal community, and the factors that may limit it.

The concept of ecosystem stability is a very important one, especially when considering the environmental impact of human activities. It describes the capacity of a particular ecosystem to return to an equilibrium state after being temporarily disturbed. The term resilience is used in this context to describe the speed of ecosystem recovery.

The land masses of the world may be divided into different biogeographical areas, known as terrestrial biomes, on the basis of floral, faunal and climatic characteristics. Examples include the tundra, temperate grasslands and tropical rainforests. Within the aquatic biome, a number of different ecosystem types are recognised, for example lakes, river estuaries and the deep oceans. It should be noted, however, that in the case of the terrestrial biomes, much of the original landscape has been changed or irretrievably lost as a result of human activities.

9.9 Problems

1 With reference to a particular habitat, e.g. a seashore rockpool or a meadow, construct a hypothetical food web. Carefully assign the organisms to the appropriate trophic level. What are omnivores and why are they difficult to allocate to one particular trophic level? Give an example of an omnivore.

2 What is meant by the term primary productivity? Discuss the factors that limit primary productivity in aquatic and terrestrial ecosystems. Why do the oceans, which cover two-thirds of the Earth's surface, contribute only one-third of its primary productivity?

3 At what three stages during the transfer of energy from one trophic level to the next is energy lost from the living community? With particular reference to herbivores, give plausible reasons for the inefficiency of energy transfer at each stage. What is the name given to the total efficiency of energy transfer and how may it be calculated?

4 Work out the surface area to volume ratio of two cubes, one with edges measuring 0.5 cm and one with edges measuring 2 cm. Which has the larger surface area to volume ratio? What implications does this have for endothermic animals of different sizes? Are young animals more vulnerable to body heat loss? Give reasons for your answer.

5 Assuming an ecological efficiency of 10%, 5% and 20% respectively (Figure 9.16), what will be the energy available at the tertiary consumer level, given a net primary productivity of $90\,000\,kJ\,m^{-2}\,a^{-1}$? What percentage is this figure of the original energy value at the primary producer level?

Figure 9.16 Diagram for Problem 5.

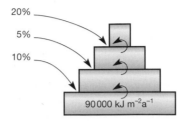

6   Describe the process of decomposition. Why is it of paramount importance to the functioning of ecosystems? How do the activities of detritivores accelerate the decomposition of dead organic matter by the decomposers? Design an experiment to illustrate this phenomenon.

7   With reference to Figure 9.1, work out the connectance of this food web.

9.10   Further reading

Begon, M., J. L. Harper and C. R. Townsend (1990) *Ecology: individuals, populations and communities* (2nd edn). Oxford: Blackwell Scientific.

Cherrett, J. M. (ed.) (1989) *Ecological concepts: the contribution of ecology to the understanding of the natural world.* Oxford: Blackwell Scientific.

Krebs, C. J. (1993) *Ecology: the experimental analysis of distribution and abundance* (4th edn). New York: HarperCollins.

Ricklefs, R. E. (1990) *Ecology* (3rd edn). New York: W. H. Freeman.

1 Satellite picture of the Earth (*NASA*). The band of thick cloud that forms at the intertropical convergence zone (ITCZ) (Section 4.2.2) can be clearly seen across equatorial Africa.

2 Violent lava fountain from the Pu'u O'o volcanic eruption, June 1986, Hawaii (*Geoscience Picture Library*). Rapid solidification of lava flows result in the formation of fine-grained extrusive igneous rocks (Section 3.1.3).

3   Soil profile (Section 3.2.3) of a brown earth (Section
    3.2.5) (*Geoscience Picture Library*).

4   Crowded street, Port-au-Prince, Haiti
    (*Mark Edwards/Still Pictures*).

5   Primary succession (Section 4.8.1): lichens colonising
    bare rock, Bamburgh beach, Northumbrland, UK
    (*photograph by Julie Jackson*).

6   Grizzly bear (*Ursus americanus*), an example of an
    omnivore (Section 9.1.1) (*Kim Heacox/Still Pictures*)

7 Tundra (Section 9.7.1), Siberia, with snowy owl (Nyctea scandiaca) (*photograph by Graham Bell*).

8 Taiga and lake during summer thaw period (Section 9.7.2), Begusin, Siberia. Subsoil still frozen by permafrost (*Geoscience Picture Library*).

9 Temperature deciduous forest (Section 9.7.3), Northumberland, UK (*photograph by Julie Jackson*).

10 Mediterranean vegetation (chaparral) (Section 9.7.4), Akamas peninsula, Cyprus (*photograph by Julia Mayne*).

11 Chilean pampas, an example of temperate grassland
(Section 9.7.5) (*photograph by Julia Mayne*).

12 African savanna, an example of tropical grassland
(Section 9.7.6) (*photograph by Julia Mayne*)

13 Desert (Section 9.7.7), Arizona, US (*photograph by Roman Kresinski*).

14 Tropical rainforest (Section 9.7.8) with tree ferns and bamboo (*Bambusa vulgaris*), St. Lucia (*Andrew D.R. Brown/Ecoscene*).

15 Coral reef (Section 9.7.9), French Polynesia (*photograph by Barbara Brown*).

16 Glacial lake (Section 9.7.10), North America (*photograph by Malcolm Rodgerson*).

17 Saltmarsh with roost of gulls and waders, Morecombe Bay, Lancs, UK, an example of a wetland ecosystem (Section 9.7.11) (*Cooper/Ecoscene*).

18 The African elephant (*Loxodonta africana*), an example of an endangered species (*photograph by Julia Mayne*).

19 Shifting cultivation (Section 11.3.2), Sarawak, Borneo (*photograph by Julia Mayne*).

20 Aral sea, Uzbekistan (Box 12.6). Excessive water abstraction for irrigation has resulted in the contraction of this inland sea and the consequential abandonment of ships (*Marco Rose/Panos Pictures*).

Biological resources

After reading this chapter, you should be able to:

- Define the terms 'biological resources' and 'genetic resources'.

- Outline the importance of biological resources to humans.

- Compare and contrast the different factors which threaten biological resources.

- Discuss the role of over-harvesting and international trafficking in endangering species.

- Understand the threats posed to native species by introduced ones.

- Describe the problem of habitat fragmentation in terms of species survival.

- Appreciate the role of conservation strategies tackling the problem of species decline.

- Outline the major international conventions related to biological resources.

Introduction

Biological resources is a general term that encompasses organisms (and parts thereof), the genetic material they contain (known more specifically as **genetic resources**), populations or any other biotic components of ecosystems with actual or potential use or value to humans. In this chapter, the emphasis is placed on organisms as biological resources, and includes reference to their genetic resources where appropriate.

Biological resources are of enormous importance to humans, providing food and medicines, together with a vast repository of genetic information (Section 10.2). Moreover, their future potential, e.g. in supplying new compounds of medicinal or pharmaceutical benefit, is huge. However, biological resources are coming under increasing pressure as a result of human activities. The threats posed by man may be broadly divided into direct threats, such as over-harvesting and the international trafficking of wild plants and animals (Section 10.3), and indirect threats, such as the introduction of exotic species (Section 10.4), and habitat degradation, loss and fragmentation (Section 10.5). Although discussed separately in this chapter, it is rare that these threats occur singly; more often than not, damaging factors act in combination to bring about the decline of a specific plant or animal species (Box 10.3 on page 227). As a result of these threats, the rate of species extinction has accelerated significantly, leading to a rapid decline in global biological diversity. In the concluding section of this chapter (Section 10.6), attempts to slow down this trend, through conservation strategies and international conventions related to biological resources, are discussed.

10.1   The nature of biological resources

The world's organisms constitute a vast and diverse biological resource, with approximately 1.75 million species named and described to date. However, it is estimated that there are many more species yet to be discovered (possibly as many as 100 million) and that the majority of these will be invertebrates, fungi and bacteria. The distribution of species throughout the world is not even. Some ecosystems, most notably the tropical forests, and biotic communities, particularly the coral reefs, have a much greater variety of species than others. This is reflected in Figure 10.1, which shows those *countries* with highest species diversity.

It is appropriate at this point to introduce the term **biodiversity** (which is the colloquial form of the term **biological diversity**). Biodiversity is used to describe the variety of life at all levels of biological organisation, from the gene through to the ecosystem. Its use is not, as is sometimes thought, restricted to the species level, although it is true that, in biodiversity assessments, species are generally accepted as being the single most useful unit to use.

In addition to those ecosystems/communities with high species diversity, there are others that are recognised by man as important because of their uniqueness. Such ecosystems, e.g. of Mediterranean vegetation, contain a proportion of **endemic** species (i.e. species that are indigenous to, and confined to, that particular location). The identification and conservation of areas rich in endemic species is an important aspect of practical biodiversity management.

The extinction of species is a natural and integral part of the evolution of biological organisms. However, the rate at which species are becoming extinct has accelerated rapidly over recent years, principally as a result of human activities (Sections 10.3, 10.4 and 10.5). The loss of biodiversity at all levels, not just species, is now a cause for global concern. This issue was addressed at the United Nations Conference on Environment and Development in Rio de Janeiro in 1992 where the Convention on Biological Diversity was opened for signature on 5 June (see Section 10.6. for further details).

10.2   The importance of biological resources

Humans derive many benefits (both actual and potential) from biological resources and therefore have a vested interest in preserving both the abundance and diversity of wild plant and animal species currently in existence.

Some of these benefits are of an aesthetic or cultural nature but many are purely practical. In the first place, wild species provide a wide variety of foodstuffs for human consumption. This is particularly important in the developing world where plants and animals harvested directly from the wild generally form a substantial part of the diet. In addition to the provision of food, a number of other important products, apart from wood and wood products, are derived from wild plant species, e.g. rubber (*Hevea* spp.), sisal (*Agave sisalana*), rattan (*Calamus* spp.) and resins. These are often exploited on a commercial basis.

Within the biological resources of the world is held a vast genetic resource. This 'genetic bank' is of immense value to the breeding of cultivated crops and domestic livestock. In the case of crops, for example, humans cultivate only a tiny fraction of the 350 000 species of flowering plants available, with an estimated half of the world's food needs being met by only three species, namely wheat (*Triticum aestivum*), rice (paddy) (*Oryza sativa*) and maize (*Zea mays*). The continued breeding of such crop species to enhance desirable traits, such as high productivity, tends to lead to a loss of genetic diversity and an increased vulnerability to, for example, outbreaks of pests or disease. Continued access to the genetic variability found in related wild strains is therefore of the greatest importance. It enables these crop species to be improved by incorporating appropriate wild traits, such as drought tolerance or parasite resistance, into their gene pool, through either breeding or genetic engineering techniques. Moreover, the huge genetic resource held amongst wild plant species is potentially useful for the future development of new crop species.

Another very important aspect of biological resources, from a human viewpoint, is their medicinal value. In many cultures, extracts from wild plants and animals form the basis of traditional medicines. This traditional use of natural products has stimulated considerable commercial interest from large companies (mainly pharmaceutical ones) and has led to the isolation of many thousands of potentially useful compounds (Table 10.1). One very important example is the rosy periwinkle (*Catharanthus roseus*) of Madagascar. Natural products derived from this native tropical tree have been used on the island for centuries, especially in the treatment of diabetes. Clinical research has led to the isolation of two alkaloids, vinblastine and vincristine, from *C. roseus*, and these have proved immensely successful as anticancer drugs. For example, the use of vincristine in the treatment of childhood leukaemia has replaced a situation of almost inevitable fatality with one of a 95% remission rate. The possibility of isolating new compounds from wild plant and animal species in the future (many of which may prove useful in disease treatment) forms a powerful argument for the conservation of *all* living species. To

Figure **10.1** Countries with highest species diversity, as estimated by the World Conservation Monitoring Centre's (WCMC) national biodiversity index. This index takes into account overall species diversity (richness and endemism) and country area data supplied by the WCMC, 1999.

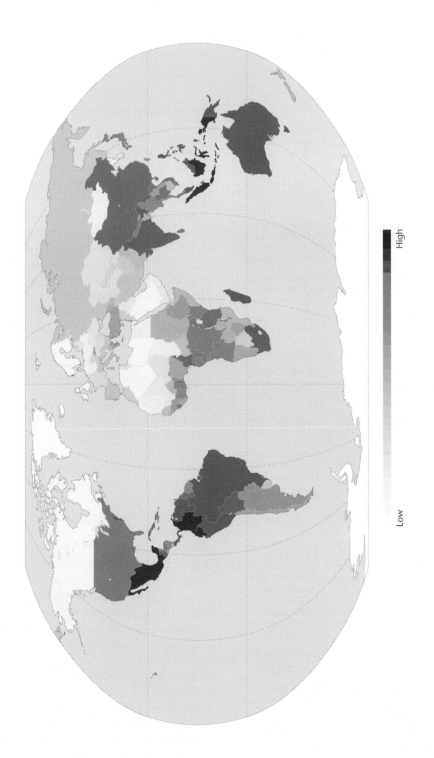

Table 10.1 Some examples of modern drugs derived from natural sources.

Drug	Source	Medical use
Aspirin	Willow (*Salix* spp.); meadowsweet (*Filipendula ulmaria*)	Painkiller (analgesic); anti-inflammatory drug
Atropine	Deadly nightshade (*Atropa belladonna*); also several other members of the potato family (Solanaceae)	Muscle relaxant
Bryostatin 1[a]	Sea mat (*Bugula neritina*)	Potential anticancer drug (trial status (1999): clinical phase II)
Curacin A[a]	*Lyngbya majuscula* (blue–green alga)	Potential anticancer drug (trial status (1999): preclinical)
Cyclomarin A/ Marinovir[a]	Marine actinomycetes (bacterium)	Potential antiviral/ anti-inflammatory drug (trial status (1999): preclinical)
Digitalin; digitoxin; digoxin	Foxglove (*Digitalis* spp.)	Treatment of heart disease; heart stimulant
Diosgenin	Certain species of yam	One of the main active ingredients used in oral contraceptives
Ecteinascidin 743[a]	Sea squirt (*Ecteinascidia turbinata*)	Potential anticancer drug (trial status (1999): clinical phase II)
Erythromycin	*Streptomyces erythreus* (bacterium)	Antibiotic
Halichondrin B[a]	*Lissodendoryx* sp. (sponge)	Potential anticancer drug (trial status (1999): preclinical)
Morphine	Opium poppy (*Papaver somniferum*)	Painkiller (analgesic)
Penicillin	*Penicillium notutum* (mould)	Antibiotic
Physostigmine	Calabar bean (*Physostigma venosum*)	Treatment of glaucoma and myasthenia gravis (disease in which muscles are weakened due to faulty transmission of nerve impulses)
Quinine	Bark of *Cinchona* spp.	Treatment of malaria
Reserpine	*Rauvolfia serpentina*	Tranquilliser
Vinblastine	Madagascar periwinkle (*Catharanthus roseus*)	Treatment of Hodgkin's disease
Vincristine	Madagascar periwinkle (*Catharanthus roseus*)	Treatment of leukaemia and Hodgkin's disease

[a] Source: Jaspars, M. (1999) Testing the water, *Chemistry and Industry*, **2**, 18 January, 51–55.

date, most such products have been derived from terrestrial organisms. However, the increasing accessibility of the marine environment in recent years (due to improvements in underwater exploration equipment) is beginning to lead to a similar exploitation of marine organisms, such as sponges (phylum Porifera) and sea squirts (class Ascidiaceae) (Table 10.1).

10.3 Direct damage to biological resources

Humans can cause direct damage to specific plant or animal species by selectively removing them from their natural habitats or, as in the case of pest control, eliminating them *in situ* (Box 11.2 on page 249). Biological species may be deliberately taken from the wild for a variety of reasons: for use as food, in medicines or fabrics, to supply the plant and pet trades, or simply for sport. Problems arise when targeted species are over-exploited and their numbers consequently become drastically reduced, in some cases to the point of extinction. In this section, the exploitation of stocks of marine fish and great whales and the international trafficking of wild plant and animal species are discussed in detail.

10.3.1 Exploitation of marine fish stocks

The majority of fish caught for human consumption is harvested from the marine environment. However, since 1950, the global catch of marine fish has increased fivefold (Figure 10.2). This trend is largely attributable to the significant advances made in fishing technology, especially those concerned with the location and capture of fish. Importantly, the actual number of marine fish species harvested for food is relatively small and this has led to the over-exploitation of a number of fish species/stocks. Moreover, good fishing grounds tend to be concentrated in areas of high biological productivity, especially those of the continental shelf regions, and these are usually fished several times each year. For example, a typical hectare of Georges Bank, a submerged mountain off the coast of New England, is trawled seven times a year. The enhanced capability of modern fishing vessels has, therefore, led not only to a serious decline in the overall numbers of certain desirable fish species but also to the 'fishing-out' of some previously rich fishing grounds. For example, over-exploitation of stocks of Atlantic cod (*Gadus morhua*) led to the collapse and subsequent closure of the Canadian Grand Banks cod fishery in 1992, with the loss of 40 000 jobs.

The current situation is one of too many fishing vessels pursuing too few fish. In order to conserve marine fish stocks in the long term, it is necessary for them to be

Figure 10.2 The global fish catch (in million metric tons) for the period 1950–94 (from Worldwatch Institute, 1996).

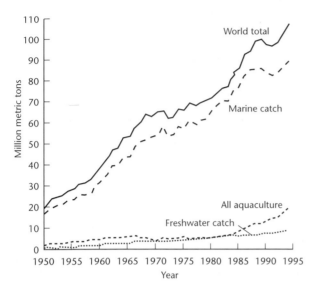

harvested in a sustainable manner, i.e. in such a way as to maintain or improve supplies, not deplete them further. There are a number of measures that can, and have, been taken to assist the recovery of declining marine fish stocks. These include a reduction in 'fishing effort' (e.g. in the number of days that vessels are allowed to put to sea), the setting and enforcement of fishing quotas (Box 10.1) and the creation of protected areas of the seabed. To give one illustrative example, large areas of Georges Bank (under US jurisdiction) were closed to fishing in 1994 in order to assist the recovery of stocks of the three main commercial fish species: yellowtail flounder (*Pleuronectes ferrugineus*), haddock (*Melanogrammus aeglefinus*) and cod (*Gadus morhua*). Concomitantly, Canada, which shares jurisdiction over Georges Bank with the US, reduced

fishing quotas for trawlers in the area. As well as directly protecting fish stocks, the exclusion of fishing from selected areas of Georges Bank enabled areas of the seafloor, previously destroyed by trawling and/or dredging, to recover. The gradual re-establishment of the diverse and complex seabed community provided fish, especially juvenile stages, with necessary food and shelter. As a result, the decline in populations of haddock and cod at Georges Bank has been halted whilst that of the yellowtail flounder has shown a significant increase.

On an international level, concern over declining fish stocks has resulted in the UN Agreement on the Conservation and Management of Straddling Fish Stocks and Highly Migratory Fish Stocks. This agreement comes under the auspices of the United Nations Convention on the Law of the Sea (10 December 1982), which 'governs all aspects of ocean spaces'. The UN Agreement on Fish Stocks was adopted on 4 August 1995 and opened for signature by UN member nations on 4 December 1995. By December 1998, it had 59 signatories but only 19 of the 30 ratifications/accessions necessary for its enforcement. Partly because of the difficulties in reaching international agreement over the sustainable management of marine fish stocks, attention is now turning more towards aquaculture for the supply of fish. It is feasible that, in the future, fish farming (Box 10.2) will raise an increasing proportion of all marine (and freshwater) fish consumed by humans.

10.3.2 Exploitation of the great whales

Within the mammalian order Cetacea, a distinction is made between the 'great whales' (otherwise known as the 'large cetaceans') and the 'small cetaceans', a group which consists of the dolphins, porpoises and smaller whale species. The twelve species of great whale (Table 10.2) face a number of

---

Further Information Box

10.1   Sustainable yield and the setting of quota

In the harvesting of marine fish, the term yield refers to the amount of fish taken over a set period of time (usually a year). The maximum amount of fish that can theoretically be harvested from a population without its depletion is known as the maximum sustainable yield (MSY). This equates to the net increase in the number of individuals in that population during a given year (i.e. the number of individuals recruited through birth or immigration minus the number lost through death or emigration).

The maximum sustainable yield can be calculated in advance

for different fish populations in different areas. However, because the MSY is a forecast (based on past figures) and because recruitment is unpredictable from year to year, catching fish at this maximal level would result in over-harvesting in many instances (i.e. in those years when recruitment levels were lower than expected). For this reason, a smaller estimate, the optimum sustainable yield (OSY), is used. This is normally calculated as half the carrying capacity of the environment for the species in question and provides the basis from which the yield quotas for commercial fisheries are worked out.

Further Information Box

10.2 Fish farming – a type of aquaculture

Aquaculture is the practice of rearing aquatic organisms, such as fish, molluscs, crustaceans and algae, for human consumption. The term fish farming is usually reserved for the rearing of fish species, both marine and freshwater. Fish farming is not a new technique. For example, in China the tradition of raising freshwater fish, such as carp, in managed ponds dates back over 5000 years, and is still found in many rural areas today.

Current methods of fish farming are highly diverse, ranging from the simple enclosure of coastal waters to protect desirable marine species from predators to the use of closely monitored and highly controlled artificial rearing systems. In fish ranching, the young are reared under controlled conditions, released from captivity to feed on natural prey and then harvested from the wild at a later date.

There has been a revived interest in fish farming worldwide during recent years, prompted by the decline in marine fish stocks. In the period 1985–95, global production from aquaculture more than doubled, reaching 21 million metric tons in 1995 (a rise of 2 million metric tons from 1994). One in five fish consumed worldwide come from farmed sources and this share of the market is likely to increase in future years. The potential for fish farming to contribute significantly to human nutrition has earned it the label 'Blue Revolution', by analogy to the Green Revolution in agriculture, which was brought about by the development of high-yielding varieties of cereal grains (Box 11.4 on page 251).

The development of fish farming has, however, led to a number of environmental problems. Farmed fish, which are typically reared in high densities, are very vulnerable to disease, which quickly spreads throughout the population. Antibiotics and pesticides used to control such outbreaks may leak into the wider environment. Another associated problem is the production of large amounts of organic waste, which have to be disposed of. This too may cause pollution problems, if not properly controlled.

In some instances, the escape of farmed species may threaten native ones. For example, between 1988 and 1998, an estimated 100 000 Atlantic salmon (*Salmo salar*) escaped from net cages along Canada's Pacific coast. Successful spawning of the farmed Atlantic salmon has already been recorded in one river in British Columbia. It is feared that the faster-growing Atlantic salmon will eventually out-compete the native Pacific salmon (*Oncorhynchus* spp.), whose numbers are already declining as a result of human activities such as logging. The construction of fish farms can involve the loss of productive agricultural land and their operative procedures may lead to the depletion of valuable freshwater supplies. Finally, the development of fish farms may not, in fact, relieve the pressure on dwindling marine stocks, since farmed species of predatory fish are generally fed on high-protein meal derived, at least in part, from marine fish species, such as Alaskan pollock.

---

major threats to their survival, the greatest of which, until recently, has been direct exploitation by man. The great whales have been hunted and killed for centuries to provide humans with a number of useful products, such as meat, baleen for whalebone, and blubber. More latterly, blubber oil derived from whale blubber (the insulating layer of fat found between the skin and muscle layer) has been used as a raw material in, for example, the manufacture of paints and cosmetics. Over-exploitation of great whale populations has led to a very serious decline in their total numbers. This has resulted in some of them, e.g. the blue whale (*Balaenoptera musculus*) and northern right whale (*Eubalaena glacialis*), being placed in the endangered category of the IUCN (International Union for the Conservation of Nature) Red List of threatened species (Table 10.2).

Conservation of great whale stocks through the regulation of commercial whaling comes under the remit of the International Whaling Commission (IWC). This was established under the International Convention for the Regulation of Whaling signed in Washington, DC, on 2 December 1946. Regulatory measures include the setting of catch quotas, the complete protection of specified species and the designation of certain areas as whale sanctuaries. To date, 40 nations have signed the 1946 Convention (1998 figure). However, the IWC has been criticised for 'lacking teeth' since any member nation who objects to a particular decision (previously agreed by the required three-quarters majority), on the grounds that it seriously affects their national interests, is not then bound by that decision. However, it has been argued that without the inclusion of this objection procedure, the Convention would probably never have been signed.

Probably the greatest obstacle to the effective management of great whale stocks is the inherent difficulty in estimating their numbers accurately and assessing their status accordingly. It was mainly for this reason that the IWC voted in 1982 for a complete moratorium on the killing of all whale species for commercial purposes from 1985/86 onwards. Exceptions were made to allow some aboriginal subsistence whaling e.g. the taking of a limited number of West Greenland fin whales (*Balaenoptera physalus*) and minke whales (*Balaenoptera acutorostrata*) by Greenlanders. Some whaling nations, however, have defied the ban and continued to harvest a limited number of great whales. These include Japan (under the guise of 'scientific research'), Iceland

Table 10.2 The 1996 IUCN Red List status of the twelve species of great whales.

Common name	Latin name	1996 IUCN Red List status[a]
Blue whale	Balaenoptera musculus	Endangered (EN)
Bowhead whale	Balaena mysticetus	Lower Risk (LR)
Bryde's whale	Balaenoptera edeni	Data Deficient (DD)
Fin whale	Balaenoptera physalus	Endangered (EN)
Gray whale	Eschrichtius robustus	Endangered (EN)/ Lower Risk (LR) (depending on population)
Humpback whale	Megaptera novaeangliae	Vulnerable (VU)
Minke whale	Balaenoptera acutorostrata	Lower Risk (LR)
Northern right whale	Eubalaena glacialis	Endangered (EN)
Pygmy blue whale	Balaenoptera musculus brevicauda	Data Deficient (DD)
Sei whale	Balaenoptera borealis	Endangered (EN)
Southern right whale	Eubalaena australis	Lower Risk (LR)
Sperm whale	Physeter catodon	Vulnerable (VU)

[a] See Table 10.3 for summary definitions of categories.

(which withdrew from the IWC) and Norway (which lodged an objection to the ban).

The 1986 moratorium on the killing of great whales currently remains in place. Its purpose, to give the great whale species a chance to recover their numbers, appears to have met with some success. Since 1986, the total population size of some of the great whale species has increased significantly. The most notable example is the minke whale (*Balaenoptera acutorostrata*) whose numbers are currently estimated at around one million. There is growing international pressure for a permanent ban on commercial whaling. It is argued that acceptable substitutes are available for all whale-derived products and that the number of jobs associated with the whaling industry is relatively small. In addition, whale-watching, a type of eco-tourism, is growing in popularity and could potentially provide an alternative source of income to whaling, in some localities.

10.3.3 The international traffic in wild plant and animal species

The international trade in wild plants and animals, and in products derived from them, poses a major threat to biodiversity. Many of the species involved in trafficking belong to threatened categories, according to the IUCN (International Union for Conservation of Nature and Natural Resources) Red Lists, e.g. the cheetah (*Acinonyx jubatus*) and the black rhinoceros (*Diceros bicornis*) (Table 10.3). Endangered species, e.g. the tiger (*Panthera tigris*) (Box 10.3), receive protection under the Convention on International Trade in Endangered Species (CITES) (Section 10.6). However, many endangered species continue to be trafficked illegally. Their rarity value means that they can fetch high prices on the black market and, as a consequence, they remain at risk from poachers.

The international trade in wild plants involves both harvested material and living specimens. Some wild species are exploited to provide cut flowers, e.g. pitcher plants (family Nepenthaceae) and orchids (family Orchidaceae), whilst others are used to provide particular substances, used in medicines, food products, etc. For example, the roots of wild orchids are dried and powdered to make salep, a health food ingredient used in specialist ice creams. Other plant species are removed alive from their natural habitat to supply the houseplant trade, e.g. cacti (family Cactaceae) and bromeliads (family Bromeliaceae). In addition, in some countries, huge quantities of bulbs, corms and tubers are dug up in the wild to supply the gardening retail trade. In Turkey, for example, millions of snowdrops (*Galanthus nivalis*), winter aconites (*Eranthus hyemalis*) and cyclamen (*Cyclamen* spp.) are uprooted annually by local villagers for this purpose.

In the traffic of wild animals, market destination determines whether individual animals are captured alive or not. A huge number of living animals, particularly fish, birds and reptiles, are taken from the wild each year to supply the exotic pet trade. The percentage of these animals that survive to be sold is very low; many perish during capture or in transit. Wild animals, especially mammals, are also taken alive to supply zoos and scientific research programmes. The methods employed in capturing wild animals can sometimes result in extensive damage to the ecosystem, beyond that caused to the target species itself. For example, the use of cyanide to obtain tropical reef fish is recognised as one of the main factors that have contributed to the deterioration of the world's coral reef ecosystem (Section 10.5.1).

Much of the international trade in wild animals involves not the living animals themselves but certain specific parts of their bodies. These 'wildlife products', as they are usually termed, may provide humans with luxury items, which are seen as desirable because of their relative scarcity and the expense involved in procuring them. Examples include the skins of big cats such as Javan leopards (*Panthera pardus melas*) and cheetahs (*Acinonyx*

Table 10.3 The 1996 IUCN Red List of Threatened Animals.

Category	Category symbol	Summary definition	Examples
Extinct	EX	No reasonable doubt that the last individual has died.	Passenger pigeon (*Ectopistes migratorius*), Falklands wolf (*Dusicyon australis*)
Extinct in the Wild	EW	No individual recorded throughout its historic range (despite exhaustive surveys) but individuals survive in cultivation, in captivity or as naturalised population(s) well outside the past range.	Przewalski's horse (*Equus przewalskii*), black-footed ferret (*Mustela nigripes*)
Critically Endangered[a]	CR	Taxon faces an extremely high risk of extinction in the wild in the immediate future.	Black rhinoceros (*Diceros bicornis*), Persian mole (*Talpa streeti*)
Endangered[a]	EN	Taxon is not Critically Endangered but faces a very high risk of extinction in the wild in the near future.	Tiger (*Panthera tigris*), European bison (*Bison bonasus*)
Vulnerable[a]	VU	Taxon is not Critically Endangered or Endangered but faces a high risk of extinction in the wild in the medium-term future.	Atlantic cod (*Gadus morhua*), Cheetah (*Acinonyx jubatus*)
Lower Risk	LR	Taxon has been evaluated, but does not satisfy the criteria for any of the categories Critically Endangered, Endangered or Vulnerable. Such taxa may be placed in one of three subcategories.[b]	Whale-headed stork (*Balaeniceps rex*) (Near Threatened (nt) subcategory), Waterbuck (antelope) (*Kobus ellipsiprymnus*) (Conservation Dependent (cd) subcategory)
Data Deficient	DD	Inadequate information available to make a direct, or indirect, assessment of taxon's risk of extinction based on its distribution and/or population status.	Giant bandicoot (*Peroryctes broadbenti*), narrow-bodied skink (*Oligosoma gracilicorpus*)
Not Evaluated	NE	Taxon not yet assessed against the criteria.	

[a] Category recognised as a threatened one.
[b] Three subcategories of Lower Risk category:
(i) Conservation Dependent (cd): Taxon subject of a continuing taxon-specific or habitat-specific conservation programme, the cessation of which would result in the taxon qualifying for one of the threatened categories (CR, EN or VU) within a period of five years.
(ii) Near Threatened (nt): Taxon does not qualify for Conservation Dependent, but is close to qualifying for Vulnerable.
(iii) Least Concern (lc): Taxon does not qualify for Conservation Dependent or Near Threatened.

jubatus) and ivory from the African elephant (*Loxodonta africana*) and the black rhinoceros (*Diceros bicornis*). Yet other wildlife products are sought because they are thought to possess medicinal or aphrodisiac properties. Traditional Chinese medicine (TCM), which is used by an estimated 25% of the world's population, makes use of a range of different body parts from a variety of animal species, e.g. tiger (*Panthera tigris*) bones and rhinoceros horn. However, the extensive and uncontrolled use of wild animal, and plant, species in TCM is, in many cases, seriously damaging wild populations and putting their long-term future at risk. For example, the loss of 95% of the world's black rhino population between 1970 and 1993 is largely attributed to the use of its horn in traditional medicine.

10.4 Introduced species

An **introduced species** may be defined as a plant or animal species which is not native to a particular geographical area and is thought to have been brought in by human agency. The terms 'exotic' and 'alien' may also be used to describe such species. The effect of introduced species on native species is usually detrimental, often resulting in the decimation or even extinction of native species of plants and

Mini Case Study

10.3 Endangered species – a profile of the tiger (*Panthera tigris*)

At the beginning of the twentieth century, there were eight subspecies of the tiger (*Panthera tigris*). However, in the past 60 years, three of these subspecies, the Bali tiger (*P. t. balica*), Caspian tiger (*P. t. virgata*) and Javan tiger (*P. t. sondaica*) have become extinct (in the 1940s, 1970s and 1980s respectively). From an estimated total population in 1900 of around 100 000, only an estimated 5000–7500 tigers remain. Details of the surviving five subspecies are given in the table opposite.

A combination of factors is responsible for the 95% decline in the tiger population since the beginning of the twentieth century. Tiger body parts are widely used in TCM (traditional Chinese medicine), e.g. as tiger plasters applied to arthritic and rheumatic joints, and, although this trade is now illegal under the Convention on International Trade in Endangered Species (CITES), poaching and smuggling continue to threaten the survival of the world's tiger population. Loss of habitat, for both tigers and their prey species, has also contributed substantially to their decline. In addition, tigers tend to occur in areas of high human population and, as they threaten livestock, conflict arises.

Subspecies of tiger	Latin name	Rough estimate of numbers[a]	1996 IUCN Red List category[b]
Amur (Siberian)	P. t. altaica	~400	Critically endangered (CR)
Bengal (Indian)	P. t. tigris	~3000	
Indo–Chinese	P. t. corbetti	~1000	
South China	P. t. amoyensis	~400	Critically endangered (CR)
Sumatran	P. t. sumatrae	~400	Critically endangered (CR)

[a] Source: WWF Tiger Status Report (1998).
[b] See Table 10.3 for summary definitions.

animals. On a global scale, introduced species are now considered by some to pose as great a threat to biodiversity as deforestation, desertification or global warming.

The introduction of exotic species into new geographical areas may be accidental or deliberate. In some cases, species are inadvertently carried from one location to another as a result of the movement of goods and people. For example, the house mouse (*Mus musculus*) and the brown rat (*Rattus norvegicus*) have been carried to all parts of the world, originally by sailing ships, and thus have achieved a worldwide distribution. The discharge of ballast water from ships has been responsible for the introduction of many exotic aquatic species. For example, in the mid-1980s, the zebra mussel (*Dreissena polymorpha*), a native of the Caspian Sea, was introduced into the Great Lakes of North America in this manner and has rapidly become established (Box 10.4).

Exotic species may be introduced deliberately for a number of diverse reasons. For example, in the nineteenth century, European settlers to North America were responsible for importing species of birds, such as the starling (*Sturnus vulgaris*) and the house sparrow (*Passer domesticus*), to remind them of home. European settlers were also instrumental in the introduction of the European rabbit (*Oryctolagus cuniculus*) into Australia for the purpose of sport shooting, an action whose devastating repercussions are still being felt today (Box 10.5). In the plant world, there are many examples of the deliberate introduction of exotic species. These are often imported for ornamental use in

parks and gardens and many have subsequently escaped and become **naturalised** (i.e. successfully established in the wild). In Britain, examples of such naturalised species include the butterfly bush (*Buddleia davidii*), a native of China, and the common rhododendron (*Rhododendron ponticum*), which originates in the Himalayas, both originally introduced as ornamentals. The introduction of exotic plant species also provides an opportunity for pest species and pathogens to simultaneously invade. For example, in the USA, the introduction of Chinese chestnut trees (*Castanea mollissima*) was responsible for importing a fungal disease called chestnut blight that subsequently decimated the native species of chestnut, American chestnut (*Castanea dentata*). In some cases, exotic animal species are deliberately introduced in order to control other introduced species of plants or animals which have reached pest proportions (Box 10.6).

The degree of damage caused by introduced species to native species of plants and/or animals varies enormously. In some cases, an introduced species fails to establish a viable population and simply dies out, with little or no effect on the local flora and fauna. However, at the other end of the scale, there are exotic species which, favoured by a lack of predation and/or competition in their new environment, are able to establish themselves with rapidity. Their population growth is explosive and typified by the J-shaped growth curve (Chapter 7, Section 7.1.4). In rare instances, such 'successful' species are benign, but more usually their impact on native species is highly

10.4 Introduced species – the zebra mussel (*Dreissena polymorpha*) in the Great Lakes of North America

The zebra mussel (*Dreissena polymorpha*) is a tiny bivalve (adult length <5 mm), indigenous to the Caspian Sea, which was first introduced into the Great Lakes of North America in the mid-1980s. Its planktonic larvae were carried from Europe in the ballast water of a cargo ship and released into the St Clair River near Detroit in 1986. The favourable conditions encountered by the zebra mussel in its new environment, including a lack of predators (namely fish and ducks), enabled it to multiply with great rapidity. It is now found throughout the Great Lakes system and from there has managed to invade the Mississippi River and its tributaries.

The life cycle of the zebra mussel consists of a microsopic, planktonic larval stage and a sessile, filter-feeding adult stage, which feeds on plankton. The adult mussels have a shell of two hinged valves (a feature typical of the class Bivalvia) and live attached to hard substrata, such as rocks, boats and piers, by means of byssal threads. Colonies of zebra mussels can reach very high densities, with figures ranging between 20 000 and 90 000 individuals per square metre. The sheer density of zebra mussels present can cause serious practical problems in some situations, especially when they clog up the water intake pipes of certain industries (e.g. municipal water supply).

From an ecological standpoint, there is much concern about the impact this exotic species will have on other species of animals, and plants, found in the Great Lakes, primarily through competition for food but also for space and dissolved oxygen.

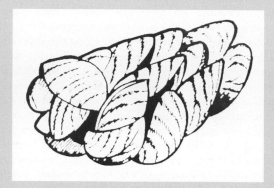

Further reading: Snyder, F.L., D. W. Garton and M. Brainard (1997) *Zebra mussels in the Great Lakes: The invasion and its implications*. Ohio Sea Grant College Program, Ohio State University.

10.5 The introduction of the European rabbit (*Oryctolagus cuniculus*) into Australia

The European rabbit (*Oryctolagus cuniculus*), originally from the Iberian peninsula, has become naturalised in numerous locations throughout the world. In 1859, the first wild rabbits were imported from England into Australia, where they were initially kept in captivity. The subsequent escape of these few individuals into the Australian outback led to a population explosion whose consequences, for farming communities and native marsupials alike, were devastating. The feeding activities of these herbivorous mammals transformed huge areas of formerly productive pastureland (used for rearing cattle and sheep) into semi-desert. They also destroyed forests by ring-barking the young trees. Between 1880 and 1950, the rabbit population, favoured by conditions that included a lack of natural predators, reached an estimated 800 million.

Over the years, a number of different methods have been used in an effort to control the Australian rabbit population,

with varying degrees of success. In the late nineteenth century, huge stretches of 'rabbit proof' fences were built in order to halt the spread of rabbits. However, as these were easily damaged, e.g. by floods and winds, they proved largely ineffectual. Other methods included gassing, trapping and poisoning. In 1950, the introduction of the species-specific virus *Myxomatosis cuniculus* proved to be a highly effective method of control. During the next three years, between 80% and 90% of the continent's rabbit population was wiped out. However, by 1955, the rabbit population had begun to show signs of resistance to the myxoma virus and started to recover. In 1996, another virus deadly to rabbits, known as calicivirus, was released in Australia to control the increasing population of wild rabbits.

Reference: Lever, C. (1994) *Naturalized animals: the ecology of successfully introduced species*. London: T & A D Poyser.

damaging. In some cases, species invasion results in the hybridisation of introduced species with native ones. For example, the North American ruddy duck (*Oxyura jamaicensis*), which originally escaped from waterfowl collections in England, has spread to a total of 13 European countries. In Turkey and Spain, it has bred with the rare white-headed duck (*Oxyura leucocephala*) and fertile hybrid offspring have been produced as a result. This interbreeding between the two species therefore threatens the survival of the native white-headed duck.

Mini Case Study

10.6   The problem of the water hyacinth (*Eichhornia crassipes*) in Africa's largest lake, Lake Victoria

The water hyacinth (*Eichhornia crassipes*) is an attractive aquatic tropical plant with spikes of blue flowers, native to Central and South America. However, its introduction, accidental or otherwise, into freshwater ecosystems throughout the world has led to a serious weed problem in a total of 53 countries, including Australia, the United States and China. Once introduced, this exotic species, with little in the way of predators or competitors to keep it in check, rapidly becomes established. With the ability to double its numbers in less than a fortnight, the water hyacinth quickly forms vast floating rafts of vegetation which choke waterways, making navigation and fishing difficult or impossible.

In the last decade, the water hyacinth has spread throughout the African continent, affecting the majority of its large water bodies. In 1989 it invaded Africa's largest lake, Lake Victoria (surface area $75\,000\,km^2$), which lies mainly in Uganda and Tanzania and partly in Kenya. Clumps of the weed, originating from the headwaters of the River Zaire, were imported into the lake by way of the River Kagera. Since then, the water hyacinth

has spread to cover in excess of 10 000 hectares, seriously impeding navigation and consequently destroying local fishing industries.

Attempts to control the water hyacinth in Lake Victoria have met with little success. Mechanical harvesters have been used to clear pathways but these are quickly recolonised by this aggressive weed. Biological control has also been tried but the introduced weevils, although successful in curbing other, less serious, infestations in other countries such as Zambia and India, have made little impact on the problem in Lake Victoria. Attention is now turning to the possible use of chemical methods of control, namely the use of the herbicides 2,4-dichlorophenoxyacetic acid (a component of Agent Orange which was used as a defoliant by the US army during the Vietnam War) and/or glyphosate.

Reference: Pearce, F. (1998) All-out war on the alien invader. *New Scientist*, 23 May, 34–38.

Oceanic islands are particularly vulnerable to species invasion, since, in many cases, native species have no natural predators. This is especially the case for indigenous species of ground-nesting birds. Introduced animals, such as cats, pigs and rats, feed on the eggs and/or young of such birds, with devastating results. For example, on the island of Guam in the western Pacific Ocean, the accidental introduction of the brown tree snake (*Boiga irregularis*) in the early 1950s led to the extinction of six of the island's 18 native bird species and severely reduced populations of the remaining 12. The ability of the brown tree snake to switch to alternative prey sources (usually small reptiles) when bird numbers are low, the absence of predators and the lack of competitors on the island were all contributory factors to its successful naturalisation.

Successful exotic species, both plant and animal, which rapidly gain a foothold in new geographical areas and quickly spread, are virtually impossible to eliminate once established. Various methods of pest control have been tried but usually with limited effect. In many cases, another exotic species is brought in, in an attempt to control the spread of the first. In the case of the water hyacinth in Africa's Lake Victoria (Box 10.6), the introduction of weevils from South America was ineffectual against this prolific weed. In this particular lake, the scale of the problem was too large and the introduction of these agents of biological control was too little and too late. Another of the difficulties with biological control methods is trying to ensure that the introduced organism will attack only the target pest

species. For example, in 1883, the small Indian mongoose (*Herpestes auropunctatus*) was deliberately introduced from Jamaica into the Hawaiian Islands to control populations of rats in sugar-cane plantations. However, although they had some success in controlling rats, they also preyed on native species such as the Hawaiian goose (*Branta sandvicensis*) and the peaceful dove (*Geopelia tranquilla*).

There are many well-documented examples of the deleterious effects that certain introduced species have on native ones. Moreover, all these individual instances of species introductions add up to a problem of global proportions. It is becoming apparent that the rate of introductions is growing, concomitant with an upsurge in world trade and travel. This is leading to an increasing threat to biodiversity (as exotic species lead to the extinction of native ones) and also to an increasing homogenisation of the world's species. For example, a comparison between the Seychelles Islands and the island of Mauritius, separated by 1500 km in the Indian Ocean, shows that they have 350 and 730 introduced species of land plants respectively and that many of these exotic species are common to both. Similarly, the Seychelles have 11 introduced species of land birds whilst Mauritius has 15, eight of which are the same alien species as found on the Seychelles.

The threat of introduced species to biodiversity, unlike other threats such as global warming and deforestation, is essentially irreversible. It has been mentioned that once introduced species have successfully established populations in the wild, they are virtually impossible to eliminate. What can be done in the future about this growing problem? Clearly, it would be best to prevent potential introductions in the first place (by tighter controls and legislation) or, if not, to deal with the introduced species as soon as they arrive, before they have the opportunity to become established. The International Union for the Conservation of Nature and Natural Resources (IUCN) has responded to the increasing threat of introduced species by setting up the Invasive Species Specialist Group (ISSG) within the Species Survival Commission (SSC). The aim of the ISSG is to increase awareness of the problems caused by the invasion of exotic species (to both native species and natural ecosystems) and to look at ways of their prevention, control and eradication.

One final point to make, which is very pertinent to this section on introduced species, is the recent development of genetically modified crops (Case study 1, page 240). It is not known what effects the introduction of these modified strains into general cultivation will have on ecosystems and the native species that they contain.

10.5 Habitat degradation, loss and fragmentation

Biological resources may be threatened by changes to habitat, which generally occur as a result of human activities. In some cases, the change takes the form of a gradual, usually detrimental, alteration in conditions, e.g. as seen in the eutrophication of a freshwater lake (Chapter 14, Section 14.2). In other instances, the habitat itself is destroyed, often in order to convert it to some other form of land use, such as agriculture or urban development. The fragmentation of a habitat through, for example, road building can severely depress the populations of wild plants and animals that live there, even to the point of extinction. This pattern of habitat loss is examined separately in Section 10.5.3.

10.5.1 Habitat degradation

The modification of habitats as a result of external factors, usually anthropogenic in origin, usually has a detrimental effect on biological resources. In many cases, particularly those involving aquatic ecosystems, habitat degradation is brought about by pollution. The adverse effects of different types of pollutant (e.g. organic oxygen-demanding wastes, mercury, lead, oil, and organochlorines such as DDT) on aquatic habitats are discussed in detail in Chapter 14. One type of aquatic ecosystem that is becoming increasingly threatened by pollution, amongst other factors, is the coral reef. A global survey carried out in 1997 found that approximately 95% of the world's coral reefs had suffered damage as a result of poisoning, dynamiting, pollution, overfishing and ships' anchors. Moreover, the phenomenon of coral bleaching has been widely reported from coral reefs across the globe (Box 10.7). Air pollution and acid deposition also have a detrimental effect on natural habitats such as lakes and forests (Chapter 14, Section 14.3.1 and Chapter 15, Section 15.2.2). Other human activities may result in the simplification of habitats. Certain practices, such as dredging streams or clearing away dead wood from forest floors, decrease habitat heterogeneity, with a resultant loss in associated species. The replacement of natural or semi-natural ecosystems with crop monocultures, or with managed forests consisting of only a few tree species, also results in habitat simplification and a decrease in species diversity.

Further Information Box

10.7 Coral bleaching

Coral reefs are submarine ridges, widely distributed in clear, shallow tropical and sub-tropical waters. They are formed by the progressive deposition of calcium carbonate by colonial corals (Cnidaria, Anthozoa). The corals contain microscopic algae (known as zooxanthellae) within their tissues, a close association that is mutually beneficial. The algae provide the corals with necessary nutrients whilst themselves making use of the metabolic waste products produced by the corals, and also receiving shelter.

However, when the corals are subjected to stress, this relationship collapses. The corals expel the tiny algae from within their tissues, becoming white or 'bleached' as a result. This phenomenon is known as **coral bleaching**. At this stage, the corals are still alive and are often capable of recovery.

However, actual coral death will result if the stress(es) involved is heightened and/or prolonged. Coral bleaching may be caused by a number of different factors, such as pollution, uncommonly high or low light levels, or unusually high or low temperatures. Of these, high temperature appears to be the causal agent in the majority of incidents.

During 1998 coral bleaching, on a global scale, was the worst recorded to date, in terms of both its geographic spread and the severity of its impact. In some areas, actual death amongst coral colonies reached 95%. Higher than average water temperatures, linked to the El Niño warm event of 1997–98 (Box 4.4, page 87), were mainly responsible for this widespread and devastating incidence of coral bleaching.

Habitat alteration may also occur through the effects of global warming (Chapter 15, Section 15.2.3). The Intergovernmental Panel on Climate Change (IPCC) has predicted that global mean temperatures may increase by 1.1°C by 2030 and 3.3°C by 2090, compared with present levels, assuming a 'business as usual' scenario. The temperature rise is expected to be greatest in the higher latitudes, especially in the Antarctic and Arctic regions. It is not known how these predicted climatic changes will influence the geographical distribution of different plant and animal species. Much depends on their ability to adapt to changing conditions and/or their capacity to alter their ranges. There is evidence that during past episodes of climate change, plant and animal species have extended and retracted their geographical ranges in response to changes in habitat suitability. This was made possible by the existence of an uninterrupted succession of biomes, each merging gradually into the next. However, these gradual changes in vegetation and habitat no longer exist over much of the Earth's surface. In many areas, human activities have replaced the natural habitat with other types of land use, e.g. agriculture and urban development. As a result, natural habitats have become dissipated into isolated fragments. This new, fractured pattern may have severe implications for those plant and animal species whose response to a changing climate is to alter their ranges.

10.5.2 Habitat loss

Habitat loss is largely caused by human activities, although, in some cases, it may be brought about by natural disasters such as mudslides. Over the centuries, progressively more of the world's natural habitats have been lost. For example, Figure 10.3 illustrates the demise of forest in Warwickshire, England, between 400 and 1960. This diagram also clearly demonstrates the process of habitat fragmentation, which is discussed further in Section 10.5.3.

There are numerous reasons for the deliberate destruction of natural habitats. In many cases, natural habitats, such as forests and wetlands, are cleared and/or drained for agricultural use or sometimes for the cultivation of trees (silviculture). To give one recent example, in Indonesia in 1997–98 large areas of the rainforest were deliberately torched in order to replace the natural forest with commercial plantations of rubber trees (*Hevea* spp.) or oil palms (Box 10.8). The need for land for urban and industrial development, together with its associated infrastructure (roads and railways), is also responsible for widespread habitat loss. The continued expansion of the world's human population, especially in

the developing world (Chapter 7, Section 7.3), and the growing need for land to meet basic requirements such as food and shelter, means that the pressure on natural habitats is unlikely to abate.

Mining activities, especially those using surface methods such as strip and opencast mining, are another cause of habitat destruction, sometimes on a very large scale. A further example of habitat loss, which has only recently come to light as a result of remote photography, concerns the ocean floor. The destruction of large tracts of this habitat has been caused by trawlers and dredgers, which scrape the seabed indiscriminately in pursuit of bottom-living fish such as Atlantic cod (*Gadus morhua*) and haddock (*Melanogrammus aeglefinus*). An analogy has been drawn between the creation of these marine deserts and the clear-cutting of forests (Chapter 11, Section 11.4). The development of aquaculture has also led, in some cases, to the loss of natural habitats. For example, in Thailand, an estimated 17% of mangrove forests were lost between 1987 and 1993 as a result of their conversion to shrimp farms. Finally, habitats may be destroyed by the commercial exploitation of their native plant species. This is the underlying reason for much of the deforestation experienced in the tropical rainforests (Chapter 11, Section 11.5.1).

10.5.3 Habitat fragmentation

The progressive fragmentation of natural habitats into smaller patches (Figure 10.3) has serious implications for the survival of wild plant and animal species. Populations of plants and animals within a particular habitat are usually present at levels at or near the carrying capacity of their environment (Chapter 7, Section 7.1.5). This means that when parts of that habitat are lost, usually as a result of human activities, the option for wild species to move into the remaining patches is not necessarily available. This leads to an overall decline in population size.

The separation of fragments of the same habitat type by, for example, canals, roads or urban development, leads to their isolation. Plant and animal species, unable to cross these barriers, become confined to particular patches. As a result, gene flow between populations of the same species is effectively stopped. This means that the genetic variability of a population within a particular patch can no longer be boosted by genetic input from individuals from outside the patch. This is especially important in light of the fact that these populations have already become reduced in size as a result of habitat fragmentation. A lessening of the genetic variability present in a small population lowers the ability of that population to adapt, in an evolutionary sense, to changing conditions. It can also lead to problems of inbreeding. The role of 'wildlife

Figure 10.3 Forest fragmentation in Warwickshire, England, from 400 to 1960 AD. Forested areas are shown in black (from Wilcove, D.S., C.H. McLellan and A.P. Dobson (1986) 'Habitat fragmentation in the temperate Zone' in *Conservation Biology: the Science of Scarcity and Diversity*, Soule, M.E. (ed), Sunderland. Mass: Sinauer Associates).

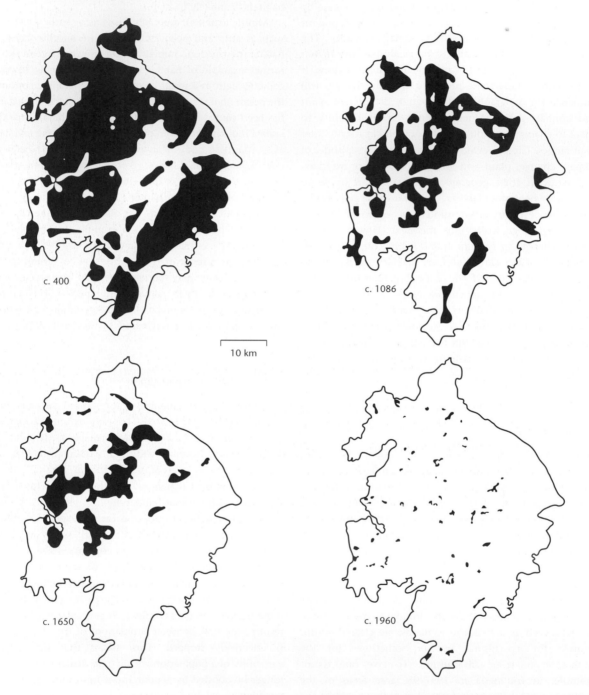

corridors' in bridging the barriers between isolated habitat fragments and facilitating the exchange of genetic material is discussed in Box 10.9.

The size of a habitat fragment is of crucial importance to the survival and recovery of the remnant populations of plant and animal species that it contains. For any particular species, the size of the habitat fragment must be sufficiently large to support a certain critical number of individuals, known as the minimum viable population (MVP) (Box 10.10). Therefore, even if the fragmentation of a habitat does not cause a significant reduction in its overall area, it can lead to population extinction by

Mini Case Study

10.8   Habitat destruction – the Indonesian forest fires of 1997–98

Indonesia, in south-east Asia, has the world's second largest area of rainforest after Brazil. During the period from August 1997 to May 1998 (with a brief interlude in December 1997 and January 1998 when the monsoon rains fell), at least 2 million hectares of this tropical rainforest were destroyed by fire. In previous incidents of uncontrolled burning, 'shifting cultivators' – local farmers who cultivate small patches of the forest in succession using the 'slash and burn' technique – have been blamed for initiating the fires. However, in this most recent incident, large-scale plantation companies, encouraged by government policies to clear large areas of rainforest for the cultivation of rubber trees (*Hevea* spp.) or oil palms, have largely been held responsible.

Conditions in the Indonesian rainforests during 1997 and 1998 were unusually dry. This situation has been attributed to the El Niño climatic event which occurred during that period (Box 4.4, page 87). The drought conditions encouraged the deliberate torching of the forests, and also assisted the fires to burn out of control. Forested peat bogs were also set on fire in a number of areas, such as central Kalimantan on the island of Borneo and the Riau area of Sumatra, either deliberately or as a result of the raging forest fires. Once alight, the peat bogs, which in many places reach depths of 20 metres or more, smouldered for weeks, producing the huge quantities of smoke that enveloped south-east Asia. The smoke caused widespread health problems, such as headaches, eye irritation and sore throats. It also had a damaging effect on the economies of south-east Asia, e.g. through a significant reduction in tourism to the region. Changes in government policy, including appropriate controls and restrictions placed on large-scale plantation companies, are needed if future instances of uncontrolled burning are to be avoided.

Reference: Pearce, F. (1998) Playing with fire. *New Scientist*, 21 March, 36–39.

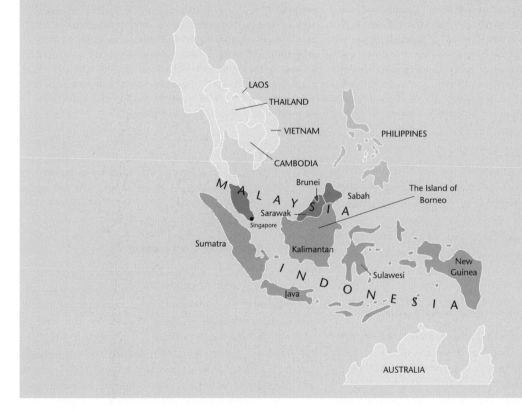

subdividing the original area into smaller, isolated patches, each of which is too small to support the MVPs of its constituent species.

Another effect of habitat fragmentation is to increase the number of edges present. This 'edge effect' may favour the survival of certain species over others. For example, in a recent study of several fragments of the Brazilian rainforest, it was found that the density of shade-tolerant seedlings (which represent the majority of the rainforest trees) decreased towards the edges of the patches. This decline was partly due to less favourable climatic conditions at the forest edge, and partly due to competition from faster-growing, light-tolerant species. The study concluded that fragments of rainforest less than

Further Information Box

10.9 Wildlife corridors

The concept of wildlife corridors (also known as green corridors or habitat corridors) is a popular one, but it is a concept that is probably misplaced. These corridors are narrow, continuous tracts of favourable habitat in otherwise unfavourable surroundings, which, theoretically, allow the free movement of animals and plants along them. Their intended purpose is to provide connecting routes between fragments of favourable habitat and thereby facilitate the exchange of genetic material between otherwise isolated populations. For this reason, wildlife corridors are often retained or even created as a conservation measure in areas undergoing some sort of development. However, their effectiveness has not yet been adequately demonstrated. In some cases, it is conceivable that their presence could prove counter-productive, should they, for example, provide conduits for the spread of introduced predators or fire. In conservation strategies, therefore, alternative approaches to the retention or creation of wildlife corridors should be considered, such as making reserves bigger (if possible) or even physically transporting some animal species between the isolated fragments.

Further Information Box

10.10 The concept of the minimum viable population (MVP)

Within any population, a certain minimum number of individuals are needed to ensure successful breeding and hence the continued survival of that population. A fall in numbers below this critical level will result in the decline and, in some cases, the extinction of that population. This critical number of individuals (which is different for each species, and sometimes for individual populations within a particular species) is known as the minimum viable population (MVP). This is usually defined as the number of individuals needed to give a population a 95% chance of surviving for a period of at least 100 years. This concept is important in conservation strategies, such as breeding programmes for rare or endangered species. Moreover, in the wild, the MVP of any species needs a certain minimum area of favourable habitat to support it. This is known as the minimum viable area (MVA) and can be calculated from the MVP. The translation of MVP into MVA is of practical importance to conservation measures that involve, for example, the creation of nature reserves.

100 hectares were unlikely to be self-sustaining. The reduced number of animal species supported by these rainforest fragments was also an important contributory factor, since animals perform a crucial role in the pollination and/or seed dispersal of the majority of tropical trees.

10.6 The conservation of biological resources

The threats faced by wild plant and animal species from human activities are many and diverse (Sections 10.3–10.5). Moreover, such threats usually occur severally, in combination or consecutively, rather than singly. As a result, species have been lost at an unprecedented rate, especially over the last few decades. In an effort to slow down the global decline in biodiversity, various conservation strategies ranging from local to global in scale have been developed. These may be carried out at localities other than the natural habitat of the species concerned (known as *ex situ* methods, Section 10.6.1) or they may occur *in situ* (Section 10.6.2). Moreover, the conservation of biological resources, and therefore of biodiversity itself, is actively supported by a number of international conventions, most of them agreed within the past 30 years (Section 10.6.3).

10.6.1 *Ex situ* conservation programmes

The essential feature of *ex situ* conservation programmes is that they take place outside the natural habitat. The type of establishments involved in these programmes include zoos and specialised breeding centres in the case of animals, and botanical gardens and research institutes in the case of plants. Originally, zoos were essentially collections of (mainly) exotic species and their purpose was primarily to entertain, not to inform. However, over the years, the educational role of zoos has become much more strongly developed. Moreover, in most modern zoos and botanical gardens, and other similar establishments, the conservation of wild species has become central to their ethos.

In *ex situ* conservation programmes, populations of plant or animal species threatened or endangered in the wild are preserved and, where possible, propagated. In some cases, zoos have preserved animal species whose populations have become extinct in the wild, e.g. the black-footed ferret (*Mustela nigripes*), Père David's deer (*Elaphurus davidianus*) and the Californian condor (*Gymnogyps californianus*). The long-term preservation of animal populations in zoos usually involves captive breeding programmes, although this approach is not possible with some groups such as bats and whales. However, since zoo populations, especially of mammals, tend of necessity to be small, continued inbreeding between relatively few individuals (even if some are imported from other establishments) can lead eventually to inbreeding depression. In this state, the vigour of a population, and thus its ability to survive and adapt, is reduced. As long-term conservation strategies, captive breeding programmes have, therefore, some serious limitations.

Ideally, groups of individuals from threatened species should be reintroduced into the wild as soon as reasonably possible in order to replenish existing populations or to establish new ones. However, in each case, reintroduction depends on the availability of suitable habitat and also the provision of appropriate ongoing protection programmes. In practice, the reintroduction of species into the wild has met with mixed results. In some cases, attempts have failed. For example, over 1500 Hawaiian geese (*Branta sandvicensis*) bred in captivity at Slimbridge, England, were reintroduced into the Hawaiian Islands in the 1970s. However, despite the apparent initial success of this operation, in less than two decades only a handful of birds remained. The failed outcome of this venture was attributed to inbreeding depression. In contrast, the reintroduction of golden lion tamarins (*Leontopithicus rosalia*) into a Brazilian reserve to restock the diminishing wild tamarin population was, on balance, successful. At the end of the seven-year reintroduction programme (1984–91), the net gain to the wild population numbered 71 individuals (either reintroduced adults or their offspring).

Whilst zoos and aquariums concentrate on the conservation of animals, botanical gardens and similar establishments perform a similar conservation role for plants. The preservation of threatened plant species generally involves the storage of plant material. In the case of flowering plants, this is usually in the form of seeds (in which case the repository is known as a seed bank). Briefly, the procedure involves the cleaning and desiccation of the seeds (to ~4% water content) and their subsequent storage at low temperatures. Stored seed remains viable for between five and 25 years, depending on species, and must therefore be periodically germinated and the new seed collected to replace the old stock. For non-flowering plants, spores and pollen can be stored and preserved in a similar way. For plants with recalcitrant seeds (i.e. those damaged by desiccation), other *ex situ* conservation methods must be employed. These may involve the use of 'field gene banks', where populations of growing plants are actively maintained, or possibly the use of tissue cultures. One final, and very important, point to make is that it is now possible to store the genetic material of both plant and animal species using recombinant DNA technology (Chapter 6, Section 6.9).

10.6.2 *In situ* conservation programmes

Whilst *ex situ* conservation programmes have a valuable role to play, *in situ* conservation, in which natural habitats are preserved, is now viewed as the most effective way of preserving biodiversity. It may well be that the presence of an endangered species focuses attention on a particular habitat in the first place. However, the use of *in situ*, rather than *ex situ*, conservation methods affords protection to all of the wild plant and animal species present, not just the 'target' species in question. The areas in which *in situ* conservation programmes operate are known as 'protected areas'. This broad definition covers a whole range of different schemes, including those in which nature conservation is combined with other activities, such as logging. The categorisation of protected areas by the International Union for the Conservation of Nature and Natural Resources (IUCN) (Table 10.4) provides a unifying framework to help classify the many different national and international schemes that exist. A special kind of

Table **10.4** IUCN protected area categories.

Category	Description
Ia	Strict nature reserve: managed mainly for science
Ib	Strict nature reserve: managed mainly for wilderness protection
II	National park: managed mainly for ecosystem protection and recreation
III	Natural monument: managed mainly for conservation of specific natural features
IV	Habitat species management area: managed mainly for conservation through management intervention
V	Protected landscape/seascape: managed mainly for landscape or seascape conservation and recreation
VI	Managed resource protected area: protected area managed mainly for the sustainable use of natural ecosystems

Source: from IUCN (1994).

10.11 Biosphere reserves

Biosphere reserves are a special type of protected area in which conservation goals are combined with sustainable human use. The concept of an international network of biosphere reserves was introduced in the 1970s, as part of UNESCO's Man and the Biosphere (MAB) Programme. The first biosphere reserve was established in 1976. By June 1995, the number of biosphere reserves had reached 328, spread across 82 different countries.

A biosphere reserve usually consists of three distinct concentric zones (see diagram). Central to the reserve is a fully protected core area from which all human activity, with the exception of some scientific study, is banned. Within this zone, endangered species are protected and the ecosystem's genetic material is conserved. The core area is surrounded by a buffer zone in which some limited human activity, e.g. ecotourism and research, is allowed. The outermost zone, the transition zone, is put to multiple use including permanent human settlements and sustainable resource use. The zoned structure of the biosphere reserve enables human needs to be integrated with conservation goals. This feature makes them especially suitable for those parts of the developing world where the needs of indigenous peoples must form part of local conservation strategies.

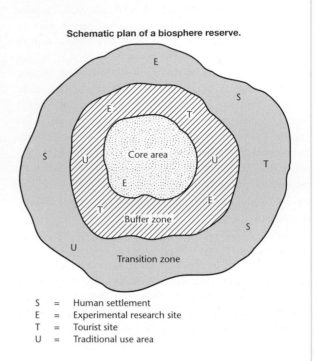

Schematic plan of a biosphere reserve.

S = Human settlement
E = Experimental research site
T = Tourist site
U = Traditional use area

---

protected area, the biosphere reserve, is discussed in more detail in Box 10.11.

The selection of any particular area of habitat for protection is dependent on many factors. The degree of species and genetic diversity contained within that habitat and the percentage of endemic species present constitute influential factors. How representative a habitat is of its own particular type, and how it complements those areas of different habitat already afforded protection, are also important considerations. Once selected, the actual design of a protected area has ramifications for its future success. As discussed previously, there is a strong connection between habitat fragmentation and species extinction. On these grounds, it might be reasonable to predict that the larger the better as far as any particular protected area is concerned. However, this is not invariably the case. For example, studies in East Africa have demonstrated that several small reserves were capable of sustaining a greater number of species of birds and mammals, compared with a single large reserve of equivalent area. On the other hand, large predators, such as tigers, need a large range for hunting, and therefore require correspondingly large reserves. The debate over the respective merits of 'single large or several small' (known by the acronym SLOSS) amongst conservationists seems set to continue.

Another aspect of conservation, and one that is coming increasingly to the fore, is that of ecological restoration (also

known as restoration ecology). This practice involves restoring altered or degraded ecosystems to a condition that is as near as possible to their original state. Ecosystems that are potentially suitable for such remedial treatment include those that have been damaged as a result of overgrazing, desertification, drainage or, in the case of lakes, eutrophication (Chapter 14, Box 14.2). One successful example of restoration ecology is that of the Danube Delta, parts of which had been drained for agricultural purposes (Box 10.12).

10.6.3 Conventions related to biological resources

In this section, the major international conventions concerning biological resources are outlined in turn. Two other relevant conventions, the UN Convention on the Law of the Sea and the International Convention for the Regulation of Whaling, have already been mentioned in Sections 10.3.1 and 10.3.2 respectively.

The Convention on Wetlands of International Importance Especially as Waterfowl Habitat

This international treaty (often referred to as the Ramsar Convention) was adopted on 2 February 1971 in Ramsar,

Mini Case Study

10.12 The ecological restoration of the Danube delta

The River Danube, which has its source in southern Germany, flows for almost 3000 kilometres eastwards across Europe before it reaches the Black Sea. At this point, the deposition of fine sediment by the river has created a huge delta with marshes and lakes, found partly in Ukraine and partly in Romania. In 1975, in Romania, long-term plans were made to drain parts of the Romanian section of the Danube delta in order to convert wetland areas into land suitable for agriculture. Huge polders were created, surrounded by protective dykes, and these were used to cultivate crops, namely wheat, maize and rice. Artificial lakes were also created for fish farming. However, the scheme was unsuccessful. The soil proved unsuitable for crop cultivation and the water in the artificial lakes simply drained away. By 1989, 14 years since the inception of the scheme, 40 000 hectares of the delta's natural wetland had been destroyed.

Since the end of the 1980s, the importance of the Danube delta as a wetland area has been internationally recognised. In 1991, under the World Heritage Convention (adopted by UNESCO in 1972), over 50% of the delta was designated a World Heritage Site. In 1992, the government of Romania assigned approximately 87% of its part of the delta as a Biosphere Reserve (under UNESCO's Man and the Biosphere Programme). Farming and fishing have been banned from the core areas of the reserve, which cover approximately 50 000 hectares.

Efforts have been made to restore those parts of the Danube delta previously destroyed by drainage. This process of ecological restoration started in 1994 with the flooding of a 2100-hectare agricultural polder called Babina. In 1996, the dykes of a 1580-hectare polder called Cernovca were similarly breached to allow the water to flow back in. The initial recovery of these wetland ecosystems has been both substantial and rapid, with plants and animals coming from other parts of the delta to recolonise. The speed of regeneration has been encouraging and is due, at least in part, to the dynamic nature of these wetland ecosystems, subjected as they are to periodic flooding. Even so, it is unlikely that these ecosystems can ever be restored completely to their pre-drainage state.

Reference: Edwards, R. (1997) Return of the pelican. *New Scientist*, 29 March, 32–35.

Iran, and entered into force in 1975. By January 1998, the number of contracting parties had reached 106. The original aim of the Ramsar Convention was to conserve wetlands, primarily as habitat for waterfowl. However, over the years, its remit has broadened considerably and the importance of wetlands as, for example, sites of biodiversity is now recognised. Under the Convention, contracting parties designate a minimum of one wetland site (selected on the basis of its significance in terms of hydrology, limnology, ecology, zoology, or botany) to be included on the 'Ramsar List' (List of Wetlands of International Importance). By February 1999, this list included 966 wetlands from all over the world, amounting to a total surface area of 70.5 million hectares.

The Convention Concerning the Protection of the World Cultural and Natural Heritage

This Convention, commonly known as The World Heritage Convention, developed from the merger of two distinct movements: one concerned with the preservation of cultural heritage, the other with natural heritage. The General Conference of UNESCO (United Nations Educational, Scientific and Cultural Organisation) adopted the Convention on 16 November 1972. By December 1998, 156 state parties had ratified the agreement. Under the Convention, a World Heritage List for properties deemed to be of outstanding universal importance was established (Table 10.5). By December 1998, 582 sites had been listed (117 of natural heritage, 445 of cultural heritage and 20 mixed) for protection and preservation.

Table 10.5 Some examples of sites from the World Heritage List (December 1998).

Site	Country	Year listed
Great Barrier Reef	Australia	1981
Hadrian's Wall	United Kingdom	1987
Peking Man Site at Zhoukoudian	China	1987
Komodo National Park	Indonesia	1991
Yosemite National Park	United States of America	1984
City of Cuzco	Peru	1983
Rio Platano Biosphere Reserve	Honduras	1982
Hwasong Fortress	Republic of Korea	1997
Lake Baikal	Russian Federation	1996
Mount Kenya National Park / Natural Forest	Kenya	1997

The Convention on International Trade in Endangered Species of Wild Fauna and Flora

This Convention, often referred to by its acronym CITES, was drawn up in 1973 in response to international concern over the threat to many species of wild plants and animals from the international wildlife trade. It came into force on 1 July 1975 and, by June 1998, had 144 member countries. Under the Convention, the international trade in wild species, and in wildlife products, is monitored and regulated and, in the case of the most endangered species, completely banned. For example, in 1990, CITES nations imposed a ban on the international trade in ivory in response to the rapid fall in numbers of the African elephant (*Loxodonta africana*) (Plate 18).

The Convention on the Conservation of Migratory Species of Wild Animals (CMS)

This Convention, also known as the Bonn Convention, was opened for signature in Bonn, Germany, on 23 June 1979 and came into force on 1 November 1983. By 1 September 1998, the number of member countries had grown to 55. This international treaty focuses on the conservation and management of migratory species (marine, terrestrial and avian) in all parts of their range. Endangered migratory species, such as the Dama gazelle (*Gazella dama*), white-tailed eagle (*Haliaeetus albicilla*) and Siberian crane (*Grus leucogeranus*), listed in Appendix I of the Convention, receive strict protection under its terms. A number of agreements have been reached under the auspices of the CMS concerning the conservation of particular groups, e.g. bats in Europe, seals in the Wadden Sea and small cetaceans in the Baltic and North Seas.

The Convention on Biological Diversity

At the United Nations Conference on Environment and Development in Rio de Janeiro in 1992 (sometimes referred to as the Earth Summit), the UN Convention on Biological Diversity was opened for signature on 5 June 1992, for a period of one year. The three main objectives of this Convention were to conserve global biological diversity (by way of national plans aimed at monitoring, conserving and sustaining national biological diversity), to use biological resources in a sustainable manner, and to share fairly and equitably the benefits accruing from the utilisation of genetic resources. The Convention entered into force on 29 December 1993, 90 days after the 30th ratification. By January 1999, the number of countries that have ratified the agreement had risen to 175. The Convention on Biological Diversity (CBD) represents the first global agreement to deal comprehensively with all aspects of biodiversity, from the gene through to the ecosystem.

10.7 Summary

Humans derive a vast array of useful and beneficial products from the Earth's biological resources, in terms of food, medicines, and, more recently, genetic material. For this reason alone (and there are others equally valid, such as the notion of stewardship), humans have a strong vested interest in preserving the vast spectrum of living organisms that constitute the world's biological resources. However, as a result of human activities, the rate of species loss has accelerated significantly, especially during the twentieth century, leading to a rapid decline in global biological diversity.

Humans may directly threaten biological resources by, for example, over-harvesting, especially of marine resources and native forests, or through the international trade (often illegal) in wild plant and animal species. Other threats may be considered to be indirect. This second category includes the introduction (accidental or otherwise) of exotic species and the degradation, loss or fragmentation of natural habitats. It is usually the case, however, that a combination of factors brings about the decline of a particular species.

The critical role played by humans in the global decline of species biodiversity is apposite to the fundamental necessity of conserving as many species as possible, for both current and future needs. In order to redress the balance, at least to some extent, conservation strategies have been initiated at a number of levels, from local to global, over the past few decades. International concern over the decline in global biodiversity led to the signature, ratification and subsequent enforcement of the UN Convention on Biological Diversity, initially presented at the United Nations Conference on Environment and Development in Rio de Janeiro in June 1992. Enshrined within this international agreement are three main objectives: to conserve global biological diversity, to use biological resources in a sustainable manner, and to share fairly and equitably the benefits accruing from the utilisation of genetic resources.

10.8   **Problems**

1   Define the terms 'biological resources' and 'genetic resources' and outline the benefits which humans derive from them.

2   Discuss the human activities that *directly* threaten biological resources. What remedial measures would you suggest?

3   The contribution of aquaculture to the future supply of marine (and freshwater) fish is set to increase. Discuss the advantages and disadvantages of rearing fish in this way.

4   In what ways do introduced species threaten native ones? Illustrate your answer with specific examples.

5   Examine the effects of habitat degradation, loss and fragmentation on species survival.

6   Discuss the relative merits of *ex situ* and *in situ* conservation programmes.

7   In the design of nature reserves, discuss the influence of size, arrangement and interconnections of habitat fragments on the probable survival of the species they contain.

10.9   **Further reading**

Allaby, M. (1996) *Basics of environmental science*. London: Routledge.

Goudie, A. (1997) *The human impact reader, Readings and case studies*. Oxford: Blackwell (especially Part V, Biological impacts).

Lever, C. (1994) *Naturalized animals: the ecology of successfully introduced species*. London: T & A D Poyser.

Mather, A. S. and K. Chapman (1995) *Environmental resources*. Harlow: Longman.

Spellerberg, I. F. (ed.) (1996) *Conservation biology*. Harlow: Longman.

Vitousek, P. M., C. M. D'Antonio, L. L. Loope, M. Rejmanek and R. Westbrooks (1997) Introduced species: a significant component of human-caused global change. *New Zealand Journal of Ecology*, **21**(1), 1–16.

Genetically modified (GM) crops

The development of genetic engineering techniques, over the last 30 years, has made it possible to alter the genetic constitution of plants and animals without the need for conventional breeding (Chapter 6, Section 6.9). Genetic modification involves the direct introduction of new genes into the genome of a selected organism. The usual aim of this procedure is to confer new, desired characteristics on the organism in question. This technique differs from traditional breeding, in which new strains are produced by crossing with close relatives, in that the genes used in genetic modification are typically obtained from *unrelated* species, in some cases from bacteria or viruses. Plants and animals that contain genes introduced from other species are termed transgenic. The newly acquired genes are then passed to successive generations through the normal mechanisms of natural heredity.

In the case of crop species, interest has focused mainly on the acquisition of herbicide tolerance and/or insect resistance, through the introduction of suitable genes from other species. For example, the common soil bacterium *Bacillus thuringiensis* (Bt) naturally produces an insecticidal toxin that is fatal to many types of caterpillar. This natural insecticide has been produced commercially and used for a number of years with great success. It is both highly specific and non-persistent in the environment. Genetic engineering has enabled the gene that encodes for the Bt toxin to be directly incorporated into a number of commercially important plant species such as cotton (*Gossypium* spp.) and maize (*Zea mays*). These Bt crops, as they are known, are able to continuously produce their own insecticide, thus reducing the need to spray with conventional insecticides.

The development of genetically modified (GM) crops for commercial use has been undertaken by multinational biotechnology companies such as Monsanto (based in St Louis, Missouri, US) and the Swiss-based company Novartis. Commercial growing of GM crops is centred on the US, where it has become well established in recent years. For example, in 1998, an estimated 27.8 million hectares of transgenic crops were planted in the United States, mainly of herbicide-resistant soya bean (*Glycine max*) and maize. Although, in terms of area, the US is the major commercial grower of GM crops worldwide, other countries, including Canada, Argentina and, most notably, China, are also significant players. The cultivation of GM crops in the US and their subsequent incorporation into food products for human consumption (so-called 'GM foods') is, apparently, acceptable practice for the majority of the American people.

Attempts to export this technology from the US to other countries, especially European ones, has met with widespread public concern. In the UK, which has recently suffered a major food scare in the form of BSE (Case study 2), public opposition both to the commercial cultivation of GM crops and to the import of GM food products has been very much in evidence. In August 1998, a controversial statement made by Dr Arpad Pusztai from the Rowett Research Institute in Aberdeen, UK, sparked intense public debate about the safety of GM foods. He claimed that feeding rats with genetically modified potatoes (containing a snowdrop gene encoded to produce a lectin) resulted in the suppression of their immune systems and damage to organs, including the liver and spleen. This particular gene is currently under investigation by a number of laboratories interested in its potential to confer resistance to sap-sucking insect pests, when genetically engineered into crops. However, at the time of writing (February 1999), Dr Pusztai's findings remain unconfirmed.

As well as food safety issues connected with the introduced genes themselves, there is also concern about the use of marker genes. These genes are used to track the transfer of other genes into genetically modified organisms (GMOs). They are usually ones that confer antibiotic resistance, a factor that can easily be checked for in the newly engineered organism. For example, a gene for an enzyme called beta-lactamase, capable of destroying ampicillin (an antibiotic of the penicillin family), has been used as a marker for two genes (one for insecticide resistance and the other for herbicide tolerance) used in a GM maize produced by Novartis. It is not known whether such antibiotic-resistant genes are capable of jumping to gut bacteria when livestock are fed on these products. The fear over this scenario is that it could lead to the spread of antibiotic-resistant bacteria, with possible risks to human health.

In addition to public anxiety over *possible* health risks associated with GM foods, a number of environmental concerns have been raised in connection with the growing of GM crops. The cultivation of herbicide-tolerant crops could encourage the widespread and indiscriminate use of herbicide sprays, leading to the loss of neighbouring wild plants and a consequential decline in overall biodiversity within the farmed environment. Moreover, it is possible that a gene conferring herbicide resistance could be spread from a GM crop species to a related wild species through cross-pollination. This could result in the development of 'superweeds' resistant to herbicide sprays. Cereal crops, with their abundance of wild relatives, might pose a particular risk with respect to this 'genetic pollution' of wild species.

Equally, the development of insect-resistant GM crops raises a number of environmental concerns. Such crops, for example the Bt crops mentioned previously, are engineered to produce pesticide continuously. This continuous supply of pesticide in GM crop plants could lead to a build-up of resistance within populations of the pest species that feed on them. In order to address this concern, the US Environmental Protection Agency (EPA) requires growers of Bt crops, e.g. Bt cotton, to provide 'pest refuges' in the form of areas of unmodified crops (of the same species). The underlying reasoning behind this idea is that non-resistant pests from these refuges will mate with surviving pests from the areas of Bt crops, thus 'watering down' the pool of resistance genes within the pest population. However, such pest refuges must be large enough *and* close enough to the Bt fields to be effectual.

There is also considerable concern about the 'knock-on' effects that insect-resistant GM crops could have on beneficial predator species. This was first demonstrated in studies carried out by Dr N. Birch (Scottish Crop Research Institute, Dundee, UK) and Dr M. Majerus (University of Cambridge, UK). They fed peach-potato aphids (*Myzus persicae*) on the sap of potatoes modified to carry a lectin from snowdrops (*Galanthus nivalis*) and found that a significant number of the aphids died as a result. In subsequent research, it was discovered that feeding two-spot ladybirds (*Adalia bipunctata*) with aphids fed on modified potatoes reduced the life span of female ladybirds by half, and that of males by five days, compared with control groups fed on aphids from normal potatoes. The percentage of viable eggs laid was also reduced (by up to 30%) if one of the parents was fed aphids from these GM potatoes. This study, and others, shows that there are risks to natural predators of insect pest species in using crops engineered for insect resistance. However, these risks must be set against the benefits to predatory insects of reduced spraying. The question is 'where does the balance lie?'.

There are many hugely complex issues involved in the debate over the development of genetically modified crops, and the desirability of, or indeed necessity for, genetically modified foods. One pertinent question to ask is 'who will benefit most from these biotechnological advances?'. The multinationals concerned naturally cite the benefits, such as the reduced need for spraying in the case of insect-resistant crops. They also claim that GM crops will help solve world food shortages. On the other hand, farmers who purchase the seed for herbicide-resistant crops must also buy the corresponding spray and this may only be available from the company supplying the seed. Moreover, the development of 'terminator seeds', i.e. seeds containing a terminator gene designed to stop transgenic plants setting their own viable seed, means that farmers must purchase new seed each year. This step is designed to protect company patents, and profits. However, it has very serious implications for poorer farmers in developing countries, who simply cannot afford to purchase fresh seed each year. The incursion of GM crops of this type into the developing world could also serve to undermine the established custom of saving seed. This practice is necessary to conserve the biodiversity contained within traditional varieties of crop species. Another consequence of the current focus on GM crops has been a major switch in the allocation of essential research funds from traditional biological pest control methods (which are often simpler, cheaper and more effective) to genetic research.

Further reading

Coghlan, A., D. Concar and D. MacKenzie (1999) Frankenfears. *New Scientist*, 20 February, 4–5.

Rifkin, J. (1998) *The biotech century*. London: Gollancz.

Schmidt, K. (1995) Whatever happened to the gene revolution? *New Scientist*, 7 January, 21–25.

Scragg, A. (1999) *Environmental biotechnology*. Harlow: Longman. (Contains an informative and accessible chapter on agrobiotechnology in general)

Several articles by various authors under the heading 'Special Report: Living in a GM world', *New Scientist*, 31 October 1998, 28–52.

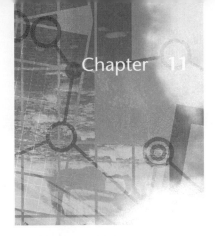

Chapter 11

Land utilisation: a focus on agriculture and forestry

After reading this chapter, you should be able to:

- Appreciate the major historical changes that have influenced patterns of land use, including the role played by urban and industrial development.

- Explain what is meant by the term 'agro-ecosystem' and compare this with the unmanaged (or natural) ecosystem.

- Compare and contrast extensive and intensive agro-ecosystems.

- Outline the main methods of pest control.

- Discuss the use of irrigation in agriculture, giving both its advantages and disadvantages.

- Define 'deforestation' and explain its underlying causes in both tropical rainforests and savanna regions.

- Describe the problem of soil erosion, how it is exacerbated by human activities, and what remedial steps may be taken.

- Understand the factors that contribute to the global problem of desertification.

Introduction

Land is essentially a finite resource. The potential use of a piece of land is influenced by its soil type, mineral resources, vegetation, topography, climate and location. However, unlike water and air, land is owned either by individuals, by groups or by the state. This means that the use of a particular area of land is often determined by what is most profitable to the owner.

Land can be used for a variety of purposes: for urban/industrial development, agriculture, forestry, strip-mining (Chapter 12, Section 12.4.1) or solid waste disposal (Chapter 16, Sections 16.2 and 16.4). In many cases, changes in land use give rise to conflict between different interest groups, for example between those who seek to exploit the resources of the tropical rainforests and the indigenous tribal peoples.

This chapter opens with a brief look at past patterns of land use. This historical sketch is followed by an examination of recent trends in urban/industrial development. This type of development has a significant impact on the wider environment, through water and air pollution and the disposal of waste materials. These issues are discussed in detail in Chapters 14, 15 and 16 respectively.

The majority of this chapter focuses on the major type of land use, agriculture, with a smaller section dedicated to forestry. The chapter concludes with a detailed examination of the direct environmental impacts of agricultural land use, concentrating on deforestation, salinisation, soil erosion and desertification.

11.1 Past patterns of land use

The beginnings of land cultivation date back to the Neolithic era (New Stone Age), approximately 12 000–10 000 years BP. Much of the evidence for the domestication of plants and animals during this period has been found in the Near East. The gradual transition from a hunter–gatherer lifestyle to one based mainly on agriculture represents a very important stage in human development. The uncertainties of food procurement by hunting were replaced by a more reliable food supply from plant cultivation and animal husbandry.

By the Bronze and Iron Ages, which followed the Neolithic era, agriculture had become common practice. The advent of metal technology, starting with copper, greatly assisted the intensification of agriculture during this period. In more arid regions, irrigation systems were developed to enhance crop production. In their role as farmers, people gained control over their own environment, using the land both for cultivation and for permanent settlements.

In recent history, as a consequence of industrialisation, there has been a diversification of land use. For example, before 1700, Britain was mainly rural and its economy was based on agriculture. However, the advent of the Industrial Revolution in the mid-eighteenth century largely swept away this rural tradition in Britain. Industry became concentrated in the towns and people moved to these urban centres to work. This period of urbanisation and industrialisation was accompanied by rapid population growth (Chapter 7, Section 7.3). The population of Britain more than doubled in the period 1700–1800, from 5 million to over 10 million. Improvements in agriculture led to increased productivity which enabled the growing population to be fed. A similar change from an economy based on agriculture to one based on industry occurred in other European countries and in North America.

more rapidly in the less-developed countries compared with the industrialised nations of Europe, North America, East Asia, Australia, and New Zealand.

In the more-developed countries, urbanisation consists of a planned combination of residential housing, service industries, transport infrastructure and industrial development. Since the 1970s, there has been a move away from traditional 'heavy' industries to 'light' industries, including electronics. This transition has important implications for land use. Heavy industries are reliant on major transport systems for the two-way traffic of raw materials and finished goods. Historically, they have been centrally sited, next to rivers, canals and railways. The newer light industries, without this constraint, are often located on out-of-town industrial estates. A similar shift from the towns into more desirable rural areas has occurred in residential housing. This has been made possible by the increased mobility of the general population, largely as a result of the rise in car ownership. Thus in the more-developed countries, urban development spreads outwards from the town and city centres and systematically encroaches on the surrounding countryside.

In the less-developed countries, the process of urbanisation tends to be less controlled. People flock to the urban centres to find work and as a result the cities become 'over-urbanised', with too many people for their resource base. This leads to enormous social and environmental problems, the latter mainly associated with pollution and inadequate sanitation. The spread of such cities tends to occur only slowly relative to the increase in their urban populations. There are several reasons for the tendency of the urban population to concentrate near city centres, including inadequate transport systems and the need for proximity to the workplace.

The increasing urbanisation of the landscape is a cause for concern, as such changes in land use are essentially irreversible. Many wildlife habitats have been lost to urban and industrial development, including woodlands and wetlands. Often the land used for urban development is productive agricultural land. For example, it is estimated that in the United States, 20% of the prime agricultural land will be lost to urban development by the year 2000, if current trends continue.

11.2 Urban and industrial development

The process of urban development (known as **urbanisation**), which started in earnest in Europe with the Industrial Revolution, is a global trend today. It is estimated that over half of the world's people will live in urban areas by the year 2000. Urbanisation is occurring

11.3 Agriculture

Agriculture, the cultivation of land for the purposes of crop production and/or the rearing of livestock, has been practised for thousands of years. The natural ('wild' or 'unmanaged') ecosystem is manipulated to produce plant and livestock products, primarily for food but also for

Table **11.1** A comparison between unmanaged (or natural) ecosystems and agro-ecosystems.

Unmanaged ecosystems	Agro-ecosystems
High species richness	Low species richness (system based on monoculture)
Many trophic levels	Few trophic levels
Complex food web	Simplified food web (exacerbated by use of herbicides and pesticides)
Strong interspecific competition between plants	Reduced competition
Complex spatial organisation	Less complex spatial organisation
Approximately closed system: nutrients recycled	Open system: nutrients exported from system as crops and livestock are 'harvested' (losses must be made good, usually by use of inorganic fertilisers)
Large amounts of dead and decaying matter	Small amounts of dead and decaying matter

clothing and shelter. This modified ecosystem, known as the **agro-ecosystem**, differs from the natural ecosystem in a number of important ways (Table 11.1).

The *intensity* of agriculture varies, and this tends to be correlated with the degree of productivity achieved (Figure 11.1). At one end of the scale lies *extensive* agriculture, namely the rough grazing of livestock and the practice of 'shifting cultivation'; whilst at the other lies *intensive* agriculture, typified by irrigation and the highly managed arable and livestock farming practised in many of the more-developed countries. In comparison with natural ecosystem types, the level of net primary productivity achieved in intensively cultivated agro-

ecosystems may be as high as that of tropical rainforests (Chapter 9, Table 9.4).

The process of cultivation

The cultivation of the soil for the production of crops involves a number of basic processes (Figure 11.2). The first of these is tillage, the physical preparation of the soil prior to sowing or planting. During cultivation, drainage and/or irrigation may be necessary to achieve an optimal air/water balance in the soil for the growing of crops. The application of fertilisers may be needed to sustain or improve nutrient levels in the soil, as lack of essential nutrients can act as limiting factors to plant growth (Chapter 9, Section 9.2.3). The protection of crops from competition from weeds and attack from pests and pathogens (disease-causing organisms) is another important aspect of crop cultivation. The cultivation process is terminated by the harvesting of the crop.

The emphasis placed on each of these cultivation stages is dependent on the type of agro-ecosystem (extensive or intensive), the requirements of the crops under cultivation and the prevailing economic and environmental conditions. Successful cultivation can be measured by the productivity of the agro-ecosystem in question (i.e. the amount produced per unit area per unit time: Chapter 9, Section 9.2.2).

Figure **11.1** Nitrogen output of agricultural systems. Black dots represent farm systems for which data are available (from Frissel, 1978).

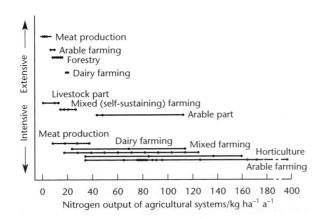

Figure **11.2** The process of cultivation.

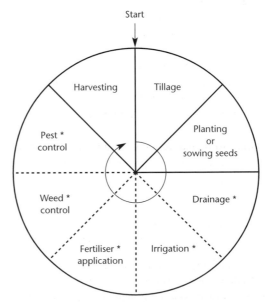

*   These agricultural practices *may* be used during the cultivation process.

It should be emphasised that successful management of the soil itself is a key factor, both in achieving maximum productivity in the short term and in maintaining long-term soil fertility. Mismanagement of the soil resource, together with exacerbating climatic conditions, can lead to severe problems of soil erosion and land degradation (Section 11.5).

11.3.2 Extensive agro-ecosystems

The active management role played by man in extensive agro-ecosystems is minimal and agricultural productivity is low, with an annual output of consumable nitrogen less than $20\,kg\,ha^{-1}$ (Figure 11.1). There are two main types of extensive agro-ecosystems: shifting cultivation and the rough grazing of livestock.

Shifting cultivation

Shifting cultivation (also known as slash and burn cultivation) has been practised in the humid tropical rainforest of Africa, South America and south-east Asia for thousands of years and it remains the most widely used agricultural practice in those regions today (Plate 19). The purpose of this type of traditional farming is to provide a continuous and adequate food supply to sustain small tribal or family groups. To achieve this, a mixture of food crops are planted to mature at different times during the year, for example maize (*Zea mays*), cassava (*Manihot esculenta*) and bananas (*Musa sapientum*).

In this method of cultivation, a small patch of the native forest is first cleared by felling the trees. The trees are then burnt to release the nutrients stored in their woody biomass. Seeds are planted in the resultant soil/ash mix using a digging stick to minimise soil disturbance. The fertility of the soil declines rapidly (within two or three years) as the levels of nutrients and soil organic matter become seriously depleted. The patch is then abandoned and the process repeated elsewhere. Reforestation of the patch is relatively rapid, usually occurring within a decade. However, without extensive periods of fallow, problems of deforestation can arise (Section 11.5).

Rough grazing of livestock

Almost half of the world's total land area is used for the rough grazing of domestic livestock on semi-natural and natural vegetation. Land used for this purpose is known as **rangeland** and is found throughout the world from the tundra to the tropics. Rangeland is not suitable for crop cultivation, for a variety of reasons. For example, in the

semi-arid and arid regions of the world, rainfall is very low and erratic and crops cannot be cultivated without irrigation.

The primary productivity of rangelands is low and the number of grazing animals which can be supported on a sustainable basis is therefore also low. The problem of overgrazing is common to rangelands throughout the world. It can lead to accelerated soil erosion and eventually desertification (Section 11.5). In addition, the widespread practice of burning in rangelands in order to stimulate new vegetative growth can exacerbate problems of land degradation.

11.3.3 Intensive agro-ecosystems

Intensive agriculture has evolved rapidly in the more-developed countries of Western Europe and North America since the Second World War. The development of this type of farming was prompted by the need for increased food production during and after the Second World War and was made possible by a combination of three major agricultural advances. These were the production of artificial fertilisers, herbicides, insecticides and pesticides; the production of new and better-performing plant and animal varieties through intensive breeding programmes, and the increasing mechanisation of agricultural practices. Intensive agro-ecosystems are characterised by high levels of management and high productivity (Figure 11.1).

Until the mid-1950s, mixed crop and livestock farming was the normal agricultural practice in temperate regions. A rotation system of cereals, root crops and grass–clover pastures was used to rear livestock on the farm. The maintenance of soil fertility was central to this type of closely integrated agro-ecosystem. It was achieved through a variety of sound cultural practices such as the return of nutrients to the soil in organic manures and the inclusion of leguminous crops, capable of nitrogen fixation, in the rotational cycle. However, the intensification of agriculture has resulted in a move away from traditional mixed farming towards increasing specialisation. This trend has led in many cases to the complete segregation of crop (arable) and livestock production.

Intensive arable farming

In modern arable farming, the traditional practices of crop rotation have largely been replaced by the continuous cultivation of crops. Cereal crops, predominantly wheat (*Triticum aestivum*), barley (*Hordeum sativa*) and maize (*Zea mays*), are the mainstay of intensive arable farming. The seed-legumes rank second in terms of yield and area planted, and of these soya bean (*Glycine max*), common field bean (*Phaseolus* spp.) and pea (*Pisum sativum*) are the most important. The development of high-yielding varieties has greatly increased the productivity of these agro-ecosystems.

The advent of intensive arable farming has had a number of environmental impacts. The development of specialised machinery for every stage of the cultivation process has made the cultivation of large tracts of land feasible and, from an economic point of view, desirable. However, this large-scale cultivation has led to the loss of many wildlife habitats. For example, in Britain, the net loss of hedgerows since the Second World War is estimated to be in the region of 17 000 km or 22%. Increasing mechanisation has brought its own problems for the farmer, including the loss of soil condition through compaction caused by increased machine-tracking. This adverse effect can be minimised by repeatedly using the same route through the arable fields for the different machines and/or by sowing seeds into unploughed fields, a process known as **zero-tillage**.

In intensive arable farming, it is necessary to supply large amounts of nutrients to replace those lost when the crops are harvested. In more-developed countries, *inorganic* fertilisers have largely replaced the use of more traditional *organic* nutrient sources, principally farmyard manure. These artificial fertilisers are usually rich in a particular element such as nitrogen, phosphorus, potassium, calcium or magnesium. The production and mode of action of inorganic phosphate fertilisers in the soil is discussed in Box 11.1.

The extensive application of fertilisers has led to the pollution of freshwater courses by nitrates and has also contributed to the contamination of fresh waters with phosphates (Chapter 14, Section 14.2).

Intensive cultivation favours the planting of **monocultures** (large areas of a single crop). Whilst economically sound, at least in the short term, this agricultural practice has a number of disadvantages. For example, monocultures greatly exacerbate the problem of pests and pathogens by providing them with an extensive, and uninterrupted, niche. When the same crop is grown year after year, this niche becomes a permanent one and the pest proliferates even further as a result. Pesticides are still widely used for pest control, although the current trend is away from conventional pesticide use (Box 11.2). Pesticides, like fertilisers, can also cause problems of water pollution (Chapter 14, Section 14.5).

Intensive livestock farming

Until the 1950s, livestock production was part of the traditional mixed farming widely practised in temperate regions. Livestock, principally cattle and sheep,

were fed with the grass, hay and root crops raised on the farm. However, like crop cultivation, livestock production has become increasingly intensified over recent years. Modern practices are geared towards achieving maximum productivity of livestock products, such as milk, meat and eggs. The use of high-quality feedstuffs, for example cereals and silage, has played a central role in increasing productivity. However, the use of animal-derived protein in ruminant animal feedstuffs is thought to have been responsible for the emergence of BSE in the British cattle population in the mid-1980s (Case study 2, page 259). Intensive breeding programmes, including the use of artificial insemination, have produced new livestock varieties able to metabolise high-concentrate diets or with an increased breeding capacity.

In some cases, the whole production process is an intensive one. For example, 'battery' hens, which are kept for egg production, spend their entire lives confined to small cages indoors. In other cases, only part of the livestock production process is intensive. This is exemplified by the American 'feedlot' system where high densities of cattle or pigs are kept in open pens and fattened before going to market. It is estimated that over 500 million head of cattle and 1 million head of pigs are kept in US feedlots. The effluent from such large concentrations of livestock inevitably poses serious problems of water pollution (Chapter 14, Section 14.1).

The use of irrigation in agriculture

The process of irrigation involves the conveyance of water from a source of supply to an area of land where it is needed for the cultivation of crops. Irrigation is a very ancient agricultural practice and was used extensively by a number of early civilisations, for example the ancient Egyptians. In recent years, there has been an upsurge in the use of irrigation to facilitate cultivation in semi-arid and arid regions (Box 11.3). Between 1970 and 1990, the total area of irrigated land in the world rose by 36% and today it accounts for one-sixth of all cultivated land. Irrigation agriculture is highly productive and provides over one-third of the world's food. Crop yields are significantly higher than those achieved on rain-fed lands with similar soil and climatic conditions (Figure 11.3).

There are a number of different types of irrigation system, ranging from the simple to the highly sophisticated. For example, gravity or surface irrigation is widely used in both traditional and modern agriculture. This method involves the intermittent discharge of large amounts of water onto land deliberately levelled to encourage water distribution. Other methods are sprinkler irrigation, which delivers the water in the form of a spray,

11.1 Inorganic phosphate fertilisers

There are extensive phosphate rock deposits in several parts of the world, including North Africa, America, and the former Soviet Union. While the phosphate content of these rocks may be high, they are of limited use as fertilisers. This is because the phosphate in these deposits is present as highly insoluble apatite minerals, most commonly fluor-apatite, $Ca_{10}(PO_4)_6F_2$.

In order to convert rock phosphate into more useful fertiliser, the solubility of its phosphate is increased. This is done either by subjecting it to heat treatments, often in the presence of other minerals, or by reacting it with mineral acids.

For example, treatment of rock phosphate with sufficient sulfuric acid yields water-soluble monocalcium orthophosphate monohydrate, $Ca(H_2PO_4)_2.H_2O$. Commercially, this process produces an impure mixture of the orthophosphate and gypsum (a by-product of the reaction). This mixture is sold as **superphosphate**.

Water-soluble phosphate-containing fertilisers react fairly rapidly with several of the constituents of soil. Most of these reactions result in the production of insoluble phosphate species, a process called **phosphate fixation**.

Take, for example, the fate of monocalcium orthophosphate monohydrate in a fertiliser granule implanted in a non-calcareous soil. Initially, water migrates into the granule by osmosis in wet soils and by vapour diffusion in drier conditions. The following reaction then occurs:

$$Ca(H_2PO_4)_2.H_2O + H_2O \rightarrow CaHPO_4.2H_2O + H_3PO_4$$

This results in a residue of solid dicalcium phosphate dihydrate ($CaHPO_4.2H_2O$), containing about 20% of the original phosphate, and a saturated solution. The solution is highly acidic (pH ~1.5) by virtue of its phosphoric acid (H_3PO_4) content. It also has a high concentration of both phosphate (~4 M) and calcium (~1.4 M) ions.

This solution migrates out of the granule, dissolving aluminium, manganese and iron from the surrounding soil.

The pH of the solution rises and within a short time the phosphates form initial precipitates with the ions dissolved from the soil. The vast majority of the phosphates therefore migrate only one or two centimetres from the point of implantation.

This process takes only about two to four days. Plants therefore do not take their phosphate from the soluble fertiliser added but from the initial products that they form on reaction with the soil.

The initial precipitates are metastable, as is the solid dicalcium phosphate dihydrate residue. These materials slowly convert to less soluble but thermodynamically more stable compounds. These include hydroxy-apatite (formed from the dicalcium phosphate dihydrate residue), strengite (formed from the initial iron phosphate precipitates) and variscite (formed from the initial aluminium phosphate precipitates).

The fates of phosphate fertilisers in soils are further complicated by fixation interactions between phosphates and solid phases present such as silicate minerals and hydrous oxides of iron, aluminium and manganese.

All of these soil-inorganic phosphate interactions exhibit a marked pH dependence. This is summarised in the figure below.

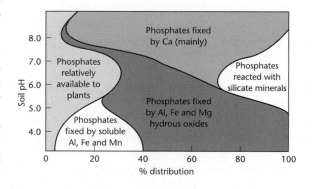

and trickle irrigation, which discharges water on or below the soil surface in the vicinity of the roots.

Surface water and ground water are the two main sources of water used in irrigation. In semi-arid and arid regions, irrigation systems rely on the import of surface water, often over considerable distances. Water is drawn from rivers and reservoirs in surrounding areas where rainfall is high and transported to the irrigated area, usually by pipeline. Ground water may be a suitable source of supply depending on its availability and the cost of pumping it to the surface. However, groundwater extraction requires careful management as over-exploitation can lead to serious problems of depletion. This is a particularly serious problem in coastal regions, where a drop in the level of the water table below that of

sea level can result in the incursion of brackish water into groundwater aquifers (Chapter 12, Section 12.5).

The main problem associated with the use of irrigation in agriculture is the inevitable increase in the salt content of the soil, a process known as **salinisation**. Salinisation reduces the fertility of the soil and depresses the yield of cultivated crops. At its extreme, it can lead to the abandonment of previously fertile land (Section 11.5.2). Another problem attributed to the use of irrigation is an increase in the number of pests, for example rats, and the incidence of vector-borne diseases such as schistosomiasis and malaria, particularly on the African continent.

It is unlikely that there will be a significant expansion of irrigated land in the future, mainly due to a shortage of suitable water. The current emphasis is on increasing the

11.2 Methods of pest control

A pest may be defined as any organism that reduces agricultural productivity as a result of damage to crops or livestock. Insects and mites constitute the largest group of pest organisms and most of these are herbivores (plant-eaters). Other pest groups include nematodes, gastropod molluscs (slugs and snails) and vertebrates, especially small mammals and birds. In some cases, it is the pests themselves that are responsible for damaging crops or destroying livestock. In other cases, further damage is caused by the introduction of pathogens (disease-causing micro-organisms) by pests. The resultant disease (bacterial, viral or fungal) may be largely responsible for the weakening and destruction of the target organism, rather than the initial pest attack.

In order to combat the damaging effects of pests on agricultural productivity, various methods of pest control have been developed. Originally, pest control methods relied almost entirely on the cultural practices used in traditional small-scale farming, such as crop rotation, fallowing and mixed cropping. However, in the 1940s and 1950s, in the more-developed Western nations, the newly developed synthetic pesticides, such as the organochlorine DDT (Chapter 14, Section 14.5.1) largely replaced cultural methods of pest control. These chemical pesticides helped to significantly raise levels of food production over the next 20+ years. However, concern over their effects on the environment and on public health led to the banning of many such pesticides in the more-developed countries during the 1970s.

In the search for more environmentally benign methods of pest control, attention has turned more towards various methods of biological control. Essentially, this involves the use of one species (the predator) to control populations of another (the prey). In some cases, the predator species is deliberately introduced from another country, with varying degrees of success. In one notable example from the late nineteenth century, the introduction of an Australian ladybird beetle (*Rodolia cardinalis*) into the citrus groves of southern California successfully controlled a very serious outbreak of cottony-cushion scale (*Icerya purchasi*). Other agents of biological control include parasites, e.g. the minute parasitic wasp *Encarsia formosa* used to control whitefly (*Trialeurodes vaporariorum*) on a range of glasshouse plants, and pathogens, e.g. the bacterium *Bacillus thuringiensis* used to control caterpillars on crops such as tomatoes (*Lycopersicon esculentum*).

Two other types of pest control considered less damaging to the environment than the use of pesticides are 'behavioural' and 'genetic' control methods. In behavioural control, use is made of certain chemical substances normally produced by a pest species, such as juvenile hormones or sex pheromones, in order to influence its behaviour. For example, the substance pyriproxyfen, which mimics the insect juvenile hormone, has been shown in tsetse fly (*Glossina morsitans*) trials to prevent the normal development of 50–75% of the larvae born to contaminated females. Tsetse flies are serious pests in parts of Africa, transmitting sleeping sickness (trypanosomiasis) to humans and a related disease, nagana, to cattle. Amongst the genetic control methods, the 'sterile insect technique' (SIT) has been successfully used for a number of insect species, e.g. the New World screwworm fly (*Cochliomyia hominivorax*) which attacks livestock in many parts of the world. In this method, large populations of the pest species are reared in the laboratory and sterilised by irradiation before being released to mate (ineffectually) with wild populations.

A further development in pest control, and one aimed at providing a long-term solution, is that of integrated pest management (IPM). This approach employs a number of different pest control techniques, including the judicial use of chemical pesticides, and has enormous potential for the effective control of many pest species. The development of disease resistance in crops, through either intensive breeding or genetic engineering (Case study 1, page 240), whilst not a pest control method *per se*, may form an important aspect of the IPM approach.

efficiency with which water is delivered to crops in areas already irrigated. Levels of wastage, mainly due to leakage, can be as high as 60%. The efficiency of irrigated agriculture could also be increased by using the irrigation system to distribute nutrients and pesticides where appropriate.

The cultivation of rice

Rice is a cereal of the tropics and sub-tropics whose distribution is limited mainly by the availability of soil water. The vast majority of rice is grown in the coastal lowland regions of the Far East and coincides with areas of very high population density. It is therefore an extremely important crop, providing the staple food for roughly half of the world's population. Rice has a very long history of cultivation and, as a result, there are almost 1500 different varieties available today. However, these are being progressively replaced by a relatively small number of high-yielding varieties (HYVs) produced by intensive breeding programmes during the 'Green Revolution' (Box 11.4).

Most rice is cultivated under wetland conditions in 'paddy fields'. The presence of standing water ensures the saturation of the soil around the roots, which is necessary for the growth of paddy rice. In Asia, the availability of low-lying deltas and flood plains combined with a tropical monsoon climate provide ideal conditions for this type of

11.3 Rice growing in the Sahel

The Sahel is a semi-desert region which lies between the Sahara desert and the tropical coast of West Africa. Millet (*Panicum miliaceum*) and sorghum (*Sorghum* spp.) are the traditional food crops of this region. However, these have been progressively replaced by paddy rice (*Oryza sativa*), grown with the aid of irrigation water from the Niger and Senegal rivers. The output of rice from the countries which make up the Sahel (Mali, Burkina Faso, Senegal, Niger and Mauritania) more than doubled between 1980 and 1992 (from 352 000 to 800 000 tonnes). Two-thirds of this increased production has been achieved by expanding the area under rice cultivation whilst the remaining third is due to the use of higher-yielding rice strains.

Rice from the Sahel accounts for about 12% of the total rice output of West Africa, although in terms of area it constitutes only 5%. However, there are signs that the recent increase in Sahelian rice productivity cannot be sustained and has been achieved at considerable cost to the environment. The main problem has been the use of poor irrigation schemes in about 20–25% of the 150 000 hectares cultivated with paddy rice. Without adequate drainage, such irrigation systems lead to the accumulation of salt in the soil (salinisation). As a result, most of the affected land is now degraded and unsuitable for further cultivation.

Figure 11.3 Size and stability of wheat field yield in irrigated and non-irrigated arid-zone agriculture (from Stanhill, 1986).

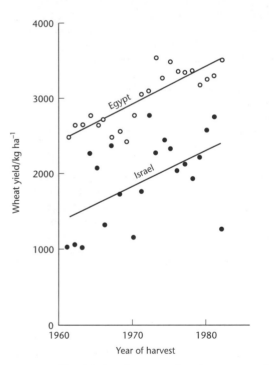

The plots show linear regression of average annual national yield in kg ha–1 on year of harvest.
Open circles: Egypt (irrigated land);
filled circles: Israel (non-irrigated land).

rice cultivation. Deep-water, or floating, varieties of rice can be successfully grown in areas subject to flooding. However, the vast majority of paddy rice is cultivated under shallow-water regimes. These depend mainly on direct precipitation, together with some surface run-off from upper terraces. Traditionally, only one rice crop is grown each year, during the summer rainy season, whilst in the dry season a different crop, such as cotton (*Gossypium* spp.), tobacco (*Nicotiana* spp.), wheat (*Triticum aestivum*) or peas (*Pisum sativa*), is cultivated. Continuous cultivation of paddy rice, perhaps with the aid of irrigation, can yield two or even three rice crops per year. However, this type of intensive agriculture requires high inputs of fertilisers and pesticides and can lead to problems of pest control.

11.4 Forestry

The natural forests of the world have all been exploited to a variable degree. In much of the more-developed world, for example Western Europe, the clearing of natural forests, a process known as **deforestation**, is mainly historical and little remains of the once-prevalent ancient woodlands. In contrast, in the developing countries, large-scale deforestation is occurring *now*. Between 1990 and 1995, the world lost an average of 11.26 million hectares of net forest area each year (Table 11.2), much of this as a result of tropical forest loss. The highest figures for annual rate loss (%) are recorded for Africa, Asia and South America (Table 11.2). There is major global concern over the rapid rate of loss of these tropical forests, especially the tropical rainforests, and the associated environmental and social problems that ensue (Section 11.5).

In many of the more-developed nations, afforestation programmes have been implemented to provide home-grown timber and wood products such as pulp and paper. **Afforestation** involves the planting of trees on land hitherto unoccupied by trees, whilst **reforestation** is used to describe the replanting of trees in areas previously cleared of their forest cover. Together, these schemes have resulted in a net gain in total forested land in a number of more-developed countries. For example, between 1990 and

Further Information Box

11.4 The Green Revolution

The **Green Revolution** is the term used to describe the success of plant-breeding programmes, instigated after the Second World War, in producing new high-yielding varieties (HYVs) of wheat, maize and rice suitable for cultivation in the tropics. In 1966, one of these programmes, carried out by the International Rice Research Institute (IRRI), resulted in a new HYV variety of rice, known as IR8, destined for use in the Philippines. This had a number of advantages over traditional varieties, including the production of higher yields within a shorter growing season in the presence of nitrogen fertilisers.

The Green Revolution has met with considerable success in increasing food production. However, the introduction of HYVs has not been universally beneficial. In order to realise their genetic potential for high yields, these new varieties require considerable inputs in the form of fertilisers, pesticides, water (in the form of irrigation) and fuel-powered machinery. Farmers with small farms and poor resources, whose need is greatest, have not been able to take advantage of this technological advance whilst more affluent landowners have undoubtedly benefited.

The widespread cultivation of HYVs has also led to a rapid decline in crop biodiversity as the genetically diverse native varieties are progressively supplanted. This is a serious cause for concern, as native varieties, by virtue of their long evolution, are inherently more resistant to attack by indigenous pests and disease than the HYVs.

Table 11.2 Change in forest cover, 1990–95 (figures given in thousand hectares).

Regions[a]	Total forest[b] 1990	Total forest[b] 1995	Total change 1990–95	Annual change	Annual change rate (%)
Africa	538 978	520 237	−18 741	−3 748	−0.7
Asia	490 812	474 172	−16 640	−3 328	−0.7
Oceania	91 149	90 695	−454	−91	−0.1
Europe	144 044	145 988	1 944	389	0.3
Former USSR	813 381	816 167	2 786	557	0.1
North and Central America	537 898	536 529	−1 369	−274	−0.1
South America	894 466	870 594	−23 872	−4 774	−0.5
World total	3 510 728	3 454 382	−56 346	−11 269	−0.3

[a] The regional groups used in this table represent the FAO's standardised regional breakdown of the world according to geographical (not economical or political) criteria.
[b] 'Total forest' is the sum of natural forest and plantations.
Source of data: *State of the world's forests 1997*, FAO, Rome.

1995, the United States gained an average of 589 000 hectares annually.

In the UK, afforestation programmes are widespread and began in earnest with the setting up of the Forestry Commission in 1919. Large tracts of upland have been converted from moorland to coniferous plantation, for example Kielder Forest in Northumberland, the largest of Britain's planted forests. The large-scale planting of these managed forests, which are usually dominated by Sitka spruce (*Picea sitchensis*), has caused a number of environmental changes. For example, the litter-fall from coniferous forests increases the acidity of the soil and consequently the acidity of the streams which drain them. This can have an adverse effect on the indigenous aquatic flora and fauna.

The management of plantations through the regulation of species composition, growth and regeneration is known as **silviculture**. The techniques used determine the level of environmental impact. One important example is the method employed to harvest the wood. In **selective cutting**, only the most mature trees are selected and removed. This minimises the impact on the forest ecosystem. In contrast, **clear-cutting** involves the wholesale felling of an even-aged stand of trees. This approach is more economical but more environmentally damaging, destroying the forest ecosystem and exposing the soil to subsequent erosion.

The contraction of the forest resource, through agricultural expansion and timber extraction, has reached a

11.5 Agroforestry

Agroforestry – the mixed cultivation of trees and other crops – has long been practised in the humid tropics, although the term is a relatively new one. One of the main advantages of this traditional and intensive method of cultivation is its sustainability. The incorporation of trees into the system provides nutrients for the herbaceous crops through a number of pathways, including litter-fall and, where applicable, nitrogen fixation. In addition, such systems guard against soil erosion and, because of their high diversity, the build-up of disease and pests.

The combination of trees with annual and perennial herbaceous crops, and, in some cases, livestock, serves to provide the farmer with a continuous supply of food/income. For example, agroforestry is practised on small farms in Sri Lanka. These are known most appropriately as 'gardens' and yield a wide array of crops including coconuts (*Cocos nucifera*), maize (*Zea mays*), breadfruit (*Artocarpus altilis*) and bananas (*Musa sapientum*). Another agroforestry technique is that of **alley-cropping**, where arable crops are cultivated between rows of planted trees and shrubs. The tree species used are usually leguminous and provide the arable crops with an enhanced nitrogen supply. This technique has been used successfully in Nigeria.

The merits of agroforestry outlined above have caused considerable interest in recent years, especially in view of the sustainable development of marginal land and the reclamation of abandoned land in the tropics. For example, in Sri Lanka, agroforestry has been used to impede soil erosion in abandoned tea plantations and, at the same time, provide new areas of productive cultivation.

---

critical level in a number of developing countries, for example Malaysia and Nigeria. Afforestation and reforestation schemes are needed on a massive scale to combat the problem of timber shortages. Notable amongst the various schemes designed to redress the balance is agroforestry, a combination of agriculture and silviculture (Box 11.5).

11.5 The impact of agriculture on the environment

In the developing world, the need to provide adequate food for a rapidly expanding population has put enormous pressure on existing productive land and brought marginal land under cultivation. This has resulted in deforestation of the tropical forests and drainage of wetland areas (Box 11.6). In semi-arid and arid regions, land has been brought into production with the use of irrigation. In many cases, this has led to an accumulation of salts in the soil (salinisation). The subsequent loss of vegetative cover leaves the land open to soil erosion and eventual desertification. Whilst these environmental problems have their greatest impact in the developing world, they are also shared to some extent by the more developed countries.

11.5.1 Deforestation

Deforestation – the removal of trees from forest or woodland areas – is currently a major environmental problem of the developing countries, most of which are in the tropics. Tropical forests account for nearly half of the world's remaining forests, covering an area of $2 \times 10^7 \, km^2$. The main regions of forest are found in Central and South America, central Africa and south and south-east Asia (Figure 11.4). In contrast, in most of the more-developed countries, the process of deforestation has been stopped and, in many cases, effectively reversed with the implementation of afforestation programmes (Table 11.2). However, it should be remembered that most of the more-developed countries were once extensively forested and what remains today is only a fraction of the original.

Deforestation in the developing countries is a problem which affects both tropical rainforest and the savanna woodlands of the drier tropical and subtropical regions. However, deforestation rates are usually highest in the tropical rainforest areas. It is estimated that about 0.6% of the world's rainforest is cleared annually *on average*. However, measuring and assessing the extent of forest cover, and the rate at which it is declining, is an enormous task, dependent on continued monitoring by organisations such as the FAO (Food and Agriculture Organisation). In the Amazon basin, the world's largest forested region, recent advances in monitoring rainforest destruction have been made with the use of satellite images provided by INPE (the space agency of Brazil).

Deforestation of the tropical rainforest is caused by a number of human activities. For example, the increase in the practice of shifting agriculture is a primary cause. This type of extensive agriculture has coexisted with tropical rainforest for thousands of years. However, in recent years, the incidence of shifting agriculture has greatly increased as peasants forced off the land by cash-cropping and ranching turn to the rainforest for sustenance. When this increased population pressure leads to a reduction in

11.6   The disappearing wetlands

Wetlands are characterised by saturated substrata and/or standing water. These productive habitats are found throughout the world in various forms and may be freshwater, brackish or salt-water, depending on their location (Chapter 9, Section 9.7.11). Wetland habitats are under threat worldwide. The global rate of wetland loss is not known but is undoubtedly high. In the United States, where the problem is well documented, one-third of the original 500 000–1 000 000 km^2 had been lost by 1950 and this figure had increased to one-half by 1985.

There are many different reasons for the destruction of wetlands. They may be drained for agricultural, urban or industrial development or to eradicate diseases, such as malaria, associated with wetland regions. Wetlands may be destroyed when the construction of dams or the diversion of water for irrigation decreases their water supply. Coastal wetlands may be converted to aquaculture. For example, in the Philippines, there has been widespread conversion of mangrove swamps to culture ponds for milkfish (*Chanos chanos*) and shrimps.

Wetlands have a number of very important biological functions. They are amongst the most productive ecosystems in the world and provide feeding grounds for millions of migratory birds. The coastal wetlands provide the spawning grounds for shellfish and fish. Wetlands play a significant role in the purification of water and in flood control. They are also important in protecting banks and shorelines from erosion.

The appreciation of wetlands as wildlife habitats and as mechanisms for natural flood and erosion control have stimulated efforts to halt their decline and preserve what remains. Under the Convention on Wetlands of International Importance Especially as Waterfowl Habitat (commonly known as the Ramsar Convention), 966 of the world's wetlands, covering a total surface area of 70 471 806 hectares, are listed for protection (February 1999 figures). However, many more remain at risk.

Figure 11.4 Percentage of land area of different countries occupied by forest and woodland (from Soussan and Millington, 1992).

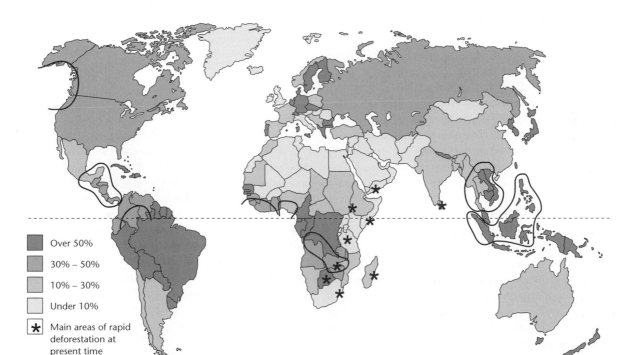

Over 50%

30% – 50%

10% – 30%

Under 10%

★ Main areas of rapid deforestation at present time

the fallow period necessary for the regeneration of cleared patches, land degradation can result.

Other agricultural practices responsible for deforestation are the establishment of plantations for cash crops, for example, rubber (*Hevea brasiliensis*) and cocoa (*Theobroma cacao*), and the use of cleared forest areas for cattle ranching. Large-scale ranching is one of the main reasons for deforestation in Central America. For example, in Costa Rica 67% of the land was forest in 1940, but by 1983 this figure had dwindled to only 17%, mainly as a result of beef cattle ranching. Other causes of deforestation are mineral extraction, the building of roads and dams and logging operations.

The causes of deforestation in savanna regions (Chapter 9, Section 9.7.6) are somewhat different from those operative in rainforest. The savanna biome covers an estimated $2.3 \times 10^7 \, \text{km}^2$ of the Earth's land surface. It separates the semi-arid and arid desert regions from the equatorial rainforest belt. Savanna consists of a mixture of grassland and a variable amount of tree and shrub cover. Deforestation is a problem in all the savanna regions of the world and has two main causes, the development of agriculture and the need for fuelwood. Deforestation of the savanna regions of Africa is particularly acute as a result of the pressures of a large and expanding population. For example, the African countries of Ethiopia and Mozambique depend almost entirely on fuelwood for cooking and warmth.

There are a number of environmental problems associated with deforestation. On a local level, the protective tree cover plays a very important role in the water cycle. The water taken up by the trees reduces the amount available for surface run-off. When deforestation occurs, surface run-off increases. This situation can lead to severe problems of accelerated soil erosion. For example, in mountainous regions of Nepal and northern India, entire hillsides, stripped of their natural tree cover, have been washed away by heavy monsoon rains. On a regional level, the increase in surface run-off associated with deforestation has caused severe downstream flooding, whilst the transport of large amounts of sediment can destroy neighbouring areas and also cause problems of siltation.

On a global scale, the burning of biomass associated with deforestation is contributing to an increase in atmospheric carbon dioxide levels. Large amounts of carbon dioxide are taken up by the forests during photosynthesis and extensive deforestation has resulted in the contraction of this important sink mechanism (Chapter 15, Section 15.1.4). Deforestation is a major contributor to the decline in global biodiversity. Tropical rainforests are estimated to contain at least half of the world's plant and animal species, although they cover only 6% of the Earth's land surface. Apart from their immense intrinsic value as wildlife habitats, they constitute a vast genetic resource of enormous importance to future medical and agricultural developments (Chapter 10).

The problem of deforestation, particularly in regard to the tropical rainforest, is recognised worldwide. However, its causes are diverse and complex and very difficult to address. To the countries which possess rainforest regions, development pressures are enormous and usually include such factors as an expanding population, poverty and huge foreign debts. However, concerted efforts to conserve rainforest regions have met with success in some cases. For example, the 'debt-for-conservation' approach has resulted in the protection of 1.5 million hectares of Amazonian rainforest in Bolivia in exchange for a US$650 000 reduction in its foreign debt. In addition, sustainable agricultural practices, notably agroforestry, have received recent attention as a means of both soil conservation and long-term maintenance of productivity in rainforest regions (Box 11.5).

11.5.2 Salinisation

The accumulation of salts (principally carbonates, chlorides and sulfates) in soil, surface water and ground water is known as **salinisation**. This process occurs naturally in arid and semi-arid regions, where high evaporation rates bring saline ground water to the surface by capillary action. As the water evaporates, salt deposits build up on the surface to form natural features such as salt flats.

The extensive use of irrigation in semi-arid and arid regions to enable crop cultivation has greatly accelerated the process of salinisation. Water brought in for irrigation tends to have a high concentration of salts, especially when ground water is the supply source. This is because the soluble mineral content of rocks in dry-land regions tends to be high. Rapid evaporation rates lead to an accumulation of these imported salts in the soil. In addition, in areas where irrigation systems are poor, problems of waterlogging and inadequate drainage contribute to the problem of salinisation (Box 11.3).

Plants vary in their tolerance to saline conditions. Amongst the cultivated grain crops, for example, wheat and barley can maintain their seed yields at the expense of vegetative growth, whilst rice is able to grow normally but fails to produce seeds. The overall effect of salinisation on crop production is a decrease in growth rate and productivity. In extreme conditions, salinisation can lead to the abandonment of previously cultivated land. It is therefore a major contributory factor to the desertification of semi-arid and arid lands.

11.5.3 Soil erosion

Soil erosion occurs when the rate of removal of soil exceeds the rate at which it can be produced by weathering of the underlying bedrock. It is a natural process, mediated by water and the wind. The rate of soil erosion is influenced by a number of factors, including climate, the degree of slope and the density of the protective vegetation cover. Human activities, primarily those involving inappropriate agricultural practices, have greatly increased the rate of soil erosion in many parts of the world, especially in dry tropical regions (Figure 11.5). It is estimated that the annual loss of soil through erosion is in the region of 75 000 million tonnes. The adverse effects of soil erosion extend far beyond the loss of productive agricultural land in the immediate area. Deposition of the soil can destroy neighbouring areas of cultivation and cause problems of sedimentation in lakes, reservoirs and rivers.

Soil erosion is a problem in both the developing and the more-developed world. In the developing world, high population pressures have resulted in the cultivation of marginal land, which is particularly vulnerable to soil erosion. Such land may be on steep slopes or it may have an inherently low soil fertility, for example on the periphery of deserts or on land made available by the clearance of tropical rainforest. Intensive cultivation of such areas without, for example, necessary periods of fallow or crop rotation can lead to a loss of soil fertility and the abandonment of the land. Without the protection of natural vegetation or crop cover, the bare soil is exposed to the forces of soil erosion. In semi-arid and arid regions, soil erosion is strongly associated with desertification.

Agricultural practices geared to long-term sustainability can enable the successful cultivation of these fragile systems, for example agroforestry (Box 11.5). However, such schemes are rare. In much of the developing world, where the need to supply food to a growing population is immediate, agricultural practices which are productive in the short term take precedence.

Soil erosion is also a serious cause for concern in the more-developed world, for example in Australia, Europe and North America. In the United States, it is estimated that the productivity of one-third of all its crop land is at risk from soil erosion. Box 11.7 describes the events which led up to the 'dust bowl' conditions experienced in the Great Plains of the USA during the 1930s, a phenomenon which still recurs today, albeit on a much reduced scale. In Europe, soil erosion was not recognised by the European Economic Community (EEC) as a major problem until as late as 1980. The intensification of agriculture since the Second World War and the concomitant rise in productivity had hitherto masked its effects on soil fertility. There are a number of agricultural practices which can be successfully employed in soil conservation. These include crop rotation, zero-tillage and the use of contour ploughing, where the furrows follow the contour of the hill and not the slope.

Figure 11.5 The global extent of soil erosion (from Mannion, 1991, after Myers, 1985).

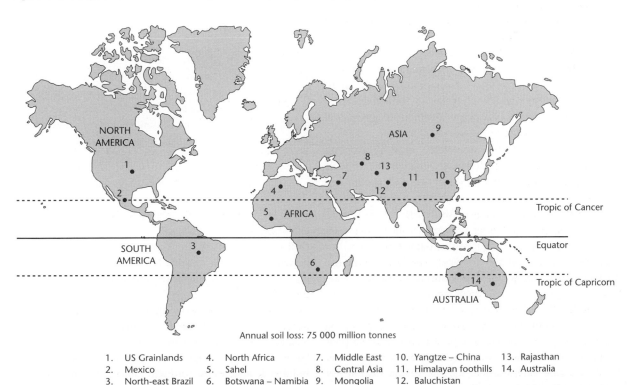

Annual soil loss: 75 000 million tonnes

1. US Grainlands
2. Mexico
3. North-east Brazil
4. North Africa
5. Sahel
6. Botswana – Namibia
7. Middle East
8. Central Asia
9. Mongolia
10. Yangtze – China
11. Himalayan foothills
12. Baluchistan
13. Rajasthan
14. Australia

255

Mini Case Study

11.7 The 'Dust Bowl' of the United States

One of the worst cases of wind-induced soil erosion occurred in the Great Plains of the USA in the 1930s, creating the infamous Dust Bowl. This semi-arid region stretches from Texas, through Oklahoma and into North Dakota. It is characterised by a highly variable rainfall and droughts every 20–25 years. However, during the Depression years of the 1930s, higher than average rainfalls encouraged the widespread agricultural development of the Great Plains. The prairie grasslands were used for grazing cattle or deep-ploughed for wheat cultivation.

The extensive and mechanised cultivation of wheat, together with overgrazing, led to a decline in soil fertility in the Plains. A succession of drought years followed and the vegetation cover was further reduced as crops failed to grow. In the summer of 1934, winds stripped the exposed topsoil from vast areas; 3.5 million hectares of farmland were destroyed and a further 30 million hectares were seriously affected. The huge dust storms which developed traversed the length of the United States, from Mexico to Canada.

This environmental disaster focused attention on the problem of soil erosion in the USA and prompted the development of soil conservation techniques. However, small-scale dust storms are still a recurrent problem in the Great Plains, suggesting that there is scope for further measures to prevent soil erosion.

Reference: Worster, D. (1979) *Dust bowl: the Southern Plains in the 1930s*. New York: Oxford University Press.

11.5.4 Desertification

Desertification describes the final stages of the process by which formerly productive semi-arid and arid land is degraded into unproductive desert, mainly as a result of human activities. The areas most at risk of desertification are the semi-arid regions adjacent to the true deserts of the world (Figure 11.6). Although desertification is a problem in parts of the more-developed world, such as Australia and the United States, it is in the developing nations, especially in sub-Saharan Africa, that it has had its greatest impact, causing widespread famines and immense loss of human life. The global rate of desertification is estimated to be about six million hectares per year.

The causes of desertification are many and complex. Natural factors such as the risk of drought and a high rainfall variability, which characterise semi-arid lands, contribute to the process of desertification. However, the problem has undoubtedly been exacerbated by a number of human activities, primarily those involving inappropriate agricultural practices. For example, years of higher than average rainfall have, on occasion, encouraged the intensification of cultivation in marginal areas already farmed, or the expansion of cultivated land into usually more arid regions. The latter process has sometimes been actively encouraged by government-aided schemes, for example the provision of boreholes in the Sahel during the 1950s and early 1960s. However, during subsequent years of drought, productivity in these areas cannot be sustained and the land is abandoned. Land made productive by the use of irrigation schemes in dry-land regions can also be subsequently lost to desertification. This occurs when poor irrigation systems cause waterlogging and salinisation of the soil to the extent where it is no longer suitable for cultivation (Box 11.3).

Approximately half of the land lost annually to desertification is rangeland, used extensively for the rough grazing of cattle. Overgrazing is thought to be the primary reason for the widespread destruction of these fragile ecosystems. Once the vegetation cover is removed, the bare soil becomes vulnerable to erosion by wind, and by water during the seasonal rains. The cattle themselves contribute further to the problem by packing the soil down with their hooves and preventing air and water from penetrating the ground. This increases surface run-off and consequently lowers the water table. Figure 11.7 illustrates how this downward spiral can lead to rangeland desertification.

The problem of desertification is a continuing one which is likely to accelerate in the developing countries, where the human population is expanding rapidly and resources to address the problem are few. The need to feed a burgeoning population puts enormous pressures on the land and this often results in the use of unsustainable agricultural methods.

11.6 Summary

During the Neolithic era, 12 000–10 000 years BP (before present), humans gradually exchanged a hunter–gatherer lifestyle for a more settled existence based on the cultivation of crops and the domestication of livestock. Since these early agrarian beginnings, land use has changed and diversified throughout the world, especially in the last two centuries. For example, in Europe in the mid-eighteenth century, the effects of the Industrial Revolution brought major changes as the twin processes of industrialisation and urbanisation

Figure 11.6 The global extent and degree of desertification (from Cunningham and Saigo, 1995).

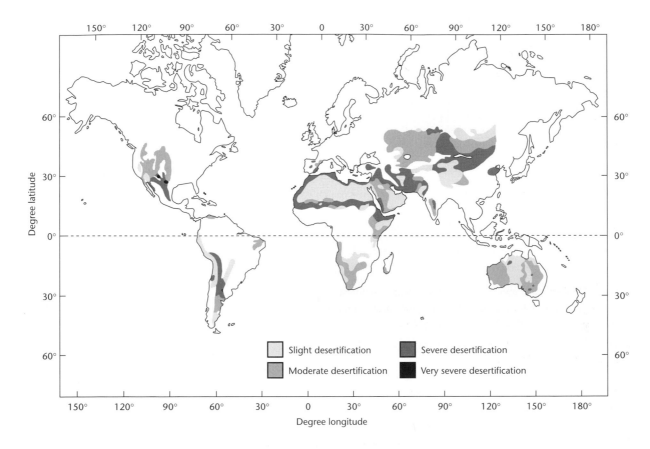

Figure 11.7 The process of rangeland desertification.

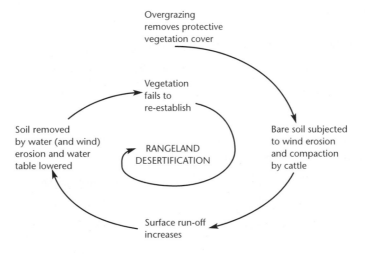

changed the face of an essentially rural landscape. This transition is still in progress today, especially in the less-developed countries.

Agriculture was the first type of land use and remains the most important one today. The fuel-powered urban–industrial systems which characterise the more-developed countries are ultimately dependent on the agro-ecosystem to feed their populations. In the developing nations, the need to provide food for a rapidly expanding population (and also to grow cash crops to earn foreign currency) has resulted in the use of marginal land for cultivation and increased the pressure on already productive land. This has caused a number of major environmental problems such as deforestation, salinisation, soil erosion and desertification. Although these problems are shared to an extent by the more-developed nations, their greatest impact has been in the developing countries, whose resources to address them are least.

11.7 Problems

1 What are the major types of land use? Briefly outline the historical development of land use, pinpointing periods of major change and their underlying causes.

2 Compare and contrast the urbanisation process in the more-developed and developing countries.

3 After the Second World War, agriculture in the more-developed Western nations became increasingly intensified to the point reached today where arable and livestock farming are largely divorced. What three major advances facilitated this intensification of agriculture? Discuss the advantages and disadvantages of intensive arable cultivation and livestock rearing.

4 What are the basic differences between extensive and intensive agriculture? Illustrate your answer with reference to specific types of agricultural practices.

5 It is estimated that about 0.6% of the world's rainforest is lost through deforestation each year. Discuss the underlying causes of rainforest clearance. What are the local, regional and global repercussions of deforestation? Suggest methods which might be used to help reverse this trend.

6 What is meant by salinisation? How may this be exacerbated by poor irrigation practices? Illustrate your answer with a specific example.

7 What are the main agents of soil erosion? Discuss how this natural process may be accelerated by inappropriate agricultural practices.

8 The global rate of desertification is estimated to be in the region of six million hectares per year. Explain what is meant by this term and which areas of the world are particularly at risk. How do human activities contribute to this process and what are the prospects for slowing down the rate of desertification in the future?

11.8 Further reading

Mannion, A. M. (1997) *Global environmental change* (2nd edn) Harlow: Longman.

Mannion, A. M. and S. R. Bowlby (eds) (1992) *Environmental issues in the 1990s*. Chichester: Wiley.

Myers, N. and G. Durrell (1994) *The Gaia atlas of planet management*. London: Gaia Books.

Tivy, J. (1990) *Agricultural ecology*. Harlow: Longman.

Tolba, M. K., O. A. El-Kholy, E. El-Hinnawi, M. W. Holdgate, D. F. McMichael and R. E. Munn (eds) (1992) *The world environment 1972–1992: two decades of challenge*. London: Chapman & Hall.

Whitmore, T. C. (1990) *An introduction to tropical rainforests*. Oxford: Oxford University Press.

BSE and the British beef crisis

BSE (bovine spongiform encephalopathy) is a neurological disease of cattle, of recent origin. It was first diagnosed in Britain in 1986 and sparked a major crisis in the British beef industry. BSE is a type of transmissible spongiform encephalopathy (TSE). TSEs are fatal neurodegenerative diseases of animals and humans in which the brain is characterised by a sponge-like appearance and deposits of protein aggregates. Other members of this group are scrapie, which affects sheep, and Creutzfeldt–Jakob disease (CJD), which affects humans. Transmissible spongiform encephalopathies have also been reported in a number of other mammals such as cats and various types of antelopes, e.g. Arabian oryx (*Oryx leucoryx*) and elk (*Alces alces*).

The typical incubation period for BSE is about five years, but it can range from $2\frac{1}{2}$ to 10 years. Initially, cattle infected with BSE showed signs of apprehension and agitation. This was followed by the appearance of obviously uncoordinated movements, such as staggering and stumbling. This loss of motor control is symptomatic of the deteriorating mental state of BSE-infected cattle, which, in turn, is caused by the development of sponge-like voids within the tissues of the brain. The symptoms shown by BSE-infected cattle have given rise to the term 'mad cow disease', a disease which invariably leads to death.

After the initial diagnosis of BSE in 1986, an epidemiological investigation was undertaken and completed by December 1987. This study concluded that the cause of BSE was the inclusion of protein derived from scrapie-infected sheep in compound cattle feed. (However, this connection has not yet been proven. Other researchers maintain that a more likely explanation is that BSE arose spontaneously within the cattle themselves and was subsequently spread by the use of protein derived from infected cattle in the cattle feed.) As a consequence of these findings, a ban on the sale of cattle feed containing ruminant protein came into force in the UK in July 1988. Figure C2.1 illustrates the annual number of confirmed cases of BSE in the UK. Numbers reached a peak in 1992 with 36 700 confirmed cases but have

Figure C2.1 The number of confirmed cases of BSE in the UK for the period 1988–97 (data from MAFF).

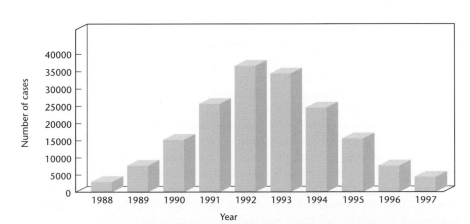

since declined year on year. This pattern of figures is consistent with the imposition of the ruminant feed ban and the incubation period of BSE.

The exact nature of the infectious agent involved in the transmission of BSE (and other transmissible spongiform encephalopathies, TSEs) is not yet clear. It is known that radiation, chemical disinfection and heat all fail to inactivate it, and that it evokes no immune response in the host organism. In these respects, it differs from bacteria and viruses. The favoured hypothesis is that the BSE agent is a proteinaceous infectious particle, or 'prion', as it is more usually known. This prion protein (PrP) exists in two forms: a normal form, known as 'prion protein cellular' (PrPC), and a rogue form, known as prion protein scrapie (PrPSc). The normal form is harmless, and, whilst its function is not known, it may play a role in the central nervous system or immune system. The abnormal form is thought to be the infectious agent involved in TSEs, causing normal prion proteins to be transformed into the rogue form. However, this protein-only hypothesis has not yet been proven and, consequently, these prions remain the subject of intense research activity and scientific debate.

The emergence of BSE within the British cattle population gave rise to public concern over the possibility of its transmission to humans. Could BSE jump the species barrier? Initially, it was thought that BSE was unlikely to affect humans. The fact that scrapie (the 'sheep equivalent' of BSE) had been endemic in British sheep for more than 200 years and never been linked to CJD in humans was partly behind government advice at the time that British beef was safe to eat.

However, in the mid-1990s, several cases of CJD were reported amongst *young* people. This rare type of TSE usually affects people over the age of 65 years, causing dementia, loss of motor control and, eventually, death. In a number of cases, it has been confused with Alzheimer's disease. Several differences in the nature of the disease became apparent between the two age groups of sufferers. For example, in the younger victims (whose average age was 27 years) the first symptoms were anxiety and depression, whilst in elderly sufferers initial signs of the disease were a tendency to be forgetful and/or behave in a peculiar manner. Also the progression of CJD took twice as long in the younger group, in comparison with the older group.

Post-mortem examinations of the young victims of CJD showed that the protein deposits in their brain tissue (a characteristic feature of TSEs) were *different* from those observed in classical CJD. This new type of CJD became known as new-variant CJD (nvCJD). In 1996, it was shown, through biochemical fingerprints of prion proteins associated with BSE and CJD, that these two diseases were related, and also that new-variant CJD was unrelated to other types of CJD described to date. This work was carried out by Professor John Collinge and co-workers at St Mary's Hospital in London. Their findings suggested that BSE had indeed jumped the species barrier from cattle to humans – probably as a result of people eating BSE-infected beef. As a result, the consumption of British beef declined sharply. Subsequent research work, both by Professor Collinge and by other research groups, has since confirmed the link between nvCJD and BSE.

In response to the findings linking nvCJD with BSE, the British government introduced the 'Over Thirty Months Scheme' (OTMS) in April 1996, as an extra precautionary measure. Under this scheme, *all* cattle over the age of 30 months had to be culled from herds. The aim of this was to ensure that no cattle over the age of 30 months entered either the human food chain or the animal feed chain. In addition to the logistics of dealing with a cull of this magnitude, this new eradication measure generated a large number of extra animal carcasses that needed to be safely disposed of. In England and Wales, responsibility for the disposal of waste, including animal-derived waste, lay with the Environment Agency. In this instance, their options included disposal to landfill and incineration. Since 1991, incineration in specially designed animal carcass incinerators has been the disposal method used for all confirmed cases of BSE. Risk assessment studies carried out by the Agency concluded that the risk of humans becoming infected with BSE through environmental pathways associated with any of the disposal options, used or considered, was extremely small.

During the BSE crises, a number of control measures were put in place by the British government (advised by the Spongiform Encephalopathy Advisory Committee (SEAC) set up in 1990) in order to eradicate BSE from the British cattle population. The ban on the sale of cattle feed containing ruminant protein (July 1988) and the 'Over Thirty Months Scheme' (April 1996) have already been mentioned. Other measures include the banning of certain specified bovine offal (SBO) for human consumption and the banning of the sale of beef on the bone (December 1997).

The BSE epidemic in the UK is now in decline (Figure C2.1). In November 1998, the European Union (EU) partially lifted its previously imposed ban on British beef exports, pending slaughterhouse inspections. On 1 August 1999, the ban was lifted completely. However, concern remains over whether BSE infection still persists in the British cattle population at a sub-clinical level. Animals may act as hidden reservoirs of BSE, capable of infecting others whilst not themselves developing the disease. Also there is evidence, from a seven-year study (1988–95) undertaken by John Wilesmith and his colleagues at the UK government's Central Veterinary Laboratory at Weybridge, that cows with BSE can pass the disease to their calves. However, the rate of maternal transmission was estimated to be in the region of 1% under field conditions and therefore not considered significant with regard to extending the epidemic.

In other countries, particularly those of continental Europe, the problem of BSE may be more widespread than is either known or acknowledged. For example, in October 1998, the EU placed an export ban on Portuguese beef after several cases of BSE suddenly came to light. There is concern too over the possibility of more cases of nvCJD emerging in the future, especially in the UK. At the time of writing (April 1999), a total of 40 people in the UK have died as a result of this disease. Sixteen deaths from nvCJD have occurred during 1998, representing a sharp rise on previous years. However, it is too soon to say if the annual number of cases will rise further. The problem is that nvCJD has a very long incubation period (10–40 years). This means that there *may* be more individuals within the population who have not yet developed recognisable symptoms but who will eventually develop nvCJD.

Crucially, a new test has recently been developed by Professor John Collinge of St Mary's Hospital, London, capable of identifying nvCJD in *living* tissue. Prior to this, the only means of identifying the presence of nvCJD in individuals was the post-mortem examination of their brain tissue. This new test, involving biopsy of material taken from the tonsils, means that this degenerative disease can now be diagnosed at a much earlier stage. It also opens the way for research, using tissues from tonsillectomies, to assess the extent of nvCJD within the general population.

Further reading

Borman, S. (1998) Prion research accelerates. *Chemical & Engineering News*, 9 February. American Chemical Society.

Environment Agency Report (June 1997) *Risks from BSE via environmental pathways*. Summary document produced by the Environment Agency (Rio House, Waterside Drive, Aztec West, Almondsbury, Bristol, BS12 4UD).

Mackenzie, D. (1998) Hard to swallow. *New Scientist*, 14 November, 22–23.

Pain, S. (1996) Mad calves fuel BSE fears. *New Scientist*, 10 August, 10–11.

Ratzan, S C. (ed.) (1997) *Mad cow crisis: Health and the public good*. London: UCL Press.

The major extractive industries

After reading this chapter, you should be able to:

- Distinguish between the terms 'resource' and 'reserve' with regard to mineral deposits.

- Define the term 'orebody', and discuss the enrichment processes by which an orebody may be formed.

- Appreciate the different stages involved in the recovery of metals from their ores.

- Outline the principal non-metalliferous mineral materials used by the construction industry, and the uses to which they are put.

- Explain how peat is formed, and discuss methods for its extraction, together with their environmental impact.

- Compare and contrast the fossil fuels – coal, oil and natural gas – in terms of their formation, extraction, associated environmental problems and current reserve status.

- Describe the effects of water extraction on both groundwater and surface water reserves.

- Discuss the advantages and disadvantages of creating reservoirs.

Introduction

Over 2000 known minerals occur within the rocks which make up the Earth's crust (Chapter 3, Section 3.1.3). The occurrence of particular minerals is associated with specific rock types, and as a result their global distribution is uneven. Mineral resources which are valued and used for human needs are referred to as **stock resources**. These include metal ores, aggregate materials used in building and road construction, and carbon and hydrocarbon fuels (coal, oil, natural gas and peat), all of which are discussed in this chapter. The final section of this chapter deals with water since much of it is extracted from deep underground aquifers, a situation analogous to the mining of fossil fuels.

Minerals are non-renewable natural resources. It is important at this early stage to distinguish between the terms 'resource' and 'reserve', especially when considering the future availability of minerals. The **resource** of a particular mineral refers to the total amount present on Earth, whether or not its location is known. The **reserve** of a mineral refers to known deposits which are recoverable under *current technological and economic conditions*. The reserve may therefore be increased by more efficient extraction techniques or when market conditions of high demand and falling supplies make the extraction of poorer grade deposits economic.

There is a marked divide between the mineral

consumption of the more-developed countries (MDCs) and that of the less-developed countries (LDCs). Even though the MDCs contain only one-fifth of the world's population, they consume approximately 75% of the non-fuel minerals. What is more, of the total production of coal, oil and natural gas, the MDCs consume about 60, 68 and 84% respectively.

The environmental impact of mining depends on a number of factors including the nature of the mineral in question, the method of extraction required (depending on the location of the deposit) and the grade of material extracted. For example, when surface methods are employed, large tracts of land are degraded by both the workings themselves and the deposition of mine-waste. In comparison, the visual impact of deep mining is generally less. However, in both cases, there may be other associated environmental costs such as the production of highly acidic waste water (either from the mines themselves or from the leaching of spoil heaps), which may eventually contaminate natural watercourses (Chapter 14, Section 14.3.2).

12.1   Metals

In nature, because of their reactivity, most metals occur as compounds rather than pure elements. These compounds are most commonly oxides, sulfides or carbonates (Table 12.1). A **metal ore** is the term used to describe a material in which the concentration of a particular metal is high enough to make its recovery economical. This definition is not absolute but dependent on the demand for a certain metal in relation to its abundance. **Orebodies** are deposits of ores which are sufficiently large to be commercially worked. They may be formed by a number of enrichment processes (Box 12.1). Ores are graded according to their metal content. It is often the case that higher grade ores become exhausted first, forcing a switch to the mining of lower grade ones.

The methods employed in the extraction of metal ores from the ground are dependent on the geology of the area, the location of the reserve and economic considerations. Deep mining and surface methods such as drift, open pit (opencast) and strip mining are all commonly used (Table 12.1 and Figure 12.1). These all have a significant impact on their immediate environment. For example, the Anaconda Mine in New Mexico is the largest open pit uranium mine in the world. It covers an area of 486 hectares, most of which is given over to enormous dump sites of mine waste and **overburden** (the soil and rocks overlying the desired ore).

When metal ores are extracted using deep mining methods, ground subsidence can be a problem. This occurs when rock layers above the excavated chambers give way

and collapse. However, the need for extensive underground excavation can be obviated (in some cases) by the *in situ* use of bioleaching (Box 12.2). In addition to the exploitation of terrestrial deposits, some metals can be recovered from river sediments, a process known as alluvial mining. In Box 12.3, the use of mercury in the capture of gold from river sediments in the Amazon Basin is examined, together with the environmental impacts of this technique.

The effects of mining are not restricted to the physical scarring of the landscape. Air, water and land pollution are all associated with the extraction of metal ores from the ground. These pollution problems are exacerbated when the processing of the metal ore (known as **extractive metallurgy**) is carried out on site. The dumping of waste material after ore processing can lead to the contamination of surface and ground water supplies through leaching of residual metal compounds. These may include traces not only of the original target metal but of other metals naturally present in the ore. For example, in Tasmania, mining for tin and tungsten has led to environmental contamination by zinc and cadmium.

After mining, the unwanted minerals, known collectively as **gangue**, are physically separated from the ore-mineral (the metal-bearing component of the ore). This initial physical separation stage is followed by the recovery of the metal itself, using an appropriate chemical or electrochemical reduction process. There are two main types of chemical processing, **pyrometallurgy** (involving the use of high temperatures) and **hydrometallurgy** (involving the use of water).

Pyrometallurgical techniques are involved in the recovery of a number of different metals from their respective metal sulfide ores by roasting. In the case of nickel, zinc and lead, the ore is initially roasted in air to yield the metal oxide, and sulfur dioxide:

$$2MS_{(s)} + 3O_{2(g)} \rightarrow 2MO_{(s)} + 2SO_{2(g)}$$

where M = Ni, Zn or Pb. The metal oxide is subsequently reduced to its elementary state using carbon, usually in the form of coke, charcoal or powdered coal:

$$MO_{(s)} + C_{(s)} \xrightarrow{\Delta} M_{(s)} + CO_{(g)}$$

where Δ represents high temperatures (Box 12.4).

In the case of copper and mercury sulfide ores, the metal is formed directly by roasting:

$$Cu_2S_{(s)} + O_{2(g)} \rightarrow 2Cu_{(s)} + SO_{2(g)}$$
$$HgS_{(s)} + O_{2(g)} \rightarrow Hg_{(l)} + SO_{2(g)}$$

The roasting of sulfide ores has serious environmental impacts because it involves the production of large amounts of sulfur dioxide, a major pollutant responsible for acid rain (Chapter 15, Section 15.2.2). For example, the

Table 12.1 The seven most common metals, plus uranium.

Metal	Ore	Main producers	Uses	Extraction method	Environmental problems
Iron (Fe)	Mainly iron oxides in form of magnetite (Fe_3O_4) and haematite (Fe_2O_3)	former Soviet Union, Brazil, Australia, USA, China	Most commonly used metal; primary use is in steel-making for construction and machinery	Deep, drift and opencast mining	Water, land and air pollution at mine and at processing plant
Aluminium (Al)	Bauxite, an impure form of aluminium oxide (Al_2O_3)	Australia, Guinea-Bissau, Jamaica, Surinam, Guyana	Second most widely used metal. Used in aircraft (light) and electrical wiring (good conductor)	Formerly deep mining, now mainly open pit	High energy requirements of the extraction of aluminium from its ore
Lead (Pb)	Lead sulfide (PbS), known as galena	USA, former Soviet Union, Australia, Canada, Peru	Battery electrodes, paint pigments and as an additive in petrol	Formerly deep mining, now mainly open pit	Production of sulfur dioxide during ore smelting; acid mine drainage
Zinc (Zn)	Zinc sulfide (ZnS), known as sphalerite	Canada, former Soviet Union, USA, Australia, Peru	In iron and steel products, chemical industry and diecasting	Formerly deep mining, now mainly open pit	Production of sulfur dioxide during ore smelting; acid mine drainage
Copper (Cu)	Formerly elemental copper, now copper sulfides such as chalcocite (Cu_2S)	USA, Chile, former Soviet Union, Canada, Zambia, Zaire	Electrical wiring and cooking utensils (good conductor of electricity and heat)	Formerly deep mining, now mainly open pit	Production of sulfur dioxide during ore smelting; acid mine drainage
Tin (Sn)	Tin oxide (SnO_2), known as cassiterite	Malaysia, Thailand, Indonesia, Nigeria	Tin-plating of steel cans, in the production of organotin, as an alloy in soldering and bronze-making	Alluvial mining (recovery of tin from river sediments)	Contamination of the surrounding area, excessive siltation in water bodies
Nickel (Ni)	Nickel sulfide (NiS)	former Soviet Union, Canada, Australia, Indonesia	In steel production; also in chemical industry for the production of dyes, catalysts and pigments	Formerly deep mining, now mainly open pit	Production of sulfur dioxide during ore smelting; acid mine drainage
Uranium (U)	Uranium oxide (U_3O_8), known as pitchblende	USA, Canada, South Africa, Namibia, Australia	Nuclear energy production	Usually extracted by open pit methods	Environmental contamination, including risk from radioactive residues to groundwater and human health

nickel and copper smelter in Sudbury, Canada, constitutes the world's largest single point source of sulfur dioxide.

In order to eliminate the roasting step, the technique of hydrometallurgy has been developed. This is basically a two-stage process. Using copper as an example, the first step converts the insoluble copper sulfide to a saturated solution of a water-soluble salt of the copper cation, Cu^{2+}:

$$2CuS_{(s)} + 4H^+_{(aq)} + O_{2(g)} \rightarrow$$
$$2Cu^{2+}_{(aq)} + 2S_{(c)} + 2H_2O_{(l)}$$

This process is known as leaching. It may be followed by additional processes which are designed to isolate a *pure* aqueous solution of the target metal salt.

In the second stage, the copper cation is reduced to pure copper by electrolysis.

$$2Cu^{2+}_{(aq)} + 2H_2O_{(l)} \rightarrow 2Cu_{(s)} + O_{2(g)} + 4H^+_{(aq)}$$

In the case of aluminium, pyrometallurgical processes are not practicable and electrochemical techniques are used instead (Box 12.4). The only economic source of aluminium is bauxite (Table 12.1). This ore contains aluminium oxide (Al_2O_3), together with impurities such as silicates and iron(III) oxide (Fe_2O_3). These must first be removed to yield pure aluminium oxide, which is extremely stable at high temperatures. The aluminium oxide is reduced to pure aluminium by electrolytic

Further Information Box

12.1   The genesis of orebodies[1]

Orebodies are deposits of minerals that contain significantly high concentrations of one or more of the useful elements and that are sufficiently large to be commercially worked.

There are a number of processes that can facilitate the enrichment necessary for the formation of orebodies. These include both those that have their origin within the Earth (endogenetic processes) and those concerned with surface phenomena (exogenetic processes). There are a variety of mechanisms by which these processes generate orebodies, the more important of which include those outlined below.

Endogenetic processes

Magmatic segregation.   If the magma of an intrusion contains significant quantities of commercially valuable elements that are capable of forming dense minerals that crystallise at high temperatures ($\sim 1000°C$), magmatic segregation deposits may be formed. For example, the chromium (Cr) content of ultrabasic and basic magmas may be high enough to allow significant quantities of chromite ($FeCr_2O_4$) to form early in the solidification process. If solidification is sufficiently slow, this dense mineral will sink through the melt, to accumulate in a layer at the foot of the intrusion.

Magmatic segregation of sulfide ores can also occur in basic rocks. While still molten, the magmas that form these rocks may produce dense beads of liquid that is essentially iron sulfide. These drops may also contain significant quantities of copper, nickel, and possibly platinum and related elements. Ultimately, because of their high density, these drops may fall to the base of the intrusion, forming an ore body.

Contact metasomatism (also called pyrometasomatism).   The movement of hot liquids and gases through country rock during an intrusion may lead to an alteration in its bulk elemental composition. Occasionally, this will generate orebodies within the contact aureole of metamorphic rock that surrounds the intrusion.

Pegmatite formation.   Pegmatites are coarse-grained deposits that are formed during the latter stages of the solidification of *acidic* intrusions. In these stages, a water-rich immiscible fluid may form within the remaining melt. Pegmatites result if this fluid is forced into cracks in the newly formed igneous rock and/or surrounding rocks, where it solidifies. While pegmatites have essentially the same mineralogy as the rest of the intrusion, they may contain significant concentrations of minerals rich in less abundant elements with large ionic radii, including, in some cases, uranium and thorium.

Hydrothermal deposition.   This can occur when hot water moves through rocks. It frequently causes minerals to be deposited as sheets (called veins) in joints or faults within the rock. The heat for this process may be of igneous origin, or from the normal geothermal gradient (Chapter 13, Section 13.3.7).

Many hydrothermal deposits do not contain commercially valuable minerals. However, orebodies may be formed if the water flows from an environment in which it can dissolve valuable metal(s) to one in which they are deposited as insoluble precipitates. For example, low-sulfide brine can dissolve metals (such as copper, Cu) from rocks as chloride complexes. If the brine then moves to a sulfide-rich area, the solubility product of the metal sulfide will be exceeded, the complexes will break down and sulfide ores (such as chalcopyrite, $CuFeS_2$) will be formed.

Hydrothermal deposition that occurs above about 400°C is called *pneumatolytic deposition.*

Exogenetic processes

Supergene deposit formation.   This occurs in the continental regions as a consequence of the processes of weathering. This process does not affect minerals that are highly resistant to chemical and physical attack. Included amongst these are some gems (e.g. diamonds and rubies) and metallic oxides, some of which are of commercial value (e.g. ilmenite, $FeTiO_3$, and cassiterite, SnO_2). As these vary in density from silicate minerals, they may form *placer deposits* if concentrated by, for example, the physical sorting action of rivers.

In hot, wet climates weathering activity is particularly intense. Under these conditions, soils are commonly so severely leached that the bulk of the more soluble minerals have been removed. This leaves a mixture of hydrated iron and aluminium oxides. Occasionally, the iron content of these soils is also low, leaving large *residual deposits* of essentially pure bauxite (hydrated aluminium oxide).

Sedimentary deposits.   These are formed when the products of weathering and erosion are laid down under large water bodies such as lakes or oceans. Most rocks formed by this process are not orebodies. However, there are significant exceptions to this. Both evaporite formation and chemical precipitation have produced deposits of commercial significance. For example, the bulk of the iron produced in the world originates from chemically precipitated minerals that were deposited between 1.7×10^9 and 3.2×10^9 years ago.

[1] You may find it useful to read Section 3.1 (Chapter 3) before considering the material in this box.

reduction. From an environmental viewpoint, the importance of this process lies with its extremely high energy requirements. In the United States, aluminium production uses a staggering 4–5% of the country's electricity supply! In comparison, aluminium recovered by the recycling of aluminium cans uses only 4% of the energy required for primary production.

It is difficult to predict accurately how long particular

Figure 12.1 Different methods of mineral extraction (not to scale): (a) deep mining (from Lambert, 1988); (b) contour strip mining, a type of surface mining.

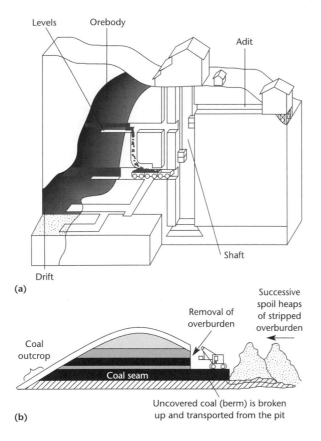

(a)

(b)

a general negative correlation between the grade of ore mined and its potential impact in terms of extraction and processing on the environment. In other words, a lower grade ore tends to cause more land disturbance, create more waste, require more energy and generate more air and water pollution (due to extra processing) in comparison with a higher grade one.

There are a number of ways in which the scarcity of metals (present or future) could be addressed. One approach could be the exploitation of new areas. The sea floor, for example, is thought to have enormous mineral deposits, mainly in the form of manganese nodules. These nodules also contain other metals such as aluminium, copper, iron and nickel. However, the utilisation of such deep-sea reserves is still at the exploratory and planning stage due to problems of cost, technological development and, not least, ownership of the sea floor!

A more immediate solution would entail the reduction of consumption, an approach particularly relevant to the industrialised nations. These are responsible for the consumption of the majority of the world's metal production, despite having only 20% of the world's population. This could be achieved by using alternative materials (substitution), by making manufactured goods lighter and smaller (miniaturisation) and/or more long-lasting (durability), by recycling waste materials and by being less acquisitive. In some cases, however, these tactics can have counter-productive effects. For example, when plastic is used as a substitute for metal, metal consumption is indeed reduced but the production of the plastic, from chemicals derived from oil and coal, has its own environmental costs.

metal stocks will last, since this is influenced by the level of future demand, the efficiency of extractive metallurgical techniques, the discovery of new reserves and, of course, economic considerations. The point has already been made that higher grade metal ores are usually exploited preferentially. When these become depleted, lower grade ores become the primary source of a particular metal. This trend has important environmental implications. There is

12.2   Building materials

The principal non-metalliferous mineral materials used by the construction industry are shales and clays, sand and gravel, and stone (Table 12.2). The distribution of

---

Further Information Box

12.2   Bioleaching

The extraction of metals from their ores using micro-organisms is known as **bioleaching**. This technique utilises bacteria known as chemolithotrophs to oxidise metal sulfides to soluble metal sulfates. The elementary metal can then be readily extracted from solution. Examples of chemolithotrophic bacteria include *Thiobacillus ferrooxidans* and *T. thiooxidans*. Bioleaching is currently used mainly for copper and uranium, although it may be extended to other metals in the future.

As well as its application in the recovery of metals from *mined* material and in the reworking of old mine dumps, bioleaching can also be used to extract metals directly from orebodies deep underground. A major advantage of applying this technique *in situ* is that it helps to minimise the environmental impact caused by extensive excavation. However, the leachate produced by bioleaching is very toxic and must be rigorously controlled to avoid land and water pollution.

Mini Case Study

12.3   Alluvial gold mining in the Amazon Basin

In the mid-1970s, gold was discovered in the river sediments of the Amazon and its tributaries. The discovery of this alluvial gold brought an influx of millions of prospectors into the Amazon Basin. Their activities have resulted in a number of serious environmental problems including widespread mercury contamination.

Mercury is used in the process of alluvial gold extraction. River sediments are flushed down a sloping sluice consisting of a series of wooden ridges interspersed with troughs of mercury. The gold is extracted from the sediments by forming a thick amalgam with the mercury. However, the eventual discharge of the processed sediments back into the river is accompanied by the loss of considerable amounts of mercury. The gold is subsequently recovered from the amalgam by heating it in an open pan. The mercury is driven off in the form of a vapour, causing additional pollution.

Mercury is very poisonous and, once in the environment, can become progressively concentrated with each successive stage of the food chain, a process known as **biomagnification**. It can be taken up by humans by eating contaminated fish or,

in the case of the gold miners, by direct inhalation of mercury vapour. Mercury poisoning poses a number of very serious health risks to humans, including mental retardation and spontaneous abortion.

The situation in Brazil, and elsewhere, could be vastly improved if two simple and inexpensive devices were incorporated into the gold mining process. These were recently designed by the German company Produkt-Consult in conjunction with Imperial College, London. The first of these is a gravity trap which, when fitted to the bottom end of the sluice, would allow the mercury, gold and amalgam to settle out prior to sediment discharge. The second device, designed to replace the traditional open pan method of gold separation, consists of a sealed crucible attached to a condenser. The mercury vapour is collected as a liquid instead of being allowed to escape into the air. Field tests have shown that when both of these simple devices are used, 95% of the mercury and some of the gold can be saved.

Further reading: Hoffman, R. (1994) Winning gold. *American Scientist*, **82**, 15–17.

---

these materials is ubiquitous and their supply, at least in the foreseeable future, is plentiful. Shales and clays are formed as the result of weathering of, for example, feldspar and mica. They are mainly used in the building industry for the production of bricks. Sand and gravel particles, 0.0625–2 mm and 4–64 mm in diameter respectively, have a number of different origins including glacial and fluvial deposition. The construction industry is the main consumer of sands and gravels, where the majority is utilised as fine and coarse aggregate in concrete-making. Stone is defined as rock which is physically but not chemically changed prior to use. The majority of quarried stone is destined for use as crushed stone. This is used primarily in road construction, followed by buildings and finally in concrete-making. Limestone dominates this category and is also the main constituent stone used in cement-making. Other types of rock such as marble, granite and sandstone are used as building stone.

There are two other non-metalliferous mineral materials which are used in the construction industry, namely asbestos and gypsum (Table 12.2). These differ from the materials previously discussed in that their distribution is much more restricted. Asbestos is the term given to several types of mineral fibre, which occur in veins of 0.5–1 cm width. The dominant form is hydrous magnesium silicate, known as chrysotile. The shorter fibres of chrysotile are used in the construction of cement pipes.

Asbestos is also used in the production of roofing materials, fireproof cloth and asbestos cement. Gypsum (hydrous calcium sulfate) is used mainly in the production of plasterboard, a finishing product used to line the interior walls of buildings.

The demand for all these materials reflects the state of the construction industry, which in turn is seen as a barometer for the economic health of a nation. For example, the recession experienced in Britain during the late 1980s was mirrored by a massive slump in the building trade and a concomitant decrease in the demand for raw materials.

The widespread availability of these non-metalliferous mineral materials means that surface deposits are usually worked in preference to deeper reserves. The materials are extracted using open pit methods. In the case of sand and gravel, the soft deposits are removed directly by specialised earth-moving machines. However, in the case of crushed stone, which is predominantly limestone, extraction involves the drilling and blasting of the rock face prior to removal. The amount of waste material generated by these extractive industries varies enormously. Asbestos is exceptional as its extraction involves the production of large amounts of waste material and, in this respect, it is more similar to metal ores.

Of all the non-metalliferous mineral materials used in construction, the unit cost of sand and gravel is the lowest because of its availability and the ease with which it can

Tool Box

12.4 The thermodynamics of carbon-based extractive metallurgy

The objective of extractive metallurgy is the production of the desired metal in its elemental form. In many cases, this is achieved by heating the appropriate metal oxide with carbon. In order to see why this reaction must, in general, be carried out at high temperatures, let us illustrate this process by examining the extraction of zinc (Zn) from its oxide (ZnO).

The reaction concerned may be represented thus:

$$ZnO + C \rightarrow Zn + CO \tag{a}$$

This can be considered to be a coupled reaction, formed by the sum of the following two processes:

$$ZnO_{(s)} \rightarrow Zn_{(s)} + \tfrac{1}{2}O_{2(g)} \tag{b}$$

$$C_{(s)} + \tfrac{1}{2}O_{2(g)} \rightarrow CO_{(g)} \tag{c}$$

Adding Equations b and c gives:

$$ZnO + C + \tfrac{1}{2}O_2 \rightarrow Zn + CO + \tfrac{1}{2}O_2 \tag{a}$$

Before considering the overall process, let us examine the thermodynamics of the individual reactions represented by Equations b and c.

The pertinent thermodynamic quantities associated with reaction b are:

$$\Delta H^{o}_{298} = 348 \, kJ \, mol^{-1}$$

$$\Delta S^{o}_{298} = 0.1002 \, kJ \, K^{-1} \, mol^{-1}$$

Recall from Chapter 2 (Section 2.1) that:

$$\Delta G = \Delta H - T\Delta S$$

Therefore, under standard conditions:

$$\Delta G^{o} = \Delta H^{o} - T\Delta S^{o}$$

Therefore, at 298 K,

$$\Delta G^{o}_{298} = 348 - 298 \times 0.1002 = +318 \, kJ \, mol^{-1}$$

As ΔG^{o}_{298} is positive the reaction is non-spontaneous under standard conditions, at 298 K. However, as both ΔH^{o} and ΔS^{o} are positive, ΔG^{o} will become less positive with increasing temperature, eventually becoming negative above a certain transition temperature, T_{trans}. Noting that neither ΔH^{o} nor ΔS^{o} varies greatly with temperature, T_{trans} can be estimated as follows. Under standard conditions, when $T = T_{trans}$, $\Delta G^{o} = 0$, therefore:

$$0 \simeq \Delta H^{o} - T_{trans}\Delta S^{o} = 348 - T_{trans} \times 0.1002$$

Rearranging:

$$T_{trans} \simeq \frac{348}{0.1002} = 3473 \, K = 3200°C$$

Temperatures of this magnitude are very difficult to attain, making the extraction of zinc from its oxide by heating alone impracticable.

Let us now turn our attention to the reaction between carbon and oxygen (Equation c). For this process,

$$\Delta H^{o}_{298} = -111 \, kJ \, mol^{-1}$$

$$\Delta S^{o}_{298} = 0.0898 \, kJ \, K^{-1} \, mol^{-1}$$

The fact that $\Delta H^{o} < 0$ and that $\Delta S^{o} > 0$ means that, under standard conditions, the reaction will be spontaneous at all temperatures (albeit *very* slow near room temperature). What is more, the value of ΔG^{o} will become more negative as the temperature rises. Therefore, if a mixture of carbon and zinc oxide is heated, a temperature (T'_{trans}) will be reached when the total free energy of reactions b and c becomes negative. At this point, the coupled reaction represented by Equation a will become spontaneous and the metal will be extracted.

For the coupled reaction,

$$\Delta H^{o}_{298} = 348 + (-111) = 237 \, kJ \, mol^{-1}$$
$$\Delta S^{o}_{298} = 0.1002 + 0.0898 = 0.1900 \, kJ \, K^{-1} \, mol^{-1}$$

Therefore:

$$T'_{trans} \simeq \frac{237}{0.1900} \simeq 1247 \, K = 974°C$$

This is much lower than the temperature required for the extraction of zinc in the absence of carbon, making this process practicable.

Similar calculations can be carried out for other metals. In most cases, the coupled reaction does not become spontaneous until temperatures appreciably above ambient are reached. In the case of the more reactive metals, the temperatures required for the reduction of the oxide with carbon are so high as to be practically unattainable. This is the case with aluminium; calculations show that the reaction represented by the following equation only becomes spontaneous above about 2000°C.

$$Al_2O_3 + 3C \rightarrow 3CO + 2Al$$

Consequently, aluminium is not extracted by reaction with carbon, but electrochemically.

be extracted. For this reason, sand and gravel pits are usually located in close proximity to urban areas, in order to minimise transport costs. For example, many are found throughout the London region in the UK. Britain is one of a number of countries which have recently started to dredge off-shore for sand and gravel. As planning restrictions progressively curtail the use of open pits in urban areas, this marine source will assume increasing importance.

The environmental impact of surface mining for building materials tends to be localised, although the area covered by these sites can be significant. The result of open pit extraction is widespread scarring of the landscape and the loss of wildlife habitats and scenic beauty.

Table 12.2 Non-metalliferous mineral materials used in the construction industry.

Class of material	Main producers	Uses
Shales and clays	USA, UK	Brick manufacture; also tiles, pipes and in cement-making
Sand and gravel	USA, UK, Mexico	Coarse and fine aggregate used in concrete-making; also in road construction and asphalt production
Crushed stone (mainly limestones)	USA, former Soviet Union, China	Road construction; building construction and in the making of concrete and cement
Building stone (granite, marble and sandstone)	Italy, France, Portugal	Exterior facing, e.g. panels for buildings; also for curbs and flagstones
Asbestos (mainly hydrous magnesium silicate)	former Soviet Union, Canada, South Africa, Zimbabwe, China	Cement pipes, flooring products; fire-proof cloth; asbestos cement and thermal insulation
Gypsum (hydrous calcium sulfate)	USA, Canada, Germany, France, Iran, former Soviet Union	Manufacture of plaster products, mainly plasterboard; also used in cement-making as a retarder

However, in a number of cases, disused quarries and gravel pits have been successfully reclaimed to provide nature reserves or recreational facilities.

12.3 Peat

Peat is an organic deposit associated with wetland areas. It accumulates when the rate of production of organic plant material exceeds the rate at which it is decomposed by micro-organisms. In waterlogged conditions, microbial decomposition is usually inhibited by a shortage of oxygen. However, other factors such as a lack of nutrients, low temperatures or low pH can also be contributory factors.

Peat deposits take thousands of years to accumulate. However, compared with other organic deposits such as oil and coal, peat is relatively new, with more than 80% of peat being less than 6000 years old. Peat is very variable in its composition, even within a single deposit. Its characteristics are determined by a wide range of interrelated factors such as the type of plants involved in its formation, the degree of decomposition achieved and its nutrient status.

Peat can be formed in three main ways (Figure 12.2). In regions of the world where the level of rainfall usually exceeds that of evaporation, the formation of blanket (bog) peat is favoured, especially where the base rock is acidic. The lack of nutrients in the precipitation and the acid litter produced by ericaceous plants, hardy grasses and *Sphagnum* moss greatly suppress the rate of decomposition and lead to the accumulation of blanket peat. In contrast, the formation of basin (fen) peat is not dependent on conditions of high rainfall. It forms where depressions allow the accumulation of drainage water and the rate of growth of grasses, sedges and trees exceeds that of plant decomposition, which is usually substantial. Fen peats are found throughout the world, although in hot, dry countries their formation is restricted to the basins and deltas of major rivers. If precipitation is substantial, fen peats can become transformed into features known as raised bogs, which are dependent on rainfall for continued plant growth. The last type of peat is marshland peat, which also has a worldwide distribution. It is formed by the gradual infill of open lakes, a process known as peatland succession (Figure 12.2(c)).

Peat deposits cover about 3% of the world's land surface. A vast tract of peatland exists in the northern hemisphere, stretching across Canada, northern Europe (including Ireland, Scotland and the Scandinavian countries) and central Russia (Figure 12.3). Significant peat deposits also occur in other countries including Indonesia, South America, China and Malaysia.

Peat is used for a number of different purposes, depending on its composition. Its main use is in agriculture and horticulture as a growing medium for plants and to improve soil condition. Raised bogs form the most important source of horticultural peat. Peat is also used as a fuel. Although globally insignificant (contributing only one-thousandth of the world's energy), peat is an important source of energy in several countries. For example, in Ireland and Finland, it contributes 10% and 5% to the country's primary energy consumption, respectively. The former Soviet Union is the largest consumer of fuel peat, although it accounts for only 0.3% of its primary energy consumption. Peat can also be used

Figure **12.2** The formation of peat.

(a) Blanket peat
This is formed in those poorly-drained upland regions where the climate is cold and wet and the soil is acidic

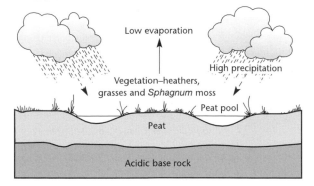

(b) Basin or fen peat
This is formed in depressions where drainage water collects and the rate of growth of vegetation exceeds that of plant decomposition

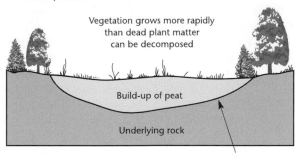

(c) Marshland peat
This is formed when open lakes become gradually infilled with peat – a process known as peatland succession

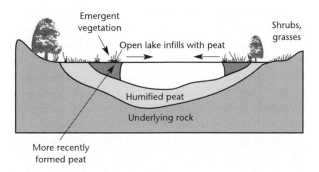

to produce a variety of useful products such as fuel gases, tars, coke and antibiotics.

Practically all peat is extracted using dry methods. These have the major disadvantage of depending on the weather. However, a suitable wet method for peat harvesting has not yet been devised. Prior to harvesting,

the peat bogs are drained to reduce the water content of the peat. This is usually done by cutting open ditches at regular intervals. After a period of 4–6 years in northern countries, the peat is ready to be harvested. Although hand-cutting persists in Ireland and Scotland, most peat extraction and its subsequent processing is highly mechanised. Peat can be either extracted from the surface and broken into granules to produce milled peat, or cut from a vertical section to produce sod peat. In both methods, once extracted, the peat is initially left to dry out as much as possible. Milled peat is used in horticulture and as a fuel in power stations, whilst sod peat is commonly used as a fuel in small boilers.

A major environmental impact of large-scale peat extraction is the destruction of unique wildlife habitats. It takes several thousand years for peat deposits to form and therefore they should be considered as non-renewable resources. Attempts are being made to conserve some peat bogs but even these may not survive if the surrounding areas are drained and the water table is consequently lowered. In Britain, gardeners are being encouraged to use alternatives to horticultural peat, for example coir from the husks of coconut shells, in a drive to reduce demand. However, it should be borne in mind that the extensive loss of peatlands has been mainly caused by drainage for agriculture and forestry and not as a result of direct peat extraction.

12.4   Fossil fuels

Coal, oil and natural gas are all classed as fossil fuels. Coal has been burnt as a fuel in Europe since the Bronze Age (4000 years ago) and its production soared with the advent of the Industrial Revolution. Oil and natural gas have only been exploited as energy sources during the last 100 years. However, reserves of these two fossil fuels when taken together are equal to only one-third of the world's current coal reserves. Whilst coal is expected to last for another three centuries, oil and natural gas supplies are forecast to become severely depleted within the next 50 years.

12.4.1   Coal

Coal is found in underground seams formed when ancient peat deposits became progressively buried under accumulating layers of sediments. During burial, the peat is compressed first into lignite, then sub-bituminous/ brown coal, then bituminous coal and finally anthracite. This succession is known as the **coal series** (Figure 12.4). It is characterised by a decrease in moisture content and

Figure 12.3 Peat resources worldwide (from Gore, 1983).

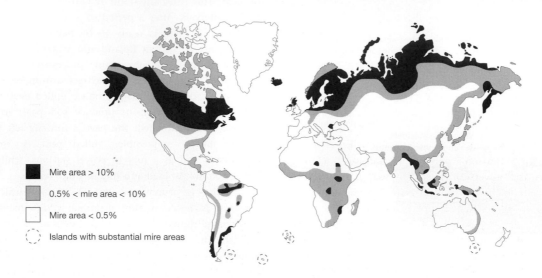

volatiles and an increase in carbon content. The progressive conversion of organic compounds within the peat to carbon is known as **carbonisation** or **coalification**. It is caused by the heat generated during the subsidence of the peat. As well as carbon, which is the main constituent of coal, variable amounts of sulfur, chlorine and nitrogen compounds are also present, together with trace amounts of heavy metals such as lead.

Coal seams were laid down during two main geological periods, the Carboniferous (from *ca.* 360 to 286 million years ago) and the Cretaceous (from *ca.* 144 to 65 million years ago). The coal associated with the more ancient Carboniferous rocks is in the form of anthracite or bituminous coal (known collectively as black or hard coal). This generally occurs in thin seams, less than 5 metres thick. Seams of brown coal (also known as sub-bituminous coal), associated with younger Cretaceous rocks, are generally thicker and easier to mine; for example, in Australia, seams 30 metres thick are common.

In terms of coal production, China is the largest single producer with 30.1% of the world total in 1997 (698 million tonnes of oil equivalent: *BP Statistical review of world energy*, 1998), followed closely by the USA with 25% of the world total in 1997 (579.3 million tonnes of oil equivalent). Other large producers are the former Soviet Union, India, Australia and South Africa with 187.6, 151.8, 142.1 and 115.2 million tonnes of oil equivalent in 1997 (*BP Statistical review of world energy*, 1998).

Coal is the most abundant fossil fuel. At the end of 1997, the world's proven reserves totalled 1031.6 billion tonnes, ~50% in the form of hard coal (i.e. anthracite or bituminous coal) and ~50% in the form of sub-bituminous (brown coal) or lignite. It is estimated that there is enough coal to supply the world for the next three centuries at present rates of use. Coal is used primarily as a feedstock for the generation of electricity (Chapter 13, Section 13.2.2). Its value as an energy source is positively correlated with its carbon content and therefore its

Figure 12.4 The coal series (from Read and Watson, 1966).

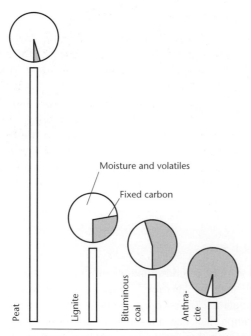

Moisture and volatiles

Fixed carbon

Peat

Lignite

Bituminous coal

Anthra-cite

During burial, moisture and volatile components are driven out and thick layers of peat are converted into thin seams of coal or anthracite

position in the coal series. Thus anthracite and bituminous coals are high-ranking coals, with a high calorific value compared with brown coal and lignite.

The method used to extract coal from the ground is determined by its location and the local geology. Coal may be deep mined or it may be extracted from nearer the surface using drift, opencast, or strip mining methods. Problems of subsidence are associated with deep mining whilst surface methods, especially strip mining, result in extensive disruption of the land surface. For example, in the Appalachian Mountains of the United States, an estimated 1.6 million hectares of land has been adversely affected by strip mining. One of the techniques used, contour strip mining, has created 40 000 km of contour benches cut into the mountainsides. The mined area, which remains unvegetated, is subject to accelerated rates of erosion and landslides. Water pollution is another environmental impact associated with coal mining. The drainage water from coal mines is usually highly acidic and this 'acid mine drainage' may play a major role in the acidification of natural waters (Chapter 14, Section 14.3.2).

12.4.2   Oil

Crude oil is a brownish-black, viscous liquid. It is composed of thousands of different organic molecules, predominantly hydrocarbons. Most oil is thought to have originated from marine sediments derived from the dead bodies of microscopic sea creatures which accumulated on the sea floor. During subsequent burial of the sediments, if conditions were suitable, the organic molecules present were converted into short-chain hydrocarbon molecules by a series of chemical reactions. Once formed, the oil may naturally seep from the sea floor into the marine environment or it may migrate under pressure into **reservoir rocks**, porous rocks capped or sealed by impermeable rock layers. Examples of the geological structures responsible for trapping oil are given in Figure 12.5.

Oil reserves are not evenly distributed throughout the world but are concentrated heavily in the Middle East. At the end of 1997, the proven oil reserves in the Middle East accounted for 65.2% of the world's total. The Middle East is the largest producer of oil, producing 1045 million tonnes in 1997 (30.1% of the world's total: *BP Statistical review of world energy*, 1998). The USA produced 379 million tonnes (10.9% of the world's total) and the former Soviet Union 363 million tonnes of oil (10.5% of the world's total) during 1997. Other major producers are Mexico, China and Venezuela, which

Figure **12.5** Examples of oil traps.

(a) Anticlinal trap
This consists of an anticline (i.e. an arch-like upfold) in which a porous rock layer containing the oil is capped by an impervious rock layer (e.g. shale)

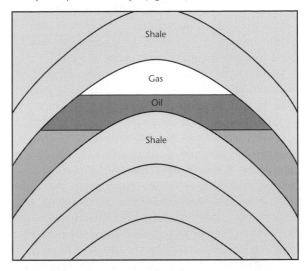

(b) Salt dome
This type of oil trap occurs when a salt dome intrudes into existing strata, allowing oil to collect in porous rocks capped by impervious rock layers (e.g. shale)

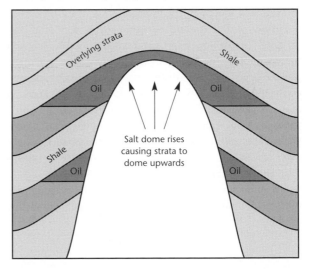

produced 171, 160 and 174 million tonnes of oil respectively in 1997.

Traditionally, oil wells were sunk into the surface of the land. However, in recent years, attention has turned to the off-shore regions of the continental shelves in the search for oil. For example, exploration led to the discovery of oil in the North Sea in 1969. This was brought ashore in the UK for the first time in 1975. From being almost wholly dependent on oil imports, the UK became self-sufficient in oil and should remain a significant producer in the foreseeable future.

There is also future potential in the extraction of heavy oils from oil-bearing shales and tar sands. The United States possesses both of these deposits whilst tar sands have also been discovered in the former Soviet Union, Canada and Africa. However, the exploitation of these oil-bearing reserves is expensive, energy-intensive and not therefore an economically viable option at present.

Crude oil is refined by the process of fractional distillation to yield a wide range of petroleum products. These include heavy fuel oil, lubricating oil, heating oil, kerosene, gasoline and propane gas. In addition, chemicals extracted from oil can be used to produce plastics and medicines, to give just two examples. There is a huge disparity in oil consumption between the more-developed and the developing countries. For example, the United States consumes almost one-third of the world's oil. Despite being one of the world's major producers, the US still needs to import considerable quantities to meet its needs. Worldwide oil reserves are estimated to be in the region of 141 billion tonnes. However, it has been forecast that oil will run out within the next 50 years or so if current rates of use continue.

There are a number of environmental problems associated with oil extraction. In the case of off-shore drilling, and indeed in the transportation of oil by tanker, pollution of the marine environment is a serious risk (Chapter 14, Section 14.6). Land-based oil extraction and transportation by pipeline can also cause pollution problems as well as disturbing natural habitats. For example, in 1994, in the Russian republic of Komi, a massive leak occurred in the Komineft pipeline, which transports oil from the Arctic to refineries in central Russia. The spill, estimated to be as high as 200 000 tonnes (over five times as much as the *Exxon Valdez* oil spill – Case study 5), caused a huge oil slick, 11 km long and up to a metre deep. It is estimated that it will take decades for the fragile tundra ecosystem to recover from this massive oil spill.

12.4.3 Natural gas

Natural gas consists mainly of methane (CH_4), the simplest of the hydrocarbons. It is released as a by-product during the natural formation of oil and is usually found in association with oil reservoirs (Figure 12.5(a)). Methane is also produced by the coalification process and may be present in the vicinity of coal seams, contained within a suitable reservoir rock. Deposits of natural gas may also occur alone. The environmental impact of natural gas extraction includes land disturbance and habitat disruption. Exploitation and transportation by pipeline also carry the risk of leakage and explosion.

Natural gas is a popular fuel, for a number of reasons. It is easy to store and transport and it is less polluting than coal and oil. The former Soviet Union and the Middle East together possess 73% of the world's proven natural gas reserves (*BP Statistical review of world energy*, 1998). The former Soviet Union is the major producer of natural gas, producing 561 million tonnes oil equivalent in 1997 (28.1% of the world's total). The USA is the next largest producer, yielding 491 million tonnes of oil equivalent in 1997 (24.5% of the world's total). Other large producers are the Middle East, Canada and the United Kingdom, which produced 150, 141 and 78 million tonnes of oil equivalent respectively in 1997.

At the end of 1997, the world's proven reserves of natual gas amounted to 144.76 trillion cubic metres, a figure which has more than doubled in the last 20 years, from 71.35 trillion cubic metres at the end of 1977 (*BP Statistical review of world energy*, 1998).

12.5 Water

Water exists in three phases: gaseous, liquid and solid. It is circulated in accordance with the hydrological cycle whereby the amount lost by evaporation from the oceans and the land is equalled by that gained by precipitation (Chapter 5, Section 5.1.1). The vast majority of the world's water (97.4%) is salt water and held in the oceans and seas which cover over 70% of the world's surface. The remaining 2.6% is fresh water. However, the vast majority of this is inaccessible, frozen solid in glaciers and in the polar icecaps. A small proportion of fresh water is held in deep underground aquifers, a source which is being increasingly utilised with the development of modern drills and pumping equipment. Only a very small proportion of fresh water is readily available for human use in the form of surface waters. Moreover, its distribution worldwide is very uneven.

Water use may be split into three different categories: agricultural, industrial and domestic. In terms of global water use, agriculture is the largest user, followed by industry and then domestic demand. In all these categories, the amount of water used is increasing (Figure 12.6). The pattern of water usage varies from region to region. For example, in Africa and Asia the vast majority of water withdrawn is used for agriculture and human usage, whilst in Europe water is used predominantly by industry.

A useful distinction is made between the *withdrawal* of water and the *consumption* of water. Withdrawn water is

Figure 12.6 Global water use, 1900–2000 (from Tolba *et al.*, 1992, after Shiklomanov, 1990).

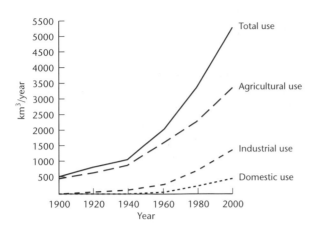

Groundwater reserves accumulate when the water from precipitation, drawn down through the soil under the influence of gravity, meets an impermeable rock layer. This type of reserve is called an **unconfined aquifer** and its upper boundary is known as the **water table** (Figure 12.7(a)). Groundwater can also become trapped in **confined aquifers** deep underground when geological formations permit. These form when a permeable rock layer is sandwiched between two layers of impermeable rock and these strata are tilted, thus allowing groundwater to seep into the central, permeable rock layer (Figure 12.7(b)). Approximately half of all groundwater occurs in these deep confined aquifers.

The fundamental difference between surface water and groundwater is that, whilst the former is usually readily replenished by precipitation, the latter is not, and this gives rise to a number of serious environmental problems. The practice of sinking wells to obtain fresh water in semi-arid regions is an ancient one. However, the development of powerful modern drills and pumps has led to the exploitation of much deeper groundwater reserves. The water in such confined aquifers may have been there for thousands of years and, once extracted, may take a similar period to be replaced. This 'fossil water' should therefore be treated as a non-renewable resource.

The over-exploitation of groundwater reserves can lead to serious problems of water depletion. For example, in the southern United States, the immense Ogallala aquifer provides water for irrigated agriculture in parts of eight states including Texas, Kansas and Nebraska. Rates of withdrawal are far in excess of rates of recharge (between one and three orders of magnitude in some parts) and this has led to an alarming drop in the water table. At current rates of use, the enormous fresh water reserves held in this aquifer will be completely depleted within the next 40–50 years.

Over-exploitation of groundwater reserves can also lead to problems of subsidence. As water is withdrawn, the rock

returned directly to its source of supply after use, whilst consumed water is irretrievably lost. For example, water used by industry may be cycled several times before it is returned to the river from where it was initially removed. On the other hand, much of the water used in irrigation is lost through evaporation into the atmosphere and therefore it is referred to as consumed.

Fresh water comes from two principal sources: it may be diverted from surface waters or it may be extracted from groundwater reserves. In addition, small amounts are obtained from the desalination of sea water (Box 12.5). Surface waters occur naturally in the form of rivers and lakes. Humans have increased this source of supply by the creation of reservoirs, artificial lakes impounded behind dams. The advantages and disadvantages of creating reservoirs are outlined in Table 12.3.

The potential supply of groundwater is much greater than that of surface water but it is much less accessible.

Further Information Box

12.5 The process of desalination

Over 97% of the water present on Earth is in the form of salt water. In exceptional cases, sea water can be drawn upon directly; for example, it can be used as a coolant in coastal electricity generating plants. However, for most purposes (agricultural, industrial and domestic), sea water is too saline and the salt must be removed prior to use. This process is known as **desalination**.

There are three main desalination techniques which can be used to produce fresh water. In one method, the salt is separated from the water by freezing. Alternatively, the salt may be removed by distillation. In this method, the sea water is heated, causing the pure water to evaporate. This is then condensed and collected. In the last method, electrolysis is used initially to remove some of the salt. This is followed by reverse osmosis, a process whereby water from the saline portion is forced through a membrane under pressure.

The disadvantage of all these techniques is that they have high energy requirements. For this reason, the implementation of desalination tends to be on a small scale and restricted to those arid regions where other sources of fresh water are not readily available.

Table 12.3 The advantages and disadvantages of creating reservoirs.

Advantages	Disadvantages
Increase in surface water supply	Flooding of large tracts of land to create reservoirs
Control of water flow and prevention of downstream flooding	Loss of seasonal floods bringing nutrient-rich sediments causes impoverishment of agricultural land bordering river
Recreational value in terms of fishing and water sports	Displacement of people, loss of homes and agricultural land
In some cases, dams are to be used for the production of hydroelectric power	Large surface area of reservoir increases water loss by evaporation and increases salinity. This may lead to land salinisation if the reservoir water is used for irrigation
	Increase in diseases which involve vector organisms that breed in standing waters
	Risk of catastrophe if dam bursts
	Eventual siltation of the reservoir, limiting its useful life

particles within the aquifer move closer together to occupy spaces hitherto taken up by the water and the aquifer becomes more compact as a result. This can lead to significant subsidence of the ground, which in turn may permanently reduce the water-holding capacity of the aquifer. For example, in the Bangkok region of Thailand, land has subsided by 20–120 cm during the past 60 years. This has been largely attributed to groundwater extraction and the compression of the depleted sub-surface aquifer. Additionally, there are regions of the world, most notably the Ganges delta (Case study 3, page 280), where abstracted groundwater is contaminated with naturally occurring arsenic. Finally, the removal of fresh groundwater can lead to the incursion of brackish water, especially in coastal regions. This problem can arise in tropical islands where the development of tourism creates an additional drain on the fresh water reserves held in underground aquifers.

There is a huge disparity in the availability and quality of water between the more-developed countries and the developing world. The majority of the inhabitants of the former have access to mains sanitation and clean piped water. However, in the developing nations, safe water is available to less than half the population. Water contaminated as a result of inadequate sanitation is responsible for the spread of many chronic and potentially fatal diseases in the developing world (Chapter 14, Section 14.1 and Table 14.2).

The outlook for the future is not promising. Whilst the amount of fresh water available is decreasing, demand continues to increase, especially in the developing countries where the population is expanding rapidly. The pressure on water resources has led to the serious depletion of many groundwater reserves. The diversion of water from surface sources has also caused serious environmental problems, as exemplified by the case of the Aral Sea in central Asia (Box 12.6). The problem of meeting future demand for water is

further exacerbated by a general deterioration in water quality. Effective water treatment (Box 12.7) and the control of water pollution must therefore be included as an integral part of water management strategies.

12.6 Summary

The exploitation of a wide array of naturally occurring mineral materials, including metals and fossil fuels, has greatly advanced the technological development of the human race. However, these non-renewable resources are now declining rapidly. Oil, for example, which took millions of years to form, has only been used as a fuel source for just over a century. However, it has been predicted that oil reserves will become severely depleted within the next 50 years, at current rates of use. The prospect of mineral shortages has prompted a number of responses including recycling, utilising low-grade ores (in the case of metals), conserving supplies and using alternative materials where possible.

The extraction of minerals, peat, fossil fuels and fossil water (from underground aquifers) all involve environmental costs. In the case of surface workings for minerals, coal and peat, large tracts of land are disturbed and natural habitats destroyed. The mining of metal ores or coal can lead to water pollution through acid mine drainage, whilst the smelting of sulfide ores causes air pollution through the production of sulfur dioxide. The exploitation of fossil water contained in underground aquifers has led, in many cases, to serious problems of depletion. On a more positive note, the environmental problems associated with the major extractive industries are now widely recognised. Increased efforts have been made, in some cases, to minimise their environmental impact and to reclaim formerly mined land in order to create nature reserves or recreational facilities.

Figure 12.7 The formation of groundwater aquifers.

(a) Unconfined aquifer

This is formed when water from precipitation is drawn down through the soil under the influence of gravity until it meets an impermeable rock layer and accumulates as a result. Its upper boundary is known as the water table.

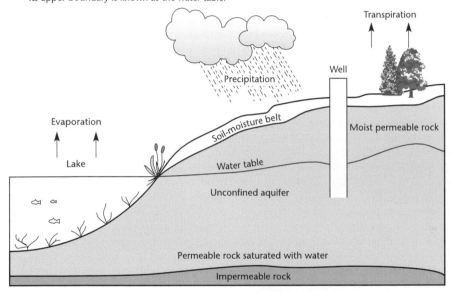

(b) Confined aquifer

This is formed when a permeable rock layer is sandwiched between two layers of impermeable rock and the strata become tilted (as a result of geological processes), allowing water to seep into the central permeable rock layer.

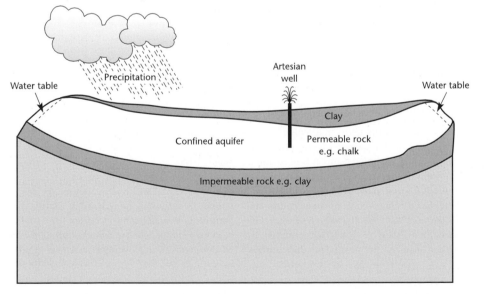

12.6 The Aral Sea

The Aral Sea in central Asia was once the fourth largest lake in the world. However, the heavy withdrawal of water from its two main tributaries, the Syr and the Amu, has reduced its area and volume dramatically in recent years (Plate 20). The ecological consequences of this rapid decline have been both disastrous and far-reaching.

Prior to the 1950s, the Aral Sea covered an area of $64\,500\,km^2$, including its many islands. Its level fluctuated between 50 and 53 m above sea level and at the latter depth it contained about $1000\,km^3$ of water. The moderately saline waters of the Aral Sea supported a number of commercially important fish species such as carp (*Cyprinus carpio*), ship sturgeon (*Acipenser nudiventris*) and roach (*Rutilus rutilus aralensis*), together with muskrats (*Ondatra zibethica*), which were trapped for their pelts. It also provided an important navigation route between the two main economic centres of the region, Muynak and Aralsk.

However, in the early 1960s, a state plan aimed at achieving cotton independence in the central Asian republics and in Kazakhstan was initiated under the banner 'Produce millions of tons of cotton at any cost'. As a result of this drive, the area of intensive, irrigated cotton cultivation rapidly expanded, covering an area of 7.6 million hectares by 1987. The water needed for irrigation was withdrawn from the Syr and Amu rivers, with disastrous consequences for the Aral Sea. Between 1960 and 1987, its level dropped by 13 m and its area decreased by 40%. By 1990, the Aral Sea had become two water bodies, separated by a wide belt of dry land. It could no longer be used as a navigation route and its once-thriving fishing industry was destroyed.

The contraction of the Aral Sea is an ecological disaster. Its salinity has increased from 10% to 27% and only one-sixth of its original 24 fish species have survived. Vast areas of the former seabed, now covered with white alkali soil (*solonchak*), are exposed to the effects of wind erosion. Huge salt dust storms result which deposit their contents on surrounding productive agricultural land, causing widespread land degradation. The Aral Sea used to have a moderating influence on the surrounding climate. With its demise, there is a trend towards continentality (higher summer and lower winter temperatures), a decrease in relative humidity and a reduction in the growing season.

The drop in the level of the Aral Sea has also lowered groundwater levels, causing problems of water supply. Moreover, water supplies, like the air and the land, are heavily contaminated with the pesticides and fertilisers used in intensive cultivation, and with salts. The health risks to local people of, for example, typhoid, hepatitis, oesophageal cancer and gastro-enteritis are abnormally high. In some localities, infant mortality is as high as 100 per 1000.

Massive changes are needed to reverse the decline in the Aral Sea, which has lost two-thirds of its water in the past 30 years. More efficient water management, the lining of leaking irrigation canals (which can lose up to 80% of their contents before reaching the crops) and a reduction in the area under cotton cultivation would all be steps in the right direction. In 1994, a pledge was made by five central Asian republics to contribute 1% of their budgets to a central fund designated to halt the decline in the Aral Sea and address the many health problems of local people. It is projected that, without effective remedial action, the Aral Sea could disappear completely by the year 2020.

References: Micklin, P. P. (1988) Desiccation of the Aral Sea: a water management disaster in the Soviet Union. *Science*, **241**, 1170–1175.

Micklin, P. P. (1992) The Aral crisis: introduction to the special issue. *Post-Soviet Geography*, **33**(5), 269–282.

12.7 Water treatment

Water for domestic consumption is taken from either surface water or groundwater sources. This raw water is rarely free from pollution and must therefore be treated before it is fit to drink. Water treatment involves the removal of harmful micro-organisms, toxic chemical species, colour, suspended solids and odour. As the level and nature of contamination of the raw water varies with location, the type and degree of treatment required also varies from place to place. For example, in general, groundwater requires less treatment than surface water. However, the conversion of raw to potable (i.e. drinkable) water is commonly accomplished by the use of some or all of the following steps:

Aeration. At this stage, air is mixed with the water by, for example, allowing it to flow over a series of weirs. The oxygen in the air coverts any iron(II) to iron(III) and reacts with the more readily oxidised organic contaminants present. Aeration also removes some offensive-smelling gases, e.g. hydrogen sulfide (H_2S), and improves the taste of the water by adding dissolved oxygen (O_2) and nitrogen (N_2).

Primary settling. This involves allowing the water to stand in a large basin, facilitating the removal, by gravity, of the larger sized particulate contaminants. During this stage, slaked lime ($Ca(OH)_2$) may be added to remove much of the hardness caused by dissolved calcium hydrogen carbonate ($Ca(HCO_3)_{2(aq)}$) and magnesium ions ($Mg^{2+}_{(aq)}$) and to reduce the concentration of both iron(III) ($Fe^{3+}_{(aq)}$) and potentially toxic heavy metal ions, thus:

$$Ca(HCO_3)_{2(aq)} + Ca(OH)_{2(aq)} \rightarrow 2CaCO_{3(s)} + 2H_2O_{(l)}$$

$$M^{n+}_{(aq)} + \frac{n}{2}Ca(OH)_{2(aq)} \rightarrow M(OH)_{n(aq)}$$

12.7   Water treatment continued

where M = Fe, Mg or heavy metal, and $n+$ = the charge on M. In some treatment works, primary settling is carried out prior to the aeration stage.

Secondary settling. After primary settlement, fine suspended solids, such as bacteria, pollen and fine calcium carbonate ($CaCO_3$), remain in the water. To remove these, a flocculating coagulant is added. This is usually either filter alum ($Al_2(SO_4)_3.18H_2O$) – sometimes added in combination with the acidic gas carbon dioxide, used to lower the pH to near 7, thereby suppressing the formation of $[Al(OH)_4]^-_{aq}$ – or iron(III) sulfate ($Fe_2(SO_4)_3$). In either case, a gelatinous precipitate of $M(OH)_{3(s)}$ (where M = Al or Fe) is formed that slowly settles from the water, taking the fine suspended contaminants with it.

Filtration though a sand bed. The water from the secondary settling phase is then clarified further by passing it through a sand filter-bed.

Final pH adjustment and disinfection. After sand filtration, the pH of the water may be re-measured and adjusted to be slightly alkaline. This decreases the rate of acid-induced water-pipe corrosion. Most importantly, the water is disinfected at this stage. This is usually achieved by the addition of chlorine (Cl_2).

In addition to the stages listed above, the water may be passed through a bed of activated charcoal (charcoal with a high specific surface area) after sand filtration. This is a relatively expensive, but effective, means of removing organic contaminants, whether natural or anthropogenic in origin.

If the raw water is brackish, an additional step, frequently reverse osmosis (Box 12.5), will be required to decrease its salinity.

12.7   Problems

1   What is meant by the term 'metal ore'? With reference to a particular metal, describe its progress from orebody to eventual recovery in its elemental form.

2   What are the major pollution problems associated with the extraction and processing of metal sulfide ores?

3   Calculate the approximate temperature above which the extraction of aluminium from its oxide by reaction with carbon becomes spontaneous. State all assumptions that you make. (See Chapter 2, Section 2.1 and Box 12.4 for help.)

Substance	$\Delta H^o_{f\,298}$/kJ mol^{-1}	$S^o_{f\,298}$/J K^{-1} mol^{-1}
$Al_2O_{3(s)}$	−1669	51.0
$Al_{(s)}$	0	28.3
$O_{2(g)}$	0	205
$C_{(s)}$	0	5.7
$CO_{(g)}$	−111	198

4   Describe the formation, characteristics and uses of peat. What are the environmental impacts of large-scale peat extraction?

5   Compare and contrast the current reserves and prospects for coal, oil and natural gas. Suggest ways in which future supplies could be supplemented.

6   What is meant by the terms 'fossil water' and 'aquifer'? Why is the exploitation of this water source a major cause for concern?

12.8   Further reading

Blunden, J. and A. Reddish (1996) *Energy resources and environment.* Hodder & Stoughton.

BP Statistical review of world energy (1998). London: The British Petroleum Company plc.

Couch, G. (1993) *Fuel peat: world resources and utilisation.* London: IEA Coal Research.

Mannion, A. M. (1997) *Global environmental change* (2nd edn). Harlow: Longman.

The future for coal. *New Scientist*, 23 January 1993, 20–41.

Arsenic in drinking water in West Bengal and Bangladesh

Tubewells, the green revolution and drinking water

In the latter half of the 1960s, an extensive programme of tubewell installation was initiated to obtain water from the alluvial Ganges aquifers of West Bengal, India and Bangladesh. This programme, much of which was paid for by the United Nations Children's Fund (UNICEF), has brought significant benefits to the region. Prior to the installation of these tubewells, the mainly rural population was dependent on rain or surface water for both irrigation and domestic purposes.

In the absence of irrigation, the monsoon climate of the region naturally limits rain-watered rice production to the wet season. The tubewells give access to aquifer water from 150 m and more below the surface of the land, providing plentiful supplies for irrigation all year round. This allows three or even four crops per year of the high-yielding rice varieties of 'the green revolution' to be grown where only one rain-watered rice harvest was possible.

Poor sanitation and inappropriate industrial waste disposal practices mean that surface water is often badly contaminated. As the tubewell water is free from both industrial contamination and sewage-derived pathogens, it was believed to be safe to drink. However, it has subsequently become apparent that this is not the case. Water from many of the tubewells is now known to be contaminated with significant levels of the highly toxic element arsenic.

Where does the arsenic come from?

It has been established that the arsenic contamination is derived from the alluvial sediments that hold the water prior to its extraction via the tubewells. However, the mechanism by which the arsenic enters the water is still a matter of debate.

Initial work[1,2] suggests that the arsenic is rendered soluble as a consequence of the lowering of the water table, following water abstraction. The argument put forward is that the falling water table enables atmospheric oxygen to enter the sediments from which the water is removed, allowing *in situ* oxidation of arsenic-rich pyrite and consequent dissolution of the poison to occur.

In contrast, more recent studies[3] suggest that arsenic enters solution as a consequence of the reduction of arsenic-rich iron-oxyhydroxide minerals in the sediments, under anaerobic conditions. It is argued that these minerals are present as a consequence of the weathering and erosion of arsenic-rich base-metal sulfides upstream in the Ganges basin and that their subsequent reduction is attributable to the presence of organic matter within the sediments.

What effect does arsenic have?

The toxicology of arsenic (symbol As) is related to its biochemical resemblance to phosphorus (P), which may be expected, as these elements are neighbours in the same group of the Periodic Table. In mammals, arsenic will replace phosphorus in key processes including oxidative phosphorylation. Arsenic also has an affinity for the thiol (—SH) groups of enzymes and tissues, to which it will reversibly bind. The speciation of arsenic has an impact on its toxicity, arsenic(III) being more toxic than arsenic(V).

Despite its toxicity, there is evidence that arsenic is an essential element in human nutrition but that it is required in tiny amounts only. Furthermore, it is believed that, when the body is confronted with a slight excess of this element, it can eliminate it by converting the arsenic to non-toxic forms. Although there is some evidence that it may be healthy to take up to 12 μg of arsenic per day, currently no-one is absolutely sure what dose rate is safe.

With this degree of uncertainty, it is not surprising that there is some disagreement about the maximum levels of arsenic that should be permitted in drinking water. Bangladesh has set its maximum at $50\,\mu g\,As\,l^{-1}$. This is in common with the current US standard and the earlier recommended maximum concentration of the World Health Organisation (WHO). This limit is now felt by many to be too high. The current WHO recommended maximum limit for drinking water is $10\,\mu g\,As\,l^{-1}$ and the US is due to revise its limit to a lower level for promulgation on 1 January 2001.

As discussed below, many millions of people in Bangladesh and West Bengal drink water that has an arsenic content above the $50\,\mu g\,l^{-1}$ limit. During long-term exposure, the amount of arsenic ingested often exceeds the level that the body can tolerate. The result is an insidious, cumulative, chronic poisoning that is often exacerbated by the effects of poor diet. Physical symptoms do not emerge until after several years of the onset of exposure. Sufferers, in the early stages of physical symptoms, show conjunctivitis and skin lesions. Further exposure can result in liver and kidney damage, a form of gangrene, and cancer that is ultimately fatal.

The effects of this arsenic poisoning are not only medical. Societal problems also occur, not only through ill health but also because of ignorance. In many instances, the symptoms are assumed to be contagious or are mistaken for those of leprosy. In either case, the sufferer may be ostracised as a result.

What is the scale of the problem?

A detailed survey of the approximately four million tubewells in the Ganges delta area has not yet been completed. Consequently, the number of tubewells that supply water contaminated above the $50\,\mu g\,As\,l^{-1}$ limit is unknown. Furthermore, reliable estimates of the number of affected wells are difficult to obtain. This is partly because, in any given village, some of the wells may be safe while others are poisoned and, without testing, no-one knows which is which.

However, the survey work that has been completed to date demonstrates that the scale of the problem is enormous, in terms of both the number of contaminated wells and the levels of contamination found. Estimates of the number of wells supplying water with $>50\,\mu g\,As\,l^{-1}$ are given variously as up to either one or two million. In some areas, concentrations of $500\,\mu g\,As\,l^{-1}$ are common and maxima of $4000\,\mu g\,As\,l^{-1}$ have been reported.

A huge number of people in the region are affected. In West Bengal, a survey of *some* of the districts suspected of suffering contamination has revealed that, in the area studied, an estimated one million people were drinking arsenic-contaminated water on a regular basis. Of these, approximately 200 000 were believed to exhibit physical symptoms of chronic arsenic poisoning. The problem in neighbouring Bangladesh is larger still. It is estimated that of the population of approximately 125 million people, 70 million are potential victims of arsenic poisoning. The proportion of these potential victims that actually develop serious health problems as a consequence of their exposure to arsenic-contaminated water is largely dependent on the success of ongoing and planned remedial work.

The possibility of environment-derived chronic arsenic poisoning is not limited to the Ganges delta area. High concentrations of arsenic in water and/or soils have been found in Taiwan, Inner Mongolia, the Lagunera region of Mexico, Antofagasta in Chile, Cordoba in Argentina, Obuasi in Ghana, and Cornwall in the UK. In the first four locations on this list, poisoning of people is known to have occurred. In some locations (e.g. Cornwall) contamination has happened when arsenic-bearing rock has been brought to the surface by mining. In other cases (e.g. Taiwan and Inner Mongolia) the cause is groundwater abstraction, just as it is in the Ganges delta region. There are many other parts of the world, particularly in the less-developed countries, where groundwater-based irrigation schemes have been installed. It remains to be seen how many of these will prove to be blighted by arsenic-contaminated water.

What can be done?

While the contamination of tubewell water with arsenic has brought misery to thousands in the Ganges delta area, the medium- to long-term prognosis is not necessarily poor. Both prevention and, in many cases, cure are possible.

Prevention could be facilitated if the extent of the contamination were known in each of the wells used to supply drinking water. In many villages some of the wells are safe while others are poisoned. A full survey of the water from the tubewells in the affected districts would enable villagers to know which water is safe to drink. It would also establish which localities have no safe wells. Here, action to remove arsenic from the water could be taken.

Laboratory-based technology for measuring arsenic levels in the $\mu g\,l^{-1}$ range in water samples is well established. However, while such laboratory provision is available within the region, the scale of the problem means that an approach based on test kits that could be used in the field would be much more practicable. Such kits already exist, although the data that they provide is fairly crude. Work to produce more reliable equipment for in-field evaluation of arsenic contamination levels is underway.

Several inexpensive means by which arsenic can be removed from contaminated well-water have been developed. One method, already employed in the region, is to dip cloth-wrapped alum $(K_2SO_4.Al_2(SO_4)_3.24H_2O)$ into the contaminated water for a few seconds. The water is left to stand overnight, during which time an arsenic-containing precipitate forms. This solid is then removed by filtering the water through cloth, thereby reportedly removing 70–80% of the original arsenic burden.

Another method (which, at the time of writing, has yet to be tested in Bangladesh) involves attaching a tube, filled with a filter-bed of sand and iron filings, to the well outlet. The water from the well is dosed with barium sulfate (unless already present) and passed though the filter. The iron in the filter medium acts as a reducing agent, reacting with the arsenic and sulfate present to form insoluble arsenopyrite (FeAsS). The arsenopyrite is then caught in the filter-bed, reportedly lowering the arsenic content of the filtered water to less than $1\,\mu g\,l^{-1}$.

In order to prevent future contamination, work to find the mechanism by which the arsenic enters the water is important, as are studies to discover the detailed composition and architecture of the sediments of the Ganges delta. Once established, this information could be drawn together to predict best practice in future tubewell installation. By doing this, locations or methodologies that are likely to lead to arsenic contamination could be avoided.

As outlined above, recent work suggests that the mechanism by which arsenic enters the water involves the reduction of arsenic-rich iron oxyhydroxides. This process also causes the iron to enter into solution. In the paper reporting this work,[3] the authors suggest that if the contaminated water were aerated, oxidation of the iron present would ensue, causing an arsenic-scavenging precipitate of iron oxyhydroxide to form. If this precipitate were removed, it would significantly lower the levels of arsenic in the water.

Cure is also possible for those individuals who are suffering from the effects of chronic arsenic poisoning, *provided* that they are free of cancer and/or kidney or liver malfunction. For those with treatable symptoms, reversal of the effects of poisoning can be brought about if they drink only uncontaminated water and take vitamin supplements and drugs (e.g. dimercaptosuccinic acid and d-penicillamine).

References

1 Das, D., G. Basu, T. R. Chowdhury and D. Chakraborty (1995) *Proc. Internat. Conf. on Arsenic in Groundwater*, Calcutta, 44–45.

2 Saha, A. K. and C. Chakrabarti (1995) *Proc. Internat. Conf. on Arsenic in Groundwater*, Calcutta, 42.

3 Nickson, R., J. McArthur, W. Burgess, K.M. Ahmed, P. Ravenscroft and M. Rahman (1998) *Nature*, **395**, 338.

Chapter 13

Energy production

Chapter Objectives

After reading this chapter, you should be able to:

- Resolve the apparent inconsistency between the implications of the first and second laws of thermodynamics and the terms energy production and energy consumption.

- Define the term energy intensity and appreciate that the peak in this parameter associated with industrialisation can be minimised by sufficient technology transfer from industrialised nations to developing counties.

- Recognise the central part played by heat-to-work transformations in the industrialised world.

- Review the means by which nuclear fuels, fossil fuels, solar energy, wind energy, wave energy, tidal energy, ocean thermal energy, hydropower, geothermal energy and biomass energy can be and are utilised.

- Discuss the means by which the efficiency of energy conversions can be maximised.

Introduction

This chapter is concerned with a description of the main ways in which energy can be transformed from a form found in nature to one that can be used in the artificial environment generated by human activity. The study of the transformations of energy is called thermodynamics. In order to derive full benefit from this chapter, you will need to understand some of the terms and concepts used in thermodynamics. It is particularly important that you are conversant with the meaning of each of the following: energy, heat, work, and the laws of thermodynamics, all of which are discussed in Chapter 2.

Arguably, it is the ability of the human race to exploit energy transformations that has set it apart from the other inhabitants of the Earth. The first transformation to be exploited was that of chemical energy to heat energy in a fire. Transformations of the mechanical energy of wind and flowing water into useful forms of work in sailing

boats, and wind and water mills were probably the next to be exploited.

The transformation of heat energy into work, however, requires much more ingenuity. There were many thousands of years between the taming of fire and the production of labour-saving heat-to-work engines. This latter development has occurred on a significant scale only in the last 200 years or so. However, it was heat-to-work transformations that made the Industrial Revolution possible and such transformations are now of major economic and environmental importance.

This chapter is largely dedicated to discussions of how heat-to-work transformations are achieved, although alternative means of energy-to-work transformations and the direct use of heat energy are also discussed. Energy transformations based on nuclear and fossil fuels are detailed in Sections 13.2.1 and 13.2.2 respectively, while

283

Tool Box

13.1   The efficiency of heat-to-work conversions

A **heat engine** is a device that converts heat into work. With *very few* exceptions, power stations are heat engines, as are internal combustion engines.

In order to convert heat energy to work both a heat source (a high temperature reservoir of heat) and a heat sink (a low temperature reservoir of heat) are required. The heat engine withdraws heat from the source, converts some of it to work and rejects the waste heat to the sink. The amount of energy available from the heat source for work depends on its heat content and the efficiency with which it can be converted. The French physicist Sadi Carnot, in 1824, derived an expression (sometimes called the **Heat Engine Rule** or **HER**) that states the thermodynamic maximum to the efficiency of heat-to-work conversions. It is usually expressed in one of two forms:

$$W/Q = (T_{source} - T_{sink})/T_{source}$$

or

$$W/Q = 1 - (T_{sink}/T_{source})$$

where, W = work output (units = N m or J)

Q = heat absorbed from source (units = J)

T_{source} = absolute temperature of heat source (units = K)

T_{sink} = absolute temperature of heat sink (units = K)

W/Q = **Carnot efficiency**, often quoted as a percentage

Clearly, either increasing the temperature of the source or decreasing the temperature of the sink will improve the Carnot efficiency of heat engines and is one of the major goals of power station engineers.

The Carnot efficiency is a *limit* that is consistent with all the laws of thermodynamics. However, many heat engines are inherently less efficient than this limit would imply; in addition, there are always unavoidable losses due to friction. Carnot efficiencies therefore are never realised. The **thermal efficiency** is an expression of the actual efficiency of a heat-to-other-energy-form conversion and is applicable to heat-to-work tranformations. It takes the form:

$$\text{thermal efficiency} = \frac{\text{useful energy output}}{\text{energy input}}$$

This parameter is often expressed as a percentage.

For power stations, thermal efficiency is taken to be the ratio of electrical power output (MW_e) to thermal power output (MW_{th}).

renewable energy sources are reviewed in Section 13.3. Maximising the efficiency with which energy transformations are carried out is the realm of energy conservation and, while this is a theme pursued throughout this chapter, it is specifically addressed in its closing pages. The efficiency of heat-to-work transformations is of particular importance and is referred to in several parts of this chapter. The efficiency of this transfer is subject to a fundamental limitation known as the Carnot efficiency; this is explained in Box 13.1 as is the term thermal efficiency.

13.1   Energy production and consumption

According to the first law of thermodynamics (Chapter 2, Section 2.1), energy can be neither created nor destroyed. It can, however, be converted from one form to another. With this in mind, the concepts of 'energy production' and 'energy consumption' are clearly false, yet they are in common use. The second law of thermodynamics informs us about the direction of spontaneous change: 'A spontaneous change will occur in a system only if the total entropy (disorder) of the universe will increase as a result'. Driving a car from home to the laboratory will involve the conversion of the chemical energy of the fuel into heat and then into motive energy, ultimately to be dissipated as heat into the surroundings. This will increase the entropy of the universe as it will cause a greater random motion of the molecules in the surroundings. The first law alone might lead us to the thought that the energy dissipated to the surroundings could be used to drive the car back home again. Clearly this is contrary to experience; it is also contrary to the second law of thermodynamics because such a conversion would involve a decrease in entropy and would therefore *not* occur spontaneously.

The terms energy production and energy consumption, although misnomers, now make more sense. The conversion of energy from a source found in nature to one that is useful may be called **energy production**. In this vein, **energy consumption** is the transformation of energy in a potentially useful form (e.g. chemical energy) to a relatively useless one (ultimately, random thermal motion at ambient temperatures). The term **primary energy consumption** is used to denote the amount of energy converted from a form found in nature. The burning of coal to generate electricity is therefore primary energy consumption; the use of the electricity generated in heating a building is not.

Figure 13.1 shows the global trends in primary energy consumption that have occurred during the recent past.

Figure **13.1** Global primary energy consumption (from *BP Amoco statistical review of world energy,* 1999)

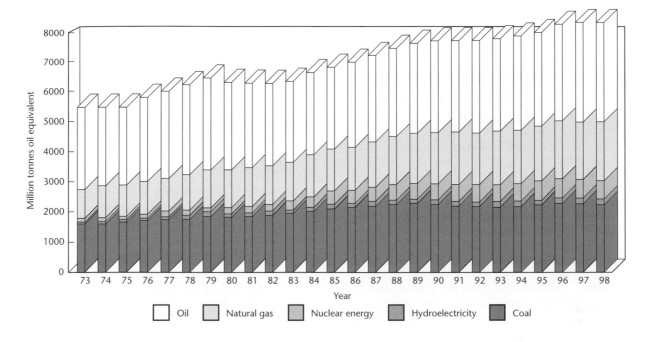

Despite a levelling in demand in the early 1990s (corresponding with the onset of falling consumption in the former Soviet Union), the overall trend is upwards. From 1972 to 1997, total energy consumption went from less than 5.3×10^{12} to 8.5×10^{12} kg oil equivalent, an increase in excess of 60%.

There are some changes that are worthy of note concerning the effectiveness of energy utilisation, the global distribution of energy consumption and the sources of primary energy that are being utilised.

Energy intensity is a measure of the effectiveness of energy utilisation. It may be defined as the amount of energy consumed per unit gross domestic product (GDP). As a country undergoes industrialisation, its need for energy increases more rapidly than its GDP; that is, its energy intensity increases. This is because economic developments that occur during industrialisation are reliant on energy-intensive heavy industry and infrastructure development. Once industrialisation has been realised, the energy intensity of a country falls. The maximum energy intensity reached during this process varies from country to country. However, because of improvements in technology that allow greater efficiency of energy use, there has been a downward trend in this maximum (Figure 13.2). If there is sufficient technology transfer between the industrialised countries and the developing nations, the industrialisation of the latter may be achieved with relatively low peaks in energy intensities.

The geographical pattern of energy consumption is far from uniform, as indicated in Figure 13.3. The industrialised nations (most of whom belong to the OECD[1]) consume many times more energy per head of population than do the developing countries. In terms of the world share of total primary energy consumption, however, the pattern is changing. Also, in absolute terms, the OECD nations consume the bulk of the total primary energy produced. For each of the years 1987 to 1997, these nations consumed between 56.5% and 58.5% of the world's primary energy supply. Taken in isolation, these figures could give a false impression of constancy. In some parts of the world, the demand for energy, as a share of the total, is changing rapidly. In 1987 the former Soviet Union consumed 18.4% of the world's primary energy production. By 1997, this had fallen to 10.5%. In contrast, over the same time period, the primary energy demand of the Asia Pacific region (which includes the OECD countries Australia, Japan and New Zealand) had increased from 20.3% to 27.9%.

[1] The Organisation for Economic Cooperation and Development (OECD) is a club that is, at the time of writing (February 1999), made up of the following 29 nations: Australia, Austria, Belgium, Canada, Czech Republic, Denmark, Finland, France, Germany, Greece, Hungary, Iceland, Republic of Ireland, Italy, Japan, Korea, Luxembourg, Mexico, The Netherlands, New Zealand, Norway, Poland, Portugal, Spain, Sweden, Switzerland, Turkey, United Kingdom and United States.

Figure 13.2 Trends in energy intensity (from Reddy and Goldemberg, 1990).

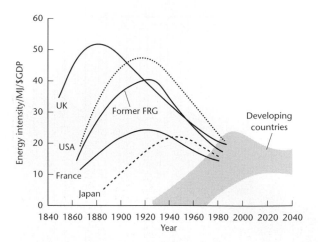

Clearly, patterns of demand for primary energy are complex and are changing with time. However, two salient features are evident. Firstly, there is a general upward trend in total consumption. Secondly, a disproportionate amount of the consumption occurs in the industrialised nations. As the developing nations become more industrialised, it can be expected that they will demand an increasing amount of primary energy and will obtain a greater share of the total produced.

13.2 Sources of energy

The major sources of primary energy are coal, oil, gas, nuclear fuels and hydropower. From Figure 13.1 it can be seen that the proportion of global primary energy demand satisfied by each of these components has been relatively constant over recent years. Oil is the single most dominant fuel. However, there is some evidence of a slight decline in its importance relative to other fuels. In 1980 it accounted for 45% of the primary energy consumption, but by 1997 this figure had fallen to 40%. A further exception to this rule is the increasing reliance on nuclear power. In the period 1980–89, the proportion of the world's energy needs met by nuclear fuels doubled from 2.5% to 5%; by 1997, this figure had risen to 7.25%. However, increasing concerns about the risks, both financial and ecological, associated with nuclear power mean that a continued high growth rate in this industry is unlikely, at least in the near future. (Case study 4 examines the impact of the nuclear accident at Chernobyl.)

13.2.1 Nuclear fuels

Nuclear reactors are the devices that are used to liberate energy from nuclear fuels, under controlled conditions. The output of these reactors is in the form of a high-temperature fluid (gas or liquid). This has the potential to be used either in the generation of electricity or as a direct source of heat for many of the more energy-intensive industries. However, civilian uses of nuclear energy are currently restricted to the production of electricity. This is because industries with high energy demands are located in areas of high population density. The risks associated with locating nuclear reactors in such areas are considered to be too great.

While nuclear fuels represent only about 7.25% (1997 data) of the total world primary energy consumption, nuclear power accounts for a significant proportion of electricity generated in the industrialised world. However, even amongst the industrialised nations, the proportion of electricity generated by this means varies enormously from country to country. France generates in the region of 77% (1995 data) of its electricity by nuclear means, while in the United Kingdom nuclear power represents about 25% (1995 data) of generating capacity, and the figure for the United States is about 19% (1995 data). There is considerable uncertainty about the proportion of electricity to be generated from nuclear energy in the future. Pressure from the increasing costs of fossil fuel consumption may increase the market share of nuclear power, as may a desire to diminish the reliance on oil. However, financial and ecological concerns about nuclear power remain, and such concerns may well curtail any significant expansion in the future. This issue is far from simple and it seems likely that different countries will adopt differing stances on the development of nuclear power in the future.

The remainder of this section is concerned with the two types of nuclear reaction that liberate significant amounts of energy: nuclear fission and nuclear fusion.

Nuclear fission

The nucleus of an atom has certain similarities to a drop of liquid. It is approximately spherical and is held together by strong forces (also known as nuclear forces). These behave in a way that is roughly analogous to the force of surface tension in a liquid drop. A nucleus with high mass number (i.e. one that contains a large number of protons and neutrons; see Chapter 1, Section 1.1) can become distorted, into a dumb-bell or more complex shape. The electrostatic repulsions between protons held in the lobes of the dumb-bell can be sufficiently high to overcome the short-range strong forces, causing the nucleus to split into two or more nuclei of similar mass. This process is called **fission**.

Figure **13.3** (a) Annual consumption of energy from commercial fuels per head of population for 1997. (b) Trends in primary energy consumption, by region, based only on those fuels that are commercially traded. Note toe = tonne oil equivalent.

(a)

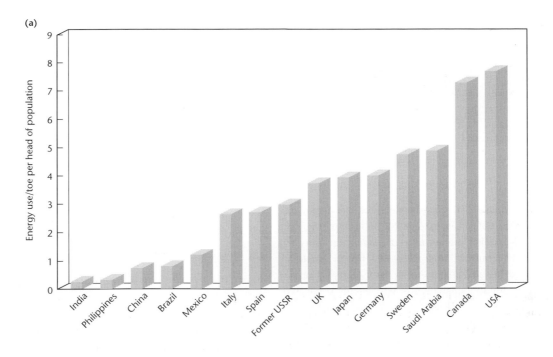

(b) Source: BP Statistical Review of World Energy, 1998.

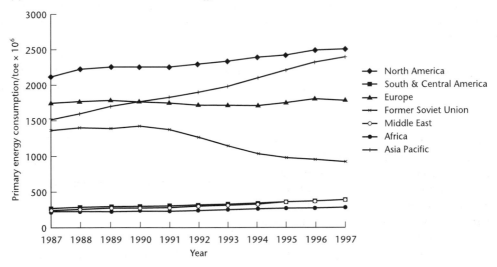

Internal oscillations can cause certain nuclei to distort sufficiently to undergo *spontaneous fission* (in this context, spontaneous means not initiated externally). For example americium-244 can disintegrate to form molybdenum-107 and iodine-134:

$$^{244}_{95}\text{Am} \rightarrow {}^{107}_{42}\text{Mo} + {}^{134}_{53}\text{I} + 3\text{n} \qquad (13.1)$$

Other nuclides will undergo *induced nuclear fission* when bombarded by neutrons. Nuclides that undergo such reactions are said to be **fissionable**. Fissionable nuclides of importance are ^{235}U, ^{238}U, ^{232}Th, ^{233}U and ^{239}Pu. A subset of these, ^{233}U, ^{235}U and ^{239}Pu, will undergo fission with low-energy (i.e. slow) neutrons; such nuclides are termed **fissile**. Indeed, fissile nuclei are more likely to be induced into fission by slow neutrons than by fast neutrons.

Uranium-235 may be used to illustrate the processes that occur on neutron bombardment of all fissile isotopes (Figure 13.4). The fission of a given nucleus will not

Figure 13.4 A slow neutron-induced fission of ^{235}U.

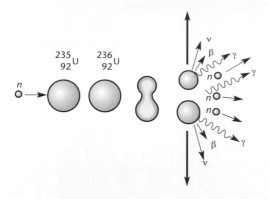

Figure 13.5 The fission spectrum of ^{235}U.

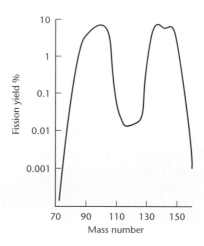

necessarily produce the same products as the fission of another nucleus of the same nuclide. Uranium-235, for example, has about 50 modes of decay, differing from one another in the number and nature of fission products produced and the amount of energy released (see Chapter 1, Section 1.7 for an explanation of why energy is released during this process). However, a typical reaction is represented in the equation below:

$$^{235}_{92}\text{U} + ^{1}_{0}\text{n} \rightarrow ^{90}_{38}\text{Sr} + ^{143}_{54}\text{Xe} + 3^{1}_{0}\text{n} \qquad (13.2)$$

As in this example, the fission process is usually asymmetrical; that is, the fission fragments usually have different, although broadly similar, mass numbers. A plot showing the percentage of the total fragments with each given mass number illustrates this phenomenon (Figure 13.5). From this it can be seen that products of symmetrical fission (i.e. two fragments with a mass number of 117) represent only about 0.01% of the total.

The fission fragments are all highly radioactive. Being neutron-rich, these decay by either beta or (more rarely) neutron emission. The daughters of these decay reactions may themselves be radioactive, as may their progeny. Hence, some fission fragments are the head of long decay series.

Each fission of a $^{235}_{92}$U nucleus produces, on average, about 200 MeV of energy and 2.5 neutrons. These neutrons can then go on to initiate further fission reactions. The fact that the fission of fissile nuclides produces more neutrons than it consumes allows a sustained **chain reaction** to occur of the type illustrated in Figure 13.6. However, neutrons can be lost from the fission process either by being absorbed by non-fissile nuclei or by being ejected from the collection of fissile material undergoing reactions. If a chain reaction occurs of the type shown in Figure 13.6, the number of neutrons produced in one generation will be greater than in the previous generation. This situation is described as **supercritical**; under these conditions the rate of reaction

will rapidly increase, possibly reaching explosive rates, as

Figure 13.6 A neutron-induced fission chain reaction.

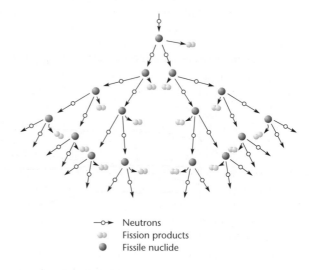

in a nuclear bomb. If the number of neutrons absorbed by the fissile material in each generation is just sufficient to maintain the reaction at a steady rate, then the number of neutrons produced in one generation will be the same as in the previous generation. This situation is said to be **critical** and is the normal running condition of a nuclear reactor. A **subcritical** condition is one in which the number of neutrons produced in one generation is less than in the previous generation. A subcritical condition will result in the eventual cessation of the fission reaction.

Thermal reactors produce energy by the fission of fissile material (predominantly ^{235}U, although ^{233}U and

^{239}Pu can also be used). During these reactions, the fissile material is consumed or 'burnt'; hence these reactors are also called **burner reactors**. The chain reaction is maintained using low-energy (slow) neutrons as these are more effectively absorbed by the fissile material than fast neutrons. These neutrons are obtained by slowing down (moderating) the fast neutrons produced by the fuel. The moderator used is either light water (i.e. normal water, $^1_1H_2O$), heavy water[2] ($^2_1H_2O$) or graphite. After moderation, the neutrons are in thermal equilibrium with the atoms of the reactor; it is for this reason that reactors of this type are called thermal reactors. Nearly all of the energy produced in the fission reaction is ultimately converted to heat by nuclear collisions (the exception being the energy associated with the neutrinos that stream harmlessly away from the reactor). This heat is carried away by a coolant which may be a gas such as carbon dioxide, or helium, or a liquid such as water.

The details of construction of nuclear power plants based on thermal reactors vary from one design type to another. However, there are essential features that are present in all such plants. These are shown in Figure 13.7.

The core is where the nuclear reaction occurs. It contains the fuel, in a matrix that includes the moderator and coolant. In many reactors, the fuel is contained in cylindrical tubes of stainless steel or other metal.

The fuel for these reactors is most commonly uranium, either in its elemental form or as the oxide UO_2. The fissile material in this fuel is ^{235}U. Fission is very effectively induced in this isotope by slow neutrons. Hence, the percentage of ^{235}U as a total of all uranium present that is required for a thermal reactor to be able to become critical is low. Some thermal reactors are designed to use uranium fuels with ^{235}U at natural abundance levels (0.715% of total U), while others require slightly enriched fuels (i.e. ^{235}U > natural abundance).

By means of pumps, the coolant is circulated through the core, usually from the bottom upwards, and the heat exchangers. There are four or more coolant loops per reactor; each has its own pump and heat exchanger system. Any one loop can be shut down for service or repair without having to shut down the reactor.

Clearly, reactors with solid (graphite) moderators must have separate coolant and moderator systems. However, if the moderator is a liquid ($^1_1H_2O$ or $^2_1H_2O$) it may or may not also act as the coolant, depending on the design details of the reactor concerned.

The reactor core also contains spaces into which control rods can be moved. These rods contain neutron-

[2] Heavy water is also known as deuterium oxide, D_2O, as the isotope of hydrogen ^2_1H is called deuterium and given the symbol D.

Figure **13.7** The essential features of a thermal reactor power plant.

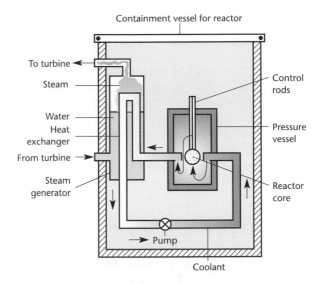

absorbing elements such as cadmium, boron or hafnium. Moving these into the reactor will cause it to become subcritical and shut down.

The core is supported in a pressure vessel that retains the coolant. Beyond this is a biological shield designed to prevent the damaging gamma and neutron radiation from escaping from the core. The shield is generally fabricated from concrete, several metres thick. In most designs, the pressure vessel is made of steel and is physically separate from the shield. There are reactors, however, in which they are one and the same steel-lined pre-stressed concrete container.

Charge/discharge machinery is often located above the core. This facilitates the replenishment of the fuel.

The heat exchanger is where the water circulating in the power cycle is heated. The steam that results is used to drive turbines and generate electricity.

There is another class of fission reactors, the **fast breeder reactor**. These have much in common with thermal reactors, for they too contain a core where the fission occurs and the heat is generated, to be carried away by a circulated coolant. As in thermal reactors, the core is supported in a pressure vessel, inside a biological shield. However, unlike thermal reactors, fast breeders do not contain a moderator; from this several other important differences flow. In fast breeder reactors:

1 The neutrons that are produced by the fuel remain fast (hence the word 'fast' in the name).

2 The fuel must contain a high proportion of fissile material for the reactor to be able to become critical. This is because fast neutrons are not

very effective at inducing fission in fissile isotopes. A typical fuel is made from oxides of either a mixture containing ~25% ^{239}Pu and ~75% depleted uranium (essentially pure ^{238}U), or highly enriched uranium (25 to 50% ^{235}U). Hence, the initial fuel costs are very high.

3 Some of the neutrons produced during the chain reaction are available for generating fissile isotopes from non-fissile ^{238}U or ^{232}Th. Such non-fissile nuclides are said to be **fertile** and their conversion to fissile material is called **breeding** (hence the word 'breeder' in the name), *the net result being the generation of more fissile material than is consumed*. Equations representing the reactions concerned are given below:

$$^{238}\text{U} + \text{n} \rightarrow {}^{239}\text{U} + \gamma \qquad (13.3)$$

The ^{239}U then undergoes the following spontaneous decay:

$$^{239}\text{U} \rightarrow {}^{239}\text{Np} + \beta^-; {}^{239}\text{Np} \rightarrow {}^{239}\textbf{Pu} + \beta^- \qquad (13.4)$$

$$^{232}\text{Th} + \text{n} \rightarrow {}^{233}\text{Th} + \gamma \qquad (13.5)$$

The ^{233}Th then undergoes the following spontaneous decay:

$$^{233}\text{Th} \rightarrow {}^{233}\text{Pa} + \beta^-; \quad {}^{233}\text{Pa} \rightarrow {}^{233}\textbf{U} + \beta^- \qquad (13.6)$$

The isotopes shown in **bold** are long-lived and fissile.

4 In order to maximise the yield of bred fissile isotopes, the reactor core is surrounded by a blanket of fertile isotopes.

5 In order to be commercially viable, these reactors must produce a higher thermal power per unit mass of fuel (referred to as **rating**) and produce more energy per unit mass of fuel per unit time (called **burnup**) than

thermal reactors. This requires a coolant with excellent thermal conductivity to remove the heat rapidly enough. In addition, the coolant must absorb little of the neutron flux if the breeding is to be maximised. Molten sodium and its potassium alloys have the desired properties for this task. Unfortunately, sodium-23 will undergo the following reaction, the product of which is radioactive:

$$^{23}\text{Na} + \text{n} \rightarrow {}^{24}\text{Na} + \gamma \qquad (13.7)$$

This means that the coolant must not be allowed outside the biological shield, necessitating the addition of an extra heat cycle between the primary coolant and the power-generating cycle (Figure 13.8) with the inevitable concomitant thermodynamic losses.

Without commercial fast breeder reactors, power production based on nuclear fission does not have a long-term future. This is because although uranium is a relatively abundant element, 99.285% of it is the non-fissile (but fertile) ^{238}U. However, uranium is currently relatively cheap and therefore the need for fast breeders, which are very expensive to build, is not pressing. While there are prototype fast breeders in France, the UK, the former Soviet Union and Germany there are few, if any, new reactors of this type planned.

The energy released per unit mass on nuclear fission is enormous when compared with the energy liberated per unit mass on the combustion of fossil fuels. As previously mentioned, the fission of a nucleus of uranium-235 releases on average about 200 MeV of energy. As 1 Mev $= 1.6 \times 10^{-13}$ J and as there are about 2.55×10^{27}

Figure 13.8 The fast breeder power station (from Porteous, 1991).

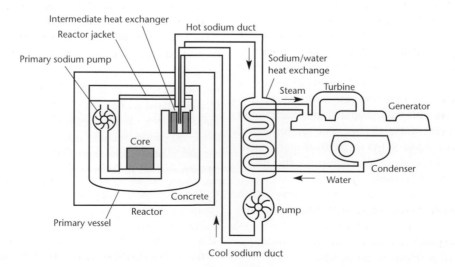

atoms per tonne of uranium-235, fission of one tonne of this nuclide will liberate 8.2×10^{13} kJ of energy, equivalent to about 2.8 million tonnes of coal!

As energy liberated by nuclear fission is ultimately in the form of heat, the *maximum* proportion of it that can be transformed into work is limited by the Carnot efficiency (Box 13.1). The ultimate heat source in a nuclear power plant is that of the coolant as it emerges from the nuclear reactor, and the ultimate sink is in the local environment of the power station. The minimum temperature of the heat sink is therefore determined by the temperature of the power station's environs.

As the power station operates, its waste heat must be absorbed by the heat sink. If this sink has a low heat capacity it will rapidly warm up, so diminishing the Carnot efficiency of the plant. For this reason, power stations are frequently built on the edges of large water bodies as this provides a convenient sink of large heat capacity. However, the disposal of waste heat to natural water bodies may lead to thermal pollution (Chapter 14, Section 14.8). Alternatively, the atmosphere provides the heat sink, cooling towers being used to transfer the waste heat from the plant. In either case, the sink temperature is usually about 30°C.

The temperature of the reactor is limited by the thermal stability of the materials that it is constructed from. Early British reactors of the magnox design had maximum coolant temperatures at the reactor outlet of 400°C to 410°C, although because of corrosion problems, operating temperatures of 370°C were used later in the lifetime of these reactors. Modern reactors have been designed to run at much higher temperatures and maximum coolant outlet temperatures in the region of 900°C have been achieved. Thus theoretical maximum (i.e. Carnot) efficiencies are typically in the range 53% to 74%. With the exception of the boiling water reactors, nuclear reactors rely on heat exchangers to transfer energy between the coolant and the working fluid of the power cycle, thus introducing inevitable thermodynamic losses beyond those predicted by the Carnot efficiency calculations. Even in the absence of heat exchangers, Carnot efficiencies are unattainable because of unavoidable losses due to friction, etc. Typically, thermal efficiencies of nuclear power stations currently in operation fall in the range 21–42%.

Nuclear fusion

Fusion of any two light nuclei, such as those of deuterium (symbol D, or $_1^2H$), tritium (T or $_1^3H$) or either of the naturally occurring lithium isotopes ($_3^6Li$ or $_3^7Li$), will yield energy (Chapter 1, Section 1.7). For example:

$$_1^2H + _1^2H \rightarrow _2^3He + _0^1n + 3.27\,\text{MeV} \qquad (13.8)$$

In order to achieve fusion, the nuclei must be brought very close to one another. This is because the nuclear forces that will bind them together after the reaction only operate over very short distances (about 10^{-13} cm). In order to bring the nuclei into such close proximity the electrostatic repulsion between them that results from their like charges must be overcome. To do this, the nuclei are made to collide with one another at very high velocities. Such velocities are generated by heating a sample of fusible atoms to the ignition temperature of the fusion reaction, about 10^8K. A gas at such a temperature is totally ionised and consists of bare nuclei in a swarm of the electrons that have been stripped from the nuclei; such a gas is called a **plasma**. A plasma in which nuclear reactions are occurring is called a **thermo-nuclear plasma**.

In order to extract useful fusion energy from a thermo-nuclear plasma, it is generally accepted that the product of its ion density (in ions m^{-3}) and confinement time (in s) must exceed 10^{20} ions s m^{-3} (this condition is called the **Lawson Criterion**). Three different approaches have been adopted in attempting to achieve this criterion, with varying degrees of success. In one approach, called magnetic confinement fusion, a magnetic field is used to contain the plasma, while a large current is applied to raise its temperature to the ignition point. In another, called inertial confinement fusion, a laser or high-energy particle beam is directed at a small, spherical capsule of fusible material. The sudden increase in temperature induced in the capsule is intended to cause it to explode. If the conditions are right, the ion density in the centre of the site of explosion will increase to reach the Lawson Criterion at temperatures at which fusion is possible. The third approach is called 'pinch' fusion. In this, effectively two concentric plasmas are established for a brief split second by the passage of a large current through them both. The current in the outer plasma generates a magnetic field that causes it to 'pinch' the inner plasma, while the massive current through the inner plasma causes its temperature to rise rapidly, causing ignition. Of these approaches, magnetic confinement fusion is currently the most popular, with research based on this technology being carried out in the US, the UK, Russia and Japan. While fusion reactions have been ignited, *none* of the above approaches has yet succeeded in generating sustainable, useful fusion power.

If fusion power is ever practicable it may well, in the first instance at least, centre around the reaction represented by the following equation, as this is the most easily ignited fusion reaction:

$$_1^2H + _1^3H \rightarrow _2^4He + _0^1n + 17.6\,\text{MeV} \qquad (13.9)$$

Most of the energy from this reaction is liberated as kinetic energy of the neutron. It has been suggested that this energy could be converted to heat in a blanket of liquid lithium surrounding the reactor by the reactions represented by the following equations:

$$_3^7\text{Li} + _0^1\text{n (fast)} \rightarrow _3^6\text{Li} + 2_0^1\text{n} \qquad (13.10)$$

$$_3^6\text{Li} + _0^1\text{n} \rightarrow _2^4\text{He} + _1^3\text{H} + 4.8\,\text{MeV} \qquad (13.11)$$

The energy in the form of heat could then be converted to work by a power cycle similar to that used in fission power plants. The tritium (which is radioactive and of very low natural abundance) produced could be used as a fuel in the fusion reactor.

Nuclear fusion is still the subject of a great deal of research effort. This is because it has several attractive qualities, among which are:

- a nigh inexhaustible supply of fuel (plentiful supplies of deuterium can be extracted from sea water, and tritium can be made from lithium as seen above);
- high energy output per unit mass of fuel;
- inherent safety compared with nuclear fission as the reactor would contain relatively little radioactive material, and virtually none of long half-life. In addition, there would be no risk of a nuclear explosion, and in the event of a breakdown the fission reaction could be stopped virtually instantaneously;
- virtually no radioactive waste disposal problems.

13.2.2 Fossil fuels

Fossil fuels (coal, natural gas and oil) account for about 90% (1997 data) of the world's primary energy consumption that is derived from commercially traded fuels (including nuclear power and hydroelectricity). They are used in the generation of electricity, the production of heat for industrial, commercial and domestic purposes, transport (especially in internal combustion engines), space heating and cooking.

The use of fossil fuels in the generation of electricity and in the internal combustion engine are of paramount economic and environmental importance and are discussed below.

Electricity generation

Very nearly all fossil fuel-fired power stations operate via power cycles that are reliant on either steam or gas turbines, typical layouts of which are illustrated schematically in Figure 13.9. Such power stations are therefore heat engines. Hence, their maximum thermodynamic efficiency (Carnot efficiency) is limited by the temperature of the heat source and heat sink (Box 13.1). Considerable gains have been made over the past century in increasing the efficiency of fossil fuel-based power generation. This has largely been achieved through an improvement in the materials used in the construction of the power plant, allowing higher source temperatures without mechanical failure and hence higher thermodynamic efficiencies. Gains in efficiency have also been achieved by better plant design, cutting losses due to friction, etc. A typical steam-based power station in 1900 would have had a thermal efficiency of 10% whereas a modern plant will have a thermal efficiency in the range 33% to 40%.

While it is possible to envisage continued improvements in the efficiency of power stations, such improvements will probably be in the order of 5 to 10 percentage points at most unless there is a radical redesign of power plant. There are several options on which such redesigns may be based, including combined heat and power plant, combined cycle plant, magnetohydrodynamic power generation, and fuel cells. The former two of these are currently in commercial operation, while the latter two are still being developed. All four of these options are outlined below.

Combined heat and power (CHP) plants (also referred to as co-generation plants) burn fuel to produce power (usually in the form of electricity) and heat (usually in the form of steam or hot water). The power cycle may be based on gas turbines, steam turbines or internal combustion piston engines. The heat delivery system represents the heat sink of the power cycle. In order to be useful, the temperature at which the heat is delivered must be appreciably above ambient. This means that the efficiency of power production is limited, because maximal efficiency for this process can only be obtained when the temperature of the heat sink is at a minimum (Box 13.1). However, the *total* fraction of fuel energy converted to useful heat *and* power is typically about 80%. This is greater than would be produced by plants producing heat and power separately.

The buildings in many Western European cities and most Scandinavian towns are warmed by large-scale district heating systems run by CHP plants. Smaller-scale CHP has found wide-ranging applicability in industry, where the heat generated is used for space heating, water heating and/or process purposes.

Combined cycle plants consist of a gas turbine system powered by either natural gas or oil. The waste heat is used to drive a steam turbine system. Both turbine systems are used to generate electricity. The total thermal efficiency of a combined cycle power station is about 50% compared with a maximum of about 40% achievable from a coal-fired steam plant.

There is considerable interest in building combined cycle power stations fuelled by gasified coal produced in

Figure 13.9 (a) Steam and (b) gas cycle power plant flow diagrams (from McGraw-Hill, 1987).

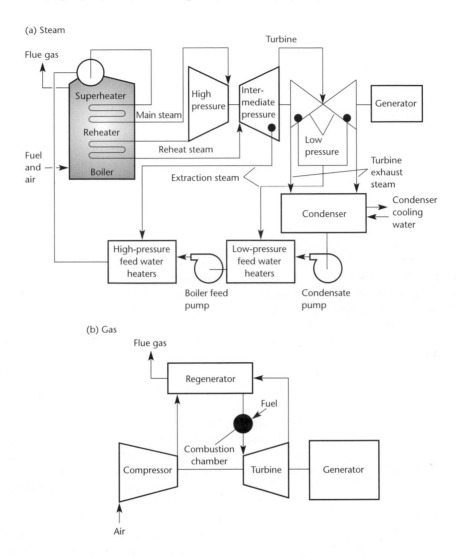

an integrated plant, and small-scale facilities of this type have been built. One of these, in Germany, delivers 170 MW of electricity with a total thermal efficiency of 36.1%, while an American station produces an electrical output of 93 MW with a total thermal efficiency of 32.6%.

Magnetohydrodynamic (MHD) power generation plants, like conventional generators, are based on the principle, discovered by Michael Faraday in 1831, that the movement of a conductor through a magnetic field generates an electric current. In the case of MHD, the conductor is a high-temperature plasma (typically at about 2500°C). This is generated by burning a fuel in a combustor and then seeding its exhaust gases with a material to induce complete ionisation (typically potassium carbonate is used for this purpose). The plasma

is then passed at high speeds through a stationary magnetic field. The electric current generated is extracted by electrodes in the channel through which the plasma is made to flow. This process can achieve efficiencies of electricity generation very close to the Carnot efficiency of the system (Box 13.1). However, the efficiency of the whole plant is considerably less than this. This is because the exhaust gases from the MHD plant are very hot and waste heat recovery is necessary if this exhaust energy is not to be wasted. Most designs employ a conventional steam turbine cycle for waste heat recovery, with concomitant inevitable efficiency loss. In addition, in order to achieve the high temperatures necessary, most designs employ either a plant for producing oxygen to enrich the air used as the oxidant, and/or a fuel-consuming device to pre-heat the gases entering the combustor. A practical problem facing MHD is the requirement for a powerful magnet. In order to consume minimal amounts of electricity such a magnet could be constructed from superconducting materials. To function, these materials must be cooled at least to liquid nitrogen temperatures, a major problem with gases at 2500°C passing nearby.

Practicable large-scale MHD plants are some time away. By the mid-1990s, a 5 MW MHD plant had been constructed near Shanghai in China. Successful though this is, it is very small when compared with the 800 MW rating of a typical thermal power plant. Other than China, countries interested in MHD include the USA, the former Soviet Union, India, Japan, the UK and Australia.

Despite the problems associated with MHD it remains attractive. It is estimated that full-scale power stations that incorporate MHD could be expected to have thermal efficiencies of between 50 and 60%.

Fuel cells are electrochemical devices that convert fuel to electricity directly, obviating the need for wasteful electromechanical devices. The cell contains an anode and a cathode. These are connected by an electrolytically conducting substance within the cell and an electrically conducting circuit outside the cell (Figure 13.10). During operation, the fuel is supplied to the anode (site of oxidation) and the oxidant to the cathode (site of reduction). The usual fuel is hydrogen and/or carbon monoxide, which can be produced from fossil fuels, while the oxidant is air. The reactions that occur within the cell produce both electricity and heat. The heat can then be used either directly (as in CHP) or to generate electricity via a conventional gas or steam power cycle. The overall thermal efficiencies of fuel cell plus turbine combined cycle plants are high, being in the range 45–58%.

There are problems associated with fuel cells, most of which are associated with the relative infancy of this technology. The long-term reliability of fuel cells is not entirely certain and they are currently expensive to make. However, a small (11 MW) facility of this type has been built on the shores of Tokyo Bay.

Transportation

Transportation accounts for about 26% of all energy demand among the OECD countries. Virtually all of the energy is supplied in the form of oil-based petroleum products and converted to motive power via internal combustion engines. Indeed, within the OECD, transport uses approximately 60% of all oil products consumed.

Internal combustion piston engines are so named to differentiate them from their predecessors, the steam piston engines that relied on an external source of heat to generate their working fluid, steam. There are two major classes of design of internal combustion engines, the Otto (spark ignition) engine and the Diesel (compression ignition) engine. These will be considered in turn.

The Otto engine. The four-stroke-cycle Otto engine operates as follows (Figure 13.11). During intake, a mixture of fuel (gasoline, petrol) and air is drawn through the inlet valve into the cylinder by the downward movement of the piston. This mixture is then compressed by the upward-moving piston and then ignited by a spark. The heat generated during the rapid burning of the fuel causes the pressure in the cylinder to rise sharply, forcing the piston back down again during the power stroke. The piston then rises during the exhaust stroke, expelling the products of the combustion reaction through the outlet valve. The following downward movement of the piston constitutes the intake stroke of the next cycle, and so on. Only the power stroke produces motive energy, some of which is stored in a flywheel and used to drive the other three strokes. The valves are operated by a cam system, also driven by the flywheel.

The Diesel engine. The four-stroke Diesel engine operates on a very similar cycle to that of the Otto engine (Figure 13.11). However, in the case of the Diesel, air only is drawn into the cylinder during intake. This air is heated by the compression stroke, at the top of which fuel is injected. The temperature of the air at this point is sufficiently high to ignite the fuel, which burns during the power stroke. The products of combustion are then ejected during the exhaust stroke.

Figure 13.10 The essential features of a fuel cell.

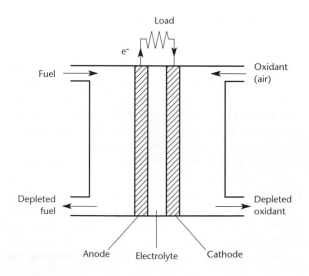

Figure 13.11 The principles of the four-stroke internal combustion engine (one cylinder, shown in cross-section).

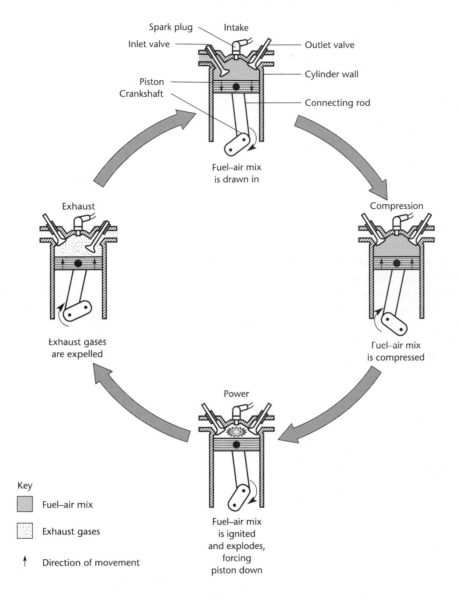

Both Otto and Diesel engines are heat-to-work devices and are therefore limited by the Carnot efficiency (Box 13.1). The temperature of the heat source (T_{source}) is the temperature of combustion, the temperature of the heat sink (T_{sink}) is that of the gases when ejected. T_{sink} is clearly above ambient, hence further work may be extracted from the exhaust gases. This is done in many Diesel engines and in some Otto engines by allowing these gases to expand in a turbine, the power output from which is used to drive the gases into the engine during intake. Engines fitted with such devices are more efficient; they are said to be turbocharged or supercharged.

The ratio of the volume of the cylinder when the piston is at the bottom of its stroke to the volume when it is at the top of its stroke is called the compression ratio of an engine. It can be shown that the Otto engine's efficiency can be improved by increasing its compression ratio. However, if this is done excessively, compression-derived heating can cause the fuel–air mixture to pre-ignite. This results in a very rapid increase in pressure in the cylinder before the piston is in a position to make maximal use of it in the power stroke. When this happens, the engine is said to be pinking, pinging or knocking. This results in a loss of efficiency, excessive noise and accelerated engine wear.

Different fuels have different propensities to pre-

Figure 13.12 Structural formulae of (a) straight-chain and (b) branched-chain alkanes typical of those found in petrol.

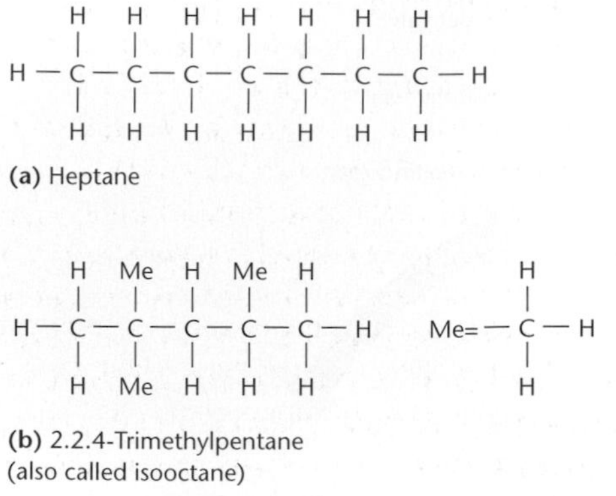

(a) Heptane

(b) 2.2.4-Trimethylpentane (also called isooctane)

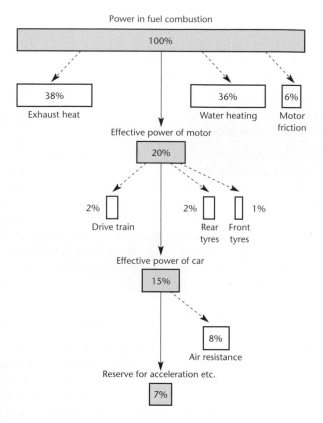

Figure 13.13 A power flow diagram for a typical vehicle propelled by an internal combustion engine. The dashed arrows represent losses.

ignition. Petrols with a low propensity to knock are said to have a high octane rating. Petrol is a mixture, containing both straight-chain and branched hydrocarbons (Figure 13.12). Of these, branched hydrocarbons are much less prone to pre-ignition. Petrol that contains a high proportion of branched hydrocarbons has a high octane rating and allows more efficient, higher compression ratio engines to be run. However, such petrol is expensive to produce. A cheaper alternative is to add chemicals that increase the octane rating of the fuel without having to increase the proportion of branched hydrocarbons that it contains. One of the most successful groups of compounds of this type are the tetraalkyl lead anti-knock agents (PbR_4, where $R = CH_3$ or CH_2CH_3). While these compounds have allowed relatively cheap fuel to be used in high compression ratio engines, they have resulted in a massive increase in atmospheric lead levels (Chapter 15, Section 15.1.6).

The compression-induced heating that causes problems in the Otto engine is made use of in the Diesel engine to ignite the fuel. Pre-ignition is avoided in Diesel engines by keeping the air and fuel separate until ignition is required. Diesel engines can therefore have higher compression ratios than Otto engines and are therefore more fuel-efficient. They can also run on a wider range of fuels. Diesel engines do have their disadvantages, however; for example, compared with Otto engines they are heavier and more expensive to build, they are slower to accelerate, they require more frequent oil changes and their fuel is more apt to freeze in cold weather.

While Diesel engines are more efficient than Otto engines, vehicles based on either have low thermal efficiencies. Typically, these fall in the range 15% (Figure 13.13) to 30%.

Improvements in the fuel efficiencies (in terms of

kilometres per litre) of vehicles can be brought about by both design and mode of use. Design parameters that affect fuel economy include:

- those that determine engine thermal efficiency (including compression ratio and the presence or absence of a turbocharger);
- the mass of the vehicle; decreasing this by minimising the amount of material it contains, substituting less dense material such as plastic and aluminium for steel, and fitting smaller, lighter engines will improve fuel economy;
- the rolling resistance of the vehicle. Power losses incurred by the continual flexing of tyres account for about 15% of the motive power produced by the engine of a typical road vehicle. This is one of the reasons why tyreless vehicles such as trains and barges are more fuel-efficient than road vehicles;
- bodywork features that affect aerodynamic drag.

The way in which a vehicle is used can markedly affect its thermal efficiency and fuel economy. Some of the actions that can be taken to improve efficiency include:

- regular servicing;
- maintaining appropriate tyre pressures (to minimise rolling resistance);
- keeping windows shut, removing roof racks and lowering speed (all of which reduce aerodynamic drag);
- carrying minimal excess baggage;
- car pooling – carrying more passengers markedly improves the fuel economy per passenger kilometre.

13.3 Renewable energy

An oil embargo imposed by some of the major oil-exporting nations in 1973 dramatically increased the price of oil and triggered a worldwide oil crisis. Industrialised nations were forced to look afresh at alternative energy sources, as well as at energy conservation (Section 13.4). Increased self-sufficiency in energy production decreases the dependence of nations on expensive oil imports, much of which come from the Middle East, an area of high political instability.

Despite the short to medium-term outlook of most energy policies, there is some awareness amongst the industrialised nations that the fossil fuels (oil, gas and coal) are not going to last for ever. Coal reserves are still considerable and are expected to last for more than 300 years. However, the supply of oil and gas is expected to be seriously diminished by the middle of the twenty-first century. The picture is further complicated by the great regional disparity in the distribution of the fossil fuel reserves. For example, the Middle East has 95 years of oil reserves remaining, whilst North America has only 10 years. Fossil fuels took millions of years to form. It seems inevitable that in only a few hundred years we will have practically exhausted them.

Another reason for the renewed interest in alternative energy sources is an increasing awareness of the very serious environmental effects associated with the production of energy from fossil fuels (Chapter 15). The **renewable energy** sources (defined broadly as those which can be harnessed without depletion) are generally regarded as being environmentally benign. The energy sources discussed in this section are solar, wind, wave, tidal, oceanic, hydropower, geothermal and biomass. With the exception of geothermal energy, renewable energy sources are derived directly or indirectly from the sun.

Despite the tremendous diversity in types of energy sources classed as renewable, they do have several characteristics in common. For example, renewable energy sources are usually intermittent, on either a predictable or an unpredictable basis. The technologies employed in exploiting them are usually costly to install but relatively cheap to run. Renewable energy sources are often used to meet localised energy demand.

13.3.1 Solar energy

The amount of energy from the sun which reaches the Earth's surface is enormous, exceeding $1 \, \mathrm{kW \, m^{-2}}$ at noon on a clear day in the tropics. However, we are only able to collect and make use of a tiny fraction of this superabundant energy source. Direct solar energy may be harnessed in a number of different ways.

Active solar heating and cooling technologies

Active solar heating makes use of pumps and/or motors to move fluids and deliver captured heat. There are a number of different active solar heating systems available. One of these is the stationary flat-plate collector system. The main application of these simple devices is to provide hot water, primarily for domestic use. In countries where the amount of solar energy reaching the Earth's surface is high, they are an economic proposition, and they are extensively used in Japan, Israel, Australia and the southern United States. Active solar technology can also be used to operate solar cooling systems.

Passive solar heating, cooling and daylighting technologies

By definition, passive solar power systems do not involve the use of motors, pumps or blowers. Their effectiveness is therefore reliant on good building design. This type of technology can play an important role in the conservation of energy (Section 13.4).

In the provision of space heating, solar radiation is transmitted through a protected glazed layer on the south side of a building (in the northern hemisphere) into a building space. It is then absorbed by containers of water or thick floors and walls (known as the thermal mass) to be subsequently released as space heat.

In passive solar cooling technologies, use is made of solar-induced climate effects such as wind and temperature differences to cool buildings. Buildings can be so designed, for example with underground walls, to take advantage of the natural convective and radiative cooling processes of the Earth at night. This enables heat which has been built up during the day to be drawn out at night. The underground walls act as a heat transfer medium and the Earth itself as a heat sink. This technique greatly reduces the need for air-conditioning in hot countries (Section 13.4).

Finally, daylighting technologies are designed to make maximum use of natural light for illuminating the interior of commercial buildings. These include such techniques as core lighting where shopping centres and office blocks have a central atrium to allow natural light to enter.

Solar thermal technologies

There are basically five different kinds of solar thermal systems, namely parabolic troughs, parabolic dishes, central receivers, hemispherical bowls and solar ponds. Most research and development has been concentrated on the first three, the so-called 'high temperature' solar thermal technologies. These are most commonly used for the generation of electricity but they can also provide high temperatures for industrial processes.

The parabolic dish and parabolic trough systems consist of many small individual units distributed on a 'dish farm'. In some systems, the individual units produce the final product, electricity, and then it is combined. In other systems, the units produce a hot heat-transfer medium (usually oil in the case of parabolic troughs) which combine to produce steam which generates electricity in a central plant. In central receiver systems (CRS), many solar collectors (known as heliostats) reflect and concentrate the sun's rays onto an elevated central receiver. The temperature of the fluid in the receiver (often water) becomes very high ($\sim$1700°C) and the steam produced drives a turbine for the production of electricity. There are several CRSs in operation, for example the Sunshine plant at Nio in Japan and Solar One at Barstow in the United States, both of which were completed in the early 1980s and use steam as their heat transfer medium.

The solar pond, a type of low-temperature thermal technology, has been under development in Israel for over three decades. In these ponds, a gradient of salt concentration is maintained to provide a dense saline bottom layer overlain by an upper layer of almost fresh water. The bottom layer heats up due to the absorption of solar radiation (to $\sim$80°C) and is drawn off to boil an organic fluid. The vapours produced drive a low-temperature turbine which produces electricity. Not surprisingly, given the number of steps involved and the relatively low starting temperature, the thermal efficiency of this process is extremely low, $\sim$1% (Box 13.1). The largest pond in operation in Israel, on the shores of the Dead Sea, covers 250 000 m^2. Its 5 MW$_e$ turbine is connected to the national grid.

Photovoltaic technologies

Photovoltaic technology involves the direct conversion of solar radiation into direct-current (DC) electricity. It was Albert Einstein who discovered that tiny particles of light known as photons (symbolised $h\nu$) can excite electrons from a lower-energy band to a higher-energy band. In this excited state, electrons can separate from parent atoms to produce an electric current. Semiconducting materials are the most effective in this process of photoconversion.

Solar cells were first used in Soviet and US space vehicles and satellites in the 1950s. These first solar cells were single crystals of silicon and were very expensive to make. However, this a rapidly developing technology. Decreasing production costs and increasing efficiency of solar cells indicate that photovoltaics could play a significant role in future electricity production. There is considerable interest in the use of photovoltaic electricity in the production of hydrogen fuel (Box 13.2).

13.3.2 Wind energy

Wind energy is the kinetic energy of moving air. The uneven absorption of solar radiation by the Earth's surface causes differences of temperature, density and pressure which produce air movements on a scale from local to global (Chapter 4, Section 4.2.2).

The harnessing of the wind's energy to provide mechanical energy, for milling corn or pumping water, has been used for centuries. The current interest in wind power is primarily for the production of electricity. Since wind is very unpredictable, one of the first challenges has been to assess potential sites accurately, averaging data collected over time.

Further Information Box

13.2   Hydrogen as a fuel

Hydrogen (H_2) can be produced by the electrolysis of water. There is considerable interest in hydrogen as a transport fuel. It has the distinct advantage over other fuel types of being a very clean fuel. On combustion, the only pollutants it produces are oxides of nitrogen (NO_x), which can be kept at safe levels fairly easily.

Hydrogen as a fuel is expensive to produce. However, recent advances in photovoltaics (the direct conversion of sunlight into electricity) mean that this source of electricity for hydrogen production is becoming progressively cheaper, bringing economic viability nearer for hydrogen as a fuel.

Solar hydrogen, as this is called, is based on the exploitation of renewable resources, i.e. water and sunlight, and on abundant materials, principally sand (which provides the silica needed for the photovoltaic cells). Solar hydrogen is not therefore resource-limited. It is possible that solar hydrogen could play an important role in meeting the world's future energy demands, without contributing to the greenhouse effect.

Resource assessments indicate that there are many potential sites in Europe. Countries currently engaged in the development of wind technology include Great Britain, the Netherlands, Greece, Spain and Denmark. Denmark leads the field and aims to provide 8% of its fuel needs from renewable sources by the year 2000, with the emphasis on wind turbines. The technology for small to medium wind systems (10–500 kW) is fairly mature (Plate 21). Nearly 90% of the world's wind-generated power is produced in the USA, primarily in California where thousands of wind turbines are concentrated on 'wind farms'.

Wind energy can meet only a tiny fraction of the world's needs. However, it could be important in supplying electricity to remote regions and, in areas of high resource, it can contribute significantly to the national grid electricity supply. It has the advantage that it is virtually pollution-free, although there are environmental objections, especially those of visual pollution.

13.3.3   Wave energy

Waves are formed as a result of the interaction of winds with the surface of the sea and involve a transfer of energy from the former to the latter. Wave energy increases with several factors including the distance over which the wind blows, i.e. the 'fetch'. Favourable areas for the exploitation of wave energy are located at the end of these fetches, especially in latitudes in the ranges 40–60°N and 40–60°S, where the winds blow strongest. These areas include the western coastlines of Norway, Scotland and the USA and the eastern coastline of Japan.

Wave technology is undergoing research but only in a very few countries, principally Norway and Japan. There are many problems in harnessing wave power including high costs, corrosion by sea water and storm damage to equipment, and the intermittent nature of this renewable energy source. The principal interest in wave energy is for the production of electricity. The only current commercial use of wave-produced electricity is to supply remote lighthouses and navigational buoys at sea; the latter are extensively used by Japan. A prototype 500 kW$_e$ land-based power station has been built north of Bergen in Norway. This station has been providing electricity for the Norwegian national grid since 1985.

13.3.4   Tidal energy

Tides are caused by the interaction of the gravitational effects of the sun and moon, and the Earth's rotation. The relative motions of these bodies produce a range of different tide cycles. The number of sites in the world suitable for harnessing tidal power is limited to about forty. The main criterion is that the mean tidal range must be greater than 5 m. Suitable sites include the Rance Estuary in France, the Bay of Fundy in Canada and the Severn Estuary in the United Kingdom.

Tidal power plants involve building a barrage equipped with sluice gates and turbines usually across a narrow neck of water. These can be designed to generate electricity on the ebb tide only, or on both the ebb and flood tides, known as 'two-way generation'. At La Rance power station on the north-west coast of France, the process of ebb generation is now favoured over the original two-way generation. La Rance is the only commercial tidal power station currently operating in the world. It has been in operation since 1968 and has a capacity of 240 MW$_e$. Another major tidal energy system is the 20 MW Annapolis Tidal Power Project in the Bay of Fundy in Canada, successfully operating since 1984.

Interest in the UK is focused once more on the feasibility of building a tidal power station on the Severn Estuary. This has a favourable tidal range of 6 m. The proposed station would have a life-span of 100 years and an installed turbine capacity of 8400 MW$_e$, and could produce a total energy output of 17 GWh per year.

However, in common with all tidal projects, very large capital investment is required. The environmental effects of such projects are considerable and must be individually assessed. They include negative effects on ports, navigation, wildlife and recreation.

13.3.5   Ocean thermal energy

Ocean thermal energy conversion (OTEC) makes use of the naturally occurring thermal gradient of the oceans. The warm water acts as a heat source whilst the cold water at about 1000 m acts as a heat sink (Box 13.1). This creates a thermal power cycle which can be used to generate electricity. The minimum difference required between the heat source and the heat sink is 20°C. Such temperature differences are only available in tropical and sub-tropical seas (within 25° of the equator).

The efficiency of OTEC is very low (<4%) but the enormous magnitude of this potential energy resource merits its investigation. In addition, OTEC could provide a *continuous* energy supply, unlike many other renewable technologies, and so could be used to provide baseload electricity. The field of OTEC research and development is led by Japan, France and the USA.

Large-scale OTEC development, if it were ever to become feasible, could have severe environmental impacts. For example, the release of carbon dioxide, formerly trapped in the ocean depths, into the atmosphere could exacerbate the greenhouse effect (Chapter 15, Section 15.2.3).

13.3.6 Hydropower

Hydropower comes indirectly from solar energy; the flowing rivers which provide the power form part of the water cycle (Chapter 5, Section 5.1.1). Hydropower has been exploited since the time of the ancient Greeks and Romans for grinding corn. Today, hydropower is used almost exclusively for the production of electricity (hydroelectric power, HEP).

Hydroelectric power can be generated directly by fast-flowing rivers but usually it involves the damming of a river and the flooding of a valley. Water flows through a pipe in the dam, driving a turbine. The efficiency of this process is very high, about 90%. However, these HEP stations have a limited life-span. The reservoir gradually fills up with sediment brought in by the river and, by the process of succession, eventually becomes land (Chapter 8, Section 8.4.2).

HEP technology is very well advanced and has been developed largely in Europe. Norway, for example, obtains all of its electricity from this renewable energy source. There are potential sites in many other countries. For example, in China, in December 1994, work was inaugurated on the world's largest hydroelectric dam project. The Three Gorges scheme will involve the building of a dam, 100 m high and almost 2 km in length, across the Yangtze river. With a generating capacity of almost 18 000 megawatts, this hydroelectric power plant will have an output *eight times* that of the Aswan Dam in Egypt.

There are serious environmental problems associated with the construction of HEP stations which involve the creation of reservoirs (Chapter 12, Table 12.3). For example, large tracts of land are lost and many people may be displaced as a result. When the Kariba Dam was built in central Africa, over 5000 km² was flooded and 50 000 people had to be resettled. In the Three Gorges scheme mentioned previously, an estimated *one million* people will be displaced by the reservoir, which will stretch 600 km upstream from the dam.

13.3.7 Geothermal energy

Geothermal energy is the thermal energy present in rocks and fluids deep within the Earth's crust. In stable geological zones, the temperature of the Earth increases by ~3°C for every 100 m depth (i.e. there is a geothermal gradient of about $30°C\,km^{-1}$), reaching about 100°C at a depth of 3 km. However, in areas of geophysical activity, characterised by volcanoes, earthquakes and rifting, hot or molten rocks are bought nearer to the Earth's surface and are therefore more accessible for exploitation.

High-enthalpy geothermal belts are associated with the edges of the Earth's crustal (tectonic) plates (Chapter 3, Section 3.1.2) (Figure 13.14). They include a major belt which skirts the Pacific Ocean (the so-called 'ring of fire'), mid-ocean ridges such as the one on which Iceland is located, and continental rift valleys, e.g. in East Africa. Low-enthalpy geothermal belts are more abundant and distributed more widely, e.g. in western Siberia and parts of central and southern Europe.

Geothermal energy is not renewable on a human time-scale but resources are vast. There are a variety of different types of geothermal resources, namely hydrothermal, geopressurised, hot dry rock, and magma (molten rock). Of these, only the first is currently exploited on a commercial basis. Hydrothermal resources can be divided into three types: dry steam deposits, wet steam deposits and hot water deposits. The first two are high-temperature deposits (>150°C) and as such are used for the generation of electricity. At Larderello in Italy, dry steam deposits are used to produce electricity, whilst at Wairakei in New Zealand, wet steam deposits are utilised. Hot water deposits are used directly for residential and commercial space and water heating, e.g. in Reykjavik, the capital of Iceland.

13.3.8 Biomass energy

Biomass energy is the energy produced by the combustion of organic matter. It is a highly diverse potential energy resource which can be separated into the following broad categories: wood and wood-processing residues, animal wastes and crop residues, energy crops, and municipal waste. Biomass of variable origins can be converted by a variety of techniques into heat, fuels (which can be substituted for petroleum or natural gas), and raw materials for the chemical industry. Table 13.1 lists some examples of biomass conversion.

Direct combustion, principally of wood, is the oldest use of biomass and currently the most prevalent in the world. In many developing countries it is the *only* source of fuel available for cooking. This has led to a fuelwood shortage crisis and severe deforestation (Chapter 11, Section 11.5.1). In more-developed countries, there is interest in short-rotation plantations of poplars, willows and conifers to provide fuel on a renewable basis for the generation of electricity. Wood-processing residues are

Figure 13.14 Global distribution of hot spots (from Summerfield, 1991, after Vogt, 1981).

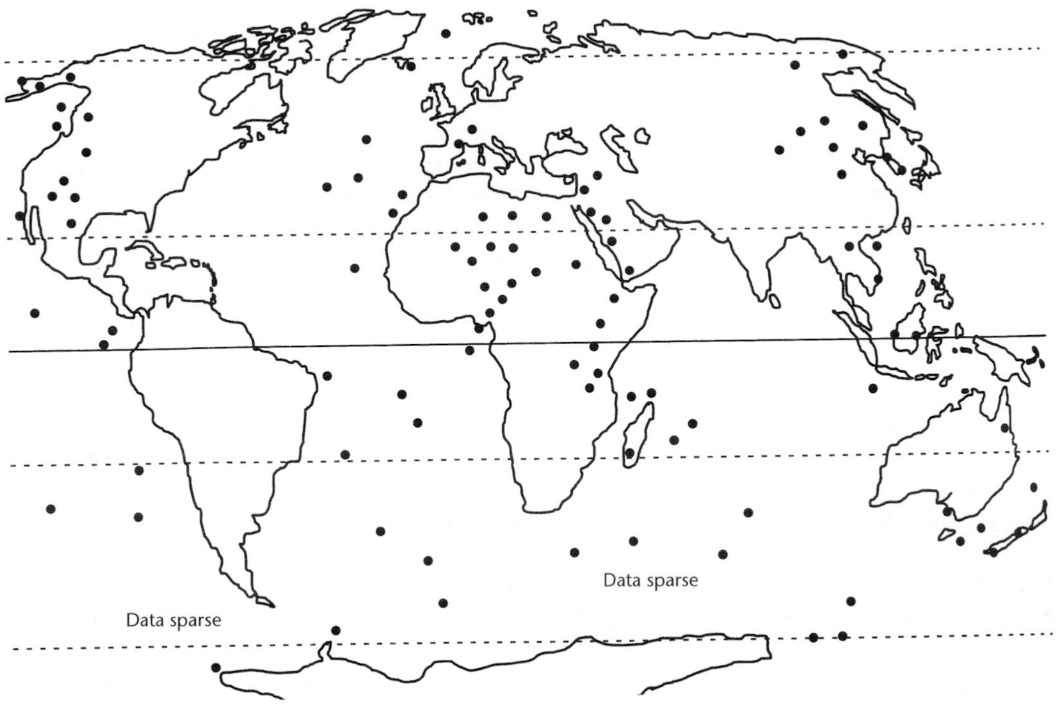

Data sparse

Data sparse

Table 13.1 Some examples of biomass conversion processes, their products and applications.

Type of biomass	Conversion process	Products	Examples of applications
Wood and wood-processing residues	Direct combustion	Heat	Electricity generation, space heating and cooking
	Pyrolysis	Char, oil and tar	To produce methanol for transportation fuel
Peat	Direct combustion	Heat	Electricity generation
Dry animal wastes and crop residues	Direct combustion	Heat	Cooking and heating
Moist animal wastes and crop residues	Anaerobic digestion	Biogas	Cooking and heating
Energy crops, e.g. maize	Fermentation	Ethanol	Petrol supplement in USA (gasohol)
Sugar cane residue	Fermentation	Ethanol	Transportation fuel in Brazil

often used to generate electricity on site; for example, Finland uses almost all of its wood waste in this way.

Energy crops, like the short-rotation plantations mentioned previously, are ones grown specifically for use as a biomass energy resource. However, it is debatable whether more energy can be obtained than is consumed in the cultivation of such crops. Potential crops, such as reeds and algae, must be assessed on an individual basis. In the United States, grain, especially maize, is grown for

fermentation into ethanol which is then used as a supplement in petrol. This is called gasohol and contains 23% ethanol. In Brazil, ethanol produced from the waste generated by the sugar cane industry is extensively used as a transportation fuel (Box 13.3).

Biomass is potentially a vast resource. However, because it is bulky, it is difficult and expensive to transport and so tends to be used to supply local needs. The future for biomass as an energy source looks promising. However,

13.3 The use of ethanol as a transport fuel in Brazil

In response to the oil crisis of the 1970s, the Brazilian government set up a huge programme called Proalcohol for the production of ethanol as an alternative transport fuel. It used the waste crop residues from its sugar cane industry to produce ethanol by fermentation.

This programme has been enormously successful. At first, the ethanol was used only as an additive, but 1979 saw the production of the first cars designed to run on pure ethanol.

Today over one-third of Brazil's 12 million cars run on ethanol produced from sugar cane. This programme has also significantly reduced the emission of greenhouse gases in Brazil, by about 20%.

However, the Proalcohol programme seems to be under threat as the present fall in world oil prices make it less economically attractive. If ethanol as a fuel is phased out, it is inevitable that Brazil's atmospheric pollution will rise dramatically.

there is concern about the atmospheric pollution associated with the direct combustion of biomass.

13.4 Energy conservation

Energy conservation can be carried out in two basic ways. Put simply, the options available are 'use less' and 'use more efficiently'. The United States is by far the greatest user of energy; with only 5% of the world's population it consumes a massive 25% of the energy used in the world. There is tremendous scope for energy saving in many countries, especially the more-developed ones, where consumption is highest.

The benefits of energy conservation are multiple. It can play a very significant role in reducing the dependence of countries on expensive oil imports. Energy conservation reduces the level of various emissions, such as carbon dioxide, into the atmosphere and helps to combat the potential problem of global warming (Chapter 15, Section 15.2.3). Conservation techniques can be rapidly put into place and to the individual, company or country can represent significant savings.

Energy conservation in buildings

In buildings, energy is used for space and water heating, lighting, air-conditioning and the operation of appliances. Most of this energy is in the form of electricity. Design features of buildings are very important in the efficient use of energy. In passive solar heating and cooling technologies (Section 13.3.1), appropriate building design can significantly reduce the need for conventional heating in winter and air-conditioning in summer. Buildings can be retro-fitted to conserve energy; for example, double-glazing windows or even lagging the hot water tank will help to prevent heat loss. Appliances differ in the amount of energy they require to run, a simple example being the contrast between low-energy light bulbs and conventional filament lamps.

Energy conservation in transportation and industry

The fuel needed for transportation of people and goods could be reduced in a variety of ways. Greater use and investment in public transport systems would reduce the number of vehicles on roads. This could also be assisted by the use of car-sharing ('car pools'). Goods could be transported in the most efficient practicable manner, for example by taking freight by rail instead of road. As outlined in Section 13.2.2, the fuel efficiency of vehicles themselves can be improved in a number of ways. Speed restrictions also have the effect of reducing fuel consumption.

In industry, there may be difficulties in the implementation of energy conservation measures as many firms do not have an 'energy budget' and therefore do not know where savings may be made. New plants can be built which are more energy-efficient but, as with the housing stock, annual turnover is minimal and therefore the response is lagged.

13.5 Summary

Energy production is the transfer of energy from a form found in nature to a useful form. Energy consumption is the transformation of energy from a potentially useful form to a relatively useless one.

The maximum efficiency of a heat-to-work conversion is limited to the Carnot efficiency, i.e. $1 - (T_{sink}/T_{source})$.

Nuclear energy can be released by either nuclear fission or nuclear fusion reactions. Of these, nuclear fission of fissile isotopes is currently the only practicable source of sustained civilian nuclear energy, all of which is currently used in the generation of electricity. There are two basic forms of nuclear fission reactor in use, the thermal and fast breeder reactors. The former are cheaper to build; the latter make more fissile material than they consume.

Fossil fuels (coal, natural gas and oil) account for about 90% of global energy consumption. Two major uses to which they are put are the generation of electricity and the propulsion of vehicles via the internal combustion engine. Current fossil fuel-based electricity generation is dominated by steam and gas cycle turbine plants, the thermal efficiency of which is about 40% for modern installations. More radical options that allow for increased efficiencies include combined heat and power plants, combined cycle plants, magnetohydrodynamic power generation and fuel cells. Of these, the first two are currently practicable. Motive power plant for vehicles is dominated by two design types of internal combustion engine, the Otto engine and the Diesel engine. Of these, the latter is operationally more efficient as it can operate at higher compression ratios.

The oil crisis of the 1970s refocused attention on renewable energy sources: solar, wind, wave, tidal, oceanic, hydropower, geothermal and biomass conversion. During this period, industrialised nations were able to cut their energy needs by up to one-third. Although some contribution was made by the exploitation of renewable energy sources, the bulk of the savings were achieved by energy conservation measures.

13.6   Problems

1   The heat rate of a power station is defined as the ratio of the heat energy consumed (in MJ) to the electrical energy produced (in kWh). If a power station has a heat rate of 9 MJ/kWh, what is its thermal efficiency? Is this an efficient power station by modern standards?

2   Consider two power stations, one located in the tropics, the other in the Arctic. Both power stations have heat sources at 350°C; however, the tropical station has a heat sink at 40°C while the other has a heat sink at 5°C. Calculate and compare the Carnot efficiencies of the two stations.

3   A heartbeat requires about 1 J of energy. How many grams of ^{235}U need to undergo fission at 200 MeV per fission in order to liberate sufficient energy for one heartbeat?

4   The equation that relates the compression ratio (cr) of an Otto engine to its ideal efficiency takes the form shown below. Use this to work out the ideal efficiency achieved with a compression ratio of infinity.

$$\text{Efficiency (\%)} = 100 \times [1 - (1/\text{cr})^{R/C_V}]$$

where R is the gas constant and C_V is heat capacity at constant volume. (Note that it is not necessary to know the values of R or C_V to complete this problem.)

5   Consider a co-generation plant with a *total* thermal efficiency of 80%. If this plant generates 26 MW of electricity and 23 MW of heat, how many tonnes of fuel must it consume to produce a total of 100 MWh of useful energy if the fuel has an enthalpy of combustion of 55 kJ g^{-1}?

6   If an active solar heating system using a flat-plate collector of 1 m^2 can convert 50% of the solar energy falling on it into useful heat, at what rate of solar energy input per unit area will it produce more useful energy than it consumes if its pumps consume 100 W of power?

7   A typical fossil fuel power station has an 800 MW$_e$ capacity. What area of solar pond would have to be used to generate the same output if the efficiency of the solar energy to electricity generation process was 3% and the solar energy supply rate was 1 kW m^{-2}?

8   Hydrogen has a specific enthalpy of combustion of 142 kJ g^{-1} while that of petrol is 48 kJ g^{-1}. At atmospheric pressure and room temperature the density of hydrogen gas is 9.1 × 10^{-5} g cm^{-3} and that of liquid petrol is 0.79 g cm^{-3}. Calculate the volume of hydrogen (in litres) required to propel a car 1 km if its petrol consumption is 12 km l^{-1}. Assume that the car has the same thermal efficiency irrespective of the fuel used.

13.7   Further reading

Boyle, G. (1996) *Renewable energy*. Oxford: Oxford University Press.

BP Statistical review of world energy (1998). London: The British Petroleum Company plc.

International Energy Agency (1998) *1998 World Energy Outlook*. The Brookings Institution.

Scragg, A. (1999) *Environmental biotechnology*. Harlow: Longman. (Chapter 6 provides useful information on renewable energy sources, especially biofuels)

Chernobyl

In the early hours of 26 April 1986, the worst accident in the history of nuclear power occurred at the V.I. Lenin nuclear power plant near Chernobyl in the Ukraine, 110 km north of Kiev. The failure to adhere to reactor safety procedures during an unauthorised experiment at low power, combined with serious design faults in the reactor itself, led to a catastrophic explosion and near-meltdown of the reactor core. The release of radioactivity into the atmosphere caused widespread contamination in the then Soviet Union and over northern Europe, affecting thousands of square kilometres.

At the time, over half of the Soviet Union's nuclear-generated electrical energy was produced by RBMK 1000 nuclear reactors, four of which were operational at the Chernobyl plant. Each reactor has the capacity to produce 3200 MW of thermal energy, which can then be converted into 1000 MW of electrical energy by the plant's turbogenerators. However, these types of reactor, which represent a modification of the design used to produce weapons-grade plutonium in the Soviet Union, have a number of serious design faults. For example, they have a potential low-power instability and, unlike US reactors, are not surrounded by a confinement shell designed to contain radioactive spills. These flaws played a key role in the Chernobyl nuclear disaster.

The fuel used in the RBMK 1000 nuclear reactor is uranium dioxide (UO_2) which is 2% enriched with ^{235}U. It is contained within 1660 zirconium alloy pressure tubes embedded in the 2000 graphite blocks which make up the reactor core. The graphite is used to convert 'fast' neutrons, produced by fission reactions and the radioactive decay of fission products, into slower, 'thermal' neutrons. This moderation process is essential to the continuation of the fission process and hence the production of power (Chapter 13, Section 13.2.1).

In the RBMK 1000 nuclear reactor, liquid water is used as the coolant, removing the large quantities of heat produced for conversion into electrical power by the plant's turbogenerators. However, in this particular design, some of the liquid water is converted into steam. This contrasts with the light-water nuclear reactors (LWRs) used in the USA, where the application of pressure maintains the water in its liquid phase. The problem with steam is that it is a less efficient absorber of neutrons than liquid water. In consequence, a rise in the temperature of the RBMK 1000 reactor increases the percentage of steam produced, thus making more neutrons available for the induction of nuclear fission. A positive feedback loop becomes established and the resultant upward spiral in temperature must be controlled, if overheating of the reactor core is to be prevented. Usually, the solid boron carbide control rods of the Control and Protection System (CPS) are automatically inserted into the reactor core to absorb the extra neutrons, should the reactor start to overheat.

The sequence of events which led up to the Chernobyl nuclear disaster began with a decision to conduct an experiment during intermediate maintenance on reactor number 4. This, the newest of the reactors, had been operational for nearly two years. At 1:00 am on 25 April 1986, the process of gradual power reduction in this reactor began. Instead of its normal thermal output of 3200 MW, an output of between 700 and 1000 MW was required for the low-power test. In the next preparatory stage, the emergency core cooling system (ECCS) was disconnected at 2:00 pm, by which time the plant was operating at half power. However, demand for electricity from the nearby city of Chernobyl necessitated the continuation of power production at this level for a further nine hours. During this period, the emergency core cooling system remained switched off.

The process of power reduction was resumed at 11:10 pm. However, instead of achieving the required level of power output for the test, the reactor power level plummeted to just 30 MW thermal. The excessive cooling of the reactor meant potential shut-down and a long interval before it could be restarted. Therefore, in order to bring the power level in reactor number 4 back up, the operators began to withdraw the control rods from the reactor core. This action contravened safety instructions. Nearly all of the 211 control rods were withdrawn within the next two hours, increasing the power level to 200 MW thermal. With only a few control rods in place and all the emergency protection systems switched off, the reactor was now in a very unstable state. Nonetheless, at 1:23 am on 26 April 1986, the planned test was initiated. Its duration was a mere 40 seconds.

At 1:23:40, the power level in reactor number 4 surged. Attempts to control the overheating by inserting the control rods proved futile. Soviet computer simulations have since shown that within 2.5 seconds, the power level in reactor number 4 had leapt to 3800 MW thermal, and within four seconds to *120 times* its normal power output of 3200 MW thermal. The hot contents from the melting fuel rods spewed into the superheated water, causing it to flash into steam. The hot steam reacted with the zirconium cladding of the fuel rods and the graphite moderator to produce hydrogen gas. The build-up of pressure inside the reactor from the excessive production of steam blasted the concrete lid off. The subsequent influx of air ignited the hydrogen and caused a massive explosion, blowing debris and radioactive material over 1000 m into the sky. Hot pieces of the core were scattered over the reactor site, starting a number of fires. Radioactive material from the fires and the blast itself poured into the atmosphere to be carried away by the prevailing winds.

In the West, the first indication that a massive release of radioactive material had occurred came when abnormally high radiation levels were recorded in Sweden on the morning of 28 April 1986. The radioactive fall-out contained isotopes characteristic of fission products from a nuclear reactor and the wind direction indicated that the Soviet Union was the source. However, it was not until the evening of that same day that news of the accident at the Chernobyl nuclear power plant was eventually broadcast from the Soviet Union. The magnitude of the disaster at Chernobyl, and its consequences, made it by far the worst accident ever to occur in the nuclear power industry.

The immediate response to the accident by the Soviet authorities was to send in local firefighters to extinguish the 30 or so fires started around the reactor complex. These external fires were extinguished by 5:00 am on 26 April, thus preventing the spread of the fire to reactor number 3. Tragically, as a result of the events of that night, 31 people lost their lives and over 200 others developed acute radiation sickness.

Within the remains of reactor number 4, the graphite fires continued to burn, sending ever more radioactive material into the atmosphere. The next priority was to prevent the escape of radiation by capping the smouldering reactor core. On 27 April helicopters began the task of dropping a total of 5000 tons of dolomite, clay, sand, boron and lead into the shell of the reactor. Together with the injection of liquid nitrogen below the reactor vault to act as a coolant, these measures eventually succeeded in covering the reactor core and decreasing the release of radiation to very low levels by 10 May 1986. Meanwhile, people living within 10 km of Chernobyl were not evacuated until 36 hours after the original accident. About a week later, this evacuation zone was extended to 30 km, bringing the total number of evacuees to about 135 000.

The total amount of radiation released as a result of the Chernobyl accident is estimated to be in the region of 50 million curies, according to Russian experts. However, Western experts believe an estimate of three times this figure to be more accurate. At first, winds from the south-east blew the radioactive cloud from Chernobyl over the Ukraine, Belarus, Latvia and Lithuania. It then passed over Poland, southern Finland and Scandinavia, eventually crossing over central Europe and Britain. The incidence of radioactive contamination in these countries was largely determined by the occurrence of heavy rain, which washed the poisonous dust out of the clouds. As a result, some areas, for example the northern and western parts of Britain, received significant amounts of radioactive fall-out. Eventually, radioactivity from Chernobyl was detected as far away as North America.

The cocktail of radionuclides released from Chernobyl contained large quantities of iodine-131, caesium-134 and caesium-137. Of these, iodine-131 posed the most immediate threat to the general population. This radioactive isotope can become concentrated in the thyroid gland, causing thyroid cancer. The main measures taken to prevent its uptake were the imposition of dietary restrictions and the administration of iodine solutions to block the absorption of the radioactive iodine. However, as the half-life of iodine-131 is only 8.02 days, this threat was relatively short-lived. In contrast, caesium-137 has a half-life of over 30 years and therefore poses a more long-term threat. Chemically it acts in a similar way to potassium and is rapidly distributed throughout the body. Long-term exposure of humans to caesium-137, to either external sources or internal sources (through the ingestion of contaminated food or water), can result in fatal cancers.

The production of caesium contamination maps in 1989, three years after the Chernobyl accident, showed that levels of radioactive caesium were as high outside the Soviet exclusion zone of 30 km as inside it. As a result, many of the original evacuees had to be re-evacuated. Further afield, in the northern parts of Norway and Sweden, the reindeer herds of the Lapp people were severely affected by the ingestion of caesium-contaminated lichen. Most of the animals slaughtered in 1986 were not fit for human consumption. In Britain, environmental contamination of upland regions used mainly for sheep-farming led to measures controlling the movement and slaughter of sheep within the affected areas.

The long-term effect of Chernobyl on the health of the general population is impossible to estimate. Hundreds of variables are involved in the assessment of individual radiation exposure such as locality, diet and whether or not it was raining when the cloud of radioactivity passed over. Estimates of the total number of cancers expected worldwide over the next 70 years as a result of Chernobyl vary from a few hundred to 100 000. However, within the former Soviet Union itself, some people continue to be exposed to radiation levels above the accepted norm, both from external sources and from the ingestion of contaminated foodstuffs.

The accident at Chernobyl was made more likely by design flaws in the RBMK 1000 reactor model and compounded by a series of operator errors, including the manual overriding of automatic safety devices. These deliberate actions demonstrated a serious lack of understanding of the processes involved in the operation of the nuclear plant and a pressing need for improved training. Radioactivity from Chernobyl spread far beyond Soviet borders, threatening the health of humans and leading to the widespread contamination of livestock and crops in a number of neighbouring countries. The Chernobyl nuclear disaster demonstrated that the unthinkable *could* happen and, in much of the world, it turned the tide of public opinion against nuclear energy as a 'safe' alternative.

Further reading

Ahearne, J. F. (1987) Nuclear power after Chernobyl. *Science*, **236**, 673–9.

Atwood, C. H. (1988) Chernobyl – what happened? *Journal of Chemical Education*, **65**(12), 1037–41.

Bojcun, M. (1991) The legacy of Chernobyl. *New Scientist*, 20 April, 30–5.

Park, C. C. (1989) *Chernobyl: the long shadow*. London: Routledge.

Rich, V. (1991) An ill wind from Chernobyl. *New Scientist*, 20 April, 26–8.

Wilson, J. and H. Apsimon (1986) Tracking the cloud from Chernobyl. *New Scientist*, 17 July, 42–5.

Pollution and waste management

The previous four chapters have reviewed the ways in which mankind utilises the natural resources upon which modern society depends. We now examine the water and atmospheric pollution that arises as a consequence of the exploitation of these resources (Chapters 14 and 15). This is followed by Chapter 16 in which we explore the technologies and strategies available for the management of waste. When taken as a whole, the next three chapters not only review the nature and causes of many of the most pressing environmental problems, they also outline the currently available means by which these problems may be ameliorated.

Water pollution

After reading this chapter, you should be able to:

- Describe the effects of organic oxygen-demanding wastes on watercourses, with special reference to the changes experienced downstream from a sewage discharge pipe.

- Outline the role of anthropogenic phosphate in the cultural eutrophication of lakes.

- Discuss the causes of acid rain and acid mine drainage, and the impact they have on natural waters.

- Relate the effects of toxic metals on water bodies and their inhabitants, with reference to mercury, lead and tin.

- Evaluate the environmental impact of organochlorines on aquatic ecosystems.

- Explain how exposure to endocrine-disrupting substances in the environment can affect certain groups of aquatic organisms.

- Understand the role of man-made radionuclides in environmental contamination.

- Discuss the effects of thermal pollution on aquatic species, especially fish.

Introduction

Water covers two-thirds of the Earth's surface, with over 97% present in the oceans and less than 1% in freshwater streams and lakes. Water is also present in the atmosphere, in solid form in the polar icecaps and as groundwater in aquifers (water-bearing rocks) deep underground. Water has many remarkable properties. It is sometimes referred to as 'the universal solvent', readily dissolving a wide range of chemical substances. It also acts as a fluid medium facilitating the dispersal of undissolved particulate matter.

Water pollution may be defined as any chemical or physical change in water detrimental to living organisms.

It can occur through natural processes, for example by sediments produced by natural erosion, but in this chapter the discussion of water pollution will be restricted to man-made pollutants.

Water bodies are a major recipient of an extensive array of wastes produced by human activity. These may be discharged directly into watercourses by sewers or pipes from factories or be washed down from agricultural or urban areas, particularly after heavy rains. Under rather exceptional circumstances, water bodies may become significantly contaminated by the atmospheric deposition of pollutants. For example, in the North Sea, an estimated $30\,000\,\mathrm{ng\,cm^{-2}}$ of aluminium and $25\,500\,\mathrm{ng\,cm^{-2}}$ of iron are transferred annually from the atmosphere to the sea surface. This indirect process of contamination is sometimes described as **cross-media pollution**.

Water pollution is a global problem and one that does not respect national boundaries. Sources of pollution may be domestic, agricultural or industrial. In less-developed countries, human and animal waste and sediments from unsound agricultural and forestry practices are the main pollutants. In more-developed countries, industrial pollutants, such as toxic metals, organic chemicals and heat, add to the water pollution problem. The level of water pollution tends to rise not only with the degree of industrialisation of countries but with increasing human population densities. The effectiveness of treating wastes prior to their release into the environment determines the balance between potential and actual pollution (Chapter 16).

In this chapter, the major types of pollutants (Table 14.1) are examined in turn. In each case, the origins, characteristics and effects of the pollutant are described, together with steps for prevention and treatment. It should be appreciated that nearly all water bodies are contaminated by *several different* pollutants. The degree to which different water bodies are effected by pollution depends on many different parameters. To give just one example, lakes are considered to be more susceptible to pollution than rivers. This is because the water in lakes may take between 10 and 100 years to be replaced. This allows pollutants to build up to hazardous levels. In contrast, rivers with their flowing waters can quickly purge themselves of pollutants, if the source of the pollution is not constant.

Table 14.1 The major types of pollutants.

Pollutant	Major sources	Effects
Oxygen-demanding wastes	Sewage effluent; agricultural run-off including animal wastes; some industrial effluents (from paper mills, food-processing, etc.)	Decomposition by aerobic bacteria depletes level of dissolved oxygen in water; flora and fauna perish; further decomposition by anaerobic bacteria produces foul-smelling toxic substances such as hydrogen sulfide
Plant nutrients	Sewage effluent including phosphates from detergents; agricultural run-off, especially nitrates from fertilisers	Algal blooms; death of submerged vegetation; production of large amounts of dead organic matter with subsequent problems of oxygen depletion (see above)
Acids	Acid rain; mine drainage; planting of extensive areas of coniferous forests, which acidify the soil	Acidification of natural waters; sharp decline in species richness; fish killed; concomitant increase in level of toxic metals in solution, for example aluminium
Toxic metals	Ore mining; associated industries; lead from vehicle exhaust emissions	Biomagnification of toxic metals with each successive stage of food chain; threat to consumers including humans
DDT (an organochlorine)	Direct application; agricultural run-off and via aerial crop-spraying	Biomagnification; top carnivores (especially birds) at risk; very persistent in the environment
PCBs (a series of organochlorines)	Sewage effluent; waste incineration; toxic dumps; landfill sites	Biomagnification; top carnivores at risk; effects on human health include joint pain, chloracne and fatigue
Oil	Drilling operations; oil tanker spills; natural seepage; waste disposal	Contamination of the aquatic environment, death of birds and mammals
Radiation	80% from natural sources; 20% from nuclear weapons testing, medical X-rays, nuclear energy industry, etc.	Degree of tissue damage and risk of death dependent on exposure; radionuclides can be biomagnified, and some are very persistent in the environment
Heat	Coolant waters from industry, principally the electricity generating industry	Change in species composition usually accompanied by a decrease in species richness; fish may migrate or be killed by suffocation; reproductive cycle of fish and other aquatic organisms disrupted

Organic oxygen-demanding wastes

The release of large quantities of oxygen-demanding organic wastes into watercourses often has disastrous effects on the indigenous flora and fauna. The primary source of organic waste released into fresh waters is sewage effluent. Other sources include run-off from urban areas and farms, and some industrial effluents. The recent intensification of livestock production, with larger herds concentrated in smaller areas, has exacerbated the problem of organic pollution from farm animal wastes (Chapter 11, Section 11.3.3). Certain industries discharge oxygen-demanding effluents into watercourses. These include paper and textile mills and the brewing and food-processing industries.

Flowing rivers are the usual recipients of organic waste, although some is discharged into lakes or offshore directly into the sea. The organic waste provides a rich substrate for bacteria. These multiply rapidly, depleting the amount of dissolved oxygen present in the water. The oxygen-depleting capacity of a given amount of organic matter can be estimated by measuring either its biochemical oxygen demand (BOD) or its total organic carbon (TOC) (Box 14.1). In extreme cases, the bacteria use up all the available oxygen and the aquatic fauna perishes. The aerobic bacteria themselves are replaced by anaerobic bacteria. These produce foul-smelling toxic products such as hydrogen sulfide and ammonia.

When the dissolved oxygen content of river water is measured downstream from the point of effluent discharge, a characteristic curve known as the **oxygen sag curve** is produced (Figure 14.1). This shows clearly that the input of organic waste severely depresses the amount of dissolved oxygen available. It also increases the turbidity of the water, thus reducing the amount of light available for photosynthesis. The deposition of organic sediments on the river bed also significantly changes the nature of the substrate.

Immediately below the point of sewage discharge, bacteria and predatory protozoans predominate. Where pollution is severe, these micro-organisms occur in association with certain fungi to form slimy filamentous colonies known as **sewage fungus**. Conditions at this point are usually suitable for only one macro-invertebrate, the tubificid worm (family Tubificidae), which is able to tolerate extremely low oxygen concentrations. Fish are unable to survive in conditions of severe organic pollution as the lack of oxygen causes them to suffocate. Algae and higher plants are also absent.

As conditions improve downstream, the colonies of sewage fungi disappear and algae, followed by higher plants, start to re-establish themselves. The tubificid or sludge worms are replaced by *Chironomus* larvae (order Diptera), which in turn are replaced by a zone dominated by the water hoglouse *Asellus* (order Isopoda). Fish usually start to reappear in the *Asellus* zone. Eventually, as the level of dissolved oxygen increases and the amount of organic sediment decreases, the clean-water flora and fauna re-establish themselves once more (Figure 14.1).

Further Information Box

14.1 Estimating the oxygen-depleting capacity of organic matter

Organic matter in aquatic ecosystems is naturally broken down by aerobic micro-organisms. However, if large amounts of organic material are introduced, for example at a sewage outfall, the dissolved oxygen present in the water can become severely depleted as it is used up by these micro-organisms.

A widely used measure of oxygen demand is the biochemical oxygen demand (BOD). It is used to assess the polluting potential of effluents. The water sample is incubated with aerobic bacteria in the dark, for a standard period (usually 5 days) and at a set temperature (normally $20°C$). The exclusion of light from the sample prevents the production of oxygen by photosynthetic organisms. The dissolved oxygen concentration is measured in the sample at the beginning and end of the incubation period. The difference is the BOD, expressed as $mg\,O_2\,l^{-1}$ of water.

The polluting potential of effluent may also be estimated by evaluating its total organic carbon (TOC). This is done by fully oxidising the sample (often in a small furnace), causing the organic carbon present to be evolved as carbon dioxide (CO_2). This gas is readily quantified, allowing the TOC content of the original water sample to be expressed as ppm of carbon. This procedure has the advantage over BOD determinations in that a period of incubation is not required.

Although BOD and TOC are useful indicators of the pollution potential of organic effluents, neither represents accurately the true oxygen demand found in the stream. For example, in the case of BOD, temperature affects the speed of oxidation of a fixed amount of oxidisable material. As the temperature at which the sample is incubated, the period of incubation and the micro-organisms used are necessarily arbitrary, BOD measurements should be treated with a degree of caution. Similarly, TOC measurements are not entirely reliable. This is because they include all of the organic carbon present in the sample, some of which may not be readily oxidised in the stream and therefore will not contribute to oxygen depletion.

Figure **14.1** Schematic representation of the changes in water quality and the populations of organisms in a river below a discharge of an organic effluent (from Hynes, 1960).

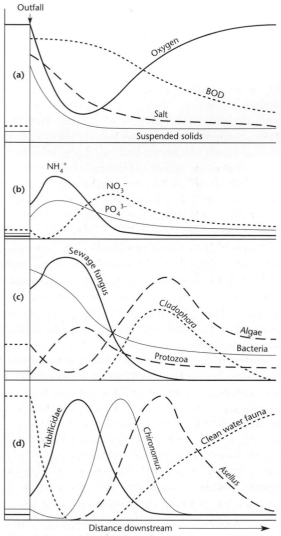

(a) Represents physical changes
(b) Represents chemical changes
(c) Represents changes in micro-organisms
(d) Represents changes in macro-invertebrates

The decomposition of organic effluent by bacteria leads to the eventual recovery of the river. This natural process is known as **self-purification**. The rapidity and effectiveness of this recovery process depends on a number of different parameters. For example, the problem of organic pollution in rivers is usually worse in the hot summer months. The rate of water-flow is slower and the volume of water carried is less, leading to an increased concentration of organic pollutants. Higher water temperatures decrease the solubility of oxygen and favour bacterial growth, thus exacerbating the problem of oxygen depletion. Moreover, many watercourses are overloaded with organic pollutants

in the first place, receiving sewage from several points of discharge along their length. This causes major pollution problems, not only for the rivers themselves but for the coastal waters where these rivers discharge. The organic waste itself often contains other pollutants such as detergents, ammonia and toxic metals.

The best approach to organic pollution is to minimise the amount discharged into watercourses in the first place through waste treatment. Such control is easier to enforce where the discharge is discrete, for example from factory pipes. The effective treatment of raw sewage is a major step, not only towards curbing organic pollution but in the elimination of water-borne pathogens (Table 14.2 and Chapter 16, Section 16.3). The spread of diseases such as cholera, typhoid and hepatitis A through water contaminated with human and animal faeces is a major problem in many less-developed countries.

14.2 Plant nutrients and eutrophication

Aquatic primary productivity is often limited by the availability of inorganic plant nutrients (Chapter 9, Section 9.2.3). In freshwater lakes and rivers, the limiting nutrient element is usually phosphorus, whilst in marine waters nitrogen is often in short supply. If small amounts of nutrients enter aquatic ecosystems where they are normally limiting, primary productivity is stimulated. However, severe problems can arise when water bodies become *over-enriched* by excessive nutrient input and consequently polluted.

The process of nutrient enrichment in water bodies is known as **eutrophication** (from the Greek *eutrophus* meaning 'well-fed'). Eutrophication is a natural aging process in lakes. It proceeds over a period of thousands or tens of thousands of years, depending on the original size and depth of the lake, the amount of sediment imported and the amount of organic matter internally generated. By this process of natural succession, the lake eventually becomes a marsh and ultimately dry land (Chapter 8, Section 8.4.2). The addition of large amounts of phosphorus (in the form of the phosphate anion, PO_4^{3-}) from a variety of man-made sources can cause **accelerated eutrophication** to occur in lakes within a few decades. This process is also known as **cultural** or **artificial eutrophication**.

Anthropogenic phosphate in the environment comes largely from domestic sewage effluent, and also from agricultural sources. Domestic sewage effluent contains significant amounts of phosphorus (and nitrogen in various forms including the nitrate anion, NO_3^-, and ammonia, NH_3), even after treatment. Much of the

Table 14.2 Examples of water-borne pathogens transmitted to humans through polluted water.

Pathogen	Disease	Effects
Bacteria		
Salmonella typhi	Typhoid fever	Severe vomiting and diarrhoea; can be fatal if untreated
Shigella dysenteriae	Dysentery	Acute diarrhoea; can be fatal to infants if untreated
Vibrio cholerae	Cholera	Severe vomiting and diarrhoea; dehydration; can be fatal if untreated
Escherichia coli	Enteritis	Vomiting and diarrhoea
Viruses		
Hepatitis virus A	Infectious hepatitis	Severe headache; fever; jaundice; enlarged liver; rarely fatal
Poliomyelitis virus	Polio	Severe headache; fever; paralysis in body and limbs; can be fatal
Parasitic protozoans		
Entamoeba histolytica	Amoebic dysentery	Severe diarrhoea; abdominal pain; chills; fever; can be fatal if untreated
Giardia lamblia	Giardia	Diarrhoea; fatigue
Parasitic worms		
Schistosoma spp. (trematode)	Schistosomiasis (bilharzia)	Debilitating illness; skin rash; anaemia; chronic fatigue; haemorrhaging; not often fatal
Anchylostoma (nematode)	Hookworm infestation	Heavy infestation causes internal haemorrhaging and anaemia; fatal in some cases

phosphate present in sewage comes from the use of modern washing powders. Phosphates are widely used as water softeners in washing powders to prevent the formation of scum in hard-water areas.

Agricultural practices such as the use of phosphate-containing fertilisers, the spreading of manure on bare fields and the intensive rearing of livestock have resulted in significant amounts of phosphates reaching watercourses through erosion and surface run-off. Certain industries, for example textiles and the phosphate industry itself, also discharge phosphates into the environment.

Anthropogenic nitrogen enters the environment in domestic sewage and in some industrial effluents, for example those from the meat-packing industry. However, the largest source of nitrate probably comes from the use of nitrogen-containing fertilisers. Since their advent in the early 1940s, nitrate fertilisers have been extensively applied by farmers in order to increase crop yields. Nitrates readily dissolve in water and are therefore rapidly leached from the soil. These may eventually contaminate ground and surface waters. Nitrogen may also contaminate natural waters through cross-media pollution from the air.

Nutrient pollution stimulates excessive growth of surface algae. These form **algal blooms**, which are usually dominated by blue-green algae (Myxophyceae), for example *Anabaena flos-aquae*. Sunlight is prevented from reaching the aquatic plants underneath and these eventually die. Large quantities of dead organic matter from the submerged vegetation and the algal blooms themselves become available for decomposition. This stimulates the growth of bacterial populations and causes the same problems of oxygen depletion as described for oxygen-demanding wastes in Section 14.1.

The eutrophication of lakes and reservoirs is a serious problem. In the United States, it is estimated that 85% of large lakes near major population centres suffer to some extent from cultural eutrophication. However, in some cases, this situation can be effectively reversed. This has been demonstrated in Lake Washington, Seattle (Box 14.2).

The role of phosphorus as the limiting factor in primary production in lake ecosystems has been vividly demonstrated by scientists at the Freshwater Institute of the Fisheries Research Board of Canada. They selected a number of lakes in Ontario to carry out field research into the effects of eutrophication. In one particular experiment, 'Lake 226' was separated into two basins by a temporary barrier. One of these basins was artificially fertilised with nitrogen, carbon *and phosphorus* and within two months had developed an algal bloom. However, the second basin, which received nitrogen and carbon *only*, failed to produce any increase in the populations of algae present.

Nitrogen, as mentioned before, is usually the limiting nutrient element in marine waters. Nitrogen-containing compounds in river water eventually end up in the sea. This has caused the production of off-shore algal blooms on a number of occasions. For example, in the summer of 1988, nutrients from fertilisers washed into the North Sea produced extensive algal blooms. These blooms had devastating effects on trout and salmon farms off the coast of Norway. European countries continue to dump in excess of 1.5 million tonnes of nitrogen annually into the North Sea, despite the fact that the link between excessive nitrates and algal blooms in the sea has been clearly established. In addition to its role in the eutrophication of marine waters, the presence of nitrates in drinking water is now a major public health concern (Box 14.3).

Mini Case Study

14.2 The recovery of Lake Washington from cultural eutrophication

Lake Washington is a large and relatively deep lake (76.5 m maximum depth) in the north-western United States. It discharges into the Pacific Ocean at Puget Sound via a series of locks and canals built in 1916. Between Puget Sound and the western shores of Lake Washington lies the city of Seattle (present population 489 000).

During the first quarter of this century, raw sewage was discharged directly into Lake Washington from Seattle (then population 50 000). Between 1926 and 1941, the 30 sewage outfalls polluting Lake Washington were redirected one by one to treatment plants and then released into Puget Sound. Pollution within the lake decreased as a result.

However, pollution by nutrients recurred when Seattle began to expand along the eastern edge of Lake Washington. By 1953, 10 treatment plants were discharging a total of 80 million litres a day of secondarily treated sewage into Lake Washington from the new eastern suburbs. Over half of the total input of phosphorus into Lake Washington was due to sewage discharge.

The level of algae in Lake Washington increased noticeably. One particular alga, the blue-green *Oscillatoria rubescens*, was found for the first time. This species has been found in other lakes, for example Lake Zürich in Switzerland, in the early

stages of lake deterioration and indicates a decline in water quality. Conditions in Lake Washington were obviously worsening. By 1962, visibility in the lake water had declined to <1 m compared with a value of 4 m in 1950.

The eutrophication of Lake Washington seriously reduced its amenity value to local residents and caused a public outcry. As a result, action was taken to redress the situation and restore Lake Washington to its former state. The effluent from the treatment plants was diverted into Puget Sound during the period 1963–67.

After this diversion, the total phosphorus level and algal biomass (as measured by chlorophyll 'a' concentration) within the lake declined significantly. This was some of the first direct evidence that phosphorus acts as a limiting factor to algal growth in fresh waters. However, the blue-green alga *O. rubescens* took several years to disappear and did not vanish until 1975. By the late 1970s, chemical and biological recovery of Lake Washington had occurred.

Reference: Gulati, R. D. (1989) Concept of stress and recovery in aquatic ecosystems. In Ravera, O. (ed.), *Ecological assessment of environmental degradation, pollution and recovery*, 81–119. Amsterdam: Elsevier.

There are a number of different ways in which the quantities of nitrates and phosphates in water could be substantially reduced. Public education concerning the role of phosphates in freshwater pollution and the provision of phosphate-free cleaning products as suitable alternatives is a major step in the right direction. The efficiency of nitrate and phosphate removal at the sewage treatment stage could, in many cases, be improved.

Further Information Box

14.3 Nitrates in drinking water

High levels of nitrate ions (NO_3^-) in drinking water can cause a severe blood disorder in babies under six months of age. In the infant intestine, bacteria, notably *Escherichia coli*, reduce the nitrate ions to nitrite (NO_2^-). The nitrite ions are absorbed into the bloodstream where they oxidise iron(II), Fe^{2+}, in the haemoglobin to iron(III), Fe^{3+}. The presence of haemoglobin containing oxidised iron (known as methaemoglobin) reduces the oxygen-carrying capacity of the blood.

Babies are more vulnerable to high nitrate levels than adults because their stomachs are less acidic. This allows *E. coli* to colonise higher up the digestive tract and convert the nitrate ions to nitrite *prior* to absorption. The use of unsterilised feeding bottles can increase the risk of methaemoglobin formation. The danger lies in the ability of the bacteria present in the feeding bottle to convert the nitrate in the water to nitrite.

A concentration of methaemoglobin in the blood above 25% causes the skin and lips of the affected infant to take on a

bluish hue (hence 'blue-baby syndrome'). Fatalities occur in the range 60–85% methaemoglobin. The World Health Organisation recorded 2000 cases of methaemoglobinaemia in Europe and North America between 1945 and 1986; of these, 160 proved fatal. Most poisonings occurred in rural areas where the drinking water was contaminated by animal wastes or domestic sewage. Cases are rarer now; the last reported case in Great Britain was in 1972.

Nitrate concentrations in drinking water should not exceed $50 \, mg \, NO_3^- \, l^{-1}$ according to European Health Standards, although water is still acceptable at levels between 50 and $100 \, mg \, NO_3^- \, l^{-1}$. In the United States, levels above $45 \, mg \, NO_3^- \, l^{-1}$ are considered unacceptable. There is a possibility that high levels of nitrate ions ($>100 \, mg \, NO_3^- \, l^{-1}$) may cause the production of carcinogenic nitrosamines in the intestines of adults. However, this link, though made in animals, has not yet been established for humans.

More difficult to control is nutrient pollution from agricultural sources, which tends to occur over a wide area. In response to this problem in Britain, the government recently launched a Nitrate Sensitive Areas (NSA) scheme to help protect selected water sources from nitrate pollution. The range of agricultural measures approved for use in NSAs include avoiding the application of fertiliser or manure in autumn and planting winter cover crops.

14.3   Acidification

Both acid rain and acid mine drainage contribute significantly to the acidification of natural waters. These two phenomena are dealt with in detail in this section. However, there are other causes of this particular type of water pollution. For example, the planting of extensive tracts of coniferous forests, usually in upland areas, results in the acidification of the soil and the waters which drain these plantations.

14.3.1   Acid rain

Acid rain is produced when sulfur dioxide (SO_2) and/or the oxides of nitrogen (NO_x) and their oxidation products are present in moisture in the atmosphere. The main acidifying species are sulfurous acid (H_2SO_3), sulfuric acid (H_2SO_4) and nitric acid (HNO_3). These acids are returned to Earth in rain or snow, a process known as wet deposition. The atmospheric chemistry of both sulfur dioxide and the oxides of nitrogen are dealt with in some detail in Chapter 15 (Sections 15.1.1 and 15.1.2). The phenomenon of acid rain is explored further in Section 15.2.2.

Normal, unpolluted rainwater is slightly acidic with a pH of about 5.6 (Chapter 3, Section 3.3.1). This is due to its equilibrium with the 350 ppm of carbon dioxide in the troposphere.

$$CO_{2(g)} + H_2O_{(l)} \rightleftharpoons H_2CO_{3(aq)} \rightleftharpoons H^+_{(aq)} + HCO_3^-_{(aq)}$$

Rain is usually classified as 'acid rain' when its pH is less than 5.

Sulfur oxides are usually the main pollutants responsible for the formation of acid rain. They are produced by burning coal, especially coal with a high sulfur content, domestically and in power stations. The other main source of sulfur dioxide comes from the roasting of metal sulfide ores, for example nickel (NiS), lead (PbS) and copper (Cu_2S), in order to recover the metal (Chapter 12, Section 12.1).

Oxides of nitrogen usually originate from power stations and from vehicle emissions. As a rule, they

contribute less to the problem of acid rain but there are exceptions where they predominate over sulfur dioxide, for example on the west coast of the United States (Chapter 15, Section 15.2.2).

Acid rain is not a new problem but it is certainly a pressing one which has received much attention in recent years. Acid rain causes a range of environmental problems but the one which concerns us here is its effect on natural waters. The susceptibility of a particular water body to acid rain depends on its capacity to act as a buffer and neutralise the effects of acidity. This capacity is determined by the underlying rock and surrounding soil type. Lakes and rivers in chalk or limestone regions are less affected by the addition of hydrogen cations (H^+) due to the presence of bicarbonate anions (HCO_3^-):

$$H^+ + HCO_3^- \rightleftharpoons H_2CO_3 \rightleftharpoons H_2O + CO_2$$

Conversely, water bodies underlain by granite, with its poor buffering capacity, are more prone to severe problems of acidification. This is the case in northern and eastern Canada, the north-eastern USA and Scandinavia.

The effect of acidification on the aquatic flora and fauna is pronounced. In general terms, both become impoverished with a sharp decline in species richness.

However, for those generalists able to withstand the acidic conditions, population densities may increase as a result of decreased competition and predation. Fish are very susceptible to changes in acidity. They may be killed directly by pulses of increased acidity, caused for example by sudden acid snow melt, or population levels may gradually decline as reproduction is adversely affected by a steady increase in acidity.

In addition to the direct effect of decreased pH itself, acidification of natural waters causes an increase in the aqueous concentration of toxic metal ions. The levels of aluminium ions, for example, rise with increased acidity. The aluminium thus brought into solution is toxic, especially to fish (Box 14.4 and Chapter 1, Section 1.6.2).

Acidification of natural waters can be reversed either by liming affected water bodies or, more effectively, by reducing emissions of sulfur and nitrogen into the atmosphere in the first place (Chapter 16, Section 16.1).

14.3.2   Acid mine drainage

The other main cause of acidification of natural waters is the acid effluent from mines, principally coal mines. The mineral iron pyrites (FeS_2) usually occurs together with coal. When exposed to air and water, this mineral oxidises to form sulfuric acid:

$$2FeS_2 + 7O_2 + 2H_2O \rightarrow 2FeSO_4 + 2H_2SO_4$$

14.4 Aluminium toxicity in fish

The solubility of aluminium in natural waters increases with acidity. At a pH below 5.5, aluminium is mobilised from the soil and the lake and stream sediments. The toxicity of aluminium has been studied mainly in fish. At concentrations less than $100\,\mu g\,l^{-1}$, it affects the osmoregulation of fish, i.e. their ability to regulate the amount of salt and water within their bodies. At concentrations greater than $100\,\mu g\,l^{-1}$, a gelatinous precipitate of aluminium hydroxide, $Al(OH)_3$, forms on the fish's gills. This interferes with respiration and the fish dies of suffocation.

The acidity of natural waters can be increased by a number of human activities, such as the planting of extensive tracts of coniferous woodland and the operational drainage of mines. This increases the amount of aluminium brought into solution.

Sometimes, aluminium is accidentally added directly to watercourses. In 1988, in Camelford, Cornwall, 20 tons of aluminium sulfate was accidentally released into the water mains. Many local residents suffered from a variety of symptoms including vomiting and muscle cramps. The public supply of polluted water was flushed out overnight into two local rivers. Many thousands of fish including brown trout (*Salmo trutta*) and salmon (*S. salar*) died as a result. Their gills were bright red, a characteristic sign of aluminium poisoning.

This reaction is speeded up by the action of specialist bacteria, such as *Thiobacillus thiooxidans*. These obtain energy from the conversion of sulfur in reduced forms to sulfate.

As well as the waste effluent from the mine itself, the leaching action of rainwater on spoil heaps of mine waste also contributes to acid pollution. As before, the high acidity causes toxic metals to come into solution. Additional problems associated with acid mine effluent occur downstream in rivers as iron precipitates out as iron(III) hydroxide, $Fe(OH)_3$. This brown slime forms a blanket over benthic algae and macrophytes and adversely effects many invertebrates, especially filter-feeders.

The fauna of waters affected by acid mine drainage is characteristically dominated by chironomid larvae. Crustaceans are rarely found and the number of species of fish present, and the size of their populations, is usually small.

In terms of acid mine drainage, abandoned mines are a greater problem than working ones (Plate 22). The recent pit closures in Great Britain mean that pollution problems from acid mine drainage could increase and must be effectively addressed. Possible approaches to controlling acid mine drainage from abandoned mines include permanently sealing and flooding the workings or filling the mine with slag.

14.4 Toxic metals

Toxic metals which pollute water bodies originate from a variety of anthropogenic sources, both from the mining of the ores themselves and from associated industries. They include mercury (Hg), lead (Pb), cadmium (Cd), zinc (Zn) and tin (Sn). The toxicity of these metallic elements depends upon their chemical form (i.e. their speciation).

In certain chemical forms, metals can be taken up directly from the water by aquatic organisms. The metallic elements can then become progressively more concentrated at each successive level of the food chain (Chapter 9, Section 9.1). This process is known as **biomagnification**. In this way, contamination of water bodies by metallic elements can ultimately pose a health risk to humans at the top of the food chain. Humans are also at risk from consuming contaminated drinking water, which ideally should be closely monitored.

Mercury and lead pollution are examined in some detail in this section. Details of a specific example of contamination by a third metal, tin, are given in Box 14.5.

14.4.1 Mercury

Public concern over mercury pollution reached its peak in the 1970s. This followed a number of incidents where the discharge of elemental mercury into watercourses was linked to fatalities and severe health problems in local residents. Details of one incident in the fishing village of Minamata in Japan are given in Box 14.6.

The main use of mercury in 1971 was in the electrolysis of brine to produce sodium hydroxide and chlorine. Since then, the use of mercury has declined and its discharge into the environment has been tightly controlled. Inorganic mercury itself is not very toxic. However, once released into the environment, bacterial action causes it to undergo methylation:

$$Hg^{2+} \xrightarrow{\text{micro-organisms}} CH_3Hg^+ \xrightarrow{\text{micro-organisms}} (CH_3)_2Hg$$

monomethyl-mercury (soluble in water)　　dimethyl-mercury (insoluble in water, volatile)

14.5 The environmental impact of tributyltin

Tributyltin (TBT) compounds belong to a group of compounds known as the organotins. They are manufactured compounds that have no counterpart in nature. TBTs are extremely toxic over a broad spectrum and are used as biocides, insecticides, fungicides, bactericides, and preservatives for wood, leather, etc. As biocides, they have been extensively used in antifouling paints. These paints are applied to the marine surfaces of ships and docks to prevent colonisation by marine organisms, such as barnacles. By 1985, it was estimated that between 20% and 30% of vessels worldwide used antifouling paints containing TBTs.

However, the use of TBTs in antifouling paints has given rise to considerable environmental concern. The tributyltins are leached from these paints directly into the aquatic environment, with the highest concentrations being found in harbours, marinas and estuaries. TBTs are very toxic indeed; concentrations as low as two parts per trillion (10^{12}) can affect marine life. For example, in marine molluscs, such as whelks, exposure to TBTs can result in endocrine disruption (Box 14.7).

Effects include the development of a condition known as imposex, in which females develop a rudimentary penis, and sterility. Also, some species of micro-organisms, bivalve molluscs, crabs and fish can bioconcentrate tributyltins to toxic levels from very low ambient concentrations, thus posing serious risks to consumers higher in the food chain.

The toxicity of TBTs has led to their use as marine antifouling agents being restricted or prohibited in some countries. For example, during the 1980s, countries bordering the North Sea banned the use of TBT paints on small boats. However, it remained in use for larger ships. In 1998, the United Nation's International Maritime Organisation responded to concern over this anomaly by agreeing to ban the use of TBT paints on commercial shipping worldwide.

The progressive restriction on the use of TBTs in antifouling paints has led to the development of alternatives, such as copper-based paints. However, concern has been expressed by some marine scientists that such substitutes may prove equally damaging to marine life in the long run.

One of the compounds produced by this natural process is monomethylmercury. This is soluble in water and very toxic. Monomethylmercury is readily absorbed by fish but slow to be eliminated. Humans consuming contaminated fish are at risk of mercury poisoning. Methylmercury is able to disrupt the blood–brain barrier. It acts as a neurotoxin and causes severe behavioural disturbances in affected individuals. Mercury is a cumulative poison and can eventually be fatal.

14.4.2 Lead

The level of lead in the environment has risen sharply since the 1950s with the rapid rise in the number of motor vehicles. Lead is used as an additive in petrol, in the form of tetraalkyl lead compounds. About 75% of this added lead is emitted into the atmosphere with the exhaust fumes. The fine particles of lead produced disperse readily and cause widespread contamination of the environment (Chapter 15, Section 15.1.6).

14.6 Mercury pollution: the Minamata disaster

In the early 1950s, the Minamata disaster in Japan sparked off widespread public concern about the pollution of the environment by mercury and other toxic metals. A local factory used mercuric oxide as a catalyst in the production of acetaldehyde (ethanal) and polyvinyl chloride. Effluent contaminated with mercury was discharged from the factory into Minamata Bay, where it was converted into the highly toxic methyl form.

The first indication of mercury poisoning was the development of a nervous disease in many local cats and dogs, with a number of fatalities. Later, local residents started to show a variety of symptoms including numbness of limbs, deafness and mental derangement. By 1958, there were over 50 reported cases of 'Minamata disease', 21 of which proved fatal.

The consumption of seafood contaminated with mercury was pinpointed as the cause and the sale of fish from Minamata Bay was banned. It was found that nearly all the victims ate fish from the bay three times a day.

However, the connection between the high levels of mercury in local fish and shellfish and the effluent discharged from the local factory was not apparently made. The factory continued to discharge mercury for another decade until economic pressures forced its closure. By 1975, the disease had claimed over 100 lives, out of a total of 800 *confirmed* cases of Minamata disease.

Reference: Kutsuna, M. (ed.) (1968) *Minamata Disease* (Minamata Report), Kumamota University, Japan.

As well as receiving lead from the atmosphere, water bodies may become polluted from industries which use lead, for example paintworks, and from the lead mines themselves. Aquatic ecosystems can also be affected by large quantities of spent lead-shot from wildfowlers and by lead weights discarded by anglers. Waterfowl such as mute swans (*Cygnus olor*) and mallards (*Anas platyrhynchos*) are most at risk from lead poisoning as they ingest the lead whilst feeding.

The risk to human health from lead comes from breathing it in or by ingesting it in contaminated food or water. Lead is a cumulative poison which builds up in the body over time. Children are particularly at risk and can suffer a variety of ill-effects such as hyperactivity, a lowered IQ and even brain damage.

Until the 1950s, lead pipes were used extensively in Britain for carrying drinking water. In soft-water areas with a pH < 5, the high solubility of lead from the pipes resulted in unacceptably high levels for human consumption. This problem has been addressed by the replacement of lead pipes with copper or plastic ones and the addition of calcium hydroxide by all water authorities to increase the pH of acid waters.

14.5 Organochlorines

Organochlorines are, as their name suggests, organic compounds containing chlorine. Manufactured organochlorines include a number of pesticides, for example DDT, and polychlorinated biphenyls, or PCBs as they are known. These two groups will be considered separately, although they do share a number of important characteristics. For example, both groups are reported to have endocrine-disrupting properties (Box 14.7 and Table 14.3).

14.5.1 Organochlorine pesticides

In 1940, the first organochlorine pesticide, DDT (dichlorodiphenyltrichloroethane) (Figure 14.2), was manufactured for Allied use in the Second World War. It met with unprecedented success against a number of insect-borne diseases, for example malaria in the tropics and typhus in Italy. It had many advantages; it was cheap to manufacture, persistent in the environment and could be applied from the air. After the war, DDT was used extensively not only to control insect populations responsible for the spread of disease but to control insect pests attacking agricultural crops. The success of DDT resulted in the development and manufacture of other organochlorine pesticides, for example lindane and dieldrin.

However, by the 1970s, public concern over the widespread use of these organochlorine pesticides led to the eventual banning of many of them in the more-developed countries. The very persistence of DDT in the environment (5–15 years) which was viewed at first as an advantage heralded its fall from public grace. For this factor, together with its high solubility in fat, meant that it became biomagnified up the food chain and eventually posed a threat to the top predators, including humans.

Aquatic ecosystems become contaminated by organochlorines from direct application and also from industrial effluents and agricultural run-off. In addition, aerial crop-spraying creates an aerosol which is widely dispersed through the atmosphere and may settle in waters some distance from the target area of application.

Carnivorous birds at the top of the food chain are particularly at risk from DDT. It interferes with their calcium metabolism and results in thin-shelled eggs which are prone to premature breakage. Contamination of human populations by organochlorine pesticides is widespread. For example, DDT has been detected in human breast milk in a number of studies in different countries. In many cases, the average concentration of DDT ($mg\,kg^{-1}$ in fat) was in excess of the maximum allowable concentration (MAC) in human foodstuffs ($0.74\,mg\,kg^{-1}$ in fat).

As mentioned previously, DDT and many other organochlorines have been banned in many developed countries. Research is now focused on producing less-persistent and more-selective insecticides. However, organochlorine pesticides continue to be used in less-developed countries.

14.5.2 Polychlorinated biphenyls (PCBs)

Unlike DDT, which is a single compound, PCBs are a chemical family of 209 congeners (Figure 14.2). Preparations of PCBs are usually mixtures. PCBs lack flammability, which makes them very suitable for use as dielectric fluids in power transformers and capacitors. PCBs were also used as plasticisers and as de-inking fluids in the recycling of newspapers.

Contamination of the aquatic environment by PCBs can originate from sewage effluent, waste incinerators, toxic dumps or landfill sites. Improper disposal of transformers and capacitors can result in leakage of the PCBs they contain. PCBs are volatile and can escape into the atmosphere, where they are widely dispersed. Alternatively, they may contaminate the groundwater directly, finding their way into rivers and eventually the sea.

Further Information Box

14.7   Endocrine-disrupting substances

The endocrine system of animals consists of a number of ductless glands that, when stimulated, secrete minute quantities of hormones directly into the blood. These 'chemical messengers' are carried round the body until they reach their target organ(s), where they interact with specific hormone receptors within the cells to produce a response. The endocrine system is a highly coordinated and complex system, linked to the nervous system, under the control of the pituitary gland (sometimes known as the 'master gland'). This system is responsible for the regulation of continuous or long-term processes such as metabolism, growth, development and reproduction.

Endocrine-disrupting substances (or 'endocrine disruptors') are exogenous substances (i.e. originating outside the organism) that interfere with the correct functioning of the endocrine system in a number of different ways. For example, the substance may act as a hormone mimic, binding to the receptor in place of the normal hormone and producing a response (known as an agonistic response/effect). Or it may act as a hormone blocker, again binding to the receptor in place of the normal hormone but in this case producing no response at all (known as an antagonistic response/effect). In the case of the female sex hormones (the oestrogens, e.g. oestrone) and the male sex hormones (the androgens, e.g. testosterone), the following terms may be used with reference to endocrine-disrupting substances: oestrogenic (mimics oestrogen), anti-oestrogenic (blocks oestrogen), androgenic (mimics androgen) and anti-androgenic (blocks androgen) (see Table 14.3).

Some substances with endocrine-disrupting properties occur naturally, e.g. the phytoestrogens present in plants, but most are man-made. The existence of such substances has been known about for years with documented examples, mainly concerning the disruption of sex hormone systems in animals, dating back over 40 years. However, over recent years, an increased amount of attention has been given to endocrine-disrupting substances in general. This heightened interest has widened the net to include substances in the environment that, apparently, disrupt other facets of the endocrine system, not just the reproductive one. The result has been a lengthening list of known endocrine disruptors that exhibit considerable diversity both in their origins and in their points of entry into the environment. Table 14.3 shows the main groups of man-made substances that cause disruption to the reproductive systems of animals.

Most of the information to date about endocrine disruptors comes from studies on aquatic animals, or those that live close to water. To give just one illustrative example, female dog whelks (Mollusca, Gastropoda) from a number of localities around the UK coast were found to have developed male characteristics and, as a result, were physically unable to lay eggs. This resulted in the decline and, in some cases, disappearance of dog whelk populations. Research work identified tributyltin (TBT) compounds, man-made substances used as biocides in marine antifouling paints (Box 14.5), as the cause of this particular manifestation of endocrine disruption. The use of paints containing TBTs is now banned on boats less than 25 m, by countries bordering the North Sea, and, as a result, affected dog whelk populations have shown some measure of recovery.

Many of the substances reported to have endocrine-disrupting properties, e.g. organochlorine pesticides and PCBs, are both persistent in the environment and subject to the process of biomagnification. It is not yet known what risk, if any, the endocrine-disrupting aspects of these environmental contaminants pose to organisms higher up the food chain, including humans. However, it is of great importance that their levels are closely monitored and controlled within all the environmental media (i.e. air, land, and especially water).

PCBs, like organochlorine pesticides, are very persistent in the environment and they are lipophilic (fat-soluble). They are therefore similarly subject to the process of biomagnification. The toxicity of PCBs varies with the types of congener present in the mixture and with the trace impurities these mixtures frequently contain. PCBs may be found in high concentrations in fish with apparently little adverse effect. Top carnivores are thought to be most at risk. For example, PCB contamination is thought to have been responsible, at least in part, for the serious decline in populations of harbour seal (*Phoca vitulina*) in the North Sea and Baltic Sea in the late 1980s (Box 14.8). Effects on humans include a persistent skin rash (chloracne), fatigue and joint pain.

The persistence of PCBs already in the environment and the potential for future contamination from unsecured toxic dumps and landfill sites means that, despite current restrictions on PCB manufacture and use, PCBs will continue to be a serious environmental problem.

14.6   Oil

Drilling for oil is one of the major extractive industries (Chapter 12, Section 12.4.2). Crude oil is a complex mixture of thousands of different organic molecules, mainly hydrocarbons (aromatics, alkanes and cyclohexanes). It is refined by the process of fractional

Table 14.3 Man-made substances with reported endocrine-disrupting properties (with regard to the reproductive systems of animals).

Category of substance	Examples	Usages	Effect on endocrine system
Organotins	Tributyltins (TBTs)[a]	As biocides in marine antifouling paints	
Organochlorine pesticides[b]	DDT, lindane, dieldrin	As insecticides (though use now banned in many more-developed countries)	Oestrogenic and anti-androgenic
Polychlorinated organic compounds	Polychlorinated biphenyls (PCBs)[b]	In plasticisers, de-inking fluids, electrical equipment (but no longer used in manufacturing processes)	Anti-oestrogenic
	Polychlorinated di-benzo-p-dioxins (PCDDs) (commonly termed dioxins)[c]	Produced as unwanted by-products during manufacturing processes, e.g. chlorine bleaching of paper; also occasionally produced during incineration	Anti-oestrogenic
Phthalates	Dibutyl phthalate (DBP)	In adhesives, paints and inks; as plasticisers in e.g. PVC	Oestrogenic
Synthetic steroids	17-β-oestradiol, ethinyl oestradiol, oestrone	In birth control pills (steroids found in activated form in treated sewage)	Oestrogenic
Alkylphenol ethoxylates (APEs)	Nonylphenol ethoxylate	In detergents used in textile processing	Oestrogenic
Alkylphenols (APs)	Nonylphenol	Formed by degradation of APEs in wastewater and the environment	Oestrogenic
Bisphenolic compounds	Bisphenol-A	In manufacture of epoxy resins, coating of steel food cans, dental fillings	Oestrogenic

[a] Box 14.5.
[b] Section 14.5 and Box 16.4, Chapter 16 (PCBs only).
[c] Box 16.3, Chapter 16.

distillation to yield a number of commercially important products such as petrol, diesel oil and tar.

Oil is a natural resource held in oil-bearing rock strata. Some oil, about 250 000 tonnes per year, is estimated to seep naturally into the oceans, particularly at the edges of tectonic plates. However, this figure is very low and accounts for only 7.7% of the oil received by the marine environment (Figure 14.3). The amount of oil produced in the world each year is enormous – 3519 million tonnes in 1998 – and over half of this is transported by tanker during its journey from well-head to consumer. Even though the proportion involved in oil pollution of the marine environment is only about 0.1% of total production, this is still a considerable amount (an estimated 3.25 million tonnes per year).

Oil pollution of the marine environment has received much more attention than that of freshwater ecosystems. This is probably due, at least in part, to the high profile given by the media to dramatic incidents of oil pollution such as the wreckage of oil tankers and blow-outs from well-heads.

The first major tanker incident was the wreck of the *Torrey Canyon* in 1967 in which 117 000 tonnes of oil were lost, causing extensive pollution of the coastlines of Brittany, France and Cornwall, UK. Since then, there have been a number of notable incidents involving oil tankers, for example the *Amoco Cadiz* in 1978 (Brittany, 233 000 tonnes, the *Exxon Valdez* in 1989 (Alaska, 38 000 tonnes) (Case study 5), and the *Sea Empress* in 1996 (Milford Haven, UK, 72 000 tonnes of crude oil lost).

Accidental oil spills from tankers constitute an estimated 12.3% of the total oil pollution received by the marine environment (Figure 14.3). A larger percentage (21.5%) originates from routine tanker operations, including the illegal dumping of contaminated sea water which has been used as ballast in the 'empty' oil tanks on return journeys. As drilling for oil beneath the ocean floor continues, pollution from this source will undoubtedly increase. Other sources of marine oil pollution include municipal and industrial wastes, atmospheric fall-out, and urban and river run-off (Figure 14.3). Most of the oil pollution in rivers comes from illegal dumping of used engine oil and surface run-off from contaminated roads. However, freshwater oil pollution may occur as the result of an accident (Box 14.9).

Figure 14.2 Chemical structure of (a) DDT and (b) PCBs.

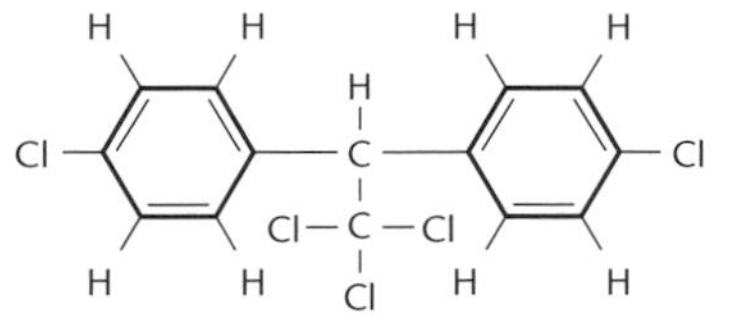

(a) DDT (single compound)

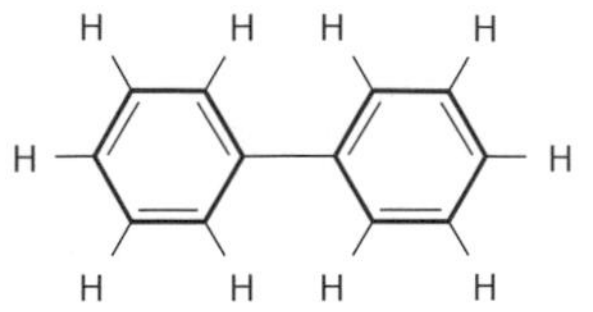

(i) Parent compound biphenyl 1. Any number of chlorine atoms can be substituted for hydrogen atoms to produce a total of 209 chlorinated biphenyls

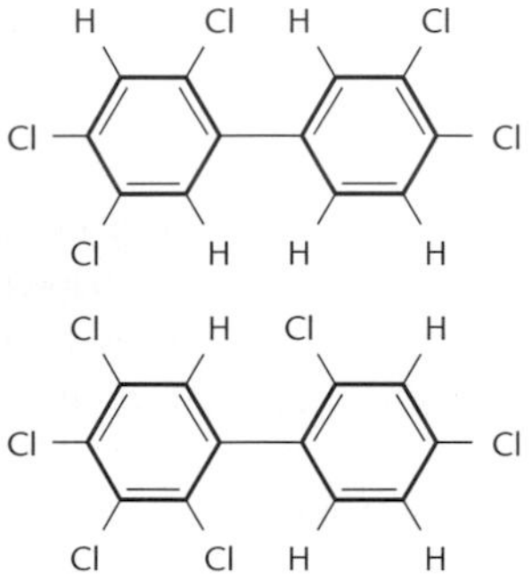

(ii) Two examples of chlorinated biphenyls

= ring of six carbon atoms

(b) PCBs (polychlorinated biphenyls)

The effects of marine oil pollution are not easy to predict as many factors are involved, for example the quantity and type of oil spilt, the distance to shore and prevailing weather conditions. However, some generalisations can be made. After an oil spill, the aromatic hydrocarbons cause the immediate death of many aquatic organisms. However, after a couple of days, these toxic chemicals largely evaporate into the atmosphere. The oil persists in globules which are naturally broken down by bacteria over a period of weeks or months, depending on the conditions.

The oil globules coat the feathers of marine birds. This causes them to lose their natural buoyancy and drown or lose their natural insulation and die of exposure. Diving birds such as puffins (*Fratercula arctica*) and guillemots (*Uria aalge*) are particularly at risk. Marine mammals, for example sea otters (*Enhydra lutris*), are also vulnerable to the adverse effects of an oil coating. The heavy

components of oil sink to the bottom of the ocean with adverse effects on the benthic community.

It is thought to take about three years for the aquatic communities of the open sea to recover from the polluting effects of a serious oil spill. However, other communities, namely those of coastal and estuarine waters and the intertidal zone of the seashore, are more seriously harmed by oil pollution and may take over a decade to recover. There is no evidence that oil pollution is harmful to human health. It does not appear that hydrocarbons are biomagnified up the food chain in the same way as DDT and some toxic metals.

The best way of addressing the problem of oil pollution is of course prevention. There are many ways in which practices could be improved to decrease the risk of pollution incidents. For example, under anti-pollution rules negotiated by the International Maritime Organisation, all new tankers constructed from 1993 must have a double-skinned hull (or equivalent method) to prevent oil leakage should they run aground.

Once an oil spill has occurred, a number of treatments, most of them not very effective, can be applied. For example, dispersants were used in the wake of the *Torrey Canyon* oil spill. Unfortunately, these proved to be more harmful to the marine community than the oil itself. Other practices include the use of booms to contain the oil, the skimming of the trapped oil and the burning of floating oil (which causes atmospheric pollution). Perhaps the most promising treatment is the inoculation of floating oil with micro-organisms to speed up the natural process of biodegradation. The provision of nutrients, usually a limiting resource in the marine environment, would further accelerate this decomposition process.

14.7   Radionuclides

In Chapter 1 (Section 1.1), the structure of the atom is discussed. To recap very briefly, it consists of a nucleus containing protons (positively charged) and neutrons (neutral), which is surrounded by a 'cloud' of electrons (negatively charged). The nuclei of the atoms of any one element all contain the same number of protons, but may differ from one another in the number of neutrons that they contain. Atoms that differ in this way are said to be different isotopes of the same element; however, all isotopes of a given element exhibit virtually identical chemistries.

Some isotopes, known as radionuclides, are unstable and achieve a more stable form by spontaneous decay (Chapter 1, Section 1.7.2). Particles or electromagnetic

---

Mini Case Study

14.8   PCBs in the environment: the case of the harbour seals (*Phoca vitulina*)

In 1988, a mysterious disease spread throughout the colonies of harbour seal (*Phoca vitulina*) of the North and Baltic Seas. The death of 12 000 individuals reduced the harbour seal population by a staggering two-thirds. This was the largest die-off of seals ever recorded. The scourge, which became known as the 'black death of the sea', is thought to have been caused by the canine distemper virus. However, many biologists believe that pollution of the marine environment was a major contributory factor to the speed and ease with which the seals succumbed.

The North and Baltic Seas are heavily polluted. Vast amounts of contaminated waste water from factories and waste treatment plants are discharged into them annually. It is thought that one group of pollutants, the PCBs (polychlorinated biphenyls), has particular relevance to the case of the harbour seals.

Seals from the North Sea have been found to be heavily contaminated with PCBs. It is known that the presence of PCBs causes suppression of the immune system, as well as adversely affecting reproduction. Pathological manifestations of immunosuppression were observed in affected seals, for example thin skin, intestinal ulcers and adrenal hyperplasia (overdevelopment of the adrenal cortex). It seems likely therefore that contamination by PCBs weakened the ability of the harbour seals to fight off the canine distemper virus.

References: Olsson, M. (1986) PCBs in the Baltic environment. In Waid, J. S. (ed.) *PCBs and the environment*, Vol. 3, 181–208. Boca Raton, FL: CRC Press.
Reijnders, P. J. H. (1985) On the extinction of the southern Dutch harbour seal population. *Biological Conservation*, **31**, 75–84.

Figure 14.3 Sources of marine oil pollution (in million t a^{-1}) (data from the Steering Committee for Petroleum in the Marine Environment Update, 1985).

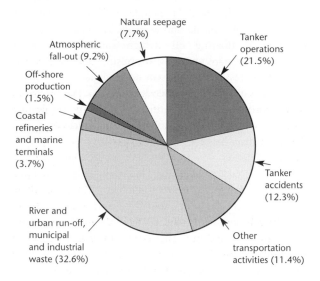

radiation are released during this process. The four main types of radiation are summarised in Table 14.4. The radioactivity of a radionuclide depends on the length of its half-life, i.e. the amount of time it takes for half of the isotope to decay. For example, the half-life of uranium-238 is 4.5×10^9 years whilst that of iodine-137 is only 24 seconds! The radioactivity of the latter is therefore more intense.

Over 80% of radiation is estimated to occur naturally. For example, the naturally occurring radionuclide, radium,

is found in soils and rocks. It undergoes α decay to produce a radioactive gas known as radon (Chapter 1, Box 1.6). The remaining 20% of radiation comes from anthropogenic sources, some from the nuclear energy industry and nuclear weapons testing. Other sources include the luminous dials on watches, television sets and X-rays used in the treatment of cancer and in the diagnosis of bone fractures.

Contamination of water bodies by man-made radionuclides can occur in a variety of ways. For example, the most common type of nuclear reactor for the production of nuclear energy is the pressurised water reactor (PWR). Such reactors are sited by large rivers or by the sea because they require large amounts of water to act as a coolant medium. Once used, the coolant water is released into the river or sea and inevitably contains small amounts of radioactive material. At present, it is not thought that these normal operational discharges of radioactive wastes pose a serious environmental problem, either directly to the aquatic organisms themselves or indirectly to humans as a result of biomagnification through the food chain.

The 'safe' disposal of radioactive wastes is a highly contentious issue (Case study 7, page 375). These may be classed as low-, intermediate- or high-level wastes, the latter being generated only by the nuclear energy industry. Various methods of disposal have been tried, including the dumping of low-level waste in steel drums at sea. There are examples of indiscriminate dumping of radioactive wastes. In the United States, tailings (wastes) from the extraction of uranium at uranium mills were spread along the banks of rivers and even used on building sites until this practice

Mini Case Study

14.9   Freshwater oil pollution: the Monongahela River incident

In January 1988, an oil storage tank sited on the banks of the Monongahela River, 37 km above Pittsburgh in Pennsylvania, collapsed. Approximately 3.5 million litres of diesel fuel were spilt. Most of this oil ended up in the Monongahela River, forming a slick over 30 km long. The oil was carried downstream into the Ohio River. As it moved past, the water intakes of cities along the Ohio River were shut off to prevent contamination of their drinking water supply. The oil slick threatened the water supplies of over a million people in four states.

Many fish and waterfowl died as a result of this oil pollution.

Effective treatment of the slick was hampered by a number of obstacles; for example the rapid flow rate of the rivers pushed the oil underneath the booms put in place to contain it. Only about 10% of the oil was successfully recovered. This example shows that serious oil pollution of fresh waters does occur on occasion, although such incidents tend to receive less media attention than their more dramatic marine counterparts.

Reference: Lemonick, M. D. (1988) Nightmare on the Monongahela. *Time*, 18 January, 34–35.

Table 14.4 Types of ionising radiation.

Radiation type	Description	Penetrating power: stopped by			
		skin	aluminium	lead	concrete
Alpha (α) particles	Helium nuclei each containing 2 neutrons and 2 protons	yes	yes	yes	yes
Beta (β) particles	Electrons ($-^{ve}$) or positrons ($+^{ve}$)	no	yes	yes	yes
Gamma (γ) rays	Short-wave electromagnetic radiation (no mass or charge)	no	no	yes	yes
Neutron radiation	Produced during spontaneous fission in nuclear reactors	no	no	no	yes

was banned in the late 1970s. It is easy to see how radionuclides can end up in water bodies through either leakage of containers or leaching of waste dumped on land.

The long half-life of some radionuclides means that it will be thousands of years before they are rendered harmless. At present, disposal of radioactive wastes in deep mines in areas of geological stability is the favoured option. However, there is always a risk of leakage from such sites and the potential for contamination of ground and surface waters.

Severe environmental contamination by radiation has occurred on a number of occasions, for example the horrific aftermath of the dropping of nuclear bombs on Hiroshima and Nagasaki in Japan at the end of the Second World War. The testing of nuclear weapons caused radioactive fall-out in a number of areas, for example in the vicinity of Bikini atoll in the South Pacific. In 1963, a test ban treaty was signed by the USSR, the USA and the UK, but the testing of nuclear weapons is still carried out by some other countries.

Perhaps the most pressing public concern with regard to nuclear energy production is the possibility of a serious accident and the ensuing radioactive pollution. Such accidents have occurred, notably at Three Mile Island,

Pennsylvania in 1979 (Box 14.10), and at Chernobyl in the Ukraine in 1986 (Case study 4).

Much of the radiation damage to body tissues is caused by the ionisation of atoms of water and other molecules (hence the term **ionising radiation**). Many radionuclides are chemically similar to, or are isotopes of, essential nutrient elements and therefore become distributed in the body in a similar fashion. Iodine-131, for example, becomes concentrated in the human thyroid gland where it may produce tumours. Another example is strontium-90, which is deposited in bones, like calcium. It has a half-life of 28 years and can cause bone cancer and leukaemia by irradiating the bone. Both of these radionuclides, once released into the environment, are taken up by grass which may be eaten by cows. The consumption of affected cows' milk means that the radionuclides are introduced into the human body through the process of bio-magnification.

14.8   Thermal pollution

Water is able to absorb large quantities of heat without appreciably increasing its own temperature or changing

---

Mini Case Study

14.10   Nuclear accidents: the Three Mile Island incident

The worst civilian nuclear accident in the United States occurred at Three Mile Island, near Harrisburg, Pennsylvania. On 28 March 1979 a series of unforeseen events took place in one of the two nuclear reactors. A combination of human operator errors and mechanical failures led to overheating of the reactor's nuclear core.

Radioactive water from the plant's emergency cooling system was released into the Susquehanna River and radioactive steam escaped into the atmosphere. Water became converted into hydrogen gas, posing the risk of explosion. At one stage, there was grave danger of a complete meltdown of the reactor's nuclear core. In the event, only a partial meltdown of the core occurred; 1% of the metal cladding containing the pellets of uranium fuel melted.

There were no injuries, deaths or serious overexposure of individuals to radioactivity in the Three Mile Island accident. However, the long-term effects on human health (cancers, genetic defects, etc.) are not yet known. The clean-up programme took over a decade to complete and cost $1.5 billion (compared with construction costs of $700 million).

The main outcome of the Three Mile Island incident was to seriously undermine public confidence in nuclear power.

References: Ford, D. F. (1982) *Three Mile Island: Thirty Minutes to Meltdown.* New York: Viking Press.
Marshall, E. (1979a) A preliminary report on Three Mile Island. *Science*, 204, 280–281.
Marshall, E. (1979b) Assessing the damage at Three Mile Island. *Science*, 204, 594–596.

---

from its liquid state. This high heat capacity means that it is extensively used as a coolant in many industries. The principal user of water as a coolant is the electricity generating industry. For example, an estimated 86% of all cooling water is used for this purpose in the United States.

The maximum efficiency of electricity generating power plants is typically less than 40% (Chapter 13, Section 13.2.2). This means that in excess of 60% of the energy converted in power stations is released into the environment as heat. A large proportion of this is absorbed by the coolant water, which is warmed as a result. Other industries which use water as a coolant include oil-refining and steel-making.

The coolant water required by industry is drawn directly from water bodies, frequently rivers. After use, the water, now warmed, is often, but not always, *directly* discharged back into the original water body. This constitutes thermal water pollution.

Thermal pollution affects aquatic ecosystems in a variety of ways. In general, the species composition changes as species tolerant of warmer waters replace those unable to adapt. This transition is often accompanied by an overall decrease in species richness. For example, attached algae in heated effluents were reported to show an increase in biomass but a decrease in the number of species represented.

Fish can be particularly susceptible to the effects of thermal pollution because their body temperature fluctuates with that of the surrounding water. For this reason, an increase in water temperature causes an increase in the metabolic rate of fish. This enhanced metabolism requires more oxygen. However, the amount of dissolved oxygen present in water is inversely related to its temperature (Figure 14.4). The lack of dissolved oxygen at higher temperatures can lead to suffocation in fish adapted to cold water conditions.

Thermal pollution can also interfere with the natural reproductive cycles of fish. For example, premature hatching of eggs by artificially raised temperatures may lead to mass mortality of the young fry through starvation. This disruption of natural life-cycles extends to other members of the aquatic community. An increased water temperature can also increase the susceptibility of aquatic organisms to parasites and disease. Toxic chemicals made more soluble by higher temperatures may present an additional hazard. Mass kills of fish and other aquatic organisms can occur when there is a very rapid change in water temperature. This is known as **thermal shock** and can occur, for example, when new power plants are made operative.

Thermal water pollution can be avoided by pre-cooling

Figure 14.4 The relationship between temperature and dissolved oxygen content of water in equilibrium with air at 1 atm. pressure.

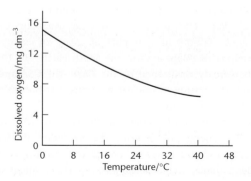

the warm water prior to its discharge. For example, cooling ponds and cooling towers are often used for this purpose in the electricity generating industry. Alternatively, the warm waste water can be effectively used by other industries. For example, it is used in the aquaculture of marine and freshwater fish and even ragworms!

14.9   Summary

Water pollution may be defined as any chemical or physical change in water that adversely effects living organisms. Although the causes of water pollution may be natural, for example the seepage of oil from the sea bed into the marine environment, the majority results from human activities. For example, oxygen-demanding wastes, often in the form of sewage effluent, can substantially deplete the amount of dissolved oxygen present in water. This problem of oxygen depletion also results from the eutrophication of natural waters which receive excessive amounts of nutrients normally limiting to plant growth. Other anthropogenic water pollutants include toxic metals, oil, organochlorines, radionuclides and heat.

Most natural waters are polluted to some extent by a number of the pollutants mentioned previously. In some cases, pollutants are discharged directly into water. For example, rivers are viewed as an effective transport medium for the removal of waste products from factory sites and sewage works. In other instances, water pollution occurs indirectly, for example through surface run-off from agricultural and urban areas and from air pollutants such as lead and oxides of sulfur.

The pollution burden of many lakes and rivers, together with certain areas of the marine environment, are a serious cause for environmental concern. The general effect of pollution on aquatic ecosystems is one of impoverishment with a sharp decline in species richness. Some environmental contaminants, such as TBTs, organochlorine pesticides and PCBs, have been reported to act as endocrine disruptors in certain groups of aquatic organisms. In some cases, the effects of water pollution are not confined to the aquatic environment. Through the process of biomagnification, some water pollutants, such as the organochlorine pesticide DDT, pose a serious risk to top-level *terrestrial* predators, including humans.

14.10   Problems

1   A pipe discharges raw sewage effluent directly into a river. Discuss the physical, chemical and biological changes you would expect to occur downstream from the discharge point.

2   What is meant by the term 'cultural eutrophication'? With reference to *lake ecosystems*, outline the causes and progression of cultural eutrophication. Suggest some methods of prevention and treatment.

3   What are the two major causes of acidification of natural waters? Choose one and describe its origins and effects in detail.

4   How can low levels of toxic metals in natural waters ultimately pose a threat to consumers at the top of the food chain, including humans? What is this process called? Illustrate your answer with specific examples.

5   What are the main sources of marine oil pollution? Discuss the effect of oil slicks on marine ecosystems. Outline the different methods of treating oil pollution and their effectiveness.

6   The development of the organochlorine pesticide DDT was hailed as a major advance in effective insect control during the Second World War. However, 30 years later, its use was banned or restricted in many countries. What were the environmental concerns which led to its demise?

7   Eighty percent of radiation comes from natural sources. What man-made sources constitute the remaining 20%? Discuss the various routes by which radionuclides can pollute natural waters.

8   Discuss the effects of thermal pollution on river ecosystems.

14.11   Further reading

Bunce, N. J. (1990) *Environmental chemistry*. Winnipeg: Wuerz.

Clark, R. B. (1997) *Marine pollution* (4th edn). Oxford: Oxford University Press.

Harper, D. (1991) *Eutrophication of freshwaters: principles, problems and restoration*. London: Chapman & Hall.

Mason, C. F. (1996) *Biology of freshwater pollution* (3rd edn). Harlow: Longman.

Welch, E. B. (1992) *Ecological effects of wastewater: applied limnology and pollutant effects* (2nd edn). London: Chapman & Hall.

Focus on oil pollution: the case of *Exxon Valdez*

On 24 March 1989, the supertanker *Exxon Valdez* ran aground on reefs in Prince William Sound, Alaska. A total of 38 000 tonnes of crude oil, about 22% of the *Exxon*'s cargo, spewed out into the pristine subarctic waters of the estuary with devastating results. This, the so-called 'Alaskan oil spill', was the worst incident of its kind to occur in United States waters.

Alaska is the 49th state of the US, separated from the lower 48 states by Canada. It is an area of outstanding natural beauty with an abundance of wildlife and a highly productive fishing industry. It also possesses a wealth of natural resources such as timber, coal, oil and natural gas. In recent years, the high energy demands of the rest of the United States have prompted the exploitation of these rich Alaskan resources, despite opposition from conservation groups. The state of Alaska benefits too from this development, at least financially. At the time of the accident, Alaska received about 80% of its revenue from the oil industry.

Oil was discovered in Alaska in 1968, in the North Slope region near Prudhoe Bay (Figure C5.1). By 1989, seven oil companies, which together constituted the Alyeska oil company, operated in the North Slope oil fields. Once extracted, the crude oil is carried 1300 km overland by the Alaskan pipeline to the port of Valdez (Figure C5.1). From the oil terminal at Valdez, tankers transport the crude oil to the ports of the west coast of the US. At the time of the *Exxon Valdez* incident, one quarter of the oil domestically produced by the US originated from the Alaskan oil fields.

In the 12 years following the opening of the Alaskan pipeline in 1977, more than 8500 oil tanker departures from the oil terminal at Valdez were made without mishap. The supertanker *Exxon Valdez* was in fact making the 8549th oil tanker journey through Prince William Sound. Soon after leaving port, en route for Long Beach, California, the ship's navigational equipment detected icebergs in the outgoing shipping lane of the sound. To avoid possible collision, the *Exxon Valdez* was permitted by the Coast Guard to change to the vacant incoming shipping lane.

Soon after this lane-switch, the *Exxon Valdez* went beyond the range of the Coast Guard's radar system. The imminent danger of collision, this time with submerged rocks off Busby Island, was not detected onshore. Once the danger was perceived on the ship, attempts were made to change its course but to no avail. The *Exxon Valdez* scraped over the submerged rocks and finally came to rest on Bligh Reef in Prince William Sound (Figure C5.1).

Eight of the ship's eleven cargo tanks and three of its seven ballast tanks were ruptured in the collision. Almost immediately, oil started to gush from the damaged tanker into the waters of Prince William Sound. Prior to the accident, the oil companies had promised that, in the very unlikely event of an oil spill, they would be able to respond within five hours with a fully equipped and trained taskforce.

However, in the event, the oil companies could not fulfil their promise. It took 14 hours, not five, for the first response team to arrive. There was insufficient equipment and trained personnel to deal with an oil spill of this magnitude. As time progressed, a catalogue of shortcomings was revealed in the oil company's contingency plans. For example, the barge needed to string together the booms, used to help contain oil slicks, had been taken out of service for repair and was not immediately available for deployment.

At first, the oil slick spread rapidly within the sheltered waters of Prince William Sound. The prevailing current in the sound runs in an anti-clockwise direction, entering through Hinchinbrook Strait and exiting through Montague Strait (Figure C5.1). This concentrated the oil slick in the south-western waters of the Sound. However, within six days, the oil slick began to spread from Prince William Sound into the Gulf of Alaska through Montague Strait.

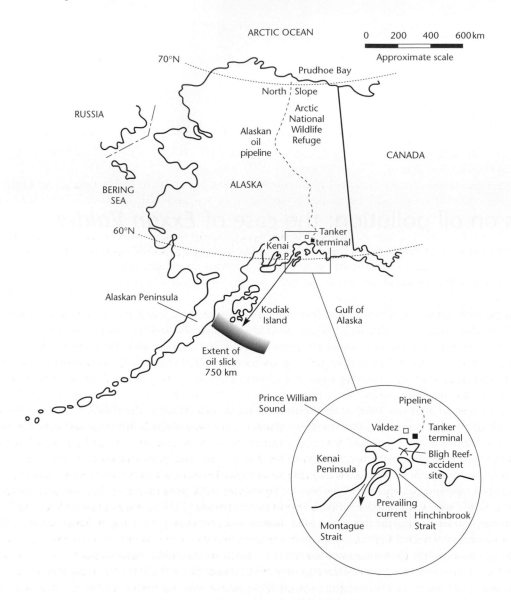

The slick travelled progressively south-westwards, threatening the coastlines of Kodiak Island and the Kenai and Alaskan Peninsulas (Figure C5.1). After 8 weeks, oil from the *Exxon Valdez* had spread 750 km down the Alaskan coastline. It is estimated that of the 38 000 tonnes of crude oil lost from the ship, 35% dispersed into the water column or evaporated within Prince William Sound, mainly within the first fortnight. A further 40% came ashore on the beaches of Prince William Sound and another 10% on those of the Gulf of Alaska and its islands.

Although the amount of oil lost from the *Exxon Valdez* was not large in comparison with many other oil spills, its effects were magnified for several reasons. Firstly, the accident occurred within a sheltered and relatively enclosed water body. Dispersal of the oil slick by the action of winds, currents and waves was not as great as it might have been in the open sea. The waters of this subarctic region are very cold and consequently the natural process of decomposition, which helps break up the oil, is slow. For this reason, it may take up to a decade for the waters of the sound to recover fully from the effects of the *Exxon Valdez* oil spill.

The coastline of this region is highly indented with many narrow fjords and inaccessible beaches. The convoluted nature of the shoreline increased the total length at risk from contamination by the oil slick. These shores and the waters of Prince William Sound were highly productive habitats, rich in the diversity and abundance of their flora and fauna.

They supported a number of commercially important species such as Pacific halibut (*Hippoglossus stenolepis*), pink salmon (*Oncorhynchus gorbuscha*), Pacific herring (*Clupen pallasii*) and clams.

The immediate effect of the oil spill was the death of numerous seabirds and marine mammals. Of the mammals, the sea otters (*Enhydra lutris*) were particularly susceptible to the effects of the oil. Sea otters have only a thin layer of body fat for insulation, and once their fur is matted with oil they are unable to conserve their body heat. Many sea otters died from hypothermia whilst others perished as a result of ingesting the oil or by inhaling toxic fumes. It is estimated that a total of 4000 sea otters died as a result of the *Exxon Valdez* oil spill, one-third of the total population of Prince William Sound.

Seabird populations were also devastated by the oil spill. In the months following the accident, 36000 dead birds were recovered, but the actual death toll is estimated to be over ten times that number. The effects of such large kills persist for generations as the offspring that these birds would have produced are also lost. In addition, the breeding of the surviving birds may be adversely affected for a number of reasons.

To take just one example, guillemots (*Uria aalge*) were particularly badly affected in the wake of the *Exxon Valdez* oil spill. Carcasses of 20000 guillemots were recovered but the figure for the actual death toll is estimated to be nearer 300000. Tragically, the breeding adults were congregating in groups on the water before travelling to their nesting sites on cliff ledges when the oil spill occurred. In the three breeding seasons after the spill, records show that the laying of guillemot eggs was delayed for, on average, 45 days. This is probably due to the predominance of young and inexperienced birds in the breeding colonies. The effect of this delay has been a serious decrease in the number of chicks fledged per pair. If this delayed breeding persists, the colonies could eventually be wiped out, and even if this aberration is a temporary one it could take 20–70 years for these colonies to recover. This example clearly illustrates that, as well as the immediate fatalities associated with the slick itself, oil spills can cause serious long-term ecological damage.

The fish populations of Prince William Sound were also severely affected by the oil spill, threatening the livelihood of many local fishermen. These highly productive waters support a number of commercially important species, including herring and pink salmon. These form the basis of a multimillion-dollar fishing industry. Local fishermen managed to protect three pink salmon hatcheries by surrounding them with booms. However, pink salmon spawn in the streams that run into Prince William Sound and it is estimated that over 200 of these streams were contaminated with oil. In 1991 and 1992, the death rate of eggs laid in such streams was twice that recorded in uncontaminated streams.

At the height of this disaster, oil from the stricken tanker covered an area of $2500 \, km^2$. Booms and skimmers were used to contain, concentrate and remove the oil from the water. The prevailing conditions precluded the widespread use of chemical dispersants and also their effectiveness when they were applied. It is widely accepted that a maximum of only 10% of the oil in a spill of this magnitude can ever be effectively recovered. In the case of the *Exxon Valdez*, there were a number of shortcomings in the response which depressed this percentage.

A total of 1700 km of shoreline was contaminated by oil from the *Exxon Valdez*. A number of time-consuming and labour-intensive techniques had to be employed to physically clean up the beaches. During the clean-up operation, a bioremediation project was carried out with promising results. Oil is a complex mixture of hydrocarbons and as such is naturally broken down by micro-organisms. However, the effectiveness of these micro-organisms is usually limited by the availability of nutrient elements, particularly nitrogen and phosphorus. Researchers sprayed selected areas of the shore with fertilisers and found an increase in the biodegradation of the oil compared with unsprayed control areas. The availability of oxygen, which can also limit microbial population growth, was not a problem in this particular study. The success of this technique could merit its inclusion in future clean-up operations.

The speed and strength of recovery of the aquatic and intertidal ecosystems affected by the *Exxon Valdez* oil spill is strongly contended between the Exxon oil company and US government agencies. In 1993, at a meeting on neutral ground in Atlanta, many differences in opinions were aired.

Essentially, Exxon claimed that recovery of the sound was almost complete. This was disputed by government agencies. Government researchers spent four years building up a dossier of the ecological impacts of the oil spill. Basically, they accused Exxon of selecting its study sites, conducting its research and using the data generated to support only its side of the case. It was implied that the aim of this approach was to minimise the perceived scale of the environmental damage of the oil spill and so help restore the public image of the Exxon Corporation. Government researchers agreed with Exxon that most of the oil had disappeared from most of the sound. However, pockets of contamination remained, a point disputed by Exxon.

It may take up to a decade for Prince William Sound to recover fully but it is likely that the legacy of the *Exxon Valdez* oil spill will extend beyond that in some cases. The plight of the guillemot populations has already been discussed in this context. Another example of the long-term effects of the oil spill is the persistence of oil in some mussel beds and its subsequent biomagnification up the food chain. This process could continue for a number of years with serious implications for the reproductive ability and general well-being of predators such as the harlequin duck (*Histrionicus histrionicus*).

The *Exxon Valdez* oil spill has received enormous publicity and been extensively studied. It has had a number of repercussions besides its devastating ecological impact. One of these has been an alteration in the public's perception of oil companies and their role as benign operators. The disaster served to strengthen the case of conservationists opposing further exploitation of Alaska, primarily within the Arctic National Wildlife Refuge (Figure C5.1).

Further reading

Buchholz, R. A. (1992) 'The big spill: oil and water still don't mix' in R. A. Buchholz, A. A. Marcus and J. E. Post, *Managing environmental issues: a casebook*. Englewood Cliffs, NJ: Prentice Hall.

Galt, J. A., W. J. Lehr and D. L. Payton (1991) Fate and transport of the *Exxon Valdez* oil spill. *Environmental Science and Technology*, **25**(2), 202–209.

Pain, S. (1993) The two faces of the *Exxon* disaster. *New Scientist*, 22 May, 11–13.

Pearce, F. (1993) What turns an oil spill into a disaster? *New Scientist*, 30 January, 11–13.

Pritchard, P. H. and C. F. Costa (1991) EPA's Alaska oil spill bioremediation project. *Environmental Science and Technology*, **25**(3), 372–379.

Wells, P. G., J. N. Butler and J. S. Hughes (eds) (1996) *Exxon Valdez oil spill: fate and effects in Alaskan waters*. American Society for Testing and Materials.

Atmospheric pollution

After reading this chapter, you should be able to:

- Define the following terms, as they apply to atmospheric pollution: primary pollutant, secondary pollutant, anthropogenic, xenobiotic, synergism and sink.

- Apply the concept of residence time to enhance your understanding of the behaviour of atmospheric pollutants.

- Summarise the main sources, sinks, levels and impacts of the individual major atmospheric pollutants.

- Describe the impacts of the major atmospheric pollutants when present in combination.

- Understand the processes that lead to, and the possible consequences of, smog, acid rain, global warming and stratospheric ozone depletion.

Introduction

The air that constitutes the atmosphere is a complex mixture of gases that is dominated by nitrogen (N_2), oxygen (O_2), argon (Ar) and variable amounts of water vapour (Chapter 4, Table 4.1). Trace gases and particulates are also found within this mixture. Many of these may be considered to be pollutants as their presence has a potentially deleterious effect on the environment.

Many atmospheric pollutants are naturally occurring substances such as carbon dioxide or methane. Human intervention in the natural environment commonly leads to an enhancement in the rate of production of these materials. For example, the burning of fossil fuels leads directly to a major increase in the rate of carbon dioxide production, adding to that naturally generated during respiration and oxidative decay (Chapter 5, Section 5.1.2).

Less direct exacerbation of natural pollution is also possible. For example, methane is produced under the

anaerobic conditions found in the digestive systems of ruminants and under flooded land. Clearly, this phenomenon is inadvertently nurtured by farming practices that include ruminant animal husbandry or paddy rice cultivation.

There are atmospheric pollutants that are not only man-made (i.e. **anthropogenic**) but are also completely unknown in biological systems (i.e. they are **xenobiotic**). Of these, the chlorofluorocarbons are probably the most important, as will be seen later.

Atmospheric pollutants may be categorised as being either primary or secondary. **Primary pollutants** are environmentally damaging materials that arise as the result of either man-made or natural processes. These substances are often susceptible to chemical change once in the environment. The products of such reactions are referred to as **secondary pollutants**. As will become evident later in this chapter, many secondary pollutants are more potent than their primary forbears.

It is rare to find one pollutant acting alone. In some cases, two or more pollutants generate a greater impact than would be expected on the basis of adding together the contributions that each pollutant would make in isolation, an effect called **synergism**. For example, there is evidence that a synergistic interaction between sulfur dioxide (SO_2), nitrogen dioxide (NO_2) and ozone (O_3) may cause greater leaf damage than would be expected on the basis of a merely additive effect.

Pollutants are continually added to the atmosphere, and yet they remain at trace levels. This is possible because in most cases there are many natural processes by which pollutants are removed from the air. These processes are referred to as **sinks** and they may be chemical or physical in nature. For example, carbon dioxide (CO_2) is chemically absorbed by green plants during photosynthesis (Chapter 9, Section 9.2.1). It is also removed from the atmosphere by physical dissolution in the waters of the oceans.

The operation of a sink mechanism may not remove the elements of a polluting compound from the atmosphere. For example, the gas hydrogen sulfide (H_2S) is oxidised in the air to sulfur dioxide (SO_2). During this process, the sulfur is transformed from one gaseous species to another and so remains in the atmosphere. Note that in this example hydrogen sulfide and sulfur dioxide are acting as primary and secondary pollutants respectively.

The total amount of a pollutant that is added to the atmosphere from its sources at the same rate as it is removed by its sinks will remain constant by virtue of a dynamic steady state. For pollutants whose behaviour approximates to this model, the concept of **residence time** is useful. This is the total amount of the pollutant in the atmosphere divided by the rate at which it is either removed from, or added to, the air. It can be seen from the data presented in Table 15.1 that residence times vary greatly from one species to another. Pollutants with relatively short residence times (less than about six months) are not uniformly mixed throughout the lower atmosphere. Hence, unless their sources and sinks are evenly distributed in time and space, local variations in concentration are to be expected.

There are very many atmospheric pollutants. Clearly, some of these are of greater significance than are others. In this chapter, we are concerned with the sources, reactions, effects and fates of the atmospheric pollutants that have most widespread impact. These are sulfur dioxide; the oxides of nitrogen and carbon; hydrocarbons (especially methane, CH_4); halogenated hydrocarbons (including chlorofluorocarbons); suspended particulates; and the secondary pollutants that these materials generate. In contrast, Case study 6 (page 357) examines the impact of a

Table **15.1** Approximate residence times for some atmospheric pollutant species.

Species	Residence time/years
N_2O	20–100
CO_2, CH_4	3
CO	0.4
SO_2	<0.02[a]
NO, NO_2	<0.01[a]
NH_3, H_2S	<0.005[a]

[a] Highly variable.

particularly severe, but localised, atmospheric pollution incident – the Bhopal accident. During this event, the toxic gas methylisocyanate escaped from a pesticide factory, rapidly killing in excess of 2500 local people and injuring hundreds of thousands more.

15.1 The major atmospheric pollutants

15.1.1 Sulfur dioxide (SO_2)

Sulfur dioxide has an unpleasant odour that is detectable at concentrations greater than about 1 ppm, although above 3 ppm the sense of smell is rapidly lost. Its tropospheric concentrations range from less than 1 ppb in locations very remote from industrial activity to 2 ppm in highly polluted areas.[1] However, concentrations of 0.1 to 0.5 ppm are more typical of urban locations in industrialised countries, while levels of around 30 ppb are the norm for rural areas in the northern hemisphere.

Sulfur dioxide is a respiratory irritant and can cause shortness of breath, enhanced likelihood of lower respiratory tract illness and chronic lung disease. Even relatively short exposure to the higher concentrations found in polluted areas can cause temporary damage to human health (Table 15.2). This pollutant is rarely found alone and its potency is frequently enhanced by synergistic interactions with other contaminants. There are indications that, in the presence of particulates, the incidence of respiratory tract disease may be increased even at concentrations as low as 30 ppb SO_2. Sulfur dioxide is a significant ingredient of the London smogs that have claimed many lives in the past (Section 15.2.1).

[1] When referring to gaseous concentrations, ppm and ppb stand for parts per million by volume and parts per billion (10^9) by volume respectively (see Chapter 2, Box 2.4).

Table 15.2 Some effects of sulfur dioxide on humans (after Wellburn, 1994).

Concentration/ ppm	Period	Effect
0.03–0.5	Continuous	Condition of bronchitic patients worsened
0.3–1	20 seconds	Brain activity changed
0.5–1.4	1 minute	Odour perceived
0.3–1.5	15 minutes	Increased eye sensitivity
1–5	30 minutes	Increased lung airway resistance, sense of smell lost
1.6–5	>6 hours	Constriction of nasal and lung passageways
5–20	>6 hours	Lung damage reversible if exposure ceases
>20	>6 hours	Waterlogging of lung passageways and tissues, eventually leading to paralysis and/or death

This gas also causes damage to plants. Clearly some plants are more susceptible than others. In extreme cases, leaf chlorosis (whitening) and necrosis (death) are obvious. However, at lower concentrations, damage resulting in reduced growth without visible lesions may occur. Significant reductions in the productivity of permanent pasture have been reported at ambient concentrations as low as 60 ppb SO_2.

Beneficial effects of sulfur dioxide have also been noted as it can act as a plant nutrient, supplying the essential element sulfur (Chapter 5, Section 5.5). In industrialised areas this commonly obviates the need for applications of sulfate-containing fertiliser, even under intensive agricultural regimes.

The principal natural sources of sulfur dioxide are vulcanism and biological activity. The latter is mainly an indirect source, providing reduced sulfur species (particularly H_2S and $(CH_3)_2S$) which are rapidly oxidised in the air to sulfur dioxide (Chapter 5, Section 5.5). Together these sources introduce about 2.3×10^{12} mol S a^{-1} into the atmosphere and provide the background concentration of sulfur dioxide of less than 1 ppb mentioned before.

Human activity is now a major contributor to tropospheric sulfur dioxide levels. Globally, anthropogenic output of this gas accounts for about 1.6×10^{12} to 2.6×10^{12} mol S a^{-1}. This is produced mainly as the result of the burning of sulfur-containing fossil fuels, particularly coal during electricity generation. Other industrial processes, notably metal sulfide ore roasting, also make a contribution (Chapter 12, Section 12.1).

There are two principal sink mechanisms for tropospheric sulfur dioxide. These are direct deposition from the gas phase onto wet or dry surfaces (a process known as **dry deposition**) and aerial oxidation to sulfur trioxide, $SO_{3(g)}$, and/or sulfuric acid, $H_2SO_{4(aq)}$ (Box 15.1). The rates at which these processes occur vary according to the prevailing conditions. However, they tend to be rapid; typically each removes between 1 and 10% of the sulfur dioxide present per hour. Consequently, sulfur dioxide has a very short residence time in the troposphere (Table 15.1). This is also true of its oxidation products (SO_3 and H_2SO_4) as they are efficiently removed from the air during precipitation (**wet deposition**), contributing to the phenomenon of acid rain (Section 15.2.2).

The short residence time of sulfur dioxide in the troposphere ensures that anthropogenic contamination of the atmosphere with this gas does not extend above the tropopause (Chapter 4, Section 4.1). However, some sulfur dioxide does reach the stratosphere as a result of natural phenomena, namely direct injection during major volcanic activity and the photochemical oxidation *in situ* of carbonyl sulfide (OCS) of marine origin (Chapter 5, Section 5.5). Once in the stratosphere the sulfur dioxide is oxidised, forming droplets of sulfuric acid. These have been implicated in the natural process of stratospheric ozone loss (Section 15.2.4).

There is an uneven distribution of the anthropogenic emissions of sulfur dioxide. In excess of 90% of discharges originate from North America, Europe, India and the Far East. This unequal distribution, coupled with the short atmospheric residence times of this gas and its oxidation products, means that its consequences are of regional rather than global significance (Sections 15.2.1 and 15.2.2). Nonetheless, there is considerable concern about the adverse effects of this pollutant. This has found expression in legislation at national level, international agreement and recent advances in emissions control technology (Chapter 16, Section 16.1).

Also, within the last 30 years, there have been a number of other factors that have tended to curb sulfur dioxide emissions. Primary amongst these are improvements in fuel use efficiency, changes in the types of fuel being consumed, and the effects of both the oil crises of 1973 and 1979 and the decrease in the industrial output of the former eastern bloc countries evident since the late 1980s. Consequently, there has been a reduction in the rate of increase of anthropogenic sulfur dioxide emissions. Indeed, there are strong indications that the absolute levels of worldwide output have stabilised since the late 1980s. Unfortunately, this situation is unlikely to be sustained into the twenty-first century, primarily

15.1 Tropospheric oxidation of sulfur dioxide (SO_2)

Sulfur dioxide is rapidly oxidised within the troposphere to form the highly damaging secondary pollutants sulfuric acid (H_2SO_4) and/or its acid anhydride, sulfur trioxide (SO_3). The phenomenon is complex and while the details of the chemistry are still a matter of debate it is clear that three distinct groups of mechanisms are involved. One of these is a heterogeneous process (i.e. it occurs at the interface between two phases), while the other two are homogeneous, one occurring in the gas phase, the other in water droplets. The main features of each of these routes are outlined below.

Heterogeneous oxidation

As indicated, the gas phase reaction represented by Equation a is thermodynamically feasible, at least when the concentrations of SO_2 and SO_3 are high and low respectively:

$$2SO_{2(g)} + O_{2(g)} \rightarrow 2SO_{3(g)}$$
$$(\Delta G^\circ_{298} = -71\,kJ\,mol^{-1} \text{ of } SO_2) \tag{a}$$

On the addition of water, this would be followed by the hydrolysis depicted by Equation b:

$$SO_{3(g)} + H_2O_{(l)} \rightarrow H_2SO_{4(aq)} \tag{b}$$

In dry and otherwise clean air at ambient tropospheric temperatures, reaction a is very slow and does not contribute significantly to the oxidation process. However, surfaces of particulate matter such as soot or fly ash appear to catalyse this reaction. The addition of moisture that allows a film of water to form around the particles may increase the rate of reaction still further. This film will allow reaction b to occur *in situ*. More importantly, it will dissolve the sulfate formed at the solid surface, transporting it away and preventing the saturation of the catalytically active sites.

It seems probable that this route reaches its maximum significance near sources of pollution, where particulates are likely to be in high concentrations.

Gas phase homogeneous oxidation

The most significant purely gas phase pathway for the oxidation of sulfur dioxide involves the hydroxyl radical (OH) (Chapter 4, Box 4.2). The initial reaction forms the $HOSO_2$ radical, thus:

$$OH + SO_2 + M \rightarrow HOSO_2 + M \tag{c}$$

where M is a third body (e.g. a molecular or solid surface). This is needed to absorb energy given out during new bond formation, so stabilising the product.

After this, the $HOSO_2$ is further oxidised to H_2SO_4. Exactly how this occurs is still not fully understood; however, the following reactions may well be significant:

$$HOSO_2 + H_2O \rightarrow HOSO_2.H_2O \tag{d}$$
$$HOSO_2.H_2O + O_2 \rightarrow H_2SO_4 + HO_2 \tag{e}$$

Interestingly, in polluted air the HO_2 may then react with NO, regenerating OH and thereby perpetuating this process:

$$HO_2 + NO \rightarrow OH + NO_2 \tag{f}$$

Aqueous phase homogeneous oxidation

Sulfur dioxide is appreciably soluble in water. Once in the aqueous phase the following equilibria are established:

$$SO_{2(aq)} + H_2O_{(l)} \rightleftharpoons H_2SO_{3(aq)} \tag{g}$$
$$\text{(sulfurous acid)}$$

$$H_2SO_{3(aq)} \rightleftharpoons HSO_3^-{}_{(aq)} + H^+{}_{(aq)} \tag{h}$$
$$\text{(bisulfite)}$$

$$HSO_3^-{}_{(aq)} \rightleftharpoons SO_3^{2-}{}_{(aq)} + H^+{}_{(aq)} \tag{i}$$
$$\text{(sulfite)}$$

There are several tropospheric oxidants that could transform these aqueous sulfur(IV) species into sulfuric acid, at significant rates. These include ozone (O_3), hydrogen peroxide (H_2O_2) and nitrogen dioxide (NO_2). Taking hydrogen peroxide as an example, the reaction concerned may be represented as follows, using $SO_{2(aq)}$ to stand for all of the sulfur(IV) species it produces in solution:

$$H_2O_{2(aq)} + SO_{2(aq)} \rightarrow H_2SO_{4(aq)} \tag{j}$$

This process is catalysed by the presence of salts of iron and other transition metals with more than one accessible oxidation state.

The hydrogen peroxide consumed by this reaction either migrates in from the gas phase or is generated *in situ*. In either case, the most significant source of this oxidant is the disproportionation of HO_2, thus:

$$2HO_2 + M \rightarrow O_2 + H_2O_2 + M \tag{k}$$

(where M has the same meaning as in equation (c) above). Clearly, the relative importance of the above three routes will be related to the prevailing atmospheric conditions at the time of the oxidation. This relationship is complex and as yet poorly understood.

because of the probable increase in the dependence on coal as a fuel (Figures 15.1 and 15.2).

15.1.2 The oxides of nitrogen

Three of the oxides of nitrogen are significant primary pollutants. These are nitrous oxide (dinitrogen oxide, N_2O), nitric oxide (NO) and nitrogen dioxide (NO_2). The atmospheric behaviour and major sources of the first of these is somewhat different from that of the other two, hence this will be considered separately.

Nitrous oxide (N_2O) is an unreactive gas found throughout the troposphere at a level of about 0.3 ppm. This concentration is rising at about 0.25% a^{-1} (0.292 ppm

Figure 15.1 Projected worldwide trends in sources of fuel (from Wellburn, 1994; data from the World Energy Conference, Cannes, 1986).

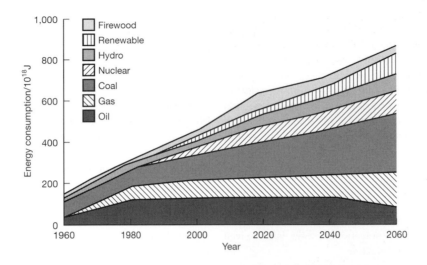

Figure 15.2 Estimated sulfur emissions for the year 2020 using assumed rates of population growth and *per capita* energy usage (from Galloway, 1989).

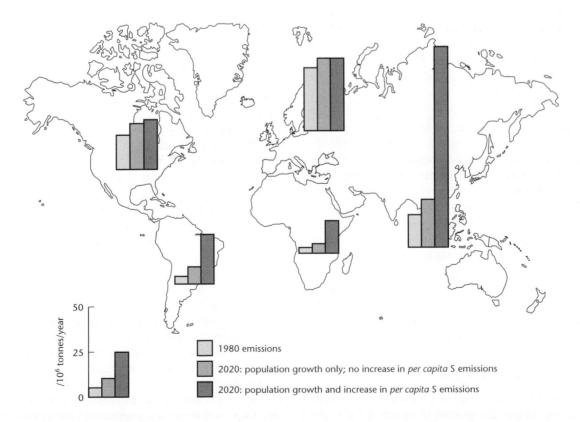

in 1961; 0.307 ppm in 1987; 0.313 ppm in 1993). The environmental consequences of this increase are not fully known. Nitrous oxide is a greenhouse gas and therefore may be contributing to global warming (Section 15.2.3). In addition, it enters the stratosphere, where it produces nitric oxide (NO) and so contributes to the mechanisms that control the concentrations of ozone (O_3) (see below and Section 15.2.4).

The main source of atmospheric nitrous oxide is probably the process of denitrification (Chapter 5, Section 5.3). This is the microbial reduction of nitrate (NO_3^-) that occurs in soils and waters with low oxygen contents. This natural phenomenon is encouraged by the use of artificial nitrogenous fertilisers, particularly if they are applied to soils that contain high concentrations of organic matter and have fluctuating levels of aeration. Similarly, the establishment of oxygen-depleted conditions in water bodies by the discharge of nutrients and/or oxygen-demanding wastes will also lead to increased rates of denitrification.

There are other sources of nitrous oxide. Relatively small amounts are generated during the burning of fossil fuels. Perhaps more importantly, it is evolved as a side product if the conversion of ammonia (NH_3) or ammonium (NH_4^+) to nitrite (NO_2^-) during the natural process of nitrification is incomplete (Chapter 5, Section 5.3). There is some evidence to suggest that this source is of considerable significance. However, this is currently a matter of debate.

The total atmospheric content of nitrous oxide is known reasonably accurately (1.1×10^{14} mol N). However, reliable assessments of the fluxes of this gas have yet to be made. This is mainly because it is difficult to establish the magnitude of oceanic denitrification. Current flux estimates are in the region of 1.1×10^{12} to 5.5×10^{12} mol N a^{-1}. This corresponds to an atmospheric residence time of about 20 to 100 years, very much longer than those of the other oxides of nitrogen (Table 15.1). This observation is in keeping with the unreactive nature of tropospheric nitrous oxide and its even global distribution.

The fact that nitrous oxide is unreactive in the troposphere means that it survives for long enough to cross the tropopause. This allows rapid stratospheric reactions to act as sinks for this gas, thus:

$$2N_2O + hv \rightarrow 2N_2 + O_2 \qquad (15.1)$$

$$N_2O + O^* \rightarrow 2NO \qquad (15.2)$$

where O^* is atomic oxygen in a highly reactive electronically excited state. This is generated as a result of the photodissociation of ozone, i.e.:

$$O_3 + hv \ (\lambda < {\sim}310\,nm) \rightarrow O^* + O_2^* \qquad (15.3)$$

The relatively long atmospheric residence time of nitrous oxide implies that the reservoir of this gas is fairly robust.

If anthropogenic additions of this gas are shown to be damaging, and control measures are introduced, they would therefore take a long time to be effective.

Nitric oxide (NO) and *nitrogen dioxide* (NO_2) are collectively referred to as NO_x. They are both highly reactive gases and therefore have extremely short tropospheric residence times (Table 15.1). As a consequence, their concentrations show great temporal and spatial variation. Levels of nitrogen dioxide vary from less than 1 ppb in remote areas to 0.5 ppm during severe periods of pollution in urban settings. Few people would be expected to show any symptomatic health changes even if exposed for short periods of time to concentrations at the higher end of this range.

While NO_x compounds are pollutants in their own right, the main problems they cause are associated with the secondary pollutants that they spawn. In the troposphere, they may be oxidised to nitric acid, a key component of acid rain (see later and Section 15.2.2). In addition, their presence is a prerequisite for the generation of photochemical smog (Section 15.2.1). Nitrogen oxides are also found in the stratosphere, partly as a result of nitrous oxide migration across the tropopause and partly from the emissions from high-flying aircraft. Once in the stratosphere, they enter into the chemistry that controls the concentration of ozone (Section 15.2.4).

The main natural sources of NO_x are biomass burning (forest fires), electrical storms, *in situ* ammonia oxidation and, in the case of nitric oxide, anaerobic soil processes. Estimates of the total flux generated vary, but are typically in the range 1.4×10^{12} to 2.7×10^{12} mol N a^{-1}. This is roughly comparable with the anthropogenic flux that results from the burning of both fossil fuels and biomass, estimated to be 2.3×10^{12} mol N a^{-1}. While there is considerable variation between countries, on a worldwide basis NO_x emissions appear to be increasing, although a peak may now have been reached.

Oxides of nitrogen form as a consequence of the high temperatures that occur during combustion. These allow the direct combination of atmospheric elemental nitrogen and oxygen, the overall reaction being:

$$N_2 + O_2 \rightarrow 2NO \qquad (15.4)$$

Additional nitric oxide may also be formed as the result of the oxidation of nitrogen compounds within the fuel. Further oxidation to nitrogen dioxide also occurs, but to a lesser degree; nitric oxide commonly accounts for in excess of 90% of the NO_x emissions from any one source.

Once within the troposphere, NO_x gases are exposed to many agents of change, the most important of which are ozone (O_3), light, hydroxyl radicals (OH), hydroperoxyl radicals (HO_2), organic molecules (including organic peroxy radicals, RO_2), moisture and particulates. Consequently, NO_x

Figure 15.3 The principal tropospheric chemical transformations of NO_x.

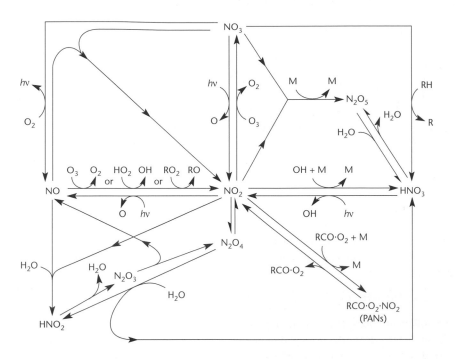

species enter into a multitude of tropospheric reactions, the more important of which are summarised in Figure 15.3. Superimposed on these chemical changes are the physical removal mechanisms of dry and wet deposition. The former of these acts as a significant sink for NO and NO_2, while the latter primarily removes PAN, HNO_3 and N_2O_5.

There is a close interplay between the levels of tropospheric ozone, and NO_x. Tropospheric ozone can oxidise nitric oxide, thus:

$$NO + O_3 \rightarrow O_2 + NO_2 \qquad (15.5)$$

This reaction is rapid. However, it does not result in the total depletion of either of the reactants.

Significantly, nitric oxide is regenerated photolytically from nitrogen dioxide:

$$NO_2 + h\nu \ (\lambda < 430\,\text{nm}) \rightarrow NO + O \qquad (15.6)$$

The oxygen atoms formed can then react with oxygen molecules, reproducing ozone:

$$O + O_2 + M \rightarrow O_3 + M \qquad (15.7)$$

where M is a third body.[2]

Reactions 15.6 and 15.7 are highly important as they are the only verified *in situ* source of tropospheric ozone (ozone also enters the troposphere by downward movement from the stratosphere).

[2] For example, M may be a molecule or solid surface. It is needed to absorb energy given out during new bond formation, so stabilising the product.

15.1.3 Hydrocarbons

As suggested by their name, hydrocarbons are compounds that contain only carbon and hydrogen. The simplest of these compounds, methane (CH_4), is best considered separately from the other hydrocarbons.

Methane

Natural sources generate a methane flux of between 6.8×10^{12} and $1.3 \times 10^{13}\,\text{mol C a}^{-1}$. This is produced almost entirely by micro-organisms under anaerobic conditions, such as those prevailing in wetlands and in the intestines of ruminant animals. Human activity produces an additional flux of between 1.9×10^{13} and $2.8 \times 10^{13}\,\text{mol C a}^{-1}$. This is primarily the result of paddy rice production, low-temperature biomass burning, cattle rearing, waste disposal and fossil fuel extraction.

There are three sinks for this methane. Some ($\simeq 5\%$) is absorbed by the soil, while a further $\simeq 7\%$ is transferred to the stratosphere, where it is oxidised. The remainder is destroyed in the troposphere primarily by the chain of reactions shown in Figure 15.4. Of major significance in this process is the attack on methane by hydroxyl radicals:

$$CH_4 + OH \rightarrow CH_3 + H_2O \qquad (15.8)$$

Human intervention may have decreased the rate at which this sink operates by depleting the air of hydroxyl radicals (OH), slowing reaction 15.8. This has happened as a

Figure 15.4 The main reactions in the day-time tropospheric oxidation of methane in the presence of NO$_x$. (Note that these reactions happen in both clean and polluted air.)

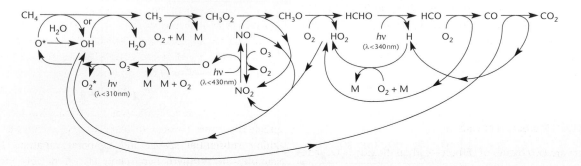

consequence of the increasing levels of tropospheric carbon monoxide (CO) (Section 15.1.4), which naturally consumes about 70% of the hydroxyl radicals via the following reaction:

$$CO + OH \rightarrow H + CO_2 \qquad (15.9)$$

Methane has a sufficiently long atmospheric residence time (about three years) to be fairly evenly distributed throughout the troposphere. Its concentration has more than doubled over the past two centuries and now stands at about 1.7 ppm (Figure 15.5(a)). Whilst the levels of this gas continue to rise (average global concentrations rose by 6% between 1984 and 1994), there is evidence of a slowdown in the rate of increase (Figure 15.5(b)).

Methane is a greenhouse gas (Chapter 4, Section 4.1) and hence may be contributing to global warming (Section 15.2.3). If this were to become established, a methane-related positive feedback mechanism may ensue. Vast quantities of this gas are trapped in ice as a clathrate compound (CH$_4$.nH$_2$O, where $n \sim 6$). Should the ice melt, this methane would enter the lower atmosphere, increasing the greenhouse effect.

Non-methane hydrocarbons (NMHCs)

As a result of several studies, in excess of 600 different airborne hydrocarbons have been identified. These include reactive materials such as isoprene and α-pinene that are released in substantial amounts by biological processes. Human activities, particularly those associated with transport and those requiring the use of organic solvents, make significant additions to the background biogenic levels of NMHCs. Anthropogenic compounds released include benzene, butanes, ethane, ethyne, hexanes, pentanes, propane and toluene. Contamination with man-made NMHCs is most acute north of 30°N.

Figure 15.5 Trends in the atmospheric concentration of methane as observed (a) over the past few hundred years (from about 1600 to 1995) (after Houghton, 1997, after Watson *et al.*, 1990) and (b) over a much smaller time-span (1983–94) (after Houghton *et al.*, 1996). Note that the lines that cross on the older data points in diagram (a) are error bars – these indicate the range of uncertainty in the data, in terms of both the date of the sample and the concentration of methane in the atmosphere that it represents.

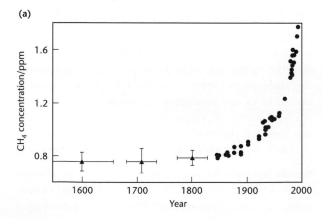

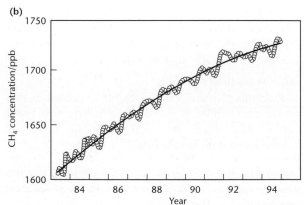

NMHCs are greenhouse gases and may therefore be implicated in global warming. Perhaps more significantly, NMHCs are oxidised in a similar way to methane within the troposphere (Figure 15.4), yielding a huge number of secondary pollutants. By this means, anthropogenic higher hydrocarbons and partially oxidised organics, such as aldehydes, play an important role in the generation of photochemical smogs (Section 15.2.1).

15.1.4 The oxides of carbon

There are two oxides of carbon – carbon dioxide (CO_2) and carbon monoxide (CO). Let us consider these in turn.

Carbon dioxide is present in the troposphere at a concentration of about 360 ppm (1997 data). Currently, this is increasing at a rate of around $0.4\%\,a^{-1}$ (Chapter 5, Figure 5.7). This is a cause for concern as carbon dioxide is a major greenhouse gas, and hence may be a contributor to global warming (Section 15.2.3).

The main sources of atmospheric carbon dioxide are respiration, oxidative decay, combustion and outgassing from the oceans. Its sinks are photosynthesis and dissolution in sea water (Chapter 5, Section 5.2). The inward and outward fluxes that these processes generate are clearly out of balance, though they are both in the region of $1.9 \times 10^{16}\,mol\,C\,a^{-1}$.

Human activity has enhanced the sources of this gas by the burning of fossil fuels and biomass (particularly during forest clearance). Estimates of these anthropogenic fluxes vary, though they are probably in the region of 4×10^{14} and $1.7 \times 10^{14}\,mol\,C\,a^{-1}$ respectively. It is possible that deforestation has also caused a significant decline in the photosynthetic sink.

The interplay between global temperatures and atmospheric carbon dioxide levels is both subtle and complex. If global warming were to become established, then both positive and negative feedback mechanisms would occur. For example, increased temperatures would cause a decrease in the solubility of carbon dioxide in water. The flux of this gas out of the oceans may thereby be increased, introducing positive feedback. On the other hand, at elevated temperatures and carbon dioxide levels photosynthesis rates may increase, removing carbon dioxide, producing negative feedback.

Carbon monoxide is generated biologically (both on land and within the oceans). It is also produced as a consequence of the atmospheric oxidation of hydrocarbons (Figure 15.4) and during the incomplete combustion of fossil fuels and biomass. Natural fluxes of this gas total about $1.8 \times 10^{13}\,mol\,C\,a^{-1}$. These are exceeded by anthropogenic emissions, which currently amount to approximately $2.7 \times 10^{13}\,mol\,C\,a^{-1}$ but are rising.

The main sinks for tropospheric carbon monoxide are transfer to the stratosphere (followed by oxidation), absorption by soil and plants and tropospheric oxidation by hydroxyl radicals. The last of these is of considerable importance as it is the major sink for these radicals: in unpolluted air, approximately 70% of OH reacts with CO, the bulk of the remainder reacting with CH_4 (Figure 15.4). The overall reaction may be represented thus:

$$OH + CO \rightarrow H + CO_2 \tag{15.10}$$

The atmospheric residence time of carbon monoxide is sufficiently short ($\sim 0.4\,a$) to allow its concentrations to exhibit substantial spatial and temporal variation. For example, the northern hemisphere is considerably more contaminated with this gas than is the southern hemisphere (Figure 15.6).

Background levels of carbon monoxide are less than 0.1 ppm. These may rise to 2–20 ppm in urban locations. More exceptionally, concentrations in excess of 100 ppm can occur in areas, such as tunnels, where road traffic and restricted air movement combine.

There are several environmental concerns associated with elevated levels of carbon monoxide. At its higher ambient concentrations, direct effects on health may be expected. Under these conditions, significant amounts of carbon monoxide combine with the blood's oxygen carrier, haemoglobin (Hb):

$$HbO_2 + CO \rightleftharpoons O_2 + HbCO \tag{15.11}$$

oxygenated   carboxyhaemoglobin
haemoglobin

This can result in an insufficient oxygen supply to vital organs, causing a decrease in behavioural effectiveness. This has been implicated in an increase in the incidence of road traffic accidents in highly polluted areas.

Figure **15.6** Latitudinal variation in carbon monoxide concentrations (from Heidt *et al.*, 1980). ITCZ = intertropical convergence zone (Chapter 4, Section 4.2.2). The boundary layer is that part of the troposphere that has its motion strongly influenced by the characteristics of the Earth's surface; this is usually taken to be the lowest 1 km of the atmosphere.

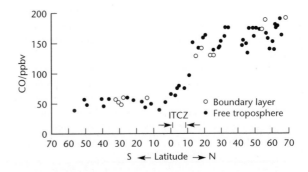

Perhaps of greater concern than these acute effects are the indirect impacts of this pollutant. Elevated emissions of carbon monoxide are likely to reduce tropospheric concentrations of the hydroxyl radical, by virtue of reaction 15.10. This, in turn, will reduce the removal rates of many other pollutants as reaction with this radical is often a major sink for these contaminants.

What is more, carbon monoxide may be a contributor to global warming as both it, and the carbon dioxide to which it is oxidised, are greenhouse gases.

15.1.5 Halogenated hydrocarbons

Structurally, halogenated hydrocarbons are generated when one or more of the hydrogen atoms of a hydrocarbon are replaced by atoms of a halogen (F, Cl, Br, I). Many of these compounds are of environmental importance; the more prominent of these are discussed below.

Chlorofluorocarbons (CFCs), as their name suggests, are compounds of carbon, chlorine and fluorine; they may also contain hydrogen. They have no natural sources and were entirely absent from the atmosphere until the 1930s, when they were introduced in the USA as a refrigerant by Du Pont and General Motors Corporation, working in collaboration.

The two most abundant compounds in this class are CFC-11 (CCl_3F) and CFC-12 (CCl_2F_2) (Box 15.2). Atmospheric concentrations of these gases are currently 0.261 ppb and 0.522 ppb respectively (1996 data). These compounds are inert, non-toxic, non-flammable and odourless, making them ideal for many industrial applications. For example, CFC-12 is a gas at room temperature (b.p. $-30°C$ at 1 atmosphere pressure) but is readily liquefied on compression, making it an optimal working fluid for refrigerators.

It was the introduction of CFCs that allowed refrigerators to become a domestic commodity. Prior to this, these machines used highly noxious working fluids (sulfur dioxide or ammonia) and were therefore only used in commercial or industrial installations. After their introduction as refrigerants, CFCs found additional applications. In particular, they were widely used as solvents, as blowing agents in the manufacture of foamed plastics and as propellants in aerosol sprays.

In view of their utility, it is not surprising that total global production of CFCs (mainly CFC-11 and CFC-12) showed a sharp upward trend between 1960 and the mid-1970s (Figure 15.7). The plateau in production that then lasted until 1982 was caused by nationally enforced restrictions on the use of these materials in aerosol sprays and the effects of economic recession. Economic recovery caused a resumption in the upward trend until a peak was reached in 1988. Since then, there has been a sustained and dramatic decline that is almost wholly attributable to the implementation of the Montreal Protocol and its revisions (Box 15.3). This effect of the Montreal Protocol has been echoed in a decline in the rate of the increase of the atmospheric concentrations of

---

Tool Box

15.2 Chlorofluorocarbon, hydrochlorofluorocarbon, hydrofluorocarbon and halon nomenclature

Chlorofluorocarbons (CFCs) are compounds of carbon, chlorine and fluorine. They may also contain hydrogen, though those that do so are usually referred to as hydrochlorofluorocarbons (HCFCs). Hydrofluorocarbons (HFCs) contain carbon, hydrogen and fluorine. Halons are brominated analogues of CFCs.

In order to find the composition of a CFC, HCFC or HFC, add 90 to the numerical part of its symbol. The three digits of the resulting number stand for the numbers of carbon, hydrogen and fluorine atoms in the molecule respectively. In the case of CFCs and HCFCs, there are remaining atoms; these are chlorine.

For example, consider CFC-11: $11 + 90 = 101$, therefore there are 1 carbon, 0 hydrogen and 1 fluorine atoms present. So far, the carbon atom has only one of its four valencies satisfied (by the fluorine). Consequently, CFC-11 must also contain three chlorine atoms. CFC-11 therefore has the formula CCl_3F.

HCFC-123 (also occasionally referred to as CFC-123) has two carbon, one hydrogen and three fluorine atoms in each of its molecules, as indicated by $123 + 90 = 213$. The two carbon atoms each have a valency of four. These are bonded together by a single bond, satisfying one of the valencies of each of the carbon atoms. The hydrogen and three fluorine atoms satisfy four of the remaining valencies, leaving two to be taken up by chlorine atoms. Its formula is therefore $C_2HF_3Cl_2$ or, as it is more commonly written, CF_3CHCl_2.

Lastly, in the case of HFC-32, adding 90 to the numerical part of this symbol gives 122. Therefore, this compound has one carbon, two hydrogen and two fluorine atoms in each of its molecules and its formula is CH_2F_2.

While there are other systems, halons are frequently given a four-digit code, prefixed by H for halon, e.g. H1211. The digits simply stand for the number of carbon, fluorine, chlorine and bromine atoms in the molecule (CF_2ClBr in this case).

Figure 15.7 Estimates of global CFC production for the period 1950–95 (source of raw data: Brown, Flavin and Kane, 1996).

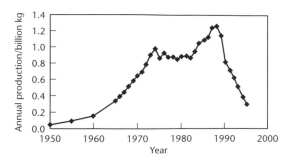

by photolysis. This reaction may be represented thus (using CFC-12 as an example):

$$CF_2Cl_2 + h\nu \ (\lambda < 250\,nm) \rightarrow CF_2Cl + Cl \qquad (15.12)$$

The chlorine atoms released then enter into catalytic cycles, destroying some of the ozone that shields the biosphere from harmful ultraviolet light (Section 15.2.4).

Hydrochlorofluorocarbons (HCFCs) and hydrofluorocarbons (HFCs). The phasing out of CFCs has led to the development and widespread introduction of alternative working practices and replacement chemicals. Amongst the substances used to replace CFCs are the HCFCs (as an

these species (Figure 15.8). Throughout the 1980s, this rate was about 5% a^{-1} but it dropped rapidly from the start of the 1990s. By 1996, it had reached zero in the case of CFC-11 and 0.6% a^{-1} in the case of CFC-12.

As a consequence of their unreactivity, the vast bulk of CFCs are not chemically altered during use and are therefore eventually released into the atmosphere. Nor are they destroyed by tropospheric reactions. Hence, they have extremely long atmospheric lifetimes (measured in tens or even hundreds of years). These gases therefore are evenly distributed throughout the troposphere and, more importantly, they pass across the tropopause into the stratosphere.

Once within the stratosphere CFCs are slowly degraded

Figure 15.8 Atmospheric concentrations of CFC-11 and CFC-12 (source: World Resources, *1998–99*).

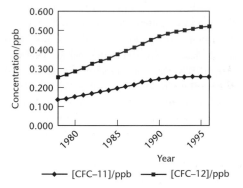

Further Information Box

15.3   The Montreal Protocol on substances that deplete the ozone layer, and its Amendments and Adjustments

The Montreal Protocol is an international agreement that was signed in 1987 and came into force in January 1989. Its main provisions were as follows. There was to be a freezing of consumption and production of CFCs 11, 12, 113, 114 and 115 and halons 1211, 1301 and 2402 at 1986 levels. This was to be achieved in 1990 in the case of the CFCs and by 2005 in the case of the halons. A commitment was also made to a reduction in the levels of CFC production and consumption to 80% of 1986 levels by 1993 and to 50% by 2000. Signatories from the developing countries had a 10-year exclusionary period.

Since then, the original protocol has been strengthened by a series of Amendments and Adjustments (The London Amendment (1990), The Copenhagen Amendment (1992), The Vienna Adjustments (1995) and The Montreal Amendment (1997)). Importantly, under the terms of the amended protocol, developed nations were obliged to have phased out the use of

CFCs in nearly all of their applications by 1996. Developing nations are to take the same action by 2010, having frozen consumption levels in 1999 at 1995–97 levels. Also, industrialised nations are to phase out the use of halons by 1994, methyl bromide by 2010 and HCFCs (except for the maintenance of existing plant) by 2020. Developing countries have until 2040 to stop using HCFCs.

There have been some difficulties with the implementation of the agreements reached. In particular, the recent economic problems experienced by many former eastern bloc countries have led a number of them, including Russia and Poland, to apply for an extension to their deadline for the phasing out of ozone-depleting substances. Also, there is evidence that a black-market in smuggled CFCs has developed. However, as exemplified by the data for CFC production presented in Figure 15.7, the Protocol has been highly successful in arresting the manufacture and use of ozone-depleting substances.

interim measure) and HFCs (as a longer-term solution) (Box 15.2). Both of these classes of compound are broken down in the atmosphere much more rapidly than CFCs. Consequently, their build-up in the atmosphere, for a given rate of production, will be lower than for CFCs. Nonetheless, they are potentially damaging to the environment.

Like CFCs, HCFCs contain chlorine. If present in the stratosphere they too can photolyse, liberating chlorine atoms and thereby facilitating stratospheric ozone depletion. However, unlike CFCs, HCFCs are broken down in the troposphere. Consequently, not all of the HCFC emitted at ground level will reach the stratosphere and therefore, on a kilogram for kilogram basis, HCFCs have a lower ozone depletion potential than CFCs. Unsurprisingly, atmospheric concentrations of HCFCs are rising. For example, the mean global concentration of HCFC-22 in 1994 was approximately 0.11 ppb but was increasing at a rate of about 5% per year.

HFCs contain no chlorine and do not have the potential to destroy stratospheric ozone. However, like CFCs and HCFCs they are greenhouse gases and may therefore contribute to global warming (Section 15.2.3).

Chlorinated hydrocarbons that do not contain fluorine also undergo photolysis in the stratosphere, liberating chlorine atoms. For this reason, there is concern about anthropogenic emissions of compounds such as carbon tetrachloride (CCl_4) and 1,1,1-trichloroethane (CCl_3CH_3, methyl chloroform).

Anthropogenic emissions of *halons* (brominated CFC analogues, Box 15.2) and *brominated hydrocarbons* are of significance. Halons are used as fire extinguishers, and like CFCs have no natural sources. In contrast, the main brominated hydrocarbon, bromomethane (CH_3Br), is mostly of natural origin, although it is used as a fumigant. As might be expected, these compounds release bromine atoms when photolysed in the stratosphere. These atoms synergistically enhance the rate of chlorine-induced ozone depletion. Rate increases of up to 20% are to be expected at a bromine concentration of 0.02 ppb. In addition, on a mole for mole basis, bromine is more catalytically efficient than chlorine. Fortunately, the concentrations of these gases are low, though rising fast in the first half of the 1990s. The concentrations of $CBrClF_2$, $CBrF_3$ and CH_3Br were 2×10^{-3} ppb (rising at 5–10% a^{-1}) (1993 data), 3×10^{-3} ppb (rising at 7% a^{-1}) (1993 data) and about 0.013 ppb (rising at 12 or 15% a^{-1}) (1992 data) respectively.

Concern about the potentially damaging implications of stratospheric ozone depletion has been sufficient to lead governments to act. Both national legislation and international agreements, most notably the Montreal Protocol (Box 15.3), are in place that aim to eliminate or severely limit the production and uses of CFCs and related materials.

Unfortunately, because of the exceedingly slow rate at which these compounds are removed from the atmosphere, curbs on their production will take a very long time to be fully effective. Even if all nations conform to the requirements of the Copenhagen Amendment to the Montreal Protocol (Box 15.3), it is estimated that full recovery of the ozone layer will not occur until approximately 2050.

Perfluorocarbons (e.g. CF_4, C_2F_6) are liberated by some industrial processes. These are of concern as they are greenhouse gases and may therefore be contributing to global warming. Furthermore, they have extremely long residence times in the atmosphere because they are chemically inert and do not photolyse even in the stratosphere.

15.1.6 Suspended particulates (aerosols) in the troposphere

A suspension of solid or liquid particles within the air is called an **aerosol**. Aerosols are generated by many natural processes including the aerial entrainment of soil, sea spray, pollen and spores by wind, volcanic activity and the burning of biomass. With the exception of the last on this list, these sources generate mainly coarse particles (i.e. with diameters of about 2.5 μm or more). These tend to be rapidly returned to the Earth's surface by sedimentation (i.e. falling) or washout (i.e. removal below clouds by rain, snow, etc.).

Human activity can increase the fluxes from some of these natural sources. For example, poor agricultural practices can lead to large-scale loss of soil by wind erosion (Chapter 11, Section 11.5.3). There are also purely anthropogenic sources of suspended particulates. Particularly important in this regard is the burning of fossil fuels and biomass. Particulates generated by combustion are mainly fine (diameters $<\sim$2.5 μm). These settle much more slowly than the coarse particulates and therefore tend to reside in the atmosphere for longer. In general, they are removed by wet deposition or, if brought into contact with surfaces by air movement, dry deposition. Aerosols can also form *in situ* within the atmosphere. For example, the aerial oxidation of sulfur dioxide produces significant quantities of sulfate particles.

There is little doubt that the twentieth century has seen an increase in the aerosol burden of the atmosphere. Evidence for this comes from several sources. For example, dust-fall onto mountain snow fields in the former USSR has increased sharply since the 1930s. In addition, turbidity measurements made over Washington, DC, USA and Davos, Switzerland have shown a marked increase (57% from 1905 to 1964 and 85% from 1920 to 1958 respectively). However, there are suggestions that, on a global basis, anthropogenic fluxes of suspended particulate matter are now being reduced. Estimated emissions have fallen from over $6.0 \times 10^{13}\,\mathrm{g\,a^{-1}}$ in 1970 to $5.7 \times 10^{13}\,\mathrm{g\,a^{-1}}$ in 1990.

Typically, urban air contains $30\text{--}40\,\mu\mathrm{m}^3\,\mathrm{cm}^{-3}$ of fine particulates and about $25\,\mu\mathrm{m}^3\,\mathrm{cm}^{-3}$ of coarse particulates. In remote continental areas these figures drop to levels at or below $2\,\mu\mathrm{m}^3\,\mathrm{cm}^{-3}$ and $5\,\mu\mathrm{m}^{-3}\,\mathrm{cm}^{-3}$ respectively (1980 data).

Elevated levels of suspended solids have chemical and physical implications. The large surface areas offered by these particles can lead to enhanced rates of chemical reaction such as the oxidation of sulfur dioxide to sulfur trioxide or sulfate (Box 15.1). Particulates also scatter or, in the case of soot, absorb light, and therefore have a complex impact on climate. Overall, the effect of anthropogenic aerosols (especially sulfate aerosols and, to a lesser extent, particulates from biomass burning) is to scatter sunlight back into space, therefore causing cooling. In addition to this direct effect, the sulfate aerosol also indirectly brings about cooling. This occurs when cloud forms in air that is contaminated with this type of particulate material. Such cloud is made up of smaller drops than normal and is therefore more effective at scattering sunlight into space than ordinary cloud. It should be borne in mind that, while these cooling effects are significant, they do not fully compensate for the warming effect that anthropogenic greenhouse gases are believed to be producing (Section 15.2.3). Furthermore, this cooling is less evenly distributed than the warming caused by greenhouse gases. This is because, unlike the main greenhouse gases, sulfate particles reside in the atmosphere for a short time (an average of about five days only). Consequently, sulfate-induced cooling is much more intense over the industrialised centres of the northern hemisphere (especially eastern USA, Europe and the Far East), where the parent sulfur dioxide is emitted in larger amounts than elsewhere on the globe. Natural aerosols can also have a cooling effect. Occasionally, large volcanic eruptions inject substantial amounts of particles into the stratosphere. While this produces a significant net cooling, the effect is transient, lasting for a few years only.

The presence of anthropogenic particulates in the troposphere has several undesirable effects on health. Long-term exposure to fine suspended solids is linked to lung diseases such as emphysema in smokers and silicosis in miners. In recent years, considerable concern has been raised over the damaging effects of the PM_{10} particles (i.e. those with diameters $\leqslant 10\,\mu\mathrm{m}$) that are found in urban air largely as a consequence of their emission from diesel road vehicles. Exposure to these particles has been linked to

deaths from both lung and heart disease. While the mechanism of their action is not fully established, it is known that they are small enough to pass deep into the lungs. Once within the lungs, they may cause irritation, changing the body's chemistry and thereby increasing the likelihood of blood clot formation and/or changes to the heart's blood vessels. Fuel smoke particulates are known to increase the health effects of other pollutants, notably sulfur dioxide in smogs (Section 15.2.1). Some particulates carry specific toxicants. Of particular importance in this regard are soot and lead compounds, which are considered below.

Soot

This is the black particulate material that is formed when either fossil fuels or biomass are incompletely burnt. It is an impure form of elemental carbon associated with which are many organic compounds. Included in these are the multi-ringed compounds known as polycyclic aromatic hydrocarbons (PAHs), of which pyrene and benzo(a)pyrene are typical examples (Figure 15.9). These are of importance because some of them are known carcinogens (i.e. can induce cancer). This property is most pronounced among the PAHs with higher molecular weights.

The yield of soot depends on both the fuel and the mode of combustion. For example, spark-ignition (Otto) engines produce about 0.1 g of elemental C per kg of fuel. Very much more is produced by compression-ignition (Diesel) engines (3 g C per kg of fuel). Diesel-engined vehicles are likely to become more popular because they are more fuel-efficient than their Otto-engined counterparts (Chapter 13, Section 13.2.2). Consequently, soot from motor vehicle emissions may become an increasing problem in the future.

Lead compounds

In excess of 90% of the lead in the atmosphere is of anthropogenic origin (1985 data). This contamination is extremely widespread as evidenced by the sudden dramatic increase in the lead levels of Greenland snow during the latter part of the twentieth century (Figure 15.10). However, it is a particular problem in urban areas

Figure 15.9 The structures of (a) pyrene and (b) benzo(a)pyrene.

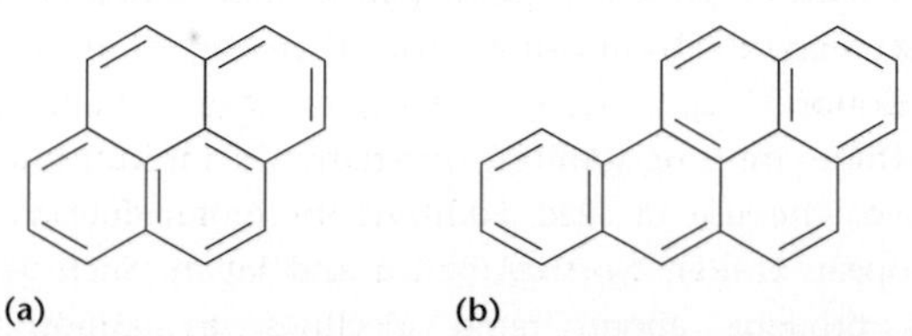

(a)   (b)

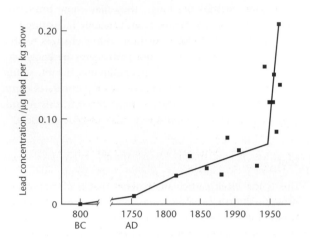

Figure 15.10 Trends in the levels of lead in Greenland snow (from Bunce, 1990, after Nriagu, 1978).

and next to main roads, where lead-containing particulates from vehicle exhausts are found in greatest concentrations.

Tetraalkyl lead compounds, especially $Pb(C_2H_5)_4$, are added to Otto engine fuels as an inexpensive means of increasing their octane ratings (Chapter 13, Section 13.2.2). In order to stop the build-up of lead residues within engines, dibromoethane and dichloroethane are also added to leaded fuel. These allow the relatively volatile compounds $PbBr_2$, $PbBrCl$ and $PbCl_2$ to be eliminated with the exhaust gases. These compounds form into particles, about one-half of which (by mass) are coarse (mass median diameter $> 5\,\mu m$) and one-third are very small (mass median diameter $< 0.5\,\mu m$). Typically, the coarse particles are deposited not far from their source. However, the finer particles remain in the atmosphere for long periods of time and may be transported great distances.

Concern has grown about the implications of leaded fuel since the 1970s; this stems from two phenomena. Firstly, lead rapidly incapacitates ('poisons') the catalytic systems fitted to vehicles in order to reduce their emissions of carbon monoxide, hydrocarbons and NO_x (Chapter 16, Section 16.1). Secondly, lead in humans acts as a cumulative poison that even at low levels may induce hyperactivity and mental retardation. Lead-containing particulates represent a significant source of this toxicant as it is absorbed following either their ingestion or their inhalation.

There are long-standing programmes for the phasing out of the use of lead additives in motor fuel in the European Union, North America and Japan. Such action has brought about rapid declines in atmospheric

concentrations of this metal. For example, in the United States the ambient lead levels measured at 189 sites declined by 87% between 1980 and 1989. What is more, there is evidence from remote regions of the world, including Antarctica, of a global decline in the levels of atmospheric lead pollution.

15.2 The impact of combinations of atmospheric pollutants

15.2.1 Smog

London-type smogs

From 5 to 10 December 1952 a combination of smoke and fog (**smog**) enveloped London. These conditions persisted because the air over the capital was virtually stationary throughout this period, trapping the pollution from the smoke of numerous coal fires close to the ground.

The lack of movement was initiated by night-time radiative cooling of the air near the Earth's surface. This caused stability because cold, dense air lay below relatively warm air – a situation known as a **temperature inversion**. The night-time cooling also decreased the moisture-carrying capacity of the air, allowing fog to form around suspended smoke particles.

There is nothing particularly unusual about this situation. Temperature inversions are common on winter nights and they frequently allow fog to form. Under normal conditions, the morning sunlight rapidly evaporates any fog and warms the ground. This then heats the air above it, breaking the inversion and allowing the air to circulate. However, unlike normal fog, the smog of December 1952 was too dense to be evaporated and the inversion, once initiated, persisted into the day to be reinforced the following night. The smog was eventually dispersed by a westerly wind that blew it into the North Sea.

At the time, smogs of this type were neither rare nor confined to London. All industrialised centres in which large amounts of coal were burnt were similarly afflicted during the nineteenth and early twentieth centuries. However, the London smog of 1952 was unusually severe. Moreover, it allowed, for the first time, an unequivocal link to be made between smog and heightened death rates (Figure 15.11). The concern that this caused moved the government to pass the 1956 Clean Air Act. This empowered local councils to establish 'smokeless zones', within which smoke-producing coal could not be burnt. These measures, together with the contemporary fashionable drift away from coal as a domestic fuel,

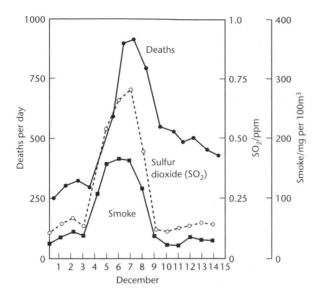

Figure 15.11 Death rates and atmospheric pollution during the London smog of 1952 (from Wilkins, 1954).

combined to remove this severe form of pollution. The last major smog in London occurred in December 1962. Further air pollution abatement legislation followed, notably the 1968 Clean Air Act. Smogs of this type are now largely restricted to parts of the developing world.

As indicated by Figure 15.11, the primary pollutants linked to deaths in London-type smogs are sulfur dioxide and smoke particulates, both formed when coal is burnt as a domestic fuel. These pollutants are respiratory irritants. What is more, when they are present together the impact of each is heightened; that is, they behave **synergistically**. There appear to be two mechanisms by which this synergism operates. Firstly, sulfur dioxide slows down the rate at which the hairs (cilia) within the lungs beat. It is this beating action that removes contaminants from the upper lungs. Impairment of this function therefore allows other irritants, such as smoke particulates, greater access to the respiratory tract. Secondly, the soot particles within the smoke offer surfaces upon which the sulfur dioxide may be oxidised to sulfuric acid, a very powerful respiratory irritant (Box 15.1). While the pH of the 1952 smog was not measured, it was probably about 1.6, much lower than vinegar (pH = 3) or lemon juice (pH = 2.2). In effect, London-type smogs are extreme examples of acid rain (Section 15.2.2).

The irritant nature of smog causes the bronchial passages within the lungs to become inflamed and to make mucus in large amounts. This prompts coughing and makes breathing difficult, particularly in individuals prone to respiratory problems. Consequently, it was primarily the

elderly who died during London's smogs, either by choking or of heart attacks brought on by the fight for breath.

Los Angeles-type smogs

There is a very different type of smog that plagues many large cities in the lower latitudes. Currently the worst afflicted are Mexico City and Baghdad, although these smogs are still called Los Angeles-type smogs[3] after the city where they were first a problem. Unlike London-type smogs, these do not form on cold winter nights in the presence of coal smoke but on warm, sunny days when traffic is busy. The main primary pollutants involved are the NO_x (chiefly NO), and unburnt hydrocarbons emitted from motor vehicles. Figure 15.12 shows how the concentrations of these pollutants and their major reaction products vary during a typical smoggy day.

As might be expected, the primary pollutants reach maximal concentrations during the morning and evening rush hours. However, the smog is at its height in the early afternoon (Plate 23). This points to secondary pollutants being the more significant active agents. What is more,

Figure 15.12 Typical daily variations in the concentrations of the major primary and secondary pollutants in Los Angeles-type smogs.

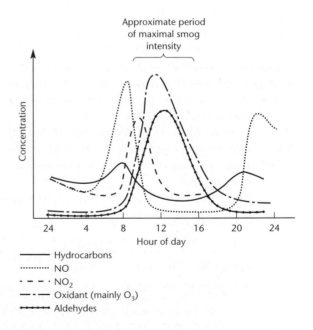

——— Hydrocarbons
··········· NO
– – – NO₂
—·—· Oxidant (mainly O_3)
——•—— Aldehydes

[3] In order to be able to differentiate between the two types of smog, those based on coal smoke are called **London-type, sulfurous** or **classical smogs**, the others being known as **Los Angeles-type smogs** or, for reasons that will become apparent, **photochemical smogs**.

there is no corresponding night-time peak in smog intensity, implicating photochemical reactions in smog generation.

The processes that occur in photochemical smogs are essentially no different from those that happen in clean air. The key to smog formation is the oxidation of the unburnt hydrocarbons, initiated by hydroxyl free radicals and maintained by photochemical reactions. This proceeds in much the same manner as the oxidation of methane in unpolluted air (Figure 15.4). Note that during this process nitric oxide (NO) is converted to nitrogen dioxide (NO_2), thus:

$$NO + RCH_2O_2 \rightarrow RCH_2O + NO_2 \qquad (15.13)$$

where $R = H$ (in the case of methane), or CH_3, CH_2CH_3, etc.

This is important because, as previously mentioned (page 337), nitrogen dioxide undergoes photolysis, yielding atomic oxygen which combines with molecular oxygen to generate ozone:

$$NO_2 + h\nu \; (\lambda < 430\,nm) \rightarrow NO + O \qquad (15.6)$$

$$O + O_2 + M \rightarrow O_3 + M \qquad (15.7)$$

It is this process that causes the increase in the concentration of tropospheric ozone that is observed on smoggy days (Figure 15.12).

Note, however, that ozone concentrations do not rise appreciably until virtually all of the nitric oxide has been consumed. This is because the following reaction is rapid:

$$NO + O_3 \rightarrow O_2 + NO_2 \qquad (15.5)$$

Paradoxically, then, in highly polluted environments, reduction in the concentration of one of the primary pollutants (NO) may worsen the smog by allowing higher concentrations of ozone to develop.

Examination of Figure 15.12 reveals that the rise in ozone concentrations is rapidly followed by a fall in the levels of nitrogen dioxide. This is primarily a consequence of the following sequence:

$$
\begin{array}{c}
\overset{h\nu}{\underset{(\lambda < 320\,nm)}{}} \quad O_2^* \qquad H_2O \\
O_3 \longrightarrow O^* \longrightarrow 2OH \\
2NO_2 + M \qquad M \\
\longrightarrow 2HNO_3 \\
\text{nitric} \\
\text{acid}
\end{array}
\qquad (15.14)
$$

Some of the nitric acid formed may undergo photolysis, regenerating NO_2 and OH. However, a significant amount is continuously removed from the atmosphere by adsorption onto particles and surfaces or by the process of wet deposition.

The organic product of reaction 15.13 may be converted to an aldehyde, thus:

$$RCH_2O + O_2 \rightarrow RCHO + HO_2 \qquad (15.15)$$

This in part accounts for the build-up of these compounds during smog formation (Figure 15.12). Aldehydes (together with ketones) are also generated as a consequence of the very rapid reaction between hydroxyl radicals and unsaturated hydrocarbons. Furthermore, they are introduced as primary pollutants for they are products of the incomplete combustion of petroleum fuels.

There are two significant ways in which aldehydes contribute to the further development of photochemical smog.

Firstly, these compounds are precursors in the production of peroxyacyl nitrates (PANs,[4] $RCO.O_2.NO_2$). Their formation may be represented thus:

$$
\begin{array}{c}
OH \qquad H_2O \qquad\qquad O_2 \\
RCHO \underset{h\nu}{\overset{\text{or}}{\longrightarrow}} RCO \longrightarrow \\
\qquad\qquad\qquad H \quad \text{acyl} \\
\qquad\qquad\qquad\quad \text{radical} \\
NO_2 + M \qquad M \\
RCO.O_2 \longrightarrow RCO.O_2.NO_2 \\
\text{peroxyacyl} \\
\text{radical}
\end{array}
\qquad (15.16)
$$

Secondly, low molecular weight compounds of this class (particularly formaldehyde (methanal), HCHO) may undergo photolysis followed by oxidation, forming CO and hydroperoxyl radicals (HO_2) (Figure 15.4). These radicals may then be reduced to regenerate hydroxyl radicals which, in turn, can initiate the attack on further hydrocarbon molecules. The introduction of extra aldehyde by inefficient catalytic converters fitted to the exhaust systems of motor vehicles may therefore inadvertently *increase* the rate of production of photochemical smog.

There are other sources of hydroxyl radicals of significance, notably:

$$O^* + CH_4 \rightarrow CH_3 + OH \qquad (15.17)$$

$$O^* + H_2O \rightarrow 2OH \qquad (15.18)$$

and

$$
\begin{array}{c}
NO + NO_2 + H_2O \longrightarrow 2HNO_2 \\
\text{nitrous} \\
\text{acid} \\
\overset{h\nu}{\underset{(\lambda < 400\,nm)}{}} \\
\longrightarrow 2OH + 2NO
\end{array}
\qquad (15.19)
$$

[4] In this text, PAN is used to represent peroxyacetyl nitrate ($CH_3CO.O_2.NO_2$) in particular, while PANs stands for peroxyacyl nitrates in general.

In generating OH, all of these help to maintain the conditions required for the aerial oxidation of hydrocarbons by reactions analogous to those shown in Figure 15.4, perpetuating the smog.

Photochemical smogs are characterised by the presence of a clearly visible aerosol that is coloured brown-yellow by the presence of nitrogen dioxide (Plate 23). Both inorganic and organic particulates are present within this, typically in roughly equal amounts (by mass) during heavy pollution.

The inorganic fraction contains ammonium (NH_4^+), nitrate (NO_3^-) and sulfate (SO_4^{2-}) ions. The first of these is generated by the protonation of atmospheric ammonia, $NH_{3(g)}$. This gas is either of biogenic origin (formed during the breakdown of animal waste) or present as the result of accidental release during the production of artificial fertilisers. Nitrate ions are produced, in the form of nitric acid (HNO_3), by the oxidation of NO_x (Equation 15.14 and Figure 15.3). Similarly, the sulfur dioxide emitted during the burning of sulfur-containing fuels is rapidly oxidised to sulfuric acid (H_2SO_4), the source of the sulfate ions (Box 15.1). The generation of considerable amounts of strong acids (mainly HNO_3, and some H_2SO_4) within photochemical smogs means that they are a significant source of acid rain (Section 15.2.2).

The organic component of the aerosol is formed, to a large part, of partially oxidised species such as alcohols, aldehydes, ketones, esters, peroxides and carboxylic acids. These have lower vapour pressures than the primary pollutant hydrocarbons from which they were derived. Consequently, they form microscopic liquid droplets within the air.

The main unwelcome aspects of photochemical smogs are ozone, PANs, NO_2 and the aerosol. Synergism between these pollutants has been observed, increasing their potency.

Effects on health primarily centre around respiratory tract and eye irritation, the main culprits for which are ozone (a respiratory irritant) and the PANs (respiratory irritants, and **lachrymators**, i.e. tear inducers). The concentrations of both of these pollutants are highly inflated in smogs (100–500 ppb O_3 and 20–70 ppb PAN) when compared with the ground level concentrations found in remote areas (<50 ppb O_3 and <0.05 ppb PAN). Respiratory impairment is measurable, although very mild at the lower end of the range of ozone concentrations found in smogs.

Plants are *extremely* sensitive to both PANs and ozone. A concentration of 100 ppb O_3 is sufficient to cut the rate of photosynthesis by more than half. Large areas of crop plants may be affected in this way because the products of photochemical smog frequently drift significant distances (150 km or more) from their point of origin. Consequently,

smog-related loss of agricultural production is of economic significance.

Finally, it is worth noting that ozone is a greenhouse gas and its presence at elevated concentrations may therefore be contributing to global warming (Section 15.2.3).

15.2.2 | Acid rain

The water of unpolluted rain, snow, hail, mist and fog is not pure H_2O. It contains small but significant concentrations of dust, dissolved solids and gases. Of particular importance is the presence of dissolved carbon dioxide as this maintains the pH of clean rainwater at about 5.6 (Chapter 3, Section 3.3.1). In other words, even *unpolluted* rain is acidic (pH < 7). The epithet **acid rain** is therefore reserved for precipitation (rain, snow, fog, etc.) that has a pH appreciably less than expected in the absence of pollution. Usually all precipitation with a pH of less than about 5 is referred to as acid rain.

The main primary pollutants that cause this phenomenon are sulfur dioxide (SO_2) and NO_x. The sources and atmospheric transformations of these pollutants were discussed earlier in this chapter (Sections 15.1.1 and 15.1.2, and Box 15.1).

In polluted urban environments, sulfur dioxide dissolved in water may cause acidification in its own right, thus:

$$SO_{2(g)} + 2H_2O_{(l)} \rightleftharpoons HSO_3^-{}_{(aq)} + H_3O^+{}_{(aq)} \qquad (15.20)$$

for which the equilibrium constant, $K = 2.1 \times 10^{-2}$ $mol^2\,l^{-2}\,atm^{-1}$. On this basis, at equilibrium, an atmospheric sulfur dioxide concentration of 0.2 ppm will give a rainwater pH of 4.2 (Chapter 2, Box 2.8).

However, it is the secondary pollutants sulfur trioxide (SO_3), sulfuric acid (H_2SO_4) and nitric acid (HNO_3) that are of greater significance as these behave as strong acids in aqueous environments:

$$SO_{3(g)} + 2H_2O_{(l)} \rightarrow HSO_4^-{}_{(aq)} + H_3O^+{}_{(aq)} \qquad (15.21)$$

$$H_2SO_{4(aq)} + H_2O_{(l)} \rightarrow HSO_4^-{}_{(aq)} + H_3O^+{}_{(aq)} \qquad (15.22)$$

$$HNO_{3(aq)} + H_2O_{(l)} \rightarrow NO_3^-{}_{(aq)} + H_3O^+{}_{(aq)} \qquad (15.23)$$

On a global scale, the major contributors to acid rain are the sulfur oxides and the sulfuric acid they generate. Nitric acid typically makes up about a third of the total acid present in air contaminated with acidic emissions. However, where traffic density is high and sulfur emissions are relatively low, nitric acid may become the dominant source of acidity. This is the case on the west coast of the USA, where there is a close link between photochemical smog and acid rain.

Figure 15.13 The global distribution of mean rainwater pH (from Wellburn, 1994).

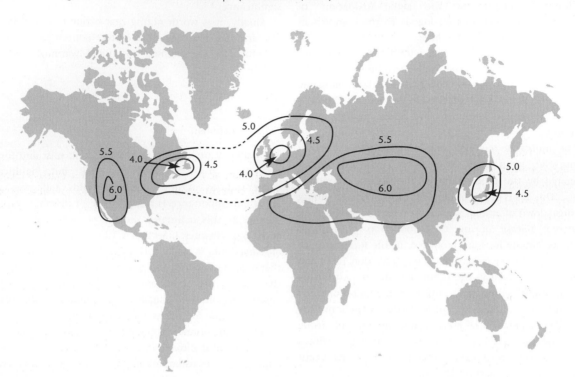

All of the species that cause acid rain are subjected to efficient sink mechanisms, including wet deposition. Consequently, they have short atmospheric residence times. This, coupled with the uneven distribution of their sources, means that acid rain is a regional rather than a global problem (Figure 15.13).

In general, acid rain has little direct measurable impact on human health, the exception being when it is present as a London-type smog (Section 15.2.1). Its main environmental impacts are on terrestrial water bodies, vegetation and buildings. The first of these is discussed in Chapter 14 (Section 14.3.1); the latter two are considered below.

The impact of acid rain on vegetation is a subject of some controversy. Pollution of this type may be a cause of lost crop productivity. More sensationally, it has been cited as the causative agent in the recent dramatic forest decline observed over large areas of Europe and North America. However, this theory remains unproven, and it is possible that other pollutants such as tropospheric ozone (O_3) and/or PAN are primarily responsible for this problem.

There is no doubt that direct acidic deposition on the leaves of plants can cause damage. Experiments using artificial acid rain have produced visible lesions on the foliage of sensitive crop plants, including soya beans and beets. However, these effects became noticeable at pH values of 3.4 and below, rather lower than normally encountered in the field. Direct acidic deposition onto the leaves of conifers may cause less spectacular damage. The stomata of these leaves are covered by waxy plugs. Acid rain may cause these plugs to crack, allowing increased water loss, enhanced frost damage and the ingress of pathogens and pollutants. Even more subtle affects may be of significance. Plants actively resist changes to the pH of their cellular fluids. During the wet deposition of acids, this process requires more energy than usual. This is obtained at the expense of growth, decreasing productivity.

More important than the direct effects of acid deposition on leaves may be the deleterious impact it has on soil. Acid rain causes the leaching of essential elements such as magnesium, while increasing the solubility and concentration of phytotoxic elements, notably aluminium. These effects are most marked in thin non-calcareous soils (i.e. those with no free calcium carbonate) with low cation exchange capacities. Such soils lack the buffering effect afforded by either of the following reactions:

$$CaCO_3 + H_3O^+ \rightarrow Ca^{2+}_{(aq)} + HCO_3^-{}_{(aq)} + H_2O_{(l)} \qquad (15.24)$$

$$(sp)M + nH_3O^+ \rightarrow (sp)(H_3O^+)_n + M^{n+} \qquad (15.25)$$

where (sp) is a soil particle and M is a non-H_3O^+ cation (e.g. K^+, Na^+, Ca^{2+}, Mg^{2+} or NH_4^+).

Acid rain has a marked impact on buildings and monuments constructed from limestone, or other carbonate-cemented sedimentary rocks. This is primarily caused by reaction 15.24 as this allows the structurally important carbonate constituents of the rock to be dissolved.

15.2.3 The greenhouse effect and climate change

The evidence available indicates that between 1860 and 1995 the global mean surface air temperature increased by between 0.3 and 0.6°C (Figure 15.14). This is important because seemingly small alterations in this average may be associated with very marked climatic changes. For example, the end of the last ice age was accompanied by a temperature increase of about 2°C. Clearly, if the trend now observed were to continue, serious perturbations in the world's climate would be expected.

The cause of this overall temperature increase is not known with complete certainty. One possibility is that it was caused by the normal pattern of variability experienced by the climate. However, another explanation is that we are entering a period of global warming brought about by anthropogenic emissions of greenhouse gases. These gases have in common the ability to absorb some of the infrared radiation emitted by the Earth that would otherwise escape into space. By doing this, current levels of greenhouse gases keep the surface of the Earth warm and hospitable (Chapter 4, Section 4.1).

The main natural greenhouse gases are water (H_2O), carbon dioxide (CO_2), methane (CH_4) and nitrous oxide (N_2O).

Tropospheric water is unlike the other main greenhouse gases in that its sources (evaporation) and sinks (precipitation) respond rapidly to changes in environmental conditions, maintaining dynamic equilibrium. If global warming were to become established, the moisture burden of the atmosphere would increase, as would the overall rates of evaporation and precipitation. The impact that this would have on global temperature is uncertain. Increased atmospheric levels of water vapour would enhance the greenhouse effect. However, the impact that increased cloud cover would have is not fully understood.

Human activity has directly caused a marked increase in the concentrations of the other major greenhouse gases (Figure 15.15), to which must be added the greenhouse effects of the halogenated hydrocarbons (Section 15.1.5), especially CFCs, which are primary pollutants, and the secondary pollutant tropospheric ozone. There is also concern over the potent greenhouse gas sulfur hexafluoride (SF_6). This is a species with an extremely long atmospheric residence time (probably >1000 years); hence, all emissions will exert their warming influence over thousands of years. If the rate of pollution with this substance rises substantially above its current low level, it will make a significant contribution to global warming in the future. It is through these changes that mankind may be altering the global climate. Concern over this issue has been sufficient to inspire international agreement (Box 15.4).

The greenhouse effect may be quantified using the concept of radiative forcing. This is the difference between the solar energy absorbed by the Earth and that radiated back into space as long-wave radiation.

The different greenhouse gases do not make equal contributions to radiative forcing. This is in part because the absolute concentrations of these gases are very different; but it is also because they differ in the effectiveness with which they can trap infrared radiation. This is complicated by the fact that the change in radiative forcing (ΔF) brought about by a given change in concentration (ΔC) is not linear for all of the greenhouse gases. However, if small changes in concentration are assumed, comparisons can be made (Table 15.3).

Despite the relatively weak greenhouse effect offered by carbon dioxide on a molecule-for-molecule basis, it is the most important single contributor to increased radiative forcing (Table 15.4). This is because its concentration, in absolute terms, is increasing *very* much more rapidly than those of the other greenhouse gases.

It is now realised that human activity also creates a *cooling* effect (i.e. a negative radiative forcing). This originates from the increased reflection into space of incoming solar radiation by aerosols, as described in

Figure **15.14** Observed recent trends in global mean surface temperatures relative to the period 1961–90. Note that the graph represents data that has been smoothed to decrease the impact of relatively large, short-lived variations and thereby more obviously portray the trends present (after Houghton *et al.*, 1996).

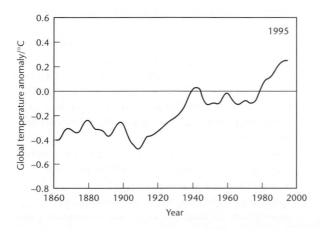

Figure 15.15 Trends in the atmospheric concentrations of the main greenhouse gases, other than water, that have both natural and anthropogenic sources (from Houghton *et al.*, 1990).

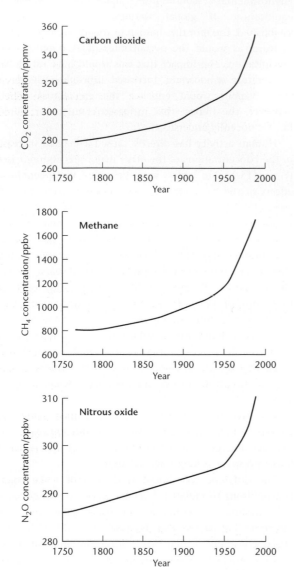

anthropogenic effects) or too short lived (in the case of the influence of volcanic eruptions) to compensate for the positive radiative forcing exerted by the greenhouse gases of anthropogenic origin. Consequently, there has been an accelerating increase in net radiative forcing in the latter half of the twentieth century. Part of this increase may be due to the relatively small effect of an increase in the output of the sun (evident from about 1850), but most is attributable to anthropogenic emissions of greenhouse gases. What is more, reliable projections indicate that unless urgent action is taken to reduce greenhouse gas emissions, a rapid rate of increase will continue into the twenty-first century (Figure 15.16). This information has been used as input data for computer models of the climatic system (Chapter 4, Section 4.2.6). While these models have severe limitations, they project, with confidence, that the radiative forcing of anthropogenic origin has led and will continue to lead to global warming (Figure 15.17). They also give some indication of the likely implications of this warming in terms of global climate change.

Perhaps the most important findings of these studies are that, on the basis of minimal curbs on output of greenhouse gases (the business-as-usual scenario):

1   Within the next century the rate of change in the global mean temperature will be larger than any seen in the last 10 000 years.
2   There will be significant rises in sea levels (Figure 15.18) caused in the main by decreases in the density of sea water and melting glaciers. These will probably lead to severe flooding problems in small islands, coastal flood plains (e.g. Bangladesh) and subsiding coastal cities (e.g. Bangkok). Even larger changes in sea level would be expected if the major ice sheets were to become unstable. Such changes seem unlikely until the twenty-second century.
3   Increased evaporation will enhance the global mean hydrological cycle, leading to increased precipitation and flooding, especially at high latitudes. However, there will also be areas that will suffer from decreased rainfall, especially in summer, and increased likelihood of drought.
4   Global warming will be neither temporally nor spatially uniform. Warming, when it happens, will generally be more intense over land than at sea, and will be particularly marked in the high northern latitudes in late autumn and winter.
5   Changes in the intensity and/or frequency of climate patterns such as the occurrence of El Niño events (Chapter 4, Box 4.4) are to be expected.
6   Tropospheric warming will be accompanied by stratospheric cooling. This is because greenhouse gases,

Section 15.1.6, and the decrease in the concentration of ozone in the stratosphere explored in Section 15.2.4. It is worth noting that neither of these effects is evenly distributed about the globe, and both can fluctuate substantially over time-scales measured in less than a year. Consequently, they will exert an uneven influence. To these should be added the substantial but transient cooling caused by the introduction of aerosols into the stratosphere by occasional large volcanic eruptions (e.g. Mt Pinatubo, June 1991).

Importantly, however, all of these factors that cause cooling are either insufficiently large (in the case of the

15.4   The United Nations Framework Convention on Climate Change and the Kyoto Protocol

There is mounting evidence that the release of greenhouse gases into the atmosphere as a result of modern human activity is causing global warming and consequent climate change. Climate models have been developed that allow predictions to be made about the nature and extent of this change. However, these models cannot predict with certainty, and there remains sufficient room for doubt to allow disagreement about the severity of the problem and need for solutions. However, few would argue that there is not cause for concern.

The United Nations Framework Convention on Climate Change (UNFCCC) is an international treaty that was born of this concern in 1992. It was designed to acknowledge that there is a problem of human-induced climate change and to establish mechanisms that would promote and allow later international agreement on how this problem should be tackled.

This convention has now been ratified by more than 160 states, called the Parties to the Convention. At the time of writing, there have been four conferences of these Parties* since the UNFCCC came into effect on 21 March 1994. Arguably, the most important of these was the 1997 meeting at Kyoto. This produced the Kyoto Protocol, an agreement that is due to come into force sometime after 2000. It will commit those countries involved to a decrease in their collective carbon dioxide equivalent emissions of a 'basket' of greenhouse gases by the period 2008–12. This basket is made up of carbon dioxide, methane, nitrous oxide, HFCs, perfluorocarbons (PFCs) and sulfur hexafluoride. Increases in the emissions of one or more of the gases in this basket will be allowed, provided that they are more than offset by decreases elsewhere.

*These are know as COP1–COP4. COP1 was held in 1995 in Berlin, COP2 in 1996 in Geneva, COP3 in 1997 in Kyoto and COP4 in 1998 in Buenos Aires. At the time of writing, COP5 is planned for 1999 in Bonn.

Table 15.3 A molecule-for-molecule comparison of changes in radiative forcing (ΔF) brought about by small changes in the concentration (ΔC) of greenhouse gases from 1990 levels.

Gas	ΔF for ΔC relative to CO_2
CFC-12	15 800
CFC-11	12 400
N_2O	206
CH_4	21
CO_2	1

Table 15.4 The contributions of the main anthropogenic greenhouse gases to the total increase in radiative forcing from 1980 to 1990.

Gas	Contribution/%
Carbon dioxide	55
CFC-11 and CFC-12	17
Methane	15
Other CFCs	7
Nitrous oxide	6

when highly dilute, as they are in the stratosphere, cause a radiative loss of energy (Chapter 4, Section 4.1). This has implications for the rate of loss of stratospheric ozone (Section 15.2.4).

7 The high rate of change will damage natural ecosystems, particularly at mid- to high latitudes.

There are a number of important issues that the models cannot address. These include:

- details of changes in local or even regional climates. For example, the incidence of tropical storms may increase while the frequency of storms in the mid-latitudes may decrease – this cannot be predicted reliably;
- the influence of unforeseeable sudden events, such as significant alterations to the operation of the oceanic conveyor belt (Chapter 4, Box 4.3) or changes to the ice sheets.

15.2.4   Stratospheric ozone depletion

Natural processes

As discussed in Chapter 4 (Section 4.1), ozone (O_3) is found at trace levels throughout the atmosphere below the stratopause. The highest concentration of this gas is found in the stratosphere in what has become known as the *ozone layer*. Even within this, its absolute concentrations are low, reaching a maximum of 8 to 10 ppm.

Stratospheric ozone is created and destroyed throughout the hours of daylight by the following naturally occurring reactions:

$$O_2 + h\nu \; (\lambda < 240 \, \text{nm}) \rightarrow 2O \quad\left.\right\} \begin{array}{l}\text{ozone} \\ \text{production}\end{array} \quad (15.26)$$

$$O + O_2 + M \rightarrow O_3 + M \quad\quad\quad\quad\quad (15.27)$$

Figure 15.16 Projected trends in radiative forcing, on the basis of the IPCC IS 92a emission scenario. This assumes no strong curbs on CO_2 emissions as a direct consequence of environmental concerns and can be thought of as an approximation of 'business-as-usual'. The 'Total non-CO_2 trace gases' line in diagram (a) is made up of the components shown in diagram (b) (from Houghton *et al.*, 1996).

Figure 15.17 Projection of the trends in global average surface air temperature on the basis of the IPCC IS 92a emission scenario. This assumes no strong curbs on CO_2 emissions as a direct consequence of environmental concerns and can be thought of as an approximation of 'business-as-usual' (after Houghton *et al.*, 1996). Note that the temperature in 1990 was about 0.5°C warmer than pre-industrial temperatures.

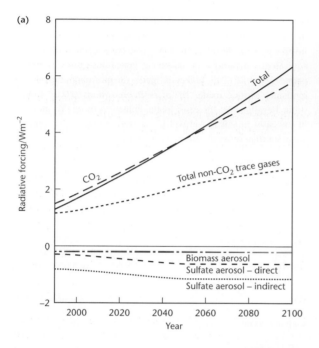

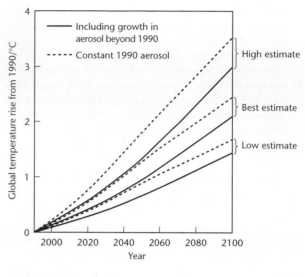

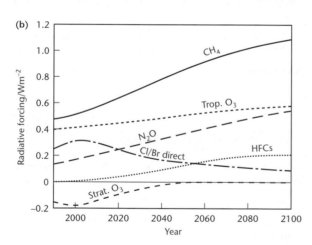

Figure 15.18 Projection of the trends in sea level on the basis of the IPCC IS 92a emission scenario. This assumes no strong curbs on CO_2 emissions as a direct consequence of environmental concerns and can be thought of as an approximation of 'business-as-usual' (from Houghton *et al.*, 1996).

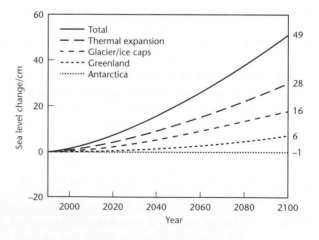

$$O_3 + hv\ (\lambda < 325\ nm) \rightarrow O_2 + O \quad \text{ozone} \quad (15.28)$$
$$O + O_3 \rightarrow 2O_2 \qquad\qquad\qquad \text{destruction} \quad (15.29)$$

where M is a third body (see footnote on page 337).

The last of these occurs both as written and via catalytic reaction cycles, thus:

$$X + O_3 \rightarrow XO + O_2 \qquad (15.30)$$
$$XO + O \rightarrow X + O_2 \qquad (15.31)$$

the net result being

$$O + O_3 \rightarrow 2O_2 \qquad (15.29)$$

where X is an odd electron species, i.e. Cl, NO, OH or H. Notice that the X consumed by reaction 15.30 is regenerated by 15.31. This means that one atom or molecule of X can destroy many thousands of molecules of O_3 before it is removed by a termination reaction with a non-ozone molecule.

These catalytic cycles are not entirely independent. For example, the following reaction removes both NO_2 (an XO species) and OH (an X species):

$$NO_2 + OH + M \rightarrow M + HNO_3 \qquad (15.32)$$

where M is a third body.[2]

This is only temporary as slow photolysis regenerates both catalytically active molecules.

Similarly, there are reactions that temporarily inactivate chlorine atoms (an X species) and chlorine monoxide (an XO species), thus:

$$Cl + CH_4 \rightarrow CH_3 + HCl \qquad (15.33)$$

and

$$ClO + NO_2 + M \rightarrow M + ClONO_2 \qquad (15.34)$$

where M is a third body (see footnote on page 337).

Compounds such as nitric acid (HNO_3), hydrogen chloride (HCl) and chlorine nitrate ($ClONO_2$) may therefore be thought of as reservoirs that temporarily store ozone-destroying catalysts.

Man-made threats to stratospheric ozone

Human activity has been responsible for an increase in the flux into the stratosphere of both nitric oxide (NO) and nitrogen dioxide (NO_2). These enhance the destruction of ozone by acting as X and XO respectively in Equations 15.30 and 15.31.

There are two main sources of this contamination. Firstly, high-flying aircraft inject NO_x (principally NO) directly into the stratosphere. Secondly, intensive agriculture is increasing the emissions of nitrous oxide (N_2O). This has no tropospheric sinks and therefore eventually migrates to the stratosphere, where some of it is converted to nitric oxide (reaction 15.2, Section 15.1.2).

More important are the anthropogenic emissions of halogenated hydrocarbons, particularly CFCs, their brominated analogues and bromomethane (CH_3Br) (Section 15.1.5). These undergo photolysis in the stratosphere to yield chlorine and/or bromine atoms, which act as X in reactions 15.30 and 15.31, destroying ozone.

Interestingly, human activity may also be responsible for *decreasing* the natural rate of stratospheric ozone *loss*. In the absence of catalytic cycles, reaction 15.29 has a relatively high activation energy. Consequently, the stratospheric *cooling* anticipated if global warming becomes established (Section 15.2.3) would decrease the rate of this reaction. Such effects are most unlikely to fully offset the effects of anthropogenic emissions of species that lead to ozone depletion. Consequently, computer simulations lead

to predictions of net average stratospheric ozone loss. These are supported by field observations that indicate that a general ozone depletion has started to occur.

In 1985, scientists of the British Antarctic Survey published results that showed a massive decline in the spring-time concentrations of ozone over the Antarctic. This is the phenomenon that became known as the **ozone hole**. Significantly, all models of stratospheric chemistry prior to that date *failed* to predict its occurrence.

Since 1985, this phenomenon has continued to be observed, with indications that it is becoming more severe with time. Intense research activity has established the factors that coincide in the Antarctic to produce the conditions necessary for the 'hole' to form.

Importantly, a stable pattern of strong circumpolar westerly winds is generated during the winter-time. This vortex extends above the tropopause and effectively isolates the air above Antarctica. Also, the winter-time temperatures of the Antarctic stratosphere are sufficiently low ($<-80°C$) to allow clouds of both nitric acid trihydrate ($HNO_3.3H_2O$), and more dilute nitric acid to form. These polar stratospheric clouds (PSCs) are highly significant, for they provide surfaces upon which two chlorine reservoir compounds can react, thus:

$$HCl + ClONO_2 \rightarrow HNO_3 + Cl_2$$

This process continues throughout the light-free winter. The nitric acid formed is dissolved by the cloud particles, leaving the chlorine molecules to accumulate in the gas phase.

On sunrise in spring, the chlorine molecules are readily photolysed, producing chlorine atoms that destroy ozone:

$$Cl_2 + h\nu \rightarrow 2Cl$$

$$Cl + O_3 \rightarrow ClO + O_2$$

At this time the concentration of stratospheric oxygen atoms (O) is very low. Consequently, the normal path leading to the regeneration of chlorine atoms (reaction 15.31) is of little significance. However, regeneration can happen by the following reactions, allowing catalytic cycles of ozone depletion to commence:

$$2ClO \xrightarrow{\text{low temperature}} ClOOCl$$

$$ClOOCl + h\nu \rightarrow 2Cl + O_2$$

or

$$ClO + BrO \rightarrow Cl + Br + O_2$$

Significantly, the formation of PSCs leads to the depletion of stratospheric NO_x. This means that the chlorine atoms released in the spring cannot be sequestered by reaction with nitrogen dioxide (Equation 15.34), leaving them free to destroy more ozone. It is therefore possible to argue that the ozone depletion directly caused by the oxides of nitrogen is more than offset by their ability to remove active chlorine of anthropogenic origin.

The polar vortex breaks up in late spring. This allows the ozone-depleted and active chlorine-enriched air of the polar stratosphere to move equatorwards. It is possible that this will cause a dilution and depletion of the ozone in lower latitudes. If this process were to happen year after year, it could eventually lead to a cumulative general loss of ozone beyond that previously expected.

The Arctic stratosphere does not get as cold as its southern counterpart, nor is it isolated in the winter by a stable circumpolar vortex. Consequently, northern polar ozone depletion is not as severe as that in the Antarctic; nonetheless it may become significant in the future.

Finally, there is evidence that the sulfuric acid and sulfate aerosols that are ubiquitous in the stratosphere may act in a similar fashion to PSCs. Therefore heterogeneous reactions that ultimately lead to ozone depletion may be significant outside the cold polar regions.

Consequences of stratospheric ozone loss

Stratospheric ozone absorbs ultraviolet light, principally in the region 230–320 nm. This is roughly coincident with the biologists' UV-B (Table 15.5). UV-B can damage a number of biological systems, including DNA.

Plants. Deleterious effects of elevated UV-B levels on crop plants are noticeable but probably not of significance, at least in the short term. This is because breeding programmes can actively select for UV-B resistant strains. The impact on phytoplankton is likely to be more severe. These floating plants are largely responsible for the primary productivity of the oceans, 70% of which occurs in the polar regions, where ozone depletion is expected to be highest. Decreases in productivity will clearly adversely affect organisms further up the food chain.

Human health. Increased levels of UV-B are expected to harm human health. The incidence of relatively trivial complaints such as sunburn, snow-blindness and enhanced ageing of skin is expected to rise. Similarly, a range of more

Table 15.5 Spectral range classification used in the biological sciences.

Wavelength/nm	Category
<290	UV-C
290–320	UV-B
320–400	UV-A
400–700	Visible

serious afflictions will become more common, including cataracts and eye and skin cancers. Furthermore, the skin's immune system is adversely affected by UV-B. Diseases that involve the skin are expected to become more problematic. These include measles, chicken pox, malaria and leprosy. Enhanced UV-B levels may well decrease the effectiveness of vaccination against these diseases.

Finally, it should be noted that ozone is a natural greenhouse gas. Its loss therefore results in a cooling of the atmosphere. As shown in Figure 15.16, this effect offsets, to some extent, the warming caused by greenhouse gases of anthropogenic origin.

15.3 Summary

The atmospheric pollutants that cause most concern are sulfur dioxide, the oxides of nitrogen and carbon, hydrocarbons, halogenated hydrocarbons (particularly CFCs), suspended particulates and the secondary pollutants that these contaminants generate.

In recent years, human activity has caused a massive increase in the amounts of these trace atmospheric constituents. What is more, some of the primary pollutants listed above are solely of anthropogenic origin. This is true of many of the hydrocarbons and their halogenated analogues (including CFCs).

The single most significant source of atmospheric pollution is the burning of fossil fuels and biomass. This causes increased emissions of sulfur dioxide, NO_x, the oxides of carbon, hydrocarbons and suspended particulates. The release of CFCs is probably the most important industrial contamination that is not related to fuel combustion. Agricultural activity is also of major significance, causing enhanced production of methane and nitrous oxide.

Some of the pollutant species have low tropospheric residence times. These include sulfur dioxide, NO_x, carbon monoxide and the larger suspended particulates. These contaminants are all rapidly removed from the atmosphere by efficient sink mechanisms. Consequently, they tend to cause local or regional problems. These include smogs and acid rain, the severity of both of which is related to the presence of secondary pollutants.

Longer-lived atmospheric species, notably carbon dioxide, methane, CFCs and nitrous oxide, tend to cause longer-term problems of global significance. All of these are greenhouse gases and may therefore be contributing to global warming. CFCs and nitrous oxide enter the stratosphere, where they contribute to the processes that control the levels of stratospheric ozone.

15.4   Problems

1 A household consumes an average of 100 units of electricity per week. Assume that this is generated in a coal-fired power station with a thermal efficiency of 33%. What mass of sulfur dioxide would be liberated into the atmosphere in one year as a result of the household's electricity consumption? Assume that the coal burnt had a sulfur content of 1.69% and a calorific value of $34\,940\,kJ\,kg^{-1}$.

Another household consumes 3 tonnes of the same coal in a year as a domestic fuel. This second household uses only an average of 85 units of electricity per week because coal rather than electricity is used to provide hot water. How do the total sulfur dioxide emissions of the two households compare?

(Note that 1 unit $= 1\,kWh$ and $1\,W = 1\,J\,s^{-1}$.)

2 (a) From the data in Table 15.1 calculate the approximate atmospheric residence times of sulfur dioxide and each of the oxides of nitrogen in weeks.

(b) Comment on the likelihood of each of these species reaching the stratosphere from the troposphere.

3 Radicals are chemical species that contain at least one unpaired electron (Chapter 1, Section 1.6.2).

(i) Why are radicals so important in atmospheric chemistry?

(ii) Why are radicals present in low concentrations in the troposphere?

(iii) Establish which of the following species are radicals. In the examples given below, this may be done by counting the number of electrons present in each; an odd number indicates a radical.

$$SO_3 \qquad HSO_3 \qquad HSO_3^-$$
$$OH^- \qquad OH \qquad H_2O \qquad HO_2$$

4 There is currently some debate about whether denitrification or nitrification is the major source of nitrous oxide (for example, contrast the writings of Wellburn, 1994, page 60 with those of Wayne, 1991, page 172). Comment on the need to resolve this debate in order to establish the likely effects on future emissions of changes in agricultural practices.

5 Why is nitrous oxide much more reactive in the stratosphere than it is in the troposphere? (This can be answered at several levels.)

6 Carbon monoxide, like unburnt hydrocarbons, can lead to tropospheric ozone production under the conditions that generate photochemical smog. Write equations that account for this observation. Would you expect carbon dioxide to have a similar effect? Justify your answer.

7 In some areas, including eastern North America, the ratio of sulfuric acid to nitric acid in acid rain is declining. Discuss the factors that may be contributing to this change. It may be useful to read Chapter 16 before answering this.

8 Comment on the likely causes and significance of the trends shown in the table below:

Date	Mean urban UK SO_2 concentrations/ $\mu g\,SO_2\,m^{-3}$	Chimney emissions of SO_2/ 10^6 tonnes		
		Tall chimneys	Low chimneys	Total
1958	188	1.4	1.7	3.1
1970	144			
1977	73	3	0.6	3.6

9 In the UK there has been a recent drift away from coal-fired power stations towards gas-fired stations. Would you expect this to result in an increase or decrease in carbon dioxide emissions?

10 Calculate the pH of otherwise pure water that is in equilibrium with air that contains 0.15 ppm sulfur dioxide and 360 ppm carbon dioxide, the relevant equations being:

$$SO_{2(g)} + 2H_2O_{(l)} \rightleftharpoons HSO_{3\,(aq)}^- + H_3O^+_{(aq)}$$

$$CO_{2(g)} + 2H_2O_{(l)} \rightleftharpoons HCO_{3\,(aq)}^- + H_3O^+_{(aq)}$$

Note that at atmospheric pressure the overall equilibrium constants for these reactions are 2.1×10^{-2} and $1.4 \times 10^{-8}\,mol^2\,l^{-2}\,atm^{-1}$ respectively.

11 Compare the rates of atmospheric sedimentation for particles that are 1.5 and 10 μm in diameter respectively. Assume that both particles have a density of 2 g cm^{-3}. If these particles were to be released into still air at an altitude of 3 km how long would it take each to reach the ground?

The equation you need to use is Stokes' law, stated thus:

$$\text{rate of sedimentation} = \frac{gd^2(\rho_{particle} - \rho_{medium})}{18\eta}$$

where g is the acceleration due to gravity (9.8 m s^{-2} at sea level), d is the diameter of the particle, $\rho_{particle}$ and ρ_{medium} are the densities of the particle and the medium in which it is falling respectively ($\rho_{air} = 1.2 \times 10^{-3}$ g cm^{-3} at 20°C and 1 atm pressure) and η is the medium's viscosity $= 1.8 \times 10^{-4}$ g cm^{-1} s^{-1}. Take care to harmonise the units prior to calculation.

12 If the total flux of lead into a given adult's blood stream is 82 μg per day, calculate the total volume of the blood in the individual, given that the residence time and concentration of lead in their blood is 30 days and 40 μg per 100 ml respectively. You may assume that the concentration of lead in the blood is held constant by virtue of a dynamic steady state.

15.5 Further reading

Brimblecombe, P. (1995) *Air composition and chemistry* (2nd edn). Cambridge: Cambridge University Press.

Elsom, D.M. (1992) *Atmospheric pollution* (2nd edn). Oxford: Blackwell Scientific.

Houghton, J. (1997) *Global warming: the complete briefing*. Cambridge: Cambridge University Press.

Houghton, J. T., L. G. Meira Filho, B. A. Callander, N. Harris, A. Kattenberg and K. Maskell (Eds) (1996) *Climate change 1995: the science of climate change*. Cambridge: Cambridge University Press.

Mannion, A.M. and S.R. Bowlby (Eds) (1992) *Environmental issues in the 1990s*. Chichester: Wiley. (Particularly Chapter 4)

Tolba, M.K., O.A. El-Kholy, E. El-Hinnawi, M.W. Holdgate, D.F. McMichael and R.E. Munn (Eds) (1992) *The world environment 1972–1992: two decades of challenge*. London: Chapman & Hall. (Chapters 1, 2 and 3 give a very useful overview of the issues)

Warneck, P. (1988) *The chemistry of the natural atmosphere*. Orlando, FL: Academic Press, a subsidiary of Harcourt Brace Jovanovich.

Wayne, R.P. (1991) *Chemistry of atmospheres* (2nd edn). Oxford: Oxford University Press. (Particularly Chapters 4 and 5)

Wellburn, A. (1994) *Air pollution and climate change: the biological impact* (2nd edn). Harlow: Longman. (Covers basic chemistry as well as biological issues)

Bhopal

The world's worst industrial disaster, in terms of fatalities, occurred in Bhopal, India, in 1984. In the early hours of the morning of 3 December, an extremely toxic gas, methylisocyanate (MIC), escaped from a local pesticide plant. Denser than air, it lingered in the vicinity of the factory, a densely populated shanty-town area. People were killed as they slept or fled from the choking gas. Within two hours, the highly poisonous gas had spread to cover an area of $60 \, \text{km}^2$. The initial death toll exceeded 2500, with hundreds of thousands injured.

The pesticide plant at Bhopal was owned by Union Carbide India Ltd (UCIL), a subsidiary of the multinational chemical company Union Carbide Corporation (UCC). UCC owns 50.9% of the stock of UCIL. The Bhopal plant was used for the production of carbamate pesticides, mainly carbaryl (brand name Sevin), together with small amounts of butylphenyl methylcarbamate and aldicarb (brand name Temik), all destined for the Indian market. The first two of these pesticides are classed as 'moderately hazardous' by the World Health Organisation whilst aldicarb is classed as 'extremely hazardous'. The extremely toxic substance methylisocyanate (MIC) is used as an intermediary in the production of these pesticides.

Methylisocyanate has the chemical formula $CH_3-N=C=O$. It is a highly volatile liquid, with a boiling point of $39°C$. It is very unstable and in the presence of certain external substances, including water, polymerises rapidly. This exothermic reaction releases large quantities of heat which in turn accelerates the polymerisation reaction (at $25°C$, polymerisation is 200 times more rapid than at $0°C$). In other countries, including Germany and the Netherlands, the storage of this toxic and unstable chemical is not allowed. However, at UCIL in Bhopal, large quantities of methylisocyanate were stored underground in three stainless steel tanks. At the time of the accident, 62 tonnes of MIC were stored at the plant, although only 5 tonnes were needed each day. Refrigeration was installed to keep the stored MIC in liquid form and help prevent a runaway polymerisation reaction from occurring.

Just after midnight on 2 December 1984, the pressure inside one of the three methylisocyanate storage tanks (tank 610) was observed to rise rapidly. The tank was equipped with a safety valve designed to rupture at 40 psi and release gas into a vent. When this burst, the safety valve within the vent itself popped, allowing methylisocyanate to escape into the atmosphere through the 33 m high vent tube.

The plant was fitted with two safety devices designed to deal with a gas escape. One of these, the vent gas scrubber, was turned on. This device consists of a tower packed with loose material through which a solution of caustic soda (sodium hydroxide) is poured in order to destroy the escaping gas. Although there is evidence to show that this system worked, it was not adequate to deal effectively with the escaping gas. The vent gas scrubber was designed to destroy only $88 \, \text{kg h}^{-1}$ of MIC whilst the gas escape was in the region of $20\,000 \, \text{kg h}^{-1}$. A second safety device, a flare tower designed to burn off escaping gas, was shut for maintenance at the time of the accident. As a result, 40–45 tonnes of highly toxic methylisocyanate gas poured into the air during the next 40 minutes before the safety valve was resealed.

The effect of the methylisocyanate gas on the local population was devastating. This substance is biologically very active and poisonous in concentrations greater than 0.02 ppm. This is the maximum level of exposure set by the US Occupational Safety and Health Administration during an 8-hour period. At 2 ppm, MIC causes nose and throat irritation in humans, whilst at 21 ppm its effect is one of suffocation. Most of the immediate deaths were caused by water from the body fluids entering the lungs, a direct result of the acute toxicity of MIC. This condition, similar in its effect to drowning, is known as pulmonary oedema.

An estimated 200 000 people were affected by the gas, many thousands of whom descended on the local hospital. Tragically, there was scant knowledge of how to treat the gas victims and many more subsequently died. Those who did survive suffered from a variety of ailments including blindness, blackouts and nausea. Little was known at the time about the long-term effects of exposure to methylisocyanate. This made effective treatment of the survivors problematic.

Investigations into the accident at Bhopal revealed that, as suspected, a runaway polymerisation reaction had occurred in one of the methylisocyanate storage tanks. This was evident from the fracturing of the concrete cladding of the tank, which indicated that the internal temperature had exceeded 300°C. The runaway reaction had been initiated by the accidental introduction of water during the cleaning of the MIC pipes, a task undertaken without proper precautions.

As enquiries proceeded, a whole catalogue of events which had contributed to the occurrence and scale of the disaster became apparent. For example, the city of Bhopal had undergone major expansion during the period 1971–81. This had led to the mushrooming of squatter settlements around the UCIL plant. These settlements were legalised by local government in 1983–84. This situation would not have been allowed to arise in more-developed countries, where strict zoning regulations are enforced with respect to the siting of industrial plants. Moreover, the local inhabitants had little appreciation of the potential danger of their industrial neighbour. The majority of the victims of the poisonous gas leak lived in these makeshift dwellings.

Within the plant itself, many failures of design, maintenance, operation and management came to light in the course of investigations. The vent gas scrubber was not adequate to deal with the leak and both the flare tower and the refrigeration system (which would have slowed down the initial stages of the runaway reaction) were not operational at the time of the accident. There were no emergency practice drills and, as a result, the reaction of the staff was one of panic when the gas did begin to leak. A warning siren was not used until 1:00 am and then only briefly. It was only sounded in earnest an hour later, at 2:00 am. Lack of preparation, information and communication played a key role in the disaster; for example, the local hospital only became aware of the accident when the first casualties began to arrive.

In the aftermath of the Bhopal catastrophe, the Indian government appointed itself sole representative of the gas victims. In 1989, after five years of legal wrangling, the government finally accepted US$470 million from the Union Carbide Corporation in full and final settlement of the case. This sum was only one-seventh of the US$3.3 billion originally sought for those injured or bereaved in the disaster. However, it was not until October 1992 that individual claims started to be processed.

Many of those claiming compensation have suffered permanent damage to their vital organs (e.g. liver, eyes and lungs) and body systems (e.g. nervous, circulatory and immune systems). As a result, many are no longer able to work and earn their living. Women affected by the gas have given birth to babies suffering from mental retardation or physical deformities. Stillbirths, abortion and sterility are also problems associated with exposure to the gas on that fateful night. Seven thousand deaths have been officially attributed to gas exposure, although pressure groups contend that a figure in excess of 16 000 is more realistic.

The human suffering caused by the gas leak at the UCIL pesticide plant in Bhopal in 1984 has been, and continues to be, immense. There are many important lessons which must be learnt from this tragedy if the risk of another accident on the scale of Bhopal is to be minimised. These include the responsibility of companies in the more-developed countries towards their subsidiaries in less-developed nations, particularly in regard to the implementation and enforcement of safety regulations. Some developing countries too may need to re-examine with urgency their policies concerning toxic substances, for example in terms of safety precautions, industrial location and crisis management.

Further reading

Bowander, B. (1985) The Bhopal accident: implications for developing countries. *The Environmentalist*, 5(2), 89–103.

Bowander, B. (1987) Industrial hazard management: an analysis of the Bhopal accident. *Project Appraisal*, 2(3), 157–68.

Shrivastava, P. (1992) *Bhopal: anatomy of a crisis* (2nd edn). London: Paul Chapman.

Weir, D. (1987) *The Bhopal syndrome*. London: Earthscan.

Waste management

After reading this chapter, you should be able to:

- Define the term waste.

- Describe the strategies that can be used to manage each of the following types of waste:
  - those formed by the combustion of fossil fuels;
  - low-hazard solid wastes;
  - sewage;
  - high-hazard wastes.

- Appreciate the value of the concepts of waste minimisation, cleaner production and integrated waste management.

Introduction

Waste is any movable material that is perceived to be of no further use and that is permanently discarded. Once in the environment, wastes frequently cause damage to ecosystems and/or human health and therefore act as pollutants (Chapters 14 and 15).

Successful waste management can largely avoid such pollution. This chapter introduces the more widely available strategies and technologies that can be effective in this area. The first three sections deal with the approaches used in the management of the relatively low-hazard wastes that are generated in bulk by industrial, commercial and domestic activity. Consideration of the options available for the safe treatment and disposal of high-hazard wastes is given in the fourth section and, in the case of radioactive waste, Case study 7 (page 375). The chapter closes with a brief introduction to the concepts of waste minimisation, cleaner production and integrated waste management. If more widely adopted, these ideas have the potential to greatly improve current waste management practices.

16.1 Wastes from fossil fuel combustion

The main wastes generated during the combustion of fossil fuels are sulfur dioxide, NO_x, carbon monoxide, unburnt hydrocarbons, particulates, residual solids (including ash) and carbon dioxide. The technologies that are available for the management of these wastes are briefly reviewed in this section.

Sulfur dioxide

Fossil fuels contain both organic sulfur (e.g. in thiophene rings) and inorganic sulfides (principally H_2S in natural gas and FeS_2 in coal). During combustion these react with atmospheric oxygen (O_2) to produce sulfur dioxide (SO_2).

The sulfur content of fossil fuels varies considerably. For example, coals and fuel oils generally contain 1–4%, and 3–4% S respectively. However, there are naturally occurring low-sulfur fuels (e.g., coals <1% S and fuel oils <0.5% S). Clearly, burning these preferentially is one of the options available for diminishing the emissions of sulfur dioxide. Unfortunately, this is of only limited applicability as supplies of these low-sulfur fuels are comparatively small.

Another alternative is the dilution and dispersion of the sulfur dioxide produced, principally by building taller chimneys. This has found favour in the past and has had noticeable success in the reduction of local levels of pollution. Unfortunately, it has had no impact on overall contamination; in effect, 'what goes up must come down'.

Fuel cleaning processes that remove sulfur are routinely applied to natural gas, oil and coal. These are now considered in turn.

Natural gas contains variable amounts of hydrogen sulfide (H_2S). This may be effectively removed by a number of processes including adsorption onto zeolites (a type of aluminosilicate mineral). The hydrogen sulfide may then be oxidised *in situ* with hot sulfur dioxide to yield sulfur vapour and regenerated zeolite adsorbent. The sulfur is then condensed and sold, while the zeolite is reused.

The desulfurisation of oils is desirable for a number of reasons that are unrelated to the lowering of sulfur dioxide emissions. These include avoiding the deactivation (poisoning) of platinum catalysts used during oil processing. Consequently, oil desulfurisation was practised before the environmental need to reduce sulfur dioxide emissions was recognised. The main process involved is hydrodesulfurisation. During this the oil is reacted with hydrogen (H_2) at elevated temperatures, under pressure and in the presence of a catalyst. This converts the sulfur to hydrogen sulfide which can then be separated as a gas.

An important consequence of oil desulfurisation is that motor spirit (petrol, gasoline) has a very low sulfur content (between 0.026% in US Premium grade and 0.040% in the UK). As a result, transport makes very little contribution to the total anthropogenic emissions of sulfur dioxide.

Coal is cleaned by the separation of the organic fuel from the inorganic ash-forming mineral impurities that it contains. This may be done on the basis of density, for the fuel has a lower specific gravity (1.1 to 1.8) than the impurities (from about 2 to about 5). In one process, the raw coal is finely ground, so that most of the mineral particles become distinct from the fuel. The ground raw coal is then agitated in a mixture of air, water, oil and surfactant. The denser particles sink, while the others are held by surface tension at the interface between the liquid and the air. The cleaned coal is then isolated in a settling tank, where the air/oil/water mixture is allowed to separate, causing the fuel to sink.

Processes such as this may remove much of the inorganic sulfur fraction (FeS_2 has a specific gravity of 4.5). In a typical British coal, about half of the sulfur is inorganic, the rest forming part of the organic matrix of the fuel. It is now technologically possible to remove some of this also, though it is currently not economically viable to do so (Box 16.1).

Vast amounts of coal are consumed worldwide (Chapter 13, Figure 13.1), particularly during the production of electricity. This, coupled with the relative inefficiency of the routine coal cleaning process, makes this fuel by far the largest single contributor to anthropogenic sulfur dioxide emissions. There is therefore considerable interest in the removal of sulfur dioxide prior to the release of the flue gases.

Further Information Box

16.1   The desulfurisation of coal by the solvent refine process

While the removal of much of the inorganic sulfur from coal can be achieved by physical separation, more drastic treatment is required to deplete it of its organic sulfur. Here we examine one means by which this can be achieved, the solvent refine process.

At the start of this process the raw coal is finely ground and mixed with a solvent oil. Hydrogen (H_2) is added to the resulting slurry which is then heated under high pressure to 45°C. This causes the dissolution of the vast bulk of the coal's carbon.

The hydrogen is added for two reasons. Firstly, it stops the re-polymerisation of the coal once in solution. Secondly, it reacts with some of the organic sulfur to yield hydrogen sulfide which can then be isolated as a gas.

After leaving the heater the coal solution is filtered to remove the mineral matter, including the pyritic sulfur (FeS_2). The solvent oil is then evaporated from the filtrate. The hot residue is allowed to cool, upon which it forms into a hard brittle fuel known as solvent refined coal (SRC).

This process has a number of advantages. It causes the sulfur and ash content of the fuel to fall dramatically, while increasing its calorific value. Unfortunately, it also causes the cost of the fuel to rise, by a factor of about three, making the process unusable on economic grounds.

Sulfur dioxide removal rates of 90% can be achieved from the combustion zone in boilers that are based on **fluidised bed combustion** (FBC) technology (Figure 16.1). In such systems, the fuel is added in a pulverised form to a bed of inert material (e.g. sand or coal ash). This is kept in a state of agitation (i.e. fluidised) by a strong updraught of air, which acts as the oxidant. Such systems allow the coal to be burnt efficiently at relatively low temperatures (~900°C). On addition of limestone (essentially $CaCO_3$), they also provide an excellent environment for the sequestering of sulfur dioxide:

$$CaCO_3 \xrightarrow{\;>700°C\;} CaO + CO_2$$
$$\tfrac{1}{2}O_2 + SO_2 \xrightarrow{\;800-900°C\;} CaSO_4$$

(16.1)

Figure **16.1** A schematic view of a fluidised bed boiler fitted with limestone-based sulfur dioxide control.

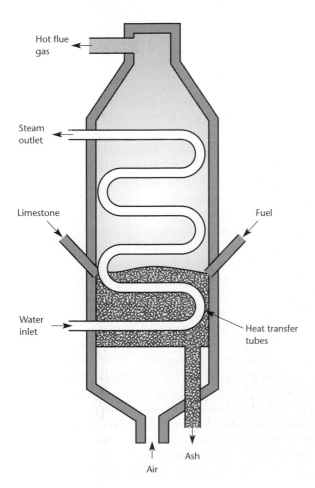

As an alternative, sulfur dioxide can be removed downstream of the boiler after the fly ash has been removed, a process called **flue gas desulfurisation** (FGD). FGD can be highly efficient: 90% removal rates are generally achievable. In a typical system, an aqueous slurry of an alkaline absorbant, commonly lime, or limestone, is passed in a fine spray through the flue gases. Sulfites and sulfates are therefore generated during this 'scrubbing' process:

$$Ca(OH)_2 + SO_2 \rightarrow CaSO_3 + H_2O$$
$$CaCO_3 + SO_2 \rightarrow CaSO_3 + CO_2$$
$$CaSO_3 + \tfrac{1}{2}O_2 \rightarrow CaSO_4$$

The last of these reactions can be encouraged by the injection of air into the sump of the scrubbing tower. This yields high-quality gypsum ($CaSO_4.2H_2O$) which can be sold for use in plasterboard and other building materials.

NO_x, carbon monoxide and unburnt hydrocarbons

The burning of fossil fuels in air produces nitric oxide (NO) and, to a lesser extent, nitrogen dioxide (NO_2); these are collectively known as NO_x. They are formed by the reaction of atmospheric oxygen with nitrogen at the high temperatures reached during combustion. The nitrogen may originate from either the air or the fuel, thereby producing thermal-NO_x and fuel-NO_x respectively.

The problem of fuel-NO_x is primarily associated with coal because it has relatively high levels of nitrogen (1–2%) compared with other fossil fuels. For example, natural gas is virtually nitrogen-free, while fuel oil contains <0.5% N.

Clearly, thermal-NO_x formation occurs whenever fuels are burnt in air. This allows transport to be a major contributor to NO_x emissions. For example, in the UK about half of NO_x is traffic-related (1994 data). The remainder originates from stationary producers, particularly electricity generating stations.

Reduction in the emissions of NO_x can be achieved by alterations to the combustion process. The reactions that produce thermal-NO_x are endothermic and are therefore favoured by high temperatures. Lowering the temperature of combustion by, for example, recycling exhaust gases will therefore diminish NO_x emissions. Unfortunately, this will also reduce the Carnot efficiency of any heat-to-work device driven by the fuel (Chapter 13, Box 13.1). If used in a motor vehicle, NO_x reduction by this method will therefore be at the expense of fuel economy.

Fuel-NO_x emissions can also be controlled by adjustments to the combustion process. Fuel nitrogen that has been oxidised to nitric oxide may then be reduced to molecular nitrogen by either fuel-derived volatiles or char, for example:

$$2NO_{(g)} + 2CO_{(g)} \rightarrow N_{2(g)} + 2CO_{2(g)}$$
$$2NO_{(g)} + 2C_{(s)} \rightarrow N_{2(g)} + 2CO_{(g)}$$

These reactions can be encouraged by allowing the early stages of the combustion process to be carried out under fuel-rich conditions, followed by an injection of air into the flame when it is more mature, allowing the char to be oxidised. This approach, called staged combustion, when used alone can result in the removal of up to 50% of NO_x in coal-fired stations.

The treatment of flue gases can also lead to NO_x removal. The approach used is dependent on whether the source is static or mobile. In the former case, either ammonia, NH_3 (with or without a catalyst), or urea, $(NH_2)_2CO$, is injected into the stack gases, causing the NO_x to be reduced:

$$6NO + 4NH_3 \rightarrow 5N_2 + 6H_2O$$

and

$$4NO + 4NH_3 + O_2 \rightarrow 4N_2 + 6H_2O$$

or

$$2(NH_2)_2CO + 6NO \rightarrow 5N_2 + 2CO_2 + 4H_2O$$

The treatment of vehicular emissions may be achieved by the catalytic reduction of NO_x to molecular nitrogen at the expense of carbon monoxide (CO) present in the exhaust gases:

$$2NO + 2CO \xrightarrow{\text{catalyst (e.g. rhodium on an inert support)}} 2CO_2 + N_2$$

Then, air may be injected and the gases allowed to pass over an oxidation catalyst such as platinum or palladium on an inert support. This will facilitate the conversion of any residual carbon monoxide to carbon dioxide and any unburnt hydrocarbons present in the waste stream to carbon dioxide and water.

Particulates

Both stationary sources and diesel-powered vehicles produce significant amounts of particulates. Where attempted, the recovery of these contaminants from the stack gases of the former source is generally very successful. The technologies used are based on cyclones, electrostatic precipitators and/or fabric filters (bag filters) (Figure 16.2).

During the operation of a cyclone, the exhaust gases enter the top of its essentially cylindrical body, at a tangent. This causes them to move downwards in a helical fashion, generating centripetal forces that drive the particulates to the walls, from where they fall, exiting the cyclone at the bottom. The cleaned gases then leave the top of the cyclone via the pipe at its centre.

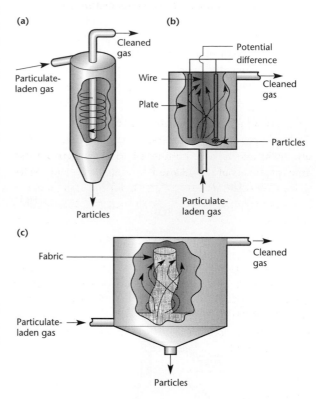

Figure 16.2 Schematic representations of particulate control devices used with static sources: (a) a cyclone, (b) an electrostatic precipitator, (c) a fabric filter.

Electrostatic precipitators (ESPs) operate by virtue of a potential difference of 30 to 60 kV between the wires and plates that they contain. This causes a very steep gradient in the electric field around the wires and a concomitant high concentration of ions. These charge the particles of the effluent stream, which are then accelerated towards the plates by the potential difference. The dust may then be dislodged from the plates by agitation, allowing it to fall into a collection hopper.

Fabric filters (bag filters) physically remove particulates from the exhaust gases that are made to pass through them. The filters may be of many designs, although tubular constructions are common. The dust burden is periodically removed by either mechanical shaking and/or the reversal of the direction of gas flow.

There is increasing concern over the sooty particulates from diesel engines, especially those with diameters $\leqslant 10 \, \mu m$ (the PM_{10}), as epidemiological studies indicate that these contaminants may cause a range of health problems including heart disease. In the UK, diesel engines account for about 20% of all PM_{10} emissions (1994 data).

Control of diesel particulates is technologically difficult, though two approaches seem promising. The first involves improving the homogeneity of the fuel–air mixture at the time of firing, so ensuring a more complete burn. The second relies on ceramic filters that may be cleaned either physically, by compressed air, or chemically, by heating in the presence of air.

Residual solids

The combustion of finely ground coal in electricity generating stations produces very large quantities of residual solids. These are ashes and, more recently, the products of limestone-based desulfurisation.

Two types of ash are generated, namely pulverised fuel ash (PFA) and furnace bottom ash (FBA); together these amount to about 12–$13\,\mathrm{Mt\,a^{-1}}$ in England and Wales alone (1990 data). PFA is collected as a particulate from the flue gases and accounts for 80% of the total. Both of these products are used in cementitious materials. Despite this, in areas where production outstrips demand, considerable quantities are sent to landfill.

As previously mentioned, lime- or limestone-based desulfurisation post PFA removal can yield high-quality gypsum ($CaSO_4.2H_2O$). Clearly this has commercial value. However, the vast amounts produced may be sufficient to swamp the market, necessitating other disposal routes including landfill.

Carbon dioxide

All fossil fuel combustion leads to the generation of carbon dioxide. Many exotic means of diminishing the contamination of the atmosphere with this gas have been suggested. Included amongst these is the possibility of increasing the primary productivity of the oceans. It is thought that this may be achieved by adding relatively small amounts of iron to areas that are deficient in this element. According to this hypothesis, the consequent increased rates of photosynthesis will result in the absorption of carbon dioxide. Recent large-scale experiments in the Pacific demonstrated that a single addition of iron salts did indeed promote productivity, at least in the short term. However, a fully concomitant net consumption of carbon dioxide did not occur. One possible explanation of this is that an increased biomass of photosynthetic plankton encouraged the activity of grazing zooplankton, and that the respiratory activity of these organisms recycled a large proportion of the carbon dioxide originally absorbed. It seems doubtful that the seeding of oceans with iron represents a feasible means of controlling atmospheric levels of carbon dioxide. A more practicable approach is to look for improved fuel efficiency. This would be of even greater efficacy if coupled with a switch to low-carbon fuels such

as methane, or even non-carbon fuels including hydrogen (H_2), which may be generated by hydroelectric power.

16.2 Low-hazard solid wastes

Solid wastes (refuse) may be categorised by source into mining, agricultural, industrial and urban (municipal) waste. The last of these includes wastes generated by commerce, local authorities and domestic households.

On a global basis, data concerning the amounts of solid waste generated are inadequate. The problem of insufficient data is compounded by variations in the definition of waste from country to country, making comparisons difficult. However, it is clear that the problem is enormous. For example, for the period of the late 1980s it has been estimated that the OECD countries generated in excess of 1.85×10^{12} kg of solid waste per year. What is more, in some respects the situation appears to be getting worse, particularly in the developing countries. For example, in the more-developed world, *municipal* solid waste generation increased from about $3.2 \times 10^{11}\,\mathrm{kg\,a^{-1}}$ in 1970 to $4 \times 10^{11}\,\mathrm{kg\,a^{-1}}$ in 1990 ($\sim$25%). During the same period, the production of refuse in the developing nations underwent an even more rapid rate of increase from $1.6 \times 10^{11}\,\mathrm{kg\,a^{-1}}$ to $3.2 \times 10^{11}\,\mathrm{kg\,a^{-1}}$ ($\sim$100%).

Most solid waste is of low intrinsic hazard. Nonetheless, if mismanaged even this has the potential to cause a diversity of problems, ranging from aesthetic deterioration of the environment through to significant increases in the incidence of disease and the pollution of drinking waters.

Of economic necessity, mining waste is usually disposed of on land near to the mine workings, often forming large spoil heaps. Agricultural solid waste, including crop residues and dung, have fertiliser and soil-conditioning value. Therefore, they are generally disposed of *in situ*. This leaves industrial and urban wastes to consider. The main disposal options for low-hazard waste from these sources are, in approximate order of increasing desirability: indiscriminate dumping, landfill (organised dumping on land), incineration (if organic) and reuse.

Indiscriminate dumping is an almost ubiquitous problem. However, it is particularly acute in many of the cities of the developing world. This is despite the relatively low *per capita* generation of domestic refuse in these cities ($\sim$145–330 kg a^{-1}) compared with the production rate in the cities of the more-developed countries ($\sim$255–655 kg a^{-1}) (1984 data). The main cause of the problem is that, in the less-developed nations, only about 50–70% of urban solid waste is collected (1992 figures). The remainder accumulates in the streets and open spaces, where it

Further Information Box

16.2 The health of waste-pickers

A very great number of people derive at least part of their livelihood from scavenging useful or saleable items from refuse tips. This practice is particularly prevalent in the developing world. The numbers of people involved in this waste-picking are not known, although some estimates have been made. For example, in the Philippines around 25 000 people take waste from the Smokey Mountain dump, Manila.

These people experience the elevated health risks associated with exposure to enhanced levels of pollution and disease vectors. A large number of the tips on which they work receive both domestic and industrial waste; many will also contain human excreta. It is unsurprising therefore that waste-pickers have a higher than normal incidence of chronic respiratory, skin and eye diseases as well as elevated levels of intestinal parasite infection.

becomes a breeding ground for vermin, spreading disease. Where collection does occur, it frequently results in the formation of open tips that support large numbers of waste-pickers who derive an income from the reusable articles that have been discarded (Box 16.2).

Unlike open tips, properly managed landfill sites are a very effective means of low-hazard solid waste disposal. If the waste is covered with soil on a daily basis, odour release is controlled and vermin are discouraged. Under these conditions, these facilities are called 'sanitary landfill' sites and need not be a source of either public nuisance or health hazard. Once full, anaerobic degradation of the material within the capped landfill occurs over a 3–10 year period. During this time, the site is of little use as the ground settles and gas is evolved. This is mainly carbon dioxide and methane, controlled removal of which is desirable as this avoids the danger of explosions.

The incineration of low-hazard solid waste with high organic contents in large purpose-built facilities is attractive for several reasons. Principal among these is the considerable reduction in the volume of solid material achieved by this process. In the case of domestic refuse this is generally about 75%. What is more, the residue does not undergo anaerobic digestion when placed in landfill; consequently, settlement and gas generation do not occur, allowing the site, once full, to be built upon.

The major drawback of incineration is the generation of flue gases and particulates. These can be minimised by the application of technologies that are essentially the same as those used to clean the stack gases of static fossil fuel burning facilities (Section 16.1).

Solid wastes sent for incineration frequently include chlorine-containing organic substances, such as polyvinylchloride (PVC). The burning of these leads to the formation of trace amounts of polychlorinated dibenzo-*p*-dioxins and polychlorinated dibenzofurans (PCDDs and PCDFs), some of which are highly toxic (Box 16.3). The presence of these materials in the emissions and ashes produced by incinerators of all kinds has generated considerable opposition to this type of waste treatment facility.

There are several ways in which low-hazard solid waste can be reused. The main processes available are the recycling of individual materials, the generation of refuse-derived fuel, composting, and thermochemical treatment.

Urban refuse from an industrialised country may be expected to have a composition that approximates to that shown in Table 16.1. Virtually all of the components listed would have a reuse value, if they were collected separately. Unfortunately, this is largely impracticable and economically unviable. However, in recent years there has been a move towards the separate collection of the more valuable items, particularly paper, glass, aluminium, steel, plastics and fabric. In the UK, this has been achieved largely by the willingness of the public to take these items to specialised receptacles ('banks'), often situated in car parks or at household waste disposal facilities.

An alternative approach is to separate the mixed waste after collection. In the case of the ferrous metals this is readily achieved by magnetic means. While the separation of the other components is more difficult, it can be achieved, to some extent, on the basis of density.

The recycling of waste has other environmental benefits besides those directly associated with direct waste reduction. Waste recycling generally consumes fewer resources and produces less pollution than the winning of materials from virgin sources (Table 16.2).

There is evidence to suggest that the recycling of some solid wastes is becoming more significant. For example, on a worldwide basis, in 1971 recycled aluminium formed about 16% of the total yearly consumption of this metal; by 1987 this had grown to over 23%. What is more, during the same period, total consumption of aluminium increased from about 1.2×10^{10} to approximately 2.2×10^{10} kg a^{-1}.

The success of recycling activity varies considerably from one country to another. For example, while the UK

Further Information Box

16.3   PCDDs and PCDFs

Major controversy surrounds the polychlorinated dibenzo-*p*-dioxins (PCDDs) and polychlorinated dibenzofurans (PCDFs). The most toxic of these compounds, 2,3,7,8-tetrachlorodibenzo-*p*-dioxin (TCDD), has been dubbed by Greenpeace as 'the world's most toxic synthetic chemical'.

PCDDs and PCDFs are known in the press as 'dioxins' and 'furans' respectively; they are not single compounds but families of congeners, the chemical structures of which may be represented thus:

[chemical structure of PCDDs]

PCDDs

[chemical structure of PCDFs]

PCDFs

The toxicity of these compounds varies greatly from one congener to another, being maximised by chlorination in the 2, 3, 7 and 8 positions. In addition, some biological species are very much more susceptible to poisoning by PCDDs or PCDFs than others. In studies using TCDD, the oral LD_{50} was found to be $0.6\,\mu\mathrm{g\,kg}^{-1}$ in male guinea pigs, compared with $1100\,\mu\mathrm{g\,kg}^{-1}$ in hamsters. The evidence available suggests that humans are much less susceptible to these toxicants than the former of these test animals.

A very wide range of sub-lethal effects have been observed in test animals dosed with TCDD. These include anorexia, cancer, immune system suppression and reproductive problems, including birth defects (i.e. TCDD is a teratogen). Epidemiological studies on humans who have been contaminated with TCDD, either voluntarily or by accident, have also been carried out. The only unequivocal finding of this work is that this compound, like many other chlorinated organics, causes persistent acne-like skin lesions (chloracne). However, there are strong indications that dioxins cause disturbances in both hormonal control mechanisms and the immune system. Among the studies carried out is recent work based on employees contaminated with TCDD during an

accident that occurred in November 1953 in BASF's Ludwigshafen plant. These workers showed highly elevated levels of infections of the respiratory and intestinal tracts, peripheral nervous system disorders and thyroid disease. Analysis of death certificates showed an abnormally high rate of death from cancers, such as lymphomas and melanoma.

Both PCDDs and PCDFs are of anthropogenic origin and are almost certainly xenobiotic. Neither is deliberately manufactured as they have no known uses. However, they are extremely widespread environmental contaminants. A study of the interior surfaces of office buildings in Boston, Massachusetts, USA, found that background levels of contamination ranged from 0.47 to 5.4 and from 2.8 to $146\,\mathrm{ng\,m}^{-2}$ for PCDFs and PCDDs respectively (1989 data).

Exposure to PCDFs and PCDDs is usually cited in terms of the equivalent amount of TCDD, because of the varying toxicity of the compounds involved. Human exposure is estimated to be about $1 \times 10^{-10}\,\mathrm{g}$ TCDD equivalent per day per person.

PCDFs and PCDDs are by-products of a number of processes. As discussed later in this chapter in Box 16.4, PCBs generate PCDFs when they are heated in the presence of air. The dioxin TCDD is formed during the alkaline hydrolysis of tetrachlorobenzene to 2,4,5-trichlorophenol. This is part of the manufacturing process making the herbicides 2,4,5-T and 'Agent Orange', hence both of these products are inevitably contaminated with trace amounts of this highly toxic substance. What is more, the hydrolysis reaction can get out of control. This has happened at least six times in the past, perhaps most notoriously on 10 July 1976 when it caused an explosion at the ICMESA works in Seveso, Italy, contaminating the surrounding area with both 2,4,5-trichlorophenol and a total of about 2 kg of TCDD.

Both PCDFs and PCDDs are formed during the combustion of materials containing organochlorine compounds, including PCBs (Box 16.4) and the common plastic, PVC. This has caused alarm over the burning of municipal waste. However, it appears that the risks are small. Even people living in the immediate locality of an incinerator will experience increases in exposure of less than 1% above background.

Finally, paper bleached with chlorine has been shown to contain traces of TCDD. This can be avoided either by using a non-chlorine bleach, such as ozone, or by leaving the paper unbleached.

recycles 14% of its glass, the Netherlands recycles 62% (1990 data). Ironically, because of the activities of waste-pickers, less-developed countries frequently have high rates of refuse reuse. This is despite the generally lower levels of valuable material contained in the solid waste of these counties.

Density-based solid waste separation can generate an inorganic fraction (containing metals and glass for recycling) and an organic fraction of sufficiently high calorific value to use as a fuel. This refuse-derived fuel may be used in either a shredded or a pelletised form. Recently, waste tyres have been used to fire cement kilns; one advantage of this process

Table 16.1 The composition of typical urban refuse derived from an industrialised country.

Component	Proportion/% by weight
Paper	35
Garden waste	16
Food waste	15
Metals	10
Glass	10
Plastics, rubber and leather	7
Rags	2
Miscellaneous	5

Table 16.2 The potential savings of recycling.

	Potential saving/%			
	Aluminium	Glass	Paper	Steel
Water used	0	50	58	40
Energy used	90–97	4–32	23–74	47–74
Mining wastes	0	80	0	97
Polluting emissions to the atmosphere	95	20	74	85
Polluting discharges to watercourses	97	0	35	76

Data from UNEP, *Environmental Data Report*, 3rd edition, Blackwell, Oxford, 1991.

is that the ash becomes integrated with the product, obviating the need for its disposal.

Composting of refuse, under aerobic conditions, offers another way of producing a useful product. The material generated finds use as a soil conditioner and low-grade fertiliser.

Finally, solid waste can be degraded by a variety of thermo-chemical processes, including pyrolysis (i.e. chemical breakdown achieved by heating in an anaerobic atmosphere). The product of most of these processes is a solid residue together with fuel gas and oil. The attraction of such processes is that they simultaneously reduce the mass of the solid that has to be disposed of, while producing fuels with good handling properties.

16.3 Low-hazard waste waters (sewage)

The water within the sewerage system of a community is called sewage. It consists of the outflow from domestic and industrial premises and, in some cases, the run-off from roads. This waste water is usually greatly diluted by the ingress of ground water through leaking pipe joints.

Only a very small fraction of sewage (0.05%) is waste material, the rest being water. Despite its apparently low waste content, the discharge of untreated sewage into surface waters can lead to gross pollution (Chapter 14, Section 14.1).

Sewage treatment is primarily aimed at lowering the pathogen content of the waste. Additional objectives include a decrease in its biochemical oxygen demand (BOD, see Chapter 14, Box 14.1) and solids content. These objectives may be achieved in a series of stages (Figure 16.3).

Preliminary treatment removes the larger objects within the raw sewage (lumps of wood, bottles, sanitary towels, toilet paper, etc.) and the grit. This may be the only treatment, if any, that is given to sewage prior to its discharge into the sea. The processes used are mechanical. Screens constructed from iron bars remove the larger objects. In addition, macerators may be used to break up the more friable lumps so that they may proceed for further treatment. Grit separation is achieved using gravity under conditions where the less dense organic matter remains in suspension.

In all but the most rudimentary plants, the effluent from preliminary treatment is then subjected to primary treatment. During this process, the sewage is allowed to slowly traverse a tank, allowing about half of the suspended solids to fall to the bottom. This produces primary sludge and settled sewage (also called primary effluent). The sludge is digested (see later) and the settled sewage then enters secondary treatment.

Secondary treatment is a biological process. Three designs of reactor are in common use, namely trickling (biological) filters, activated sludge tanks and oxidation (stabilisation) ponds. The last of these is only appropriate in warm climates.

A trickling filter is a tank filled with inert solid particles, typically in the size range 3.8–5.0 cm in diameter. These are covered with a mixed, essentially microbiological community, mainly developed from the sewage. Settled sewage is sprinkled over the top of the tank via moving booms. The sewage percolates down the filter, where its organic content is largely oxidised by organisms established on the solid support. Oxygen for this process is provided by air that is passively drawn into the tank. In contrast, activated sludge tanks are actively aerated. In these, the settled sewage is oxidised by a suspension of micro-organisms.

Both trickling filters and activated sludge tanks produce secondary sludge that is removed downstream in final settlement tanks. In the case of the activated sludge

Figure 16.3 The sewage treatment process.

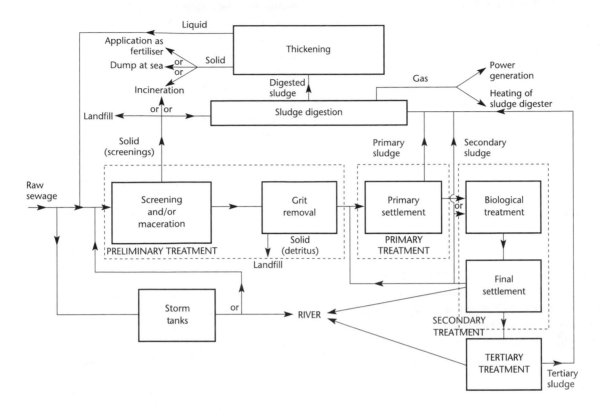

process most of this is returned to the aerated tank in order to maintain its biological community. The remainder may be added to the primary settlement tank, as may all of the sludge from trickling filters.

Oxidation ponds are large shallow (~1 m in depth) tanks through which settled sewage may slowly pass. Microbial action releases nutrient species (CO_2, NH_3, NO_3^-) that sustain algal growth. The algae generate molecular oxygen during photosynthesis, which sustains the activity of the bacteria. An anaerobic sludge forms on the bottom of the ponds in which methane is produced. An advantage of oxidation ponds is that they can be harvested. The algae generated can be fed to animals or burnt. What is more, oxidation ponds can be used to raise fish, although there is a risk of pathogen transfer if the fish are used for human consumption.

The preliminary, primary and secondary treatments outlined above are highly successful. When in combination, they are capable of producing an effluent with less than 30 mg l^{-1} of suspended solids and a BOD of less than 20 mg l^{-1} (typical sewage contains 600 mg l^{-1} of total solids, of which 200 mg l^{-1} are suspended, and has a BOD of 3000 mg l^{-1}). Pathogen populations are also greatly reduced. For example, the population of *Salmonella paratyphi* can be decreased by 84–99% by the use of trickling filters.

The final effluent from the treatment works is discharged into a river, lake or sea. Tertiary treatment is seen as desirable in locations where the degree of dilution of the effluent is small, or where potable water is to be withdrawn downstream for treatment and distribution. The purpose of this treatment is to further reduce the BOD and/or concentrations of suspended solids, nutrients, toxicants (such as heavy metals or poisonous organics) and/or pathogens. A wide range of technologies have been developed to facilitate the desired improvements, including oxidation ponds, sand filters, microstrainers, adsorption onto activated carbon, ion exchange, chemical precipitation, microfiltration, and disinfection. None of these, when operated alone, can bring about the desired reductions in all of the parameters listed above.

Conventional sewage treatment generates sludge from both the primary and secondary stages, to which may be added any sludge produced during tertiary treatment. These are mixed and digested in a two-stage process, the aim of which is to produce a material of reduced volume and acceptable odour that does not attract harmful insects or rodents. The first stage is anaerobic and is carried out at 27–35°C. It produces a gas that is approximately 72% methane and 28% carbon dioxide; this may be collected

Waste management

and used to generate heat (to warm the digester) and electricity.

The second stage is carried out in the open. The sludge is allowed to settle (thicken), producing the final product, digested sludge. Disposing of this is problematic. Options include dumping at sea, incineration, landfill, and use on land as a fertiliser/soil conditioner. The last of these is restricted by both transport costs and the heavy metal burden of the sludge. Landfill sites are increasingly scarce and dumping at sea is becoming restricted by legislation; in the US this practice was banned in 1991, and in the UK it ceased in 1998. Therefore the percentage of sludge that is sent for incineration appears likely to increase, at least in the more-developed countries.

For economic reasons, many households are not connected to mains sewerage systems. A commonly practised, but inferior, alternative is waste water treatment based on the septic tank. This acts as a combined sedimentation tank and anaerobic digester. The liquid effluent is allowed to soak away into the soil, while the sludge is periodically removed from the tank to be treated in a conventional sewage treatment plant.

Despite the existence of well-established technologies for the treatment and disposal of sewage, these are denied to many people. Estimates indicate that the number of people without sanitation facilities has reached 1880 million and this number seems likely to rise.

For example, estimates of South Korean hazardous waste production for 1985 and 1989 are 1.2×10^{10} and 2.1×10^{10} kg a^{-1} respectively.

In addition to the hazardous wastes currently being produced, considerable amounts have been inappropriately disposed of in the past. Consequently, a large number of sites have been contaminated and are potentially hazardous. For example, 32 000 such sites have been identified in the USA alone (1991 data). The remedial treatment of these is likely to be extremely costly.

There is also a legacy of materials that are now known to be hazardous, but that were once in common usage. Disposal of these substances is likely to cause problems for some time to come. Notable amongst these are the polychlorinated biphenyls (PCBs), which found extensive use as dielectrics in transformers (Box 16.4 and Chapter 14, Section 14.5.2) and asbestos, which was widely used as a building material.

For the purposes of the discussion here, high-hazard wastes may be considered to be those that, when released in relatively small amounts, are capable of producing severe and/or long-lasting damage to human health or the environment. Included in our definition are materials that contain pathogens or radioactive isotopes, along with substances that are corrosive, toxic, flammable, violently reactive or explosive.

Treatment and disposal

Strategies for the treatment of high-hazard wastes can be divided into those aimed at reuse, at destruction or at immobilisation.

Options for reuse include purification followed by recycling. This approach is frequently applied to solvents, as recovery of pure material from waste solvent is often achievable by distillation. An alternative approach is to use the waste from one process as a feedstock for another. For example, some waste oils may be mixed with fuel oils and burnt in industrial boilers.

There are instances where the waste from one process can be used to treat the waste from another. For example, prior to painting or electroplating, the oxide coat on steel is removed using acidic pickling liquors. Once spent, these may be reused as precipitating agents, removing phosphate from waste waters.

Reuse within the facility that generated the waste is desirable as the need for transport is minimised. However, this is not always possible. In such cases, certain types of waste, including metals and solvents, may be passed on to commercial reclaimers. These then treat the wastes and sell them on as useful products. Alternatively, the wastes generated by one manufacturing

16.4 High-hazard wastes

Assessment of the amount of high-hazard waste generated on a global basis is problematic. This is in part because of inadequate record keeping, but also because there is no uniformly accepted definition of high-hazard waste. This makes international comparisons very difficult as some countries use definitions that are much more all-embracing than others. By way of illustration, it is interesting to note that 41% of the solid industrial waste generated in the USA is categorised as hazardous. This compares with 33.5% in Hungary, 3% in the UK and 0.3% in Japan and Italy (1992 data). To a considerable degree, the enormous disparity between these figures reflects the differing regulatory frameworks within which the data were collected.

There are strong indications, however, that the production of high-hazard wastes is vast and expanding, both absolutely and as a proportion of industrial wastes as a whole. Global production of hazardous waste is estimated to be at least 3.38×10^{11} kg a^{-1} (1991 data), about 80% of which is generated in the USA. In some countries, the rate of increase appears to be phenomenal.

368

Further Information Box

16.4   PCBs

Polychlorinated biphenyls (PCBs) are a group of anthropogenic compounds that share the following structure:

PCBs

Commercial production of these compounds started in 1929. It peaked in 1970 at about $1.0 \times 10^8\,\mathrm{kg\,a^{-1}}$, followed by a rapid decline, with production ceasing later in the same decade.

These compounds were used as dielectric fluids in electrical transformers and capacitors. They also found uses in other essentially closed systems, namely vacuum pumps, compressors, hydraulic equipment and heat exchangers. Applications where these materials were open to the environment were also developed. These included their use in dirt-road dust-control agents, cutting oils, de-inking agents in newsprint recycling, and plasticiser and carbonless copy-paper production.

There have been two incidents in which large numbers of people have suffered from symptoms of organochlorine poisoning after consuming rice oil contaminated with PCBs from leaking heat exchangers. The first (the Yusho incident) occurred in Japan, involved about 1800 people and was initially recognised in 1968. The second (the Yu-Cheng incident) occurred in Taiwan in 1978–79.

In the acute sense, PCBs do not appear to be highly toxic; rodent oral LD_{50} values are about 1 g per kg of body weight. In humans, sub-lethal exposure to PCBs has been linked to the unpleasant skin rash known as chloracne, joint pain, fatigue and headaches. More alarmingly, the Yusho and Yu-Cheng incidents appeared to be linked to rises in the rates of miscarriage and birth defects. It now believed that the toxicity of the PCBs involved in these incidents was greatly elevated by the presence of PCDFs, which are formed when PCBs are heated in the presence of air (Box 16.3).

The fact that PCBs were widely used in power transformers leads to further concern. Malfunctions of such facilities may well be followed by fire. At the high temperatures reached, the PCBs will be oxidised forming, among other products, highly toxic PCDFs and PCDDs (Box 16.3).

PCB disposal represents a considerable problem. Much of the total production has now found its way to landfill. Given the longevity of these materials in the environment, this may well not be the best means of disposal. A wide range of chemical and biological treatments aimed at the total destruction of PCBs have been devised. Currently the best option appears to be incineration with a large excess of fuel oil. Clearly, care must be taken to avoid the production of PCDDs and PCDFs. The conditions required to do this include prolonged exposure of the waste (residence time $\sim 2\,\mathrm{s}$) to temperatures in excess of $1000\,^\circ\mathrm{C}$.

---

company may be used directly by another. In some areas this has been encouraged by the establishment of 'waste exchanges'. These produce databases that list the wastes available in a given region, so facilitating trade in these commodities.

Destruction of high-hazard wastes is only applicable to those that are hazardous by virtue of molecules that they contain rather than their constituent elements. For example, the cyanide ion (CN^-) is found in wastes from metal processing industries. It is highly toxic even though both of its constituent elements are essential for life (Chapter 5). It is toxic by virtue of its affinity for the active sites of enzymes involved in respiration. Consequently, ingestion of sufficient amounts of this ion results in rapid death. Wastes containing this species may be detoxified by treatment with chlorine (Cl_2), thus:

$$CN^-_{(aq)} + H_2O_{(l)} + Cl_{2(aq)} \rightarrow OCN^-_{(aq)} + 2HCl_{(aq)}$$
$$\text{cyanate}$$

followed by

$$OCN^-_{(aq)} + H_3O^+_{(aq)} \rightarrow NH_{3(aq)} + CO_{2(aq)}$$

Compare this process with the approach used in the treatment of waste waters containing toxic metals. These are generated by a number of industries including mining, metal-plating and ceramics manufacture. Unlike cyanide, metals cannot be destroyed. Consequently, treatment of waste streams contaminated with these elements involves the removal of metals from the aqueous phase. Clearly, the contaminants vary from source to source; however, they may include copper, nickel, cadmium, lead, chromium, mercury and/or zinc. These and many other heavy metals can be largely removed from the water by the addition of an anion that causes the precipitation of the metal as an insoluble salt. Anions used for this purpose include sulfate (SO_4^{2-}), sulfide (S^{2-}) and hydroxide (OH^-).

As in the case of cyanide destruction, discussed above, many of the destructive treatment methods are waste specific. However, there are others of more general applicability, notably thermo-chemical and biological processes.

The main thermo-chemical treatment used is incineration. In the case of wholly organic wastes, this method is also a means of complete waste disposal as the products are relatively harmless gases, principally $CO_{2(g)}$

and $H_2O_{(g)}$, which are subsequently vented into the air. The high temperatures reached also result in sterilisation. This is seen as a great advantage in the disposal of materials, such as hospital wastes, that may be contaminated with pathogens.

Incineration of high- and low-hazard wastes share the same drawback, namely potential air pollution. However, this may be minimised by a combination of:

- high-temperature combustion (ideally >1000°C);
- a long residence time of the waste in a hot oxidising environment (>2 or 3 seconds, depending on the waste);
- rapid stack gas cooling (to avoid the formation of toxic dioxins and furans: Box 16.3);
- flue gas cleaning.

By such means, modern plant is capable of achieving burnouts in excess of 99.99%.

Unfortunately, there are still a great number of incinerators that do not incorporate all of the features listed above. This has led to concern in recent years. In the UK, much of this has centred on the incineration of clinical waste as, until April 1991, this fell outside the reach of all environmental law.

The incorporation of organic high-hazard wastes into the input stream of cement kilns has been used for many years as an ultimate disposal system. This has several advantages including high-temperature incineration with long residence times and the incorporation of any ash into the cement product, thus avoiding disposal costs.

Other thermo-chemical treatments applicable to high-hazard wastes include pyrolysis (mentioned in Section 16.2) and wet air oxidation. The latter of these involves heating the waste in a water slurry at high temperatures and pressures in the presence of air or pure oxygen (O_2). The products of this process are similar to those generated by combustion.

Biological methods of high-hazard waste disposal have been used for some time. In one system, known as land farming, oily wastes are spread onto the soil. Decomposition may be enhanced by the addition of inorganic fertilisers and the periodic disturbance of the land using conventional agricultural implements. This generates the right conditions for the breakdown of the wastes by the naturally occurring soil micro-organisms.

Wastes that are neither recycled nor destroyed must be disposed of. This can be done with much greater safety if the waste is immobilised first. The technologies used to do this involve either the incorporation of the waste into a solid matrix or its encapsulation within an impermeable polymeric cover. In addition to immobilisation, these processes are variously referred to as stabilisation, solidification or fixation.

Solid matrices within which waste can be incorporated may be formed of cementitious or organic polymeric material. Alternatively, inorganic wastes may be turned into a glass (vitrified) or incorporated into ceramic artifacts such as bricks. Vitrification involves the formation of a melt at around 1300°C and is therefore highly expensive. Consequently, it is generally reserved for the treatment of highly hazardous materials and may become the preferred option for the treatment of highly radioactive wastes (Case study 7, page 375, considers the disposal of radioactive waste in some detail).

Historically, the bulk of high-hazard waste has been disposed of to landfill, often with little or no pretreatment. In 1985, in the UK about $2.75 \times 10^9 \, kg \, a^{-1}$ of chemical waste was sent to landfill; this compares with a total of about $4.2 \times 10^8 \, kg \, a^{-1}$ that was treated chemically, fixed or incinerated.

It is clear that ill-considered landfill practices have caused and continue to cause environmental damage at a large number of sites. Nonetheless, when carefully managed, landfill is still seen as a highly appropriate means of disposal for many high-hazard wastes.

Modern secured landfill facilities are located in areas where groundwater contamination is unlikely. They are covered and lined with impermeable membranes and leachates are collected, monitored and treated (Figure 16.4). The site is divided into a number of areas called cells, into which wastes of known characteristics are placed. This avoids the co-disposal of incompatible materials and facilitates future removal of waste for recycling or further treatment. Ideally, an extensive programme of air and groundwater monitoring should be undertaken prior to the establishment of the facility and during and after its operation.

Heightened public concern and the increased commercial pressure on land means that the continued use of landfill as the primary means of high-hazard waste management seems in doubt, at least in the more-developed countries. Programmes of waste minimisation and waste treatment are likely to become more prevalent.

Other procedures that are used for the disposal of high-hazard wastes include dumping at sea. This has been a matter of controversy for some time. In *relative* terms the amounts of waste disposed of by this means are small; nonetheless, the absolute quantities are significant. For example, in 1985 the UK disposed of about $2.3 \times 10^8 \, kg \, a^{-1}$ of chemical wastes in this way. However, there have been political moves to curb this practice. It was agreed by the 13th Consultative Meeting of the London Dumping Convention (1972) that all sea-dumping of non-inert industrial waste should have ceased by 31 December 1995.

High-hazard wastes have also been disposed of by placement at depth within the Earth, well out of the reach

Figure 16.4 Systems suitable for (a) the lining and (b) the capping of secured landfill sites.

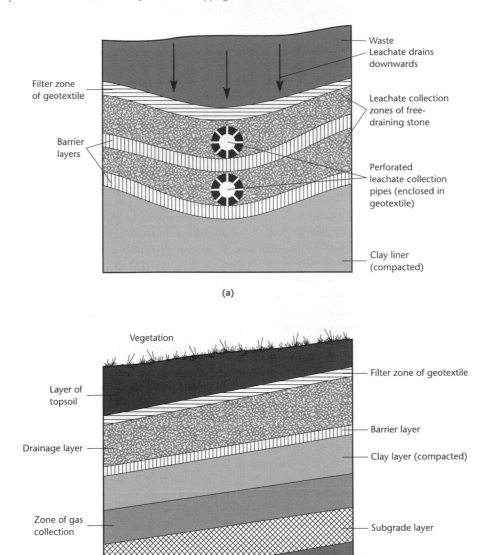

of potable aquifers. This has been done both within disused mines and by deep-well injection.

International trade in high-hazard wastes

In recent years, in the more-developed countries, there has been a progressive tightening of the legal frameworks that regulate the disposal of high-hazard wastes. In many cases this has increased the financial cost of disposal within the countries of origin, spawning an international trade in noxious waste. For example, legal exports of hazardous waste from Europe to less-developed countries total about 1.2×10^8 kg a^{-1} (1991 data).

In some cases, waste is imported by countries that have appropriate facilities for its treatment and disposal. For example, in 1992, clinical waste was imported by the UK from Germany for incineration in a specialised facility near Heathrow airport. Unfortunately, there have been a number of instances where high-hazard waste has been exported to countries that do not have the necessary facilities to deal with it adequately.

16.5 Waste minimisation, cleaner production and integrated waste management

Historically, industrial waste producers have relied on the cheapest means of disposal. This frequently involved discharges of untreated noxious material into water bodies or dumping on unsecured landfill sites. It is now evident that such inappropriate waste disposal practices have left a legacy of problems. The consequent economic, environmental and social costs are huge, but difficult to estimate. Most of these costs have been absorbed by society as a whole. However, there is evidence that attitudes are changing as the 'polluter pays' principle becomes more widely established.

Appropriate treatment and disposal of wastes can greatly ameliorate their environmental impact. However, this 'end-of-pipe' technology cannot reduce the amount of waste generated. This can only be achieved by in-process modifications targeted at cleaner production. The concept of cleaner production involves the application of integrated strategies aimed at avoiding unnecessary waste production and ensuring that the remaining wastes produced are innocuous. In order to be fully effective, this concept must be applied throughout the life-cycle of a product, from the extraction of the raw materials from which it is made through to its ultimate disposal.

Large manufacturing organisations are under increasing legislative and consumer pressure to limit the impact of their operations on the environment. There are now many examples of corporate initiatives that are aimed both at waste minimisation through cleaner production and at appropriate waste treatment. These can have direct economic as well as environmental benefits. For example, the 3M Corporation introduced its Pollution Prevention Pays, or '3P', programme in 1975. This concentrates on waste reuse and the reduction of pollution at source. The corporation believes that between its inception and 1989 the 3P programme directly resulted in a saving of US$408 million. Other examples include Polaroid's TUWR (Toxic Use and Waste Reduction) programme, started in 1987, and Dow's WRAP (Waste Reduction Always Pays) policy initiated the year before; excellent accounts of these measures are given by Buchholz *et al.* (1992) (see Section 16.8, Further reading).

Since the mid-1970s national and international agencies have been instrumental in promoting responsible waste reduction, treatment and disposal. The then EEC took an early interest, organising in 1976 one of the first meetings to discuss 'Low and Non-Waste Technologies' (LNWT). By 1978 compendia of these technologies were available. Other initiatives include PRISMA (Project on Industrial Successes with Waste Prevention) in the Netherlands, the Environmental Management Company (CETESB) in Brazil, and UNEP's International Cleaner Production Information Clearing House (IPIC). For further information about these and other schemes, see Tolba *et al.* (1992), pages 357 to 364.

Clearly, there is still enormous scope for improvement. In many cases, this can be achieved by simple means, such as waste segregation. To cite but one example, in Britain each hospital bed generates about 18 kg per week of waste. This includes everything from used dressings to flowers, all of which is classified as clinical and incinerated as if it were hazardous. In Germany, by careful segregation of truly hazardous materials from the rest, the amount of clinical waste is reduced to about 18 kg *per year* per bed (1992 data).

16.6 Summary

Virtually all human activity produces materials that are discarded as useless. These wastes include the gases and solids generated during fossil fuel combustion (primarily SO_2, NO_x, CO, CO_2, unburnt hydrocarbons, suspended particulates and ash), the solid wastes generated by mining, agricultural, industrial, commercial and domestic activity, and waste waters (sewage).

All of these wastes, whether intrinsically highly hazardous or not, are potentially damaging to the environment. This threat may be reduced by the appropriate use of the technologies that are outlined in this chapter. These aim to decrease either the production of waste or its environmental impact.

In recent years there has been a wider acceptance of waste management strategies based on the concept of cleaner production. This entails the minimisation of both the formation of waste and the level of its intrinsic hazard at all stages in the life-cycle of a product.

16.7 Problems

1 A coal with a calorific value of 3.4×10^4 kJ kg^{-1} and a sulfur content of 2% (w/w) generated the same amount of sulfur dioxide per kJ of energy released as an oil with a sulfur content of 3% (w/w). What is the calorific value of the oil?

2 Drax power station in North Yorkshire, UK, burns 1.1×10^{10} kg a^{-1} of coal.
  (a) At what rate would this produce sulfur dioxide assuming that no attempt was made to reduce emissions of this gas?
  (b) If flue gas desulfurisation (FGD) were used, based on the production of gypsum (CaSO$_4$.2H$_2$O) from limestone, how much stone would be consumed per year and how much gypsum would be produced? Assume that this process removed 90% of the SO$_2$, that limestone is pure CaCO$_3$ and that the product is pure CaSO$_4$.2H$_2$O.
  (c) Under the conditions posed in (b) above, how much extra carbon dioxide would be generated per year as a consequence of FGD? How does this compare with the rate of carbon dioxide production in the absence of FGD?
  Express your answers in kg a^{-1}. Assume that the coal burnt contained 2% (w/w) S and 87% (w/w) C and that the introduction of FGD had no effect on the efficiency of the plant.

3 Oxidation catalysts are fitted to vehicles to cut the emissions of carbon monoxide and hydrocarbons. Write balanced equations to represent the overall reactions that occur. Use methane to represent the unburnt hydrocarbon.

4 If one were to use methane (CH$_4$) instead of octane (C$_8$H$_{18}$) as a fuel, what percentage saving in carbon dioxide emissions would be expected? You may assume that there would be no alteration in the thermal efficiency with which these fuels can be used. Note that the standard enthalpies of combustion of methane and octane are -890 and -5471 kJ mol^{-1} respectively.

5 One of the main inspirations behind suggestions of hydrogen (H$_2$) as a transport fuel is the potential saving in the emissions of the greenhouse gas carbon dioxide. Is the product of hydrogen combustion a greenhouse gas? Would increased output of this product be a cause for concern?

6 The main driving force behind a move to the incineration of domestic refuse is the reduction in waste volume that this achieves. List as many other advantages of this process as you can think of. Does it have any disadvantages?

7 Each volume of raw sludge digested yields about 10 volumes of sludge gas.
  (a) If this is converted to electricity with an overall efficiency of 25%, how much sludge must be digested to generate 1 kJ of electricity?
  (b) If the raw sludge is 96% water by weight and the untreated sewage had an organic content of 200 mg l^{-1}, how much raw sewage must be treated to generate 1 kJ of electricity? Assume that half of the organic matter in the raw sewage is removed as sludge.
  Express your answers in litres and state all of the assumptions that you make. Note that the enthalpy of combustion of methane is -890 kJ mol^{-1}, that one mole of gas occupies 22.4 litres at 0°C and 1 atmosphere pressure, and that sludge gas is ~65% methane.

8 Why are oxidation ponds unsuitable for use in cooler climates?

9 What types of reaction are involved in the destruction of cyanide by the method outlined in the text? (See page 369.)

10 Lead(II) may be removed from aqueous waste by the addition of hydrogen sulfide gas (H$_2$S). Calculate the concentration of this gas that must be maintained in solution in order to achieve a maximum lead concentration in the treated effluent of 10 ppm at both pH 2 and pH 7. At what pH would the reaction between lead(II) and hydroxide ions obviate the need for the treatment with hydrogen sulfide? State all of the assumptions that you make during your calculations. Note that K_{sp} for PbS $= 7 \times 10^{-29}$ and for Pb(OH)$_2 = 2.8 \times 10^{-16}$, and that K_a for H$_2$S $= 1.1 \times 10^{-7}$ and for HS$^- = 1 \times 10^{-14}$.

11 Co-disposal of metal sulfides and sludge contaminated with sulfuric acid is most inadvisable. Why? (Hint: see Problem 10.)

12 The US Environmental Protection Agency estimates that an intake of PCDDs and PCDFs of 6×10^{-15} g TCDD equivalent per day per kilogram of body weight will enhance the chances of contracting cancer by 1 part in a million. This is considered to be acceptable. Are you consuming these contaminants at an acceptable rate? Assume that your intake is the same as the average cited in Box 16.3.

13 From a cleaner production point of view, is flue gas desulfurisation a good idea? Include in your answer a review of the other options that are available.

16.8   Further reading

Buchholz, R. A., A. A. Marcus and J. E. Post (1992) *Managing environmental issues; a casebook*. Englewood Cliffs, NJ: Prentice Hall. (Particularly good on corporate response to waste management)

Bunce, N. J. (1990) *Environmental chemistry*. Winnipeg: Wuerz. (Gives some of the scientific background to the technologies discussed in this chapter)

La Grega, M. D., P. L. Buckingham and J. C. Evans (1994) *Hazardous waste management*. New York: McGraw-Hill. (Highlights technical details, concentrates on the US experience)

Scragg, A. (1999) *Environmental biotechnology*. Harlow: Longman. (An accessible book with good coverage of sewage treatment and biological approaches to clean technology and the treatment of domestic, industrial and agricultural wastes)

Tolba, M. K., O. A. El-Kholy, E. El-Hinnawi, M. W. Holdgate, D. F. McMichael and R. E. Munn (Eds) (1992) *The world environment 1972–1992; two decades of challenge*. London: Chapman & Hall. (Includes some discussion of many of the wider issues associated with waste management)

Williams, P. T. (1998) *Waste treatment and disposal*. Chichester: John Wiley & Sons.

The disposal of radioactive waste

According to the International Atomic Energy Agency (IAEA), radioactive waste is defined as 'any material that contains a concentration of radionuclides greater that those deemed safe by national authorities, and for which no use is foreseen'. A radionuclide is an unstable atomic nucleus, which undergoes spontaneous radioactive decay, emitting radiation and usually eventually changing from one element to another (Chapter 1, Section 1.7). Radionuclides pose very serious risks, both to the environment and to human health. Importantly, exposure to radiation can lead to the development of cancer. However, radioactive elements vary greatly in their toxicity. The duration of the threat posed by a given radioisotope (the term for a radioactive isotope) depends in part on its half-life, i.e. the time required for the radioactive decay of half the original amount of material. This differs enormously between radioisotopes, e.g. the half-life of iodine-131 is only 8.02 days whilst that of plutonium-239 is 24 390 years.

Radioactive waste (also called nuclear waste) is generated by a number of different industries and services, from both the civilian and military sectors. Sources include nuclear power generation, nuclear weapons production and, to a lesser extent, medical and scientific research applications involving radionuclides. In this case study, attention is focused on the major producer of non-military radioactive waste, the nuclear power industry, and, in particular, the nature and destination of the wastes generated by the final stages of the nuclear fuel cycle (Figure C7.1). For further information on the processes involved in nuclear energy production, including the different types of reactors used, the reader is referred to Chapter 13, Section 13.2.1.

The generation of significant amounts of electricity using nuclear fuel dates back to the 1960s. On a global scale, the electrical generating capacity of nuclear power plants increased considerably in the period between the early 1970s and the late 1980s, since when it has remained largely constant (Figure C7.2). This plateau is attributable to a number of factors, notably a loss of public confidence after the nuclear accident at Chernobyl in 1986 (Case study 4), the high cost of reactor decommissioning and the problems associated with the disposal of radioactive waste.

Radioactive waste is primarily classified on the basis of its radioactive content. Such waste may be in either solid or liquid form. According to the IAEA scheme, as revised in 1994, three principal classes of radioactive waste are recognised. These are exempt waste (EW) (for waste whose radionuclide level is considered too low to pose a radiological hazard), low- and intermediate-level waste (LILW) (grouped together) and high-level waste (HLW). Within the LILW class, a distinction may be made between 'short-lived' wastes, which contain radionuclides with a half-life of less than 30 years, and 'long-lived' wastes, which contain radionuclides with a half-life greater than 30 years. Most of the LILW from nuclear power plants is classified as short-lived, although long-lived LILW arises from the reprocessing of spent nuclear fuel. High-level waste (HLW) is highly radioactive, contains long-lived radionuclides and is the only class of nuclear waste to continue to generate heat. BNFL (British Nuclear Fuels plc) uses a slightly different classification system, in which the following three classes are recognised: low-level waste (LLW), intermediate-level waste (ILW) and high-level waste (HLW). Table C7.1 outlines the main sources of nuclear waste, using the BNFL classification scheme.

The disposal methods used for the different categories of nuclear waste are largely determined by the level of radioactivity present, together with the longevity of the constituent radionuclides. Low-level and intermediate-level short-lived wastes are, in many cases, treated and then conditioned prior to disposal. The object of the treatment procedure is to reduce waste volume, e.g. by compaction or incineration, whilst conditioning involves the immobilisation of the waste in substances such as polymers or concrete.

Figure C7.1 The nuclear fuel cycle. This encompasses the various stages associated with nuclear energy production, from uranium extraction through to the disposal of radioactive waste. The data presented is given in tonnes (t) and relates to the average annual fuel requirements of a typical 1000 MW light water reactor (after Cunningham and Saigo, 1995).

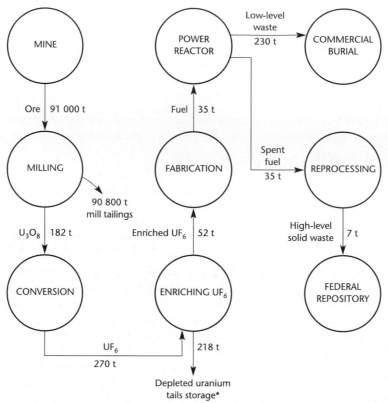

* Not required for reactor, but must be stored safely. Has value for future breeder reactor blanket.

Figure C7.2 Worldwide capacity (in gigawatts, GW) for electricity generation from nuclear fuels. Source: Vital Signs 1997–1998.

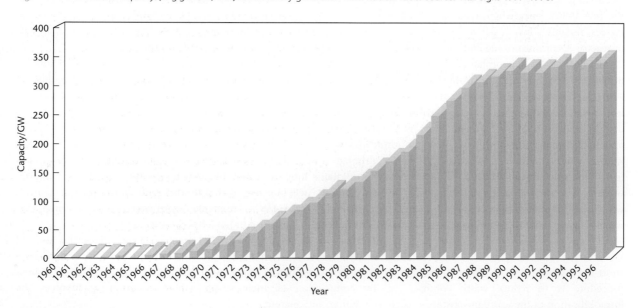

Table C7.1 The main sources of nuclear waste (using the BNFL classification system).

Type of nuclear waste	Sources associated with the nuclear power industry	Other sources
Low-level waste (LLW)	Cooling water from nuclear reactors; protective clothing, gloves, paper towels, packaging, etc., used in the vicinity of radioactive materials; material from decommissioned reactors	Certain practices/processes involving radionuclides carried out in hospitals, scientific research establishments and some industries
Intermediate-level waste (ILW)	Sludge from various treatment processes; fuel element cladding; contaminated equipment	
High-level waste (HLW)	Spent nuclear fuel rods	Obsolete nuclear weapons

At present, much of this type of less hazardous nuclear waste is disposed of to near-surface facilities. For example, low-level waste from the nuclear plant at Sellafield, Cumbria, UK (formerly Windscale) is deposited in containers inside a concrete vault at nearby Drigg. However, in the future, it is likely that disposal to repositories deep underground will become the method increasingly favoured for the disposal of LLW and ILW. This disposal method is already utilised by some countries, e.g. Finland. In the past, both the US and Europe have used dumping at sea as a disposal option for LLW and/or ILW. This practice was ended in 1970 by the US and in 1983 by European countries. However, a number of other countries continue to use the world's oceans as a receptacle for their nuclear waste.

Within the nuclear power industry, high-level waste is generated in the form of spent nuclear fuel rods. These are removed from the reactor core once their useful life is over. There are two options for dealing with the used nuclear fuel: reprocessing (in order to regenerate more fuel) or direct disposal. Reprocessing separates out the following fractions: uranium (96%), plutonium (1%) and waste (3%). According to BNFL, for each tonne of used nuclear fuel reprocessed, approximately $4\,m^3$ of LLW, $1\,m^3$ of ILW and $0.1\,m^3$ of HLW are isolated. These contain approximately 0.001%, 1% and 99% of the used fuel's total radioactivity, respectively. The high-level waste that arises from this reprocessing is in liquid form. This may be converted into a glassy solid, a process known as **vitrification**. Vitrified waste has a number of advantages over its liquid counterpart. For example, the volume of the HLW is reduced by up to one-third of the original, and handling, storage, transport, etc., are made safer and easier as a result.

In Western Europe, there are three reprocessing plants, one each at La Hague and Marcoule, both in France, and one at Sellafield, UK. All of these plants deal with both foreign and domestic fuel rods. There are also reprocessing plants in the former Soviet Union, which will accept back fuel rods that they have manufactured. However, reprocessing is not an option for all spent nuclear fuel. Reasons include the relatively large quantity of spent fuel generated worldwide (with an estimated 10 000 tonnes added each year) and the high expenditure involved in reprocessing, including transportation costs. In the US, which is the highest consumer of nuclear energy worldwide (Table C7.2), there has been no commercial spent fuel reprocessing since 1977.

The alternative for spent nuclear fuel not ultimately destined for reprocessing (and also for the HLW isolated by reprocessing itself) is direct disposal. However, the problem of finally disposing of such highly radioactive material safely has not yet been adequately addressed. Currently, used nuclear fuel remains in interim storage, usually in special storage ponds at the reactor sites where it was produced. The favoured option is burial in repositories deep underground, to a

Table C7.2 Nuclear energy consumption.

Country	Consumption (million tonnes oil equivalent) (1997)	Share of world total (1997)
United States	170.9	27.7%
France	102.1	16.5%
Japan	83.4	13.5%
Former Soviet Union (total)	52	8.4%
Germany	43.9	7.1%
United Kingdom	25.5	4.1%

Source: BP Statistical Review of World Energy, 1998.

depth of several hundred metres, within stable geological formations. However, to be considered for this purpose, rock formations must show no evidence of groundwater leaching or seismic (earthquake) or volcanic activity within the last 10 000 years. On this basis, it is inferred that they will remain stable for the next 10 000 years. Location (in relation to major centres of population) and accessibility (by road and rail links) are also factors which must be taken into account.

At present, several nuclear countries, notably the US, UK and Germany, are actively seeking suitable sites for the deep disposal of nuclear waste. However, such investigations have met with considerable public opposition, especially from communities in the vicinity of proposed sites. For example, local opposition to the proposal for a national repository at Yucca Mountain in Nevada, USA (for an estimated 40 000 tonnes of high-level nuclear waste), has brought a temporary halt to the proceedings, until the year 2010. No country yet disposes of high-level nuclear waste to deep underground repositories. However, some countries, for example Sweden, have established interim storage facilities, called monitored retrievable storage (MRS) facilities, to accommodate spent fuel rods for a period of 30–40 years, until they can be disposed of to a deep geologic repository. In the Swedish case, this is located within a rock cavern. There are calls in the US for the Department of Energy to adopt a similar system whilst the Yucca Mountain project remains on hold.

The need to find a *long-term* solution to the disposal of HLW, however, remains a pressing one. The amount of spent nuclear fuel requiring disposal (i.e. that not ultimately destined for reprocessing) is fast outstripping storage facilities at reactor sites. Moreover, many nuclear power stations are now reaching the end of their useful lives (after about 20 years in operation), with the majority having been constructed before 1986. Decommissioning these obsolete plants will further add to the stockpile of nuclear waste.

Further reading

Edwards, R. (1998) The world's dustbin. *New Scientist*, 31 January, 11.

Edwards, R. (1999) It's got to go. *New Scientist*, 27 March, 22–23.

Pickering, K. T. and L. A. Owen (1997) *An introduction to global environmental issues* (2nd edn). Chapter 6: Nuclear issues. London and New York: Routledge.

Brief answers to selected end of chapter problems

Chapter 1

1 (i)   2.
  (ii)   2.4.
  (iii) 2.8.6.
  (iv) 2.5.

2 Complete octets are attained if each oxygen is considered to be O^{2-} (electronic structure 2.8) and each titanium is considered to be Ti^{4+} (electronic structure 2.8.8).

3 All of the bonds present are single bonds.

4 (b) Hydrogen sulfide (H_2S can form intermolecular hydrogen bonds, silane cannot).

5 Equations (ii), (iii), (iv) and (v) are not balanced as given in the question. Balanced versions of these equations are given below:

  (ii) $MgCO_{3(s)} + 2H^+_{(aq)} \rightarrow Mg^{2+}_{(aq)} + H_2O_{(l)} + CO_{2(g)}$
  (iii) $CO_{2(g)} + H_2O_{(l)} \rightarrow H_2CO_{3(aq)}$
  (iv) $2SO_{2(g)} + O_{2(g)} \rightarrow 2SO_{3(g)}$
  (v) $SiO_4H_{4(aq)} \rightarrow SiO_{2(s)} + 2H_2O_{(l)}$

6 (i)   0.
  (ii)   −III.
  (iii) −III.
  (iv) V.
  (v)   III.
  (vi) III.

7

Eqn	Acid	Conjugate base	Base	Conjugate acid
(ii)	HNO_2	NO_2^-	H_2O	H_3O^+
(iii)	H_2S	S^{-II} (in FeS)	H_2O	H_3O^+
(iv)	H_2O	OH^-	CO_3^{2-} (in Na_2CO_3)	HCO_3^- (in $NaHCO_3$)
(v)	H_2O	OH^- (in $Fe(OH)_3$)	O^{2-} (formed from O_2)	OH^- (in $Fe(OH)_3$)
(vii)	H_2O	OH^-	NH_3	NH_4^+

8

Eqn	Reducing agent	Species reduced
(i)	HNO_2	O_2
(v)	Fe^{2+}	O_2

9 (iii), (v).

10 (ii), (iii), (iv), (v), (vi), (vii).

11 (vi) $Cu(H_2O)_6^{2+}$ contains dative bonds between the water molecules and the copper(II). (vii) NH_4^+ contains a dative bond. Equations (ii) and (iii) may also be considered as representations of complexation reactions as H_3O^+ contains a dative bond.

12 (i) 4.54×10^{-12} J/nucleus.
  (ii) 2.68×10^9 kJ mol^{-1}.
  (iii) 7.12 MeV/nucleon.

Chapter 2

1 (a) $\Delta H^o = -1429\,\text{kJ}\,\text{mol}^{-1}$.
   $\Delta S^o = 47.5\,\text{J}\,\text{K}^{-1}\,\text{mol}^{-1}$.
   $\Delta G^o = 1415\,\text{kJ}\,\text{mol}^{-1}$.
   (b) Specific enthalpy of ethane $= 47.5\,\text{kJ}\,\text{g}^{-1}$. Octane will produce more CO_2 than ethane on a joule for joule basis.

2 $16\,832\,\text{kJ}\,\text{dm}^{-3}$.

3 (a) 273 K (to three significant figures).
   (b) No.

4 As temperature increases gases become less soluble.

5 (a) $K = K_{sp}/K_a = 125$.
   (b) In acid rain.
   (c) Approximately $2.5 \times 10^3\,\text{ppm}$ or $6.3 \times 10^{-2}\,\text{mol}$ dm^{-3}, assuming that all $Ca^{2+}_{(aq)}$ and $HCO_3^-{}_{(aq)}$ ions originate from the interactions of H_3O^+ with calcium carbonate, and that $[Ca^{2+}_{(aq)}] = [HCO_3^-{}_{(aq)}]$.

6 pH $\simeq 3.8$, ignoring any contribution made by dissolved CO_2.

7 $1.9 \times 10^3\,\text{s}$ (to two significant figures).

8 $k^* = k[O_2]$.

9 0.53, assuming dry air.

Chapter 3

1 3.

2 Olivine (most easy), hornblende, biotite, quartz.

3 (a) (i)   loamy sand.
       (ii) sandy silt loam.
       (iii) clay.
   (b)

Textural class	% Sand		% Silt		% Clay	
	Max.	Min.	Max.	Min.	Max.	Min.
Clay loam	50	20	62	20	35	18
Silty clay	20	0	65	45	55	35
Sand	100	85	14	0	10	0

6 pH $\simeq 5.0$, assuming that, in the soil atmosphere, the partial pressure of $CO_{2(g)} = 6.4 \times 10^{-3}$ atm.

8 4°C.

9 No, because no inverse stratification.

Chapter 4

6 (a) $0\,\text{m}\,\text{s}^{-2}$.
   (b) $2.182 \times 10^{-3}\,\text{m}\,\text{s}^{-2}$.
   (c) $2.182 \times 10^{-3}\,\text{m}\,\text{s}^{-2}$.
   (d) $7.461 \times 10^{-4}\,\text{m}\,\text{s}^{-2}$.

Chapter 5

5 $2H_2O + NH_4^+ \rightarrow NO_2^- + 6e^- + 8H^+$
   $4H^+ + O_2 + 4e^- \rightarrow 2H_2O$

6 $4NO_3^- + 5CH_2O + 4H^+ \rightarrow 2N_2 + 7H_2O + 5CO_2$

9 $2.8 \times 10^{13}\,\text{dm}^3$.

11 *Approximate* atmospheric residence times for:
    $N_2 = 1.45 \times 10^7$ years,
    $SO_2 = 0.022$ years.

12 (a) 6.9 to 69 hours.
    (b) For a first order process, after ten half-lives less than 0.1% of the original sample remains. In this case this would take between 69 and 690 hours.

14 Troilite: $-$II.
    Pyrites: $-$I.

15 $0.90\,\text{mol}\,\text{kg}^{-1}$ or $2.6\,\text{mol}\,\text{dm}^{-3}$.

17 (a) $t_{1/2} = 0.6931\tau$.
    (b) 9.2 years.

Chapter 7

1 154.

3 The estimated population of yeast cells at 5, 10 and 15 hours is 122, 1484 and 18 080, respectively.

Chapter 9

4 The surface area to volume ratios of cubes with edges measuring 0.5 cm and 2 cm are 12 to 1 and 3 to 1 respectively.

5 $90\,\text{kJ}\,\text{m}^{-2}\,\text{a}^{-1}$; 0.1%.

7 0.17.

Chapter 12

3 $2.0 \times 10^3\,°\text{C}$ (to two significant figures).

Chapter 13

1 Thermal efficiency = 36%.

2 Tropics: 49.75%.
Arctic: 55.36%.

3 Approximately 1.2×10^{-11} g.

4 100%.

5 8.2 tonnes.

6 $>200\,J\,s^{-1}\,m^{-2} > 200\,W\,m^{-2}$.

7 $2.7 \times 10^7\,m^2$.

8 244.5 litres.

Chapter 15

1 First household: $54.8\,kg\,SO_2\,a^{-1}$.
Second household: $148\,kg\,SO_2\,a^{-1}$.

2 (a) $SO_2 < 1.04$ weeks.
$N_2O = 1040$ weeks.
NO, $NO_2 < 0.52$ weeks.

3 (iii) The following are radicals: HSO_3, OH, HO_2.

10 Approximately, pH = 4.2, assuming that the contribution to the $[H_3O^+]$ from the reaction between water and carbon dioxide is negligible.

11

Particle diameter/μm	Sedimentation rate[a]/ m s^{-1}	Time to fall 3 km[a]
1.5	1.4×10^{-4}	2.2×10^7 s
10	6.0×10^{-3}	5.0×10^5 s

[a]At terminal velocity

12 6.15 litres.

Chapter 16

1 $5.1 \times 10^4\,kJ\,kg^{-1}$.

2 (a) $4.4 \times 10^8\,kg\,SO_2\,a^{-1}$.
(b) Rate of limestone consumption, assuming that the stone need not be present in excess = $6.2 \times 10^8\,kg\,a^{-1}$. Rate of gypsum production = $1.1 \times 10^9\,kg\,a^{-1}$.
(c) Extra CO_2 production due to FGD = $2.7 \times 10^8\,kg\,CO_2\,a^{-1}$. CO_2 production without FGD = $3.5 \times 10^{10}\,kg\,CO_2\,a^{-1}$, assuming all of the carbon is transformed to CO_2 on combustion.

4 23.2%.

7 (a) 0.15 litres.
(b) 6.2 litres.

10 At pH 2, $1.3 \times 10^{-7}\,mol\,dm^{-3}$.
At pH 7, $1.3 \times 10^{-17}\,mol\,dm^{-3}$.
No H_2S needed at pH 8.4 and above.

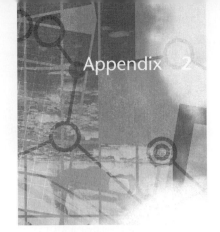

Units and molar constants

A	Conversion factors between units in common usage

Units of mass

Exact conversions:

	Grams (g)	Kilograms (kg)	Tonnes (t)
1 gram (g)	1	1×10^{-3}	1×10^{-6}
1 kilogram (kg)	1×10^3	1	1×10^{-3}
1 tonne (t)	1×10^6	1×10^3	1

The relationship between mass and chemical amount

The mass expressed in grams (symbol g) of a pure substance is related to the chemical amount expressed in moles (symbol mol) of that substance by the following equation (see Chapter 2, Box 2.4 for more information):

$$\text{moles} = \frac{\text{mass}}{\text{molar mass}}$$

Units of energy and work

Conversion data to five significant figures, except for those printed in *italics*, which are approximate:

	Joules (J)	calories (cal)	Kilowatt hours (kWh)	Electron volts (eV)
1 joule (J)	1	0.23885	2.7778×10^{-7}	6.2418×10^{18}
1 calorie (cal)	4.1868	1	1.1630×10^{-6}	2.6133×10^{19}
1 kilowatt hour (kWh)	3.6×10^6	8.5984×10^5	1	2.2470×10^{25}
1 electron volt (eV)	1.602×10^{-19}	3.8265×10^{-20}	4.4503×10^{-26}	1

Units of energy and work continued

	Joules (J)	British Thermal Units (btu or BTU)	Tonnes coal equivalent (tce)	
			UK	EU, non-UK
1 joule (J)	1	9.4781×10^{-4}	4.2×10^{-11}	3.4×10^{-11}
1 British Thermal Unit (btu or BTU)	1055.1	1	4.4×10^{-8}	3.6×10^{-8}
1 tonne coal equivalent (tce), UK definition	2.4×10^{10}	2.3×10^{7}	1	0.82
1 tonne coal equivalent (tce), EU, excluding UK, definition	2.93×10^{10}	2.8×10^{7}	1.2	1

Units of energy and work (continued)

	Joules (J)	Tonnes oil equivalent (toe)
1 joule (J)	1	2.3×10^{-11}
1 tonne oil equivalent (toe)	4.4×10^{10}	1

Note: 1 joule = 1 watt second, 1 therm = 1×10^5 btu.

Absolute temperature and the Celsius scale

Where absolute temperatures are required, the kelvin (K) scale is used in this book. To convert temperature in °C to temperature in K, add 273.15.

Units of concentration

See Chapter 2, Box 2.4.

Units of pressure

Conversion data to six significant figures:

	Atmospheres (atm)	Bars (bar)
1 atmosphere (atm)	1	1.01325
1 bar	0.986923	1

Units of area

Conversion data to six significant figures:

	Square metres (m²)	Square kilometres (km²)	Hectares (ha)	Acres
1 square metre (m²)	1	1×10^{-6}	1×10^{-4}	2.47105×10^{-4}
1 square kilometre (km²)	1×10^{6}	1	100	247.105
1 hectare (ha)	1×10^{4}	0.01	1	2.47105
1 acre	4046.86	4.04686×10^{-3}	0.404686	1

B   Prefixes that indicate multiples of units

Prefix	Symbol	Multiple
tera	T	10^{12}
giga	G	10^{9}
mega	M	10^{6}
kilo	k	10^{3}
hecto	h	10^{2}
deca	da	10
deci	d	10^{-1}
centi	c	10^{-2}
milli	m	10^{-3}
micro	μ	10^{-6}
nano	n	10^{-9}
pico	p	10^{-12}

C   Molar constants

The **Avogadro constant** (Avogadro's number) (symbol L or N_A) is the number of particles in one mole, i.e. $6.02252 \times 10^{23}\ \text{mol}^{-1}$.

The **molar gas volume** is the volume occupied by one mole of a gas. For any ideal gas, at 1 atmosphere pressure and 0°C, this is $22.415\ \text{dm}^3$. Note that this volume can be related to the volume of the ideal gas at any temperature (in K) and pressure, by the following expression:

$$\frac{P_1 V_1}{T_1} = \frac{P_2 V_2}{T_2}$$

where P_1, V_1 and T_1 represent the initial pressure, volume and temperature respectively, and P_2, V_2 and T_2 stand for the final pressure, volume and temperature.

Glossary

For a much more extensive listing of terms, see Lawrence, E., A. R. W. Jackson and J.M. Jackson (1998) *Longman dictionary of environmental science*. Harlow, UK: Addison Wesley Longman Ltd.

acid rain   rain, or precipitation in general (rain, snow, hail, etc.), that is contaminated with acidifying pollutants (principally $SO_{2(aq)}$, $H_2SO_{4(aq)}$ and $HNO_{3(aq)}$).

aerosol   a suspension of solid or liquid particles within a gas.

agroecosystem   an ecosystem that develops on farmed land and that includes the indigenous micro-organisms, plants and animals, and the crop species.

agroforestry   term used for the mixed cultivation of trees and herbaceous crops, long practised in the humid tropics.

air mass   a large body of air that shows relatively little horizontal variation in temperature or humidity. An air mass may be classified on the basis of characteristics dictated by its source region, e.g. polar continental, tropical maritime.

algal bloom   excessive growth of aquatic algae, often blue-green algae (Myxophyceae).

alpha decay   a spontaneous partial nuclear disintegration reaction, undergone by certain unstable nuclides, that is characterised by the emission of a fast-moving helium nucleus (an alpha particle, symbol α, $^4_2\alpha$ or $^4_2He^{2+}$).

anion   any negatively charged ion (i.e. contains more electrons than protons).

anthropogenic   produced or caused by human activity.

anticyclone   area of high atmospheric pressure.

aquifer   an underground layer of water-bearing rock.

atoms   the smallest units of matter that are capable of entering into chemical reactions.

autotroph   any organism able to utilise inorganic sources to synthesise its organic substances, using either light (photoautotroph) or inorganic chemicals (chemoautotroph) as a source of energy.

beta decay   a spontaneous partial nuclear disintegration reaction, undergone by certain unstable nuclides, that is characterised by the emission of a fast-moving electron (a beta particle, symbol β, β^- or $^0_{-1}e$).

biodiversity   term used to describe the variety of life at all levels of biological organisation, from the gene through to the ecosystem, although most commonly used with reference to the species level. The colloquial expression for biological diversity.

bioelements   those chemical elements that are required for the normal growth of organisms.

bioleaching   extraction of metals (mainly copper and uranium) from their ores using micro-organisms.

biological control   a pest control method in which, usually, one species of organism is used to control populations of another.

biological resources   a general term applied to all genetic resources, organisms (or parts thereof), populations or any other biotic components of ecosystems with actual or potential use or value to humans.

biological speciation   the process by which new species evolve.

biological species   a group of interbreeding individuals reproductively isolated from other groups.

biomagnification   increase in concentration of pollutants, e.g. DDT, in the bodies of living organisms at successively higher levels in the food chain.

biome   a major biogeographical division, characterised by its distinctive vegetation and climate. Examples include tundra, taiga, tropical rainforest and desert.

bioprospecting   the investigation of wild species of plants and animals for 'natural products' potentially useful to humans, e.g. through the development of pharmaceutical drugs.

bioremediation any technique used to enhance the recovery of a contaminated site by the use of living organisms.

biosphere reserve a specific type of protected area which, by its zoned structure, integrates human usage with conservation goals.

bovine spongiform encephalopathy (BSE) a type of degenerative neurological disease of cattle.

box model a method of portraying the biogeochemical cycle of an element or chemical species. In this system, each individual reservoir is represented by a box, while the direction of fluxes between reservoirs is indicated by arrows connecting the boxes.

BSE (bovine spongiform encephalopathy) a type of degenerative neurological disease of cattle.

cation any positively charged ion (i.e. contains fewer electrons than protons).

CFCs (chlorofluorocarbons) compounds of carbon, chlorine and fluorine; may also contain hydrogen.

chemical speciation the collection of chemical species in which an element is found in a given environmental system.

chemical species an atom, ion or molecule.

chlorofluorocarbons (CFCs) compounds of carbon, chlorine and fluorine; may also contain hydrogen.

chloroplasts organelles found in the cytoplasm of cells of all green plants and photosynthetic algae, which contain light-sensitive pigments and whose main function is to trap light energy from the sun for photosynthesis.

CHP plant see *combined heat and power (CHP) plant*.

CJD (Creutzfeldt–Jakob disease) a type of degenerative neurological disease of humans.

climate the long-term view of the weather patterns of a particular location, generally defined in terms of either its average weather conditions and/or the frequency of occurrence of a particular atmospheric feature, such as thunderstorms.

cloning the process by which any number of genetically identical individuals, or cells, are produced from a single individual, or cell, by repeated asexual divisions.

combined cycle plant installation that consists of a gas turbine powered by either natural gas or oil, the waste heat from which is used to drive a steam turbine. Both turbine systems are used to generate electricity.

combined heat and power (CHP) plant installation that burns fuel to produce power (usually in the form of electricity) and heat (usually in the form of steam or hot water).

compound [noun] a material that contains more than one element and that has been formed by chemical

reaction. Separation of the elements that are present cannot be achieved by purely physical processes, as compounds contain atoms and/or ions that are held together by chemical bonds.

coral bleaching the phenomenon in which corals under stress, from, e.g., uncommonly high water temperatures or pollution, expel the tiny algae that live symbiotically within their tissues and become bleached in appearance as a result.

Creutzfeldt–Jakob disease (CJD) a type of degenerative neurological disease of humans.

decomposer organism (usually a micro-organism, fungus or small invertebrate) that feeds on dead plant and animal matter, resulting in its physical and chemical breakdown.

deforestation complete and permanent removal of forest or woodland.

demographic transition the transition from high birth and death rates to low birth and death rates, usually associated with the general development and industrialisation of a society.

denitrification 1. the reduction of nitrate to elemental nitrogen and/or nitrous oxide; 2. the reduction of nitrates to nitrites and ammonia, as in plant tissues.

deoxyribonucleic acid see *DNA*.

depensation process by which the population level of a particular species falls to a level too low to facilitate effective reproduction. This may be caused, e.g., through over-harvesting and can lead to the progressive decline and eventual extinction of the affected population.

depression an essentially circular area of low atmospheric pressure, with diameter up to 3000 km, which usually develops at a front and typically lasts for 4–7 days.

detritivore organism (usually an invertebrate) that feeds on detritus (small fragments of dead and decaying matter derived from plants and animals, and their wastes).

dioxins a colloquial term for polychlorinated dibenzo-*p*-dioxins (PCDDs).

DNA (deoxyribonucleic acid) a long-chain molecule that carries the genetic information in all cells, found, as a major component, within the chromosomes.

dry deposition the direct deposition from the gas phase onto wet or dry surfaces.

dynamic equilibrium a state that represents a system at a thermodynamic minimum, i.e. $\Delta G = 0$, in which no net change is observable over time and that is maintained by a balance between equal and opposite processes.

dynamic steady state the maintenance of an apparently static condition by the operation of equal and opposite processes.

ecological efficiency the efficiency with which energy is transferred from one trophic level to the next.

ecological niche a term used to describe the role of an organism in a community, taking into account its effect on the environment, its interactions with other organisms present and the parameters of the habitat itself.

ecological restoration the process by which ecosystems damaged by human activities, such as overgrazing by livestock or drainage, are restored to a condition approaching, as near as possible, their original state.

El Niño a warm current that periodically flows along the western coast of South America.

El Niño–Southern Oscillation (ENSO) a cyclic climatic phenomenon that is centred on the tropical Pacific.

element a collection of atoms, each of which contains the same number of protons and electrons as the other atoms present.

endemic species species indigenous to, and restricted to, a particular region or part of a region.

endocrine-disrupting substances substances, e.g. tributyltin (TBT) compounds, which, when released into the environment, interfere with the correct functioning of the endocrine system in certain types of organisms.

energy the capacity to do work or supply heat.

energy consumption a commonly used term that is a misnomer as the destruction of energy would contravene the first law of thermodynamics. However, this term can be taken to mean the transformation of energy in a potentially useful form to a relatively useless one (ultimately, random thermal motion at ambient temperatures).

energy intensity a term used in environmental economics to express the effectiveness of energy utilisation. For a country, it may be defined as the amount of energy consumed (see *energy consumption*) per unit gross domestic product.

energy production a commonly used term that is a misnomer as the production of energy would contravene the first law of thermodynamics. However, this term can be taken to mean the conversion of energy from a source found in nature to one that is useful.

ENSO (El Niño–Southern Oscillation) a cyclic climatic phenomenon that is centred on the tropical Pacific.

essential elements those chemical elements that are required for the normal growth of organisms.

eukaryotes organisms (e.g. protozoans, algae, fungi, plants and animals) made up of eukaryotic cells. These cells are characterised by the presence of a membrane-bound nucleus and other specialised membrane-bound organelles, such as mitochondria.

eutrophication the nutrient enrichment of water bodies, especially lakes.

evapotranspiration loss of water from soil as a consequence of evaporation from the surface and transpiration from plants growing therein.

extratropical cyclone an essentially circular area of low atmospheric pressure, with a diameter up to 3000 km, which usually develops at a front and typically lasts for 4–7 days.

fast breeder reactor nuclear reactor that uses fast neutrons to maintain induced nuclear fission in fissile material. Some of the neutrons produced during fission are used to transform non-fissile uranium-238 or thorium-232 into fissile material (a process called breeding).

first law of thermodynamics if mass is taken to be a form of energy, the first law of thermodynamics can be stated thus: the total energy content of the universe is constant. If mass is not considered to be a form of energy, then this law may be formulated as: the total energy content on an isolated system of constant mass can be neither increased nor decreased.

fissile adjective applied to materials that undergo nuclear fission when bombarded with slow neutrons.

fissionable adjective applied to materials that undergo nuclear fission when bombarded with neutrons.

fitness a measure of the relative contribution of individuals to the genetic make-up of the next generation.

free radical molecular fragment, usually short lived, that contains one or more unpaired electrons.

front [noun] zone of rapid temperature change across the horizontal plane, formed when two air masses with different temperature characteristics meet.

fuel cell an electrochemical device that directly produces electricity from the oxidation of fuel (usually hydrogen and/or carbon monoxide). The oxidant is most commonly air. Fuel cells also produce heat.

furans a colloquial term for polychlorinated dibenzofurans (PCDFs) (see Box 16.3).

gamma decay the emission of a photon of electromagnetic radiation of extremely short wavelength (1×10^{-10} to 1×10^{-13} m) from certain radionuclides. Streams of such photons are called gamma rays, symbol γ.

gangue unwanted minerals and rock material in a mined ore deposit that is physically separated from the ore mineral prior to processing.

genetically modified (GM) crop crop which contains genes deliberately introduced from other (usually unrelated) species using genetic engineering techniques, in order to confer desirable traits such as herbicide tolerance or pesticide resistance.

genotype the genetic make-up of an organism.

global warming the increase in the temperature of the lower atmosphere that has occurred over the past 100 years and that is considered to result, principally, from the increased emission of CO_2 into the atmosphere as a result of fossil fuel burning and deforestation.

GM crop   see *genetically modified (GM) crop*.

greenhouse effect   the warming of the atmosphere (especially near ground level) caused by the absorption of terrestrial radiation (i.e. radiation given out by the Earth) by greenhouse gases.

greenhouse gases   those gases capable of absorbing terrestrial radiation (i.e. radiation given out by the Earth). With respect to their influence on climate, the main greenhouse gases are water vapour, carbon dioxide, methane, nitrous oxide and CFCs.

habitat   the place where an organism normally lives.

habitat fragmentation   the breaking-up of a continuous area of habitat into progressively smaller and more isolated patches, as a result of, e.g., urban or agricultural development.

half-life ($t_{\frac{1}{2}}$)   the time taken for the concentration, or amount, of a chemical species or radioactive isotope to drop to half its original value.

heat   energy that is transferred by virtue of a difference in temperature.

heterotroph   any organism that obtains its energy through the consumption of organic material.

horizon   in the study of soils, a horizon is any one of the distinct, essentially horizontal bands that are evident in the majority of soil profiles.

humus   that part of soil organic matter that is resistant to microbial decay.

hydrolysis reaction   reaction that involves water as one of the reactants.

hydrosphere   the waters of the Earth's surface.

hydrothermal vent community   a unique type of marine benthic community, composed largely of tubeworms and bivalve molluscs, found at great depths in the vicinity of the volcanic vents of the mid-ocean ridges.

igneous rock   rock formed on the solidification of molten rock material.

insect parasitoids   insects, usually of the order Hymenoptera or Diptera, that parasitise members of other insect orders, causing the death of their host organisms.

interaction   in thermodynamic analysis, an interaction has occurred when an observable change in one part of the universe is accompanied by a corresponding change in another.

interspecific competition   competition between members of different species for the same resource.

intertropical convergence zone (ITCZ)   zone near the equator where the north-east and south-east trade winds converge. This low-pressure belt of rising air produces a wide cloud and precipitation band that can be seen from space (Plate 1).

intraspecific competition   competition between members of the same species for the same resource (e.g. food, territory or mates).

introduced species   species not native to a particular region, thought to have been brought in (accidentally or deliberately) by humans.

ion   an atom or molecule that is electrically charged because the number of electrons it contains does not equal the number of protons present.

isotopes   atoms of any given element that differ in the number of neutrons that they contain. Each of the vast majority of naturally occurring elements is made up of a mixture of isotopes.

ITCZ (intertropical convergence zone)   zone near the equator where the north-east and south-east trade winds converge. This low-pressure belt of rising air produces a wide cloud and precipitation band that can be seen from space (Plate 1).

K-species   species whose characteristics, e.g. relatively large size, long generation time and few offspring, best suit them to stable habitats.

Le Chatelier's principle   if a system at dynamic equilibrium is perturbed by changes in concentration, pressure or temperature, it will alter its composition so as to minimise the change.

lentic ecosystem   freshwater ecosystem characterised by standing water, e.g. a lake.

Lindeman efficiency   the efficiency with which energy is transferred from one trophic level to the next.

lithosphere   the coherent solid layer of the Earth made up of the crust and the upper part of the mantle.

lotic ecosystem   freshwater ecosystem characterised by running water, e.g. a stream.

low [noun]   an essentially circular area of low atmospheric pressure, with a diameter up to 3000 km, which usually develops at a front and typically lasts for 4–7 days.

macro-nutrient elements   the nine essential elements that are required in relatively large amounts by living organisms, being major constituents of living matter, i.e. oxygen (O), hydrogen (H), carbon (C), nitrogen (N), calcium (C), phosphorus (P), sulfur (S), potassium (K) and magnesium (Mg).

matter   anything that takes up space.

meiosis   a type of nuclear division, which takes place in the formation of sex cells (gametes) during sexual reproduction, in which the resultant daughter nuclei contain half the number of chromosomes of the parent nucleus.

metamorphic rock   rock formed by the alteration of existing rock by the action of extreme heat and/or pressure and/or permeating hot gases or liquids.

mineral reserve   known deposits of a particular mineral, which are recoverable under current technological and economic conditions.

mineral resource   the total amount of a particular mineral present in the Earth's crust, whether or not its location is known.

mitochondria   organelles present in the cytoplasm of eukaryotic cells, which are the sites of cell respiration.

mitosis   a type of nuclear division, which occurs in asexual reproduction and in the growth of body tissues, in which the daughter nuclei produced contain exactly the same number of chromosomes as the parent nucleus (as a result of chromosomal duplication prior to division) and are genetically identical to it, and to each other. Mitosis is generally followed by cell division.

monoculture   an extensive area planted with a single crop variety.

monsoon   seasonal reversal in wind direction, which affects the climate of much of tropical Africa, Asia and Australasia.

mycorrhiza   a mutually beneficial association formed between certain fungi and plant roots, found in many shrubs, trees and herbaceous plants.

nitrification   the oxidation of ammonium to nitrite and of nitrite to nitrate, that occurs as a consequence of microbiological activity in aerobic soils.

nitrogen fixation   the reduction of elemental nitrogen to ammonia.

nuclear binding energy   the energy or work required to completely separate, from each other, all of the nucleons of a given atomic nucleus.

nuclear fission   the splitting of a heavy atomic nucleus into two or more nuclei of similar mass, with the simultaneous ejection of rapidly moving neutrons and liberation of nuclear energy.

nuclear fusion   a type of nuclear reaction that occurs when two light nuclei collide with such force that their mutual electrostatic repulsion is overcome. This reaction produces a heavier nucleus and liberates nuclear energy.

nuclear reaction   process that leads to a change in the number, nature or energy of the nucleons from which the nucleus of an atom is made.

nuclide   an atom, or the nucleus of that atom, that has specific values for both its mass number and its atomic number.

nutrient   any one chemical species that is actively taken up by an organism and used to maintain its bodily functions.

omnivore   any animal that consumes food from a variety of different sources, both plant and animal in origin.

orebody   deposit of ore that is sufficiently large to be commercially worked.

organochlorines   organic compounds containing chlorine. This group contains a number of important pollutants such as the pesticide DDT and PCBs (polychlorinated biphenyls).

oxidising agent   a chemical species that accepts one or more electrons in a redox reaction.

oxygen sag curve   typical curve produced when dissolved oxygen levels are plotted against distance downstream from a discharge point of organic material, e.g. a sewage outlet.

ozone hole   a substantial drop in the concentration of stratospheric ozone observed in the springtime over Antarctica and, to a lesser degree, the Arctic.

ozone layer   the band of relatively concentrated (but still very dilute) ozone found in the stratosphere.

pathogen   any disease-causing organism (usually a micro-organism).

PCBs   polychlorinated biphenyls.

PCDDs   polychlorinated dibenzo-p-dioxins.

PCDFs   polychlorinated dibenzofurans.

peat   organic deposit consisting of partly decomposed plant material associated with wetland areas and formed when the rate of production of vegetation exceeds that of microbial decomposition.

phenotype   the physical appearance of an organism, produced as a result of the interaction between its genotype and its environment.

photosynthesis   the complex chemical process that occurs in green plants in which light energy from the sun is used to convert water and carbon dioxide (from the atmosphere) into simple sugars, releasing oxygen as a by-product.

plagioclimax community   a plant community that is maintained in a subclimax stage of succession as a result of human, or animal, activities.

plate tectonics   a widely accepted theory that the Earth's surface is divided into a series of essentially rigid plates of lithosphere and that the plastic nature of the underlying asthenosphere allows these plates to move relative to one another.

PM$_{10}$ particle with diameter $\leqslant 10\,\mu$m.

population dynamics   the changes in population structure, in terms of, e.g., sex ratio or relative age, over time.

prey switching   behaviour pattern exhibited by predatory animals in which prey species are targeted preferentially when their numbers are most abundant.

primary energy consumption   energy conversion, by human endeavour, from a form found in nature. The burning of coal to generate electricity is therefore primary energy consumption; the use of the electricity generated in the heating of a building is not.

primary pollutants   environmentally damaging substances (whether natural or man-made) that are present in the chemical form in which they were released into the environment.

primary productivity   the rate, with respect to time, at which primary producers (autotrophs) produce new biomass per unit area.

primary succession   sequence of different plant communities developing over time, initiated when new, uncolonised habitats are created.

prion   proteinaceous infectious particle, thought to be the infective agent involved in transmissible spongiform encephalopathies, such as BSE.

prokaryotes   unicellular organisms, including bacteria and cyanobacteria, which are small in size ($1-10\,\mu$m) and simple in structure, containing no membrane-bound nucleus or other specialised membrane-bound organelles, such as mitochondria.

radioactive decay   the spontaneous disintegration of any unstable nuclide with the emission of alpha particles or beta particles and/or gamma rays.

radioactive waste   as defined by the International Atomic Energy Agency, 'any material that contains a concentration of radionuclides greater than those deemed safe by national authorities, and for which no use is foreseen'.

radioactivity   the disposition of some nuclides to undergo radioactive decay.

radioisotope   an unstable isotope, the atomic nuclei of which undergo radioactive decay.

radionuclide   an unstable atomic nucleus that undergoes radioactive decay.

radon   (symbol Rn) a naturally occurring radioactive gas.

rate of reaction   in a chemical reaction products are formed from reactants. The rate of reaction is the rate, with respect to time (t), of the disappearance of the reactants or appearance of the products, each divided by their coefficient of stoichiometry. That is, for the reaction $aA + bB \rightarrow cC + dD$,

$$\text{rate} = -\frac{d[A]}{a \times dt} = -\frac{d[B]}{b \times dt} = +\frac{d[C]}{c \times dt} = +\frac{d[D]}{d \times dt}$$

where d stands for 'infinitesimal change in' and $[\,] =$ concentration of the species in the brackets.

recombinant DNA technology   collectively, the techniques used to isolate, analyse and manipulate individual genes found on the chromosomal DNA, in order to produce artificially genetically modified micro-organisms, organisms and cells, together with the various applications of this biotechnology.

redox reaction   reaction that involves the complete transfer of one or more electrons from one chemical species to another.

reducing agent   a chemical species that loses one or more electrons in a redox reaction.

regolith   the mantle of unconsolidated material that covers the surface of virtually all rocks.

renewable energy   useful energy derived from resources that are not depleted as a result. Hydropower, solar, wind, wave, tidal, ocean thermal, biomass and geothermal energy are all usually included in this category.

reservoir   as used in box models, this term refers to a 'store' of material that is separate from other such stores on the grounds of physical location and/or chemical speciation.

residence time   the ratio of the amount of material in a reservoir to the total flux in or out of it.

restoration ecology   1. the process by which ecosystems damaged by human activities, such as overgrazing by livestock or drainage, are restored to a condition approaching, as near as possible, their original state; 2. the study of 1.

rocks   the non-living, naturally occurring solid materials that form the Earth's crust.

r-species   species, e.g. bacteria and annual plants, whose characteristics, e.g. rapid rate of reproduction, small size and good dispersal, allow them to successfully exploit new or disturbed habitats, or those that are temporary or generally unpredictable in character.

salinisation   the progressive deposition of large amounts of soluble mineral salts in the soil, making it unfit for cultivation, often associated with unsound irrigation techniques.

second law of thermodynamics   the entropy (disorder) of an isolated system can either remain constant or increase.

secondary pollutant   any environmentally damaging substance that is not released directly into the environment but forms as the result of the chemical alteration of, or interactions between, primary pollutants.

secondary productivity   the rate, with respect to time, at which secondary producers (herbivores) produce new biomass per unit area.

secondary succession   sequence of different plant communities developing over time, initiated when the existing vegetation is abruptly removed, as a result of either natural disasters or human activities such as strip mining.

sedimentary rock   rock formed by the compression, compaction and cementation of sediments; can originate from the fragments produced during weathering and erosion, as a result of dissolved material precipitating from water, or as a consequence of biological activity.

shifting cultivation   a type of cultivation (also known as slash and burn cultivation), widely practised in Africa, South America and south-east Asia, in which a patch of rainforest is first felled and then burnt. The resultant clearing is planted with a variety of crops until, after 2–3 years, the nutrients become exhausted. At this stage, the patch is abandoned in favour of a new one.

silviculture   the cultivation of trees and the management of forests and woodlands for timber.

sink   any process, chemical or physical in nature, that results in the loss of a pollutant from a given part of the environment.

smog   a mixture of *sm*oke and f*og*. There are two distinct categories of smog: London-type smogs (also called sulfurous or classical smogs) and Los Angeles-type smogs (also called photochemical smogs).

soil   that part of the terrestrial crust that has been altered by biological activity.

soil profile   a vertical section through a soil.

speciation, biological   the process by which new species evolve.

speciation, chemical   the collection of chemical species in which an element is found in a given environmental system.

species, biological   a group of interbreeding individuals reproductively isolated from other groups.

species, chemical   an atom, ion or molecule.

species diversity   the number and relative abundance of different species present in a particular area or community.

species richness   the number of different species present in a particular area or community.

system   in thermodynamic analysis, the portion of the universe that is under consideration. It is encapsulated by a real or imaginary boundary that separates it from its surroundings. Both matter and energy can cross the boundary of an open system. The boundary of a closed system can be traversed by energy but not matter. Isolated systems allow neither matter nor energy to cross their boundaries.

temperature inversion   an atmospheric condition in which warmer air lies above cooler, denser air. This condition is the norm in the stratosphere but occurs only as a temporary phenomenon in the troposphere.

thermal reactor   nuclear reactor that uses slow (i.e. thermal) neutrons to maintain induced nuclear fission in fissile material.

thermal shock   rapid change in water temperature that results in mass kills of fish and other aquatic organisms.

thermodynamics   the study of energy transformations.

transgenic organism   organism that contains genetic material deliberately introduced from another species by genetic engineering.

transmutation   the change, via a nuclear reaction, of the nuclei of one element into those of another.

transpiration   the evaporation of water through stomata of plant leaves and stem.

urbanisation   the process of urban development.

waste   any moveable material that is perceived to be of no further use and that is permanently discarded.

water table   upper boundary of the zone of saturation, below which all available pores in soil and rock are filled with water.

weather   the physical condition of the atmosphere (particularly the troposphere) at a specific time and place with regard to wind, temperature, cloud cover, fog and precipitation (the collective word for rain, hail, snow, etc.).

weathering   the *in situ* physical and/or chemical breakdown of rocks by external agents, such as frost, percolating rainwater and biological activity.

wet deposition   the removal of material from the atmosphere by its incorporation into rain or other precipitation, both within clouds (known as rainout) and/or beneath clouds (known as washout).

wetland   an area habitually saturated with water, which may be partly or wholly covered permanently, periodically or occasionally by fresh, brackish or salt water (static or flowing) up to a depth of 6 metres.

wildlife corridor   a strip of natural habitat left intact, in an area undergoing some type of development, whose purpose is to connect otherwise isolated areas of similar habitat and to allow the free movement of wildlife between patches.

work   any interaction between two bodies, or any system and its surroundings, that is neither heat nor the transfer of matter.

xenobiotic [adjective]   1. not found in nature, i.e. entirely man-made; 2. foreign to a living organism (applied to, e.g., a drug); 3. applied to micro-organisms capable of degrading foreign organic compounds, e.g. man-made organic pesticides.

zero tillage   the sowing of crop seeds into unploughed fields.

Index